Buyer's Guide
to New Zealand
Wines

2011

Hodder Moa

A catalogue record for this book is available from the National Library of New Zealand

ISBN 978-1-86971-207-5

A Hodder Moa Book
Published in 2010 by Hachette New Zealand Ltd
4 Whetu Place, Mairangi Bay
Auckland, New Zealand

Text © Michael Cooper 2010
The moral rights of the author have been asserted.
Design and format © Hachette New Zealand Ltd 2010

All rights reserved. No part of this publication may be reproduced or transmitted in any form or by any means, electronic or mechanical, including photocopying, recording, or any information storage and retrieval system, without permission in writing from the publisher.

Designed and produced by Hachette Livre NZ Ltd
Printed by Griffin Press, Australia

Reviews of the latest editions

'The absolute bible of New Zealand wines.'
– *Newstalk ZB*

'The *Buyer's Guide* is an essential book for anyone wishing to cut through the fluff and get a fast, honest appraisal of practically any wine made in New Zealand. If a wine doesn't rate well, Cooper tells you why, and if it gains five stars his praise is lavish. … This is a book for the novice and the connoisseur, the wine student and wine professional, the collector and the drinker.'
– *New Zealand House & Garden*

'An essential reference for anyone bemused by the hundreds of labels on supermarket or wine-shop shelves, or puzzling over something for a special occasion.'
– *Otago Daily Times*

'The indispensable guide for New Zealanders.'
– *Marlborough Express*

'Whenever I stand in front of the Chardonnay section at my local Glengarry's wine store and feel overwhelmed by the hundred or so New Zealand Chardonnays on display there, I wonder how I could ever make a choice if I didn't have with me the current edition of Cooper's invaluable guide. I never buy wine without having it with me. It is totally indispensable and the best guide on the market by a country mile.'
– *Beattie's Book Blog*

'Cooper's is the definitive work.'
– *Sunday Star-Times*

Michael Cooper is New Zealand's most acclaimed wine writer, with 34 books and several major literary awards to his credit, including the Montana Medal for the supreme work of non-fiction at the 2003 Montana New Zealand Book Awards for his magnum opus, *Wine Atlas of New Zealand*. In the 2004 New Year Honours, Michael was appointed an Officer of the New Zealand Order of Merit for services to wine writing.

Author of the country's biggest-selling wine book, the annual *Michael Cooper's Buyer's Guide to New Zealand Wines*, now in its 19th edition, he was awarded the Sir George Fistonich Medal in recognition of services to New Zealand wine in 2009. The award is made each year at the country's largest wine competition, the New Zealand International Wine Show, to a 'living legend' of New Zealand wine. The weekly wine columnist for the *New Zealand Listener*, he is also New Zealand editor of Australia's *Winestate* magazine and chairman of its New Zealand tasting panel.

In 1977 he obtained a Master of Arts degree from the University of Auckland with a thesis entitled 'The Wine Lobby: Pressure Group Politics and the New Zealand Wine Industry'. He was marketing manager for Babich Wines from 1980 to 1990, and since 1991 has been a full-time wine writer.

Cooper's other major works include the much-extended second edition of *Wine Atlas of New Zealand* (2008); *Classic Wines of New Zealand* (second edition 2005); *The Wines and Vineyards of New Zealand* (published in five editions from 1984 to 1996); and *Pocket Guide to Wines of New Zealand* (second edition 2000). He is the New Zealand consultant for Hugh Johnson's annual, best-selling *Pocket Wine Book* and the acclaimed *World Atlas of Wine*.

Contents

The Winemaking Regions of New Zealand	6
Preface	7
Vintage Charts	8
2010 Vintage Report	9
Best Buys of the Year	15
Update on the Wine Glut	17
Classic Wines of New Zealand	21
Cellar Sense	26
Cellaring Guidelines	28
How to Use this Book	29

White Wines 32

Arneis	32	Pinot Blanc	157
Branded and Other White Wines	34	Pinot Gris	159
Breidecker	40	Riesling	219
Chardonnay	41	Sauvignon Blanc	266
Chenin Blanc	130	Sauvignon Gris	358
Flora	132	Sémillon	359
Gewürztraminer	133	Verdelho	360
Grüner Veltliner	154	Viognier	361
Müller-Thurgau	155	Würzer	371
Muscat	156		

Sweet White Wines 372

Sparkling Wines 395

Rosé Wines 411

Red Wines 429

Branded and Other Red Wines	429	Merlot	474
Cabernet Franc	450	Montepulciano	508
Cabernet Sauvignon and Cabernet-predominant blends	453	Pinotage	511
		Pinot Noir	514
Carmenère	468	St Laurent	629
Chambourcin	468	Sangiovese	629
Dolcetto	469	Syrah	630
Gamay Noir	469	Tempranillo	659
Malbec	470	Zinfandel	660
Marzemino	473	Zweigelt	660

Index of Wine Brands 661

The Winemaking Regions of New Zealand

Area in producing vines 2011 (percentage of national producing vineyard area)

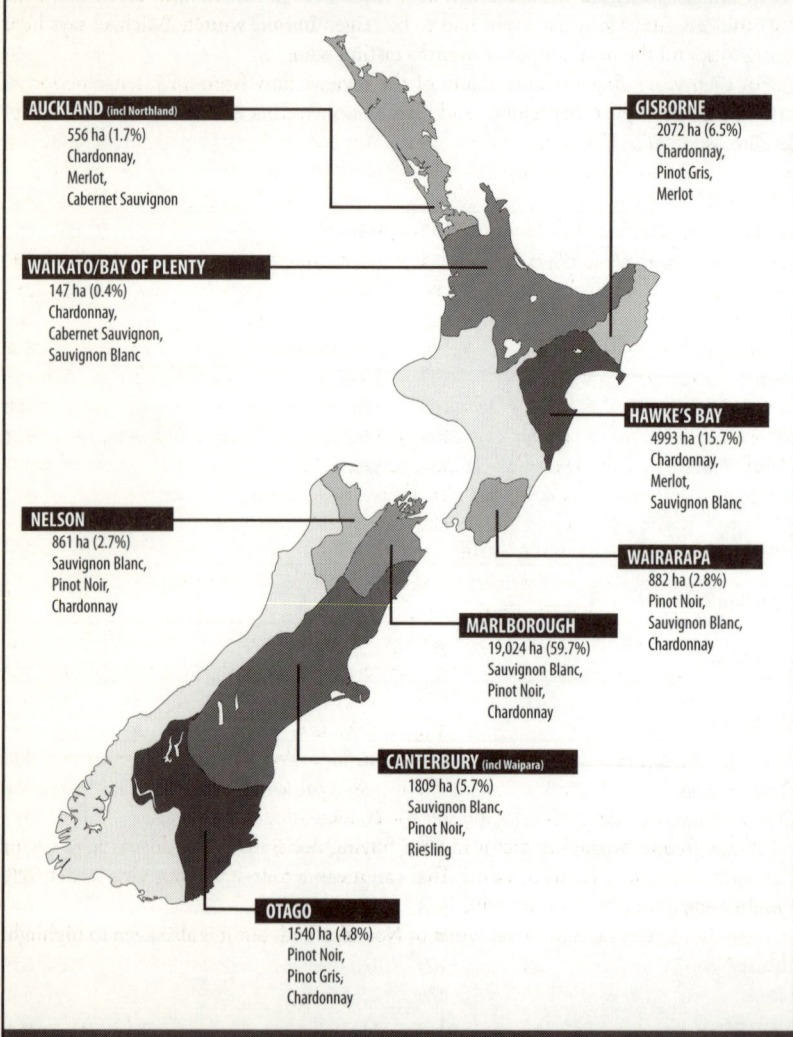

AUCKLAND (incl Northland)
556 ha (1.7%)
Chardonnay,
Merlot,
Cabernet Sauvignon

WAIKATO/BAY OF PLENTY
147 ha (0.4%)
Chardonnay,
Cabernet Sauvignon,
Sauvignon Blanc

NELSON
861 ha (2.7%)
Sauvignon Blanc,
Pinot Noir,
Chardonnay

GISBORNE
2072 ha (6.5%)
Chardonnay,
Pinot Gris,
Merlot

HAWKE'S BAY
4993 ha (15.7%)
Chardonnay,
Merlot,
Sauvignon Blanc

WAIRARAPA
882 ha (2.8%)
Pinot Noir,
Sauvignon Blanc,
Chardonnay

MARLBOROUGH
19,024 ha (59.7%)
Sauvignon Blanc,
Pinot Noir,
Chardonnay

CANTERBURY (incl Waipara)
1809 ha (5.7%)
Sauvignon Blanc,
Pinot Noir,
Riesling

OTAGO
1540 ha (4.8%)
Pinot Noir,
Pinot Gris,
Chardonnay

These figures are extracted from the *New Zealand Winegrowers Statistical Annual*, published by New Zealand Winegrowers. During the five-year period 2007 to 2012 the total area of producing vines is projected to expand from 25,355 to 33,600 hectares – a rise of nearly 33 per cent.

Preface

At a tasting I presented a few months ago, there were lots of envious looks when the host told his guests why the event had to be staged in mid-winter. 'Michael says he is going to spend the next couple of months tasting wine . . .'

In each year's *Buyer's Guide*, many of the reviews flow from an intense period of tasting during August, September and early October. This ensures the book is as up-to-date as possible. These tastings in late winter and early spring attract a multitude of wines from the new season (2010), together with older wines still in the pipeline but scheduled for release over the coming year, such as 2009 Chardonnays and Pinot Noirs, or top-end Hawke's Bay reds from 2008.

Every day, the wines are tasted in two periods, generally between 11 a.m. and midday, and later from 5 p.m. to 6 p.m. Six to 10 wines are tasted at a time, grouped by variety or style. A typical tasting might be eight Pinot Gris or Syrah.

But the tastings for the *Buyer's Guide* take place year-round. *Winestate*'s annual regional tastings of wines from Marlborough, Hawke's Bay, Canterbury/Otago, Nelson/Wairarapa and the Upper North Island are a key source of tasting notes, as are *Winestate*'s bi-monthly tastings of Recent Releases. Other samples are sent for review in my weekly column in the *New Zealand Listener*. Many other wines are tasted when their producers visit Auckland, or I visit them in the regions.

When writing the book, I often find I've tasted a particular wine several times – frequently 'blind' (label hidden), but sometimes with its label revealed; occasionally with food, but more often by itself. And the wine itself is changing over time. Every time you taste it, you get to know it better.

Wine lovers often see the task of tasting 3000-plus wines each year as Herculean. But if you taste about 10 wines daily – easy for a professional taster – the numbers add up swiftly.

I like to score wines on a star-rating system that includes the use of half stars. Three, four and five stars (equivalent to bronze, silver and gold medals) are useful, but these bands of quality can be broad. Wine judges often talk about a 'high bronze' or 'low silver' wine. Half stars offer a taster the chance to be more precise.

Value should be the key factor in your buying decisions. Who doesn't love a wine that over-delivers, in terms of value? That can mean a four-star Pinot Gris under $20, or a five-star Pinot Noir under $40.

This book celebrates the great wines of New Zealand, but it is also keen to highlight the best buys.

– Michael Cooper

Vintage Charts 2001–2010

WHITES

WHITES	Auckland	Gisborne	Hawke's Bay	Wairarapa	Nelson	Marlborough	Canterbury	Otago
2010	7	6–7	7	6	7	7	6	6
2009	4	6–7	4	5	6	5	6	3–5
2008	5–6	3–4	3–5	5–7	4	2–5	3–6	5–6
2007	6	7	6	4–5	5	5–6	5–6	4–6
2006	6–7	4–5	6	5	5	4–5	5	5–6
2005	7	5	4	3	4	4–5	5	3–4
2004	6	5–6	5–6	5	5	6	3–6	3
2003	5–6	4	3–4	6	5–6	5	4–6	5
2002	6	7	6	6	6–7	4–6	4–7	5–7
2001	3–5	4	4–5	5	6	6–7	6	4–6

REDS

REDS	Auckland	Gisborne	Hawke's Bay	Wairarapa	Nelson	Marlborough	Canterbury	Otago
2010	7	6	6	5	6	6–7	5	5–6
2009	5	6–7	6	5	6	6	6	3–5
2008	5–7	3–4	3–5	5–7	4	2–5	3–6	5–6
2007	3–5	7	6	4–5	5	4–6	5–6	4–6
2006	4–5	4–5	4–5	5	5	4–5	5	5–6
2005	7	5	4–6	3	4	4–5	5	4–5
2004	5–7	6	5–6	5	4	4–5	4–6	3–4
2003	4–6	4	3–4	7	5–7	5	4–7	5–6
2002	6	7	5–6	4	5–7	4–7	3–6	5–6
2001	4–5	4	4	6	6	5–7	7	6

7 = Outstanding 6 = Excellent 5 = Above average 4 = Average 3 = Below average 2 = Poor 1 = Bad

2010 Vintage Report

Thanks to the Indian summer, you can look forward to some memorable wines from this year's harvest. '2010 will go down as one of Marlborough's top vintages,' says Mike Just, of Clayridge Vineyards. 'A long, dry, sunny autumn allowed us to pick lovely, clean, ripe fruit at our leisure.'

It didn't always look that way. The country's coldest October since 1945 was followed by a dismally wet January in Hawke's Bay and Gisborne. But in February the weather settled, drought spread and the grapes basked in unusual warmth and dryness right through into the key harvest month of April.

New Zealand Winegrowers, grappling with the industry's worst oversupply since the mid-1980s, in February predicted a 2010 grape crop of 265,000 to 285,000 tonnes (compared to the glut-inducing 285,000 tonnes harvested in 2008 and 2009), from a producing area of 33,000 hectares of vineyards, up from 31,000 hectares in 2009. In April, it revised its estimate to the lower end, noting that 'a smaller vintage this time will help rebalance people's stock'.

The final figures revealed a 2010 harvest of 266,000 tonnes from 33,200 hectares – 7 per cent lighter than 2009. It was a low-cropping year – the vines' average yield of 8 tonnes of grapes per hectare was significantly below 2009 (8.9 tonnes/hectare) and 2008 (9.7 tonnes/hectare), and the lowest since 2005. The decline even led some companies to search for extra fruit, triggering a lift in the prices of grapes sold on the 'spot' market and bulk-wine prices.

Of the three major regions, Marlborough dominated as usual, accounting for 69.3 per cent of the national grape harvest, ahead of Hawke's Bay (14.8 per cent) and Gisborne (7 per cent). In terms of the key grape varieties, Sauvignon Blanc was equally dominant, with 66 per cent of the crop, followed by Chardonnay (10 per cent), Pinot Noir (9 per cent), Pinot Gris (5 per cent) and Merlot (3 per cent).

The icy start to the season and damp mid-summer slowed ripening, leading many growers to wonder if their grapes would ever ripen fully. But February was settled, bringing hot, dry weather to most of the country, and in March the rain stayed away.

By April, drought had been officially declared in Northland, Auckland, Waikato and Otago. Liam McElhinney, winemaker at Marisco Vineyards, in Marlborough, told *New Zealand Winegrower* that due to the ongoing warmth and dryness, the weather did not influence harvest dates. 'We could literally drive around the vineyard in the morning, taste and then decide to pick or not. It was luxury, absolute luxury.'

Northland

So rare is Northland wine, less than 0.1 per cent of the country's 2010 grape harvest was grown in the region. The total crop of 178 tonnes was heavier than in 2009 (only 148 tonnes) but lighter than the 2005, 2006, 2007 and 2008 vintages, and equates to little more than 13,000 cases.

After an exceptionally dry November and sunny, dry December, by year's end a total fire ban was in force. 'The vines are shutting down,' Rod MacIvor, of Marsden Estate, reported in late January. 'All that energy and sugar is going straight into the berries.'

Longview Estate, near Whangarei, harvested its White Diamond grapes in mid-February – the earliest ever. During the four-month period, January to April, Northland received just one-third of its normal rainfall.

Ben Dugdale, winemaker at Karikari Estate, reported 'a very good season', with small berries and grape flavours exhibiting 'classical varietal notes'.

Auckland

Auckland's harvest of 1325 tonnes of grapes was 18 per cent smaller than in 2009 and 17 per cent smaller than in 2008, but looks likely to yield outstanding Chardonnays and reds.

'Spring commenced with two weeks of warmth and bud-burst,' says Te Whau, 'followed by the coolest, wettest six weeks in memory.' The combination of spring frosts and poor weather during flowering slashed the size of the potential grape crop.

Summer, however, was 'spectacularly sunny', according to Kumeu River. February was warm and extremely dry, with less than 10 per cent of the average rainfall. 'We started picking on 29 February with Pinot Gris, then Chardonnay and Viognier,' Cable Bay reported in late March. 'It's looking a dream so far.'

Only 56.6 mm of rain fell in Auckland during January, February and March – the driest quarter for at least 50 years. April was close to average, in terms of temperatures and sunshine hours – and the weather stayed dry.

Kumeu River, renowned for Chardonnay, views 2010 as 'truly remarkable. The warm weather allowed the grapes to ripen evenly with great concentration from the low yield.'

On Waiheke Island, Te Whau harvested a small crop of Chardonnay and Merlot. 'The Cabernets [Sauvignon and Franc] and the Syrah were the big beneficiaries of the big dry – small berries with very focused, rich flavours and abundant, ripe tannins.' Cable Bay praised 2010 as 'maybe the best vintage yet for the island'.

Waikato

Waikato growers picked 118 tonnes of grapes, their smallest crop in a decade and 41 per cent less than in 2009. The tiny harvest is equivalent to just 9000 cases of wine, but quality expectations are high.

Drought was widespread in the Waikato by late summer. In April, Vilagrad reported a marvellous crop. 'It's not good for farmers, but when the Waikato has a drought, we have the best grapes ever.'

Gisborne

Gisborne growers harvested 18,316 tonnes of grapes – a 21 per cent drop on 2009 and the smallest crop since 2006. However, favourable weather during late summer and autumn should produce some top-flight wines.

In spring, bud-burst was 'right on the dot', according to The Millton Vineyard. October brought cool, extremely wet weather, but November was warm and very dry. 'Flowering was interrupted a little due to a southerly which came through,' said Pernod Ricard NZ, 'and it looks like this has affected the vines to give smaller bunches.' Gewürztraminer was especially hard hit.

Summer got off to a good start with a warm, dry December but was followed by one of the coolest, cloudiest, wettest Januarys on record, with more than triple the average January rainfall. Near the end of the month, a storm caused widespread slips and flooding.

However, February brought warm, very dry weather (with 31 per cent of normal rainfall), and for the rest of the growing season the weather gods kept smiling. A warm, extremely dry March was followed by a dry April with the second highest sunshine hours since 1905.

After three weeks of 'truly exceptional weather', James Millton reported in late March that the grapes were 'in very good condition, with no botrytis or mildew'. He forecast the 2010 wines would possess 'balanced acids for freshness and lower than normal alcohols'.

'We've had what I'd say was the best possible first vintage we could have had,' enthused Warwick Bruce, of Gro Co. Kirkpatrick Estate reported 'exceptional' Gewürztraminer and 'wonderful' Merlot and Malbec. Wine giant Pernod Ricard NZ described its 2010 Gisborne Chardonnay as 'outstanding'.

Hawke's Bay

Hawke's Bay's grape harvest of 38,860 tonnes was 5 per cent lighter than in 2009, but still the third-largest ever. 'It has shades of 2002 all over again,' declared winemaker Gordon Russell of Esk Valley, 'a poor summer followed by an Indian summer, saving the vintage.'

Spring was cold – but not frosty. After the hottest August on record, bud-burst was two weeks early, says Te Mata. However, September proved cooler than average; October was the coldest since the Second World War and extremely wet; and November brought average temperatures, with little rainfall.

Hawke's Bay Winegrowers reported 'a challenging, cool summer'. After a cool, fairly damp December, January was 'the wettest for 100 years, so we were very pessimistic by the end of January,' says John Hancock, of Trinity Hill. But as February wore on, the rain eased and temperatures climbed.

In early March, ripening was running two to three weeks late, according to Te Mata. However, after a warm, dry March and notably sunny, dry April, Rod McDonald, chairman of Hawke's Bay Winegrowers, described autumn as 'amazing'.

Te Mata reported its white wines show slightly below-average alcohol levels. Trinity Hill praised 2010 as 'the best Chardonnay vintage we have seen since 2002 – the fruit is pretty special'.

Hugh Crichton, winemaker at Vidal, sees 2010 as a 'classic year for Chardonnay and Syrah'. Te Mata closed the vintage by picking Cabernet Sauvignon from its 1892 Vineyard on 6 May, 'as late as we have ever experienced'. Trinity Hill predicts its 2010 reds will be 'sensational'.

Wairarapa

Wairarapa growers picked 3942 tonnes of grapes – 11 per cent less than in 2009, but still the third-largest crop on record. After a cool, late-ripening season, the prospects are for good wines with relatively low alcohol levels.

'The season got off to a very slow start, with cool temperatures prevailing through October and November,' reported Nga Waka. Flowering was delayed by two weeks, according to Dry River. 'This was a blessing, as a short but settled period of warmer weather occurred right at the critical time of flowering.'

When summer arrived, the temperatures stayed low. Martinborough recorded an all-time December low of 1.4°C. In January, the total number of sunshine hours was the lowest since records began in 1986. 'November through to January was very cold,' says Dry River. 'January compounded this "sin" by also being very wet.'

However, the cool, wet spring and summer gave way to the sunniest March on record. In April, the weather stayed unusually warm and sunny, and Masterton experienced record low rainfall. 'Mid-March to late April brought a seemingly endless procession of fine, warm autumn days,' reported Nga Waka.

Overall, the October to April growing season was cooler than 2008, 2006 and 2005, but similar to 2009 and 2007. 'The fruit has ripened well,' observed Gladstone Vineyard. 'The weather has been magnificent ... enabling us to pick when we want to optimise flavours and ripeness. The longer, cooler ripening period encourages good flavour development in the grapes at lower potential alcohol levels.'

Urlar reported 'absolutely wonderful' Sauvignon Blanc and 'promising' Pinot Gris and Pinot Noir. Borthwick Vineyard described its white wines as having 'wonderful flavours' and its Pinot Noir as 'very good'.

Nelson

At the end of a challenging season, Nelson's winegrowers celebrated one of their finest vintages. At 5963 tonnes, the harvest was 23 per cent smaller than in 2009, but was still the third largest to date and is widely expected to yield exceptional wines.

After a cool, wet October and warm, dry November, early to mid-summer was also variable, with a cool, dry December followed by a slightly warmer than average, but wet, January. Phil Gladstone, of Neudorf, reported 'the worst spring and early summer that Nelson has had since 1946'.

However, a settled late summer and autumn rescued the season. Near the end of a warm, dry February, Agnes Seifried said the harvest was 'looking a bit late, but the weather is now very hot and dry, so might catch up a bit.'

At the start of autumn, Woollaston enthused that 'the canopy is the healthiest it has ever looked; the fruit is clean and free of disease'. March, warm and dry, was followed by an exceptionally dry, hot April – the mean maximum air temperature of 19.8°C in April was the highest since records began in 1943.

Seifried harvested its lightest crop since 2007. After a '"California" summer with fine, settled weather right through to harvest,' Phil Gladstone rated 2010 as 'possibly the best vintage that Nelson has had for a very long time'.

Blackenbrook Vineyard reported its greatest harvest to date: 'The fruit is fully ripe with sugar levels up to [a soaring] 26 brix and the taste is incredible – amazingly intense.'

Marlborough

After a near-average growing season – in terms of warmth and sunshine hours – but less rain than usual, Marlborough growers picked 182,658 tonnes of grapes. The crop was 5 per cent lighter than in 2009 but still nearly 70 per cent of the national total.

A cool spring, with well below average temperatures, slowed the vines' development. A sunny, cool September was followed by the coldest October since 1992, with below-average sunshine hours and the fifth-highest rainfall for 80 years. After a cloudy but dry November, with average temperatures, Framingham reported, 'We are approximately two weeks behind in growth.'

'Summer has been a little slow in getting here this time around,' Clayridge declared in December. 'Seems like we've had one helluva long spring, but the grapes are finally flowering.' After a cool and cloudy start, December turned sunny and warm, with little rain. A warm, dry but cloudy January was followed by a slightly cool and cloudy but notably dry February – the fourth month in a row with below-average rainfall.

Autumn kicked off with a warm, dry March, followed by a hot, sunny and dry April – the sixth warmest since 1932. From January to April 2010, the rainfall was just 45 per cent of the long-term average.

Overall, the growing season was fractionally warmer and sunnier, but much drier, than average, according to Rob Agnew, of Plant & Food Research. Cloudy Bay and Fromm reported flavour ripeness in the berries at moderate sugar levels, suggesting some 2010 wines from Marlborough will not be high in alcohol, but other winemakers reported Sauvignon Blancs with up to 14 per cent alcohol.

'The fruit is excellent, clean, and particularly in the Chardonnay and Riesling, there are some wonderful flavours,' says grower Chris Simmonds. Clayridge, which also picked 'wonderful' Pinot Noir, praised 2010 as 'one of Marlborough's top vintages'.

Jamie Marfell, winemaker for Pernod Ricard NZ, described Stoneleigh and Stoneleigh Rapaura Series Sauvignon Blancs as 'fantastic, showing ... some great intensity of flavours and big aromas'. Liam McElhinney, of Marisco, described his company's Sauvignon Blancs in *New Zealand Winegrower* as 'pristine, precise, focused and expressive'.

Canterbury

After a chilly start to the season but a favourably warm, dry autumn, Canterbury growers picked 5870 tonnes – 7 per cent more than in 2009 and the region's second biggest grape harvest to date.

In spring, October was extremely cold (with temperatures 2.1°C below average) and wetter than usual. *New Zealand Winegrower* reported that a severe October frost damaged many vineyards on the Canterbury Plains. November was cold but relatively dry.

In early to mid-summer, the temperatures stayed low, but December and January were also drier than usual, bringing drought to coastal areas. As summer wore on, February brought more dry weather and temperatures climbed to the long-term average.

Autumn got off to a good start with a warm, notably dry March. At Waipara, Torlesse noted in early March that 'we are finally getting our summer – now that we are in autumn'. Black Estate reported on 19 March that 'we have lately enjoyed some beautiful, hot North Canterbury weather'.

In April, the weather stayed sunny, warm and dry, with less than half the normal rainfall. 'Temperatures picked up and a very warm April set the scene for substantial late season ripening with the best flavour development in several years, particularly for Riesling,' enthused Tony Rutherford, of Mount Brown Vineyard, in *New Zealand Winegrower*.

Glen Creasy, of the Centre for Viticulture and Oenology at Lincoln University, reported that for Canterbury growers, 'the payoff comes in a season like this, when you get great ripe flavours in lower alcohol wines'.

Otago

After a cold spring, favourably warm and dry summer, but wetter than average autumn, Otago growers picked 6196 tonnes of grapes – an almost identical crop to 2009's 6218 tonnes. The official figure took many winemakers – who had predicted a much smaller harvest – by surprise.

Spring was cold and wet, according to Greg Hay, of Peregrine. At Alexandra, Grasshopper Rock reported a warm start to the season and an early bud-burst, but from October to December, 'we lost ground and, most importantly, this coincided with flowering. As a result of the cold, fruit set was mixed.'

In the Waitaki Valley, viticulturist Steve Harrop reported a normal bud-burst in October and frost damage in unprotected vineyards. 'This frost period was followed by an unseasonably cool October and November, which resulted in very slow growth.'

'Summer was generally warm,' according to Grasshopper Rock, 'and rainfall was well below average – a one-in-10-year low…' Rockburn reported snow in mid-January and 'the cold and wet weather hasn't done much for our tans', but in February, the weather turned hot and dry.

'The vines finally saw some real Waitaki Valley heat at the end of January, on through February and into March,' says Harrop. Nick Mills, of Rippon Vineyard, summed up the Central Otago summer as 'amazing'.

Autumn was warm but wet, with a hot, cloudy, damp April. 'This year the fruit is absolutely beautiful,' Mills reported in mid-April. 'The white wines are some of the most fragrant I've seen,' enthused Hay, in late April.

Mt Difficulty and Mount Edward reported a 25 per cent volume drop, compared to 2009. Misha's Vineyard says 2010 will be 'fantastic in terms of wine quality', with small bunches and small berries yielding intense, well-structured reds. But Grasshopper Rock noted that 'the quality of fruit picked in the last week of April and early May will be mixed, with the wet and cold weather experienced then.'

Best Buys of the Year

Best White Wine Buy of the Year

Villa Maria Private Bin Marlborough Sauvignon Blanc 2010
★★★★☆, $21 (but widely available at $11.99)

The first thing you need to know about this delicious wine is that its suggested retail price is just under $21. At that price, it offers above-average value. The second thing to know is that the vast majority is sold on 'promotion' at around $11.99. At that price, given its excellent quality, it's an absolute 'steal' – and winner of the Best White Wine Buy of the Year Award.

From one vintage to the next, this large-volume label offers impressive quality and great value. The 2010 is mouthfilling, fleshy and finely textured, yet also very fresh and zingy, with sweet-fruit delights and rich, ripe melon, lime and capsicum flavours, crisp and lingering. When I tasted it in October alongside one of Marlborough's most expensive and prestigious Sauvignon Blancs, it held its own well.

For such a low-priced wine, Villa Maria Private Bin Marlborough Sauvignon Blanc 2010 has already made a strong impact on the show circuit, winning a silver medal at the New Zealand International Wine Show 2010, then gold at the New World Wine Awards 2010. At the Royal Perth Wine Show 2010, it performed even more impressively, scooping the trophy for champion Sauvignon Blanc.

Grown in vineyards across the Wairau and Awatere valleys, the grapes were harvested at varying levels of ripeness over a three-week period, providing an array of flavours and blending options. The juice was cool-fermented at 12–14°C in tanks, retaining its most delicate aromas and flavours. Made in a basically dry style (3.5 grams/litre of residual sugar), it was bottled early to maximise its freshness and vibrancy.

Villa Maria recommends drinking this punchy yet also hugely drinkable Sauvignon Blanc anytime from now until 2012. In terms of garden freshness and sheer aromatic intensity, it's likely to be at its peak this summer and during 2011. Villa Maria suggests serving it with grilled seasonal vegetables and seafood or chicken, but served gently chilled, it's also a great apéritif.

Best Red Wine Buy of the Year

Church Road Hawke's Bay Merlot/Cabernet Sauvignon 2008
★★★★☆, $26 (but widely available under $15)

How many classy reds can you buy under $15? This dark, densely flavoured wine won a gold medal at the Royal Easter Show Wine Awards 2010, a four-star rating in *Winestate*, and five stars from *Cuisine* (ahead of several high-profile, $50 reds). Its recommended retail price is $26, but in supermarkets, where it is almost entirely sold on 'promotion', the average sale price is under $15. That's stunning value – worthy of the Best Red Wine Buy of the Year award.

Church Road Hawke's Bay Merlot/Cabernet Sauvignon is consistently a richly flavoured, complex, distinctly Bordeaux-like red. The 2008 vintage is dark, fragrant, mouthfilling and concentrated, with blackcurrant, plum and spice flavours, showing good, savoury complexity, and excellent warmth and density.

For winemaker Chris Scott, this popular red is "one of the most challenging and exciting wine styles to produce. There is a synergy between Merlot and Cabernet Sauvignon which, when blended in the right proportions, produces arguably the most complete, complex, fragrant and satisfying style of red wine in the world." I agree.

Church Road Hawke's Bay Merlot/Cabernet Sauvignon 2008 is a blend of Merlot (45 per cent), Cabernet Sauvignon (42 per cent) and Malbec (13 per cent). Most of the grapes (75 per cent) were grown in the Gimblett Gravels - with smaller components from the company's vineyards in The Triangle and at Havelock North - and the wine was matured for a year in French and Hungarian oak barriques (30 per cent new.)

Satisfyingly full-bodied and rich, Church Road Hawke's Bay Merlot/Cabernet Sauvignon 2008 is already highly enjoyable, but should reward cellaring for several years, gaining in complexity and downright drinkability. The winery suggests serving it as "the ultimate match for savoury game and red meat dishes". Try char-grilled, herbed veal chops.

If you want to buy this great-value red, move quickly, because stocks are getting low and the 2009 vintage will be released before Christmas. If you miss out, I was given a 'sneak preview' of the 2009. From the hottest season for the last decade and the driest since 1973, it's even better. Grab it.

Other shortlisted wines

Whites
Church Road Hawke's Bay Chardonnay 2009 (★★★★, $27
   – but widely available around $15)
Mission Vineyard Selection Chardonnay 2009 (★★★★★, $18)
Montana Marlborough Sauvignon Blanc 2010 (★★★☆, $18
   – but widely available under $10)
Palliser Estate Martinborough Riesling 2008 (★★★★, $16)

Reds
Brightside Nelson Pinot Noir 2009 (★★★☆, $18)
Rua Central Otago Pinot Noir 2009 (★★★★, $25)
Te Mata Estate Woodthorpe Vineyard Merlot/Cabernets 2008 (★★★★, $19)
Vidal Hawke's Bay Merlot/Cabernet Sauvignon 2009 (★★★★☆, $19.95)
Wild South Marlborough Pinot Noir 2009 (★★★☆, $19)

Update on the Wine Glut

Good New Zealand wine has never been cheaper. A 2009 Sauvignon Blanc from Nelson was stacked in one of my local supermarkets this year at $6.99, after an export order went off the rails. Villa Maria's consistently attractive Private Bin wines were snapped up around the country at $8.99.

Murdoch James offered its Martinborough Pinot Gris 2009, bearing *personalised* labels, for $120 per case, plus freight. You could buy a white wine from a fashionable variety and a highly rated wine district, with *your* name emblazoned on the label, for just over $10.

'There are a lot of new labels out there at very cheap prices and some established brands at very cheap prices too,' says a highly regarded Pinot Noir producer. 'These prices are not sustainable. I know how much it costs to make the wine. It is very easy to work the retail price back and figure out that a lot of this wine is being sold way below cost. It is a very good time for the consumer to snap up these bargains...'

Half of the country's wineries haven't raised their prices for at least five years, according to a recent survey by New Zealand Winegrowers. A third – without prompting – said they had *lowered* their prices. Winery failures have been at an all-time high this year, while others are visibly struggling.

Winemakers with long memories recall the early 1980s, when overplanting of vineyards created a wine glut of then-record proportions. Simultaneously, demand for wine was slashed by the 1984 Budget, which almost doubled the sales tax on table wines.

A decision by the giant Cooks/McWilliam's group to unload its surplus stocks set alight a ferocious price war in 1985–86. The government intervened with an offer of up to $10 million to fund a vine-uprooting programme, but the industry's travails resulted in a severe loss of investor confidence and sweeping ownership changes at Montana, Penfolds, Villa Maria/Vidal, Cooks/McWilliam's and Delegat's.

This time around, small-scale producers are the worst hit. Most New Zealand wineries are still making money, according to a survey by Deloitte, the international accounting and consulting firm. But the global economic recession, and the country's bumper 2008 and 2009 harvests, have led to 'a clear downward profitability trend'. The survey also noted fast-rising debt levels.

Most at risk are small – but not tiny – wineries, with an average annual output of 20,000 cases and turnover of $1 million to $5 million. Last year, before tax, they averaged a 6.7 per cent *loss*.

The crisis for small producers is described vividly by Deloitte. 'Translating total revenue into a 12-bottle case and tying this back to profit per case, the two largest companies [in the survey] get to keep approximately two of their 12 bottles as profit, the $0–$1 million and $5 million–$10 million categories can enjoy approximately one of their 12 bottles as profit, while the $1 million–$5 million category has to go and buy an additional bottle and give it away.'

Smallish wineries are no longer Ma and Pa outfits, but they lack any major economies of scale. During the 2009 financial year, their average revenue per case plummeted from $153 to $99. Now, with the value of their wine stocks and vineyard land falling, bankers are losing confidence in those producers who cannot pay their interest bills.

Yet we are drinking more New Zealand wine than ever. Last year, our adult consumption per capita of domestic wine soared to 13.9 litres – well above the previous record of 12.2 litres in 2007. As New Zealand wine gets cheaper and cheaper on the shelves, we buy more of it. Wine imports have plummeted to the lowest level for a decade.

But export prices are falling, too. Receipts hit a lofty $1 billion last year and volumes are still growing, but Mike Spratt, of Destiny Bay, a red-wine producer on Waiheke Island, has pointed out that 'the inflation-adjusted price per litre is on a steady decline. In 2001 that price was $13.40. In 2009, it had dropped by 35 per cent to $8.81, and by July of this year [2010] it had further eroded to $7.25. If this rate continues, by 2025 New Zealand will be shipping over 250 million litres of wine overseas for free.'

Is it time New Zealand's 675 wine producers, until recently focused on relentless growth, slowed down?

For 20 years, New Zealand's wine exports have risen at a compounding annual growth rate of 24 per cent. Between 2009 and 2014, New Zealand Winegrowers predicts that shipments will surge from 113 million litres (equivalent to 12.5 million cases) to 175 million litres (over 19 million cases).

New Zealand 'is cementing its position as a producer of decent quality cheap wine,' says Spratt, who believes the industry has paid a huge price for its success in breaking the $1 billion export barrier. Spratt, who has a doctorate in psychology from the University of California at Berkeley, was previously a senior partner in PricewaterhouseCoopers' global mergers and acquisitions consulting business.

'What attractive wine categories can New Zealand be first in?' he wrote in *New Zealand Winegrower*. 'The answer is not Sauvignon Blanc that tastes grassy. New Zealand might lead in making that wine, but it is not a financially attractive category. It has limited price elasticity, is not regarded as a premium variety that commands lofty prices, and New Zealand is ill-equipped to be the low-cost producer.'

Spratt believes that New Zealand, as a small-scale producer, should shift its focus to the top end of the world's wine markets. 'New Zealand should be the leader in penetrating prestigious restaurants and in cultivating relationships with influential writers. ... This is a far more sensible investment of marketing resources than convention centre shows for high-volume distribution outlets.'

The global marketing strategy of New Zealand Winegrowers is designed to 'meet the requirements of small, medium and large wineries' by mounting promotions that support restaurants, independent retailers and multiple retailers. Last year, promotions were organised with groups of top restaurants in the UK, US and Japan. In Australia, blind tastings of New Zealand wines, with international benchmarks, were organised for sommeliers.

Chris Yorke, global marketing director of New Zealand Winegrowers, agrees with Mike Spratt that New Zealand is not suited to the profitable production of low-priced wine. In Australia, Yorke points out, New Zealand wine trades at an average price premium of 35 per cent, and in UK off-licence retailers, New Zealand's white wines sell for 40 per cent more than the average price.

Yorke defends New Zealand Winegrowers' marketing activities on the grounds that over 250 wineries, accounting for more than 95 per cent of exports, support them. 'The predominantly user-pays system of funding ... means that our programme has to be a cost-effective use of a winery's scarce marketing dollars. Where it is, wineries will join; where it is not, they won't.'

Has the recent heavy discounting of Marlborough Sauvignon Blanc hurt New Zealand's wine image? 'New Zealand has bastardised its reputation in the UK in the past year,' reports wine importer David Gleave, of Liberty Wines.

Some argue that the recent tidal wave of low-price Kiwi Sauvignon Blanc has not hurt the sales of established, higher-priced brands. Consumers buying the cheap stuff don't care where the wine comes from; they just want a bargain.

In the UK, New Zealand has staked out a profitable territory in the middle–upper price categories, achieving good volume sales while preserving profitable prices. A future challenge will be to fend off other, fast-improving Sauvignon Blanc producers, notably Chile and South Africa.

Exports of bulk wine are a more pressing concern. Over the past two years, of the total growth in wine exports of 40 million litres, bulk wine accounted for 30 million litres.

'That means 75 per cent of New Zealand's wine export growth has been in bulk wine,' says Philip Gregan, CEO of New Zealand Winegrowers. 'We have handed control or are in the process of handing control over to the buyers of that bulk wine and, in Australia and the UK, those buyers are largely supermarkets. We are in the process of turning supermarkets from our very important customers into our competitors.'

Should bulk wine exports be banned? Gregan says no. 'The government just wouldn't do it.' And if the surplus wine couldn't be exported in bulk, it would end up flooding the domestic market.

David Cox, Europe director for New Zealand Winegrowers, like Mike Spratt has called on the industry to reinvent its wine brand. Cox favours the 'masstige' approach, where you 'take a prestige brand and make it available to the greater mass market through distribution points, but without going into commodity areas.'

That would position New Zealand as a sort of BMW of the wine world – or maybe the Jack Daniel's.

Five small wineries recently formed a marketing alliance, The Specialist Winegrowers of New Zealand, in a bid to 'escape the commodity trap'. Most wineries, to attract as many customers as possible, produce a diverse array of wines – but not those in TSWNZ. 'We are true specialists,' says Nick Nobilo, of Vinoptima, 'intent on making the very best wine from our one chosen variety or style, which has led each of us to a level of dedication that borders on the obsessive.'

The gang of five includes two producers who focus exclusively on a single grape variety (Vinoptima, a Gisborne-based Gewürztraminer specialist; and The Hay Paddock, committed to Syrah, grown on Waiheke Island); two producers who specialise in a single style (Destiny Bay, also on the island, with Bordeaux-style reds; and No. 1 Family Estate, Daniel Le Brun's Marlborough-based bubbly venture); and

Wooing Tree, one of the best Pinot Noir producers in Central Otago.

Gerry Brownlee, Minister for Economic Development, this year announced a government plan to boost wine exports, including $1.2 million backing for an initiative to push high-end wine into the US. At promotions in New York, San Francisco and Chicago, Pinot Noir will lead the charge. Project chairman Steve Smith, of Craggy Range, says: 'We have given ourselves two years to convince the sommeliers, wine buyers, collectors and media that New Zealand makes some of the finest wines in the world.'

The 21 wineries in the initiative will match the government's financial contribution. The selected producers were able to convince a panel that they had enough time and money to put into the US market, had existing distribution channels, and were champions of 'must have' regions or wine styles.

Setting out to seduce America's finest palates are: Kumeu River (Auckland); Vinoptima (Gisborne); Craggy Range, Trinity Hill (Hawke's Bay); Ata Rangi, Escarpment, Palliser (Martinborough); Neudorf (Nelson); Cloudy Bay, Nautilus, Saint Clair, Seresin, Spy Valley, Vavasour, Villa Maria (Marlborough); Muddy Water, Pegasus Bay (Waipara); and Amisfield, Felton Road, Mt Difficulty and Quartz Reef (Central Otago).

Philip Gregan believes the industry has the potential to double the value of its exports over the next decade, from $1 billion to $2 billion. He believes the current tough times will last for another two or three years, but from 2013 onwards, the outlook is rosier. The plan is to maintain the industry's current production base of 33,000 hectares of vineyards, while stimulating greater demand for New Zealand wine in northern Europe, Asia and the US.

'The wines are getting better as far as I can see,' says one of Marlborough's top boutique producers. 'As long as we work hard, demand versus supply will eventually balance itself. It is just a matter of who will be around when it does!'

Classic Wines of New Zealand

A crop of one new Super Classic (Forrest Estate Botrytised Riesling), six new Classics and 27 Potential Classics are the features of this year's revised list of New Zealand wine classics.

What is a New Zealand wine classic? It is a wine that in quality terms consistently ranks in the very forefront of its class. To qualify for selection, each label must have achieved an outstanding level of quality for at least three vintages; there are no flashes in the pan here.

By identifying New Zealand wine classics, my aim is to transcend the inconsistencies of individual vintages and wine competition results, and highlight consistency of excellence. When introducing the elite category of Super Classics, I restricted entry to wines which have achieved brilliance in at least five vintages (compared to three for Classic status). The Super Classics are all highly prestigious wines, with a proven ability to mature well (even the Sauvignon Blancs, compared to other examples of the variety).

The Potential Classics are the pool from which future Classics will emerge. These are wines of outstanding quality which look likely, if their current standards are maintained or improved, to qualify after another vintage or two for elevation to Classic status. All the additions and elevations on this year's list are identified by an asterisk.

An in-depth discussion of New Zealand's greatest wines (what they taste like, how well they mature, the secrets of their success) can be found in the second edition of my book, *Classic Wines of New Zealand* (Hodder Moa, 2005), which grew out of the *Buyer's Guide*'s annually updated list of New Zealand wine classics.

Super Classics

Branded and Other White Wines
Cloudy Bay Te Koko

Chardonnay
Ata Rangi Craighall; Clearview Reserve; Clos de Ste Anne Naboth's Vineyard; Kumeu River Estate; Kumeu River Mate's Vineyard; Neudorf Moutere; Sacred Hill Riflemans; Te Mata Elston

Gewürztraminer
Dry River; Lawson's Dry Hills Marlborough

Pinot Gris
Dry River

Riesling
Dry River Craighall Vineyard; Felton Road; Pegasus Bay

Sauvignon Blanc
Cloudy Bay; Palliser Estate; Saint Clair Wairau Reserve; Seresin Marlborough

Sweet Whites
Dry River Late Harvest Craighall Riesling; ***Forrest Estate Botrytised Riesling; Villa Maria Reserve Noble Riesling

Branded and Other Red Wines
Esk Valley The Terraces; Goldwater Goldie; Stonyridge Larose Cabernets; Te Mata Coleraine

Merlot
Esk Valley Reserve Merlot-predominant blend

Pinot Noir
Ata Rangi; Dry River; Martinborough Vineyard; Pegasus Bay; Villa Maria Reserve Marlborough

Syrah
Te Mata Estate Bullnose

Classics

Chardonnay
Babich Irongate; Church Road Reserve; Cloudy Bay; Dog Point Vineyard; Dry River; Esk Valley Reserve [Winemakers]; Fromm Clayvin Vineyard; Martinborough Vineyard; [Ormond Estate] Montana 'O' Ormond; Pegasus Bay; Seresin Reserve; Stonecroft Hawke's Bay; Te Whau Vineyard Waiheke Island; Vidal Reserve; Villa Maria Reserve Barrique Fermented Gisborne; Villa Maria Reserve Marlborough

Chenin Blanc
Millton Te Arai Vineyard

Gewürztraminer
Johanneshof Marlborough; Stonecroft Old Vine

Pinot Gris
Martinborough Vineyard; Villa Maria Single Vineyard Seddon

Sauvignon Blanc
Lawson's Dry Hills Marlborough; **[Ormond Estate] Montana 'B' Brancott Marlborough; Nga Waka; **Staete Landt Marlborough; Te Mata Cape Crest; Villa Maria Reserve Clifford Bay; Villa Maria Reserve Wairau Valley

Sweet Whites
Forrest Estate Botrytised Riesling; Glazebrook Regional Reserve Noble Harvest Riesling

Bottle-fermented Sparklings
Deutz Marlborough Cuvée Blanc de Blancs; Deutz Marlborough Cuvée Brut NV; Nautilus Cuvée Marlborough; Pelorus

Branded and Other Red Wines
Babich The Patriarch; Craggy Range Le Sol; Newton Forrest Cornerstone; Unison Selection

***New Super Classic **New Classic

Cabernet Sauvignon-predominant Reds
Brookfields Reserve Vintage ['Gold Label'] Cabernet/Merlot; Te Mata Estate Cabernets/Merlot; Villa Maria Reserve Hawke's Bay Cabernet Sauvignon/Merlot

Merlot
**Sacred Hill Brokenstone; Vidal Reserve Hawke's Bay Merlot/Cabernet Sauvignon; **Villa Maria Cellar Selection Hawke's Bay Merlot/Cabernet Sauvignon; Villa Maria Reserve Hawke's Bay

Pinot Noir
Felton Road Block 3; **Felton Road Block 5; **Fromm Clayvin Vineyard; Gibbston Valley Reserve; Greenhough Hope Vineyard; Neudorf Moutere; Neudorf Moutere Home Vineyard; Palliser Estate; Wither Hills Marlborough

Syrah
Mills Reef Elspeth; Passage Rock Reserve; Stonecroft

Potential Classics

Branded and Other White Wines
Craggy Range Les Beaux Cailloux

Chardonnay
Corbans Cottage Block Hawke's Bay; Mission Jewelstone; Ngatarawa Alwyn; Odyssey Reserve Iliad; *Spy Valley Envoy Marlborough; Te Awa; Trinity Hill Hawke's Bay [Black Label]; Villa Maria Single Vineyard Keltern

Gewürztraminer
Cloudy Bay; Villa Maria Single Vineyard Ihumatao; Vinoptima Ormond Reserve

Pinot Gris
*Blackenbrook Vineyard Nelson; Escarpment Martinborough

Riesling
Carrick Josephine Central Otago; Framingham Classic; Muddy Water Growers' Series James Hardwick Waipara; Neudorf Moutere; *Rippon

Sauvignon Blanc
Astrolabe Voyage Marlborough; Clifford Bay Awatere Valley Marlborough; Clos Henri Marlborough; Greenhough Nelson; Highfield Marlborough; *Jackson Estate Stich Marlborough *Vavasour Awatere; Whitehaven Marlborough; *Wither Hills Single Vineyard Rarangi

Viognier
Clos de Ste Anne Les Arbres; Trinity Hill Gimblett Gravels; Villa Maria Single Vineyard Omahu Gravels Vineyard

**New Classic *New Potential Classic

Sweet White Wines
Cloudy Bay Late Harvest Riesling; Ngatarawa Alwyn Winemaker's Reserve Noble Harvest Riesling; *Pegasus Bay Aria Late Harvest Riesling

Bottle-fermented Sparklings
Quartz Reef Méthode Traditionnelle Vintage

Rosé
Esk Valley Merlot/Malbec Rosé

Branded and Other Red Wines
*Alluviale; Benfield & Delamare; Clearview Enigma; *Clearview Old Olive Block; *Clearview The Basket Press; Craggy Range Sophia; Craggy Range The Quarry; *Obsidian; Puriri Hills Reserve; Te Awa Boundary; Tom; *Trinity Hill The Gimblett

Cabernet Sauvignon-predominant Reds
*Babich Irongate Cabernet/Merlot/Franc; *Church Road Reserve Hawke's Bay Cabernet/Merlot; Mills Reef Elspeth Cabernet/Merlot; Mills Reef Elspeth Cabernet Sauvignon; Sacred Hill Helmsman Cabernet/Merlot

Malbec
*Stonyridge Luna Negra

Merlot
*Craggy Range Gimblett Gravels; Hans Herzog Spirit of Marlborough Merlot/Cabernet Sauvignon; *Ngatarawa Alwyn Merlot/Cabernet; *Providence Private Reserve Merlot/Cabernet Franc/Malbec; *Vidal Hawke's Bay Merlot/Cabernet Sauvignon

Montepulciano
Hans Herzog Marlborough

Pinot Noir
*Akarua Reserve; *Amisfield Central Otago; Bannock Brae Barrel Selection; *Bell Hill; Carrick Central Otago; Dog Point Vineyard Marlborough; *Felton Road Central Otago; Hans Herzog Marlborough; Kaituna Valley The Kaituna Vineyard Canterbury; *Mondillo Central Otago; Mt Difficulty Single Vineyard Pipeclay Terrace; Muddy Water Slowhand; Olssen's Slapjack Creek; Pegasus Bay Prima Donna; Peregrine Central Otago; Pisa Range Estate Black Poplar Block; Quartz Reef Bendigo Estate Vineyard; Quartz Reef Central Otago; Terravin Hillside Reserve; Villa Maria Cellar Selection Marlborough; Villa Maria Single Vineyard Seddon; *Wooing Tree Central Otago

Syrah
Bilancia La Collina; *Church Road Reserve Hawke's Bay; Craggy Range Gimblett Gravels Vineyard; *Kennedy Point; Passage Rock; *Stonyridge Pilgrim Syrah/Mourvedre/Grenache; Trinity Hill Homage; Vidal Reserve

New Potential Classic

The following wines are not at the very forefront in quality terms, yet have been produced for many vintages, are extremely widely available and typically deliver good to excellent quality and value. They are all benchmark wines of their type – a sort of Everyman's classic.

Chardonnay
Church Road Hawke's Bay;
Stoneleigh Marlborough

Gewürztraminer
Seifried Nelson

Riesling
Seifried Nelson

Sauvignon Blanc
Montana Marlborough; Oyster Bay Marlborough; Shingle Peak Marlborough; Stoneleigh Marlborough; Villa Maria Private Bin Marlborough

Sparkling
Lindauer Brut; Lindauer Special Reserve

Merlot
Church Road Hawke's Bay
Merlot/Cabernet

Pinot Noir
Villa Maria Private Bin Marlborough

Cellar Sense

Someone gives you a good bottle of Chardonnay, Riesling, Pinot Noir or Merlot, but it's only a year or two old. Should you drink it or cellar it?

Surveys show that most wine in New Zealand is drunk on the day it is bought and only 1 per cent is cellared for more than a year. Everyone relishes the idea of a personal wine cellar, packed with vintage wines maturing slowly to their peak – but few of us actually do it. Instead, it's three or four bottles in a little rack perched on top of the fridge.

To enjoy many wines at the peak of their powers, you do need to lay them down. Some people keep wine far too long. They *worship* their famous bottles, picking them up from time to time, fondling them, talking about them, but they never get around to opening them – until they are well past their best.

A friend called me over a few years ago to sort out his cellar, acquired in a burst of enthusiasm 20 years earlier. His interest in wine later faded and the bottles had been lying under his house ever since. 'Bring a corkscrew. I can't find mine any more.'

It was hard going. After several bottles, it was clear that most New Zealand wines don't repay keeping for 20 or 30 years. Nor do most of the world's wines. But another tasting revealed that good New Zealand wines can certainly mature well for a decade.

Opened five years ago, 22 highly rated whites from the 1990 to 1994 vintages, although stored in an uncomfortably hot office, yielded some delicious surprises. Most were still alive, nine were enjoyable and four were magical: Matua Valley Reserve Sauvignon Blanc 1994, grown in West Auckland; Neudorf Moutere Riesling 1994; Dry River Craighall Estate Riesling 1994, from Martinborough; and Dry River Gewürztraminer 1994.

The oldest New Zealand wine I've ever tasted was McWilliam's Hawke's Bay Cabernet Sauvignon 1965. I snapped up a bottle for $20 at an auction several years ago, knowing that the wine once acclaimed as New Zealand's greatest-ever red would be well past its best. A mellow, faded conversation-piece, it was still alive – just.

Others have had more exciting experiences. In 1892, William Beetham planted a 1.2-hectare vineyard at Masterton, mostly in Pinot Noir, Pinot Meunier and Syrah. In 1985, Beetham's descendants broached a rare bottle of his Lansdowne Claret 1903. Geoff Kelly, then the wine columnist for *National Business Review*, enthused that the 82-year-old wine was 'alive and well ... with the oak standing firm, yet amazing fruit, body and freshness for the age. The finish is superb, long and lingering.'

For my book, *Classic Wines of New Zealand* (second edition 2005), I conducted vertical tastings of over 100 of New Zealand's top wines. In a vertical tasting, several – perhaps all – vintages of a wine are tasted side by side, allowing you to assess the overall quality of a wine, the evolution of its style, the impact of vintage variation and its maturation potential.

One insight from the tastings was that the best South Island Chardonnays age just as well as those from the most prestigious Chardonnay region – Hawke's Bay. Fromm Clayvin Vineyard Chardonnay, from Marlborough, and Neudorf Moutere

Chardonnay, from Nelson, blossom in the bottle for a minimum of five years – every bit as long as such Hawke's Bay classics as Te Mata Elston Chardonnay and Sacred Hill Riflemans Chardonnay.

Another trend in the Chardonnay section was for the wines from cooler vintages to mature better than those from warmer seasons. Crisp, firmly structured Chardonnays may be less seductive in their youth than fleshy, soft models, but they often perform better over the long haul.

Central Otago winemakers sent me a dozen of their 2002 vintage Pinot Noirs to assess, when the wines were more than five years old. How well had they matured?

Overall, pretty well. All of the wines were alive and most were attractive, showing good, bottle-aged complexity. Whether the wines were more enjoyable then than when they were released four years earlier was a matter of debate. Many drinkers enjoy Pinot Noir in its youth, with garden-fresh, vibrant fruit flavours to the fore, while others prefer the savoury, mellow notes that come with maturity.

So which wines most repay cellaring? First, forget the idea that all wines improve with age. Many New Zealand wines are best drunk young.

I suggest drinking fine-quality New Zealand Sauvignon Blancs at six months to two years old. The good news is that screwcaps are preserving the wines' freshness markedly better than corks did, so that Sauvignon Blancs that are several years old can still offer pleasure. Sauvignon Blancs bottled with corks typically tasted past their best before they reached two years old.

Most Pinot Gris, Gewürztraminers and Viogniers are at their best between one and three years old; fine-quality Chardonnays at two to five years old; and top Rieslings at three to seven years old. Some outstanding examples will flourish for longer, but if you buy a case, it pays to check regularly.

Pinot Noirs and Merlots typically drink well at two to five years old. No one knows yet how well Syrah, the hot new red-wine variety, will mature, but the best should reward cellaring for five to 10 years. The top Cabernet/Merlot blends from Hawke's Bay and Waiheke Island are still the safest bet for long-term cellaring.

Cellaring Guidelines

Grape variety	Best age to open

White
Sauvignon Blanc

(non-wooded)	6–24 months
(wooded)	1–3 years
Gewürztraminer	1–3 years
Viognier	1–3 years
Pinot Gris	1–4 years
Sémillon	1–4 years
Chenin Blanc	1–5 years
Chardonnay	2–5 years
Riesling	2–7+ years

Red

Pinotage	1–3 years
Malbec	1–3 years
Cabernet Franc	2–5 years
Merlot	2–5+ years
Pinot Noir	2–5+ years
Syrah	2–5+ years
Cabernet Sauvignon	3–7+ years
Cabernet/Merlot	3–7+ years

Other

Sweet whites	2–5 years
Bottle-fermented sparklings	
(vintage-dated)	3–5+ years

How to Use this Book

It is essential to read this brief section to understand how the book works. Feel free to skip any of the other preliminary pages, but not these.

The majority of wines have been listed in the book according to their principal grape variety, as shown on the front label. Lawson's Dry Hills Marlborough Sauvignon Blanc, for instance, can be located simply by turning to the Sauvignon Blanc section. Wines with front labels that do not refer clearly to a grape variety or blend of grapes, such as Cloudy Bay Te Koko or Tom, can be found in the Branded and Other Wines sections for white and red wines.

Most entries are firstly identified by their producer's names. Wines not usually called by their producer's name, such as Drylands Marlborough Sauvignon Blanc (from Constellation New Zealand), or Triplebank Awatere Valley Marlborough Pinot Noir (from Pernod Ricard NZ), are listed under their most common name.

The star ratings for quality reflect my own opinions, formed where possible by tasting a wine over several vintages, and often a particular vintage several times. *The star ratings are therefore a guide to each wine's overall standard in recent vintages*, rather than simply the quality of the latest release. However, to enhance the usefulness of the book, in the body of the text I have also given a *quality rating for the latest vintage of each wine*; sometimes for more than one vintage. (Since April 2010 wineries have been able to buy stickers to attach to their bottles, based on these ratings.)

I hope the star ratings give interesting food for thought and succeed in introducing you to a galaxy of little-known but worthwhile wines. It pays to remember, however, that wine-tasting is a business fraught with subjectivity. You should always treat the views expressed in these pages for what they are – one person's opinion. The quality ratings are:

★★★★★	Outstanding quality (gold medal standard)
★★★★☆	Excellent quality, verging on outstanding
★★★★	Excellent quality (silver medal standard)
★★★☆	Very good quality
★★★	Good quality (bronze medal standard)
★★☆	Average quality
★★	Plain
★	Poor
No star	To be avoided

These quality ratings are based on comparative assessments of New Zealand wines against one another. A five-star Merlot/Cabernet Sauvignon, for instance, is an outstanding-quality red judged by the standards of other Merlot/Cabernet Sauvignon blends made in New Zealand. It is not judged by the standards of overseas reds of a similar style (for instance Bordeaux), because the book is focused solely on New Zealand wines and their relative merits. (Some familiar New Zealand wine brands in recent years have included varying proportions of overseas wine. To be featured in this book, they must still include at least some New Zealand wine in the blend.)

Where brackets enclose the star rating on the right-hand side of the page, for example (★★★), this indicates the assessment is only tentative, because I have tasted very few vintages of the wine. A dash is used in the relatively few cases where a wine's quality has oscillated over and above normal vintage variations (for example ★–★★★).

Super Classic wines, Classic wines and Potential Classic wines (see page 21) are highlighted in the text by the following symbols:

Super Classic	Classic	Potential Classic

Each wine has also been given a dryness-sweetness, price and value-for-money rating. The precise levels of sweetness indicated by the four ratings are:

DRY	Less than 5 grams/litre of sugar
MED/DRY	5–14 grams/litre of sugar
MED	15–49 grams/litre of sugar
SW	50 and over grams/litre of sugar

Less than 5 grams of sugar per litre is virtually imperceptible to most palates – the wine tastes fully dry. With between 5 and 14 grams, a wine has a hint of sweetness, although a high level of acidity (as in Rieslings or even Marlborough Sauvignon Blancs, which often have 4 to 6 grams per litre of sugar) reduces the perception of sweetness. Where a wine harbours over 15 grams, the sweetness is clearly in evidence. At above 50 grams per litre, a wine is unabashedly sweet.

Prices shown are based on the average price in a supermarket or wine shop (as indicated by the producer), except where most of the wine is sold directly to consumers from the winery, either over the vineyard counter or via mail order or the Internet.

The art of wine buying involves more than discovering top-quality wines. The real challenge – and the greatest satisfaction – lies in identifying wines at varying quality levels that deliver outstanding value for money. The symbols I have used are self-explanatory:

–V	=	Below average value
AV	=	Average value
V+	=	Above average value

The ratings discussed thus far are all my own. Many of the wine producers themselves, however, have also contributed individual vintage ratings of their own top wines over the past decade and the 'When to drink' recommendations. (The symbol **WR** indicates Winemaker's Rating, and the symbol **NM** alongside a vintage means the wine was not made that year.) Only the producers have such detailed knowledge of the relative quality of all their recent vintages (although in some cases, when the information was not forthcoming, I have rated a vintage myself). The key point you must note is that *each producer has rated each vintage of each wine against his or her highest quality aspirations for that particular label, not against any absolute standard*. Thus, a 7 out of 7 score merely indicates that the producer considers that particular vintage to be an outstanding example of that particular wine; not that it is the best-quality wine he or she makes.

The 'When to drink' (**Drink**) recommendations (which I find myself referring to constantly) are largely self-explanatory. The **P** symbol for PEAKED means that a particular vintage is already at, or has passed, its peak; no further benefits are expected from aging.

Here is an example of how the ratings work:

Kumeu River Estate Chardonnay ★★★★★

This wine now ranks fourth in the company's hierarchy of five Chardonnays, after three single-vineyard labels, but is still outstanding. Grown at Kumeu, in West Auckland, it is powerful, with rich, beautifully interwoven flavours and a seductively creamy texture, but it also has good acid spine. The key to its quality lies in the vineyards, says wine-maker Michael Brajkovich: 'We manage to get the grapes very ripe.' Grown in several blocks around Kumeu, hand-picked, fermented with indigenous yeasts and lees-aged (with weekly or twice-weekly lees-stirring) in Burgundy oak barriques (typically 25 per cent new), the wine also normally undergoes a full malolactic fermentation. Tasted in April 2010, the 2006 vintage (★★★★★) is probably currently at its peak, while the 2007 (★★★★★) is still developing. The 2008 vintage (★★★★★) is very open and expressive. Weighty and rich, showing lovely fruit sweetness, it offers highly concentrated stone-fruit flavours with finely integrated oak and fresh, appetising acidity. Peachy and mealy, with a hint of butterscotch, it's a lush, generous wine, already delicious.

Vintage	08	07	06	05	04	03	02	DRY $36 AV
WR	6	7	7	7	7	6	7	
Drink	10-14	10-14	10-13	P	P	P	P	

The winemaker's own ratings indicate that the 2008 vintage is of excellent quality for the label, and is recommended for drinking between 2010 and 2014.

Describes 'Classic' status, ranging from 🍇🍇🍇 for Super Classic, 🍇🍇 for Classic to 🍇 for Potential Classic. This is a wine that in quality terms ranks in the forefront of its class.

Dryness-sweetness rating, price and value for money. This wine is dry in style (below 5 grams/litre of sugar). At $36 it is average value for money.

Quality rating, ranging from ★★★★★ for outstanding to no star (–), to be avoided. This is generally a wine of outstanding quality.

White Wines

Arneis

Still rare here – so rare it is not listed separately in *New Zealand Winegrowers Statistical Annual 2009* – Arneis (pronounce the 'neis' as in 'place') is a traditional grape of Piedmont, in north-west Italy, where it yields soft, early-maturing wines with slightly herbaceous aromas and almond flavours. First planted in New Zealand in the late 1990s at the Clevedon Hills vineyard in South Auckland, its potential is now being explored by Pernod Ricard NZ, Trinity Hill and several other producers. Coopers Creek released the country's first varietal Arneis from the 2006 vintage.

Clevedon Hills Arneis ★★★☆

Estate-grown in South Auckland, the 2008 vintage (★★★) is full-bodied and dry, with ripe, citrusy, slightly spicy flavours, showing good depth. The more powerful 2009 (★★★★☆) is a big step up, showing excellent freshness and concentration. Attractively scented, it is fleshy and vibrantly fruity, with rich, peachy, spicy flavours, a hint of pineapple, and a dry, rounded finish. Delicious drinking from now onwards.

DRY $30 –V

Coopers Creek SV Gisborne Arneis The Little Rascal ★★★★

Who would have thought Arneis would perform so well in Gisborne? The 2009 vintage (★★★★) is scented and gently sweet (6 grams/litre of residual sugar), with mouthfilling body, strong, peachy, spicy, vaguely nutty flavours, a slightly oily texture and a well-rounded finish.

Vintage	09	08
WR	5	6
Drink	10-13	10-12

MED/DRY $20 V+

Doctors', The, Marlborough Arneis ★★★★

The 2009 vintage (★★★★) from Forrest is floral, fresh and full-bodied, with a basket of ripe fruit flavours, suggestive of peaches, pears and spices. Off-dry (5 grams/litre of residual sugar), it shows excellent depth. The 2010 (★★★★) is weighty, fleshy and rounded, with ripe, citrusy, spicy flavours showing very good depth. A dryish wine, it's already drinking well.

Vintage	09
WR	5
Drink	11-15

MED/DRY $25 AV

Matawhero Gisborne Arneis (★★★★)

Fleshy and smooth, the debut 2009 vintage (★★★★) was harvested in the Bell vineyard, at Hexton, at a ripe 24.2 brix. Delicious young, it's a high-alcohol style (over 14 per cent) with good concentration of peach, pear and lychee flavours, a hint of herbs and a dryish, finely textured finish.

MED/DRY $30 –V

Montana Showcase Series Gisborne Arneis (★★★★)
The debut 2008 vintage (★★★★), grown at Patutahi, is a distinctive wine with lemon, apple and spice aromas. Fleshy and slightly minerally, with a dry feel and excellent flavour depth, it is reminiscent of Italian Arneis and a good all-purpose wine.

DRY $24 AV

Trinity Hill Hawke's Bay Arneis ★★★★
A consistently good buy. The 2009 vintage (★★★★) was estate-grown and hand-harvested in the Gimblett Gravels, and fermented in tanks and old barrels. The bouquet is fresh, lifted and strongly varietal; the palate is mouthfilling, with ripe pineapple, herb and spice flavours, and an appetisingly crisp, dry finish.

DRY $20 V+

Villa Maria Cellar Selection Hawke's Bay Arneis (★★★★)
The debut 2010 vintage (★★★★) was hand-picked at three sites and matured on its yeast lees in tanks for two months. Highly fragrant, it is mouthfilling, with fresh, ripe tropical-fruit and spice flavours, and a finely poised, bone-dry finish.

Vintage	10
WR	6
Drink	10-12

DRY $24 AV

Branded and Other White Wines

Cloudy Bay Te Koko, Craggy Range Les Beaux Cailloux, Dog Point Vineyard Section 94 – in this section you'll find all the white wines that don't feature varietal names. Lower-priced branded white wines can give winemakers an outlet for grapes like Chenin Blanc, Sémillon and Riesling that otherwise can be hard to sell. They can also be an outlet for coarser, less delicate juice ('pressings'). Some of the branded whites are quaffers, but others are highly distinguished.

Alluviale Blanc ★★★☆

Weighty and restrained, the 2009 vintage (★★★☆) was grown at Mangatahi, in Hawke's Bay. A blend of Sauvignon Blanc (93 per cent) and Sémillon (7 per cent), partly French oak-fermented, it is ripely scented and mouthfilling, with tropical-fruit flavours, gently seasoned with biscuity oak, and a crisp, dry finish. Very fresh and tightly structured, it needs time; open mid-2011+.

DRY $24 AV

Alpha Domus The Aviatrix (★★★★)

The 2009 vintage (★★★★) is a blend of Sauvignon Blanc (60 per cent), Chardonnay (27 per cent) and Viognier (13 per cent). Estate-grown in Hawke's Bay and fermented in tanks (60 per cent) and new French oak barrels (40 per cent), it's a skilfully crafted wine, mouthfilling, peachy and smooth, with fresh, ripe, vibrant fruit flavours to the fore and complexity from barrel fermentation and lees-aging. Fleshy and harmonious, it's immediately appealing.

Vintage	09
WR	6
Drink	10-15

DRY $23 V+

Artisan Betty Davis ★★★☆

Grown in the Tara Vineyard at Oratia, in West Auckland, the 2008 vintage (★★★☆) is a barrel-fermented blend of Pinot Gris (85 per cent) and Viognier (15 per cent). Softly mouthfilling, it's a straw-coloured wine with ripe sweet-fruit flavours of peaches, apricots and spices, and very good depth. Drink now to 2011.

DRY $25 –V

Bellbird Spring Home Block White ★★★★

Showing greater complexity than most young aromatic whites, the 2009 vintage (★★★★) is a single-vineyard, Waipara blend of Pinot Gris, Riesling, Muscat and Gewürztraminer, hand-picked and fermented and lees-aged in old oak barriques. Instantly attractive, it's a weighty, distinctly medium style (32 grams/litre of residual sugar), highly perfumed and full of personality, with rich, peachy, citrusy, spicy flavours, showing excellent concentration, complexity and charm, and a deliciously soft finish.

MED $31 –V

Clearview Endeavour (★★★★★)

New Zealand's most expensive white wine is estate-grown at Te Awanga, in Hawke's Bay, and bottled in magnums. Hand-picked from 24-year-old vines and matured for two and a half years in new French oak casks, the 2007 vintage (tasted prior to bottling, and so not rated) is a richly fragrant, powerful wine, sweet-fruited, with highly concentrated flavours of grapefruit, peach and nectarine, and a biscuity, mealy complexity. It should be long-lived.

Vintage	07
WR	7
Drink	12-15

DRY $250 (1.5L) –V

Cloudy Bay Te Koko ★★★★★

Te Koko o Kupe ('The oyster dredge of Kupe') is the original name for Cloudy Bay; it is also the name of the Marlborough winery's intriguing oak-aged Sauvignon Blanc. The 2007 vintage (★★★★★) was grown at five sites around the Wairau Valley and harvested at an average of 22.7 to 23.4 brix. Fermented with indigenous yeasts in French oak barrels (less than 10 per cent new, to ensure a subtle oak influence), it was matured in wood on its yeast lees until September 2008, and all the blend went through a softening malolactic fermentation. Delicious now, it is fleshy and rich, with concentrated, ripe tropical-fruit flavours and a dry, well-rounded finish. A very non-herbaceous style, it is finely textured, weighty, sweet-fruited and harmonious. Te Koko lies well outside the mainstream regional style of Sauvignon Blanc but is well worth discovering.

Vintage	07	06	05	04	03
WR	7	7	7	6	6
Drink	11-15	10-13	10-12	P	10-11

DRY $50 AV

Craggy Range Les Beaux Cailloux ★★★★★

Craggy Range's flagship Chardonnay is an unusually complex Hawke's Bay wine with loads of personality and great texture, mouthfeel and depth. Based on low-yielding Gimblett Gravels vines, it is fermented with indigenous yeasts and lees-aged for up to 17 months in French oak barriques (45 per cent new in 2008), with a full, softening malolactic fermentation. The 2008 vintage (★★★★★) is a quietly classy wine, showing real weight and concentration. Powerful (14.5 per cent alcohol), it has an inviting, highly complex, citrusy, mealy bouquet. Creamy textured, with fresh, rich, grapefruit-like flavours seasoned with well-integrated oak, it's still very youthful; open 2012+.

Vintage	08	07
WR	7	7
Drink	11-15	10-14

DRY $60 AV

Dada (★★★★☆)

Labelled simply as 'a blended, dry white wine from New Zealand' but expensive, Dada 1 2007 (★★★★☆) is from a Hawke's Bay producer. It is not labelled as Sauvignon Blanc because that would 'automatically pigeonhole the wine and the benchmark default to Marlborough Sauvignon Blanc'. Full of personality, it is dry, peachy, spicy and slightly toasty, in a complex style with a long finish. Alluviale Blanc (above) is from the same winemakers.

DRY $50 –V

Dog Point Vineyard Section 94 ★★★★☆

Looking for 'texture, rather than rich aromatics', winemaker James Healy and his partner, Ivan Sutherland, fermented and lees-aged their 2008 vintage (★★★★★) Sauvignon Blanc for 18 months in seasoned French oak casks. Hand-picked in Sutherland's Dog Point Vineyard (for which 'Section 94' was the original survey title) and fermented with indigenous yeasts, it's a very elegant, tight, minerally, dry wine with a slightly 'funky' bouquet. Fresh, ripe flavours of grapefruit and guava are gently seasoned with oak, and the wine shows good acid spine, excellent delicacy and length.

Vintage	08	07	06	05	04	03
WR	6	5	6	6	5	6
Drink	10-14	10-13	10-13	10-12	10-11	P

DRY $33 AV

Hans Herzog Marlborough Heavenly Seven (★★★★☆)

The 'glorious, mighty' – according to the back label – 2009 vintage (★★★★☆) is a blend of seven grape varieties, late-harvested, co-fermented and matured for a year in French oak puncheons. The bouquet is fragrant and spicy; the palate is full-bodied and dry, with an array of peachy, citrusy, slightly spicy and honeyed flavours, finely textured and concentrated. Best drinking mid-2011+.

Vintage	09
WR	7
Drink	10-14

DRY $44 –V

John Forrest Collection The White ★★★★

With his uniquely diverse blend, winemaker John Forrest is after a 'full-bodied, dry style with fruit intensity and acid definition, but no excess of wood, malolactic fermentation or sugar'. It is billed as an 'uninhibited' marriage of up to seven grape varieties (Viognier, Sauvignon Blanc, Pinot Gris, Chenin Blanc, Riesling, Chardonnay and Gewürztraminer) drawn from Marlborough, Hawke's Bay, Central Otago and the Waitaki Valley. Building up well with bottle-age, the 2007 (★★★★) was made with 'more Chenin Blanc than usual'. It's a fleshy, full-bodied wine with an array of fruit characters, very good flavour depth and a fresh, smooth finish (7 grams/litre of residual sugar).

Vintage	07	06
WR	6	6
Drink	11-20	11-20

MED/DRY $50 –V

Kaipara Estate Nine Lakes ★★★☆

Estate-grown on the South Head peninsula of the Kaipara Harbour, in Auckland, the 2008 vintage (★★★☆) is a blend of Chardonnay (73 per cent), Pinot Gris (20 per cent), Arneis (5 per cent) and Viognier (2 per cent). Floral and fruity, with fresh flavours of citrus fruits and pears and finely balanced acidity, it could easily be mistaken for a Viognier. The 2007 (★★★☆) is more Chardonnay-like (85 per cent), with lots of ripe, peachy, slightly toasty and buttery flavour, showing some complexity.

DRY $22 AV

Kidnapper Cliffs Hawke's Bay Solan (★★★★)

From Te Awa, the debut 2009 vintage (★★★★) is a blend of Sauvignon Blanc (88 per cent) and 'chalky, slaty' Sémillon (12 per cent), fermented in tanks (56 per cent) and barrels. It's a very youthful wine, weighty, with rich, ripe sweet-fruit flavours of melons and limes, and a tight, dry finish. Open mid-2011+.

DRY $35 –V

Marsden Estate Duo (★★★)

The 2009 vintage (★★★) was made from Flora grapes, grown at Kerikeri, in Northland, and matured for a year in seasoned oak puncheons. Harvested at over 25 brix, it's a fleshy, bone-dry wine with substantial body, lots of peachy, slightly spicy flavour, showing some complexity, and a rounded finish.

Vintage	09
WR	5
Drink	10-12

DRY $20 –V

Millton Les Trois Enfants Clos Monique (★★★★☆)

The 2007 vintage (★★★★☆) is a single-vineyard Gisborne blend of Gewürztraminer, Pinot Gris and Riesling, grown together at Clos Monique, picked together and fermented together. The bouquet is complex, peachy and distinctly spicy; the palate is impressively full and concentrated, with unobtrusive sweetness (12 grams/litre of residual sugar) and fresh acidity. The Gewürztraminer makes its presence well felt, but the blend possesses more weight, richness and complexity than most 'straight' Gewürztraminers, with a lingering, spicy finish. The 2009 is a slightly drier style (7 grams/litre of residual sugar).

Vintage	07
WR	6
Drink	P

MED/DRY $26 V+

Paritua Grace ★★★☆

The 2008 vintage (★★★☆) is a medium-bodied Hawke's Bay blend of Sauvignon Blanc and Sémillon, barrel-fermented and oak-aged for 10 months. Fresh, crisp and minerally, it is slightly creamy and nutty, with very good depth and complexity, firm acid spine and a tight, dry finish.

Vintage	08
WR	7
Drink	10-13

DRY $30 –V

Rippon Vineyard Ralph Hotere White Wine ★★☆
Grown on the shores of Lake Wanaka, in Central Otago, this wine is made 'for summer drinking, not sipping'. Made from Osteiner (a crossing of Riesling and Sylvaner), it typically tastes like a restrained Riesling – tangy, with light body and slightly sweet lemon, apple and lime flavours cut with fresh acidity.

MED/DRY $17 –V

Seresin Chiaroscuro (★★★★☆)
The debut 2007 vintage (★★★★☆) is a full-bodied, finely textured dry blend of 42 per cent Chardonnay (for 'structure'), 32 per cent Pinot Gris (for 'texture'), 19.5 per cent Riesling (for 'fruity acidity') and 6.5 per cent Pinot Meunier ('spicy interest'). Grown organically in the Home Vineyard at Renwick, in Marlborough, the grapes were hand-picked and co-fermented with indigenous yeasts in French oak barriques. Oak-aged for 17 months, and given a full, softening malolactic fermentation, it's a light yellow, peachy, lemony and spicy wine, with complexity, sweet-fruit delights and a faintly buttery, lingering, well-rounded finish.

DRY $60 –V

Terravin Te Ahu ★★★★★
The delicious 2009 vintage (★★★★★) is a single-vineyard Marlborough Sauvignon Blanc, hand-picked on the south side of the Wairau Valley at 24.6 brix and fermented with indigenous yeasts in French oak puncheons. Barrel-aged for nearly a year, it's a 'serious', full-bodied wine with fresh, concentrated flavours of tropical fruits and nuts, showing notable richness and complexity. A powerful wine with a strong presence, it should mature well.

Vintage	09	08	07
WR	7	5	5
Drink	11-15	10-12	11-13

DRY $36 AV

Te Whare Ra Toru ★★★★
This Marlborough blend of three ('toru') varieties – Gewürztraminer, Riesling and Pinot Gris – is hand-picked and tank-fermented. It is typically an attractively perfumed, softly mouthfilling wine with ripe pear, spice and slight ginger flavours, a gentle splash of sweetness, and very good texture, harmony and depth.

MED/DRY $22 V+

Vynfields Peche De Noire (★★★☆)
Estate-grown organically in Martinborough, this dry white is made from Pinot Noir and partly barrel-fermented. The 2009 vintage (★★★☆) is pale pink, with plenty of fresh, peachy, strawberryish, spicy flavour and a hint of apricot, in a crisp, refreshing style.

DRY $26 –V

Waimea Nelson Edel (★★★★)

The 2009 vintage (★★★★) is a seductive blend of three aromatic varieties – Riesling (47 per cent), Pinot Gris (38 per cent) and Gewürztraminer (15 per cent). Mouthfilling and rich, it's a slightly sweet wine with concentrated, peachy, spicy flavours.

Vintage 09
WR 6
Drink 10-12

MED/DRY $22 V+

White Cloud Medium White Wine ★★

From Constellation NZ (formerly Nobilo), this was once a huge seller, here and abroad – a sort of New Zealand version of Blue Nun. However, despite the name 'White Cloud' and a picture of what looks like the Southern Alps on the label, it is sometimes blended from New Zealand and imported wines. It's typically a soft, medium-bodied wine with a distinct splash of sweetness amid its simple, lemony, slightly peachy flavours.

MED $9 AV

White Wire ★★☆

From Mount George, a subsidiary of Paritua, the 2008 vintage (★★★) was made mostly from Gisborne and Hawke's Bay Chardonnay, blended with Gewürztraminer (5 per cent), Riesling (5 per cent) and Sauvignon Blanc (4 per cent). It's a good, easy quaffer, fruity, tasty and smooth (6.5 grams/litre of residual sugar), with citrusy, peachy, slightly spicy flavours.

MED/DRY $15 AV

Wooing Tree Blondie ★★★

This is a *blanc de noir* – a white (or rather faintly pink) Central Otago wine, estate-grown at Cromwell. The 2010 vintage (★★★☆) was made from Pinot Noir grapes; the juice was held briefly in contact with the skins and then fermented in a mix of tanks (30 per cent) and seasoned French oak barrels (70 per cent). Very pale pink, it is fresh, crisp and aromatic, with gentle strawberry, peach and spice flavours, showing a touch of complexity. A good summer thirst-quencher.

DRY $25 –V

Breidecker

A nondescript crossing of Müller-Thurgau and the white hybrid Seibel 7053, Breidecker is rarely seen in New Zealand. There were 32 hectares of bearing vines recorded in 2003, but only 7 hectares in 2010. Its early-ripening ability is an advantage in cooler regions, but Breidecker typically yields light, fresh quaffing wines, best drunk young.

Hunter's Marlborough Breidecker ★★★

A drink-young charmer, 'for those who are new to wine'. Grown in the Wairau Valley, it is floral, fresh, light and lively, with a distinct splash of sweetness (19 grams/litre of residual sugar in 2009), gentle acidity and ripe flavours of lemons and apples. Very easy to gulp.

Vintage	09
WR	5
Drink	P

MED $18 –V

Chardonnay

New Zealand Chardonnay has yet to make the huge international impact of our Sauvignon Blanc. Our top Chardonnays are world class – Sacred Hill Riflemans Chardonnay 2007 was joint winner of the trophy for Best Fuller Bodied Dry White Table Wine at the 2010 Sydney International Wine Competition – but so are those from numerous other countries in the Old and New Worlds. In the year to mid-2010, Chardonnay accounted for 3.7 per cent by volume of New Zealand's wine exports (far behind Sauvignon Blanc, with 82 per cent, and also Pinot Noir with 5.8 per cent).

There's an enormous range to choose from. Most wineries – especially in the North Island and upper South Island – make at least one Chardonnay; many produce several and the big wineries produce dozens. The hallmark of New Zealand Chardonnays is their delicious varietal intensity – the leading labels show notably concentrated aromas and flavours, threaded with fresh, appetising acidity.

Yet Chardonnay is less popular than a few years ago, when it was the country's most prestigious white-wine variety. Sauvignon Blanc now decisively outsells Chardonnay in supermarkets and in restaurants, while Pinot Gris is flying high.

The price of New Zealand Chardonnay ranges from under $10 to $250 (for a magnum of Clearview Endeavour). The quality differences are equally wide, although not always in relation to their prices. Lower-priced wines are typically fermented in stainless steel tanks and bottled young with little or no oak influence; these wines rely on fresh, lemony, uncluttered fruit flavours for their appeal.

Recent vintages have brought a surge of unoaked Chardonnays, as winemakers with an eye on overseas markets strive to showcase New Zealand's fresh, vibrant fruit characters. Without oak flavours to add richness and complexity, Chardonnay handled entirely in stainless steel tanks can be plain – even boring. The key to the style is to use well-ripened, intensely flavoured grapes.

Mid-price wines may be fermented in tanks and matured in oak casks, which adds to their complexity and richness, or fermented and/or matured in a mix of tanks and barrels. The top labels are fully fermented and matured in oak barriques (normally French, with varying proportions of new casks); there may also be extended aging on (and regular stirring of) yeast lees and varying proportions of a secondary, softening malolactic fermentation (sometimes referred to in the tasting notes as 'malo'). The best of these display the arresting subtlety and depth of flavour for which Chardonnay is so highly prized.

Chardonnay plantings have been far outstripped in recent years by Sauvignon Blanc, as wine producers respond to overseas demand, and in 2011 will constitute 12.1 per cent of the bearing vineyard. The variety is spread throughout the wine regions, particularly Hawke's Bay (where 30 per cent of the vines are concentrated), Marlborough (28.1 per cent) and Gisborne (27.6 per cent). Gisborne is renowned for its softly mouthfilling, ripe, peachy Chardonnays, which offer very seductive drinking in their youth; Hawke's Bay yields sturdy wines with rich grapefruit-like flavours, power and longevity; and Marlborough's Chardonnays are slightly leaner in a cool-climate, more appley, appetisingly crisp style.

Chardonnay has often been dubbed 'the red-wine drinker's white wine'. Chardonnays are usually (although not always, especially cheap models) fully dry, as are all reds with any aspirations to quality. Chardonnay's typically mouthfilling body and multi-faceted flavours are another obvious red-wine parallel.

Broaching a top New Zealand Chardonnay at less than two years old can be infanticide – the finest of the 2008s will offer excellent drinking during 2011. If you must drink Chardonnay when it is only a year old, it makes sense to buy one of the cheaper, less complex wines specifically designed to be enjoyable in their youth.

3 Stones Hawke's Bay Unoaked Chardonnay (★★☆)

From Ager Sectus (which also owns Crossroads, The Crossings and Southbank Estate), the 2007 vintage (★★☆) is sturdy and smooth, with plenty of flavour. A solid quaffer, still on the market in 2010, it is now slightly past its best.

Vintage	07
WR	7
Drink	P

DRY $20 –V

Akarua Central Otago Chardonnay ★★★☆

This is consistently one of the region's best Chardonnays. Estate-grown at Bannockburn and fermented and matured in French oak barriques (30 per cent new), the 2008 vintage (★★★☆) is a finely balanced wine, fresh and crisp, with ripe, citrusy, slightly nutty flavours that linger well.

Vintage	08	07	06	05
WR	6	6	6	6
Drink	10-14	10-11	P	P

DRY $27 –V

Ake Ake Chardonnay Reserve (★★★☆)

The 2008 vintage (★★★☆) was hand-picked at Kerikeri, in the Bay of Islands, and fermented and matured in a mix of tanks and new American oak barriques, with weekly lees-stirring. It's a mouthfilling wine with very good depth of fresh, ripe, slightly buttery flavours in a moderately complex style, worth cellaring.

Vintage	08
WR	5
Drink	10-11

DRY $29 –V

Alana Estate Martinborough Chardonnay ★★★★☆

This winery produces consistently stylish Chardonnays that mature well. Hand-harvested and fermented and matured in French oak casks, the 2007 vintage (★★★★☆) has a complex, slightly peachy bouquet. Weighty, with impressively rich stone-fruit flavours, gently seasoned with biscuity oak, it shows good richness, texture and harmony, with a long finish.

Vintage	08	07
WR	5	7
Drink	10-16	10-13

DRY $42 –V

Alexandra Wine Company Feraud's Chardonnay ★★★☆

The 2007 vintage (★★★☆) was grown at Alexandra, in Central Otago. Fermented in French oak casks (20 per cent new), it is weighty and finely textured, with a fragrant, creamy bouquet and lemony, slightly appley and nutty flavours, showing good drive and immediacy.

Vintage	08	07	06
WR	5	6	5
Drink	10-11	P	P

DRY $21 AV

Alexia Hawke's Bay Chardonnay ★★★
The 2009 vintage (★★★) from Jane Cooper, winemaker at Matahiwi Estate, under her own label, is full-bodied, fresh, fruity and smooth, with ripe, peachy flavours offering good, easy drinking.

DRY $20 –V

Allan Scott Marlborough Chardonnay ★★★☆
This label began as a fruit-driven style, but in recent years has shown greater complexity and is now consistently satisfying. Grown at four sites at Rapaura, the 2009 (★★★☆) is a fully barrel-fermented wine (30 per cent new oak), with vibrant, citrusy, peachy flavours to the fore, slightly buttery, toasty notes adding complexity and a smooth, dry finish. It has plenty of drink-young appeal.

Vintage	09	08	07	06	05	04
WR	5	5	6	6	6	6
DRINK	10-14	10-13	10-13	10-12	10-11	P

DRY $22 AV

Allan Scott Wallops Marlborough Chardonnay ★★★★☆
This single-vineyard wine is typically rich, creamy and complex. Barrel-fermented with indigenous yeasts and given a full, softening malolactic fermentation, the 2009 vintage (★★★★☆) is a highly fragrant, full-bodied style with a strong presence. A drink-now or cellaring proposition, it is generous, with concentrated, ripe stone-fruit flavours, buttery, toasty notes adding complexity and a lasting finish.

Vintage	09	08	07
WR	6	7	7
Drink	10-14	10-14	10-13

DRY $30 AV

Alpha Domus AD Chardonnay ★★★★☆
This is a single-vineyard Hawke's Bay wine, hand-picked, fermented with indigenous and cultured yeasts, and lees-aged, with stirring, for 10 months in French oak barriques (55 per cent new in 2007). The 2007 vintage (★★★★☆) – the first since 2004 – is very fragrant, with mouthfilling body and ripe grapefruit and nut flavours, showing excellent delicacy and concentration. A very tightly structured and elegant wine, with good acid spine, it should be long-lived.

Vintage	07	06	05	04
WR	7	NM	NM	7
Drink	10-11	NM	NM	P

DRY $30 AV

Alpha Domus Barrique Fermented Chardonnay ★★★☆
This is the Hawke's Bay winery's middle-tier Chardonnay. Fermented and lees-aged in a 4:1 mix of French and European oak barrels (25 per cent new), the 2009 vintage (★★★) is an upfront, high-flavoured style, peachy and toasty, with substantial body and an ultra-smooth (5.5 grams/litre of residual sugar) finish.

Vintage	09	08	07	06	05
WR	6	7	6	6	6
Drink	10-14	10-13	10-11	P	P

MED/DRY $23 AV

Alpha Domus The Pilot Hawke's Bay Chardonnay (★★☆)

The 'lightly oaked' 2009 vintage (★★☆) is an off-dry style (5 grams/litre of residual sugar) with mouthfilling body and decent depth of peachy, slightly limey and honeyed flavours.

Vintage 09	
WR 6	
Drink 10-13	

MED/DRY $20 –V

Anchorage Nelson Chardonnay ★★★

Estate-grown at Motueka, the 2009 vintage (★★★) is a weighty, creamy, single-vineyard wine, given a full, softening malolactic fermentation. A good drink-young style, it is citrusy and slightly appley, with a hint of toasty oak (French and American), satisfying body and a dry, well-rounded finish.

DRY $19 AV

Anchorage Reserve Chardonnay (★★★☆)

Maturing well, the 2008 vintage (★★★☆) is a Nelson wine, hand-picked from first-crop vines and fermented initially in tanks, then in French oak barrels (100 per cent new). Savoury, with peachy, citrusy, slightly toasty and buttery flavours, and considerable complexity, it shows very good depth.

DRY $22 AV

Anchorage Unoaked Chardonnay ★★☆

From Motueka, the 2009 vintage (★★☆) is a fresh, lively Nelson wine, made without oak or malolactic fermentation. It's a straightforward, fruit-driven wine with lemony, appley flavours, fresh, dry and crisp.

DRY $16 AV

Artisan Kauri Ridge Oratia Chardonnay ★★★★

Grown in the Kauri Ridge Vineyard in West Auckland, the fleshy, rich 2007 vintage (★★★★) was fermented in French oak casks (40 per cent new). Bright, light yellow/green, it is vibrant and sweet-fruited, with excellent depth of ripe grapefruit-like flavours, finely balanced nutty oak and considerable elegance. It's drinking well now.

DRY $25 AV

Ascension The Ascent Reserve Matakana Chardonnay ★★★☆

Estate-grown and barrel-fermented, this is typically a full-bodied wine with ripe, peachy, slightly buttery and nutty flavours, smooth and rich. Mouthfilling and toasty, the 2008 (★★★) is slightly less fresh and vibrant than in top vintages, but shows some mealy complexity.

DRY $35 –V

Ashwell Chardonnay ★★★★

The 2008 vintage (★★★★) is a barrel-fermented Martinborough wine, elegant and youthful, with ripe sweet-fruit characters, citrusy, mealy flavours and a deliciously creamy texture. Drink now or cellar.

Vintage	09	08	07	06
WR	6	6	6	7
Drink	10-15	10-13	10-12	P

DRY $25 AV

Ashwell Martinborough Chardonnay ★★★★

The 2008 (★★★★) is elegant and youthful, with ripe sweet-fruit characters, citrusy, mealy flavours and a deliciously creamy texture. Barrel-fermented, the 2009 vintage (★★★★) is fragrant, with fresh, strong peach, grapefruit and toast flavours, creamy-textured and complex. Drink now or cellar.

Vintage	09	08	07	06
WR	6	6	6	7
Drink	10-15	10-13	10-12	P

DRY $24 V+

Askerne Hawke's Bay Chardonnay ★★★

Estate-grown near Havelock North and fully barrel-fermented, the 2009 vintage (★★★) is mouthfilling, with ripe, citrusy, slightly biscuity and buttery flavours and a smooth finish. It's still youthful.

Vintage	09	08
WR	6	6
Drink	10-13	10-13

DRY $20 –V

Aspire Chardonnay ★★★

From Matariki, this Hawke's Bay wine is estate-grown in the Gimblett Gravels and at Havelock North. It's typically fresh and crisp, with citrusy flavours and a subtle twist of oak – the 2007 vintage (★★★), still on sale, was matured in tanks and seasoned oak barrels. It's a mid-weight style with fresh, ripe, citrusy flavours to the fore, a hint of toasty oak and good depth.

Vintage	07	06
WR	6	6
Drink	10-12	10-11

DRY $20 –V

Astrolabe Voyage Marlborough Chardonnay ★★★★

The 2008 vintage (★★★★) was hand-picked, fermented and matured for 10 months in oak barrels, and given a full, softening malolactic fermentation. It's an elegant, fleshy wine, lemony and buttery, slightly peachy and toasty, with finely balanced acidity and good complexity. It should age well.

Vintage	08	07
WR	6	6
Drink	10-12	10-14

DRY $26 AV

Ataahua Waipara Chardonnay (★★★★)

From vines over 20 years old, the 2009 vintage (★★★★) is a refined, barrel-fermented wine with substantial body, strong, ripe, citrusy fruit flavours, a subtle seasoning of wood (all seasoned French) and fresh acidity. Tight and youthful, very fresh and vibrant, with a slightly oily richness, it should be at its best mid-2011+.

Vintage	09
WR	6
Drink	10-13

DRY $26 AV

Ata Rangi Craighall Chardonnay ★★★★★

This consistently memorable Martinborough wine has notable body, richness, complexity and downright drinkability. Made from a company-owned block of low-yielding, mostly over 20-year-old Mendoza clone vines in the Craighall Vineyard, it is hand-picked, whole-bunch pressed and fully fermented in French oak barriques (typically 25 per cent new). The 2008 (★★★★★) is richly fragrant, sturdy and creamy-textured, with concentrated flavours of stone-fruit, butter and toast. A notably ripe-tasting and well-rounded vintage (akin to the Chardonnay style more often found in Hawke's Bay), it shows real power and richness.

Vintage	08	07	06	05	04	03	02
WR	7	7	7	6	6	7	7
Drink	10-16	10-15	10-12	10-11	P	P	P

DRY $38 AV

Ata Rangi Petrie Chardonnay ★★★★

This single-vineyard wine is grown south of Masterton, in the Wairarapa. It's not in the same class as its Craighall stablemate (above), but the price is lower. It is typically fragrant and creamy, with rich peach and grapefruit characters, a distinct touch of butterscotch and a well-rounded finish. From a top vintage, the 2008 (★★★★☆) was hand-picked and fermented and lees-aged for seven months in French oak barriques (25 per cent new), with 30 per cent malolactic fermentation. It's an elegant, rich wine, slightly creamy, with finely balanced acidity and concentrated, peachy, sweet-fruit flavours. Delicious from the start.

DRY $28 AV

Auntsfield Cob Cottage Marlborough Chardonnay ★★★★

A consistently rewarding wine. Estate-grown on the south side of the Wairau Valley, hand-picked and fermented (partly with indigenous yeasts) in French oak barriques (40 per cent new), the 2008 vintage (★★★★) is full-bodied and youthful, with rich, ripe, peachy, slightly creamy flavours, good texture and obvious cellaring potential.

Vintage	08	07	06	05	04
WR	6	7	7	6	6
Drink	10-16	10-15	10-14	10-13	10-11

DRY $34 –V

Auntsfield Orchard Hill Chardonnay (★★★)

Sold only at the cellar door, the 2008 vintage (★★★) is a fruit-driven style, mostly handled in tanks; 15 per cent of the blend was barrel-aged. Fresh and vibrant, it has good body, a touch of complexity and good depth of smooth, citrusy, appley flavours.

DRY $21 –V

Awa Valley Chardonnay ★★★☆

This consistently enjoyable wine is priced sharply. Estate-grown in West Auckland, hand-harvested and barrel-fermented, it is typically full-bodied, with sweet oak aromas and ripe grapefruit and peach flavours. The 2008 vintage (★★★☆), American oak-aged, is fleshy, with grapefruit and toast flavours, showing some mealy complexity. The 2009 (★★★☆) is similar – mouthfilling and citrusy, with some mealy, toasty complexity and a smooth finish.

DRY $16 V+

Awa Valley Unoaked Chardonnay (★★★)

Estate-grown at Huapai, the 2009 vintage (★★★) is fresh and lively, with plenty of ripe, peachy, citrusy flavour. Good value.

DRY $15 V+

Awaroa Reserve Chardonnay (★★★☆)

From a Waiheke Island-based winery, the 2009 vintage (★★★☆) was hand-harvested in the Stell Vineyard at Te Awanga, in Hawke's Bay, and fermented and matured for nine months in French oak casks (mostly new). It's a robust, slightly oaky wine, offering ripe, citrusy, peachy, slightly buttery flavours, showing good richness. It needs time; open mid-2011+.

DRY $28 –V

Awhitu Peninsula Chardonnay ★★★☆

Maturing very gracefully, the 2007 vintage (★★★★) was estate-grown on the shores of the Manukau Harbour, in Auckland, and fermented and lees-stirred for 10 months in barrels. It's a refined, full-bodied wine with strong, ripe grapefruit and peach flavours, a subtle seasoning of biscuity oak, good complexity and texture, and a tight, dry finish. Drink now to 2012.

DRY $25 –V

Babich Gimblett Gravels Hawke's Bay Chardonnay ★★★

Fermented in tanks (mostly) and casks, this is designed as a fruit-driven style. The 2008 vintage (★★★) is vibrant and crisp, with citrusy, peachy, slightly biscuity flavours, balanced for easy drinking.

Vintage	08
WR	4
Drink	10-12

DRY $20 –V

Babich Irongate Chardonnay ★★★★★

Babich's flagship Chardonnay. A stylish wine, Irongate has traditionally been leaner and tighter than other top Hawke's Bay Chardonnays, while performing well in the cellar, but the latest releases have more drink-young appeal. It is based on hand-picked fruit from the shingly Irongate Vineyard in Gimblett Road, fully barrel-fermented (about 20 per cent new), and lees-matured for up to nine months. Malolactic fermentation was rare up to the 2002 but is now a growing influence. The 2007 (★★★★★) is a top vintage. Very sweet-fruited and rounded, it has deep peach and grapefruit flavours, hints of nuts and biscuits, and excellent complexity and fragrance. The 2008 (★★★★☆) is powerful (14.5 per cent alcohol), with ripe, stone-fruit flavours. Already quite open, it is vibrant, generous, soft and rich, in a drink-now or cellaring style.

Vintage	08
WR	7
Drink	10-23

DRY $33 V+

Babich Lone Tree Unoaked Chardonnay ★★★

Made with no 'intrusion' of oak, this wine is handled in tanks, with 'a bit of malolactic fermentation and lees-stirring' to add complexity. It is typically finely balanced, with fresh, citrusy flavours showing good delicacy and depth. The 2008 vintage (★★☆), grown in Hawke's Bay, is lemony and crisp, fruity and slightly honeyed, in a pleasant, drink-young style.

DRY $16 V+

Bascand Marlborough Chardonnay (★★★)

Partly oak-aged, the 2008 vintage (★★★) is a light yellow, mouthfilling wine, made in an upfront style with smooth, peachy, slightly buttery and honeyed flavours. It's drinking well now.

DRY $17 AV

Beach House Hawke's Bay Chardonnay ★★★☆

The barrel-fermented 2009 vintage (★★★☆) has ripe citrus and stone-fruit flavours, a hint of butterscotch and a rounded finish. It's a youthful, slightly creamy wine with some elegance and good length.

DRY $24 AV

Bensen Block Chardonnay ★★★

The 2008 vintage (★★★) from Pernod Ricard NZ, grown in Gisborne, was made in a fruit-driven style. It's a flavoursome wine, ripe, slightly buttery and creamy, balanced for easy drinking.

DRY $17 AV

Black Barn Barrel Fermented Chardonnay ★★★★

Grown on the Havelock North hills, hand-picked, fermented with some use of indigenous yeasts in French oak barriques and given a full, softening malolactic fermentation, this is typically a classy wine, in a classic regional style. The 2007 vintage (★★★★) is elegant and vibrantly fruity, with a strong seasoning of toasty oak (60 per cent new) but concentrated fruit flavours to match. It's maturing very gracefully, with a harmonious, long, rich finish.

Vintage	07	06
WR	7	6
Drink	10-14	P

DRY $35 –V

Black Barn Hawke's Bay Chardonnay ★★★☆

The 2009 vintage (★★★☆) is fragrant and smooth, with ripe citrus-fruit characters to the fore, slightly toasty and buttery notes adding complexity, and mouthfilling body. It's a finely textured wine with good length.

DRY $28 –V

Black Barn Unoaked Chardonnay (★★☆)

The 2008 vintage (★★☆) is a mouthfilling, dry Hawke's Bay wine with ripe, grapefruit-like flavours. It's a solid wine, but lacks a bit of freshness and vibrancy.

DRY $20 –V

Black Estate Omihi Waipara Chardonnay ★★★★

The 2009 vintage (★★★★) is an upfront style, hand-picked from mature vines and fermented with indigenous yeasts in barrels (30 per cent new). The bouquet is strong, peachy and toasty; the palate is concentrated, with a hint of butterscotch, fresh acidity and lots of personality. Drink now or cellar.

DRY $31 –V

Blackenbrook Nelson Chardonnay ★★★☆

Enjoyable now, the 2008 vintage (★★★☆) was estate-grown, hand-picked at over 24 brix and matured for a year in seasoned American and French oak barrels. Pale yellow, it is sturdy (14.5 per cent alcohol) and smooth, with very good depth of fresh peach and grapefruit flavours, moderately complex and slightly buttery. (The Reserve Chardonnay from 2009 was matured entirely in French oak.)

Vintage	09
WR	6
Drink	10-13

DRY $24 AV

Bloody Bay Gisborne Chardonnay (★★★)

From wine distributor Federal Geo, the 2009 vintage (★★★) is an enjoyable, drink-young style. Pale yellow, it is full-bodied, with ripe, peachy, slightly toasty flavours, showing good depth, and a smooth, dry finish.

DRY $17 AV

Blue Ridge Marlborough Chardonnay ★★★★

From West Brook, the fully barrel-fermented 2007 vintage (★★★★) is an upfront style with strong flavours of grapefruit and pears. It's a sweetly oaked wine with a fully dry, slightly creamy finish.

Vintage	07
WR	7
Drink	10-12

DRY $25 AV

Boatshed Bay by Goldwater Marlborough Chardonnay ★★★☆

Fresh, fruity and slightly creamy, with ripe, citrusy flavours, the 2008 vintage (★★★) was mostly handled in tanks; 10 per cent of the blend was French oak-aged. It's an enjoyable, easy-drinking style, with a touch of complexity.

Vintage	08	07
WR	6	6
Drink	10-11	P

DRY $17 V+

Borthwick Vineyard Wairarapa Chardonnay ★★★☆

The 2009 vintage (★★★☆), grown at Gladstone, was fermented in French (65 per cent) and American oak casks (25 per cent new). It's a smooth, easy-drinking wine with good weight and depth of stone-fruit flavours, a hint of butterscotch and a rounded, very harmonious finish.

DRY $25 –V

Bouldevines Marlborough Chardonnay ★★★★

From the south side of the Wairau Valley, the 2008 vintage (★★★★) is a single-vineyard wine, harvested at 24.5 brix and 'aged on a mixture of new and old French oak'. A high-flavoured style, it is mouthfilling, citrusy, buttery and toasty, with excellent weight, complexity and richness. It's drinking well now.

DRY $25 AV

Boundary Vineyards Tuki Tuki Road Hawke's Bay Chardonnay ★★★☆

Pernod Ricard NZ's wine is grown at a 'semi-coastal' site at Te Awanga. Fermented in Hungarian oak barriques (25 per cent new), with over 60 per cent of the blend given a softening malolactic fermentation, the 2008 vintage (★★★☆) is a generous, full-bodied wine with ripe stone-fruit flavours, nutty oak adding complexity, and a well-rounded finish. The 2009 (★★★☆) is generous, ripe and smooth, with tropical-fruit flavours, slightly toasty and creamy, and very good texture and depth.

DRY $20 AV

Brancott Estate 'O' Ormond Chardonnay ★★★★★

Up to and including the 2007 vintage, this wine was branded Montana (see the entry for Montana 'O' Ormond Chardonnay), but the 2008 (★★★★☆) is labelled Brancott Estate. It is the flagship Gisborne Chardonnay from Pernod Ricard NZ, made for cellaring. The 2008 vintage (★★★★☆) is fleshy, with concentrated, ripe, peachy, nutty flavours, showing excellent complexity and harmony. It's already drinking well.

DRY $33 V+

Brancott Estate Reserve Chardonnay – see Montana Reserve Chardonnay

Brightside Brightwater Chardonnay ★★☆

From Kaimira Estate, the 2009 vintage (★★★) was grown at Brightwater, in Nelson, and lightly oaked. It's an attractive wine, mouthfilling, with fresh, citrusy flavours, slightly creamy and biscuity notes, good depth and a fully dry finish.

Vintage	09	08	07
WR	5	5	6
Drink	10-12	10-11	10-11

DRY $16 AV

Brightwater Vineyards Lord Rutherford Barrique Chardonnay ★★★★
The creamy-textured 2008 vintage (★★★★) is a single-vineyard Nelson wine, hand-picked and fermented in French oak barriques (25 per cent new). Oak-aged for 10 months, it is rich, with peachy, citrusy, slightly buttery and toasty flavours in a concentrated, upfront style for drinking now or cellaring.

Vintage	08	07	06
WR	5	6	6
Drink	10-14	10-11	10-11

DRY $30 –V

Brookfields Bergman Chardonnay ★★★☆
Named after the Ingrid Bergman roses in the estate garden, this wine is grown alongside the winery at Meeanee, in Hawke's Bay, hand-picked, and fermented and matured on its yeast lees in seasoned French and American oak casks. The 2009 vintage (★★★☆) is mouthfilling and smooth, with ripe, peachy, moderately complex flavours, balanced acidity, and good freshness, depth and harmony.

Vintage	09	08	07	06
WR	7	7	7	7
Drink	10-14	10-13	10-12	10-11

DRY $19 V+

Brookfields Marshall Bank Chardonnay ★★★★☆
Brookfields' top Chardonnay is named after proprietor Peter Robertson's grandfather's property in Otago. Grown in a vineyard adjacent to the winery at Meeanee and fermented and matured in French oak barriques (50 per cent new in 2009), it is a rich, concentrated Hawke's Bay wine. The 2009 vintage (★★★★☆), oak-aged for eight months, with weekly lees-stirring, is a fresh, elegant, very youthful wine with a mealy complexity, good texture and strong yet delicate, citrusy, slightly buttery, well-rounded flavours. Best drinking 2012+.

Vintage	09
WR	7
DRINK	11-15

DRY $30 AV

Brookfields Unoaked Hawke's Bay Chardonnay (★★★☆)
Delicious from the start, the estate-grown 2009 vintage (★★★☆) is fresh-scented, with vibrant, ripe stone-fruit flavours, a hint of spice, and a very smooth (5 grams/litre of residual sugar) finish. A good example of the unwooded style, it offers very easy drinking.

Vintage	09
WR	7
Drink	10-12

MED/DRY $19 V+

Brunton Road Gisborne Chardonnay ★★★☆

The 2008 vintage (★★★☆) of this single-vineyard wine was grown at Patutahi. A barrel-fermented style with fresh, ripe, peachy flavours seasoned with perfumed, toasty oak (French and American) and a creamy-smooth finish, it is moderately complex, with good depth and drink-young appeal.

DRY $25 –V

Bushmere Estate Classic Gisborne Chardonnay ★★★★

A good buy. Enjoyable now, the 2008 (★★★☆) is full-bodied, with generous, peachy flavours, slightly honeyed and toasty, and a smooth finish. The 2009 vintage (★★★★) was hand-picked and fermented and lees-aged for nine months in French oak casks (20 per cent new). Poised and finely textured, it has concentrated peach and slight grapefruit flavours, hints of toast and butterscotch, and obvious cellaring potential.

DRY $23 V+

Bushmere Estate Gisborne Chardonnay/Viognier (★★★☆)

The 2009 vintage (★★★☆) is a 70:30 blend with strong upfront appeal. Fermented in seasoned French casks, it's an off-dry style (6 grams/litre of residual sugar), with plenty of peachy, slightly buttery flavour and a seductively smooth finish.

MED/DRY $25 –V

Cable Bay Reserve Waiheke Island Chardonnay (★★★★☆)

The 2009 vintage (★★★★☆) is a single-vineyard wine, grown at Church Bay and matured in French oak barriques. It's an elegant, complex wine, showing lovely concentration, delicacy and texture. Still very youthful, with a strong, nutty oak influence and deep grapefruit and peach flavours, it shows great potential, but needs more time to achieve balance; open mid-2011+.

Vintage	09
WR	7
Drink	10-15

DRY $56 –V

Cable Bay Single Vineyard Waiheke Chardonnay (★★★★☆)

Only 1001 bottles were produced of the 2007 vintage (★★★★☆). Handled without oak, it's an elegant, youthful wine, bright, light lemon/green, with penetrating grapefruit, peach and lime flavours, slightly minerally and tightly structured. It's a finely poised wine, built to last.

Vintage	07
WR	6
Drink	10-12

DRY $49 –V

Cable Bay Waiheke Chardonnay ★★★★☆

Blended from five sites at the western end of the island, this tightly structured wine opens out well with bottle-age. Hand-picked, it is fermented (partly with indigenous yeasts) and matured for 10 months in French oak barriques (around 15 per cent new), with no use of malolactic fermentation. The 2008 vintage (★★★★☆) is mouthfilling and subtle, slightly creamy and biscuity, with ripe stone-fruit flavours, a mealy complexity and a dry, finely textured, sustained finish. Best drinking mid-2011+.

Vintage	08	07	06	05	04
WR	7	7	6	7	7
Drink	10-15	10-14	10-11	10-11	P

DRY $33 AV

Cable Station Marlborough Chardonnay ★★★
From Cape Campbell, the 2007 vintage (★★★) is a lightly wooded style: '50 per cent of the wine had oak contact for seven months'. Vibrantly fruity, with grapefruit characters to the fore, a touch of creaminess and a soft finish, it's enjoyable young.

DRY $19 AV

Cadwalladers Riverside Hawke's Bay Chardonnay ★★★
The 2007 vintage (★★★) is full-bodied, peachy and faintly honeyed, in a fruity, soft style with drink-young appeal.

DRY $15 V+

Cape Campbell Limited Edition Reserve Marlborough Chardonnay ★★★★
A rich, upfront style. The 2007 vintage (★★★★☆) was grown in the Kernick Vineyard at Rapaura and the Turner Vineyard at Blind River, and fermented in new and once-used American oak casks. The bouquet is mealy and sweetly oaked; the palate is toasty, with good weight and depth of peachy, slightly buttery flavour.

Vintage	07
WR	6
Drink	10-11

DRY $25 AV

Cape Campbell Marlborough Chardonnay ★★★☆
Grown at Rapaura, on the north side of the Wairau Valley, and partly American oak-aged, the 2008 vintage (★★★) is fresh and vibrant, with good depth of citrusy, slightly toasty flavours, finely balanced for early drinking.

DRY $18 V+

Carrick Cairnmuir Terraces EBM Chardonnay ★★★★☆
From a region that has struggled to produce top Chardonnay, this wine is one of the best. The 2008 vintage (★★★★☆), grown at Bannockburn, was fermented and matured for 18 months (EBM means 'extended barrel maturation') in French oak barriques (20 per cent new). Still youthful, it is mouthfilling, concentrated and minerally, with grapefruit-like flavours, hints of biscuits and butterscotch, a mealy complexity, and a long, finely balanced finish.

Vintage	08	07	06	05	04	03
WR	6	7	6	6	6	7
Drink	10-15	10-15	10-12	10-12	P	P

DRY $33 AV

Carrick Central Otago Chardonnay ★★★★
A tight, elegant, cool-climate style, this wine is grown at Bannockburn and matured for a year in French oak barriques (15 per cent new). The 2008 vintage (★★★★) shows good complexity, with peach and grapefruit flavours, hints of spices and nuts, a minerally streak and a crisp, lengthy finish.

DRY $26 AV

Catalina Sounds Marlborough Chardonnay ★★★☆
The 2008 vintage (★★★) is a single-vineyard wine, hand-picked in the upper Wairau Valley and barrel-fermented. It's a medium-bodied style (12.5 per cent alcohol) with fresh acidity and citrusy, creamy, moderately complex flavours.

DRY $22 AV

Cathedral Cove Hawke's Bay Chardonnay (★★)
From One Tree Hill Vineyards, a division of Morton Estate, the non-vintage wine on sale in 2010 (★★) is a moderately flavoursome wine, smooth, creamy and slightly honeyed. It's ready to roll.

DRY $8 AV

Chard Farm Closeburn Chardonnay ★★★
The winery's second-tier Chardonnay is typically a fresh, vibrant Central Otago wine with appetising acidity. Handled entirely in tanks, it offers fresh, crisp, citrusy flavours, with minerally, buttery notes adding interest.

DRY $22 –V

Chard Farm Judge and Jury Chardonnay ★★★★
Named after a rocky outcrop overlooking the Gibbston (Central Otago) winery, this wine was in the past a very fresh, elegant, cool-climate style, fully barrel-fermented, with rich citrusy and peachy flavours, showing a good balance of oak and acidity. The 2009 vintage (not yet tasted) is lower-priced than past releases and was mostly handled in tanks (15 per cent French oak-aged).

Vintage	09
WR	6
Drink	11-17

DRY $28 AV

Charles Wiffen Marlborough Chardonnay ★★★
Charles and Sandy Wiffen own a vineyard in the Wairau Valley, but their wine is made at West Brook in West Auckland. The 2007 vintage (★★★☆) was French oak-aged for 10 months. It's a vibrantly fruity style with ripe grapefruit, pear and spice flavours, finely integrated oak and a fresh, smooth finish.

DRY $23 –V

Cheeky Little White East Coast Chardonnay (★★☆)
From Babich, the medium-bodied 2009 vintage (★★☆) is fresh and lively, with citrusy, slightly peachy flavours, crisp and dry. A simple, fruit-driven style, it's priced sharply.

DRY $10 V+

Church Road Cuve Chardonnay ★★★★
This label was originally reserved for rare wines, made in 'a more Burgundian, less fruit-driven, less oaky' style of Hawke's Bay Chardonnay than its lush and (at that stage) relatively fast-maturing Church Road Reserve stablemate. However, since the 2006 vintage – hand-picked, fermented with indigenous yeasts in French oak barriques (28 per cent new), and barrel-aged for over a year – its production has been expanded and the price reduced significantly. The 2008 vintage (★★★★) is a classic regional style, rich and sweet-fruited, with ripe, lemony, peachy flavours, plenty of oak and substantial body. It's a complex, creamy wine with a lingering finish.

DRY $27 AV

Church Road Hawke's Bay Chardonnay ★★★★
This typically mouthfilling, rich wine is made by Pernod Ricard NZ at the Church Road winery in Hawke's Bay. The 2008 vintage (★★★★) was fermented, partly with indigenous yeasts, in French (70 per cent) and Hungarian (30 per cent) oak barriques (a third new), and barrel-aged for 10 months on its full yeast lees, with fortnightly stirring. Fleshy and rounded, it has substantial body and ripe stone-fruit flavours showing good texture, complexity and depth. Already delicious, the 2009 (★★★★) is weighty, rich, creamy and very harmonious, with concentrated, ripe stone-fruit flavours and nutty, biscuity notes adding complexity. At its average retail price in supermarkets of around $15, this is a great buy.

Vintage	09	08
WR	7	5
Drink	10-12	10-11

DRY $27 AV

Church Road Reserve Hawke's Bay Chardonnay ★★★★★
This classy wine is based on the 'pick' of Pernod Ricard NZ's Hawke's Bay Chardonnay crop. It is hand-harvested, fermented with indigenous yeasts in French oak barriques (about 50 per cent new), and stays on its yeast lees for the total time in barrel (up to 14 months), with frequent lees-stirring. In recent years, the wine has become more elegant, less 'upfront' in style, and should mature longer. The 2008 vintage (★★★★★) has a rich, complex bouquet. Full-bodied and concentrated, with deep, stone-fruit flavours, well seasoned with toasty oak, it is powerful and full of personality, with a strong oak influence – but the fruit to carry it. Well worth cellaring.

Vintage	08	07	06	05	04	03	02
WR	6	6	7	6	6	NM	7
Drink	10-12	10-11	P	P	P	NM	P

DRY $37 AV

Church Road Tom Chardonnay (★★★★★)
Released in late 2009, the debut 2006 vintage (★★★★★) is a great wine – one of the most memorable New Zealand Chardonnays yet. Grown in Hawke's Bay and fermented with indigenous yeasts in French oak barriques (new and two years old), it has an arrestingly rich and complex bouquet. Powerful and weighty (14.5 per cent alcohol), it is sweet-fruited, with an array of stone-fruit, citrus and nut flavours, slightly buttery and notably concentrated. An exciting mouthful.

DRY $70 AV

C.J. Pask Declaration Hawke's Bay Chardonnay ★★★★☆

The Hawke's Bay winery's top Chardonnay is grown in Gimblett Road and fermented and matured in all-new French oak barriques, with weekly lees-stirring. The 2007 vintage (★★★★) is a classic regional style, with rich, ripe stone-fruit flavours seasoned with French oak and fresh acidity keeping things lively. The 2008 (★★★★☆) is highly fragrant, with rich stone-fruit flavours, slightly nutty and creamy, and excellent complexity. Weighty, concentrated and long, it's drinking well now.

Vintage	07	06	05	04
WR	7	7	6	7
Drink	10-11	P	P	P

DRY $32 AV

C.J. Pask Gimblett Road Hawke's Bay Chardonnay ★★★☆

This second-tier Chardonnay is designed to highlight vibrant fruit characters, fleshed out with restrained wood. The 2008 vintage (★★★☆) is still youthful, with a hint of oak (25 per cent of the blend was barrel-aged), and fresh, delicate, citrusy fruit flavours shining through.

DRY $20 AV

C.J. Pask Roy's Hill Hawke's Bay Unoaked Chardonnay ★★☆

Grown in Gimblett Road and handled in stainless steel tanks, the 2009 vintage (★★☆) is a medium-bodied, fruit-driven style with fresh, peachy, slightly limey flavours and a crisp, dry finish. Priced right.

DRY $15 AV

Clearview Beachhead Chardonnay ★★★☆

This Hawke's Bay winery has a reputation for powerful Chardonnays, and top vintages of its second-tier label are no exception – big and rich. The lighter 2008 (★★★) was hand-picked at Te Awanga and fermented in seasoned French oak casks. It's a fruit-driven style, fresh-scented, with vibrant, grapefruit-like flavours to the fore, a subtle oak influence and moderate complexity.

Vintage	09	08
WR	6	6
Drink	10-15	10-14

DRY $23 AV

Clearview Reserve Chardonnay ★★★★★

For his premium Hawke's Bay Chardonnay label, winemaker Tim Turvey aims for a 'big, grunty, upfront' style – and hits the target with ease. It's typically a hedonist's delight – an arrestingly bold, intense, savoury, mealy, complex wine with layers of flavour. Based on ultra-ripe fruit (hand-harvested at 24–25 brix from Te Awanga vines, up to 21 years old), the 2009 vintage (★★★★★) is a highly scented, very vibrant wine. Barrel-fermented, it is very poised and elegant, with fresh, rich, grapefruit and peach flavours, seasoned with toasty French (mostly) and American oak (50 per cent new). Weighty and concentrated, with lovely harmony and immediacy, it's still very youthful; open mid-2011+.

Vintage	09	08	07	06	05	04
WR	7	7	7	7	7	7
Drink	10-19	10-18	10-14	10-12	10-11	P

DRY $35 AV

Clearview Unwooded Chardonnay ★★★☆
This Hawke's Bay wine is a tank-fermented style, simple but full-flavoured. The 2008 vintage (★★★☆) was hand-picked at Te Awanga, on the coast, cool-fermented and lees-stirred, with 30 per cent malolactic fermentation. Instantly appealing, it's a full-bodied wine, not complex, but offering loads of fresh, vibrant, peachy flavour, dry, ripe and smooth.

Vintage	09	08	07
WR	5	7	6
Drink	10-13	10-15	P

DRY $19 V+

Clos de Ste Anne Chardonnay Naboth's Vineyard ★★★★★
Millton's flagship Chardonnay is based on mature vines in the steep, north-east-facing Naboth's Vineyard in the Poverty Bay foothills, planted in loams overlying sedimentary calcareous rock. Grown biodynamically and hand-harvested, it is fermented in mostly second-fill French oak barrels, and in most vintages it is not put through malolactic fermentation, 'to leave a pure, crisp mineral flavour'. The 2008 (★★★★★) is full of personality. Highly concentrated, it has grapefruit and peach flavours, with buttery and nutty notes adding complexity, a creamy texture and a slightly minerally streak. It's already quite open and expressive. Certified organic.

Vintage	08	07	06	05	04	03	02
WR	6	7	7	7	7	6	7
Drink	10-17	10-17	10-16	10-15	10-14	P	10-12

DRY $54 AV

Cloudy Bay Chardonnay ★★★★★
A powerful Marlborough wine with impressively concentrated, savoury, lemony, mealy flavours and a proven ability to mature well over the long haul (at least four years and up to a decade). The grapes, mostly hand-picked, are sourced from numerous company-owned and growers' vineyards in the Wairau and Brancott valleys. All of the wine is fermented (with a high proportion of indigenous yeasts) in French oak barriques (about 20 per cent new) and lees-aged in barrels for up to 15 months, and most goes through a softening malolactic fermentation. The 2008 vintage (★★★★★) is a powerful yet very elegant, cool-climate style with impressive richness, complexity and harmony. The bouquet is fragrant, biscuity and mealy; the palate is full-bodied, with concentrated, citrusy, slightly buttery and nutty flavours, and good acid spine. Drink now or cellar.

Vintage	08	07	06
WR	5	6	7
Drink	11-16	10-14	10-14

DRY $38 AV

Coniglio Hawke's Bay Chardonnay ★★★★★

Launched by Morton Estate from 1998, Coniglio is one of New Zealand's most expensive Chardonnays. A Rolls-Royce version of the company's famous Black Label Chardonnay, it is typically an arresting wine, powerful and concentrated. Grown in the cool, elevated (150 metres above sea level) Riverview Vineyard at Mangatahi, Hawke's Bay, it is hand-picked from mature vines and fermented and lees-aged in all-new French oak barriques, with malolactic fermentation according to the season. Harvested at a very ripe 25 brix, the bright yellow 2004 vintage (★★★★★) is a refined wine with a highly fragrant, citrusy, nutty bouquet. Mouthfilling and sweet-fruited, with a fine thread of acidity, it's a rich, elegant wine, maturing gracefully and now probably at its peak. (There is no 2005.)

Vintage	05	04	03	02	01	00
WR	NM	7	NM	7	NM	6
Drink	NM	10-12	NM	P	NM	P

DRY $80 –V

Coopers Creek Gisborne Chardonnay/Viognier (★★★)

Still on sale, the 2007 vintage (★★★) is a very easy-drinking style, full-bodied and fruity, with ripe, peachy flavours and a smooth (off-dry) finish.

Vintage	07
WR	7
Drink	10-11

MED/DRY $17 AV

Coopers Creek Reserve Gisborne Chardonnay ★★★★

Designed as a 'full-bodied, oak-influenced style', this wine is fermented and matured for nine months in partly new French oak barriques. The classy 2009 vintage (★★★★☆) has a fragrant, toasty, mealy bouquet, leading into a complex palate with ripe grapefruit-like flavours. A finely textured wine, it is rich and youthful.

Vintage	09
WR	6
Drink	10-12

DRY $25 AV

Coopers Creek SV The Limeworks Hawke's Bay Chardonnay ★★★★

This single-vineyard, Havelock North wine is a 'full-on' style with rich grapefruit-like flavours, well seasoned with toasty American oak, and a creamy-soft texture. The 2009 vintage (★★★☆) is citrusy and slightly creamy, with sweet, nutty, American oak aromas and some freshness, elegance and richness.

Vintage	09	08	07	06
WR	6	6	5	7
Drink	10-12	10-12	10-11	P

DRY $20 V+

Coopers Creek Swamp Reserve Chardonnay ★★★★☆

Based on the winery's best Hawke's Bay Chardonnay fruit, this is typically a lush, highly seductive wine with a finely judged balance of rich, citrusy, peachy fruit flavours and toasty oak. Hand-picked in the company's Middle Road Vineyard at Havelock North, it is fully fermented and matured for 10 months in French oak barriques (33 to 50 per cent new). The 2009 vintage (★★★☆) is youthful, with good weight and depth of ripe, citrusy flavours, seasoned with toasty oak, a creamy texture and a finely balanced, well-rounded finish. It's well worth cellaring. The 2008 (★★★★☆) is mouthfilling and slightly creamy, with strong, ripe, grapefruit and biscuity oak flavours, mealy, complex and rich. Drink now onwards.

Vintage	09	08	07	06	05	04
WR	6	7	7	6	6	6
Drink	11-14	10-13	10-11	P	P	P

DRY $29 V+

Coopers Creek Unoaked Gisborne Chardonnay ★★★☆

Coopers Creek no longer matures its popular, moderately priced Gisborne wine in wood, but the recipe still includes maturation on its yeast lees. The 2009 vintage (★★★☆) is full-bodied and vibrantly fruity, with fresh, tight, peachy, citrusy flavours and lively acidity.

Vintage	09	08	07	06
WR	6	6	6	5
Drink	10-12	10-11	P	P

DRY $17 V+

Corazon Single Vineyard Chardonnay ★★★☆

Grown at Kumeu, in West Auckland, the 2009 vintage (★★★★) is a single-vineyard wine, hand-picked at 23.5 brix and fermented in French oak casks (20 per cent new). Biscuity and mealy, with ripe, peachy fruit flavours, considerable complexity and a crisp, dry finish, it's a good food wine, worth cellaring.

DRY $23 AV

Corbans Cottage Block Hawke's Bay Chardonnay ★★★★★

A consistently classy wine from Pernod Ricard NZ. The superb 2007 (★★★★★) was hand-picked in three company-owned vineyards, fully barrel-fermented with indigenous yeasts, and matured for a year in French oak barriques (new and one year old). A classic regional style, it has a fragrant, complex, nutty, creamy bouquet, leading into a generous, finely textured palate with ripe grapefruit and smoky oak flavours, showing lovely delicacy, complexity and length. The 2009 vintage (★★★★☆) is again rich and refined, with fresh, tight, grapefruit-like flavours and earthy, nutty, smoky notes adding real complexity. One for the cellar.

Vintage	07	06	05
WR	7	7	6
Drink	10-12	10-11	P

DRY $36 AV

Corbans Homestead Hawke's Bay Chardonnay (★★☆)

From Pernod Ricard NZ, this dry wine is made without oak in a simple, fruit-driven style. The 2008 vintage (★★☆) is a faintly honeyed style with decent depth of ripe, peachy, slightly buttery flavour.

Vintage	08	07
WR	5	6
Drink	P	P

DRY $17 –V

Corbans Private Bin Hawke's Bay Chardonnay ★★★★

Hand-picked and barrel-fermented, with indigenous yeasts adding absorbing 'funky' notes, this is typically a great buy. The 2007 vintage (★★★★☆) is weighty and rich, with concentrated, peachy, toasty, nutty flavours, moderate acidity and a slightly creamy texture.

Vintage	07	06	05	04
WR	7	6	6	7
Drink	10-12	P	P	P

DRY $24 V+

Corbans White Label Chardonnay (★★☆)

From Pernod Ricard NZ, the 2008 vintage (★★☆) is a regional blend with citrusy and peachy flavours in a simple style with a smooth, slightly buttery finish.

MED/DRY $10 V+

Couper's Shed Hawke's Bay Chardonnay (★★★)

From Pernod Ricard NZ, the 2009 vintage (★★★) is a fruit-driven style, full-bodied, with plenty of ripe, peachy flavour and a rounded, dryish finish. It has lots of drink-young charm.

DRY $20 –V

Crab Farm Chardonnay ★★★☆

Grown in Hawke's Bay, the 2007 vintage (★★★☆) is a fruit-driven style, handled without oak. It's a full-bodied wine (14.5 per cent alcohol) with ripe, grapefruit-like flavours, a slightly creamy texture and good immediacy.

Vintage	07	06
WR	6	6
Drink	P	P

DRY $17 V+

Crab Farm Reserve Chardonnay ★★★★

The 2008 vintage (★★★★) from this small Hawke's Bay winery was hand-picked and aged for eight months in new oak barrels. It is mouthfilling and sweet-fruited, with rich, vibrant, peachy, citrusy flavours, oak complexity and good acid spine.

Vintage	08
WR	7
Drink	10-11

DRY $25 AV

Craggy Range Gimblett Gravels Vineyard Chardonnay ★★★★☆

This stylish Hawke's Bay wine is mouthfilling, complex and savoury, with biscuity, nutty characters from fermentation and maturation in French oak barriques (23 per cent new in 2009). The 2009 vintage (★★★★☆) is a refined, very youthful wine, with substantial body and ripe, citrusy flavours, seasoned with biscuity oak. Concentrated, savoury and complex, it's a classy, tightly structured wine, well worth cellaring.

Vintage	09	08	07	06
WR	6	6	6	6
Drink	10-14	10-13	10-13	P

DRY $30 AV

Craggy Range Kidnappers Vineyard Hawke's Bay Chardonnay ★★★★☆

Made using 'the traditional techniques of Chablis', the 2009 vintage (★★★★☆) is a gently oaked style, full of interest. Grown near the coast at Te Awanga, and fermented in a mix of tanks (91 per cent) and French oak barriques and puncheons (9 per cent), it is weighty and sweet-fruited, with very fresh and vibrant, grapefruit and peach flavours, slightly mealy and leesy, surprising complexity, and a lengthy finish. It's a subtle style of Chardonnay, yet very refined and satisfying.

Vintage	09	08	07
WR	5	6	6
Drink	10-13	10-13	10-12

DRY $23 V+

Craggy Range Les Beaux Cailloux – see the Branded and Other White Wines section

Crawford Farm Chardonnay ★★☆

From Constellation NZ, the 2008 vintage (★★★) is fruity, peachy, slightly buttery and spicy, in a smooth, easy-drinking style, enjoyable now.

DRY $22 –V

Crazy by Nature Shotberry Chardonnay (★★☆)

From Millton, the 2008 vintage (★★☆) is a fruity, easy-drinking Gisborne wine with fresh, citrusy flavours and a very smooth finish. Certified organic.

DRY $20 –V

Croft Vineyard Martinborough Chardonnay ★★★★☆

The 2006 vintage (★★★★☆) is a refined wine, maturing gracefully, and the 2008 (★★★★☆) offers equally good value. Harvested at 24 brix and fully barrel-fermented (in 30 per cent new oak), mostly with indigenous yeasts, it is elegant, with youthful, concentrated peach, grapefruit and nut flavours, showing good complexity, and a finely balanced, long finish. Priced sharply.

DRY $24 V+

Croney Three Ton Marlborough Chardonnay (★★★)

This is an 'oak-free' style, recommended for enjoying with food and friends, 'or just drink it alone in your room'. Hand-picked, tank-fermented and lees-aged, the 2008 vintage (★★★) has a slightly creamy bouquet leading into a full-bodied wine with good depth of ripe, citrusy, peachy flavour and a smooth, dry finish. Fine value.

DRY $15 V+

Crossroads Hawke's Bay Chardonnay ★★★★

A consistently good buy. The 2008 vintage (★★★★☆) is a weighty, softly structured wine, handled partly in tanks, but a 'large portion' was barrel-fermented. Mouthfilling, with strong, ripe flavours, slightly biscuity and creamy, it's a rich, harmonious wine, offering great value. The 2009 (★★★☆) is full-bodied, peachy and slightly nutty, with generous, ripe-fruit flavours, showing some mealy complexity, and a creamy-smooth finish.

DRY $20 V+

Crowded House Chardonnay (★★★☆)

Drinking well now, the 2008 vintage (★★★☆) is a fruit-driven style, blended from Nelson and Marlborough grapes, and 20 per cent fermented in seasoned oak casks. Mouthfilling, smooth and slightly creamy, it has good depth of grapefruit and spice flavours and a faintly nutty, dry finish.

DRY $18 V+

Culley Marlborough Chardonnay ★★☆

Produced by Neill Culley, a partner in the Cable Bay winery on Waiheke Island, the 2007 vintage (★★☆) is a fruit-driven style with citrusy, appley flavours, fresh and uncomplicated.

DRY $20 –V

Cypress Hawke's Bay Chardonnay ★★★

The 2008 vintage (★★★) was tank-fermented, with 'some French oak influence', but was not barrel-aged. Full-bodied, fresh and fruity, with ripe, peachy flavours and a smooth, dry finish, it slips down very easily. Ready.

Vintage	08	07
WR	6	5
Drink	10-11	P

DRY $20 –V

Cypress Terraces Hawke's Bay Chardonnay (★★★★)

From a sloping, 2-hectare vineyard, the 2008 vintage (★★★★) is a barrel-fermented wine, sturdy (14.5 per cent alcohol) and very ripe-tasting, with sweet-fruit delights of peaches and melons, buttery, toasty notes (French oak, 60 per cent new), gentle acidity, and good complexity and texture. Drink now or cellar.

Vintage	08
WR	6
Drink	10-12

DRY $30 –V

Dashwood Marlborough Chardonnay ★★★

Vavasour's lower-tier Chardonnay. The 2008 (★★★) offers easy drinking, with peachy flavours and slightly toasty, creamy notes adding a touch of complexity. The 2009 vintage (★★★☆) is a fleshy, upfront style with stone-fruit, spice and butterscotch characters and plenty of flavour.

Vintage	08
WR	6
Drink	10-11

DRY $17 AV

Delegat Hawke's Bay Chardonnay ★★★

For Delegat's lower-tier Chardonnay, the idea is: 'let the fruit do the talking'. The 2008 vintage (★★★☆), fermented in tanks and barrels, is flavoursome, peachy and citrusy, in a ripe, vibrantly fruity style, creamy-textured, with strong drink-young appeal.

Vintage	08	07	06
WR	6	7	5
Drink	10-14	10-14	P

DRY $16 V+

Delegat Reserve Hawke's Bay Chardonnay ★★★★

The fine-value 2007 vintage (★★★★), grown in the inland Crownthorpe district, was fully barrel-fermented. It's a very elegant, fragrant wine with citrusy, nutty flavours, showing good delicacy and richness, fresh acidity and a lingering finish.

Vintage	08	07	06	05
WR	6	7	6	5
Drink	10-14	10-14	10-12	10-11

DRY $20 V+

Discovery Point Judd Vineyard Selection Chardonnay (★★★★)

From wine distributors Bennett & Deller, the 2008 vintage (★★★★) was grown at the Judd Estate vineyard in Gisborne, fermented with indigenous yeasts in seasoned oak barrels and lees-stirred for 14 months. Delicious now, it's a full-bodied, generous wine with strong peach, grapefruit and nut flavours, showing good complexity, and a well-rounded finish.

DRY $30 –V

Distant Land Hawke's Bay Chardonnay (★★☆)

From Lincoln, the 2007 vintage (★★☆) was grown in the Dartmoor Valley, lees-aged and handled without oak. It's a full-bodied, slightly sweet wine (6 grams/litre of residual sugar) with ripe, citrusy flavours, offering easy drinking.

MED/DRY $20 –V

Distant Land [Reserve] Hawke's Bay Chardonnay ★★★★

Note: the word 'reserve' appears only on the back label. The 2007 vintage (★★★★) is an elegant wine, with rich grapefruit and peach flavours, slightly toasty, finely balanced and smooth.

DRY $28 AV

Dog Point Vineyard Marlborough Chardonnay ★★★★★

This consistently classy, single-vineyard wine is grown on the south side of the Wairau Valley, fermented with indigenous yeasts, matured for 18 to 20 months in French oak barriques (15 to 25 per cent new), and given a full, softening malolactic fermentation. The 2008 vintage (★★★★☆) is tightly structured and crisp, with substantial body (14.5 per cent alcohol) and strong, ripe citrus and tropical-fruit flavours, gently seasoned with oak. A vibrantly fruity, minerally wine with firm acid spine, it is still very fresh and youthful; open mid-2011+.

Vintage	08	07	06	05	04	03
WR	6	6	6	5	6	5
Drink	10-14	10-12	10-13	10-12	10-11	P

DRY $33 V+

Dolbel Estate Hawke's Bay Chardonnay ★★★★☆

The generous, sophisticated 2008 vintage (★★★★☆) was estate-grown, hand-harvested and fully barrel-fermented (French, 57 per cent new). It's a sturdy, fleshy wine with concentrated, ripe stone-fruit flavours, dry, savoury and complex, a slightly toasty oak influence and a creamy-smooth finish. It's drinking well now.

Vintage	08	07
WR	6	6
Drink	10-12	10-11

DRY $30 AV

Domaine Georges Michel Golden Mile Marlborough Chardonnay ★★★

Named after 'the central route of the Rapaura area', this wine is tank-fermented and then matured in seasoned French oak casks. It is typically full-bodied and crisp, offering easy, no-fuss drinking. The 2007 vintage (★★★☆) is mouthfilling and vibrantly fruity, with good depth of ripe, peachy flavours, subtle toasty oak and a rounded, creamy-smooth finish.

DRY $20 –V

Domaine Georges Michel La Reserve Chardonnay ★★★☆

Grown at Rapaura, in Marlborough, this wine is tank-fermented and then matured for a year in new and one-year-old French oak barriques. Maturing well, the 2006 vintage (★★★★) is a mouthfilling, distinctly creamy wine with fresh acidity and strong grapefruit and nut flavours, showing considerable complexity.

Vintage	06	05
WR	6	6
Drink	10-12	10-11

DRY $25 –V

Drylands Marlborough Chardonnay ★★★★

From Constellation NZ, this enjoyable wine is an upfront style – fragrant, creamy and full of flavour. The 2007 vintage (★★★★), 'fermented predominantly in French oak barriques', has a toasty bouquet leading into a fleshy, smooth wine with stone-fruit and citrus-fruit flavours, creamy and toasty. Showing good concentration, it's drinking well now.

DRY $22 V+

Dry River Chardonnay ★★★★★

Elegance, restraint and subtle power are the key qualities of this Martinborough wine. It's not a bold, upfront style, but tight, savoury and seamless, with rich grapefruit and nut flavours that build in the bottle for several years. Based on very low-cropping (typically below 5 tonnes/hectare) Mendoza clone vines, it is hand-harvested, whole-bunch pressed and fermented in French oak hogsheads (averaging 25 per cent new). The proportion of the blend that has gone through a softening malolactic fermentation has never exceeded 15 per cent. The 2009 vintage (★★★★★) is typically subtle and complex, with a fragrant, slightly creamy and mealy bouquet leading into a refined, very fresh and youthful wine with fresh grapefruit-like flavours, subtle biscuity notes and a tight, slightly minerally finish. A very harmonious wine with excellent delicacy and structure, it's a classic cellaring style, best kept for at least a couple of years.

Vintage	09	08	07	06	05	04	03	02
WR	7	7	7	7	6	6	7	7
Drink	13-20	11-17	12-18	10-14	10-13	10-11	10-11	P

DRY $52 AV

East Coast Chardonnay (★★)

Made for 'Foodstuffs Own Brands' and sold cheaply in supermarkets, the 'cleanskin' 2009 vintage is a no-fuss quaffer with straightforward, lemony, peachy flavours and a very smooth finish. Priced right.

DRY $9 AV

Elephant Hill Chardonnay (★★★★☆)

Grown near the coast at Te Awanga, in Hawke's Bay, the 2008 vintage (★★★★☆) is rich, complex and full of personality. Hand-harvested, fermented with indigenous yeasts in French oak barriques (50 per cent new) and lees-aged in oak for 10 months, with no use of malolactic fermentation, it's a sophisticated wine with sweet-fruit delights, highly concentrated grapefruit and stone-fruit flavours seasoned with toasty oak, and a fresh, finely balanced finish. Drink now or cellar.

DRY $26 V+

Elephant Hill Hawke's Bay Chardonnay (★★★★☆)

The stylish 2008 vintage (★★★★☆) was estate-grown at Te Awanga, hand-picked and fermented with indigenous yeasts in French oak casks (half new). It's a sophisticated wine, sweet-fruited, with fresh, concentrated grapefruit and stone-fruit flavours, finely integrated toasty oak, and excellent complexity, texture and richness. Drink now or cellar.

DRY $26 V+

Emeny Road Tauranga Reserve Chardonnay ★★★☆

This rare Bay of Plenty wine is grown at Plummers Point, 17 kilometres west of Tauranga. The powerful 2007 vintage (★★★☆) is mouthfilling, with concentrated stone-fruit flavours, toasty oak, a hint of honey and firm acid spine. Drink now.

DRY $23 AV

Escarpment Chardonnay ★★★★

Due to the light crop in Martinborough, the 2007 vintage (★★★★) is a blend of Martinborough and Hawke's Bay grapes. Fermented and matured in French oak barriques (30 per cent new), it has very satisfying body and depth of grapefruit and peach flavours, seasoned with toasty oak. Finely balanced, with fresh acidity, it's a complex style, likely to age well.

Vintage	07	06
WR	5	7
Drink	10-11	P

DRY $35 -V

Esk Valley Hawke's Bay Chardonnay ★★★★

Top vintages offer fine value. The 2009 (★★★☆) was partly handled in tanks, but 71 per cent of the blend was fermented (partly with indigenous yeasts) in French oak barrels (15 per cent new). It's a full-bodied wine, very lively and refreshing, with ripe tropical-fruit flavours to the fore, a subtle seasoning of oak, good harmony and a dry, well-rounded finish.

Vintage	10	09	08	07	06
WR	6	6	7	7	6
Drink	11-13	10-12	10-11	10-12	P

DRY $24 V+

Esk Valley Winemakers Hawke's Bay Chardonnay ★★★★★

Often one of the region's most distinguished Chardonnays, this wine was called 'Reserve' rather than 'Winemakers', prior to the 2008 vintage. The 2008 (★★★★☆) is a blend of grapes from two sites – 85 per cent from Bay View, on the coast (which gives 'lush' fruit characters), and 15 per cent from the Gimblett Gravels (which yields a more 'flinty' style). Hand-picked, fermented with indigenous yeasts and matured for a year in French oak barriques (35 per cent new), it is sturdy (14.5 per cent alcohol), with rich peach and grapefruit flavours, complex, deliciously nutty and creamy. The 2009 vintage (★★★★☆) is fleshy, with rich, ripe tropical-fruit flavours, hints of butterscotch and toast, and fresh, vibrant acidity. It's still very youthful; open 2012+.

Vintage	09	08	07	06	05	04	03	02
WR	7	7	7	7	7	7	7	7
Drink	11-15	10-13	10-14	10-12	10-11	10-12	10-12	10-11

DRY $32 V+

Fairhall Downs Single Vineyard Marlborough Chardonnay ★★★★

Grown and hand-picked in the Brancott Valley, this wine shows rising form and the 2008 vintage (★★★★) is one of the best yet. Fermented with indigenous yeasts and matured for 10 months in French oak barriques, it's a very open, expressive and well-rounded wine with mouthfilling body and citrusy, peachy, slightly toasty and nutty flavours, showing good complexity.

Vintage	08	07	06	05	04
WR	6	7	7	NM	7
Drink	10-15	10-13	10-12	NM	P

DRY $30 –V

Fall Harvest Chardonnay (★★★)

From Constellation NZ, the 2007 vintage (★★★) is not identified by region, but made from New Zealand grapes. It shows good body, with plenty of peachy, slightly spicy flavour, ripe and smooth, and even a touch of complexity.

DRY $13 V+

Farmers Market Gisborne Chardonnay (★★★☆)

The attractive 2009 vintage (★★★☆) is a single-vineyard wine, not oak-aged. Medium to full-bodied, it is peachy, ripe and vibrantly fruity, with very good flavour depth and a slightly buttery, rounded finish. Drink 2010–11.

DRY $20 AV

Farmgate Hawke's Bay Chardonnay ★★★☆

From the Ngatarawa winery, this brand is sold directly to consumers via the Farmgate website. The 2008 vintage (★★★) was barrel-aged for 10 months. Full-bodied, with a biscuity bouquet and moderately concentrated flavours, it is peachy and smooth, with a fractionally off-dry finish.

Vintage	08	07	06
WR	7	NM	7
Drink	10-13	NM	P

MED/DRY $22 AV

Felton Road Block 2 Chardonnay ★★★★

The 2008 vintage (★★★★☆), estate-grown at Bannockburn, in Central Otago, was matured for 18 months in French oak casks (12 per cent new). Highly refined and mouthfilling, it has grapefruit-like flavours, slightly nutty and buttery, in a finely poised, very elegant style, likely to be long-lived.

Vintage	08
WR	7
Drink	10-18

DRY $42 –V

Felton Road Central Otago Chardonnay ★★★☆

Estate-grown at Bannockburn, this wine is matured in French oak barriques (with limited use of new oak – 12 per cent in 2008). The 2008 vintage (★★★★) is toasty and creamy, with mouthfilling body, cool-climate vigour and strong, citrusy, slightly buttery flavours, woven with fresh acidity. It should mature well.

Vintage	08	07	06	05	04
WR	6	7	6	6	6
Drink	10-18	10-13	10-12	10-11	P

DRY $32 –V

Felton Road Elms Central Otago Chardonnay ★★★★

The finely poised 2009 vintage (★★★★) is full of interest for Chardonnay lovers. Handled without oak, it is weighty and full-flavoured, citrusy and faintly buttery, with balanced acidity and excellent harmony in a very pleasant style, not at all brash but quietly satisfying, and enjoyable from the start.

Vintage	09
WR	6
Drink	10-17

DRY $24 V+

Fiddler's Green Waipara Chardonnay ★★★☆

The 2008 vintage (★★★☆) is a distinctly cool-climate style, fermented with indigenous yeasts in French oak barrels (20 per cent new). It offers fresh, strong, peachy, citrusy flavours, slightly toasty and honeyed, with good acid spine and some mealy complexity.

DRY $25 –V

Five Flax Chardonnay ★★★

A drink-young style, priced right. Made by Pernod Ricard NZ and handled without oak, but lees-aged and lees-stirred, it is typically fresh and smooth, in a vibrantly fruity style, balanced for easy drinking. The 2008 vintage (★★☆) is ripe and peachy, slightly buttery and creamy.

DRY $15 V+

Forrest Marlborough Chardonnay ★★★☆

John Forrest favours a gently oaked style, looking to very ripe grapes and extended lees-aging to give his wine character. It typically matures well. The 2007 vintage (★★★☆), released in mid-2010, was mostly handled in tanks, but a third of the blend was barrel-fermented. Enjoyable now, it's a fresh, fruit-driven style, balanced for easy drinking, with citrusy, slightly buttery flavours, showing some mealy complexity, and good harmony and depth.

DRY $20 AV

Fossil Ridge Nelson Unoaked Chardonnay ★★★
The 2007 vintage (★★★) is fruity and smooth, with plenty of citrusy, slightly limey flavour and a crisp finish.

DRY $17 AV

Foxes Island Marlborough Chardonnay ★★★★☆
This deeply flavoured, finely balanced Chardonnay is consistently impressive. The 2006 vintage (★★★★☆), fully fermented in French oak barriques, has concentrated, grapefruit-like flavours and a subtle seasoning of oak in a tightly structured, complex, minerally style.

Vintage	07	06	05	04
WR	6	6	6	6
Drink	10-15	P	P	P

DRY $35 –V

Framingham Marlborough Chardonnay ★★★★
Consistently attractive, in a subtle, satisfying style. Grown at several sites in the Wairau Valley, it is fermented in a 50:50 split of tanks and French oak barriques, with lees-aging and some malolactic fermentation. The 2009 vintage (★★★★) is already delicious. An elegant wine, it is full-bodied, with vibrant, peachy, citrusy, slightly buttery flavours, showing good richness and harmony, and a rounded finish.

Vintage	09	08	07	06
WR	6	6	6	6
Drink	10-15	10-13	10-12	10-11

DRY $23 V+

Frizzell Hawke's Bay Chardonnay (★★★)
Winemaker Rod McDonald set out to make a 'gutsy' style 'but without too much oak'. The debut 2008 vintage (★★★) was given a full, softening malolactic fermentation. A mouthfilling wine, it lacks complexity, but has generous, peachy, slightly buttery flavours, with a well-rounded finish.

Vintage	08
WR	5
Drink	10-12

DRY $22 –V

Fromm Brancott Valley Chardonnay (★★★★☆)
This stylish wine is grown in the Brancott Valley, on the south side of the Wairau Valley, fermented with indigenous yeasts in French oak casks (a low percentage new), and barrel-aged for well over a year. The 2006 vintage (★★★★☆) has buttery, biscuity aromas leading into a mouthfilling, creamy-textured wine with concentrated grapefruit-like flavours, mealy notes adding complexity, fresh underlying acidity and a tight, dry finish.

Vintage	08	07	06	05
WR	6	6	6	6
Drink	10-14	10-13	10-12	10-11

DRY $42 –V

Fromm Clayvin Vineyard Chardonnay ★★★★★

Fromm's top Chardonnay is grown on the southern flanks of the Wairau Valley, where the clay soils, says winemaker Hätsch Kalberer, give 'a less fruity, more minerally and tighter character'. Top vintages mature well for up to a decade. Fermented with indigenous yeasts in French oak barriques, with little or no use of new wood, it is barrel-aged for well over a year. The superb 2006 vintage (★★★★★) is rich and elegant, with a fragrant, complex bouquet and beautifully concentrated, grapefruit and slight spice flavours, showing a subtle oak/lees influence, and a long, finely balanced finish.

Vintage	08	07	06	05	04	03	02
WR	6	7	7	7	6	5	5
Drink	11-16	10-15	10-14	10-13	10-12	P	P

DRY $56 AV

Gem Gisborne Chardonnay ★★★★

Drinking well now, the 2006 vintage (★★★★) is a mature wine, softening and probably at its peak. Fermented with indigenous yeasts in French oak casks (one-third new), it is deep yellow, fleshy and rounded, with rich, peachy flavours. The 2007 is youthful and elegant, with peachy, slightly toasty flavours, showing excellent richness, delicacy and complexity. Best drinking mid-2011+.

Vintage	07	06
WR	7	6
Drink	10-17	10-15

DRY $30 –V

Gibbston Highgate Estate Heartbreaker Chardonnay ★★★

The 2008 vintage (★★★) was harvested at 24.8 brix in Central Otago and mostly tank-fermented; 20 per cent of the blend was fermented and lees-aged in new and older French oak casks. It's a distinctly cool-climate style, reminiscent of Chablis, with citrusy, appley flavours, crisp and lively. The 2009 (★★★) is fresh, vibrant and lemony, with a touch of creamy, toasty complexity and firm acid spine.

Vintage	09	08	07	06
WR	6	6	5	6
Drink	11-16	10-15	10-12	10-12

MED/DRY $29 –V

Gibbston Valley Reserve Chardonnay ★★★★

This is a more complex style than its stablemate under the Greenstone brand (below). Estate-grown in the Chinaman's Terrace Vineyard at Bendigo, in Central Otago, the 2008 vintage (★★★★) was fermented and lees-aged in French oak barriques (20 per cent new). It's a rich, mouthfilling, slightly creamy wine with citrusy, peachy and spicy flavours, showing good texture, complexity and harmony. The 2009 (★★★★) is richly fragrant, with vibrant stone-fruit flavours seasoned with toasty oak. Fresh, concentrated and harmonious, it should be at its best mid-2011+.

Vintage	09	08	07
WR	7	7	6
Drink	10-15	10-14	10-12

DRY $32 –V

Giesen Marlborough Chardonnay ★★★
The 2008 vintage (★★★), grown in the Wairau Valley, was mostly handled in tanks, but 35 per cent was barrel-fermented and all of the final blend was lees-aged, with 60 per cent malolactic fermentation. It's a mouthfilling wine with plenty of ripe, peachy flavour, a very subtle oak influence and a soft, rounded finish.

DRY $17 AV

Giesen The Brothers Marlborough Chardonnay (★★★★)
Drinking well now, the 2007 vintage (★★★★) was grown at two Wairau Valley sites and fermented and lees-aged for a year in barrels (45 per cent new). Still youthful in colour, with a fragrant, creamy, slightly toasty bouquet, it is mouthfilling, with rich, ripe grapefruit-like flavours, well-integrated oak, good complexity and a soft, well-rounded finish.

DRY $24 V+

Glazebrook Regional Reserve Chardonnay ★★★☆
Ngatarawa's second-tier Chardonnay is named after the Glazebrook family, formerly partners in the Hawke's Bay venture. Grown in The Triangle district and fermented and matured for 11 months in French oak barrels (15 per cent), the 2007 vintage (★★★★) is one of the best yet and maturing well. Full-bodied, it's an elegant wine with citrusy flavours showing good richness, finely integrated oak, and slightly mealy, buttery notes adding complexity.

Vintage	07	06	05
WR	7	6	6
Drink	10-12	10-11	P

DRY $27 –V

Goldridge Estate Gisborne Chardonnay ★★☆
The 2009 vintage (★★☆) was partly barrel-fermented. A single-vineyard wine, it is fresh and lively, in a fruit-driven style with peachy, smooth flavours.

DRY $16 AV

Goldridge Estate Premium Reserve Chardonnay ★★★
The easy-drinking 2008 vintage (★★★) is a blend of Matakana (70 per cent) and Hawke's Bay (30 per cent) grapes, fermented and lees-aged for 10 months in predominantly French oak barriques (30 per cent new). Fleshy and smooth, it has plenty of ripe, peachy, slightly toasty and buttery flavour, with a well-rounded finish. Ready.

DRY $19 AV

Goldridge Estate Premium Reserve Hawke's Bay Chardonnay ★★★★
The 2009 vintage (★★★★) is a great buy. A single-vineyard wine, fermented and matured on its yeast lees for 10 months in predominantly French oak barriques (30 per cent new), it has a nutty bouquet leading into a full-bodied palate with peachy, slightly creamy flavours, showing considerable complexity. Fleshy, weighty and well-rounded, it's already delicious.

DRY $19 V+

Goldwater Marlborough Chardonnay ★★★★

Typically a finely scented, weighty, vibrantly fruity wine with tropical-fruit characters and subtle use of oak in a highly attractive style. Partly French oak-fermented, the 2008 vintage (★★★★) is a full-bodied style with strong ripe-fruit flavours, a touch of butteriness and a dry, well-rounded finish. Drinking well in its youth, it shows excellent delicacy, texture, complexity and harmony.

Vintage	08	07	06	05	04
WR	6	7	7	6	6
Drink	10-13	P	P	P	P

DRY $21 V+

Goldwater Zell Waiheke Island Chardonnay ★★★★☆

Grown in the hillside, clay-based Zell Vineyard on Waiheke Island, this is a rich, complex wine with the ripeness and roundness typical of northern Chardonnays. It is hand-picked, whole-bunch pressed and fermented with indigenous yeasts in French oak casks (30 to 40 per cent new), with full malolactic fermentation in 2008. The 2008 vintage (★★★★★), barrel-aged for a year, is one of the finest yet. A lovely, tightly structured wine, it is highly fragrant, with rich stone-fruit flavours, a hint of butterscotch, and excellent vigour, delicacy and length. It should mature well.

DRY $34 AV

Gravitas Reserve Marlborough Chardonnay ★★★★☆

The 2007 vintage (★★★★☆) was hand-picked and fermented with indigenous yeasts in French oak barriques. Fragrant, with a complex, slightly biscuity bouquet, it is sweet-fruited and rich, with concentrated peach and slight butterscotch flavours woven with fresh acidity.

Vintage	07	06
WR	7	6
Drink	10-11	P

DRY $29 V+

Greenhough Hope Vineyard Chardonnay ★★★★★

This impressive wine is estate-grown at Hope, in Nelson, hand-picked and fermented and matured for a year in French oak casks (36 per cent new in 2008). The 2008 (★★★★★) is very refined and highly concentrated. Still youthful, it has sweet-fruit delights, very generous, citrusy flavours, a hint of butterscotch, mealy, biscuity complexities and a long, rounded finish.

Vintage	08	07	06	05	04
WR	6	7	6	6	6
Drink	10-15	10-13	10-12	10-12	P

DRY $32 V+

Greenhough Nelson Chardonnay ★★★★

This consistently enjoyable wine is fermented and matured in seasoned French oak casks. The 2008 vintage (★★★☆) is fresh and vibrantly fruity, with good body and depth of lemony, appley flavours and a subtle seasoning of oak.

Vintage	08	07
WR	7	6
Drink	10-13	10-12

DRY $22 V+

Greenstone Central Otago Chardonnay ★★★

Past vintages were called 'Gibbston Valley Greenstone Chardonnay'. The 2009 (★★★) is an attractive example of 'fruit-driven' Chardonnay – vibrant, with fresh, lemony, appley flavours, showing good immediacy.

DRY $24 –V

Greystone Waipara Chardonnay (★★★★☆)

The excellent 2009 vintage (★★★★☆) was hand-picked and mostly (75 per cent) fermented in tanks, but all the blend was matured in French oak barrels (25 per cent new). A fleshy, weighty, complex wine with rich stone-fruit flavours and a hint of butterscotch, it has lovely texture and depth.

Vintage	09
WR	7
Drink	10-14

DRY $34 AV

Grove Mill Marlborough Chardonnay ★★★☆

Typically an attractive, skilfully balanced, flavoursome wine with a subtle oak influence and fresh, crisp acidity. The 2007 (★★★★), fermented in a mix of tanks and barrels (new to five years old), is an elegant, weighty, vibrantly fruity wine with strong grapefruit and slight lime flavours, balanced acidity and a twist of oak. Subtle but not simple, it's a top vintage, enjoyable from the start.

Vintage	08	07
WR	6	6
Drink	10-13	10-12

DRY $18 V+

Gunn Estate Chardonnay ★★★

The 2009 vintage (★★★) is a New Zealand wine, not identified by region and handled without oak. Pale straw, it is mouthfilling, ripe, peachy and smooth, with plenty of flavour and a slightly spicy, rounded, dry finish. Good, easy drinking.

DRY $18 AV

Gunn Estate Skeetfield Chardonnay ★★★★☆

From Sacred Hill, the 2007 vintage (★★★★) was hand-picked in Hawke's Bay and fermented and lees-aged for 10 months in new and one-year-old French oak barriques. A tight, elegant style, it has rich, citrusy, slightly limey flavours, showing good complexity, and a fresh, crisp and lively finish.

Vintage	07	06	05	04
WR	7	6	6	7
Drink	12-14	10-11	P	P

DRY $33 AV

Hans Herzog Marlborough Chardonnay ★★★★☆

At its best, this is a notably powerful wine with layers of peach, butterscotch, grapefruit and nut flavours and a long, rounded finish. The 2008 (★★★★☆) was hand-picked at 24 brix, fermented with indigenous yeasts in 500-litre French oak puncheons and given a full, softening malolactic fermentation. Oak-aged for a year, it is weighty, rich and sweet-fruited, with concentrated, citrusy flavours, a subtle oak influence, good texture and a rounded finish. It's a forward vintage, already drinking well.

Vintage	09	08
WR	7	7
Drink	10-20	10-19

DRY $44 –V

Hay Maker Hawke's Bay Chardonnay (★★☆)

From Mud House, the 2007 vintage (★★☆) is a fruit-driven style with decent depth of vibrant, citrusy flavours and a dry finish.

DRY $17 –V

Highfield Marlborough Chardonnay ★★★★

A consistently classy wine. The 2008 vintage (★★★★☆) has a fragrant bouquet, citrusy and biscuity. Mouthfilling, it's a rich, elegant wine, tightly structured, with grapefruit-like flavours, slightly nutty, mealy and buttery, and a dry, minerally finish. It should be long-lived. Still very youthful, the 2009 (★★★☆) was grown in the Omaka Valley and fully barrel-fermented. Citrusy, with fresh acidity and some mealy complexity, it needs more time; open mid-2011+.

Vintage	09	08	07	06
WR	6	5	6	6
Drink	11-15	10-14	10-11	P

DRY $33 –V

Hinchco Barrel Fermented Matakana Chardonnay (★★★)

Hand-picked and fermented and lees-aged in new American oak, the 2008 vintage (★★★) is a peachy, nutty wine with good body and freshness, but less oak would have been better.

DRY $30 –V

Hitchen Road Chardonnay (★★★★)

The 2009 vintage (★★★★) is a great buy. Grown at Pokeno, in North Waikato, hand-picked, barrel-fermented and wood-aged for over a year, it is mouthfilling, fresh, youthful and creamy-textured, with ripe peach, fig, grapefruit and nut flavours, slightly nutty and mealy, and good delicacy and harmony. Best drinking mid-2011+.

Vintage	09
WR	6
Drink	10-14

DRY $15 V+

Hitchen Road Pokeno Unwooded Chardonnay (★★★☆)

Priced sharply, the 2009 vintage (★★★☆) was estate-grown at a 'summer-dry' site at Pokeno, in northern Waikato. Fleshy (14.4 per cent alcohol), ripe and rounded, it's a very good example of the unoaked style, with sweet-fruit characters and good depth of stone-fruit flavours, soft and forward.

Vintage	08
WR	6
Drink	10-12

DRY $15 V+

Huia Marlborough Chardonnay ★★★★

This full-bodied, creamy-textured wine is hand-picked, fermented with indigenous yeasts and matured in French oak casks, emerging with citrusy, slightly nutty flavours. Understated in its youth, it typically matures well for several years, offering smooth, very satisfying drinking. The 2007 vintage (★★★★) is mouthfilling and rounded, with ripe, grapefruit-like flavours, a gentle oak influence, slightly buttery notes, and good harmony and texture. It's a subtle, satisfying wine with a lingering finish.

Vintage	07	06
WR	7	6
Drink	10-15	10-11

DRY $34 –V

Huntaway Reserve Gisborne Chardonnay ★★★☆

From Pernod Ricard NZ, this wine is made in a high-impact, creamy-rich style. The 2008 vintage (★★★☆) was fermented in French oak casks and lees-stirred weekly, with a 'huge' percentage of malolactic fermentation. A weighty, overtly oaky wine with ripe-fruit flavours, it is peachy, creamy and nutty, with considerable complexity. Tasted before bottling (and so not rated), the 2009 is rich and ripe, with grapefruit and nut flavours, showing good complexity.

DRY $24 AV

Hunter's Marlborough Chardonnay ★★★☆

This wine places its accent on fresh, vibrant fruit flavours, overlaid with subtle, mealy barrel-ferment characters. About 40 per cent of the blend is fermented and lees-aged in new French oak barriques (medium toast); the rest is tank-fermented and then matured in one and two-year-old casks. It is a proven performer in the cellar. The 2008 (★★★☆) is creamy and smooth, with satisfying fullness and depth of grapefruit-like flavours, a slightly nutty complexity and good texture.

Vintage	08	07	06
WR	6	6	6
Drink	10-13	10-11	P

DRY $20 AV

Hyperion Helios Matakana Chardonnay ★★★☆

The 2008 vintage (★★★☆) was estate-grown, hand-picked and fermented and lees-aged for six months in French oak barriques (one year old). It's a weighty wine with ripe stone-fruit and toasty oak flavours, balanced acidity, fractional sweetness (6 grams/litre of residual sugar) and very good depth.

Vintage	08
WR	6
Drink	10-14

MED/DRY $27 –V

Instinct Hawke's Bay Chardonnay (★★★)

From C.J. Pask, the easy-drinking 2007 vintage (★★★) was grown in Gimblett Road and mostly tank-fermented, with 'some' barrel fermentation. Mouthfilling, with a citrusy bouquet, it has lemony flavours to the fore, with hints of toast and butterscotch, lively acidity and a smooth finish.

DRY $17 AV

Isabel Marlborough Chardonnay ★★★★

This producer is after 'a tight, restrained style'. Clearly the best vintage for several years, the 2006 (★★★★☆) was tank-fermented and then matured for 10 months in seasoned barrels. It is fragrant, minerally and slightly creamy, with mouthfilling body, generous, ripe-fruit flavours and a finely textured, lingering finish.

Vintage	06	05
WR	7	7
Drink	10-17	10-15

DRY $28 AV

Ivicevich Signature Reserve Waimauku Chardonnay ★★★★☆

This is West Brook's estate Chardonnay, grown in West Auckland. The 2007 vintage (★★★★☆) is fleshy, with fresh, very delicate pear, grapefruit and spice flavours, gentle acidity and lovely texture.

DRY $39 –V

Jackson Estate Shelter Belt Marlborough Chardonnay ★★★☆

The 2008 vintage (★★★☆) was estate-grown in the Homestead Vineyard and fully barrel-aged (20 per cent new). Creamy and slightly biscuity on the nose, it is mouthfilling and rounded, with citrusy, peachy flavours, a hint of butterscotch, and very good complexity and depth.

Vintage	08	07	06
WR	6	6	6
Drink	10-14	10-15	10-12

DRY $23 AV

Johner Wairarapa Chardonnay (★★★☆)

Grown at Gladstone, in the northern Wairarapa, the 2009 vintage (★★★☆) is youthful, with mouthfilling body and very good depth of fresh, vibrant, peachy, citrusy flavours, slightly buttery and crisp.

DRY $24 AV

John Forrest Collection Marlborough Chardonnay ★★★★☆

The debut 2004 vintage (★★★★) is still very alive, with youthful colour, rich grapefruit and spice flavours, slightly minerally and crisp, and a slightly toasty finish. There is no 2005, but the 2006 vintage (★★★★★) is very classy. Fermented and matured in French oak casks (over half new), it's a highly refined wine with concentrated, citrusy flavours, nutty, mealy notes adding richness and complexity, and good harmony and length.

DRY $50 –V

John Forrest Collection Waitaki Valley North Otago Chardonnay (★★★★☆)

Fully fermented in French oak barriques (all older) and given a full, softening malolactic fermentation, the debut 2008 vintage (★★★★☆) has a fragrant, creamy bouquet leading into a weighty, citrusy, toasty and buttery wine, with good richness and a rounded finish. It's hard to pin down any distinctive regional characters, but it's a complex wine, maturing well.

Vintage	08
WR	6
Drink	10-12

DRY $50 –V

Kahurangi Estate Moutere Chardonnay ★★★

The 2007 vintage (★★★) is a crisp Nelson wine, mouthfilling (14 per cent alcohol), with peachy, slightly honeyed and toasty flavours, and a hint of butterscotch. It's an upfront style, ready to roll.

DRY $22 –V

Kaimira Estate Brightwater Chardonnay ★★★☆

Estate-grown in Nelson and fermented and matured for nine months in French oak casks (20 per cent new), the 2009 vintage (★★★) is a fresh, fruit-driven style with vibrant, citrusy aromas and flavours and a slightly buttery finish.

Vintage	09	08	07	06	05
WR	5	5	5	5	6
Drink	10-12	10-12	10-12	10-11	P

DRY $22 AV

Kaipara Estate Nine Lakes Chardonnay ★★★☆

Estate-grown on the South Head peninsula of the Kaipara Harbour, in Auckland, the 2007 vintage (★★★☆) is an elegant wine, still youthful, with strong, citrusy flavours, slightly buttery and toasty, and a crisp finish. The 2008 (★★★☆) is mouthfilling, with ripe stone-fruit flavours, slightly buttery notes, a strong seasoning of toasty oak and a rounded finish. It's already drinking well.

DRY $25 –V

Kaituna Valley Canterbury The Kaituna Vineyard Chardonnay ★★★

Grown on Banks Peninsula, this is always a characterful wine. The 2007 vintage (★★★) was estate-grown in the Kaituna Valley, hand-picked at 24 to 25 brix, and fermented in French oak casks (30 per cent new). Enjoyable now, it's a mellow wine with grapefruit-like flavours, some 'funky' indigenous yeast notes adding interest, and a slightly creamy texture.

DRY $22 –V

Karikari Estate Karikari Peninsula Chardonnay ★★★★

From New Zealand's northernmost vineyard and winery, this sturdy wine reminds me of a white from the Rhône Valley. The 2007 vintage (★★★★) was fermented and matured for nine months in predominantly French oak barriques. The toasty, creamy bouquet leads into a mouthfilling wine with fresh acidity and ripe sweet-fruit flavours, showing excellent depth.

Vintage	07
WR	7
Drink	10-12

DRY $34 –V

Kawarau Estate Reserve Chardonnay ★★★★

Certified organic, this consistently excellent, single-vineyard wine is grown at Pisa Flats, north of Cromwell in Central Otago. The 2007 (★★★★) was fermented with indigenous yeasts in French barriques, oak-aged for 10 months and given a full, softening malolactic fermentation. Invitingly fragrant, it is a weighty wine with ripe, concentrated flavours, slightly creamy, harmonious and persistent. The refined 2008 vintage (★★★★) is fresh, lemony and dry, with mouthfilling body, crisp, minerally acidity and nutty oak adding complexity.

Vintage	08	07	06
WR	5	6	5
Drink	10-11	10-11	P

DRY $30 –V

Kemblefield The Distinction Chardonnay ★★★★

This has been the key wine in the Kemblefield range, although it now has a low profile in New Zealand. Estate-grown in the slightly elevated, relatively cool Mangatahi district of Hawke's Bay, French oak-fermented and matured on its yeast lees for up to 14 months, it is typically made in an upfront style with rich toast and butterscotch aromas, substantial body and strong, peachy, toasty flavours.

DRY $22 V+

Kennedy Point Chardonnay Cuvée Eve (★★★★)

The debut 2008 vintage (★★★★) was grown in the Oakura Bay Vineyard on Waiheke Island, and fermented (with indigenous yeasts) and matured for 15 months in French oak barriques. It's a full-bodied, rich wine with concentrated, ripe, stone-fruit flavours, showing good freshness and complexity.

DRY $38 –V

Kerr Farm Limited Release Kumeu Chardonnay ★★★

Estate-grown in West Auckland and fermented and matured in French and American oak casks, the 2007 vintage (★★★) is pale gold, with mouthfilling body and peachy, slightly toasty flavours, crisp and dry. Maturing solidly, with some complexity, it's ready for drinking.

DRY $25 –V

Kerr Farm Thelma Grace Chardonnay (★★☆)

Made in a 'very lightly oaked' style, the easy-drinking 2009 vintage (★★☆) of this Kumeu, West Auckland wine is pleasantly fruity, with ripe, citrusy, peachy flavours and a smooth finish.

DRY $20 –V

Kidnapper Cliffs Hawke's Bay Chardonnay (★★★★★)

From Te Awa, the debut 2009 vintage (★★★★★) was estate-grown in the Gimblett Gravels, fermented with cultured yeasts and matured in French oak casks of varying sizes (225 to 500 litres, 15 to 20 per cent new). It's a classy, immaculate wine, weighty and rich, with ripe grapefruit-like flavours and finely integrated, biscuity oak. Built for cellaring, it is very refined, with fresh, vibrant fruit flavours shining through and lovely depth, texture and length.

DRY $45 AV

Kim Crawford New Zealand Unoaked Chardonnay ★★★

Blended from Gisborne, Hawke's Bay and Marlborough grapes, the 2008 vintage (★★☆) is an easy-drinking style with simple, vibrantly fruity, faintly honeyed flavours and a rounded finish. Ready.

DRY $23 –V

Kim Crawford SP Tietjen Gisborne Chardonnay ★★★★

Made in an upfront style, this is one of the region's boldest Chardonnays, with rich ripe-fruit flavours, strongly seasoned with perfumed, toasty oak. Fermented in American oak casks, it is given a full, softening malolactic fermentation. Less lush than some vintages, the 2007 (★★★☆) is mouthfilling (14.5 per cent alcohol), with ripe, peachy, citrusy, toasty flavours, showing some complexity and very good depth. Ready.

DRY $33 –V

Kina Beach Vineyard Reserve Chardonnay ★★★★☆

This single-vineyard, coastal Nelson wine possesses strong personality. The 2007 vintage (★★★★☆) was grown at Kina Beach and fermented and matured in French oak barriques (one-third new). Weighty and rich, it is slightly tighter, more elegant and complex than some past vintages, with finely integrated oak and impressive concentration, delicacy and length. The 2008 (★★★★★) is the best yet. A stylish wine, it is very fresh and vibrant, with concentrated, ripe grapefruit-like flavours, a subtle seasoning of oak and a slightly creamy, long finish.

Vintage	08	07	06	05	04
WR	7	7	7	7	7
Drink	10-15	10-15	10-15	P	P

DRY $30 AV

Kirkpatrick Estate Reserve Chardonnay (★★★☆)

Grown at Patutahi, in Gisborne, the 2009 vintage (★★★☆) was barrel-aged for 16 months in oak casks (20 per cent new). It's an upfront style, full-bodied, fleshy and soft, with strong, ripe, citrusy flavours strongly seasoned with toasty oak. It's already enjoyable; drink now or cellar.

Vintage	09
WR	5
Drink	10-13

DRY $26 –V

Kono Gisborne Unoaked Chardonnay (★★★)

From Tohu Wines, the 2007 vintage (★★★) is a smooth, fruit-driven style with lively, citrusy, appley flavours and slightly creamy notes. It offers easy, enjoyable drinking.

DRY $18 AV

Kumeu River Coddington Chardonnay ★★★★★

Launched from the 2006 vintage, this wine is grown in the Coddington Vineyard, between Huapai and Waimauku. The grapes, cultivated on a clay hillside, achieve an advanced level of ripeness (described by marketing manager Paul Brajkovich as 'flamboyant, unctuous, peachy'). Powerful, complex and slightly nutty, it's a lusher, softer wine than its Hunting Hill stablemate (below), but the finish is tight-knit, promising plenty of scope for development. Tasted in April 2010, the 2006 (★★★★★) and 2007 (★★★★★) vintages are both unfolding well, showing notable power and concentration. The 2008 (★★★★★) is highly fragrant, with rich, ripe stone-fruit flavours, biscuity, mealy notes adding complexity, good acid spine and a long finish. Still youthful, it's well worth cellaring.

Vintage	08	07	06
WR	6	7	7
Drink	10-14	10-14	10-13

DRY $43 AV

Kumeu River Estate Chardonnay ★★★★★

This wine now ranks fourth in the company's hierarchy of five Chardonnays, after three single-vineyard labels, but is still outstanding. Grown at Kumeu, in West Auckland, it is powerful, with rich, beautifully interwoven flavours and a seductively creamy texture, but it also has good acid spine. The key to its quality lies in the vineyards, says winemaker Michael Brajkovich: 'We manage to get the grapes very ripe.' Grown in several blocks around Kumeu, hand-picked, fermented with indigenous yeasts and lees-aged (with weekly or twice-weekly lees-stirring) in Burgundy oak barriques (typically 25 per cent new), the wine also normally undergoes a full malolactic fermentation. Tasted in April 2010, the 2006 vintage (★★★★★) is probably currently at its peak, while the 2007 (★★★★★) is still developing. The 2008 vintage (★★★★★) is very open and expressive. Weighty and rich, showing lovely fruit sweetness, it offers highly concentrated stone-fruit flavours, with finely integrated oak and fresh, appetising acidity. Peachy and mealy, with a hint of butterscotch, it's a lush, generous wine, already delicious.

Vintage	08	07	06	05	04	03	02
WR	7	7	7	7	7	6	7
Drink	10-14	10-14	10-13	P	P	P	P

DRY $36 AV

Kumeu River Hunting Hill Chardonnay ★★★★★

Launched from the 2006 vintage, this single-vineyard wine is grown on the slopes above Mate's Vineyard, directly over the road from the winery at Kumeu. Marketing manager Paul Brajkovich describes the site's Chardonnay fruit characters as 'floral'. A stylish, elegant wine, in its youth it is less lush than its Coddington stablemate (above), but with good acidity and citrusy, complex flavours that build well across the palate. Tasted in April 2010, the 2006 vintage (★★★★★) is outstanding – a very 'complete' wine – while the very refined, tightly structured 2007 (★★★★★) is still unfolding. Very fresh and youthful, the 2008 (★★★★★) is highly fragrant, with generous grapefruit, peach and nut flavours and a tight-knit finish. A very classy wine, it should be long-lived.

Vintage	08	07	06
WR	7	7	7
Drink	10-14	10-14	10-13

DRY $45 AV

Kumeu River Mate's Vineyard Kumeu Chardonnay ★★★★★

This extremely classy single-vineyard wine is Kumeu River's flagship. It is made entirely from the best of the fruit harvested from Mate's Vineyard, planted in 1990 on the site of the original Kumeu River vineyard purchased by Mate Brajkovich in 1944. Strikingly similar to Kumeu River Estate Chardonnay, but slightly more opulent and concentrated, it offers the same rich and harmonious flavours of grapefruit, peach and butterscotch, typically with a stronger seasoning of new French oak. For winemaker Michael Brajkovich, the hallmark of Mate's Vineyard is 'a pear-like character on the nose, with richness and length on the palate after two to three years'. Tasted in April 2010, the 2006 (★★★★★) is powerful, rich and harmonious, with good freshness and vigour; the 2007 (★★★★★) is superb now, with concentrated stone-fruit flavours and a long, slightly buttery finish. The 2008 vintage (★★★★★) is highly fragrant and finely poised, with rich, youthful flavours of stone-fruit and toast, showing lovely depth and complexity. It's already approachable, but best cellared to at least mid-2011.

Vintage	08	07	06	05	04	03	02
WR	6	7	7	6	7	6	7
Drink	10-14	10-14	10-13	10-11	P	P	P

DRY $50 AV

Kumeu River Village Chardonnay ★★★☆

Kumeu River's lower-tier, drink-young wine is made from heavier-bearing Chardonnay clones than the Mendoza commonly used for the top wines, and is fermented with indigenous yeasts in a mix of tanks (principally) and seasoned French oak casks. The 2008 vintage (★★★☆) is mouthfilling, with good depth of ripe, peachy, slightly spicy flavours, fresh, crisp and dry.

DRY $18 V+

Kupe by Escarpment Martinborough Chardonnay ★★★★☆

The 2008 vintage (★★★★☆) is Escarpment's top Chardonnay. A single-vineyard wine, it was fermented with indigenous yeasts and lees-aged for a year in French oak barriques (30 per cent new). Deliciously rich and sweet-fruited, with fresh, vibrant flavours of stone-fruit and toasty oak, and good acid spine, it's an elegant, tightly structured wine, well worth cellaring.

DRY $55 –V

Lake Chalice Flight 42 Unoaked Marlborough Chardonnay ★★★

Typically a fresh, vibrant wine with good depth of citrusy, appley flavours, balanced for easy drinking. The 2009 vintage (★★★), grown in the Wairau and Awatere valleys, is mouthfilling, slightly buttery and smooth, with fresh, lemony aromas and flavours.

DRY $20 –V

Lake Chalice Marlborough Chardonnay ★★★☆

This 'black label' wine is fresh, vibrant and creamy, with drink-young appeal. The 2007 vintage (★★★☆) was fermented in a mix of tanks and barrels, and given a full, softening malolactic fermentation. Buoyantly fruity, it is citrusy and appley, with a gentle twist of oak, mouthfilling body and a well-rounded finish.

DRY $20 AV

Lake Chalice Platinum Marlborough Chardonnay ★★★★

This lush, rich, complex wine is estate-grown in the Falcon Vineyard at Rapaura. Hand-picked, it is fermented in French and American oak barriques, lees-aged and given a full malolactic fermentation. It typically offers strong, nutty, mealy flavours and a very creamy texture in a fragrant, full-blown Chardonnay style. The powerful 2007 vintage (★★★★) has deep grapefruit and nut flavours, with a hint of butterscotch.

Vintage	07
WR	6
Drink	P

DRY $29 AV

La Strada Marlborough Chardonnay (★★★★)

Fromm's unoaked Chardonnay, described by winemaker Hätsch Kalberer as 'very Chablis-like', is given extensive aging on lees and a full, softening malolactic fermentation, but no barrel maturation. The 2007 vintage (★★★★) is weighty and concentrated, with citrusy, slightly spicy flavours, finely balanced acidity and a long finish.

Vintage	08	07	06
WR	6	6	6
Drink	10-14	10-13	10-12

DRY $31 –V

Lawson's Dry Hills Marlborough Chardonnay ★★★★
This is typically a characterful wine with concentrated, peachy, toasty flavours. Released at up to four years old, it gives a rare opportunity to buy a mature Chardonnay, at its peak. The 2007 vintage (★★★☆) is a single-vineyard wine, harvested in the Wairau Valley at a ripe 24 brix, and fermented and matured for nine months in French oak casks. Light gold, it has crisp, slightly developed grapefruit and toast flavours, showing very good complexity and depth. Ready.

Vintage	07	DRY $27 AV
WR	6	
Drink	10-11	

Lawson's Dry Hills Unoaked Marlborough Chardonnay ★★★☆
Grown in the company-owned Chaytors Road Vineyard in the Wairau Valley, this wine is cool-fermented in tanks, with daily stirring of its yeast lees 'to add a creamy texture', but malolactic fermentation is avoided. The 2008 vintage (★★★) is mouthfilling and dry, with citrusy, appley aromas and flavours in an uncomplicated but very fresh and vibrant, highly enjoyable style.

Vintage	09	08	DRY $20 AV
WR	6	7	
Drink	P	P	

Lochiel Estate Mangawhai Chardonnay (★★★★)
The skilfully crafted, powerful, creamy-textured 2008 vintage (★★★★) was estate-grown in Northland, in the foothills of the Brynderwyn Range, and 80 per cent barrel-fermented (French, 30 per cent new). Light yellow, with a fragrant bouquet mingling ripe-fruit aromas and toasty oak, it is sturdy (14.5 per cent alcohol), with concentrated stone-fruit flavours, good complexity and a rounded finish. A bold, upfront style, it's drinking well now.

Vintage	08	DRY $25 AV
WR	6	
Drink	10-12	

Lonestone Hawke's Bay Chardonnay ★★★☆
Produced by Auckland-based wine distributor Bennett & Deller, the 2007 vintage (★★★★) was French oak-aged for six months. Delicious now, it's a very harmonious wine, only moderately complex but concentrated, with strong grapefruit and peach flavours and a creamy-smooth texture.

Vintage	07	06	DRY $20 AV
WR	7	7	
Drink	10-12	10-11	

Longbush Chardonnay ★★★
This 'bird series' label is enjoyable young. Grown in Gisborne and French oak-aged for 10 months, the 2008 vintage (★★★) is full-bodied, with a slightly buttery and toasty bouquet, and satisfying depth of peachy, toasty, well-rounded flavour.

Vintage	08	07	DRY $18 AV
WR	6	5	
Drink	10-14	P	

Longridge Hawke's Bay Chardonnay ★★★

Part of the Pernod Ricard NZ portfolio, this wine showcases fresh, ripe fruit characters. The 2007 vintage (★★★), partly French and American oak-aged, is an easy-drinking wine with citrusy, slightly buttery flavours, fresh and smooth.

Vintage	07	06	05
WR	6	6	5
Drink	P	P	P

DRY $18 AV

Longview Estate Northland Chardonnay (★★)

Estate-grown just south of Whangarei, this wine is matured for five months in French and Hungarian oak barriques. Most vintages I have tasted have been full-bodied and dry, but lacked a bit of freshness and vibrancy.

DRY $18 –V

Mahi Marlborough Chardonnay ★★★★☆

The great value 2009 vintage (★★★★☆) was hand-picked and fermented with indigenous yeasts in French oak barriques. It's a mouthfilling, creamy-textured wine with strong, ripe stone-fruit and toast flavours, a fine thread of acidity, a distinct hint of butterscotch and a rich, rounded finish. Showing excellent harmony, delicacy and richness, it's already delicious.

Vintage	09
WR	6
Drink	10-15

DRY $24 V+

Mahi Twin Valleys Vineyard Marlborough Chardonnay ★★★★☆

The 2008 vintage (★★★★☆) was grown and hand-picked in the Twin Valleys Vineyard, at the junction of the Wairau and Waihopai valleys. Fermented with indigenous yeasts and matured for 10 months in French oak barriques, it's a fleshy, creamy wine with rich grapefruit and nut flavours, showing good complexity. Delicious from the start, it's a very harmonious wine, for drinking now or cellaring.

Vintage	08	07	06
WR	6	6	6
Drink	10-16	10-12	10-12

DRY $35 –V

Mahurangi River Field of Grace Chardonnay ★★★☆

Grown at Matakana, the 2009 vintage (★★★★) was fermented and matured for a year in seasoned French oak barrels. Pale yellow, it's weighty and complex, with generous peachy, slightly spicy flavours, a hint of honey, and a rich, rounded finish. Showing strong personality, it's already drinking well. The 2008 vintage (★★☆) is also mouthfilling and full-flavoured, but slightly rustic. The more enjoyable 2007 (★★★☆) is weighty and complex but now slightly past its best.

DRY $39 –V

Chardonnay

Mahurangi River Field of Grace Reserve Chardonnay (★★★)

Grown at Matakana and fermented with indigenous yeasts in French oak casks (all new), the 2009 vintage (★★★) is straw-coloured, with substantial body and lots of peachy, slightly spicy and honeyed flavour. It shows considerable development for such a young wine; drink now to 2011.

DRY $54 –V

Maimai Creek Hawke's Bay Chardonnay ★★☆

The 2009 vintage (★★☆) is a fruit-driven style, with simple, lemony aromas and flavours and mouthfilling body.

DRY $20 –V

Main Divide Waipara Valley Chardonnay ★★★☆

The Main Divide range is from Pegasus Bay. The 2008 vintage (★★★☆), the first to be grown at Waipara, was fermented with indigenous yeasts and lees-aged for a year in French barriques (with no new oak). Drinking well now, it has fresh acidity and generous, peachy, slightly honeyed flavours, showing considerable complexity and richness.

Vintage	08	07	06
WR	6	5	6
Drink	10-12	10-11	P

DRY $20 AV

Man O' War Valhalla Waiheke Island Chardonnay ★★★★

Grown at the far, eastern end of the island in Auckland's Hauraki Gulf and matured for a year in French oak casks (40 per cent new), the bright, light yellow 2009 vintage (★★★★☆) is a tightly structured, very youthful wine with good acid spine and rich, citrusy, peachy flavours, slightly nutty, minerally and long. Showing good intensity and poise, it's one for the cellar.

Vintage	09
WR	7
Drink	11-13

DRY $40 –V

Man O' War Waiheke Island Chardonnay ★★★★

Fermented in tanks (70 per cent) and seasoned oak barrels (30 per cent), the 2009 vintage (★★★★) is a quite powerful wine, sturdy, with concentrated, peachy, citrusy flavours, a subtle oak influence, a minerally streak, considerable complexity and a crisp, long finish.

Vintage	09
WR	7
Drink	11-13

DRY $28 AV

Map Maker Marlborough Chardonnay Pure (★★★)

Described by the producer, Staete Landt, as a 'Chablis style', the 2008 vintage (★★★) was grown at Rapaura, hand-picked, fermented in old French barriques and then matured in stainless steel tanks. Mouthfilling, it is citrusy and crisp, with a very subtle oak influence, good vigour and a dry finish.

Vintage	08
WR	6
Drink	10-12

DRY $25 –V

Marble Point Hanmer Springs Chardonnay ★★★☆

The 2008 (★★★★), grown in North Canterbury, is an elegant, distinctly cool-climate style with a lemony, biscuity, fragrant bouquet. Refined and youthful, with citrusy fruit flavours, barrel-ferment complexity and good acid spine, it's an auspicious debut, worth cellaring. The 2009 vintage (★★★), harvested at 25 brix and barrel-fermented, has strong, peachy, toasty flavours, a hint of butterscotch and a crisp, dry finish, but when tasted in mid to late 2010 was still coming together.

Vintage	09
WR	6
Drink	12-16

DRY $25 –V

Margrain Martinborough Chardonnay ★★★☆

The 2009 vintage (★★★★) was fermented and matured for 10 months in French oak casks (10 per cent new). An elegant, cool-climate style, with crisp, lemony, peachy flavours, slightly minerally and tight, it's a subtle, fairly complex, food-wine style that should mature well.

Vintage	09	08
WR	6	6
Drink	10-13	10-13

DRY $28 –V

Marsden Bay of Islands Black Rocks Chardonnay ★★★★

This Kerikeri, Bay of Islands, wine is outstanding in favourable vintages – sturdy, with concentrated, ripe sweet-fruit flavours well seasoned with toasty oak, in a lush, creamy-smooth style. The 2008 (★★★☆), fermented in French (70 per cent) and American oak barriques, is slightly honeyed, with peachy, toasty flavours, showing some complexity and richness. The 2009 vintage (★★★★) is very fragrant and fresh, with butterscotch and sweet oak aromas. Still youthful, it is rich, ripe, peachy and toasty, in a high-impact style, likely to be at its best from mid-2011+.

Vintage	09	08	07	06
WR	6	4	5	7
Drink	10-15	10-14	P	P

DRY $35 –V

Marsden Bay of Islands Estate Chardonnay ★★★

This Northland wine is estate-grown at Kerikeri, in the Bay of Islands, and made without any oak or malolactic fermentation. The 2007 vintage (★★★☆) is a weighty, rounded northern style, full-bodied and fleshy, with moderate acidity and very satisfying depth of ripe stone-fruit flavours.

Vintage	07	06
WR	5	7
Drink	P	P

DRY $25 –V

Martinborough Vineyard Chardonnay ★★★★★

Mouthfilling, peachy, citrusy and mealy, this is a powerful, harmonious wine, rich and complex. Made entirely from grapes grown on the gravelly Martinborough Terrace, including the original

Mendoza clone vines planted in 1980, it is hand-picked, fully fermented (with indigenous yeasts) and lees-aged for a year in French oak barriques (typically 25 per cent new). The 2008 vintage (★★★★☆) has a fragrant, classy bouquet, leading into a rich, elegant palate with ripe grapefruit and nut flavours, showing excellent delicacy and depth. A creamy-textured wine, it offers delicious drinking from now onwards.

Vintage	08	07	06	05	04
WR	7	7	7	6	6
Drink	10-14	10-13	10-12	10-11	P

DRY $40 AV

Matahiwi Estate Hawke's Bay Chardonnay (★★★☆)

The 2008 vintage (★★★☆) is full-bodied, with strong, citrusy flavours, a gentle seasoning of nutty oak, and a slightly creamy finish. Drink now onwards.

Vintage	08
WR	5
Drink	10-11

DRY $19 V+

Matahiwi Estate Holly Wairarapa Chardonnay (★★★★)

The 2008 vintage (★★★★) is a single-vineyard wine, fermented and lees-aged for 10 months in barrels (35 per cent new). It's a full-on style, still youthful, with fresh acidity and concentrated, grapefruit-like flavours, slightly minerally, buttery, nutty and toasty.

Vintage	08
WR	6
Drink	10-12

DRY $26 AV

Matakana Estate Matakana Chardonnay ★★★★

Estate-grown north of Auckland, this wine has shown excellent form recently. The 2009 vintage (★★★★) was hand-picked and fermented and lees-aged for 10 months in French oak barriques (35 per cent new). A distinctly northern style, it is fleshy and ripe-tasting, with powerful body, sweet-fruit delights and stone-fruit and nut flavours showing good richness.

DRY $27 AV

Matariki Aspire Chardonnay – see Aspire Chardonnay

Matariki Hawke's Bay Chardonnay ★★★★

This is a consistently rewarding wine. It is grown in Gimblett Road (principally), with a smaller portion of fruit cultivated in limestone soils on the east side of Te Mata Peak giving 'a flinty, lime character'. Partly French oak-fermented and fully barrel-aged, the 2006 vintage (★★★★) is a tightly structured, complex wine with fresh acidity and strong grapefruit and peach flavours, slightly nutty and toasty.

Vintage	07	06	05	04
WR	7	6	6	6
Drink	10-12	10-11	P	P

DRY $27 AV

Matariki Reserve Chardonnay ★★★★☆

This often outstanding Hawke's Bay wine is grown at the company's sites in the Gimblett Gravels and at Te Mata Peak (see above) and fermented (partly with indigenous yeasts) in French oak barriques (92 per cent new in 2006). The 2006 vintage (★★★★☆) has a fragrant, citrusy, biscuity bouquet. Mouthfilling and slightly creamy, it is very refined, with a core of ripe grapefruit-like flavours, hints of butterscotch and toasty oak, and excellent richness and elegance.

Vintage	07	06	05	04
WR	7	6	7	7
Drink	10-12	10-11	P	P

DRY $36 –V

Matawhero Gisborne Chardonnay (★★★☆)

A drink-young style, the 2009 vintage (★★★☆) was grown in the Tietjen Vineyard, at Ormond. Moderately complex, it has creamy, buttery aromas and flavours, peachy and spicy, with fresh acidity enlivening the finish.

DRY $30 –V

Matua Valley Ararimu Chardonnay ★★★★☆

Ararimu ('Path to the Forest') is Matua Valley's premier Chardonnay. It is usually based on low-cropped, hand-picked grapes at Judd Estate in Gisborne, and fermented and matured, with regular lees-stirring, in French oak barriques (55 per cent new in 2007). The delicious 2007 vintage (★★★★☆) is fragrant, complex, rich and rounded. It's a very harmonious wine, concentrated, nutty and creamy, with a long finish.

Vintage	07
WR	7
Drink	10-12

DRY $40 –V

Matua Valley Gisborne/Hawke's Bay Chardonnay (★★☆)

The 2009 vintage (★★☆) is light and lively, with vibrant fruit flavours, citrusy, peachy and smooth. An enjoyable quaffer.

DRY $11 V+

Matua Valley Judd Estate Chardonnay ★★★★

Hand-picked in the company-owned Judd Estate Vineyard, this is a softly mouthfilling Gisborne wine with good complexity and the ability to age well. The 2007 vintage (★★★★), fermented and matured for 10 months in French oak barriques (35 per cent new), has a fragrant, ripe, slightly nutty bouquet, leading into a finely textured wine, mouthfilling and smooth, with vibrant peach and grapefruit flavours, slightly toasty, creamy and concentrated.

Vintage	07
WR	6
Drink	10-12

DRY $25 AV

Matua Valley Reserve Chardonnay (★★★☆)

The 2007 vintage (★★★☆) was mostly grown and hand-picked at Judd Estate Vineyard, in Gisborne, and fully barrel-fermented. A tightly structured, full-bodied wine with smooth, citrusy, appley flavours, it shows good delicacy, with toasty, creamy notes adding a degree of complexity.

DRY $20 AV

Maude Mt Maude Family Vineyard Chardonnay (★★★★)

The fleshy, elegant 2009 vintage (★★★★) was grown in the Mt Maude Vineyard at Wanaka. Matured in seasoned French oak casks, it is very fresh and youthful. Creamy-textured, with citrusy, slightly mealy and biscuity flavours, it has very good complexity and potential.

DRY $25 AV

Michelle Richardson Central Otago Chardonnay (★★★★☆)

The elegant 2008 vintage (★★★★☆) is one of the region's best Chardonnays yet. 'Chablis with oak' was the style goal. Grown in the Pisa/Lowburn district, it was mostly (90 per cent) tank-fermented, with indigenous yeasts, and all barrel-aged (10 per cent new). Highly fragrant, it is rich and citrusy, with sweet-fruit delights, fresh acidity, and excellent concentration, texture and complexity.

DRY $35 –V

Mill Road Hawke's Bay Chardonnay ★★

Priced right, Morton Estate's bottom-tier, non-vintage Chardonnay typically offers lively, citrusy fruit characters in an uncomplicated style, fresh and crisp. The wine on the market in 2010 (★★) has a slightly honeyed bouquet, with fresh, lemony flavours, offering simple, easy drinking.

DRY $13 AV

Mills Reef Elspeth Chardonnay ★★★★☆

Mills Reef's flagship Hawke's Bay Chardonnay is consistently rewarding and a classic regional style. The 2008 vintage (★★★★☆) is a single-vineyard wine, hand-picked and fermented and matured for 11 months in French oak barriques (80 per cent new). Mouthfilling and rounded, it has concentrated, ripe grapefruit and peach flavours, with a hint of butterscotch (50 per cent malolactic fermentation), and excellent texture, complexity and length.

DRY $32 AV

Mills Reef Hawke's Bay Chardonnay ★★★

Mills Reef's bottom-tier Chardonnay is an easy-drinking Hawke's Bay wine. Grown at Meeanee, the 2009 vintage (★★★) was mostly handled in tanks, but 43 per cent of the blend was briefly barrel-aged. It's a mouthfilling, fruity and flavoursome wine, ripe, peachy and smooth (3.7 grams/litre of residual sugar), with a touch of toasty oak and lots of drink-young appeal.

DRY $19 AV

Mills Reef Reserve Hawke's Bay Chardonnay ★★★★

Mills Reef's middle-tier Chardonnay. The 2009 vintage (★★★☆) was grown in relatively cool, coastal vineyards at Meeanee. About 80 per cent of the blend was barrel-fermented and it was all barrel-matured (in French and American oak, only 8 per cent new). A full-bodied, peachy, ripely flavoured wine, it shows considerable complexity, but is also quite oaky in its youth and needs time; open mid-2011+.

DRY $25 AV

Millton Clos de Ste Anne Chardonnay – see Clos de Ste Anne Chardonnay

Millton Gisborne Chardonnay Opou Vineyard ★★★★

This is Millton's middle-tier Chardonnay, barrel-fermented and certified organic. The 2008 vintage (★★★☆) is a fresh, citrusy, vibrantly fruity wine with a subtle seasoning of oak, very good balance and vigour, and a crisp, dry finish.

Vintage	08	07	06	05	04
WR	6	7	6	6	7
Drink	10-14	10-14	10-12	P	P

DRY $27 AV

Millton Gisborne Chardonnay Riverpoint Vineyard ★★★

The 2008 vintage (★★★) was grown organically near the sea, hand-picked and lightly oaked. It's a medium-bodied, easy-drinking wine, fruity and harmonious, with good depth of ripe, peachy flavours, a vague hint of honey and a well-rounded finish.

Vintage	08	07	06
WR	6	6	5
Drink	10-11	P	P

DRY $20 –V

Mission Hawke's Bay Chardonnay ★★★☆

Hawke's Bay winemaker Paul Mooney knows how to make Chardonnay taste delicious at just a few months old. The 2008 vintage (★★★★) is a great buy. Tank-fermented and lees-aged for six months, it's a citrusy, fruit-driven, lightly oaked style with mouthfilling body and a slightly buttery finish. Freshly scented, it has excellent flavour depth, balance and length, and is unfolding well with bottle-age.

DRY $17 V+

Mission Jewelstone Hawke's Bay Chardonnay ★★★★★

This wine has shone since the super-stylish 2002 vintage (★★★★★), grown in Central Hawke's Bay. The 2007 (★★★★★), grown at Te Awanga, near the coast, is powerful and tightly structured, with highly concentrated stone-fruit flavours woven with appetising acidity, and lovely length. The 2008 vintage (★★★★), grown in the Gimblett Gravels, was fermented and lees-aged for 18 months in French oak casks (40 per cent new). It's a stylish wine, but still very fresh and youthful, with mouthfilling body, strong, ripe, tropical-fruit flavours, biscuity oak and a tight, crisp finish. It needs more time; open mid-2011+.

Vintage	08	07	06	05	04
WR	5	6	5	6	5
Drink	10-16	10-13	10-11	10-11	P

DRY $34 V+

Mission Reserve Chardonnay ★★★★

For Mission's middle-tier Chardonnay, the style goal is a Hawke's Bay wine that 'emphasises fruit characters rather than oak, but offers some of the benefits of fermentation and maturation in wood'. Grown at Ohiti Road, the 2009 vintage (★★★★) was fermented and lees-aged for 10 months in French oak barriques (25 per cent new). It's a fragrant, complex wine, rich, ripe and rounded, with peachy, slightly buttery flavours, already delicious. Drink now or cellar.

Vintage	09	08	07	06	05	04
WR	7	7	7	5	5	5
Drink	11-15	10-15	10-11	P	P	P

DRY $24 V+

Mission Vineyard Selection Chardonnay ★★★★

Grown in the Gimblett Gravels, the 2008 (★★★☆) is mouthfilling, with strong grapefruit-like flavours, hints of limes and honey, and good complexity. The 2009 vintage (★★★★) is a wonderful buy. Grown on limestone soils in Middle Road, Central Hawke's Bay (25 kilometres south of Hastings), it was tank-fermented and matured for eight months on its yeast lees in tanks, using 'oak adjuncts', rather than barrels. Fleshy and weighty, it has concentrated citrus and stone-fruit flavours, enriched by hints of nutty oak and butterscotch. Creamy, with some flinty, minerally notes and a rounded, dry finish, it offers delicious drinking from now onwards.

DRY $18 V+

Moana Park Vineyard Selection Grange Block Chardonnay (★★☆)

The 2008 vintage (★★☆) was grown in Hawke's Bay and mostly handled in tanks, but 30 per cent of the blend was barrel-fermented. Mouthfilling, fruity and smooth, it's an uncomplicated wine with fresh, citrusy, appley flavours. A drink-young style, priced right.

Vintage	08
WR	5
Drink	09-12

DRY $15 AV

Moana Park Vineyard Tribute Chardonnay ★★★★

The impressive 2009 vintage (★★★★☆) was hand-picked in the Gimblett Gravels, Hawke's Bay, and fermented – mostly with indigenous yeasts – in French oak barriques (30 per cent new). A powerful wine, already drinking well, it is fragrant and full-bodied, with concentrated, ripe flavours of stone-fruit, butterscotch and nuts, buttery, mealy notes adding complexity, and a rich, rounded finish.

DRY $30 –V

Momo Marlborough Chardonnay (★★★☆)

From Seresin, the 2008 vintage (★★★☆) was grown organically and fermented with indigenous yeasts in seasoned oak barrels. Enjoyable from the start, it is fruity and softly textured, with the slightly earthy aromas of 'wild' yeasts and plenty of citrusy, slightly nutty flavour.

Vintage	08
WR	6
DRINK	10-12

DRY $20 AV

Monkey Bay Gisborne Chardonnay ★★☆
From Constellation NZ, the 2008 vintage (★★☆) was made without oak aging or malolactic fermentation, 'to ensure a vibrant, fruit-driven flavour profile'. It's an easy-drinking, simple wine with lemony, appley flavours and a very smooth finish.

MED/DRY $17 –V

Montana Gisborne Chardonnay ★★☆
From Pernod Ricard NZ, this long-popular Chardonnay is an undemanding style, fresh, fruity and smooth. The 2008 vintage (★★☆) was tank-fermented, with no oak, but 4 per cent Viognier was added for its 'lovely apricot flavours' and 'enticing texture'. It's a lemony, appley, faintly honeyed wine in a straightforward style, crisp, fresh and dry. (Note: at its average price in supermarkets of under $10, it delivers fine value.)

DRY $18 –V

Montana Living Land Series Marlborough Chardonnay (★★★☆)
The debut 2009 vintage (★★★☆) was grown in the Wairau Valley and fermented in tanks (30 per cent) and French oak barrels (70 per cent). It's a very easy-drinking wine, mouthfilling, citrusy and smooth (4.9 grams/litre of residual sugar), with buttery and biscuity notes adding complexity and good depth.

DRY $20 AV

Montana 'O' Ormond Chardonnay ★★★★★
(Note: the 2008 vintage is branded as Brancott Estate, rather than Montana – see that entry.) This is the flagship Gisborne Chardonnay from Pernod Ricard NZ, made for cellaring. Grown at three sites, two at Ormond and the third at Patutahi, it is hand-harvested, whole-bunch pressed, fermented in French oak barriques (40 to 50 per cent new) and matured on its yeast lees for 10 to 11 months. It has a proven ability to age well for a decade. The 2007 vintage (★★★★★) is rich and poised, with grapefruit and peach flavours, slightly creamy and toasty, and good drive and complexity.

DRY $33 V+

Montana Reserve Chardonnay ★★★☆
Past releases were sourced from Marlborough, but the 2007 vintage (★★★★) was from Hawke's Bay and since 2008 the grapes have been sourced from Gisborne. The 2008 (★★★☆) was partly tank-fermented, but 60 per cent of the blend was fermented in French and Hungarian oak barriques (25 per cent new). It's a mouthfilling wine, crisp and elegant, with good depth of ripe-fruit flavours and a subtle seasoning of oak. The 2009 (★★★★) is a top vintage – fleshy, with fresh, strong, grapefruit-like flavours, seasoned with nutty oak, and a tight, sustained finish. (Fine value at its average supermarket price of $13.)

DRY $23 AV

Montana Showcase Series Stuart Block Gisborne Chardonnay ★★★★
(Past vintages were labelled 'Terroir' rather than 'Showcase Series'.) Grown in the relatively cool Patutahi district and barrel-fermented, the 2008 vintage (★★★★) is delicious now, with rich, ripe, peachy, nutty flavours, showing excellent complexity and depth.

DRY $29 AV

Morton Estate Black Label Hawke's Bay Chardonnay ★★★★☆

Grown principally in the company's cool, elevated Riverview Vineyard at Mangatahi, this can be a very classy Chardonnay, although some of the latest releases did not achieve the standard of a decade ago. At its best, it's a powerful wine, robust and awash with flavour, yet also highly refined, with beautifully intense citrusy fruit, firm acid spine and the structure to flourish with age. It is fully barrel-fermented, and given the wine's concentrated fruit characters, the French oak barriques are 100 per cent new. The 2002 was the first to include fruit from Matapiro – over the river from Riverview. The 2006 vintage (★★★★) has strong peach and grapefruit flavours, hints of honey and toast, and a slightly oily richness. The 2007 (★★★★) is the best since 2002. Youthful in colour, it is very elegant, sweet-fruited and finely poised, with rich grapefruit and nut flavours, a minerally thread, and a long, harmonious finish.

Vintage	07	06	05	04	03	02
WR	7	5	NM	6	NM	7
Drink	10-14	10-12	NM	P	NM	P

DRY $35 –V

Morton Estate Coniglio Chardonnay – see Coniglio Hawke's Bay Chardonnay

Morton Estate Private Reserve Hawke's Bay Chardonnay ★★★

The 2008 vintage (★★★☆) is the best since 2002. The bouquet is creamy and nutty, with some complexity; the palate is mouthfilling and smooth, with ripe, peachy, nutty flavours, showing good harmony. It's enjoyable now.

Vintage	08
WR	6
Drink	10-14

DRY $21 –V

Morton Estate Three Vineyards Hawke's Bay Chardonnay ★★★

The 'three vineyards' include Tantallon, Morton's warmest vineyard, down on the Heretaunga Plains (which gives 'a more tropical, fruit-forward style'), and the cooler Kinross and Riverview vineyards. The 2008 vintage (★★☆) is light yellow, with mouthfilling body and citrusy, slightly honeyed flavours, showing a clear botrytis influence. Drink young.

Vintage	08	07
WR	6	6
Drink	10-13	10-12

DRY $20 –V

Morton Estate White Label Hawke's Bay Chardonnay ★★★☆

Morton Estate's best-known Hawke's Bay Chardonnay is typically a good buy. Fermented and lees-aged in French oak barriques, the 2008 (★★★) is mouthfilling and smooth, with peachy, citrusy, slightly honeyed flavours, showing good depth, and a touch of biscuity oak adding complexity. It's a forward vintage, ready to roll.

Vintage	08
WR	6
Drink	10-12

DRY $18 V+

Mother Clucker's Unoaked Gisborne Chardonnay (★★★)

From Chookhouse Wines (Coopers Creek), the 2008 vintage (★★★) is a mouthfilling, vibrantly fruity wine, fresh and crisp, with satisfying depth of ripe, citrusy, peachy flavours, balanced for easy drinking.

DRY $17 AV

Mount Maude Central Otago Chardonnay ★★★

The 2007 vintage (★★☆) is a single-vineyard Wanaka wine, fermented with indigenous yeasts and matured for 10 months in oak puncheons. It's a very lightly wooded wine with straightforward, citrusy, appley flavours and appetising acidity.

DRY $25 –V

Mount Michael Bessie's Block Central Otago Chardonnay ★★★☆

Estate-grown on a site overlooking Cromwell, the 2007 vintage (★★★) is mouthfilling and crisp, with vibrant, citrusy, appley flavours, showing good depth, but only moderate complexity.

DRY $27 –V

Mount Riley Marlborough Chardonnay ★★★

The 2009 vintage (★★★☆) is an elegant, fruit-driven style, fermented in an even split of tanks and French oak casks. Lees-aged for seven months, it's delicious young, with vibrant, peachy flavours to the fore, a hint of butterscotch and fresh, appetising acidity.

DRY $18 AV

Mount Riley Seventeen Valley Marlborough Chardonnay ★★★★

The 2009 vintage (★★★★★) is the best yet. Hand-picked, fermented with indigenous yeasts in new and seasoned French oak casks, with extensive lees-stirring and full malolactic fermentation, it is classy and concentrated, with a rich bouquet and lovely depth of ripe, peachy, slightly appley and spicy flavours, a distinct hint of butterscotch, and notable complexity and harmony.

Vintage	09
WR	7
Drink	10-16

DRY $30 –V

Moutere Hills New Zealand Chardonnay (★★★★)

The 2007 vintage (★★★★) is a tight, Chablis-style Nelson wine with a minerally bouquet. Barrel-fermented, it is weighty and dry, with firm acidity threaded through its citrusy, appley, mealy, biscuity flavours, flinty and tautly structured.

DRY $38 –V

Mt Hector Hawke's Bay Chardonnay (★★☆)

From Matahiwi, the 2007 vintage (★★☆) is full-bodied and fruity, with decent depth of citrusy, slightly limey flavours in a solid, no-fuss style, priced right.

DRY $13 V+

Mudbrick Vineyard Reserve Waiheke Island Chardonnay ★★★★☆

The 2009 vintage (★★★★☆) was fermented and matured in French oak barriques (25 per cent new). It's a tightly structured, elegant wine with ripe, youthful flavours of grapefruit and peaches, finely integrated oak and excellent richness. Drink mid-2011+.

Vintage	09	08
WR	7	7
Drink	10-13	10-12

DRY $42 –V

Muddy Water Growers' Series Fitzgerald Vineyard Chardonnay (★★★☆)

Grown at Waipara, hand-picked and fermented with indigenous yeasts in French oak casks (10 per cent new), the 2008 vintage (★★★☆) has firm acid spine, strong, lemony flavours and a subtle oak influence in a distinctly cool-climate, minerally, flinty style. Worth cellaring to 2011+.

Vintage	08
WR	6
Drink	10-16

DRY $23 AV

Muddy Water Waipara Chardonnay ★★★★

The 2008 vintage (★★★★) was fermented with indigenous yeasts and lees-aged for 11 months in French oak barrels (10 per cent new). A lemony, slightly buttery wine with good intensity and drive, it's tight-knit with good acid spine and complexity. The bolder 2009 (★★★★☆) is unusually robust and fleshy, with high alcohol (14.5 per cent) and strong grapefruit and peach flavours, ripe and rounded. It's approachable already, but should be long-lived.

Vintage	09	08	07	06	05	04
WR	7	6	7	7	7	6
Drink	10-22	10-18	10-15	10-12	10-12	P

DRY $32 –V

Mud House Swan Marlborough Chardonnay ★★★★

The 2007 vintage (★★★★) was fermented and lees-aged for 10 months in French oak barriques. A high-impact style, offering concentrated, stone-fruit flavours strongly seasoned with toasty oak, it is mouthfilling, rich, peachy and slightly creamy, with loads of personality.

DRY $25 AV

Murdoch James Blue Rock Chardonnay ★★★

Grown in Martinborough, the 2009 vintage (★★★) is an unwooded style. Estate-grown in the Blue Rock Vineyard and lees-stirred in tanks, it is fresh and full-bodied (14.5 per cent alcohol), with pleasant, lemony, peachy flavours, crisp underlying acidity and a smooth finish.

DRY $25 –V

Nautilus Marlborough Chardonnay ★★★★☆

This stylish wine has fresh, strong, citrusy flavours and finely integrated oak. The quietly classy 2009 vintage (★★★★★) is outstanding. Hand-harvested, fermented and lees-aged in French oak barriques (20 per cent new), it's a slightly creamy, beautifully textured wine with layers of rich, ripe, citrusy, slightly nutty and toasty flavours, a minerally streak and notable depth and harmony.

Vintage	09	08	07	06	05	04
WR	7	7	7	6	6	6
Drink	10-14	10-13	10-12	10-11	P	P

DRY $29 V+

Nest, The, Marlborough Chardonnay (★★★)

From Lake Chalice, the debut 2008 vintage (★★★) is an easy-drinking style, grown in the Wairau Valley and fermented in a mix of tanks and barrels (French and American). Given a full, softening malolactic fermentation, it is creamy and faintly nutty, with citrusy, slightly peachy flavours and a well-rounded finish.

DRY $20 –V

Neudorf Moutere Chardonnay ★★★★★

Superbly rich but not overblown, with arrestingly intense flavours enlivened with fine acidity, this rare, multi-faceted Nelson wine enjoys a reputation second to none among New Zealand Chardonnays. Grown in clay soils threaded with gravel at Upper Moutere, it is hand-harvested from vines up to 30 years old, fermented with indigenous yeasts, and lees-aged for up to a year in French oak barriques (typically 45 per cent new). The 2008 vintage (★★★★★) has a rich, citrusy fragrance. A very refined, vibrant wine with intense, youthful, grapefruit and biscuity oak flavours, it's built to last. Tasted in June 2010, the 2002 (★★★★★) is now in full stride, with a Burgundian intensity and finesse.

Vintage	08	07	06	05	04	03	02	01	00
WR	6	7	7	6	6	7	6	6	6
Drink	10-16	10-15	10-16	10-15	10-14	10-13	10-13	10-11	P

DRY $55 AV

Neudorf Nelson Chardonnay ★★★★☆

Overshadowed by its famous stablemate (above), this regional blend is a fine Chardonnay in its own right. Grown at Upper Moutere (mostly), but also at Kina, on the coast, and at Brightwater, on the Waimea Plains, it is fermented with indigenous yeasts in French oak casks (18 per cent new in 2008), and given a full, softening malolactic fermentation. The 2008 vintage (★★★★) is weighty and concentrated, with good acid spine, strong peachy, citrusy flavours, and hints of butterscotch and toast. It's a youthful, generous wine, for drinking now or cellaring.

Vintage	08	07	06	05	04
WR	6	6	7	7	6
Drink	10-16	10-15	10-14	10-13	10-12

DRY $29 V+

Ngatarawa Alwyn Chardonnay ★★★★★

Ngatarawa's flagship Hawke's Bay Chardonnay is based on estate-grown, hand-picked grapes, supplemented since 2000 with fruit from a neighbouring grower's vineyard. Fermented and lees-aged for a year in French oak barriques, with no use of malolactic fermentation, it is typically an arrestingly bold, highly concentrated wine that takes years to reveal its full class and complexity. The 2007 vintage (★★★★★) has very rich, stone-fruit flavours, balanced toasty oak and a bone-dry, finely structured finish. It's a finely poised wine, for drinking now or cellaring. There is no 2008.

Vintage	08	07	06
WR	NM	7	7
Drink	NM	10-12	10-11

DRY $35 AV

Ngatarawa Silks Chardonnay ★★★

The 2008 vintage (★★★) is basically a Hawke's Bay wine (with 8 per cent Gisborne fruit). Ready to roll, it is full-bodied, with fresh, citrusy, peachy flavours, a touch of biscuity oak and a slightly off-dry finish.

Vintage	08	07	06
WR	7	6	6
Drink	10-12	10-11	P

MED/DRY $20 –V

Ngatarawa Stables Chardonnay ★★★

Ngatarawa's lower-tier Chardonnay is made for easy drinking. The 2009 vintage (★★☆) is an East Coast blend of Hawke's Bay and Gisborne grapes, fresh and fruity, with pleasant, peachy flavours and a smooth finish.

Vintage	08	07	06
WR	6	6	6
Drink	10-11	P	P

DRY $16 V+

Ngatarawa Stables Reserve Hawke's Bay Chardonnay (★★★☆)

Made in a fruit-driven style, the 2008 vintage (★★★☆) has strong, citrusy flavours to the fore and subtle oak and butterscotch notes adding a touch of complexity.

DRY $22 AV

Nga Waka Home Block Chardonnay ★★★★☆

This single-vineyard Martinborough wine is based on mature vines and fermented and lees-aged in French oak barriques. At its best, it is an authoritative wine, weighty and concentrated, with grapefruit and toast flavours, a fresh, minerally character and great personality. The pale yellow 2007 vintage (★★★★☆) is a very elegant, cool-climate style with citrusy, slightly toasty and buttery flavours, a minerally streak and a rounded finish. It's delicious now.

Vintage	07	06
WR	7	7
Drink	10+	10+

DRY $35 –V

Nga Waka Martinborough Chardonnay ★★★★☆

Following the launch of the flagship label (above), the price of this consistently rewarding wine was trimmed and it now offers great value. Hand-harvested and French oak-fermented, the 2009 vintage (★★★★★) is a wonderful buy. Already delicious, it is full-bodied and highly concentrated, with a strong presence. It has sweet-fruit delights, with deep stone-fruit flavours, fresh acidity, finely integrated oak and lovely harmony. Drink now or cellar.

Vintage	09	08
WR	7	7
Drink	11+	10+

DRY $25 V+

Nikau Point Reserve Hawke's Bay Chardonnay ★★★

The 'One Tree Hill Vineyards' in small print is a division of Morton Estate. The 2008 vintage (★★★☆) is fresh and vibrant, with strong grapefruit and peach flavours and a slightly creamy texture. The 2009 (★★☆) is fresh, crisp and lemony, in a simple, but vibrantly fruity and lively, style.

Vintage	09	08
WR	6	7
Drink	10-13	P

DRY $16 V+

Nikau Point Unoaked Hawke's Bay Chardonnay ★★☆

The 2007 vintage from Morton Estate (★★☆) is fresh and fruity, with pleasant, simple, citrusy flavours.

DRY $16 AV

Nobilo Regional Collection Gisborne Chardonnay (★★★)

Tank-fermented and matured 'on' oak, with some malolactic fermentation and lees-aging, the 2008 vintage (★★★) is a creamy-textured wine, offering enjoyable, early drinking. Mouthfilling and fresh, it is ripe, peachy and slightly buttery, with plenty of flavour and a smooth finish.

DRY $17 AV

Northfield Frog Rock Waipara Chardonnay ★★★☆

Maturing well, the 2007 vintage (★★★☆) is an upfront style, peachy, spicy and creamy, with a seasoning of sweet oak (French and American), some mealy complexity and a well-rounded finish. The 2009 (★★★) has buttery aromas leading into a peachy, slightly honeyed, full-flavoured wine, with a sweet, toasty oak influence and fresh acidity.

DRY $21 AV

Oak Hill Matakana Chardonnay (★★★☆)

The fleshy, barrel-fermented 2009 vintage (★★★☆) has a powerful, nutty oak influence (French, one-third new). It offers very good depth of ripe stone-fruit flavours and a well-rounded texture, but needs time; open mid-2011+.

DRY $24 AV

Obsidian Waiheke Island Chardonnay ★★★★☆

Well worth cellaring, the 2009 vintage (★★★★☆) is a single-vineyard wine, hand-picked and fermented and lees-aged for eight months in French oak barriques (25 per cent new). It's a very refined, elegant wine, mouthfilling and finely textured, with youthful peach and grapefruit flavours, showing excellent ripeness, delicacy and freshness, a slightly creamy richness and lovely harmony.

Vintage	09	08	07
WR	6	6	6
Drink	10-15	10-14	10-12

DRY $35 –V

Odyssey Gisborne Chardonnay ★★★

A drink-young style, this is typically a crisp, fruity, often slightly honeyed wine, flavoursome and smooth. The 2008 vintage (★★★), grown in the Kawatiri Vineyard and mostly handled in tanks (10 per cent barrel-fermented), is peachy and faintly honeyed, with fresh acidity, a touch of complexity and mouthfilling body.

Vintage	08	07
WR	6	6
Drink	10-11	P

DRY $19 AV

Odyssey Reserve Iliad Gisborne Chardonnay ★★★★★

Top vintages represent Gisborne Chardonnay at its finest. Hand-picked in the Kawatiri Vineyard at Hexton and fermented and lees-aged in French oak barriques (30 per cent new), the 2008 (★★★★) is a generous, full-bodied wine with ripe, concentrated, peachy flavours, fresh acidity and balanced toasty oak. It shows good complexity; drink now onwards.

Vintage	08	07	06	05	04
WR	6	7	6	6	7
Drink	11-13	10-12	P	P	P

DRY $35 AV

Ohinemuri Estate Reserve Patutahi Chardonnay ★★★☆

Fermented in barrels (72 per cent) and tanks, and barrel-aged for six months, the 2009 vintage (★★★★) is full of promise. Mouthfilling, with vibrant, ripe stone-fruit and pear flavours, it is still slightly oaky, but powerful and sweet-fruited, with excellent weight, freshness and depth.

Vintage	09
WR	6
Drink	11-15

DRY $24 AV

Okahu Chardonnay ★★★☆

The 2007 vintage (★★★☆) was estate-grown in Northland and 60 per cent barrel-fermented (in French and American oak, partly new). Mouthfilling, with a rich, slightly toasty bouquet, it has ripe, citrusy, slightly nutty flavours, showing very good depth, fresh acidity and considerable complexity.

DRY $27 –V

Okahu Chardonnay/Viognier Unoaked (★★☆)

Grown in Northland, the 2007 vintage (★★☆) is 'unhindered by oak'. It's a solid but fairly plain wine, appley, slightly peachy, mouthfilling and dry, with fresh acidity.

DRY $26 –V

Old Coach Road Nelson Chardonnay ★★★

Tank-fermented and mostly American oak-matured, with lots of lees-stirring, this affordable wine from Seifried Estate is an upfront, high-flavoured style that slides down very easily. The 2008 vintage (★★★) is full-bodied and slightly creamy, with plenty of citrusy, peachy, slightly toasty flavour and a well-rounded finish. The 2009 (★★★) is fresh, lemony and flavoursome, with a smooth finish and drink-young appeal.

Vintage 08	DRY $17 AV
WR 7	
Drink 10-14	

Old Coach Road Unoaked Nelson Chardonnay ★★☆

Seifried Estate's low-priced Chardonnay typically appeals for its freshness and vigour. The 2009 vintage (★★☆) is vibrantly fruity, fresh and crisp, appley and limey. The 2010 (★★☆) is mouthfilling, with fresh, fruity, lemony flavours, lively and direct.

Vintage 10	DRY $15 AV
WR 6	
Drink 10-12	

Olssen's Charcoal Joe Chardonnay ★★★☆

Named after a nineteenth-century gold miner, this wine is hand-picked at Bannockburn, in Central Otago, and fermented and matured in French oak barriques (15 per cent new in 2009). The 2009 vintage (★★★★) is one of the best yet. Fleshy, with ripe grapefruit-like flavours, showing oak-derived complexity, it has a hint of butterscotch and very good depth.

Vintage 09	DRY $33 –V
WR 6	
Drink 15-18	

Omaka Springs Falveys Marlborough Chardonnay ★★★

The 2008 vintage (★★☆), lees-aged for a year in French oak barriques, is lemony and toasty, with a soft, slightly buttery finish.

Vintage 08	DRY $22 –V
WR 7	
Drink 10-12	

Omihi Road Waipara Chardonnay ★★★☆

Still on sale, the 2006 vintage (★★★☆) of this barrel-fermented wine from Torlesse is a cool-climate style with mouthfilling body, citrusy, slightly peachy flavours, threaded with fresh acidity, and some minerally complexity. It's maturing well.

Vintage 06	DRY $20 AV
WR 6	
Drink 12-19	

One Tree Hawke's Bay Chardonnay ★★★
Made by Capricorn Wine Estates (a division of Craggy Range), the 2007 vintage (★★★☆) is a fruit-driven style with mouthfilling body, a slightly creamy texture and strong, peachy flavours. Good value.

Vintage	07			
WR	6			
Drink	P			

DRY $16 V+

Onyx Reserve Hawke's Bay Chardonnay (★★★★☆)
From wine distributor Bennett & Deller, the 2007 vintage (★★★★☆) is full of personality. French oak-aged for a year, it is mouthfilling and concentrated, with vibrant, sweet-fruit flavours, a hint of butterscotch, a fine thread of acidity, and excellent delicacy and richness.

Vintage	07
WR	7
Drink	10-11

DRY $29 V+

Opihi Vineyard South Canterbury Chardonnay (★★☆)
The 2009 vintage (★★☆) is rare – only 44 cases were produced. Hand-harvested and handled without oak, it is pale, with some creamy notes, moderately ripe, appley flavours, fresh acidity and a crisp, dry finish.

DRY $22 –V

Orinoco Vineyards Nelson Chardonnay (★★★☆)
The 2007 vintage (★★★☆) is a creamy, upfront style, fermented in a 50:50 split of tanks and barrels. Peachy, with toast and butterscotch characters, it has underlying acidity and very good depth.

DRY $20 AV

Oyster Bay Marlborough Chardonnay ★★★☆
From Delegat's, this wine sets out to showcase Marlborough's pure, incisive fruit flavours. Only 50 per cent of the blend is barrel-fermented, but all of the wine spends six months in casks (mostly French), with weekly lees-stirring. It typically offers ripe grapefruit-like flavours, slightly buttery and crisp, with creamy, toasty elements adding complexity.

DRY $20 AV

Palliser Estate Martinborough Chardonnay ★★★★
Rather than sheer power, the key attributes of this wine are delicacy and finesse. A celebration of rich, ripe fruit flavours, it is gently seasoned with French oak, producing a delicious wine with subtle winemaking input and concentrated varietal flavours. The 2008 vintage (★★★★) is creamy-textured, with concentrated, citrusy, peachy flavours to the fore, a subtle, biscuity oak influence and excellent harmony.

Vintage	08	07	06	05
WR	7	6	6	5
Drink	10-12	10-12	10-11	P

DRY $28 AV

Palliser Pencarrow Chardonnay – see Pencarrow Martinborough Chardonnay

Paritua Hawke's Bay Chardonnay ★★★★☆
The 2008 vintage (★★★★) was hand-picked and fermented (60 per cent with indigenous yeasts) in French oak barriques (60 per cent new). Fragrant, with a toasty, nutty bouquet, it is weighty and concentrated, with ripe stone-fruit flavours, strongly seasoned with oak, and a well-rounded finish. It shows good complexity, texture and richness.

Vintage	08
WR	6
Drink	10-13

DRY $30 AV

Parr & Simpson Limestone Bay Barrique Fermented Chardonnay ★★★★
From a site overlooking Golden Bay, in Nelson, this is a wine with strong personality. The 2008 vintage (★★★★) is a refined wine, citrusy, nutty and slightly buttery, with excellent complexity, texture and length. The 2009 (★★★★☆) is even better. Hand-picked at 23.8 brix and fermented and lees-stirred for 10 months in French oak barriques (partly new), it is tightly coiled and concentrated, lemony and mealy, with finely integrated oak, crisp, minerally notes and a dry, long finish. A label worth discovering.

DRY $22 V+

Passage Rock Waiheke Island Chardonnay (★★★★)
The 2008 vintage (★★★★) is a powerful wine with an oaky bouquet, substantial body and ripe grapefruit and peach flavours, slightly nutty and youthful.

DRY $30 –V

Peacock Sky Chardonnay (★★★☆)
Grown on Waiheke Island and matured for five months in new French and American oak casks, the 2009 vintage (★★★☆) is an upfront style with generous, ripe flavours, very toasty and buttery, and a creamy-smooth finish.

Vintage	09
WR	5
Drink	10-12

DRY $30 –V

Pegasus Bay Chardonnay ★★★★★
Strapping yet delicate, richly flavoured yet subtle, this sophisticated wine is one of the country's best Chardonnays grown south of Marlborough. Muscular and taut, it typically offers a seamless array of fresh, crisp, citrusy, biscuity, complex flavours and great concentration and length. Estate-grown at Waipara, it is based almost entirely on mature Mendoza clone vines, fermented with indigenous yeasts, given a full, softening malolactic fermentation and matured for a year on its yeast lees in barrels (French oak puncheons, 30 per cent new in 2008). The 2008 vintage (★★★★) is still very youthful. Tightly structured, with mouthfilling body and strong, vibrant, grapefruit-like flavours, it is woven with fresh acidity, with mealy, nutty notes adding complexity. Open mid-2011+.

Vintage	08	07	06	05	04
WR	6	6	6	6	6
Drink	10-15	10-16	10-14	10-12	10-11

DRY $36 AV

Pegasus Bay Virtuoso Chardonnay ★★★★★

The 2006 vintage (★★★★☆) represents the 'four best barrels' made from the company's 22-year-old Mendoza clone vines at Waipara. Fermented with indigenous yeasts, lees-aged for a year in French oak puncheons (30 per cent new), then matured in tanks on light lees for a further six months before bottling, it was then bottle-aged prior to its release in 2009. Youthful in colour, with a complex bouquet, it is tightly structured, very crisp and vibrant, with peachy, citrusy, nutty flavours, firm acid spine and unusual complexity. A slightly austere, thought-provoking wine, it should be very long-lived; open 2011 onwards.

Vintage	06	05
WR	6	7
Drink	10-18	10-13

DRY $49 AV

Pencarrow Martinborough Chardonnay ★★★☆

Pencarrow is Palliser Estate's second-tier label. The 2009 (★★★☆), released in the year of vintage, is a fleshy wine with ripe, citrusy, slightly toasty flavours, showing some complexity. Fine value.

DRY $15 V+

Penny Lane Pure Chardonnay ★★☆

From Morton Estate, the easy-drinking 2009 vintage (★★☆) is a Hawke's Bay wine, lemon-scented, with fresh, smooth flavours. A pleasant quaffer.

Vintage	09
WR	6
Drink	P

DRY $15 AV

Peregrine Central Otago Chardonnay ★★★★

The 2009 vintage (★★★★) was hand-picked and fermented in French oak casks (45 per cent new). Mouthfilling and slightly creamy, with ripe, citrusy, appley, spicy flavours showing good immediacy, it is a finely balanced, subtle wine, crisp, tight and lingering.

DRY $25 AV

Poderi Crisci Chardonnay (★★★)

Grown on Waiheke Island, the 2009 vintage (★★★) is fresh, crisp and lively, with lemony, appley flavours, showing some complexity.

DRY $42 –V

Pukeora Estate Chardonnay (★)

Grown at Pukeora Estate, in Central Hawke's Bay, this wine was previously sold under the San Hill label. The 2009 vintage (★), which includes Sémillon (4 per cent), was mostly barrel-fermented and oak-aged for nine months. A dry wine, it lacks freshness and vibrancy.

Vintage	09
WR	5
Drink	10-13

DRY $18 –V

Ra Nui Marlborough Chardonnay ★★★☆

The 2007 vintage (★★★☆) was mostly handled in tanks, but 10 per cent of the blend was fermented in new barrels. It's a mouthfilling, easy-drinking wine, with peachy, citrusy flavours, slightly mealy and nutty, and good harmony and depth.

DRY $20 AV

Rapaura Springs Marlborough Chardonnay (★★★★)

The 2008 vintage (★★★★) was barrel-fermented and lees-aged for six months. Mouthfilling and vibrantly fruity, it has generous, sweet-fruit flavours, a subtle oak influence and a rounded, slightly buttery finish.

Vintage	08
WR	5
Drink	10-12

DRY $22 V+

Redmetal Vineyards Hawke's Bay Chardonnay (★★★☆)

Made in an easy-drinking style, the 2007 vintage (★★★☆) is full-bodied and vibrantly fruity, with a 'minimal' oak influence. It offers plenty of ripe, peachy, citrusy flavour, with fresh acidity to keep things lively and a smooth finish.

Vintage	07
WR	6
Drink	P

DRY $20 AV

Renato Nelson Chardonnay ★★★★

Estate-grown on the Kina Peninsula, hand-picked and fully barrel-fermented (French, 25 per cent new), the 2009 vintage (★★★★) is a single-vineyard wine with fresh, strong, citrusy flavours, vibrant and crisp, and buttery, toasty notes adding complexity and richness. It's an upfront style, for drinking now or cellaring.

Vintage	09	08	07
WR	7	6	NM
Drink	10-14	10-12	NM

DRY $24 V+

Revington Vineyard Estate Chardonnay ★★★

Fresh and lively, the 2007 vintage (★★★☆) is a Gisborne wine with plenty of ripe, peachy, toasty, faintly honeyed flavour and a smooth finish.

Vintage	07
WR	7
Drink	10-14

DRY $23 –V

Richardson Central Otago Chardonnay – see Michelle Richardson Central Otago Chardonnay

Richmond Plains Nelson Chardonnay ★★★

The 2008 vintage (★★★) is a crisp, fruit-driven style with satisfying depth of fresh, dry, citrusy, appley flavours. Certified organic.

Vintage	08	07	06
WR	5	6	5
Drink	10-12	10-11	P

DRY $20 –V

Rimu Grove Nelson Chardonnay ★★★★☆

This wine is always full of personality. Estate-grown near the coast in the Moutere hills and fermented and lees-aged in French oak casks, the 2008 vintage (★★★★☆) is weighty and rich, with generous peachy, buttery and toasty flavours and a rounded, long finish.

Vintage	08	07	06	05	04
WR	6	7	7	7	7
Drink	10-17	10-21	10-20	10-12	P

DRY $30 AV

Riverby Estate Marlborough Chardonnay ★★★★☆

This single-vineyard wine is grown in the heart of the Wairau Valley. Harvested from 20-year-old vines, the 2008 vintage (★★★★) was fully fermented and lees-aged in French oak barrels (30 per cent new), and 50 per cent went through a softening malolactic fermentation. It's a powerful wine (14.5 per cent alcohol), with ripe, peachy, toasty flavours, good complexity and a creamy, rounded finish.

Vintage	08	07	06
WR	6	7	7
Drink	10-12	10-11	P

DRY $25 V+

River Farm Godfrey Road Marlborough Chardonnay (★★★★)

The full-bodied, creamy-smooth 2009 vintage (★★★★) is a single-vineyard wine, hand-picked at 24.7 brix, fermented with indigenous yeasts in French oak barriques, and barrel-aged for 11 months. It's a weighty, complex wine with concentrated, peachy, biscuity flavours, a hint of butterscotch (from 100 per cent malolactic fermentation) and a dry, finely balanced finish. Worth cellaring.

Vintage	09
WR	6
DRINK	10-15

DRY $29 AV

Riverstone Chardonnay (★★☆)

From Villa Maria, the non-vintage wine (★★☆) I tasted in 2009 was fresh and fruity, with plenty of smooth, slightly honeyed flavour, balanced for easy drinking.

MED/DRY $12 V+

Road Works Waiheke Island Chardonnay (★★★☆)

The 2008 vintage (★★★☆) is lemon-scented, with substantial body and strong, citrusy, slightly toasty flavours. A sturdy wine with fresh acidity and some oak complexity, it delivers good value.

DRY $19 V+

Rockburn Central Otago Chardonnay ★★★

Grown at Parkburn, in the Cromwell Basin, and at Gibbston, this is a distinctly cool-climate style with a crisp, minerally streak. The 2008 vintage (★★☆), hand-picked and mostly handled in tanks (14 per cent of the blend was barrel-fermented), is a fruit-driven style with uncomplicated, citrusy, appley flavours, dry, fresh and lively.

Vintage	09	08	07
WR	5	5	7
Drink	11-14	10-14	10-14

DRY $25 –V

Rock Ferry Marlborough Chardonnay (★★★★)

Grown in the Corners Vineyard, in conversion to organic, the 2007 vintage (★★★★) was fermented, mostly with indigenous yeasts, in French oak barriques (50 per cent new). Light yellow, it is mouthfilling and rich, with peachy, slightly nutty flavours, showing good concentration and complexity and a rounded finish. It's drinking well now.

Vintage	07
WR	5
Drink	10-14

DRY $32 –V

Rongopai East Coast Chardonnay ★★☆

From Babich, the 2009 vintage (★★★) is a vibrant, fruit-driven style with ripe melon and peach flavours, showing good depth. Medium-bodied, with fresh acidity, it's finely balanced for easy, enjoyable drinking.

DRY $14 AV

Ruben Hall Chardonnay (★★★)

From Villa Maria, the non-vintage bottling (★★★) I tasted in 2009 is a blend of New Zealand and Australian wines. It's a very satisfying quaffer, mouthfilling and slightly creamy, with ripe, tropical-fruit aromas and flavours, and even a hint of toasty oak. Worth buying.

DRY $11 V+

Ruby Bay Vineyard SV Chardonnay ★★★☆

The 2007 vintage (★★★☆) was grown at a coastal site in Nelson, hand-picked and handled in a mix of tanks (75 per cent) and new French oak (25 per cent). It's an elegant, fruit-driven style with lively acidity, fresh, vibrant, grapefruit-like flavours and a subtle seasoning of oak.

DRY $24 AV

Sacred Hill Halo Hawke's Bay Chardonnay (★★★☆)

Worth cellaring, the debut 2008 vintage (★★★☆) was French oak-fermented. Fresh, crisp and dry, it has grapefruit-like flavours, woven with fresh acidity, and a subtle seasoning of oak.

DRY $26 –V

Sacred Hill Hawke's Bay Chardonnay ★★★☆

(Up to and including the 2008 vintage, this wine was labelled 'Barrel Fermented'.) The 2009 (★★★☆) was estate-grown, fermented 'with French oak' and lees-aged for six months. A fresh, vibrantly fruity wine with some elegance, it is full-bodied, with ripe, peachy, slightly nutty flavours and a rounded finish. A very harmonious wine, it's already drinking well.

Vintage	09	08	07
WR	7	6	7
Drink	10-12	10-11	10-12

DRY $21 AV

Sacred Hill Riflemans Chardonnay ★★★★★

Sacred Hill's flagship Chardonnay is one of New Zealand's greatest – powerful yet elegant, with striking intensity and outstanding cellaring potential. Grown in the cool, inland, elevated (100 metres above sea level) Riflemans Vineyard in the Dartmoor Valley of Hawke's Bay, it is hand-picked from mature, own-rooted, Mendoza clone vines and fermented with indigenous yeasts in French oak barriques (new and one year old), with some malolactic fermentation. There is no 2008. The 2009 vintage (★★★★★) is very classy and finely structured. Pale yellow, it is highly concentrated, with grapefruit, peach and nut flavours and a crisp, minerally streak, building across the palate to a lasting finish. A very complete wine, it's built to last.

Vintage	09	08	07
WR	7	NM	7
Drink	11-14	NM	10-12

DRY $54 AV

Sacred Hill The Wine Thief Series Hawke's Bay Chardonnay ★★★★☆

A classic regional style, the 2008 vintage (★★★★☆) was hand-harvested in the Ohiti Valley, barrel-fermented and lees-aged for a year. Full-bodied, with fresh, ripe citrus and stone-fruit flavours, seasoned with toasty French oak (50 per cent new), and a finely textured, rounded finish, it's developing good complexity and is delicious now.

Vintage	08	07
WR	7	7
Drink	10-12	10-12

DRY $30 AV

Saint Clair Marlborough Chardonnay ★★★☆

This smooth, full-flavoured, early-drinking wine is fermented and lees-aged in a mix of tanks and new and older French and American oak casks. The 2008 (★★★★) is a top vintage. Delicious from the start, it is mouthfilling, with fresh, ripe peach and grapefruit flavours, finely integrated, biscuity oak and a well-balanced, dry finish.

Vintage	08	07
WR	6	6
Drink	10-12	P

DRY $21 AV

Saint Clair Omaka Reserve Marlborough Chardonnay ★★★★☆

A proven show-stopper, this is a fat, creamy wine, weighty and rich, in a strikingly bold, upfront style. It is hand-picked, mostly in the company's vineyard in the Omaka Valley, and fermented and lees-aged in American oak casks, with a full, softening malolactic fermentation. The 2008 vintage (★★★★★) has a creamy, toasty bouquet. Weighty and concentrated, with ripe, peachy fruit characters and a clear but not dominating oak influence, it's a better balanced wine than some past vintages, with good texture and harmony, and a long finish.

Vintage 08
WR 7
Drink 10-12

DRY $33 AV

Saint Clair Pioneer Block 4 Sawcut Marlborough Chardonnay ★★★★

Grown in the Ure Valley, half-way between Blenheim and Kaikoura, the 2008 vintage (★★★★) was hand-picked, fermented with indigenous yeasts and lees-aged for 10 months in French oak casks (50 per cent new). Weighty, it's an elegant, very harmonious wine with fresh acidity, good concentration of citrusy, peachy flavours and a creamy-smooth finish.

Vintage 08 07
WR 7 7
Drink 10-13 10-11

DRY $30 –V

Saint Clair Pioneer Block 10 Twin Hills Marlborough Chardonnay ★★★★☆

The outstanding 2008 vintage (★★★★★) is a single-vineyard, Omaka Valley wine, hand-picked and fermented and matured for nine months in French oak casks (50 per cent new). Mouthfilling, with excellent concentration of ripe, peachy, toasty flavours, it is finely textured, biscuity and creamy, with notable depth and complexity.

Vintage 08 07
WR 6 6
Drink 10-13 10-11

DRY $30 AV

Saint Clair Pioneer Block 11 Cell Block Marlborough Chardonnay ★★★★

Grown in the 'slightly cooler' Dillons Point district, east of Blenheim, the 2008 vintage (★★★★) shows exuberant use of oak – it was matured for 10 months in French oak casks, 100 per cent new. Fresh, ripe, citrusy, peachy, nutty and buttery, with impressively concentrated fruit flavours, it's a rich, upfront style.

Vintage 08 07
WR 7 7
Drink 10-11 P

DRY $30 –V

Saint Clair Pioneer Block 13 B & B Block Marlborough Chardonnay (★★★★)

Made in an 'old world style', the debut 2007 vintage (★★★★) was grown on the seaward side of Rapaura, fermented with indigenous yeasts and handled entirely without oak. Fresh and vibrant, it's an age-worthy wine with delicate, citrusy, appley flavours that build well across the palate to a slightly minerally and nutty finish. There is no 2008.

Vintage	08	07
WR	NM	7
Drink	NM	P

DRY $30 –V

Saint Clair Unoaked Marlborough Chardonnay ★★★

This refreshing wine is cool-fermented in tanks, using malolactic fermentation to add complexity and soften the acidity. The 2008 vintage (★★★) is fleshy, with citrusy, buttery, creamy flavours, showing a distinct 'malo' influence. It's an easy-drinking style with a well-rounded finish.

Vintage	08	07
WR	6	6
Drink	10-11	P

DRY $21 –V

Saint Clair Vicar's Choice Marlborough Chardonnay ★★★

The very user-friendly 2009 vintage (★★★) is a lightly oaked style, full-bodied, with peachy, slightly biscuity and buttery flavours and a fresh, smooth finish.

Vintage	09	08	07
WR	6	6	6
Drink	10-12	10-11	P

DRY $19 AV

Saints Gisborne Chardonnay ★★★☆

From Pernod Ricard NZ, this ripe, creamy-smooth wine is always enjoyable. The 2008 vintage (★★★☆), grown at Patutahi and Ormond, was fermented and matured for six months in French (70 per cent) and American oak casks (16 per cent new). With sweet oak aromas, it's an upfront style, peachy, citrusy, toasty and crisp, with moderate complexity and plenty of flavour. The 2009 (★★★☆) is similar – peachy, nutty and buttery, with loads of flavour in a bold, upfront style.

Vintage	09	08	07
WR	6	5	6
Drink	10-11	P	P

DRY $20 AV

Salvare Hawke's Bay Chardonnay (★★★)

The 2007 vintage (★★★) was estate-grown and hand-harvested in The Triangle and handled with 'delicate oak'. Maturing solidly, it's a full-bodied wine with peachy, citrusy, slightly biscuity flavours and a fully dry finish.

DRY $25 –V

Salvare Unoaked Hawke's Bay Chardonnay (★★★)

Hand-picked in The Triangle, the 2008 vintage (★★★) is fresh and mouthfilling, with peachy, citrusy, slightly spicy flavours and a dry, rounded finish. It's drinking well now.

Vintage	08
WR	5
Drink	10-13

DRY $20 –V

Scott Base Central Otago Chardonnay (★★★☆)

From Allan Scott, the 2009 vintage (★★★☆) is a single-vineyard Cromwell wine, fermented with indigenous yeasts in French oak puncheons (partly new) and given a full, softening malolactic fermentation. Full-bodied, with strong, lemony flavours, slightly buttery and crisp, it's fleshy, youthful and worth cellaring.

Vintage	09
WR	6
Drink	10-14

DRY $30 –V

Sears Road Chardonnay (★★☆)

From Maimai Creek, this Hawke's Bay quaffer is priced sharply. The 2009 vintage (★★☆) is fleshy and lemony, gutsy and slightly spicy. A no-fuss, drink-young style.

DRY $12 V+

Secret Stone Marlborough Chardonnay ★★★☆

From Foster's, which also owns Matua Valley, the 2008 vintage (★★★☆) is mouthfilling, creamy and buttery, with citrusy, slightly limey and nutty flavours, showing very good texture and depth. The 2009 (★★★☆) is also highly enjoyable. Mouthfilling and smooth, it's a very harmonious, fresh and lively wine with ripe, grapefruit-like flavours, hints of nuts and spices, and a slightly buttery finish.

DRY $20 AV

Seifried Nelson Chardonnay ★★★☆

Always enjoyable. Fermented in a mix of tanks and American oak barriques (new to two years old), the 2009 vintage (★★★☆) is pale yellow, with lots of smooth, peachy flavour, a toasty oak influence and some mealy complexity. Drink now or cellar.

Vintage	09	08	07	06
WR	6	6	6	6
Drink	10-16	10-14	10-13	P

DRY $21 AV

Seifried Winemakers Collection Barrique Fermented Chardonnay ★★★★

This is always a bold style, concentrated and creamy, with lashings of flavour. The 2008 vintage (★★★★), grown in the Rabbit Island Vineyard, adjacent to the winery, was fermented and lees-aged for a year in French and American oak barriques (one year old). It's a rich, toasty wine, weighty and peachy, with excellent freshness, vigour and depth. The 2009 (★★★★) was matured for a year in American oak barriques (new and one year old). Pale yellow, it has fresh, strong grapefruit and peach flavours, seasoned with toasty oak, and good acid spine. Worth cellaring.

Vintage	09
WR	6
Drink	10-16

DRY $28 AV

Selaks Founders Reserve Hawke's Bay Chardonnay ★★★★☆
The 2007 vintage (★★★★★), estate-grown in Constellation NZ's Corner 50 Vineyard, was fermented in French oak barriques, partly with indigenous yeasts, and lees-aged in oak for nine months. A notably refined and rich wine, it has a fragrant, complex, savoury bouquet, with rich, grapefruit-like flavours, tight, mealy and finely balanced with toasty oak. It shows excellent delicacy, complexity and length.

DRY $28 V+

Selaks Winemaker's Favourite Hawke's Bay Chardonnay ★★★★
This smooth, richly flavoured wine from Constellation NZ is a bargain. The 2009 vintage (★★★★), grown at Bay View and Haumoana, was French oak-fermented – mostly with indigenous yeasts – and 85 per cent of the blend went through a softening malolactic fermentation. A generous wine with ripe, stone-fruit flavours seasoned with nutty oak and a hint of butterscotch, it is creamy-textured, with good harmony.

DRY $21 V+

Seresin Chardonnay ★★★★☆
This stylish Marlborough wine is designed to 'focus on the textural element of the palate rather than emphasising primary fruit characters'. It is typically a full-bodied and complex wine with good mouthfeel, ripe melon/citrus characters shining through, subtle toasty oak and fresh acidity. The 2008 vintage (★★★★) was hand-picked in the Home and Raupo Creek vineyards, fermented with indigenous yeasts in French oak barriques (25 per cent new), and lees-aged for 11 months, with full malolactic fermentation. A complex style, mouthfilling and concentrated, with strong, ripe stone-fruit flavours, a hint of butterscotch, and a slightly honeyed richness, it's drinking well now.

Vintage	08	07	06
WR	6	6	7
Drink	10-15	10-12	P

DRY $28 V+

Seresin Chardonnay Reserve ★★★★★
Finesse is the keynote quality of this classy Marlborough wine. Estate-grown at Renwick and in the Raupo Creek Vineyard, hand-picked, French oak-fermented with indigenous yeasts and lees-aged in barriques (25 per cent new in 2008) for a year, it is typically a powerful wine, toasty and nutty, with citrusy, mealy, complex flavours of great depth. The 2008 vintage (★★★★☆) has a fragrant, complex bouquet. Tight and elegant, with lovely fruit flavours of grapefruit and peach shining through, finely integrated oak and a long finish, it's still unfolding.

Vintage	08	07	06	05	04
WR	6	7	7	6	7
Drink	10-15	10-13	10-12	P	P

DRY $39 AV

Shaky Bridge Central Otago Chardonnay ★★☆
The 2008 vintage (★★☆) was estate-grown at Alexandra. Hand-picked, it was mostly handled in tanks, then blended with 'a small amount of lightly oaked wine'. It's a fruity, simple wine, smooth, lemony and appley, with crisp acidity and a fractionally off-dry finish.

DRY $20 –V

Shepherds Ridge Marlborough Chardonnay ★★★☆
From Wither Hills, the 2008 vintage (★★★☆), 60 per cent French oak-aged, is mouthfilling, fresh and fruity, with vibrant, citrusy, slightly toasty and buttery flavours, showing a touch of complexity and very good depth.

DRY $20 AV

Shingle Peak Chardonnay ★★★
The 2008 vintage (★★★) no longer features the Matua Valley logo and is no longer identified as a Marlborough wine. 'New Zealand' in origin, it is fruity, citrusy, fresh and simple, in an easy-drinking style with reasonable depth.

DRY $18 AV

Shipwreck Bay New Zealand Chardonnay ★★☆
The 2008 vintage (★★☆) from Okahu Estate is a blend of Gisborne (80 per cent) and Northland grapes. 'Uncluttered by oak', it's a medium-bodied wine, fresh and fruity, with straightforward, lemony, appley flavours and a crisp finish.

DRY $18 –V

Sileni Cellar Selection Hawke's Bay Chardonnay ★★☆
Partly French oak-fermented, the 2009 vintage (★★☆) is vibrantly fruity, citrusy and smooth, in a medium-bodied style offering fresh, easy, no-fuss drinking.

Vintage	09	08	07
WR	5	4	5
Drink	10-12	10-11	P

DRY $20 –V

Sileni Exceptional Vintage Hawke's Bay Chardonnay ★★★★☆
Sileni's flagship Hawke's Bay Chardonnay. The 2007 vintage (★★★★☆) was fermented in French oak barriques, given a full, softening malolactic fermentation and matured on its yeast lees in oak for 10 months. Mouthfilling and creamy-smooth, it shows excellent complexity, with rich, ripe, peachy, mealy, toasty flavours, a fine thread of acidity and a tight, slightly minerally finish. Drink now or cellar.

Vintage	07
WR	5
DRINK	10-12

DRY $50 –V

Sileni The Lodge Hawke's Bay Chardonnay ★★★★
Estate-grown at the Plateau Vineyard at Maraekakaho and hand-picked, this wine gets the works in the winery, including fermentation and lees-aging in French oak barriques. The 2008 vintage (★★★★) is a creamy-textured, mouthfilling wine with ripe stone-fruit and toast flavours, showing excellent complexity and depth. Fleshy and rounded, it has good presence. The 2009 (★★★★☆) is a classy young wine, fragrant, citrusy and slightly nutty, with substantial body, a subtle oak influence, and excellent delicacy, texture and complexity. It's built to last; open mid-2011+.

Vintage	09	08	07	06
WR	5	4	5	6
Drink	11-14	10-12	10-12	10-11

DRY $30 –V

Soho Carter Waiheke Island Chardonnay ★★★★
Delicious from the start, the 2009 vintage (★★★★) was fermented and matured in French oak barriques (50 per cent new). A creamy-textured wine with strong stone-fruit and nut flavours, showing good complexity, it's a very ripe and rounded style, with excellent depth and harmony.

DRY $38 –V

Soljans Barrique Reserve Chardonnay ★★★★
The 2009 vintage (★★★★) was hand-harvested in Hawke's Bay and barrel-aged for 11 months. Fresh, weighty and smooth, it's still very youthful, in a creamy, finely textured style with peach, pear, spice and toast flavours, showing excellent ripeness, delicacy and depth. Best drinking mid-2011+.

Vintage	09
WR	6
Drink	10-20

DRY $25 AV

Southbank Estate Hawke's Bay Chardonnay ★★★☆
Maturing well, the 2007 vintage (★★★★) was mostly (80 per cent) matured for eight months in French oak casks (25 per cent new). It's a mouthfilling wine with a fragrant, citrusy bouquet and ripe grapefruit and nut flavours. Slightly creamy, it shows excellent delicacy, complexity and length.

Vintage	07	06	05
WR	7	6	6
Drink	10-12	10-12	P

DRY $20 AV

Southern Cross Hawke's Bay Chardonnay ★★☆
From One Tree Hill Vineyards, a division of Morton Estate, the 2008 vintage (★★★) is an easy-drinking style with peachy, buttery flavours and a very smooth finish.

Vintage	08	07
WR	6	6
Drink	P	P

DRY $13 V+

Spinyback Nelson Chardonnay ★★★☆
From Waimea Estates, the 2009 vintage (★★★) is a creamy-textured, fruit-driven style with fresh, vibrant, peachy flavours and a crisp finish. Enjoyable young.

DRY $15 V+

Spy Valley Envoy Marlborough Chardonnay ★★★★★
Launched from the 2005 vintage (★★★★★), this distinguished wine is estate-grown in the Waihopai Valley, hand-picked, fermented with indigenous yeasts and lees-aged in French oak barriques (mostly seasoned) for up to 18 months. The 2007 (★★★★★) is again very classy. The bouquet is fragrant, mealy and complex; the palate is very refined, full-bodied and seamless, citrusy and slightly creamy, with a fine thread of acidity and a long finish. One of the region's greatest Chardonnays, it's delicious now.

Vintage	07	06	05
WR	7	7	7
Drink	10-13	10-12	10-11

DRY $40 AV

Spy Valley Marlborough Chardonnay ★★★☆

A consistently attractive wine. The 2008 vintage (★★★☆) was hand-picked, 90 per cent barrel-fermented (with 50 per cent indigenous yeasts), and lees-aged for 10 months in French oak barrels. Fresh and lively, it is citrusy and nutty, with some savoury complexity, good depth and a well-rounded finish.

Vintage	09	08	07	06
WR	6	6	6	6
Drink	11-13	10-12	10-12	10-11

DRY $23 AV

Spy Valley Marlborough Unoaked Chardonnay ★★★

The 2009 vintage (★★★☆), estate-grown and lees-aged for five months, is a fruit-driven style, ripely scented, fleshy, fresh and full-flavoured, with good immediacy and a slightly off-dry, smooth finish.

Vintage	09	08	07
WR	7	5	6
Drink	10-12	P	P

MED/DRY $19 AV

Squawking Magpie Gimblett Gravels Chardonnay ★★★★

Squawking Magpie is the label of Gavin Yortt, co-founder of the Irongate Vineyard in Gimblett Road, Hawke's Bay. Also grown in Gimblett Road, the 2007 vintage (★★★★) is a savoury style, full and rich, with melon and grapefruit flavours and finely integrated oak adding complexity.

DRY $33 –V

Staete Landt Marlborough Chardonnay ★★★★☆

This consistently impressive, single-vineyard wine is grown in the Rapaura district, hand-picked and fermented with partial use of indigenous yeasts in French oak barriques (10–15 per cent new in 2008). The 2008 vintage (★★★★) is fleshy and slightly creamy, with rich, ripe peach and grapefruit flavours, layered with cashew notes from finely integrated oak. A complex, well-rounded wine, it's delicious now.

Vintage	08	07	06
WR	7	6	6
Drink	10-17	10-13	10-12

DRY $29 V+

Stafford Lane Estate Nelson Chardonnay ★★★

Handled in tanks, with some exposure to oak, the estate-grown 2007 vintage (★★★) is a fleshy, weighty wine (14.5 per cent alcohol) with crisp, lemony, slightly buttery flavours, not highly complex, but showing some elegance and richness.

DRY $20 –V

Stone Bridge Gisborne Chardonnay (★★★★☆)

Estate-grown, the 2007 vintage (★★★★) was fermented in a 50:50 split of seasoned French and new French and American oak barrels. Mouthfilling, with excellent concentration and complexity, it is peachy and toasty, with sweet-fruit delights, in a generous, upfront but also refined style.

DRY $24 V+

Stone Bridge Unoaked Chardonnay ★★☆
The 2007 vintage (★★☆) of this Gisborne wine was matured on its yeast lees for three months in tanks. It's a solid but simple, lemony, appley, crisp wine.

DRY $20 –V

Stonecroft Hawke's Bay Chardonnay ★★★★★
Alan Limmer aimed for a 'restrained style of Chardonnay with elegance and complexity which ages well'. His wine (sold at $38) also had impressive weight and flavour richness. The 2007 (★★★★★) is concentrated and seamless, with a power and complexity reminiscent of a good Meursault. Due to frost, the new owners, Andria Monin and Dermot McCollum, bought grapes from Eskdale Winegrowers for their 2009 vintage (★★★★) – and lowered the price substantially. Fermented and matured for eight months in seasoned French oak casks, it's still an impressive wine, fleshy and creamy, with mouthfilling body and ripe stone-fruit flavours, showing good complexity and concentration.

Vintage	09	08	07	06
WR	6	NM	7	6
Drink	NM	10-16	10-16	10-15

DRY $25 V+

Stonecroft Old Vine Chardonnay ★★★★★
The 2007 vintage (★★★★★) is fleshy and rich, with deep flavours of peaches and grapefruit, subtle, integrated oak and finely balanced acidity. Concentrated and finely structured, with richness through the palate, it's a classic cellaring style. There is no 2008, but the very refined and harmonious 2009 vintage (★★★★★) will be released in early 2011. Fermented and matured for a year in French oak casks (partly new), it is weighty, concentrated and rounded, in a rich, complex style with sweet-fruit delights, generous, peachy, mealy flavours, a hint of butterscotch, and a long, seamless finish.

DRY $45 AV

Stoneleigh Marlborough Chardonnay ★★★☆
Made by Pernod Ricard NZ, this wine is typically highly enjoyable. Fermented in a mix of tanks (40 per cent) and French oak casks (60 per cent), the 2008 vintage (★★★☆) is fresh, mouthfilling and smooth, with grapefruit and peach flavours, a subtle oak influence, moderate complexity, and good body and depth. The 2009 (★★★☆) is fresh, lemony and vibrant, with finely integrated oak. It's not highly complex, but shows very good depth and harmony.

Vintage	09	08	07
WR	6	5	6
Drink	10-11	P	P

oDRY $22 AV

Stoneleigh Rapaura Series Marlborough Chardonnay ★★★★☆
Since the 2007 vintage, this wine has moved to a more 'fruit forward' style, involving briefer oak maturation. Fermented and lees-aged for four months in new and one-year-old French oak casks, the 2008 (★★★★) is rich, mealy and finely textured, with generous, ripe-fruit flavours, creamy, cashew notes and a long finish. It's still a complex style, with excellent harmony and immediacy.

DRY $27 V+

Stone Paddock Hawke's Bay Chardonnay ★★★

From Paritua, the 2009 vintage (★★★☆) is already enjoyable. A fruit-driven style with a touch of class, it is mouthfilling, with very good depth of fresh, ripe, peachy flavours, a hint of oak (35 per cent barrel-fermented) and a well-rounded finish.

Vintage	09	08
WR	7	7
Drink	10-13	10-12

MED/DRY $20 –V

Stop Banks Hawke's Bay Chardonnay (★★★)

From a Marlborough-based producer, the 2008 vintage (★★★) is a fruit-driven style with ripe, peachy flavours, not complex, but vibrant and well-rounded. Drink young.

DRY $18 AV

Summerhouse Marlborough Chardonnay ★★★★

This single-vineyard label is worth discovering. The 2009 vintage (★★★★) was fully fermented and lees-aged for 10 months in French oak barriques. It's a full-bodied (14.5 per cent alcohol), well-rounded wine with strong, peachy, gently toasty and buttery flavours. Concentrated, with a slightly oily richness, it's an upfront style, already drinking well.

DRY $27 AV

Tasman Bay New Zealand Chardonnay ★★★☆

This soft, creamy-smooth wine is delicious young. Fermented in tanks, with a full, softening malolactic fermentation, it is not barrel-aged, but oak staves are immersed in the wine. It typically has a fragrant, sweetly oaked bouquet and strong, smooth, slightly buttery and toasty flavours.

DRY $20 AV

Te Awa Chardonnay ★★★★★

Top vintages of this Hawke's Bay wine are very classy. Hand-harvested in the Gimblett Gravels, the 2007 vintage (★★★★☆) was fermented and lees-aged for a year in French oak hogsheads and puncheons (25 per cent new). It's a powerful wine (14.5 per cent alcohol), very sturdy and ripe, with a fragrant, creamy bouquet and deep grapefruit, pear and spice flavours, slightly biscuity and toasty. The 2009 (★★★★) is refined and youthful. Mouthfilling, with ripe grapefruit and subtle oak flavours, it is weighty and finely textured, and likely to unfold well during 2011.

DRY $30 V+

Te Awa Left Field Hawke's Bay Chardonnay ★★★☆

The fresh, easy-drinking 2009 vintage (★★★☆) is an unoaked style, fermented in small stainless steel 'barrels', lees-aged for six months, and blended with 3 per cent Viognier. Mouthfilling and vibrantly fruity, it is a ripe, peachy, slightly spicy wine, showing good weight, flavour depth and texture.

DRY $25 –V

Te Henga The Westie Chardonnay (★★★)

From Babich, the 2007 vintage (★★★) is an unoaked style, mouthfilling and smooth, with good depth of ripe, peachy flavours and a dry finish. Fine value.

DRY $13 V+

Te Kairanga Casarina Reserve Chardonnay ★★★★

Estate-grown in the Casarina Block at Martinborough, the 2007 vintage (★★★★) was harvested at 23.8 brix and fermented and lees-aged for 10 months in French oak barriques (34 per cent new). Light yellow, it's a refined, citrusy wine with a slightly nutty bouquet. Savoury and slightly minerally, it is woven with fresh acidity, with good fruit/oak balance and a lingering finish.

Vintage	08	07	06	05
WR	7	6	6	5
Drink	10-14	10-13	10-12	10-11

DRY $29 AV

Te Kairanga Gisborne Chardonnay ★★☆

This is typically a drink-young style with vibrant fruit characters and restrained oak. The 2008 vintage (★★★) is ripely scented, with fresh, peachy flavours and a crisp finish.

Vintage	08
WR	6
Drink	10-12

DRY $19 –V

Te Kairanga Martinborough Chardonnay ★★★☆

Te Kairanga's second-tier Chardonnay. The 2007 vintage (★★★★) was fermented and matured for 10 months in French oak barriques (20 per cent new). A crisp, slightly minerally style, drinking well now, it has a toasty, citrusy bouquet, showing some development, and a rich, flavoursome palate, with grapefruit and peachy characters and deftly judged, nutty oak.

Vintage	07	06	05
WR	6	4	6
Drink	10-13	10-12	P

DRY $21 AV

Te Kairanga Runholder Martinborough Chardonnay (★★★★☆)

The 2008 vintage (★★★★☆) is a powerful, fully barrel-fermented style (nine months in French oak barriques, 30 per cent new), with substantial body and concentrated, ripe peach and grapefruit flavours, mealy, toasty, slightly minerally and complex. It shows excellent weight and richness, with a crisp, dry, long finish.

Vintage	08
WR	7
Drink	10-14

DRY $29 V+

Te Mania Nelson Chardonnay ★★★

The 2008 vintage (★★☆) is an easy-drinking style, lightly oaked, with fresh, lemony scents and flavours and a crisp, smooth finish.

Vintage	08	07	06
WR	5	7	6
Drink	10-12	P	P

DRY $20 –V

Te Mania Reserve Nelson Chardonnay ★★★☆

Typically a powerful wine with heaps of oak seasoning concentrated, ripe-fruit flavours, and a creamy-smooth texture. The 2008 vintage (★★★☆), fermented and matured for 10 months in French and American oak barriques (30 per cent new), is mouthfilling, with strong, citrusy flavours wrapped in toasty oak.

Vintage	08	07
WR	5	7
Drink	10-13	10-12

DRY $28 –V

Te Mata Elston Chardonnay ★★★★★

One of New Zealand's most illustrious Chardonnays, Elston is a stylish, intense, slowly evolving Hawke's Bay wine. At around four years old, it is notably complete, showing concentration and finesse. The grapes are grown principally at two sites in the Te Mata hills at Havelock North, and the wine is fully fermented in French oak barriques (35 per cent new), with full malolactic fermentation. The 2008 vintage (★★★★★) is weighty, generous and complex, with rich, ripe peach and slight fig flavours showing excellent delicacy, a fine thread of acidity, well-integrated oak and a tight, long finish. It's a highly concentrated wine, likely to be long-lived.

Vintage	09	08	07	06	05	04
WR	7	7	7	7	7	7
Drink	10-14	10-13	10-12	10-11	P	P

DRY $34 V+

Te Mata Estate Woodthorpe Chardonnay ★★★★

This bargain-priced Hawke's Bay wine is grown in the company's inland Woodthorpe Vineyard in the Dartmoor Valley. Fermented and lees-aged in a mix of tanks (50 per cent) and French oak barrels, it is typically a harmonious wine with ripe grapefruit characters enriched with biscuity oak and very good richness and complexity. The 2009 vintage (★★★☆) is mouthfilling, sweet-fruited and rounded, with fresh, vibrant fruit flavours, a slightly creamy texture, moderate complexity, and very good harmony and depth.

Vintage	09	08
WR	7	7
Drink	10-14	10-11

DRY $19 V+

Terrain East Coast Chardonnay ★★★

Produced for Foodstuffs supermarkets (New World and PAK'nSAVE), the 2007 vintage (★★★) is drinking well now. It tastes like a typical Gisborne style (as past releases were labelled), with mouthfilling body, an attractively creamy texture and plenty of flavour, peachy, citrusy and smooth.

MED/DRY $11 V+

Chardonnay 117

Terravin Chardonnay ★★★★☆

The debut 2007 vintage (★★★★☆) was grown in the Omaka Valley, in Marlborough, hand-picked and fermented with indigenous yeasts in seasoned French oak puncheons. It is powerful, with mouthfilling body, very ripe, peachy, citrusy flavours, good fruit/oak balance and a rich, harmonious finish.

DRY $35 –V

Te Whau Vineyard Waiheke Island Chardonnay ★★★★★

For its sheer vintage-to-vintage consistency, this is Te Whau's finest wine. Full of personality, it has beautifully ripe fruit characters showing excellent concentration, nutty oak and a long, finely poised finish. Hand-picked and fermented and lees-aged for a year in French oak barriques (one-third new), the 2009 vintage (★★★★☆) has a fragrant bouquet with slightly 'funky', indigenous yeast notes. Rich and tightly structured, it has concentrated stone-fruit and nut flavours, excellent texture and complexity, and a well-rounded finish. An elegant wine with obvious potential, it's still very youthful; open 2012.

Vintage	09	08	07
WR	6	7	7
Drink	10-15	10-15	10-12

DRY $70 –V

Thornbury Gisborne Chardonnay ★★★★

From Villa Maria, the 2009 vintage (★★★★) was fermented and matured for six months in a mix of tanks and barrels (French, 20 per cent new). Creamy-textured and already delicious, it's a fleshy wine with plenty of fresh, ripe, citrusy fruit flavour, hints of toast and butterscotch, and a rich, well-rounded finish.

Vintage	10	09
WR	7	6
Drink	10-14	10-15

DRY $21 V+

Three Paddles Martinborough Chardonnay (★★★)

From Nga Waka, the 2009 vintage (★★★) has vibrant fruit aromas, good body and plenty of peachy, slightly limey and spicy flavour. Crisp and lively, it has a Sauvignon Blanc-like freshness and immediacy.

Vintage	09
WR	7
Drink	10+

DRY $18 AV

Timara Chardonnay (★★☆)

The 2008 vintage (★★☆) from Pernod Ricard NZ is a fresh, fruit-driven style with ripe, peachy flavours, balanced for smooth, easy drinking. Good value.

DRY $11 V+

Ti Point Hawke's Bay Chardonnay (★★★)

The 2009 vintage (★★★), grown in the Dartmoor Valley, was mostly fermented with indigenous yeasts in tanks, but 20 per cent of the blend was fermented in seasoned French oak barrels. It's a mouthfilling, moderately complex wine with fresh, stone-fruit flavours, a hint of toasty oak, balanced acidity and a dry finish.

DRY $21 –V

Tiritiri Reserve Chardonnay ★★★★☆

Duncan and Judy Smith's tiny (0.27-hectare), organically managed vineyard is in the Waimata Valley, 25 kilometres from the city of Gisborne. Enjoyable now, the 2008 vintage (★★★★) is full-bodied and rounded, slightly creamy and nutty, in a fleshy, sweet-fruited style, finely balanced, soft and generous ($39). The 2009 ($49), fermented and lees-aged for 10 months in French oak barriques, should blossom with cellaring. Refined, elegant and youthful, it's a sophisticated, immaculate wine, with grapefruit, peach and subtle oak flavours and a rich, slightly creamy finish.

Vintage	09	08	07
WR	6	4	6
Drink	12-16	12-15	10-11

DRY $49 –V

Tohu Gisborne Unoaked Chardonnay ★★★

Made in a drink-young style, the 2007 vintage (★★★) was handled entirely in stainless steel tanks. It's a fresh, lively wine with mouthfilling body and satisfying depth of ripe, citrusy, peachy flavours.

DRY $19 AV

Tohu Marlborough Unoaked Chardonnay ★★★

The 2009 vintage (★★★) is a drink-young style, mouthfilling and dryish (5 grams/litre of residual sugar). Given a full, softening malolactic fermentation, it is fleshy and fruity, with a slightly creamy texture and a well-rounded finish.

MED/DRY $19 AV

Toi Toi Marlborough Unoaked Chardonnay (★★★)

The 2009 vintage (★★★) is a single-vineyard wine, grown in the lower Wairau Valley and hand-picked at 24 brix. Fruity and fresh, it is medium-bodied, with pure, citrusy, appley flavours and a smooth finish.

DRY $16 V+

Tolaga Bay Estate Tolaga Bay Unoaked Chardonnay (★★★)

Enjoyable young, the 2009 vintage (★★★) is a single-vineyard wine from the East Cape, north of Gisborne. Fleshy, it is ripe and rounded, with very satisfying depth of peachy, slightly spicy flavour.

DRY $18 AV

Torlesse Waipara Chardonnay ★★★
Fresh, fruity and smooth, the 2008 vintage (★★★) is a medium-bodied style with vibrant, peachy, slightly limey flavours and a very subtle seasoning of oak (25 per cent barrel-fermented).

Vintage	08	07
WR	5	5
Drink	12-15	10-12

DRY $18 AV

Torrent Bay Nelson Chardonnay (★★☆)
From Anchorage, the 2008 vintage (★★☆) was grown at Motueka and fermented in French and American oak casks. It's a lemony, appley, slightly honeyed wine, with a slightly sweet (6 grams/litre of residual sugar) finish. The 2009 is fully dry.

MED/DRY $16 AV

Tranquillity Bay Nelson Chardonnay (★★☆)
From Anchorage, the 2009 vintage (★★☆) was grown at Motueka. It's a lemony, appley wine in a very fruit-driven style, offering fresh, easy drinking.

DRY $13 V+

Trinity Hill Hawke's Bay Chardonnay [Black Label] ★★★★★
(Up to and including the 2008 vintage, this wine was labelled 'Gimblett Gravels'.) The flagship Chardonnay from John Hancock, it is typically very stylish, intense and finely structured. The 2009 vintage (★★★★★) was grown at two sites in the Gimblett Gravels and two sites 'in a cooler part of Hawke's Bay'. Hand-picked, barrel-fermented and matured on its yeast lees for 10 months in French oak barriques (partly new), it is lemon-scented, with lovely fruit sweetness, delicacy, texture and length. Showing very elegant fruit flavours and good acid spine, it is vibrant and seamless, with strong cellaring potential.

Vintage	09	08	07	06	05	04
WR	7	5	6	6	5	5
Drink	11-14	10-12	10-13	10-12	10-12	P

DRY $35 AV

Trinity Hill Hawke's Bay Chardonnay ★★★☆
The 2009 vintage (★★★☆) was mostly handled in tanks, but 20 per cent of the blend was French oak-fermented. A good example of the fruit-driven style, it is mouthfilling, with a citrusy bouquet, very good depth of grapefruit and peach flavours, a touch of nutty oak and a dry, rounded finish.

DRY $20 AV

Trinity Hill Hawke's Bay Chardonnay/Viognier (★★★)
The debut 2008 vintage (★★★) is a fruit-driven blend of Chardonnay (86 per cent) and Viognier (14 per cent). Slightly honeyed, it has fresh fruit aromas, subtle citrus and melon flavours, enlivened by fresh acidity, and a dry finish.

DRY $19 AV

Tukipo River Estate Fat Snapper Central Hawke's Bay Chardonnay (★★★)
Grown at Takapau, the 2009 vintage (★★★) is full-bodied, with creamy aromas and good depth of citrusy, appley flavours, fresh, fruity and crisp.

DRY $20 –V

Tukipo River Estate Fat Trout Central Hawke's Bay Chardonnay ★★★☆
Grown at Takapau, the 2009 vintage (★★★★) is a 'full-on' style, with excellent concentration of stone-fruit flavours, seasoned with toasty oak. Fleshy and creamy-textured, with balanced acidity and slightly buttery notes, it's drinking well now.

DRY $28 –V

TW CV Chardonnay/Viognier ★★★
The 2008 vintage (★★★☆) is a Gisborne blend of Chardonnay (70 per cent) and Viognier (30 per cent), partly handled in old oak casks. Full-bodied, fruity and smooth, with peach, pear and slight spice flavours, it is a soft, very easy-drinking style, showing good freshness, depth and charm.

DRY $20 –V

TW Gisborne Chardonnay ★★★★
'TW' stands for Paul Tietjen and Geordie Witters, vastly experienced Gisborne grape-growers. Typically excellent, this wine is fermented and matured in French and American oak barriques, with partial malolactic fermentation. The 2007 vintage (★★★★☆) is a lovely wine, with ripe peach and pear flavours, showing excellent delicacy and depth, finely integrated oak and impressive complexity.

Vintage	07
WR	7
Drink	10-17

DRY $27 AV

Twin Islands Marlborough Chardonnay ★★★☆
From Nautilus Estate, this lightly wooded, drink-young style offers top value. The 2009 vintage (★★★☆), fermented in tanks (85 per cent) and barrels (15 per cent), is fruity and smooth, peachy, slightly spicy and buttery, with good vibrancy and texture, and greater complexity than you'd expect in its humble price range.

DRY $15 V+

Two Tracks Marlborough Chardonnay ★★★☆
From Wither Hills, the 2008 vintage (★★★☆) was mostly handled in tanks, but 20 per cent of the blend was wood-aged. It's a fruit-driven style, fresh, crisp and lively, with peachy, slightly toasty flavours, showing very good vigour and depth.

Vintage	08
WR	5
Drink	09-11

DRY $20 AV

Vavasour Anna's Vineyard Chardonnay ★★★★★
Named after Peter Vavasour's late wife, this is the company's top wine, produced intermittently. Released in late 2009, the 2006 vintage (★★★★★) was grown in the original vineyard in the Awatere Valley, hand-picked, barrel-fermented with indigenous yeasts, and lees-aged for 10 months in French oak casks (75 per cent new). A complex style, it's delicious now, with peach, grapefruit and nut flavours. Fragrant, with rich, ripe sweet-fruit characters, it is very pure, silky and finely textured.

DRY $40 AV

Vavasour Awatere Valley Chardonnay ★★★★☆
A powerful Marlborough wine, rich and creamy. The 2008 vintage (★★★★☆) was hand-picked, fermented with indigenous yeasts in French oak barriques (35 per cent new), and oak-aged for nine months, with weekly lees-stirring. Fleshy and rich, it's mouthfilling (14.5 per cent alcohol), with deep stone-fruit and toasty oak flavours, finely balanced acidity, and excellent complexity and harmony. The 2009 (★★★★☆) is highly fragrant and big-bodied (14.5 per cent alcohol), with concentrated peach and slight butterscotch flavours, showing excellent complexity. Rich and rounded, it's a high-impact wine, already delicious.

Vintage	09	08	07	06
WR	6	6	7	7
Drink	10-14	10-13	10-12	10-12

DRY $26 V+

Vidal Hawke's Bay Chardonnay ★★★☆
Typically a fruit-driven style with a touch of class. The 2009 vintage (★★★☆) was fermented in a near-even split of tanks and French oak barriques (only 10 per cent new). It has ripe peach and passionfruit-like flavours, fresh, crisp and lively, with some mealy complexity and a fully dry finish.

Vintage	09	08
WR	7	6
Drink	10-13	10-11

DRY $21 AV

Vidal Reserve Hawke's Bay Chardonnay ★★★★★
At its best, this is one of Hawke's Bay's finest Chardonnays, with a string of top wines stretching back to the mid-1980s. The 2009 vintage (★★★★★) was hand-picked, mostly in the Gimblett Gravels but also at Maraekakaho and Ohiti, and fermented, entirely with indigenous yeasts, in French oak barriques (45 per cent new). It's a beautifully rich and complex wine, highly refined, with deep, ripe stone-fruit flavours, a slightly creamy texture, and excellent harmony and length. Drink now or cellar.

Vintage	09	08	07	06
WR	7	6	7	7
Drink	10-15	10-13	10-12	10-12

DRY $32 V+

Villa Maria Cellar Selection Hawke's Bay Chardonnay ★★★★
Typically rich and good value. The 2007 vintage (★★★★) was hand-picked and fermented in a mix of tanks and French oak barriques (new and seasoned); all components were lees-aged and stirred. It's a refined wine, fragrant and finely balanced, with ripe, concentrated, stone-fruit flavours, slightly buttery and toasty, and a long finish.

Vintage	07	06	05	04
WR	6	7	7	7
Drink	10-12	10-12	10-11	P

DRY $23 V+

Villa Maria Cellar Selection Marlborough Chardonnay ★★★★
A stylish, good-value wine. The 2008 vintage (★★★★) is instantly likeable, with mouthfilling body and strong, ripe citrusy flavours. Fresh and vibrant, with toasty, creamy notes adding considerable complexity, it has excellent balance for early drinking. The 2009 (★★★★), a blend of Marlborough (89 per cent) and Hawke's Bay (11 per cent) grapes, mostly hand-picked, was fermented and aged for 10 months in oak barriques. Fragrant, it is rich and rounded, with stone-fruit and butterscotch flavours, showing excellent depth.

Vintage	09	08	07	06
WR	6	6	6	6
Drink	10-14	10-14	10-12	10-12

DRY $23 V+

Villa Maria Private Bin East Coast Chardonnay ★★★☆
A drink-young, fruit-driven style with a touch of class. The 2008 vintage (★★★☆) was mostly grown in the North Island regions of Gisborne and Hawke's Bay, but a small portion of the blend came from Marlborough. Mostly lees-aged in tanks, but partly barrel-aged, it has ripe stone-fruit flavours, slightly honeyed and toasty, with good depth and a well-rounded, dry finish.

Vintage	08	07	06
WR	5	6	6
Drink	10-12	10-11	P

DRY $18 V+

Villa Maria Reserve Barrique Fermented Gisborne Chardonnay ★★★★★
This acclaimed wine is grown mostly in the company's Katoa and McDiarmid Hill vineyards. The 2008 vintage (★★★★★) is concentrated and creamy, with delicious depth of peachy, slightly buttery flavours, dry, rounded and rich. The 2009 (★★★★★) – which also includes fruit from the McIldowie Block, a relatively warm site at Patutahi – was hand-picked, given a full, softening malolactic fermentation, and fermented and matured for 10 months in French oak casks (43 per cent new). A very elegant, rich wine, tight and youthful, it is creamy-textured, with grapefruit, peach and nut flavours showing impressive delicacy, complexity and depth. Refined and immaculate, it's still in its infancy.

Vintage	09	08	07	06
WR	6	6	7	7
Drink	11-14	10-13	10-16	10-15

DRY $37 AV

Villa Maria Reserve Hawke's Bay Chardonnay ★★★★☆

Hand-picked in the Waikahu Vineyard at Maraekakaho, the 2008 (★★★★★) is an authoritative wine, fleshy and forward, with substantial body (14.5 per cent alcohol) and highly concentrated stone-fruit flavours, rounded and creamy. The 2009 vintage (★★★★☆) was grown at three sites, in Maraekakaho, Te Awanga and the Gimblett Gravels. Fermented and matured in French oak barriques (43 per cent new), it is fragrant, with peach and butterscotch aromas and flavours. Weighty and finely textured, it's a youthful, elegant wine, best cellared until 2012.

Vintage	09	08
WR	7	7
Drink	11-15	10-14

DRY $32 AV

Villa Maria Reserve Marlborough Chardonnay ★★★★★

With its rich, slightly mealy, citrusy flavours, this is a distinguished wine, very concentrated and finely structured. A marriage of intense, ripe Marlborough fruit with premium French oak, it is one of the region's greatest Chardonnays. It is typically grown in the warmest sites supplying Chardonnay grapes to Villa Maria, in the Awatere and Wairau valleys. The grapes are hand-picked and the wine is fermented with cultured and indigenous yeasts in French oak barriques (20 per cent new in 2007). Built to last, the 2007 vintage (★★★★★) is a classy wine with subtle grapefruit and nutty oak flavours, showing lovely delicacy, poise and length. The 2008 (★★★★☆) is a sophisticated wine, weighty, with a complex bouquet and rich, citrusy, creamy and nutty flavours.

Vintage	09	08	07	06	05	04
WR	7	6	7	7	7	7
Drink	10-15	10-15	10-14	10-13	10-12	10-12

DRY $32 V+

Villa Maria Single Vineyard Ihumatao Chardonnay ★★★★☆

This impressive wine is estate-grown in South Auckland and fermented with indigenous yeasts in French oak barriques (30 per cent new in 2008). The 2008 vintage (★★★★☆) is tightly structured and elegant, with strong grapefruit, peach and nutty oak flavours, very harmonious and long. The 2009 (★★★★☆) is powerful and creamy-textured, with ripe, peachy, nutty flavours, showing excellent complexity and harmony.

Vintage	09	08	07	06	05
WR	6	6	7	7	7
Drink	11-14	10-13	10-14	10-13	10-12

DRY $37 –V

Villa Maria Single Vineyard Keltern Chardonnay ★★★★★

Grown at the Keltern Vineyard, a warm, inland site east of Maraekakaho in Hawke's Bay, this wine is hand-picked, fermented with indigenous yeasts and lees-aged in French oak barriques (40 per cent new in 2009). The 2008 (★★★★☆) is powerful and tightly structured, with mouthfilling body and concentrated, peachy, toasty flavours showing excellent ripeness and complexity. The 2009 vintage (★★★★☆) is savoury and creamy, with very ripe, peachy flavours, subtle, complex and smooth.

Vintage	09	08	07
WR	6	6	7
Drink	11-16	10-16	10-17

DRY $37 AV

Villa Maria Single Vineyard Taylors Pass Chardonnay ★★★★
Grown in the company's Taylors Pass Vineyard in Marlborough's Awatere Valley, this wine is hand-picked and fermented and matured for a year in French oak barriques (28 per cent new in 2007). The refined 2007 vintage (★★★★) is a mouthfilling wine with subtle, delicate flavours of peaches, grapefruit and slight butterscotch, woven with fresh acidity.

Vintage	07	06	05
WR	7	7	7
Drink	10-13	10-12	10-11

DRY $36 –V

Voss Reserve Chardonnay ★★★★☆
This powerful, richly flavoured Martinborough wine is typically fragrant and mouthfilling, with ripe grapefruit flavours, hints of nuts and butterscotch and a creamy, rounded finish. The 2008 vintage (★★★★☆) was hand-picked at two sites from vines up to 20 years old, and fermented and matured for a year in French oak barriques (25 per cent new). Youthful and refined, creamy-textured and long, it has rich, peachy, slightly mealy and biscuity flavours, showing excellent delicacy and complexity.

DRY $28 V+

Waimarie Gisborne Chardonnay [Yellow Label] (★★★☆)
Grown in the Judd Estate Vineyard, hand-picked and two-thirds barrel-fermented (French, 20 per cent new), the 2008 vintage (★★★☆) is mouthfilling, with very good depth of ripe citrus and stone-fruit flavours, well-integrated nutty oak and fresh acidity.

Vintage	08
WR	6
Drink	10-12

DRY $20 AV

Waimarie Muriwai Valley Chardonnay (★★★★☆)
Grown at Waimauku, in West Auckland, the rare 2008 vintage (★★★★☆) was hand-picked and fermented with indigenous yeasts in a single one-year-old French oak barrel. It is weighty and rich, with ripe, peachy, sweet-fruit flavours and excellent complexity. A powerful wine, already drinking well, it should also reward cellaring.

Vintage	08
WR	6
Drink	10-13

DRY $48 –V

Waimata Cogniscenti Chardonnay (★★★★)
The finely poised 2008 vintage (★★★★) is a fragrant, creamy-textured Gisborne wine, fermented in French oak (25 per cent new) with indigenous yeasts, lees-aged for eight months and given a full, softening malolactic fermentation. It offers rich, citrusy, nutty flavours, showing excellent delicacy and complexity.

DRY $28 AV

Waimea Bolitho SV Nelson Chardonnay ★★★★

Still on sale, the 2005 vintage (★★★☆) is a single-vineyard wine, grown on the coast at Kina and barrel-fermented with indigenous yeasts. Mouthfilling (15 per cent alcohol) and peachy, with crisp acidity and some complexity, it is developed and ready.

Vintage	05	04	03
WR	5	5	7
Drink	P	P	P

DRY $25 AV

Waimea Nelson Chardonnay ★★★★

The 2008 vintage (★★★★) was grown on the Kina Peninsula, hand-picked, barrel-fermented with indigenous yeasts, and given a full, softening malolactic fermentation. It's a full-bodied wine (14.5 per cent alcohol) with strong, peachy, citrusy, toasty flavours, good complexity and a slightly buttery finish. The 2009 (★★★★), fully barrel-fermented, has lots of toasty oak in evidence, in a mouthfilling, rich style with strong, peachy flavours woven with fresh acidity.

Vintage	09	08
WR	6	6
Drink	10-14	10-13

DRY $22 V+

Waipara Hills Marlborough Chardonnay (★★★★)

Drinking well now, the 2007 vintage (★★★★) was grown at several sites in the Wairau Valley. It's a stylish wine, showing some development, with ripe, grapefruit-like flavours to the fore, creamy, biscuity notes adding complexity and a dry, lasting finish.

DRY $22 V+

Waipara Hills Soul of the South Waipara Chardonnay (★★★☆)

The 2008 vintage (★★★☆) was grown in the Glasnevin Vineyard, behind the winery, and matured in seasoned oak barrels, with no use of malolactic fermentation. It's an elegant, gently wooded wine with ripe grapefruit and slight spice flavours, showing good concentration, and fresh acidity.

DRY $21 AV

Waipara Hills Southern Cross Selection Waipara Chardonnay (★★★☆)

Fully fermented and matured for five months in French oak barrels (partly new), the 2008 vintage (★★★☆) was grown behind the winery, in the Glasnevin Vineyard. It's a fresh, vibrantly fruity wine with grapefruit, peach and toasty oak flavours, showing very good depth.

DRY $29 –V

Waipara Springs Reserve Premo Chardonnay (★★☆)

The 2008 vintage (★★☆) was harvested from 29-year-old vines and French oak-fermented with indigenous yeasts. Light gold, it is peachy and honeyed, with marmalade-like characters that point to early drinking.

DRY $24 –V

Waipara Springs Waipara Chardonnay ★★★
The 2008 vintage (★★★☆) is a full-flavoured wine, maturing very solidly, with peachy, slightly honeyed flavours, showing a touch of complexity. Drink now to 2011.

DRY $19 AV

Waipara West Unoaked Chardonnay (★★★☆)
A good example of the unoaked style, the 2008 vintage (★★★☆) has plenty of peachy, slightly spicy and limey flavour, very fresh and vibrant.

DRY $19 V+

Waipipi Wairarapa Chardonnay ★★☆
Grown at Opaki, north of Masterton, and matured in new French oak barriques, the 2007 vintage (★★★) is a bright yellow, mouthfilling, peachy wine, slightly honeyed and toasty, in an upfront style, now ready.

Vintage	07	06
WR	5	5
Drink	10-12	P

DRY $22 –V

Wairau River Home Block Marlborough Chardonnay (★★★★)
Grown on the northern side of the Wairau Valley and barrel-matured for nine months, the 2007 vintage (★★★★) is an elegant, mouthfilling wine, sweet-fruited, with ripe, citrusy, slightly nutty flavours, showing excellent harmony, roundness and depth. It's delicious now.

Vintage	07
WR	6
Drink	10-11

DRY $28 AV

Wairau River Marlborough Chardonnay ★★★☆
The 2008 vintage (★★★) was mostly handled in tanks, but 30 per cent was oak-aged. It's a fruit-driven style with vibrant, lemony, slightly biscuity flavours, showing good freshness and depth.

Vintage	08
WR	5
Drink	10-11

DRY $20 AV

Wairau River Reserve Marlborough Chardonnay (★★★★)
Grown at two sites adjacent to the Wairau River, on the north side of the valley, the 2009 vintage (★★★★) was matured for 10 months in seasoned French oak puncheons. Fresh and dry, with a slightly creamy texture, it's an elegant, gently oaked style with grapefruit-like flavours and nutty, mealy notes adding complexity. Well worth cellaring.

DRY $30 –V

West Brook Barrique Fermented Marlborough Chardonnay ★★★★

The 2008 vintage (★★★★), fully barrel-fermented, is a powerful, rich wine, finely balanced, with ripe grapefruit and slightly mealy flavours, showing sensitive use of oak, and good complexity and harmony. Fine value.

DRY $20 V+

West Brook Waimauku Estate Chardonnay ★★★★☆

This stylish, complex wine is estate-grown in West Auckland. Hand-harvested and fermented in French oak casks (35 per cent new), the 2008 vintage (★★★★★) has a very fragrant, slightly smoky bouquet. Creamy-textured, with ripe grapefruit and stone-fruit flavours and finely integrated, nutty oak, it's a deliciously rich, very harmonious wine.

DRY $29 V+

Whitecliff Chardonnay (★★★)

From Sacred Hill, the 2007 vintage (★★★) is an above-average quaffer. Fresh, vibrantly fruity and smooth, with good depth of peachy, citrusy flavour in an easy-drinking style, it offers top value.

DRY $10 V+

Whitehaven Marlborough Chardonnay ★★☆

The 2008 vintage (★★★), French and American oak-aged, is an easy-drinking, fruit-driven style with an attractive, fleshy texture and ripe, peachy, slightly buttery flavours, showing decent depth.

Vintage	08	07	06
WR	5	6	6
Drink	10-14	10-11	P

DRY $20 –V

Wicked Vicar, The, Chardonnay ★★★

The 2007 vintage (★★★) was grown at Waipara and matured in French oak casks (10 per cent new). It's a lemony, buttery, slightly toasty wine, full-flavoured, in a slightly austere style with flinty acidity.

Vintage	07	06
WR	6	6
Drink	10-13	10-12

DRY $26 –V

Wild Rock Hawke's Bay Chardonnay (★★★☆)

Sold only in supermarkets, the 2008 vintage (★★★☆) is mouthfilling and vibrantly fruity, with ripe, peachy, citrusy flavours gently seasoned with toasty oak, a slightly creamy texture, and a rounded finish.

DRY $19 V+

Wild Rock Pania Hawke's Bay Chardonnay ★★★★
Wild Rock is a division of Craggy Range. Partly barrel-fermented, the 2009 vintage (★★★★) is a mouthfilling, well-rounded wine with a fragrant, nutty bouquet. Sweet-fruited, with ripe stone-fruit flavours, it is peachy, toasty and rich, with an attractively creamy texture.

Vintage	09	08	07
WR	6	7	6
Drink	10-13	10-12	10-11

DRY $20 V+

Wild Rock Wild Ferment Chardonnay (★★★☆)
The creamy, well-rounded 2007 vintage (★★★☆) is a Hawke's Bay wine with vibrant, ripe, peachy flavours and a hint of butterscotch. It's a moderately complex style with good texture and drinkability.

DRY $20 AV

Wild South Marlborough Chardonnay ★★★
The 2009 vintage (★★★) from Sacred Hill was handled entirely in tanks. Still very youthful, it is mouthfilling and vibrantly fruity, with citrusy, peachy flavours, very crisp and dry, appetising acidity and some nutty, creamy notes.

DRY $19 AV

Wishart Reserve Chardonnay ★★★☆
Still on sale, the 2005 vintage (★★★☆) is a powerful Hawke's Bay wine, hand-picked and barrel-fermented. Deep yellow/green, with a developed bouquet, it has rich grapefruit and toast flavours, leading to a rounded, slightly honeyed finish. It's an upfront style, ready now.

DRY $25 –V

Wishart Te Puriri Chardonnay ★★☆
Still on sale, the 2006 vintage (★★☆) was grown in Hawke's Bay and partly barrel-fermented. It's a smooth wine with ripe, citrusy, peachy, slightly buttery flavours and some bottle-aged complexity. Ready.

DRY $20 –V

Wishart Te Puriri Unoaked Chardonnay ★★★
Still on sale, the 2007 vintage (★★★) was estate-grown at Bay View, in Hawke's Bay, and lees-aged for six months. It's a medium-bodied wine with citrusy, slightly spicy flavours, and an emerging hint of honey.

DRY $19 AV

Wither Hills Wairau Valley Marlborough Chardonnay ★★★★
This consistently attractive wine was formerly produced in a rich, peachy, toasty, creamy style and sold at $29, but is now made with less new oak and lees-stirring, in the search for a more refined, less upfront style. Already drinking well, the 2009 vintage (★★★★) is a fleshy, generous wine with a fragrant bouquet of peachy fruit and a subtle, biscuity oak influence. Mouthfilling, with fresh, stone-fruit flavours to the fore, it's a finely textured wine with good complexity and richness. Top value at $20.

Vintage	09	08
WR	7	7
Drink	10-14	10-13

DRY $20 V+

Wooing Tree Central Otago Chardonnay ★★★☆
The 2008 vintage (★★★☆) was hand-picked at Lowburn and fermented in French oak barriques. It's a fleshy, rounded wine with a creamy, slightly toasty bouquet and lots of peachy, toasty flavour, showing good complexity.

DRY $28 –V

Chenin Blanc

Today's Chenin Blancs are far riper, rounder and more enjoyable to drink than the typically thin, sharply acidic and austere wines of the 1980s, when Chenin Blanc was far more widely planted in New Zealand. Yet this classic grape variety is still struggling for an identity in New Zealand. In recent years, several labels have been discontinued – not for lack of quality or value but lack of buyer interest.

A good New Zealand Chenin Blanc is fresh and buoyantly fruity, with melon and pineapple-evoking flavours and a crisp finish. In the cooler parts of the country, the variety's naturally high acidity (an asset in the warmer viticultural regions of South Africa, the United States and Australia) can be a distinct handicap. But when the grapes achieve full ripeness here, this classic grape of Vouvray, in the Loire Valley, yields sturdy wines that are satisfying in their youth yet can mature for many years, gradually unfolding a delicious, honeyed richness.

Only three wineries have consistently made impressive Chenin Blancs over the past decade: Millton, Margrain and Esk Valley. Many growers, put off by the variety's late-ripening nature and the susceptibility of its tight bunches to botrytis rot, have uprooted their vines. Plantings have plummeted from 372 hectares in 1983 to 47 hectares of bearing vines in 2011.

Chenin Blanc is the country's eleventh most widely planted white-wine variety (behind even Reichensteiner, a bulk-wine variety), with plantings concentrated in Gisborne and Hawke's Bay. In the future, winemakers who plant Chenin Blanc in warm, sunny vineyard sites with devigorating soils, where the variety's vigorous growth can be controlled and yields reduced, can be expected to produce the ripest, most concentrated wines. New Zealand winemakers have yet to get to grips with Chenin Blanc.

Esk Valley Hawke's Bay Chenin Blanc ★★★★

This is one of New Zealand's best (and few truly convincing) Chenin Blancs, with the ability to mature well for several years. A single-vineyard wine, grown at Moteo Pa, the 2009 vintage (★★★★) was partly fermented and lees-aged in tanks, but 55 per cent of the blend was fermented and matured in seasoned French oak barriques and larger, 600-litre *demi-muids*. Still very fresh and youthful, it's an elegant, medium-bodied wine with tight, lemony flavours, showing some barrel-ferment complexity, and obvious cellaring potential. Best drinking 2012+.

Vintage	10	09	08	07	06
WR	6	6	7	7	6
Drink	11-15	10-14	10-14	10-14	10-12

MED/DRY $24 AV

Farmgate Hawke's Bay Chenin Blanc (★★★☆)

Grown in the Gimblett Gravels and partly barrel-fermented, the 2008 vintage (★★★☆) is a mouthfilling, minerally wine with good depth of pear, citrus-fruit and apple flavours and a crisp, dry finish. Finely balanced, it should mature well. (Sold directly to consumers by Ngatarawa from the Farmgate website.)

Vintage	08
WR	6
Drink	10-14

DRY $22 AV

Forrest Marlborough Chenin Blanc ★★★
This is an extremely rare beast – a Chenin Blanc grown in the South Island. The 2009 vintage (★★★) is an easy-drinking style, grown in the Wairau Valley, with a sliver of sweetness and very decent depth of lemon, apple, slight pear and spice flavours. A medium-bodied, slightly creamy wine, fruity and smooth, it's still unfolding.

Vintage	09	
WR	6	MED/DRY $30 –V
Drink	11-20	

Margrain Martinborough Chenin Blanc ★★★★
When Margrain bought the neighbouring Chifney property in 2001, they acquired Chenin Blanc vines now around 30 years old. The 2008 vintage (★★★★) is medium-bodied, fresh and vibrant, with good harmony of ripe citrus, melon and pineapple flavours, a splash of sweetness (18 grams/litre of residual sugar) and appetising acidity. It's enjoyable now, but should blossom with cellaring.

Vintage	08	
WR	7	MED $30 –V
Drink	10-19	

Millton Chenin Blanc Te Arai Vineyard ★★★★★
This Gisborne wine is New Zealand's greatest Chenin Blanc. It's a richly varietal wine with concentrated, fresh, vibrant fruit flavours to the fore in some vintages (2006, 2007), nectareous scents and flavours in others (2005, 2008). The grapes are grown organically and hand-picked at different stages of ripening, culminating in some years ('It's in the lap of the gods,' says James Millton) in a final harvest of botrytis-affected fruit. Fermentation is in tanks and large, 620-litre French oak casks, used in the Loire for Chenin Blanc. The 2008 (and 25th) vintage (★★★★☆) is already very expressive. Highly scented, it has distinctly pineappley, slightly honeyed flavours, woven with fresh acidity, a subtle seasoning of oak, and excellent complexity and richness. Drink now or cellar.

Vintage	08	07	06	05	04	03	02
WR	6	7	7	6	7	5	7
Drink	10-15	10-15	10-20	P	10-14	P	10-12

MED/DRY $30 AV

Flora

A California crossing of Gewürztraminer and Sémillon, in cool-climate regions Flora produces aromatic, spicy wine. Some of New Zealand's 'Pinot Gris' vines were a few years ago positively identified as Flora, but the country's total area of bearing Flora vines in 2011 will be just 2 hectares.

Artisan Kauri Ridge Oratia Flora ★★★☆

Estate-grown in the Kauri Ridge Vineyard at Oratia, in West Auckland, the 2009 vintage (★★★☆) is a distinctly medium style (25 grams/litre of residual sugar), medium-bodied, with ripe tropical-fruit flavours, showing very good depth, and a rounded finish. Very gluggable.

MED $20 AV

Ascension The Rogue Flora ★★★

Grown at Matakana, this is typically a floral, weighty wine with grapey, slightly sweet and spicy flavours in a smooth, easy-drinking style.

MED/DRY $27 –V

Omaha Bay Vineyard The Impostor Matakana Flora ★★★☆

The 2008 vintage (★★★★) is the best yet. A full-bodied wine (over 13 per cent alcohol), it is gently sweet, with generous, citrusy, spicy flavours, a hint of apricots and a tight finish. Showing good weight and depth, it should mature well.

Vintage	08	07	06
WR	6	6	6
Drink	10-12	10-12	P

MED $27 –V

Gewürztraminer

Only a trickle of Gewürztraminer is exported (18,000 cases in the year to mid-2010, 0.1 per cent of total wine shipments), and the majority of New Zealand bottlings lack the power and richness of the great Alsace model. Yet this classic grape is starting to get the respect it deserves from grape-growers and winemakers here.

For most of the 1990s, Gewürztraminer's popularity was on the wane. Between 1983 and 1996, New Zealand's plantings of Gewürztraminer dropped by almost two-thirds. A key problem is that Gewürztraminer is a temperamental performer in the vineyard, being particularly vulnerable to adverse weather at flowering, which can decimate grape yields. Now there is proof of a strong renewal of interest: the area of bearing vines has surged from 85 hectares in 1998 to 313 hectares in 2011. Most of the plantings are in Gisborne (34 per cent of the national total), Marlborough (27 per cent) and Hawke's Bay (19 per cent).

Slight sweetness and skin contact were commonly used in the past to boost the flavour of Gewürztraminer, at the cost of flavour delicacy and longevity. Such outstanding wines as Dry River have revealed the far richer, softer flavours and greater aging potential that can be gained by reducing crops, leaf-plucking to promote fruit ripeness and avoiding skin contact.

Gewürztraminer is a high-impact wine, brimming with scents and flavours. 'Spicy' is the most common adjective used to pinpoint its distinctive, heady aromas and flavours; tasters also find nuances of gingerbread, freshly ground black pepper, cinnamon, cloves, mint, lychees and mangoes. Once you've tasted one or two Gewürztraminers, you won't have any trouble recognising it in a 'blind' tasting – it's the most forthright, distinctive white-wine variety of all.

Allan Scott Marlborough Gewürztraminer ★★★★

The 2008 vintage (★★★★) is a perfumed, softly mouthfilling wine, fermented in tanks and old barrels. It offers impressively ripe lychee and spice flavours, with a hint of ginger, some complexity, and very good delicacy and depth.

Vintage	08
WR	10-15
Drink	6

MED/DRY $18 V+

Anchorage Nelson Gewürztraminer ★★★

Grown at Motueka, the 2009 vintage (★★★) is a gently perfumed, medium-bodied wine with good depth of fresh lychee and spice flavours, gentle acidity and a dry (2.9 grams/litre of residual sugar) finish.

DRY $20 –V

Artisan Eight Rows Gisborne Gewürztraminer ★★★

Grown in the Makauri Vineyard, the 2007 vintage (★★★☆) is from a block originally of eight rows, now expanded to 16 – but the name survives. Bright, light yellow, with a gingery bouquet and flavours, it's a mouthfilling, full-flavoured wine, ripe, peachy and spicy, with bottle-aged complexity. Ready.

MED/DRY $20 –V

Askerne Hawke's Bay Gewürztraminer ★★★☆

This small winery has an excellent track record with Gewürztraminer. The 2009 vintage (★★★) was estate-grown, hand-picked and mostly handled in tanks; 15 per cent of the blend was fermented in old French oak casks. It's a full-bodied wine with spicy, gingery flavours, a slightly oily texture and good depth.

Vintage	09	08	07	06
WR	6	6	7	7
Drink	10-12	10-11	10-11	P

DRY $20 AV

Askerne Reserve Hawke's Bay Gewürztraminer (★★★★)

Delicious now, the exotically perfumed 2008 vintage (★★★★) was harvested at 27 brix and 15 per cent barrel-fermented. It has concentrated, slightly gingery and honeyed flavours in a forward, gently sweet style (22 grams/litre of residual sugar), rich, rounded and ready.

Vintage	08
WR	6
Drink	10-12

MED $25 AV

Astrolabe Voyage Marlborough Gewürztraminer ★★★★

The richly scented 2009 vintage (★★★★), grown at Grovetown and in the Waihopai Valley, has a gentle splash of sweetness (9.8 grams/litre of residual sugar). Exotically perfumed, it's a rich wine with a slightly oily texture and concentrated flavours of lychees, spices and pears, ripe and rounded.

Vintage	09	08
WR	6	6
Drink	12-13	10-13

MED $22 V+

Ataahua Waipara Gewürztraminer ★★★☆

The softly mouthfilling 2009 vintage (★★★★) was hand-picked and fermented and matured for six months in seasoned oak barrels. The bouquet is spicy and perfumed; the palate is full-bodied, with ripe, strongly varietal flavours of peach, lychee and ginger and a distinctly spicy, dry (4.5 grams/litre of residual sugar) finish.

DRY $20 AV

Babich Gimblett Gravels Gewürztraminer ★★★☆

Grown in the company's vineyard in Gimblett Road, Hawke's Bay, and fermented and lees-aged for 11 months in old French oak puncheons, the 2008 vintage (★★★★) is fleshy and full of personality. It has gingery, spicy aromas leading into an intensely varietal wine, strongly flavoured, slightly sweet (8 grams/litre of residual sugar), ripe and rounded, with good complexity.

Vintage	08	07	06	05
WR	5	7	6	6
Drink	10-15	10-15	10-14	10-13

MED/DRY $20 AV

Beach House Hawke's Bay Gewürztraminer ★★★☆

Grown at Te Awanga, the 2009 vintage (★★★☆) is floral and fresh, with good weight and depth of lychee and spice flavours, leading to a well-spiced, dryish, finely balanced finish.

DRY $22 AV

Bird Marlborough Gewürztraminer ★★★

Mouthfilling and smooth, the 2008 vintage (★★★) is a single-vineyard wine, grown in the Omaka Valley. Vibrantly fruity, slightly sweet (5.9 grams/litre of residual sugar) and crisp, it has a ripe, spicy bouquet and good depth of lychee, pear and spice flavours.

Vintage	08	07	06
WR	6	4	5
Drink	10-12	P	P

MED/DRY $23 –V

Blackenbrook Vineyard Nelson Gewürztraminer ★★★★☆

A consistently delicious wine. The estate-grown, exotically perfumed 2009 vintage (★★★★☆) is an Alsace style, hand-picked very ripe (over 24 brix), with substantial body and just a sliver of sweetness (7 grams/litre of residual sugar). Richly scented, it is mouthfilling, with peachy, spicy flavours showing excellent delicacy and depth, considerable complexity, gentle acidity and a long, spicy finish.

Vintage	09	08	07	06
WR	7	7	NM	7
Drink	10-13	10-11	NM	P

MED/DRY $27 AV

Blackenbrook Vineyard Nelson Reserve Gewürztraminer ★★★★☆

The powerful, softly mouthfilling (14.5 per cent alcohol) 2010 vintage (★★★★☆) was harvested at 25.2 brix. It is still very youthful, but pure and delicate, with lychee, pear, peach and spice flavours, a slightly oily texture and soft, long finish. Best drinking 2012+.

Vintage	10
WR	7
Drink	10-14

MED $31 –V

Bladen Marlborough Gewürztraminer ★★★☆

Hand-picked in the Tilly Vineyard, the 2009 vintage (★★★☆) is ripely perfumed and mouthfilling, with plenty of ripe, peachy, spicy, slightly gingery flavour and a gently sweet (9.5 grams/litre of residual sugar) finish.

Vintage	09
WR	6
Drink	10-12

MED/DRY $23 –V

Bouldevines Marlborough Gewürztraminer (★★★☆)

Ripely scented and mouthfilling, the 2009 vintage (★★★☆) is a single-vineyard, finely textured wine with good depth of lychee and spice flavours, gentle acidity and a dryish finish.

MED/DRY $25 –V

Brancott Estate 'P' Patutahi Gisborne Gewürztraminer ★★★★☆

In the past branded as Montana, but since 2009 as Brancott Estate, at its best this wine is full of personality, with a musky perfume and lush lychee and spice flavours. The 2009 vintage (★★★★★) is one of the best – mouthfilling, with a heady fragrance and very rich, citrusy, spicy flavours. It's deliciously weighty, concentrated and well-rounded.

MED $36 –V

Brennan Gibbston Gewürztraminer (★★★☆)

Grown at Gibbston, in Central Otago, the 2008 vintage (★★★☆) is aromatic, mouthfilling and gently sweet (13 grams/litre of residual sugar), with very good depth of citrus fruit, lychee and spice flavours and a rounded finish. It's drinking well now.

MED/DRY $28 –V

Brookfields Gewürztraminer ★★★☆

Grown in stony soils in Ohiti Road, inland from Fernhill, this is typically a weighty Hawke's Bay wine with plenty of character. The 2008 vintage (★★★☆), harvested at 24 brix, is very full-bodied (14.5 per cent alcohol), with soft, ripe lychee and spice flavours in a creamy-textured, relatively dry style (5 grams/litre of residual sugar) with a well-rounded finish.

Vintage	08	07	06
WR	7	7	7
Drink	10-12	10-11	P

MED/DRY $20 AV

Brunton Road Gisborne Gewürztraminer ★★★☆

Grown in the Searle Vineyard at Patutahi, the 2008 vintage (★★★) was hand-harvested and stop-fermented in an off-dry style (5 grams/litre of residual sugar). It's a mouthfilling wine (14 per cent alcohol) with ripe lychee, pear and spice flavours, gentle acidity and a slightly gingery, rounded finish.

MED/DRY $23 –V

Bushmere Estate Gisborne Gewürztraminer ★★★★

The 2009 vintage (★★★★) is a medium-dry style (8 grams/litre of residual sugar), hand-harvested at 23.5 brix. Exotically perfumed, with good body and concentrated, ripe flavours of peaches, spices, lychees and ginger, it's drinking well now, but also worth cellaring.

MED/DRY $22 V+

Cable Bay Marlborough Gewürztraminer ★★★☆

The 2008 vintage (★★★☆) was grown at the Brentwood Vineyard, in the warm Rapaura district. It's a mouthfilling wine with smooth, ripe flavours of citrus fruits, lychees and spices, showing good delicacy, depth and harmony.

Vintage	08	07
WR	6	7
Drink	P	P

MED/DRY $25 –V

Charles Wiffen Marlborough Gewürztraminer (★★★☆)

The mouthfilling 2009 vintage (★★★☆) shows some richness of ripe, lemon/spice flavours, fresh acidity and good harmony.

DRY $24 –V

Clearview Estate Gewürztraminer ★★★

The 2009 vintage (★★★), grown at Te Awanga, in Hawke's Bay, is perfumed, with dry pear, citrus fruit and spice flavours. It's not concentrated, but shows good varietal character and freshness.

Vintage	09	08	07
WR	7	6	7
Drink	10-15	10-12	P

DRY $19 AV

Cloudy Bay Marlborough Gewürztraminer ★★★★★

Top vintages of this wine are distinctly Alsace-like – highly perfumed, weighty, complex and rounded. The 2008 (★★★★☆), fermented and matured in old French oak barrels, is full-bodied, rich and complex, in a medium-dry style (8 grams/litre of residual sugar) with concentrated, citrusy, spicy flavours, showing lovely depth and harmony.

Vintage	08
WR	6
Drink	11-13

MED/DRY $30 AV

Coopers Creek Gisborne Gewürztraminer ★★★☆

The bargain-priced 2009 vintage (★★★★) has a floral, spicy, musky bouquet. Mouthfilling, with ripe, moderately intense lemon, spice and slight apricot flavours, it is fresh, slightly sweet (7.5 grams/litre of residual sugar) and smooth, with good delicacy and potential.

Vintage	09	08	07
WR	5	NM	6
Drink	10-12	NM	P

MED/DRY $17 V+

Corbans Private Bin Hawke's Bay Gewürztraminer ★★★★☆

The 2007 vintage (★★★★) from Pernod Ricard NZ has a perfumed, musky bouquet, good weight and concentrated flavours, soft and rich. The 2008 (★★★★), grown at Haumoana, is mouthfilling and rounded, with ripe, spicy, gingery flavours, a sliver of sweetness and good length.

Vintage	08	07	06
WR	6	7	6
Drink	10-11	10-11	P

MED/DRY $24 V+

Crab Farm Hawke's Bay Gewürztraminer ★★★☆

The 2008 vintage (★★★☆) has a spicy bouquet, leading into a medium to full-bodied wine (12 per cent alcohol) with very good depth of citrus fruit, lychee, pear and spice flavours, slightly sweet and crisp.

Vintage	08
WR	7
Drink	10-12

MED/DRY $17 V+

Crossroads Hawke's Bay Origin Vineyard Gewürztraminer (★★★★)

Perfumed, mouthfilling and soft, the estate-grown 2007 vintage (★★★★) is developing good complexity with bottle-age. Full-bodied, with strong lychee, spice and ginger flavours and a slightly sweet (16 grams/litre of residual sugar), well-rounded finish, it's a finely textured, harmonious wine, delicious now.

MED $20 V+

Curio D'Auvergne Vineyard Wairau Valley Marlborough Gewürztraminer (★★★★★)

From Mud House, the lovely 2008 vintage (★★★★★) was harvested at a very ripe 24.6 brix and made with some use of indigenous yeasts and barrel fermentation. Enticingly scented, it is concentrated and complex, with rich lychee, spice and ginger flavours in a medium style (16.5 grams/litre of residual sugar), delicious now.

MED $28 V+

Darling, The, Marlborough Gewürztraminer ★★★★☆

The 2009 vintage (★★★★☆) is a single-vineyard wine, grown at Rapaura. Concentrated, ripe and rounded, it's an Alsace-style, medium-dry wine, barrel-fermented (partly with indigenous yeasts) and lees-aged. Full of personality, weighty and finely textured, it shows excellent complexity and richness. The 2010 (★★★★☆) is dry (4 grams/litre of residual sugar) and richly scented, with an oily texture and concentrated citrus-fruit, spice and slight ginger flavours. Handled in tanks (40 per cent) and old oak casks (60 per cent), it shows considerable complexity; open mid-2011+.

Vintage	10
WR	6
Drink	10-13

MED/DRY $24 V+

Dry Gully Central Otago Gewürztraminer (★★★)

From an Alexandra-based producer, the 2009 vintage (★★★) is mouthfilling and smooth, with satisfying depth of pear, lychee and spice flavours, fresh acidity and a slightly gingery finish.

Vintage	09
WR	4
Drink	10-13

MED/DRY $20 –V

Dry River Gewürztraminer Dry River Estate ★★★★★

This intensely perfumed and flavoured Martinborough Gewürztraminer is one of the country's finest. Medium-dry or medium in most years, in top vintages it shows a power and richness comparable to Alsace's *vendange tardive* (late-harvest) wines. Always rich in alcohol and exceptionally full-flavoured, it is also very delicate, with a tight, concentrated, highly refined palate that is typically at its most seductive at two to four years old, although it can mature well for more than a decade. The 2009 vintage (★★★★☆) is mouthfilling (14 per cent alcohol), ripe and slightly sweet, with fresh, pure, intensely varietal flavours of stone-fruit and spices, showing excellent depth and harmony. Drink now or cellar.

Vintage	09	08	07	06	05	04
WR	6	7	NM	6	NM	6
Drink	10-16	10-15	NM	10-12	NM	P

MED/DRY $48 AV

Dry River Lovat Vineyard Gewürztraminer ★★★★★

Grown in the Lovat Vineyard in Martinborough, a few hundred metres down the road from the winery, the 2009 vintage (★★★★☆) is highly perfumed, mouthfilling and soft, with fresh lychee and spice flavours, a distinct splash of sweetness (24 grams/litre of residual sugar) and a soft, rich finish. It's already delicious.

Vintage	09	08
WR	7	7
Drink	10-14	10-15

MED $39 AV

Ellero Central Otago Gewürztraminer (★★★☆)

From vines nearly 20 years old, the 2009 vintage (★★★☆) was hand-picked at Bannockburn and two-thirds of the blend was barrel-fermented (in one old puncheon). Weighty (14.4 per cent alcohol), with a full-bloomed fragrance, it has ripe lychee and spice flavours, showing some 'funky' notes, and an off-dry, soft, well-balanced finish.

MED/DRY $27 –V

Farmgate Hawke's Bay Gewürztraminer ★★★☆

From Ngatarawa, the 2008 vintage (★★★☆) is a mouthfilling, ripely perfumed wine with lychee, spice and ginger flavours in a medium-dry style with very good varietal character and depth.

Vintage	08	07
WR	7	7
Drink	10-13	10-11

MED $22 AV

Forrest The Valleys Wairau Gewürztraminer ★★★★

The 2008 vintage (★★★★) was grown in the middle of the Wairau Valley and in the Brancott Valley. Full-bodied and smooth, it has concentrated, delicate flavours of lychees, pears and spices, gentle sweetness (14 grams/litre of residual sugar) and lovely harmony. The 2009 (★★★★☆) is a top vintage, enticingly scented, with an array of fresh, vibrant, beautifully ripe peach, lychee and spice flavours, a sliver of sweetness and a soft, rich finish.

Vintage	09	08	07	06
WR	6	6	7	7
Drink	10-15	10-15	P	P

MED/DRY $25 AV

Fossil Ridge Nelson Gewürztraminer ★★★☆

From an elevated site at Richmond, the 2008 vintage (★★★★) is perfumed and full-bodied, with a distinct splash of sweetness (14 grams/litre of residual sugar) and very good depth of ripe lychee, pear, spice and slight ginger flavours. Full of personality, it's delicious now.

MED/DRY $20 AV

Framingham Marlborough Gewürztraminer ★★★★☆

This label has shown excellent form of late. A single-vineyard wine, made in an off-dry style, it is mostly handled in tanks, but part of the blend is aged in old barrels. A top vintage, the 2009 (★★★★★) was 30 per cent barrel-fermented. Exotically perfumed, it is weighty and concentrated, with gentle sweetness (16 grams/litre of residual sugar) and rich peach, lychee, ginger and spice flavours, fresh, vibrant and long.

Vintage	09	08	07	06
WR	7	7	6	6
Drink	10-14	10-13	10-11	P

MED $28 AV

Gibbston Valley La Dulcinee The Expressionist Series Gewürztraminer (★★★★☆)

Just 35 cases were made of the 2008 vintage (★★★★☆), from 'old', company-owned vines at Gibbston. Richly perfumed and weighty (14 per cent alcohol), it has concentrated, peachy, spicy, faintly buttery flavours, with a slightly sweet finish (12 grams/litre of residual sugar), offering delicious drinking from now onwards.

Vintage	08
WR	7
Drink	10-15

MED/DRY $45 –V

Gibson Bridge Reserve Marlborough Gewürztraminer ★★★☆

Fleshy and softly textured, the hand-picked 2009 vintage (★★★★) is a weighty wine, ripely perfumed, with strong lychee, pear and ginger flavours and a lingering, well-rounded, spicy finish.

MED/DRY $25 –V

Greenhough Nelson Gewürztraminer ★★★★

Grown at Hope and Moutere, the 2009 vintage (★★★★) is richly perfumed and mouthfilling, with concentrated peach, lychee and spice flavours, and an off-dry (8 grams/litre of residual sugar), finely balanced finish. Drink now or cellar.

Vintage	09	08	07	06
WR	7	7	6	5
Drink	10-14	10-12	10-11	P

MED/DRY $22 V+

Greystone Waipara Gewürztraminer ★★★★☆

The 2009 vintage (★★★★☆) is a medium style (19 grams/litre of residual sugar), hand-harvested at 24.7 brix. Perfumed and mouthfilling, with fresh, concentrated lychee, pear and spice flavours, a hint of ginger, a slightly oily texture and a lasting finish, it's an intensely varietal wine, refined and rich.

MED $28 AV

Huia Marlborough Gewürztraminer ★★★☆

This is a consistently characterful wine. The 2008 vintage (★★★☆) is a fully dry style, mostly handled in tanks; 10 per cent of the blend was fermented in old French oak casks. Full-bodied (14 per cent alcohol), it is softly textured, with some complexity and good depth of pear and spice flavours.

Vintage	08	07	06	05	04
WR	7	6	6	5	6
Drink	10-19	10-13	10-11	P	P

DRY $28 –V

Huntaway Reserve Gisborne Gewürztraminer ★★★★

The 2007 vintage (★★★★) from Pernod Ricard NZ was grown at Riverpoint. Most of the blend was fermented initially in tanks, then in a large oak cuve, but 24 per cent was fermented in seasoned French oak barrels. Perfumed, with excellent weight and harmony, it's a mouthfilling wine with ripe lychee and spice flavours, showing some complexity, a slightly oily texture and a smooth, dryish finish (5.9 grams/litre of residual sugar). The 2009 (★★★★) is also highly attractive, in a distinctly Alsace style with considerable complexity and rich, soft flavours.

MED/DRY $24 AV

Hunter's Marlborough Gewürztraminer ★★★★☆

Hunter's produces a consistently stylish Gewürztraminer, with impressive weight, flavour depth and fragrance. A beautifully scented, fleshy wine with a rich, oily texture and concentrated lychee and spice flavours, ripe and finely balanced, the 2009 vintage (★★★★★) is a great buy.

Vintage	09	08	07	06
WR	7	7	6	5
Drink	10-13	10-12	P	P

MED/DRY $23 V+

Johanneshof Marlborough Gewürztraminer ★★★★★

This beauty is one of the country's most gorgeous Gewürztraminers. The 2009 vintage (★★★★★) is a medium style with lovely richness, delicacy and harmony. Finely poised, with gentle acidity, it has beautifully ripe lychee and spice flavours and a heady, musky bouquet.

Vintage	10	09	08	07	06	05	04	03
WR	7	6	6	7	6	7	7	6
Drink	10-20	10-17	10-16	10-17	10-15	10-15	10-14	10-12

MED $31 AV

Kaimira Estate Brightwater Gewürztraminer ★★★

The 2008 vintage (★★★) is a dryish (5.3 grams/litre of residual sugar) Nelson wine, attractively perfumed, with substantial body (14 per cent alcohol) and plenty of spicy, slightly gingery flavour. (The 2009 is a distinctly medium style.)

MED/DRY $20 –V

Kirkpatrick Estate Patutahi Gisborne Gewürztraminer ★★★☆

The 2009 vintage (★★★☆) is a medium-dry (10 grams/litre of residual sugar), slightly honeyed wine, peachy and spicy, with good flavour depth and harmony. The promising 2010 (★★★☆) is fragrant and full-bodied, with soft, ripe flavours showing very good delicacy and richness.

Vintage	09
WR	5
Drink	10-13

MED/DRY $25 –V

Konrad Marlborough Gewürztraminer (★★★)

From first-crop, hand-harvested vines in the Waihopai Valley, the 2009 vintage (★★★) is mouthfilling and ripe, with slightly sweet (6 grams/litre of residual sugar), citrusy, spicy flavours and a hint of ginger.

MED/DRY $19 AV

Lawson's Dry Hills Marlborough Gewürztraminer ★★★★★

This is consistently one of the country's most impressive Gewürztraminers. Grown near the winery in the Lawson's Dry Hills and nearby Woodward vineyards, at the foot of the Wither Hills, it is typically harvested at over 24 brix and mostly cool-fermented in stainless steel tanks, but a small component (7.5 per cent in 2008) is given 'the full treatment', with a high-solids, indigenous yeast ferment in seasoned French oak barriques, malolactic fermentation and lees-stirring. The 2008 (★★★★☆) is fleshy and soft, with ripe lychee, ginger and spice flavours, pure, intensely varietal and very harmonious, but fractionally less intense than in a top vintage.

Vintage	08	07	06	05	04
WR	7	7	7	6	7
Drink	10-13	10-12	10-11	P	P

DRY $27 V+

🍇🍇🍇

Lawson's Dry Hills The Pioneer Marlborough Gewürztraminer (★★★★★)

The debut 2009 vintage (★★★★★) was estate-grown, harvested at an average of over 25 brix, with some botrytis shrivel, and partly barrel-fermented. The bouquet is rich and highly spiced; the palate is powerful, very soft and concentrated, with deep lychee, spice and ginger flavours, considerable complexity, and strong drink-young appeal.

MED $32 AV

Leaning Rock Central Otago Gewürztraminer (★★★)

Still youthful in colour, the 2007 vintage (★★★) was estate-grown at Alexandra. Enjoyable now, it's a medium-bodied wine with citrusy, spicy, gingery, clearly varietal flavours and a slightly sweet, crisp finish.

MED/DRY $25 –V

Longbush Gewürztraminer [Bird Series] (★★★)

The 2008 vintage (★★★) is a full-bodied Gisborne wine (14.4 per cent alcohol) with gently sweet (10 grams/litre of residual sugar) lychee and spice flavours, fresh and lively. It's drinking well now.

Vintage	08
WR	6
Drink	10-12

MED/DRY $18 AV

Longbush Gisborne Gewürztraminer (★★★)

The 2008 vintage (★★★) is mouthfilling, with plenty of spicy, gingery flavour, off-dry (8 grams/litre of residual sugar), and drink-young appeal.

Vintage	08	
WR	5	
Drink	10-11	

MED/DRY $13 V+

Mahi Twin Valleys Marlborough Gewürztraminer ★★★★

The bone-dry 2009 vintage (★★★★) was grown at the Fareham Lane junction of the Wairau and Waihopai valleys, hand-picked and fermented with indigenous yeasts in tanks and seasoned French oak barriques. Mouthfilling and soft, it's a creamy-textured wine with strong, citrusy, spicy, slightly gingery flavours, showing good complexity.

Vintage	09
WR	6
Drink	10-15

DRY $24 AV

Maimai Creek Hawke's Bay Gewürztraminer ★★★☆

The 2009 vintage (★★★) is a mouthfilling (14.5 per cent alcohol) wine with plenty of spicy flavour and a dryish, gingery finish.

MED/DRY $20 AV

Matawhero Gisborne Gewürztraminer ★★★★

The 2009 vintage (★★★★) is the first for many years under one of the most famous wine brands of the 1970s and 1980s, now under new ownership. Grown mostly in the Patutahi district, inland from Matawhero, it is a full-bodied, dry style with a perfumed, gingery bouquet. Mouthfilling, with good concentration of peachy, gingery, spicy flavour, ripe and rounded, it's already drinking well.

DRY $30 –V

Misha's Vineyard The Gallery Central Otago Gewürztraminer ★★★★☆

The 2009 vintage (★★★★☆) was hand-picked at Bendigo at over 26 brix and mostly handled in tanks, but 30 per cent was fermented with indigenous yeasts in seasoned oak casks. It's a mouthfilling (14.3 per cent alcohol), medium-dry style (10 grams/litre of residual sugar), perfumed and soft, with fresh lychee, pear and spice flavours, showing excellent delicacy and concentration, a sliver of sweetness, an oily texture and a rich, very harmonious finish.

Vintage	09	08
WR	6	7
Drink	10-12	10-12

MED/DRY $28 AV

Mission Hawke's Bay Gewürztraminer ★★★☆

Typically great value. The 2010 vintage (★★★★) has a perfumed, spicy bouquet. Light and lively, with fresh, delicate lemon, apple and spice flavours, a sliver of sweetness (6 grams/litre of residual sugar), and excellent balance and length, it's full of youthful promise.

MED/DRY $17 V+

Moana Park Vineyard Tribute Taché Gewürztraminer (★★★☆)

The faintly pink 2008 vintage (★★★☆) is a powerful wine with strong, peachy, slightly gingery and spicy flavours, fresh and vibrant. Fully dry, it shows good body (14 per cent alcohol) and depth.

Vintage	08
WR	6
Drink	10-12

DRY $20 AV

Montana 'P' Patutahi Gisborne Gewürztraminer ★★★★

Full of character, at its best this is a mouthfilling wine with a musky perfume and intense pepper and lychees-like flavours, delicate and lush. Grown mostly hard against the hills inland from the city of Gisborne, at Patutahi, supplemented by fruit from Riverpoint Estate, the 2007 vintage (★★★★) was hand-picked at 24.8 brix and stop-fermented in a medium style (17 grams/litre of residual sugar). It's a soft, rich wine with abundant sweetness and strong pear, lychee and spice flavours, showing good delicacy and texture. (The 2009 vintage is labelled as Brancott Estate 'P' Gewürztraminer – see that entry.)

MED $36 –V

Montana Reserve Gisborne Gewürztraminer ★★★☆

The 2008 (★★★) was lees-aged for several months. Fresh, with citrus-fruit and lychee flavours, slightly spicy and gingery, it's an easy-drinking, dryish wine with good depth, but lacks the richness of a top vintage.

MED/DRY $24 –V

Montana Terroir Series McLoughlin Block Gewürztraminer ★★★☆

Grown at Patutahi, further from the sea and cooler at night than Riverpoint (see below), the 2007 vintage (★★★☆) has a perfumed, spicy bouquet leading into a finely balanced Gisborne wine with very good depth of citrusy, spicy flavours, ripe and gently sweet.

Vintage	07	06	05
WR	7	6	6
Drink	P	P	P

MED/DRY $24 –V

Montana Terroir Series Riverpoint Gewürztraminer ★★★★☆

Grown on the same site (now owned by Pernod Ricard NZ) as Denis Irwin's original Matawhero Gewürztraminers of the 1970s, the finely textured 2007 vintage (★★★★☆) is a richer Gisborne wine than its McLoughlin Block stablemate (above). Perfumed and ripe, it has lush, concentrated lychee, apricot and spice flavours, a splash of sweetness and a soft finish.

Vintage	07
WR	7
Drink	P

MED/DRY $25 V+

Morton Estate White Label Hawke's Bay Gewürztraminer ★★★☆

The 2009 vintage (★★★☆) is a powerful wine (14.5 per cent alcohol), ripely perfumed, with strong pear, lychee, ginger and spice flavours, quite open and expressive.

Vintage 09
WR 7
Drink 10-11

MED/DRY $19 V+

Mud House Marlborough Gewürztraminer (★★★☆)

The 2009 vintage (★★★☆) is an easy-drinking, full-flavoured wine, fresh, citrusy, spicy and gingery, with a touch of sweetness and substantial body.

MED/DRY $20 AV

Ohinemuri Estate Matawhero Gewürztraminer ★★★☆

The pale yellow 2009 vintage (★★★☆) was grown in Gisborne and mostly fermented in tanks, but 18 per cent of the blend was barrel-fermented. It's a medium style (18 grams/litre of residual sugar), with mouthfilling body and plenty of gingery, spicy flavour, crisp and strong.

Vintage 09 08 07 06
WR 5 6 7 6
Drink 10-14 10-11 10-11 P

MED $23 –V

Old Coach Road Nelson Gewürztraminer ★★★☆

The 2010 vintage (★★★☆) from Seifried Estate has an inviting, musky perfume. Already enjoyable, it is mouthfilling and gently sweet (10 grams/litre of residual sugar), with very good depth of citrusy, spicy flavours and a smooth finish.

MED/DRY $19 V+

Olssen's Central Otago Gewürztraminer ★★★

Estate-grown at Bannockburn, the 2009 vintage (★★★☆) was picked at a very ripe 24.7 brix and tank-fermented. Attractively perfumed, it's a very easy-drinking style with fresh, moderately concentrated pear, lychee and spice flavours, showing good delicacy and varietal character, a touch of sweetness (8.4 grams/litre of residual sugar), gentle acidity and a soft finish.

Vintage 09
WR 6
Drink 10-18

MED/DRY $25 –V

Omihi Road Waipara Gewürztraminer ★★★★

The generous 2008 vintage (★★★★) from Torlesse is exotically perfumed, with mouthfilling body, an oily texture and strong, slightly sweet flavours of citrus fruits, lychees and spices, ripe and smooth. The 2009 (★★★★☆) is rich, intensely varietal, weighty and very youthful. Slightly oily, with concentrated peach, lychee and spice flavours, gentle sweetness and fresh acidity, it's best cellared to 2011+.

Vintage 08
WR 6
Drink 10-12

MED/DRY $24 AV

Passage Rock Gisborne Gewürztraminer (★★★)

The 2008 vintage (★★★) from this small, Waiheke Island-based producer has an attractively perfumed bouquet. It's a medium-bodied, gently sweet wine with lychee, spice and ginger flavours, balanced for easy drinking.

MED $20 –V

Pegasus Bay Gewürztraminer ★★★★★

The memorable 2009 vintage (★★★★★) is from vines planted at Waipara in the 1970s. Hand-picked at 28 brix and fermented with indigenous yeasts in old French barrels, it has a ravishingly full-bloomed bouquet, perfumed and complex, leading into a weighty palate (14 per cent alcohol) with superbly concentrated, spicy, gingery flavours. Made in a medium style (26 grams/litre of residual sugar), it's a commanding, deliciously harmonious wine with a powerful presence.

Vintage	10	09
WR	6	6
Drink	10-14	10-12

MED $35 AV

Pyramid Valley Growers Collection Orton Vineyard Hawke's Bay Gewürztraminer (★★★★★)

From 30-year-old vines, since uprooted, the 2007 vintage (★★★★★) was hand-picked, fermented with indigenous yeasts in French oak puncheons (20 per cent new), and bottled unfined and unfiltered. Light gold, it's a striking wine, full-bodied (14.5 per cent alcohol), with an intensely spicy perfume and flavours. Very powerful and concentrated, with a rounded, dry finish (1.7 grams/litre of residual sugar), it's drinking superbly now.

DRY $39 AV

Ra Nui Wairau Valley Marlborough Gewürztraminer ★★★☆

The 2009 vintage (★★★★) is a distinctive, dry style. Hand-picked in the Cob Cottage Vineyard, it is attractively perfumed and fleshy, with ripe lychee and spice flavours, showing good harmony and concentration. The 2010 (★★★☆) is dry (4 grams/litre of residual sugar) with fresh, moderately concentrated flavours of lychees, spices, lemons and apples that linger to a smooth, well-spiced finish.

DRY $24 –V

Revington Vineyard Gisborne Gewürztraminer ★★★★

The Revington Vineyard in Gisborne's Ormond Valley yields a rare wine that has ranked among the country's finest Gewürztraminers. Full of personality, the 2007 vintage (★★★★☆) has a scented, gingery bouquet, showing good complexity. It is mouthfilling (14 per cent alcohol), with concentrated, spicy, gingery flavours, a hint of honey, and a slightly sweet (16 grams/litre of residual sugar) finish.

Vintage	07
WR	7
Drink	10-14

MED $30 –V

River Farm Godfrey Road Marlborough Gewürztraminer (★★★★)
Full of interest, the 2009 vintage (★★★★) was hand-picked at 24.5 brix, partly fermented with indigenous yeasts in seasoned French oak casks, and made in a fully dry style. Mouthfilling (14.5 per cent alcohol), it is fleshy and ripe, with strong citrus-fruit, lychee and spice flavours, showing a touch of complexity, and excellent harmony.

Vintage	09
WR	6
Drink	10-14

DRY $20 V+

Rockburn Central Otago Gewürztraminer ★★★
The bone-dry 2008 vintage (★★★) was grown at Parkburn, in the Cromwell Basin, and fermented and lees-aged in tanks. It's a sturdy wine (14.4 per cent alcohol) with a perfumed, musky bouquet, ripe lychee and spice flavours and a fully dry finish.

Vintage	08
WR	5
Drink	10-11

DRY $24 –V

Saint Clair Pioneer Block 12 Lone Gum Gewürztraminer ★★★★
Grown in a warm site in Marlborough's lower Omaka Valley, the 2008 vintage (★★★★) was late-harvested and made in a medium-dry (13.8 grams/litre of residual sugar) style. Softly seductive, it is perfumed and full-bodied, with rich, ripe lychee and spice flavours and a well-rounded finish.

Vintage	08	07
WR	6	6
Drink	10-12	10-12

MED/DRY $23 AV

Saint Clair Reserve Godfrey's Creek Gewürztraminer ★★★☆
Grown in the Godfrey's Creek Vineyard, in the Brancott Valley, the 2008 vintage (★★★☆) is a distinctly medium style (28 grams/litre of residual sugar), harvested from first-crop vines. Rich and soft, it's a gently perfumed wine with ripe peach, lychee and spice flavours, gentle acidity and drink-young appeal.

Vintage	08
WR	6
Drink	10-11

MED $27 –V

Saints Gisborne Gewürztraminer ★★★☆
Grown at Patutahi, at its best Pernod Ricard NZ's wine is rich and flavour-packed. Already drinking well, the 2009 vintage (★★★☆) is a slightly sweet style with strong, ripe flavours of stone-fruit and spice.

MED/DRY $20 AV

Sanctuary Marlborough Gewürztraminer (★★☆)

From Grove Mill, the debut 2008 vintage (★★☆) is a medium-bodied style with solid depth of lemon, lychee and slight apple flavours. Fresh and smooth, it lacks intensity, but is a well-balanced, easy-drinking style (10 grams/litre of residual sugar).

Vintage	08
WR	7
Drink	P

MED/DRY $17 –V

Seifried Nelson Gewürztraminer ★★★★

Typically a floral, well-spiced wine, of excellent quality and value. Unfolding well with bottle-age, the 2009 vintage ★★★★ is enticingly perfumed, with a distinct splash of sweetness amid its strong, ripe peach and slight apricot flavours. The intensely varietal 2010 (★★★★) is exotically scented, in a medium style (16 grams/litre of residual sugar) with rich, peachy, gingery, spicy flavours.

Vintage	10	09
WR	6	6
Drink	10-15	10-13

MED $21 V+

Seifried Winemaker's Collection Nelson Gewürztraminer ★★★★☆

This is typically a rich wine with loads of personality. Grown at Brightwater, the 2009 vintage (★★★★☆) is faintly pink and exotically perfumed. Delicious from the start, it is concentrated, slightly oily and gently sweet (8.6 grams/litre of residual sugar), with moderate acidity and soft peach, apricot and spice flavours, rich, ripe and rounded. The 2010 (★★★★☆) is a medium style (22 grams/litre of residual sugar), perfumed, rich and oily-textured, with concentrated stone-fruit and spice flavours, a hint of apricot and real harmony. Already lovely.

Vintage	10	09	08	07	06
WR	6	6	6	6	7
Drink	10-15	10-14	10-12	P	P

MED $23 V+

Selaks The Favourite Marlborough Gewürztraminer (★★★★)

The 2007 vintage (★★★★) from Constellation NZ is a single-vineyard wine, made in a basically dry style (4 grams/litre of residual sugar). Perfumed and mouthfilling, with ripe, citrusy, spicy, slightly gingery flavours, showing a touch of complexity, it's intensely varietal, with impressive richness and a smooth finish.

DRY $21 V+

Seresin Marlborough Gewürztraminer ★★★☆

This wine is hand-picked in the Raupo Creek Vineyard, in the Omaka Valley. The 2008 vintage (★★★☆) is a medium-dry style (7 grams/litre of residual sugar), partly fermented in old French oak barriques. A mouthfilling wine with a touch of complexity, it is fleshy and ripe, with peachy, spicy flavours, showing very good depth, and a soft, creamy texture.

Vintage	08
WR	6
Drink	10-13

MED/DRY $29 –V

Shaky Bridge Central Otago Gewürztraminer ★★★

Grown at Alexandra, the 2008 vintage (★★☆) was hand-picked in the Pioneer Vineyard. It's a pleasant, dry style (4 grams/litre of residual sugar) with solid depth of lychee, pear and spice flavours and a soft finish.

Vintage	08
WR	5
Drink	10-13

DRY $25 –V

Shaky Bridge Pioneer Series Central Otago Gewürztraminer (★★★)

The 2008 vintage (★★★) was estate-grown in the Alexandra Basin and hand-picked. Made in a slightly sweeter style (11 grams/litre of residual sugar) than its stablemate (above), it's a perfumed, moderately concentrated wine with lychee, spice and slight ginger flavours, drinking well now.

MED/DRY $19 AV

Soljans Gisborne Gewürztraminer ★★★

Drinking well now, the 2006 vintage (★★★☆) is a medium style (26 grams/litre of residual sugar), with good depth of lychee and spice flavours, ripe and rounded.

MED $20 –V

Spy Valley Envoy Marlborough Gewürztraminer ★★★★☆

Still on sale, the 2007 vintage (★★★★), estate-grown in the lower Waihopai Valley, was hand-picked at over 25 brix, and fermented and lees-aged for seven months in large German oak ovals. Restrained in its youth but opening out now, it has soft citrus-fruit, lychee, spice and orange flavours, a splash of sweetness (19 grams/litre of residual sugar), gentle acidity and good weight, complexity and texture.

Vintage	09	08	07	06
WR	7	6	6	6
Drink	10-14	10-13	10-12	10-11

MED $30 –V

Spy Valley Marlborough Gewürztraminer ★★★★☆

Estate-grown in the Waihopai Valley, this wine consistently offers great value. The 2009 vintage (★★★★) was harvested at 22.2 to 27.8 brix and partly fermented in seasoned oak barrels. Fleshy and rich, with a slightly gingery bouquet, it is slightly sweet (13.9 grams/litre of residual sugar), soft and forward, with an oily texture and concentrated ginger and spice flavours, ripe and rounded.

Vintage	10	09	08	07	06
WR	6	7	6	6	6
Drink	11-13	10-12	10-11	P	P

MED/DRY $23 V+

Stafford Lane Nelson Gewürztraminer (★★☆)

The 2009 vintage (★★☆) is a medium-bodied wine, fresh, crisp and lively, with decent depth of lemon, apple and spice flavours and an off-dry (6.7 grams/litre of residual sugar) finish.

MED/DRY $19 –V

Stone Bridge Gisborne Gewürztraminer ★★★

The 2007 vintage (★★★) was harvested at 24 brix and stop-fermented with 11 grams per litre of residual sugar, creating a slightly sweet style. It's a medium-bodied wine with clear-cut varietal character and plenty of gently spicy flavour.

DRY $23 –V

Stonecroft Hawke's Bay Gewürztraminer ★★★★

The 2009 vintage (★★★★) was made from grapes purchased from the Eskdale Vineyard in the Esk Valley. It's a mouthfilling wine, gently sweet (7.5 grams/litre of residual sugar), with fresh acidity and peachy, spicy flavours that linger well. The youthful, highly promising 2010 vintage (★★★★☆) is partly barrel-fermented (unusual for this wine). Full-bodied, well-spiced and rich, it shows excellent weight and concentration, with deep, ripe, peachy, slightly gingery flavours, an oily texture and impressive complexity.

Vintage	10	09
WR	7	6
Drink	10-20	10-20

MED/DRY $25 AV

Stonecroft Old Vine Gewürztraminer ★★★★★

The Gewürztraminers from this tiny Hawke's Bay winery are striking and among the finest in the country. This 'Old Vine' wine, introduced from the 2004 vintage, is made entirely from grapes hand-picked from the original Mere Road plantings in 1983. The 2009 vintage (★★★★★), handled entirely in tanks, makes a powerful statement. An authoritative wine with a voluminous, spicy, gingery, slightly honeyed fragrance, it is weighty and complex, with superbly rich, peachy and spicy flavours, fresh and lasting.

Vintage	09
WR	6
Drink	10-20

MED/DRY $45 AV

Summerhouse Marlborough Gewürztraminer ★★★☆

The 2009 vintage (★★★☆) is a single-vineyard wine, weighty, with ripe pear, lychee and spice flavours showing good delicacy and depth. The 2010 (★★★☆) is mouthfilling and soft, with moderately concentrated flavours, showing good texture, delicacy and freshness.

DRY $27 –V

Te Kairanga Six Sons Gisborne Gewürztraminer (★★★★)

Drinking well now, the 2008 vintage (★★★★) is ripely scented, with mouthfilling body and fresh, finely balanced lychee, ginger and spice flavours. It's a medium-dry style (12 grams/litre of residual sugar), with excellent depth.

Vintage	08
WR	6
Drink	10-12

MED/DRY $21 V+

Te Whare Ra Marlborough Gewürztraminer ★★★☆
This was once an arrestingly powerful, hedonistic wine that crammed more flavour into the glass than most other Gewürztraminers from the region. The wines I have tasted in recent years have been attractive but less exciting.

MED $32 –V

Torlesse Waipara Gewürztraminer ★★★★
The 2008 (★★★★) is a perfumed, gently sweet wine with excellent body, texture and richness of lychee, pear and spice flavours. The 2009 vintage (★★★★) is fresh and lively, in an intensely varietal style with a distinct splash of sweetness (16 grams/litre of residual sugar) and spicy, concentrated flavours.

Vintage	09
WR	6
Drink	12-15

MED $20 V+

Villa Maria Private Bin East Coast Gewürztraminer ★★★★
This deservedly popular wine is a vibrantly fruity, well-spiced, medium-dry style, bargain-priced. The 2009 vintage (★★★★) has a perfumed, intensely varietal bouquet of lychees and spices. Weighty and rounded, it has excellent body and depth of fresh lychee, pear and spice flavours, dryish (7.5 grams/litre of residual sugar) and lingering.

Vintage	10	09	08	07
WR	6	6	6	6
Drink	10-13	10-12	10-11	P

MED/DRY $20 V+

Villa Maria Single Vineyard Ihumatao Gewürztraminer ★★★★★
The 2009 vintage (★★★★) was estate-grown at Mangere, in South Auckland, and 40 per cent of the blend was fermented with indigenous yeasts in seasoned French oak barriques; the rest was handled in tanks. Ripely perfumed, it is mouthfilling and soft, with lychee, pear and spice flavours, showing good complexity, and a long, slightly gingery, dryish finish. The 2010 (★★★★☆), 30 per cent barrel-fermented, is highly promising, with fresh, strong, slightly sweet flavours (7 grams/litre of residual sugar), showing lovely delicacy, purity and length. Open 2012+.

Vintage	10	09
WR	7	5
Drink	11-15	10-13

MED/DRY $32 AV

Vinoptima Ormond Reserve Gewürztraminer ★★★★★
Launched from 2003, this memorable wine flows from Nick Nobilo's vineyard at Ormond, in Gisborne, devoted exclusively to Gewürztraminer, and is partly fermented in large, 1200-litre German oak ovals. The lovely 2006 vintage (★★★★★) is mouthfilling and rich, with notable delicacy, spiciness, concentration and harmony. The 2004 (★★★★★) is the other outstanding vintage to date.

Vintage	06	05	04	03
WR	6	5	7	5
Drink	10-17	10-12	10-12	P

MED $55 –V

Waimea Nelson Gewürztraminer ★★★★

Estate-grown on the Waimea Plains, the 2008 vintage (★★★★) was hand-picked at 23–26 brix. It's a full-bodied (14.5 per cent alcohol) wine, exotically perfumed, with fresh acidity, rich, well-spiced, slightly gingery flavours, showing some complexity, and an off-dry (6.3 grams/litre of residual sugar), smooth finish.

Vintage	08
WR	6
Drink	10-11

MED/DRY $22 V+

Waipara Hills Soul of the South Waipara Gewürztraminer (★★★★)

Estate-grown in the Mound Vineyard, the 2009 vintage (★★★★) is ripely scented and mouthfilling, fresh and rich, with crisp, vibrant flavours of citrus fruits and spices, excellent delicacy, and a medium-dry (11 grams/litre of residual sugar), finely balanced finish.

MED/DRY $21 V+

Waipara Springs Premo Gewürztraminer (★★★★☆)

Maturing gracefully, the 2008 vintage (★★★★) is a medium style (25 grams/litre of residual sugar), full-bodied and finely textured, with fresh, very ripe peach, spice and slight apricot flavours, showing a touch of complexity and impressive concentration, and a well-rounded finish.

MED $24 V+

Wairau River Marlborough Gewürztraminer ★★★☆

The 2009 vintage (★★★★) is a medium style. Ripely scented, it has good weight and texture, with rich lychee, pear, apricot and spice flavours, showing excellent delicacy, roundness and depth. The 2010 (★★★★) is an off-dry style (7 grams/litre of residual sugar), 10 per cent oak-matured. Richly perfumed, with lychee and spice aromas, it is full-bodied (14.5 per cent alcohol), with strong lychee, pear and spice flavours, showing very good delicacy and purity, and a fresh, lingering finish.

Vintage	10	09	08
WR	6	6	5
Drink	10-13	10-12	P

MED/DRY $25 –V

West Brook Marlborough Gewürztraminer (★★★☆)

The 2009 vintage (★★★☆) is an easy-drinking wine, full-bodied and fresh, with strong peach, lychee, spice and ginger flavours and a soft, gently sweet finish (27 grams/litre of residual sugar).

MED $26 –V

Whitehaven Marlborough Gewürztraminer ★★★★

The 2009 vintage (★★★★) is mouthfilling and soft, with indigenous yeast fermentation in old barriques for part of the blend adding a touch of complexity. Already delicious, it has strong lychee, spice and slight ginger flavours, fresh and ripe, in an off-dry style (9 grams/litre of residual sugar) with lovely texture.

Vintage	09	08
WR	7	5
Drink	10-14	10-12

MED/DRY $20 V+

Yealands Estate Marlborough Gewürztraminer ★★★
Estate-grown at Seaview, in the Awatere Valley, the 2009 vintage (★★☆) is citrusy, spicy and slightly limey, with green edges, fresh acidity and a slightly sweet (8 grams/litre of residual sugar) finish.

MED/DRY $24 –V

Grüner Veltliner

Grüner Veltliner, Austria's favourite white-wine variety, is now arousing interest in New Zealand, where the first vines have been established in Marlborough and Gisborne. Central Otago growers are also excited by the prospects for 'Grü-Vee'. In Austria, this fairly late-ripening grape yields medium-bodied wines, fruity, crisp and dry, with a spicy, slightly musky aroma. Most are drunk young, but the finest wines, with an Alsace-like substance and perfume, are more age-worthy. Coopers Creek produced New Zealand's first Grüner Veltliner from the 2008 vintage, but according to the latest national vineyard survey, just 1 hectare of Grüner Veltliner vines will be bearing in 2011.

Coopers Creek SV The Groover Gisborne Grüner Veltliner ★★★☆

The 2009 (★★★☆) is a fresh, medium-bodied wine with citrusy, peachy, slightly spicy flavours. It's enjoyably fruity and smooth, but not highly distinctive. The 2010 vintage (★★★★) is the best yet. Mouthfilling and finely textured, it's an off-dry style (5 grams/litre of residual sugar), fleshy, ripe, peachy and spicy, with gentle acidity and a well-rounded finish.

Vintage	10	09	08
WR	6	6	5
Drink	10-13	10-12	10-11

MED/DRY $20 AV

Doctors', The, Marlborough Grüner Veltliner (★★★★)

From Forrest Estate, the debut 2010 vintage (★★★★) was made from infant, two-year-old vines at Renwick, in the Wairau Valley. A weighty, dryish, fruity wine with very good depth of peach, pear, lychee and spice flavours and a rounded finish, it's not highly distinctive, in terms of varietal character, but a delicious mouthful.

MED/DRY $25 AV

Seifried Nelson Grüner Veltliner (★★★☆)

The debut 2010 vintage (★★★☆) of a variety famous in Hermann Seifried's homeland was made in a fully dry style. Mouthfilling, with peachy, slightly spicy and lemony flavours, it's a vibrantly fruity wine with fresh acidity, for drinking mid-2011+.

Vintage	10
WR	5
Drink	10-13

DRY $21 AV

Müller-Thurgau

New Zealand's most common variety 20 years ago, Müller-Thurgau is an endangered species.

Most likely a crossing of Riesling and Sylvaner, Müller-Thurgau became extremely popular in Germany after the Second World War, when it was prized for its ability to ripen early with bumper crops. In New Zealand, plantings started to snowball in the early 1970s, and by 1975 it was our most widely planted variety. Today, however, there are only 78 hectares of bearing vines – down from 1873 hectares in 1983. Two-thirds of the vines are clustered in Gisborne.

Müller-Thurgau should be drunk young, at six to 18 months old, when its garden-fresh aromas are in full flower. To attract those who are new to wine, it is typically made slightly sweet. Its fruity, citrusy flavours are typically mild and soft, lacking the crisp acidity and flavour intensity of Riesling.

Corbans White Label Müller-Thurgau ★★★

This cheap, easy-drinking wine from Pernod Ricard NZ is smooth and lemon-scented, with gentle sweetness balanced by moderate acidity in a light-bodied style with greater character and depth than most Müller-Thurgaus of the past. The 2008 vintage (★★★) is light (10.5 per cent alcohol) and lively, with citrusy, limey flavours, showing good depth and harmony.

MED $9 V+

Opihi Vineyard South Canterbury Müller-Thurgau ★★★

Estate-grown and hand-picked, the 2009 vintage (★★☆) is light, with lemony, appley flavours, gentle sweetness (9 grams/litre of residual sugar) and crisp acidity keeping things lively.

MED/DRY $16 –V

Muscat

Muscat vines grow all over the Mediterranean, but Muscat is rarely seen in New Zealand as a varietal wine, because it ripens late in the season, without the lushness and intensity achieved in warmer regions. Of the country's 125 hectares of bearing Muscat vines in 2010, 99 hectares were in Gisborne. Most of the grapes were used to add an inviting, musky perfume to low-priced sparklings, modelled on the Asti Spumantes of northern Italy.

Blackenbrook Vineyard Nelson Muscat (★★★★)

The debut 2010 vintage (★★★★) is a breakthrough – the South Island's first Muscat. Estate-grown, hand-picked at 23.4 brix and lees-aged in tanks, it's a finely scented – although not overwhelmingly musky – wine, fresh and finely poised, with delicious, citrusy flavours, hints of oranges and spices, gentle sweetness (20 grams/litre of residual sugar) and mouthfilling body.

Vintage	10
WR	7
Drink	10-12

MED $23 AV

Leaning Rock Central Otago Rosa Muskat (★★★★)

Grown at Alexandra, the attractively perfumed 2008 vintage (★★★★) is not a true Muscat, but based on a variety – also called Schönburger – bred by crossing Pinot Noir, Chasselas and Muscat Hamburgh. Full of charm, it's a juicy, gently sweet, medium-bodied wine with distinct hints of oranges and pineapples, none of the earthiness typical of most white wines made from Pinot Noir, gentle acidity and very good depth. Worth trying.

MED $20 V+

Millton Te Arai Vineyard Muskats @ Dawn ★★★

Modelled on Moscato d'Asti, the 2008 vintage (★★★) of this Gisborne wine was handled entirely in stainless steel tanks and stop-fermented with low alcohol (9.3 per cent) and plentiful sweetness (40 grams/litre of residual sugar). Perfumed, Muscat aromas lead into a fresh, light wine with lemony, appley, lively flavours, showing good delicacy and liveliness. Easy, summer sipping.

Vintage	08
WR	7
Drink	P

MED $28 –V

Tolaga Bay Estate Tolaga Bay Muscat ★★★

Grown on the East Cape, north of Gisborne, the 2009 vintage (★★★) tastes like Asti Spumante – without the bubbles. Light and lively, it's a low-alcohol wine (10 per cent), gently perfumed, with a touch of *spritzig* and fresh, attractive, citrus-fruit and orange flavours, slightly sweet and smooth.

MED $20 –V

Pinot Blanc

If you love Chardonnay, try Pinot Blanc. A white mutation of Pinot Noir, Pinot Blanc is highly regarded in Italy and California for its generous extract and moderate acidity, although in Alsace and Germany, the more aromatic Pinot Gris finds greater favour.

With its fullness of weight and subtle aromatics, Pinot Blanc can easily be mistaken for Chardonnay in a blind tasting. The variety is still rare in New Zealand, but in 2010 there were 17 hectares of bearing vines, mostly in Canterbury and Central Otago.

Bracken's Order Central Otago Pinot Blanc (★★★★)

The 2008 vintage (★★★★) was grown at Gibbston and mostly handled in tanks, but 30 per cent of the blend was fermented in new French oak casks. Fleshy, with some complexity, it is scented and lively, with citrusy, slightly spicy flavours, a sliver of sweetness and good acid spine.

MED/DRY $20 V+

Clayridge Marlborough Pinot Blanc ★★★★

The 2008 vintage (★★★★), 30 per cent fermented with indigenous yeasts in seasoned French oak barriques, is a basically dry style (4.5 grams/litre of residual sugar), with mouthfilling body and peach, pear and slightly spicy flavours, showing a touch of complexity and good concentration.

Vintage	08
WR	6
Drink	P

DRY $24 AV

Gibbston Valley Central Otago Pinot Blanc ★★★☆

The 2008 vintage (★★★☆) was estate-grown at Bendigo, fermented – 50 per cent with indigenous yeasts – in old French oak casks, and lees-aged for nine months. It's a mouthfilling, rather Chardonnay-like wine, peachy and dry, with good acid spine and aging potential. The 2009 (★★★★) tastes like a cross of Chardonnay and Pinot Gris. Delicious now, it's fresh and full-bodied, with rich, peachy, slightly spicy and toasty flavours.

DRY $27 –V

Greenhough Hope Vineyard Pinot Blanc ★★★★☆

From vines planted at Hope, in Nelson, in the late 1970s, the 2009 vintage (★★★★★) is engrossing. Fermented and matured in seasoned French oak barriques and produced in a slightly off-dry style (5 grams/litre of residual sugar), it's very full-bodied (14.5 per cent alcohol), weighty, complex and rich, with deep peach, pear and spice flavours, slightly buttery and savoury. Sweet-fruited and highly concentrated, it's a very harmonious wine, for drinking now or cellaring.

Vintage	09	08	07	06
WR	6	7	7	6
Drink	10-15	10-13	10-12	10-12

MED/DRY $32 –V

Kerner Estate Marlborough Pinot Blanc (★★★☆)
Hand-picked and barrel-fermented with indigenous yeasts, the 2008 vintage (★★★☆) is mouthfilling and soft, with pear and spice, slightly buttery flavours, showing good depth and complexity. It tastes like a cross of Pinot Gris and Chardonnay.

DRY $25 –V

Mt Rosa Central Otago Pinot Blanc (★★★★)
Still unfolding, the 2009 vintage (★★★★) is a dry wine, barrel-fermented and matured on its yeast lees for nine months. Attractively scented, with the confectionery notes typical of this variety, it is very fresh, with lively acidity and peachy, gently oaked flavours, showing excellent delicacy and depth.

DRY $22 V+

Pyramid Valley Vineyards Growers Collection
Kerner Estate Vineyard Marlborough Pinot Blanc ★★★★
Grown in the Waihopai Valley, the light yellow 2008 vintage (★★★★☆) was hand-picked and fermented with indigenous yeasts in old French barrels. It's a sturdy wine (14.6 per cent alcohol), with rich, peachy, citrusy flavours, slightly buttery and biscuity notes adding complexity, and a well-rounded, fully dry finish. A slightly Chardonnay-like wine, it offers delicious drinking now onwards.

DRY $29 –V

Whitestone Waipara Pinot Blanc ★★★☆
The 2009 vintage (★★★★) is a mouthfilling, partly barrel-fermented wine with good weight and concentrated, ripe citrus-fruit and peach flavours. It's a finely textured wine with a long finish.

DRY $24 –V

Pinot Gris

Pinot Gris has soared in popularity in recent years, making this one of the fastest-growing sections of the *Buyer's Guide*. The wines are also starting to carve out an international reputation. Over 300,000 cases were exported in the year to mid-2010 – more than 10 times the volume shipped five years ago.

At *Winestate* magazine's 2009 Wine of the Year Awards, in Australia, the trophy for champion Pinot Gris was awarded to Spy Valley Marlborough Pinot Gris 2009. The top five Pinot Gris of the year also included Gibbston Valley Central Otago Pinot Gris 2008, as runner-up, Blackenbrook Nelson Pinot Gris 2008, in third place, and Greystone Waipara Pinot Gris 2008, fifth.

The variety is spreading like wildfire – from 130 hectares of bearing vines in 2000 to 1725 hectares in 2011 – and accounts for over 5 per cent of the total producing vineyard area. New Zealand's third most extensively planted white-wine variety, with plantings now almost double those of Riesling, Pinot Gris is trailing only Sauvignon Blanc and Chardonnay.

A mutation of Pinot Noir, Pinot Gris has skin colours ranging from blue-grey to reddish-pink, sturdy extract and a fairly subtle, spicy aroma. It is not a difficult variety to cultivate, adapting well to most soils, and ripens with fairly low acidity to high sugar levels. In Alsace, the best Pinot Gris are matured in large casks, but the wood is old, so as not to interfere with the grape's subtle flavour.

What does Pinot Gris taste like? Imagine a wine that couples the satisfying weight and roundness of Chardonnay with some of the aromatic spiciness of Gewürztraminer. As a refined, full-bodied, dryish white wine – most New Zealand versions are fractionally sweet – that accompanies a wide variety of dishes well, Pinot Gris is worth getting to know.

In terms of style and quality, however, New Zealand Pinot Gris vary widely. Many of the wines lack the enticing perfume, mouthfilling body, flavour richness and softness of the benchmark wines from Alsace. These lesser wines, typically made from heavily cropped vines, are much leaner and crisper – more in the tradition of cheap Italian Pinot Grigio.

Popular in Germany, Alsace and Italy, Pinot Gris is now playing an important role here too. Well over half of the country's plantings are concentrated in Marlborough (42 per cent) and Hawke's Bay (21 per cent), but there are also significant pockets of Pinot Gris in Gisborne, Otago, Canterbury, Nelson, Auckland and Wairarapa.

3 Stones New Zealand Pinot Gris (★★★)

From Ager Sectus (which also owns Crossroads, The Crossings and Southbank), the 2008 vintage (★★★) is a regional blend. It's a smooth, medium-bodied wine with decent depth of citrusy, slightly spicy flavours, rounded and ready.

MED/DRY $20 –V

3 Terraces Pinot Gris (★★★★)

From Gladstone Vineyard, the 2009 vintage (★★★★) was grown in the northern Wairarapa. A medium-dry style, it shows good richness and harmony, with ripe peachy flavours and a creamy-smooth finish. Ready to roll.

MED/DRY $18 V+

36 Bottles Central Otago Pinot Gris ★★★☆

From Mt Aspiring Wines, the 2009 vintage (★★★★) is rare – just 110 cases were produced. Hand-picked at Lowburn, in the Cromwell Basin, it has good immediacy, with mouthfilling body and fresh, vibrant peach, pear and spice flavours in an off-dry style, deliciously strong and lively.

MED/DRY $25 –V

12,000 Miles Wairarapa Pinot Gris ★★★☆

From Gladstone Vineyard, the 2009 vintage (★★★☆) was grown in the northern Wairarapa, tank-fermented and lees-aged. It's a full-bodied wine with good depth of ripe stone-fruit and spice flavours, a hint of ginger and a soft, dry (3.9 grams/litre of residual sugar) finish.

DRY $22 AV

Akarua Central Otago Pinot Gris ★★★☆

Estate-grown at Bannockburn, the 2009 vintage (★★★☆) was mostly handled in tanks, but 15 per cent was fermented and lees-stirred weekly for six months in old oak barriques. Fresh, crisp and finely balanced for easy drinking, it's a pale, youthful wine, moderately concentrated, with mouthfilling body, a sliver of sweetness (9 grams/litre of residual sugar), and vibrant apple, pear, lychee and spice flavours.

Vintage	09	08
WR	6	6
Drink	10-12	10-11

MED/DRY $25 –V

Ake Ake Vineyard Pinot Gris (★★★★)

The 2010 vintage (★★★★) was hand-picked at 24 brix from first-crop vines at Kerikeri, in Northland, tank-fermented and bottled early. It's an auspicious debut – full-bodied, with strong stone-fruit and spice flavours, showing a touch of lees-aging complexity. Weighty, rich and dry, it's a distinctly northern style, with gentle acidity and a ripe, well-rounded finish.

Vintage	10
WR	5
Drink	10-12

DRY $24 AV

Alexia Wairarapa Pinot Gris (★★★★)

Delicious young, the 2010 vintage (★★★★) was grown in the northern Wairarapa and partly barrel-fermented. Finely scented, it's an instantly attractive wine with mouthfilling body and a sliver of sweetness amid its rich, ripe peachy flavours, enlivened by fresh, appetising acidity.

MED/DRY $18 V+

Allan Scott Marlborough Pinot Gris ★★★

The 2008 vintage (★★★) is a medium-bodied style, with a sliver of sweetness (7 grams/litre of residual sugar). It was mostly handled in tanks, but 10 per cent was matured in old oak. Peachy and smooth, it's a softly textured wine, moderately concentrated, offering very easy drinking.

Vintage	08
WR	5
Drink	10-13

MED/DRY $18 AV

Allan Scott Omaka Marlborough Pinot Gris (★★★★)

The debut 2009 vintage (★★★★) is an Alsace-style, single-vineyard wine, tank-fermented and matured in old oak barrels, with regular lees-stirring. Worth cellaring, it's a mouthfilling, off-dry wine (6 grams/litre of residual sugar), with stone-fruit, pear and spice flavours, showing very good delicacy, complexity and depth, and a slightly creamy texture.

Vintage	09				
WR	6				
Drink	10-14				

MED/DRY $29 –V

Amisfield Central Otago Pinot Gris ★★★★

The 2009 vintage (★★★☆) was estate-grown in the Cromwell Basin, harvested at 20 to 23 brix, and mostly fermented in tanks; part of the blend was fermented with indigenous yeasts in large (600-litre) French oak casks. It is a youthful, easy-drinking wine with good depth of ripe peach, pear and spice flavours, a touch of complexity and an off-dry (7.3 grams/litre of residual sugar) finish.

Vintage	10	09	08	07	06
WR	6	5	7	5	4
Drink	12-15	11-14	10-20	10-12	10-11

MED/DRY $30 –V

Anchorage Nelson Pinot Gris ★★★

The 2009 vintage (★★★) is a medium-bodied style, still very fresh and youthful, with crisp, slightly sweet (11 grams/litre of residual sugar) flavours of lychees, pears and spices, and good depth.

MED/DRY $18 AV

Ant Moore Marlborough Pinot Gris (★★★★☆)

Estate-grown in the Waihopai Valley, the 2009 vintage (★★★★☆) is richly scented and mouthfilling, with fresh, slightly sweet stone-fruit, pear and spice flavours, showing good concentration. Crisp, youthful and tightly structured, it's an intensely varietal, very harmonious wine, worth cellaring.

MED/DRY $22 V+

Artisan The Far Paddock Marlborough Pinot Gris ★★★☆

The 2009 vintage (★★★☆) is a dryish style (5 grams/litre of residual sugar) with substantial body (14.5 per cent alcohol), fresh, strong flavours of peaches and apricots and a strongly spicy finish.

MED/DRY $20 AV

Ashwood Estate Gisborne Pinot Gris (★★★★)

One of Gisborne's finest Pinot Gris to date, the 2008 vintage (★★★★) is from a partnership between grower Murray McPhail and winemaker Nick Nobilo, of Vinoptima. It's a weighty wine with concentrated peach and slight apricot flavours, an oily texture and a slightly sweet (8 grams/litre of residual sugar), distinctly spicy, lingering finish.

MED/DRY $25 AV

Askerne Hawke's Bay Pinot Gris ★★★★

The 2010 vintage (★★★★☆) was estate-grown near Havelock North and fermented in tanks (90 per cent) and old French oak barrels (10 per cent). Delicious from the start, it is highly scented and mouthfilling, with vibrant flavours of peaches, apricots and spices, a touch of complexity and a soft, slightly sweet (10 grams/litre of residual sugar), rich finish.

Vintage	10	09
WR	6	6
Drink	10-12	10-11

MED/DRY $20 V+

Astrolabe Discovery Awatere Pinot Gris (★★★☆)

Hand-picked in the lower Awatere Valley, the 2008 vintage (★★★☆) is a full-bodied (14.5 per cent alcohol), moderately concentrated wine with fresh citrus-fruit, pear and spice flavours, showing good delicacy and purity, a slightly oily texture and a crisp, dryish (5.6 grams/litre of residual sugar) finish.

Vintage	08
WR	6
Drink	10-13

MED/DRY $24 –V

Astrolabe Discovery Kekerengu Coast Pinot Gris (★★★☆)

Grown between the Awatere Valley and Kaikoura, the 2009 vintage (★★★☆) is a floral and fleshy, slightly oily wine with good texture, delicacy and depth of pear, lychee and spice flavours and an off-dry (8.8 grams/litre of residual sugar) finish.

Vintage	09
WR	6
Drink	10-12

MED/DRY $25 –V

Astrolabe Experience The Rocks Pinot Gris (★★★☆)

Grown in the lower Awatere Valley, the 2008 vintage (★★★☆) was hand-picked and barrel-fermented, with frequent lees-stirring. It's a slightly Chardonnay-like wine, fleshy and creamy-textured, with stone-fruit and spice flavours, plenty of toasty oak in evidence (arguably a bit too much) and a dry (4 grams/litre of residual sugar) finish.

Vintage	08
WR	6
Drink	10-12

DRY $37 –V

Astrolabe Voyage Marlborough Pinot Gris (★★★)

Grown in the Waihopai and Awatere valleys, the 2008 voyage (★★★) is a mouthfilling, off-dry style (6.2 grams/litre of residual sugar) with fresh acidity and good depth of pear, lychee and spice flavours.

Vintage	08
WR	6
Drink	10-13

MED/DRY $21 –V

Ata Rangi Lismore Pinot Gris ★★★★☆

Grown in the Lismore Vineyard in Martinborough, 400 metres from the Ata Rangi winery, the intensely varietal 2009 vintage (★★★★☆) is a mouthfilling, gently sweet wine (11 grams/litre of residual sugar) with deep, peachy flavours, hints of pears and spices, and lovely vibrancy and harmony.

Vintage	09	08	07	06
WR	7	6	6	7
Drink	10-13	10-12	P	P

MED/DRY $28 AV

Aurora Vineyard Bendigo Pinot Gris (★★★☆)

The fleshy, distinctive 2008 vintage (★★★☆) was estate-grown at Bendigo and 75 per cent barrel-fermented. Mouthfilling (14.5 per cent alcohol), it's a slightly Chardonnay-like wine with strong, ripe stone-fruit flavours and creamy, leesy notes adding complexity.

DRY $28 –V

Aurum Central Otago Pinot Gris ★★★☆

Estate-grown at Lowburn, the 2009 vintage (★★★★) is the best yet. A distinctly medium style (19 grams/litre of residual sugar), it is mouthfilling, very fresh and youthful, with rich, ripe peach and pear flavours and appetising acidity. A finely balanced, vibrantly fruity wine, it's well worth cellaring.

Vintage	09	08	07
WR	6	5	6
Drink	10-13	10-12	P

MED $25 –V

Awatere River Marlborough Pinot Gris (★★★★)

The 2008 vintage (★★★★) is an attractively scented blend of Awatere Valley and Wairau Valley grapes, with excellent delicacy and depth. Hand-picked and partly handled in seasoned French oak barriques, it is mouthfilling, ripe and rounded, with an oily texture and pear/lychee flavours, slightly sweet and rounded.

MED/DRY $22 V+

Babich Black Label Marlborough Pinot Gris (★★★★☆)

Sold in restaurants, the distinctive 2009 vintage (★★★★☆) was partly barrel-fermented. Full-bodied (14 per cent alcohol), it is vibrant, with rich pear, lychee and spice flavours, good texture, a touch of oak complexity and an unusually dry (2.8 grams/litre of residual sugar) but finely balanced finish. Fleshy and youthful, it's still unfolding; open mid-2011+.

DRY $25 V+

Babich Marlborough Pinot Gris ★★★☆

Grown in the Wairau and Waihopai valleys and partly barrel-fermented, the 2009 vintage (★★★★) is an Alsace-style wine, with mouthfilling body and strong stone-fruit, pear and spice flavours. A medium-dry style, it is deliciously harmonious, with a rich, well-rounded finish.

MED/DRY $20 AV

Bald Hills Pinot Gris ★★★

From a small block of vines at Bannockburn, in Central Otago, the 2008 vintage (★★★☆) has gently spicy aromas. Enlivened by fresh acidity, it's a dry style (3.4 grams/litre of residual sugar) with a slightly creamy texture and vibrant, citrusy, slightly appley and spicy flavours, showing good depth.

Vintage	09	07	06
WR	7	6	5
Drink	10-14	11-13	10-12

DRY $25 –V

Bascand Marlborough Pinot Gris ★★☆

Faintly pink, the very easy-drinking 2009 vintage (★★☆) is full-bodied, with pear and spice flavours, gentle sweetness (10 grams/litre of residual sugar) and a soft, creamy texture.

MED/DRY $17 –V

Bellbird Spring Block Eight Pinot Gris (★★★★)

Grown at Waipara, the 2009 vintage (★★★★) is a single-vineyard wine, hand-harvested and fermented and lees-aged in old oak casks. Mouthfilling, it's a medium-sweet style (40 grams/litre of residual sugar), with concentrated, ripe lychee, pear, spice and apricot flavours, a hint of oak and a softly textured finish.

MED $30 –V

Bensen Block Pinot Gris (★★★)

The 2008 vintage (★★★) from Pernod Ricard NZ is not identified by region, but the grapes were grown in Gisborne. Full-bodied, it offers plenty of citrusy, slightly appley and spicy flavour, with a dryish (6.5 grams/litre of residual sugar), crisp finish.

MED/DRY $17 AV

Bijou Estate Double Bridges Pinot Gris (★★)

The copper-hued 2008 vintage (★★) was grown at Opaki, just north of Masterton, in the Wairarapa. Partly barrel-fermented, it lacks a bit of freshness and vibrancy.

DRY $22 –V

Bilancia Hawke's Bay Pinot Gris ★★★★

From Lorraine Leheny and Warren Gibson (winemaker at Trinity Hill), the 2008 vintage (★★★★) is a dry style (3 grams/litre of residual sugar) with a peachy, spicy bouquet, good weight (14 per cent alcohol) and strong, ripe peach, pear and spice flavours. A generous, finely textured wine, showing excellent depth and harmony, it's drinking well now.

Vintage	08
WR	6
Drink	10-14

DRY $25 AV

Bilancia Reserve Pinot Gris ★★★★★

Grown at Haumoana, near the Hawke's Bay coast, this is a vineyard selection of grapes from the most heavily crop-thinned, later harvested vines. The classy 2008 vintage (★★★★★) is mouthfilling (14.5 per cent alcohol), with deep stone-fruit and spice flavours, gentle acidity, a sliver of sweetness (7 grams/litre of residual sugar), a slightly oily texture and lovely harmony. It's a distinctly Alsace-style wine, for drinking now or cellaring.

Vintage	08
WR	7
Drink	10-16

MED/DRY $35 AV

Bird Marlborough Pinot Gris ★★★☆

Very pale pink, the 2008 vintage (★★★) is a mouthfilling wine with strawberry and spice aromas, a hint of apricots, plenty of flavour and a dry (3 grams/litre of residual sugar) finish.

Vintage	08	07	06
WR	6	4	4
Drink	10-11	P	P

DRY $23 –V

Bishops Head Waipara Valley Pinot Gris (★★★☆)

The 2008 vintage (★★★☆) is a citrusy, slightly peachy wine, medium-bodied, with very good depth of flavour, slightly sweet and crisp.

MED/DRY $20 AV

Black Barn Vineyards Hawke's Bay Pinot Gris ★★★★

The 2009 vintage (★★★★) was hand-harvested at two sites in the Te Mata district and briefly lees-aged. Fleshy and finely textured, it's a medium-dry style (12 grams/litre of residual sugar), with very good delicacy and richness of pear, lychee and spice flavours, fresh, pure and vibrant. It's already delicious.

MED/DRY $25 AV

Black Cottage Marlborough Pinot Gris (★★★)

From Two Rivers, the 2010 vintage (★★★) is a good buy. Mouthfilling, it's a very easy-drinking style with good depth of vibrant, peachy, slightly spicy flavours, gently sweet and smooth.

MED/DRY $15 V+

Blackenbrook Vineyard Nelson Pinot Gris ★★★★★

An emerging classic. The estate-grown 2009 vintage (★★★★★) is a powerful, Alsace-style, very ripely scented wine with fresh, rich flavours of stone-fruit, lychees and spices, gentle sweetness and balanced acidity. The 2010 (★★★★★) was hand-picked at 25.7 brix. Harbouring 15 per cent alcohol, it is beautifully floral, with fresh, very vibrant peach, pear and spice aromas and flavours, a hint of ginger, slight sweetness (20 grams/litre of residual sugar), and lovely purity, delicacy and richness.

Vintage	10	09	08	07	06
WR	6	6	7	7	6
Drink	10-13	10-12	10-12	P	P

MED $27 V+

Black Stilt Pinot Gris (★★★)

The 2009 vintage (★★★), grown in the Waitaki Valley, North Otago, is a fresh, light, Pinot Grigio style with pear and green-apple flavours threaded with crisp acidity.

DRY $27 –V

Bladen Marlborough Pinot Gris ★★★

The 2009 vintage (★★★) was estate-grown and hand-picked. Vibrantly fruity and smooth, it is balanced for easy drinking, with a sliver of sweetness (5.7 grams/litre of residual sugar) and satisfying depth of pear, lychee and spice flavours.

Vintage 09
WR 6
Drink 10-12

MED/DRY $23 –V

Bloody Bay Marlborough Pinot Gris (★★★)

From wine distributor Federal Geo, the 2009 vintage (★★★) is a powerful (14.5 per cent alcohol), upfront style with gingery, very spicy, slightly honeyed flavours and a smooth finish.

DRY $17 AV

Boreham Wood Single Vineyard Awatere Valley Pinot Gris ★★★★

The 2009 vintage (★★★★) is an Alsace-style, fleshy, dryish (6 grams/litre of residual sugar) and well-rounded. It has strong, ripe peach, pear and spice flavours, showing some complexity, and excellent texture, richness and downright drinkability.

Vintage 09 08
WR 7 6
Drink 10-14 10-12

DRY $24 AV

Bouldevines Marlborough Pinot Gris ★★☆

The 2009 vintage (★★) is pale, with citrusy, slightly appley aromas and flavours, lacking real ripeness and richness.

MED/DRY $25 –V

Boundary Vineyards Paper Lane Waipara Pinot Gris (★★★☆)

From Pernod Ricard NZ, the 2008 vintage (★★★☆) is a mouthfilling Waipara wine with vibrant pear and spice flavours, showing clear-cut varietal characters, and a splash of sweetness (7.9 grams/litre of residual sugar) giving easy-drinking appeal.

MED/DRY $20 AV

Brancott Estate Living Land Series Marlborough Pinot Gris ★★★☆

The 2010 vintage (★★★☆), tasted in its infancy, looked highly promising, with satisfying body and ripe, slightly sweet flavours, showing very good depth.

MED/DRY $20 AV

Brancott Estate North Island Pinot Gris ★★★
Up to the 2008 vintage, this wine was sold under the Montana brand. The 2009 (★★★) is medium-bodied, with fresh, vibrant pear and spice flavours, showing good balance and drink-young appeal.

MED/DRY $18 AV

Brennan Gibbston Pinot Grigio (★★★☆)
Maturing well, the 2008 vintage (★★★☆) is a mouthfilling, lemony Central Otago wine with hints of spices and apricots, and a crisp, dry finish.

DRY $18 V+

Brick Bay Matakana Pinot Gris ★★★☆
At its best, this wine is impressively weighty, rich and rounded. Hand-picked, lees-aged and made in an off-dry style, the 2009 vintage (★★★☆) is medium-bodied (12 per cent alcohol), very fresh and vibrant, with lemon, apple and spice flavours. The 2010 (★★★★) is ripely scented and mouthfilling, with rich, ripe, peachy, slightly spicy flavours, showing excellent freshness, purity and depth.

Vintage	10	09	08	07	06
WR	7	7	7	7	7
Drink	10-15	10-14	10-11	P	P

MED/DRY $32 –V

Brightside Nelson Pinot Gris ★★★
From Kaimira Estate, the 2009 vintage (★★★) is full-bodied, with fresh, gently sweet (9 grams/litre of residual sugar) flavours, ripe, peachy and gently spicy, in a very easy-drinking style.

MED/DRY $16 V+

Brightwater Vineyards Lord Rutherford Pinot Gris (★★★★☆)
Set to unfold well, the 2010 vintage (★★★★☆) is highly scented, mouthfilling and gently sweet (13 grams/litre of residual sugar), with ripe citrus-fruit, peach and spice flavours. It's an elegant wine with a touch of complexity and good texture.

Vintage	10
WR	5
Drink	10-12

MED/DRY $30 –V

Brightwater Vineyards Nelson Pinot Gris (★★★★)
Attractively scented, the 2009 vintage (★★★★) has fresh, rich lychee, citrus-fruit and lime flavours. A distinctly medium style (20 grams/litre of residual sugar), it is vibrantly fruity, with balanced acidity and excellent texture and harmony.

Vintage	10
WR	5
Drink	10-12

MED $25 AV

Bronte by Rimu Grove Nelson Pinot Gris ★★★★

Rimu Grove's second-tier Pinot Gris – but it's still rewarding. The 2009 vintage (★★★☆) was hand-picked in the Moutere hills and mostly handled in tanks, but 15 per cent of the blend was fermented and lees-aged for four months in seasoned French oak barrels. Fresh, vibrant and slightly sweet (13 grams/litre of residual sugar), it is tight and citrusy, with a touch of complexity and very good texture and depth.

Vintage	09	08
WR	6	6
Drink	10-14	10-13

MED/DRY $24 AV

Brookfields Robertson Hawke's Bay Pinot Gris ★★★

The 2009 vintage (★★★) is a slightly sweet wine (11 grams/litre of residual sugar), full-bodied, with peachy, appley, spicy flavours, in an easy-drinking style with a smooth finish.

Vintage	09	08
WR	7	7
Drink	10-13	10-11

MED/DRY $19 AV

Brunton Road Gisborne Pinot Gris ★★★

A single-vineyard wine, grown at Patutahi, the 2008 vintage (★★★) is a mouthfilling, pleasantly fruity wine, citrusy, slightly appley and spicy, with a fresh, crisp, dryish (4 grams/litre of residual sugar) finish.

DRY $21 –V

Burnt Spur Martinborough Pinot Gris ★★★★

A single-vineyard wine from Martinborough Vineyard, the 2009 vintage (★★★★★) was estate-grown in the Burnt Spur Vineyard, hand-picked, and lees-aged in tanks. Instantly attractive, it is a medium style (16 grams/litre of residual sugar), rich and soft, with mouthfilling body, an oily texture and concentrated, deliciously ripe stone-fruit and spice flavours.

Vintage	09	08	07
WR	7	7	7
Drink	10-14	10-13	10-12

MED $22 V+

Butterfish Bay Northland Pinot Gris (★★★☆)

The debut 2009 vintage (★★★☆) was hand-harvested on Paewhenua Island, a peninsula reaching into Mangonui Harbour. Enjoyable from the start, it's a medium to full-bodied wine, freshly aromatic, with good depth of ripe peach, pear and lychee flavours, a sliver of sweetness (9 grams/litre of residual sugar) and a well-rounded finish.

Vintage	09
WR	6
Drink	10-11

MED/DRY $28 –V

Camshorn Waipara Pinot Gris ★★★★
Grown in Pernod Ricard NZ's hillside vineyard in North Canterbury, the easy-drinking 2008 vintage (★★★★) is an enticingly scented wine, oily and rich, with strongly varietal pear, lychee and spice flavours, pure, gently sweet and smooth.

Vintage	08	07
WR	5	5
Drink	P	P

MED/DRY $27 –V

Cape Campbell Marlborough Pinot Gris ★★★☆
The 2008 vintage (★★★☆) is fresh and lively, with a floral bouquet, medium body and slightly sweet pear and spice flavours that linger well.

Vintage	08	07	06
WR	6	7	6
Drink	10-11	P	P

MED/DRY $19 V+

Carrick Central Otago Pinot Gris ★★★★
The stylish 2010 vintage (★★★★) was grown at Bannockburn and 20 per cent fermented in very old casks; the rest was handled in tanks. It's a scented, mouthfilling wine (14 per cent alcohol), with just a hint of sweetness (5.7 grams/litre of residual sugar) amid its citrusy, slightly spicy flavours, which show excellent freshness, depth and harmony. The 2009 (★★★☆) is full-bodied, with satisfying depth of lemony, appley flavours, slightly creamy and buttery notes, and fresh acidity.

MED/DRY $25 AV

Castaway Bay Marlborough Pinot Gris (★★☆)
From Maven, the 2008 vintage (★★☆) was hand-harvested in the Wairau and Omaka valleys, and part of the blend was fermented with indigenous yeasts in seasoned French oak barriques. It's a medium-bodied wine, slightly sweet, with moderate depth of flavour, a slightly creamy texture and a soft finish.

MED/DRY $15 AV

Catalina Sounds Marlborough Pinot Gris ★★★
Still youthful, the 2009 vintage (★★★☆) is a single-vineyard wine, hand-picked in the Waihopai Valley and mostly handled in tanks; 4 per cent was barrel-fermented. It's a dry style (3.3 grams/litre of residual sugar), mouthfilling and vibrantly fruity, with moderately concentrated peach, pear and spice flavours, woven with fresh acidity, and good harmony.

DRY $26 –V

Chard Farm Central Otago Pinot Gris ★★★★
Hand-picked in Cromwell vineyards, the 2009 vintage (★★★★) is ripely scented, mouthfilling and fleshy, with strong, ripe, peachy, citrusy, slighty spicy flavours, an oily texture and a well-rounded, off-dry finish.

MED/DRY $28 –V

Charles Wiffen Marlborough Pinot Gris ★★★★
The 2009 vintage (★★★★) is medium-bodied, with fresh, ripe stone-fruit and pear flavours, a gentle splash of sweetness and finely balanced acidity. It's a very harmonious wine, delicious from the start.

MED/DRY $23 AV

Church Road Cuve Hawke's Bay Pinot Gris ★★★★☆
Grown 300 metres above sea level in Pernod Ricard NZ's cool, inland site at Matapiro, the 2008 vintage (★★★★) is a scented, distinctly medium style with good weight and concentrated, ripe, slightly honeyed flavours. It's drinking well now. The 2009 (★★★★☆) is even better, with beautifully ripe, peachy flavours, an oily texture and a rich, well-rounded finish.

MED/DRY $27 AV

Church Road Hawke's Bay Pinot Gris ★★★☆
Grown mostly at Pernod Ricard NZ's cool, elevated, inland site at Matapiro, this wine is mostly lees-aged in tanks; a small portion is fermented in seasoned French oak barrels. The 2009 vintage (★★★☆) is a strongly varietal wine, mouthfilling, with fresh, gently sweet, peachy flavours and a creamy-smooth finish.

MED/DRY $26 –V

Clark Estate Single Vineyard Awatere Valley Marlborough Pinot Gris (★★★☆)
Harvested at 23.5 brix from young, second-crop vines, the 2009 vintage (★★★☆) is freshly scented, mouthfilling and vibrantly fruity, with pear and lychee flavours, slightly spicy and limey. It's an off-dry style (6.3 grams/litre of residual sugar) with good delicacy and varietal character.

MED/DRY $20 AV

Clayridge Excalibur Marlborough Pinot Gris (★★★★★)
Showing real personality, the 2008 vintage (★★★★★) was barrel-fermented with indigenous yeasts. It's a powerful, dryish wine (5 grams/litre of residual sugar) with rich, peachy, spicy flavours, notably complex and concentrated.

MED/DRY $33 AV

Clayridge Marlborough Pinot Gris ★★★★☆
The 2008 vintage (★★★★☆) was grown at two sites and part of the blend was fermented with indigenous yeasts and lees-aged in seasoned French oak barriques. Scented and mouthfilling, it's a dryish wine (5.8 grams/litre of residual sugar) with stone-fruit and spice flavours, faintly honeyed and rich.

Vintage	08	07
WR	7	7
Drink	10-12	10-12

MED/DRY $24 V+

Clifford Bay Marlborough Pinot Gris (★★★☆)

From Vavasour, the debut 2010 vintage (★★★☆) is mouthfilling, with clear-cut varietal character. Still very youthful, it has fresh pear and spice flavours, showing very good depth, and an off-dry, crisp finish.

MED/DRY $16 V+

Clos St William Waipara Pinot Gris (★★★★)

The 2009 vintage (★★★★) was hand-picked at 25 brix and given some exposure to old oak. Fleshy, it's a medium-dry style with well-ripened pear, spice and stone-fruit flavours, a slightly oily texture, and excellent harmony and richness.

MED/DRY $20 V+

Cloudy Bay Marlborough Pinot Gris (★★★★)

The 2008 vintage (★★★★) was handled in a mix of tanks (30 per cent) and seasoned French oak barrels (70 per cent). Mouthfilling and smooth, with pear, spice and lychee aromas and flavours, it's a moderately concentrated wine, off-dry (5.3 grams/litre of residual sugar) with a touch of complexity, good texture and length. The very similar 2009 (★★★★) is full-bodied and vibrant, with strong, fresh pear and spice flavours, good complexity and harmony, and a well-rounded, dryish (5 grams/litre of residual sugar) finish. Open mid-2011+.

Vintage	09
WR	7
Drink	11-12

MED/DRY $30 –V

Coney Piccolo Martinborough Pinot Gris ★★★★

The 2009 vintage (★★★★) is a tight, youthful wine with rich, vibrant pear, lychee and spice flavours and a crisp, off-dry (6.5 grams/litre of residual sugar) finish. It shows good freshness, weight and concentration, with some cellaring potential.

MED/DRY $24 AV

Coopers Creek New Zealand Pinot Gris ★★★

The early releases were estate-grown at Huapai, in West Auckland, then Gisborne grapes were added, and the 2008 vintage (★★★) also includes Marlborough fruit. It's an easy-drinking, medium to full-bodied wine with decent depth of citrus-fruit, pear and spice flavours, slightly sweet and crisp. The 2009 (★★☆) is mouthfilling, with citrusy, slightly spicy flavours, a touch of sweetness (5.5 grams/litre of residual sugar) and reasonable depth.

Vintage	09	08	07	06
WR	5	6	7	6
Drink	10-12	P	P	P

MED/DRY $17 AV

Coopers Creek SV The Pointer Marlborough Pinot Gris ★★★★

The 2009 vintage (★★★☆) is fleshy and slightly creamy, with very good depth of vibrant pear, lychee and spice flavours, slightly sweet (8.3 grams/litre of residual sugar), fresh and rounded.

Vintage	09	08
WR	6	7
Drink	10-12	10-11

MED/DRY $20 V+

Corazon Single Vineyard Pinot Gris (★★★)

Grown in Marlborough and partly barrel-fermented, the 2008 vintage (★★★) is full-bodied, with ripe pear and lychee flavours, oaky, leesy notes adding a touch of complexity and good depth.

MED/DRY $24 –V

Corbans Homestead Gisborne Pinot Gris ★★★

The 2008 vintage (★★★) from Pernod Ricard NZ was lees-aged for four months in tanks and stop-fermented in a medium-dry style. Offering very easy drinking, it's medium to full-bodied, with soft, peachy flavours, showing good depth.

MED/DRY $17 AV

Corbans Private Bin Hawke's Bay Pinot Gris ★★★☆

The 2007 vintage (★★★☆) was picked in Pernod Ricard NZ's inland, elevated Matapiro Vineyard, and 50 per cent of the blend was fermented in seasoned French oak barriques. A mouthfilling wine with an oily texture, good depth of peach, pear and spice flavours and a dryish (8 grams/litre of residual sugar) finish, it is scented, with good vigour and a touch of complexity.

Vintage	07	06
WR	6	5
Drink	P	P

MED/DRY $24 –V

Couper's Shed Hawke's Bay Pinot Gris (★★★★)

The invitingly perfumed 2009 vintage (★★★★) was grown by Pernod Ricard NZ at Matapiro and 35 per cent of the blend was fermented with indigenous yeasts in old French oak barriques; the rest was tank-fermented and lees-aged. It's a full-bodied, medium-dry style (13.2 grams/litre of residual sugar) with ripe stone-fruit, spice and ginger flavours, a slightly oily texture and excellent delicacy and richness.

MED $20 V+

Cracroft Chase Single Vineyard Grey Pearl Canterbury Pinot Gris ★★☆

Grown in the Port Hills at Christchurch, the 2009 vintage (★★☆) is an off-dry wine (6 grams/litre of residual sugar), lees-aged in tanks. It's a pleasant, Pinot Grigio style, light and lemony, with a slightly spicy, crisp finish.

Vintage	09
WR	6
Drink	10-13

MED/DRY $15 AV

Cracroft Chase Wood's Edge Pinot Gris ★★★

The 2008 vintage (★★★) was estate-grown in Canterbury and lees-aged in tanks and barrels. A dry style (3.4 grams/litre of residual sugar), it is still youthful, with crisp, vibrant, citrusy flavours and a touch of complexity.

DRY $20 –V

Craggy Range Otago Station Vineyard Waitaki Valley Pinot Gris ★★★☆

The 2009 vintage (★★★★) is lemon-scented and fleshy, with ripe, peachy, citrusy flavours, fresh and strong, a slightly creamy texture and a harmonious, off-dry (6 grams/litre of residual sugar) finish.

Vintage	09	08
WR	6	6
Drink	10-15	10-14

MED/DRY $35 –V

Crater Rim, The, Waipara Pinot Gris ★★★★

Already delicious, the 2009 vintage (★★★★☆) is a single-vineyard wine, fermented with indigenous yeasts and partly barrel-fermented. The bouquet is fragrant, spicy and faintly honeyed; the palate is full-bodied and rich, with peach and apricot flavours, fresh, concentrated and well-rounded. It shows lovely harmony; drink now onwards.

MED/DRY $28 –V

Crawford Farm New Zealand Pinot Gris (★★★)

The 2008 vintage (★★★) from Constellation NZ is a regional blend. A medium to full-bodied style with a splash of sweetness amid its lemon, apple and spice flavours, it's a smooth, easy-drinking wine with decent depth. Ready.

DRY $22 –V

Crossroads Hawke's Bay Pinot Gris ★★☆

The 2009 vintage (★★☆) is a fully dry style (1 gram/litre of residual sugar) with peachy, slightly gingery aromas and flavours, showing moderate depth.

DRY $20 –V

Crowded House Marlborough Pinot Gris (★★★☆)

Offering fine value, the 2008 vintage (★★★☆) is mouthfilling and clearly varietal, with very good depth of pear and spice flavours, hints of peaches and nectarines, and a basically dry finish.

DRY $18 V+

Culley Marlborough Pinot Gris (★★★)

The debut 2008 vintage (★★★) has fresh pear, spice and apricot flavours, slightly sweet and crisp. It's a clearly varietal, moderately concentrated wine, enjoyable from the start.

MED/DRY $19 AV

Curio Horrell Vineyard Nelson Pinot Gris (★★★☆)

From Mud House, the 2008 vintage (★★★☆) is scented, mouthfilling and well-rounded, in a medium-dry style with plenty of ripe, peachy, spicy flavour, balanced for easy drinking. Ready.

MED/DRY $28 –V

Cypress Hawke's Bay Pinot Gris ★★★☆
The 2009 vintage (★★★☆) was hand-picked and tank-fermented. It's a good food wine, mouthfilling and dry (4 grams/litre of residual sugar), with citrusy, slightly peachy and spicy flavours, showing good depth and roundness.

Vintage	09	08
WR	6	6
Drink	10-12	10-11

DRY $25 –V

Darling, The, Marlborough Pinot Gris ★★★★☆
The 2009 vintage (★★★★☆) is a single-vineyard wine, grown at Rapaura, in the Wairau Valley, and mostly handled in tanks; 20 per cent was barrel-fermented with indigenous yeasts. It's an intensely varietal wine, mouthfilling, with pure, ripe peach, lychee and spice flavours, showing excellent concentration. Weighty and finely textured, it's an impressive debut. The 2010 (★★★★☆), 20 per cent oak-aged, has strong personality. Mouthfilling, with strong peach, lychee and spice flavours, fresh and pure, it is slightly sweet (7 grams/litre of residual sugar), with an oily texture and excellent depth and harmony.

Vintage	10
WR	7
Drink	10-13

MED/DRY $23 V+

Dashwood Marlborough Pinot Gris (★★★★)
Grown in the Awatere Valley, the 2008 vintage (★★★★) is scented and softly mouthfilling, with vibrant, pure pear, citrus-fruit, lychee and spice flavours, gentle sweetness (8 grams/litre of residual sugar), and very good depth.

MED/DRY $21 V+

Dawn Ghost Central Otago Pinot Gris (★★★☆)
From an Alexandra-based company, the 2009 vintage (★★★☆) is full-bodied, fresh and smooth, with very good depth of peachy, citrusy, slightly spicy flavour. It's drinking well now.

MED $20 AV

Desert Heart Central Otago Pinot Gris (★★)
Grown at Bannockburn, the 2008 vintage (★★) was matured for five months in old oak barrels. It has light lemon, apple and pear flavours, but lacks real fragrance, ripeness and richness.

MED/DRY $25 –V

Devil's Staircase Central Otago Pinot Gris ★★★
From Rockburn, the 2009 vintage (★★☆) is a slightly rustic wine, mouthfilling (14 per cent alcohol), with dryish, crisp, citrusy, spicy flavours that lack real ripeness and richness.

MED/DRY $20 –V

Distant Land Marlborough Pinot Gris ★★★☆

The 2008 vintage (★★★☆) from Lincoln was grown in the Wairau Valley and 10 per cent of the blend was fermented in old French barrels. It's a mouthfilling, ripely scented wine with soft, peachy, slightly spicy flavours, showing very good depth. The 2009 (★★★★), not oak-aged, is delicious from the start, with an attractively scented bouquet and fresh, rich nectarine and pear flavours, showing good harmony.

MED/DRY $20 AV

Domain Road Vineyard Central Otago Pinot Gris (★★★★)

The 2010 vintage (★★★★) is an excellent debut. Partly (35 per cent) barrel-fermented, it's a medium-dry style (11.5 grams/litre of residual sugar), fresh, mouthfilling and rounded, with ripe peach, pear, lychee and spice flavours, a very subtle seasoning of oak and good texture, complexity and potential. Drink mid-2011+.

MED/DRY $24 AV

Drumsara Central Otago Ventifacts Block Pinot Gris ★★★★

The 2008 vintage (★★★★), estate-grown at Alexandra, has strong personality. Hand-picked at 23.5 brix, it's a dry wine (3.9 grams/litre of residual sugar), with a scented bouquet, moderate acidity and ripe stone-fruit flavours, showing good concentration.

Vintage	09	08
WR	6	5
Drink	10-13	10-12

DRY $28 –V

Dry Gully Walkers Block Central Otago Pinot Gris (★★★☆)

Grown at Alexandra, the 2008 vintage (★★★☆) is a fleshy, sturdy (14.5 per cent alcohol) wine, attractively scented, with peach, pear, lychee and spice flavours, showing very good depth, and a dry finish.

Vintage	08
WR	5
Drink	10-12

DRY $20 AV

Dry River Pinot Gris ★★★★★

From the first vintage in 1986, for many years Dry River towered over other New Zealand Pinot Gris, by virtue of its exceptional body, flavour richness and longevity. A sturdy Martinborough wine, it has peachy, spicy characters that can develop great subtlety and richness with maturity (at around five years old for top vintages, which also hold well for a decade). It is grown in the estate and nearby Craighall vineyards, where the majority of the vines are over 25 years old. To avoid any loss of varietal flavour, it is not oak-aged. At a tasting in late 2009 of the 2004–2007 vintages, the star was the richly perfumed, oily-textured, highly concentrated 2007 (★★★★★), from an ultra-low-cropping (1.7 tonnes/hectare) season. The very youthful 2009 (★★★★★) is fleshy, with ripe stone-fruit and spice flavours, a sliver of sweetness and lovely depth, delicacy and harmony. It needs time; open mid-2011+.

Vintage	09	08	07	06	05
WR	7	7	7	7	7
Drink	10-19	10-18	10-17	10-18	10-13

MED/DRY $50 AV

Durvillea Marlborough Pinot Grigio (★★★)
From Astrolabe, the 2009 vintage (★★★) is floral, fresh, light and crisp, in a dry, Pinot Grigio style.

DRY $14 V+

Edge, The, Martinborough Pinot Gris ★★★
From Escarpment, the 2009 vintage (★★★☆) is an easy-drinking style, full-bodied and slightly sweet, with fresh, vibrant flavours of lychees, pears and spices, showing very good depth.

MED/DRY $19 AV

Eradus Awatere Valley Marlborough Pinot Gris ★★★
Enjoyable young, the 2009 vintage (★★★☆) is a mouthfilling, rounded wine, freshly aromatic, with very good depth of peachy, slightly spicy flavours, slightly sweet (10 grams/litre of residual sugar) and balanced for easy drinking.

Vintage	09
WR	5
Drink	10-11

MED/DRY $19 AV

Escarpment Martinborough Pinot Gris ★★★★★
This distinctive, 'Burgundian inspired' Pinot Gris is barrel-fermented. The 2008 vintage (★★★★) is mouthfilling, with rich, peachy, spicy, slightly honeyed flavours, subtle oak and a smooth, off-dry finish. The 2009 (★★★★★) is already delicious. An authoritative wine, it is fleshy and rich, with concentrated stone-fruit and pear flavours, finely integrated oak and a finely textured, smooth (5 grams/litre of residual sugar) finish. Drink now or cellar.

MED/DRY $29 V+

Esk Valley Hawke's Bay Pinot Gris ★★★★
Maturing very gracefully, the 2009 vintage (★★★★) was hand-picked in the Esk Valley and at Maraekakaho, and mostly handled in tanks; 40 per cent was fermented in old casks. Very fresh and vibrant, it's a weighty, easy-drinking style with strong, slightly sweet flavours of citrus fruits, apples and pears, a hint of honey, and a well-rounded finish.

Vintage	10	09	08	07	06
WR	7	7	6	7	6
Drink	11-13	10-14	10-13	10-12	P

MED/DRY $24 AV

Fairhall Downs Single Vineyard Marlborough Pinot Gris ★★★☆
Grown in the Brancott Valley, the 2009 vintage (★★★☆) was mostly tank-fermented; 23 per cent was handled in seasoned French oak casks. Enjoyable from the start, it is mouthfilling and well-rounded, with vibrant, ripe pear, lychee and spice flavours, fresh acidity and a dry, finely textured finish.

DRY $25 –V

Farmers Market Grower's Mark Marlborough Pinot Gris (★★★☆)

The 2009 vintage (★★★☆) is a blend of Pinot Gris (90 per cent), Gewürztraminer (5 per cent) and Riesling (5 per cent). It's an attractively perfumed, creamy-textured wine with very good depth of lemon, apple and lychee flavours, soft and round.

MED/DRY $25 –V

Farmers Market Marlborough Pinot Gris (★★★★)

Grown in the Awatere and Wairau valleys, the good-value 2009 vintage (★★★★) is a generous, ripe-tasting blend of Pinot Gris (90 per cent), Riesling (5 per cent) and Gewürztraminer (5 per cent). A full-bodied wine in the Alsace mould, it offers strong stone-fruit, apple and spice flavours, fresh and finely textured, with a spicy, floral, slightly honeyed bouquet.

MED/DRY $20 V+

Fiddler's Green Waipara Pinot Gris (★★★☆)

The 2008 vintage (★★★☆) was fermented with indigenous yeasts and lees-aged in tanks. It's a medium-dry style (10 grams/litre of residual sugar), softly textured, with peachy, slightly buttery flavours, offering very easy drinking.

Vintage	08
WR	6
Drink	10-12

MED/DRY $23 –V

Five Flax Pinot Gris (★★☆)

A blend of New Zealand and Australian wines, the 2008 vintage (★★☆) from Pernod Ricard NZ is a very easy-drinking style with pear, spice and slight honey flavours, smooth and ready.

MED/DRY $15 AV

Forrest Marlborough Pinot Gris ★★★☆

The 2009 vintage (★★★☆) has a strongly spiced, Gewürztraminer-like bouquet and good weight and depth of fresh peach and pear flavours. Slightly sweet (10 grams/litre of residual sugar) and soft, it's an easy-drinking style, enjoyable young.

Vintage	09
WR	5
Drink	10-15

MED/DRY $25 –V

Framingham Marlborough Pinot Gris ★★★★

The 2009 vintage (★★★★) was mostly handled in tanks, but 30 per cent was fermented in a mix of old oak casks and small, stainless steel 'barrels'. It's a mouthfilling wine, slightly sweet (10 grams/litre of residual sugar), with an array of peach, pear, lychee and spice flavours, a slightly oily texture, and good concentration and harmony.

Vintage	09	08	07	06
WR	7	6	7	6
Drink	10-12	10-12	10-11	P

MED/DRY $28 –V

Freefall Waipara Pinot Gris (★★★)

Ready to roll, the 2008 vintage (★★★) is a medium style (15 grams/litre of residual sugar) with mouthfilling body and ripe, citrusy, peachy, spicy flavours. It's a slightly honeyed wine, offering smooth, easy drinking.

MED $24 –V

Frizzell Pinot Gris (★★★☆)

Grown in Marlborough, the 2009 vintage (★★★☆) was fermented and lees-aged in tanks, with some use of indigenous yeasts. It has fresh, vibrant, pear-like aromas and flavours, a hint of spices, good weight and a crisp, dry finish. Still very youthful, it's likely to be at its best 2011+.

Vintage	09
WR	6
Drink	10-13

DRY $22 AV

Gibbston Highgate Estate Dreammaker Pinot Gris ★★★

From a vineyard at Gibbston, in Central Otago, the 2009 vintage (★★★) was fermented and lees-aged for two months in a tank. It's a medium-dry style (9 grams/litre of residual sugar) with crisp, lemony, slightly spicy flavours, showing a distinctly cool-climate freshness and vibrancy.

Vintage	09	08
WR	6	5
Drink	10-13	10-12

MED/DRY $21 –V

Gibbston Valley Central Otago Pinot Gris ★★★★

At its best, this wine is full of personality. The 2009 vintage (★★★★) was grown at Bendigo (principally) and Gibbston, and mostly handled in tanks; 15 per cent was fermented in old oak barrels. Fresh, lively and full-bodied (14 per cent alcohol), it's a finely scented, dry wine (4.1 grams/litre of residual sugar), with very good depth of pure peach, lychee and spice flavours, cool-climate vivacity and a well-rounded finish. Worth cellaring.

Vintage	09	08	07	06
WR	7	7	7	6
Drink	10-15	10-12	10-11	P

DRY $28 –V

Gibbston Valley Dulcinee The Expressionist Series Pinot Gris ★★★★★

The 2008 vintage (★★★★★) was grown in the School House Vineyard at Bendigo, in Central Otago, and handled in stainless steel 'barriques'. A medium-dry style (7 grams/litre of residual sugar), it is powerful, weighty and rounded, with highly concentrated peach, pear and spice flavours, showing excellent complexity, balanced acidity and a long finish. Drink now or cellar.

Vintage	09	08	07
WR	7	7	7
Drink	11-20	12-16	10-15

MED/DRY $35 AV

Gibson Bridge Cellar Selection Marlborough Pinot Gris ★★★☆

The highly impressive 2009 vintage (★★★★☆) was hand-picked at Renwick and mostly handled in tanks, but a small portion of the blend is barrel-aged wine from the 2007 vintage.

Beautifully perfumed, with ripe pear and lychee aromas showing excellent varietal definition, it is a weighty, Alsace style with deep yet delicate flavours and a gently spicy, softly textured finish.

MED/DRY $30 –V

Gibson Bridge Reserve Marlborough Pinot Gris ★★★★

Estate-grown at Renwick, the 2009 vintage (★★★★) was fermented and lees-aged in tanks. Mouthfilling and creamy-textured, it has excellent depth of stone-fruit and pear flavours, with a slightly gingery, distinctly spicy finish.

MED/DRY $29 –V

Gibson Bridge Single Vineyard Marlborough Pinot Gris (★★★☆)

The easy-drinking 2009 vintage (★★★☆) is full-bodied, with very good depth of stone-fruit and pear flavours, a hint of ginger and a fresh, distinctly spicy, smooth finish.

MED/DRY $24 –V

Gladstone Vineyard Pinot Gris ★★★★

The 2009 vintage (★★★★☆) is one of the finest yet. Grown in the northern Wairarapa, it was hand-picked and mostly fermented and lees-aged in tanks, but 30 per cent of the blend was fermented and matured in old French barrels. Beautifully scented, it is rich and finely textured, with concentrated stone-fruit and spice flavours, complexity from the subtle oak handling and a deliciously smooth, dry finish (4.6 grams/litre of residual sugar). It's already drinking well.

Vintage	09
WR	5
Drink	10-13

DRY $25 AV

Glasnevin Pinot Gris ★★★★☆

From a company owned by Fiddler's Green, the 2008 vintage (★★★★☆) is a rich Waipara wine, fermented with indigenous yeasts and matured for nine months in French oak barriques (20 per cent new). It's a concentrated wine with peachy, spicy flavours showing excellent complexity, an oily texture, and a finely balanced, dry (4 grams/litre of residual sugar), well-rounded finish.

Vintage	08
WR	7
Drink	10-14

DRY $28 AV

Glazebrook Regional Reserve Hawke's Bay Pinot Gris ★★★☆

From the Ngatarawa winery, the 2008 vintage (★★★☆) was grown at Bridge Pa, in The Triangle district, and tank-fermented to dryness. Fresh, crisp and mouthfilling, with very good depth of citrus and stone-fruit flavours and a hint of spice, in style it sits half-way between the classic Pinot Gris of Alsace and the Pinot Grigio of northern Italy. The 2009 (★★★) is fresh and lively, with satisfying depth of citrusy, slightly appley flavours, crisp and dry.

Vintage	09	08	07	06
WR	6	5	6	6
Drink	10-12	10-11	P	P

DRY $22 AV

Golden Hills Estate Nelson Pinot Gris (★★★★)

Grown on the Waimea Plains, the 2009 vintage (★★★★) is a good buy. Hand-picked at over 23 brix and tank-fermented, it's an intensely varietal wine with a sliver of sweetness (8.7 grams/litre of residual sugar) amid its rich stone-fruit and spice flavours, balanced by fresh acidity.

MED/DRY $20 V+

Goldridge Estate Pinot Gris (★★☆)

Grown 'predominantly' at Matakana and partly barrel-aged, the 2008 vintage (★★☆) is a smooth, easy-drinking wine, citrusy, slightly peachy and honeyed, with moderate flavour depth.

MED/DRY $16 AV

Goldridge Estate Premium Reserve Matakana Pinot Gris ★★★

The 2008 vintage (★★★) is a dry Matakana wine with refreshing acidity and good depth of citrusy, slightly honeyed flavour.

DRY $19 AV

Grass Cove Marlborough Pinot Gris (★★★☆)

Drinking well now, the 2008 vintage (★★★☆) has fresh, pear-like aromas leading into a mouthfilling wine with crisp, dryish flavours of lychees, pears and spice, showing very good varietal character and depth.

MED/DRY $18 V+

Greenstone Central Otago Pinot Gris (★★★)

From Gibbston Valley, the 2008 vintage (★★★) is a fresh, full-bodied wine, dryish, citrusy and slightly spicy, with clear-cut varietal character and decent depth.

MED/DRY $18 AV

Greystone Waipara Pinot Gris ★★★★☆

Benchmark stuff, the 2009 vintage (★★★★★), harvested at over 25 brix, is beautifully scented, rich and rounded. Mouthfilling, fresh and finely poised, it's a gently sweet style (15 grams/litre of residual sugar), vibrantly fruity, with excellent concentration of peach, pear and spice flavours, showing lovely richness and harmony.

Vintage	10	09
WR	6	7
Drink	10-13	10-13

MED $29 AV

Greystone Winemaker's Series Waipara Pinot Gris (★★★★)

Powerful, with rich stone-fruit flavours, the 2008 vintage (★★★★) was fermented in a 50:50 mix of tanks and barrels and fully barrel-aged. Weighty and soft, with a slightly oily texture, it's drinking well now.

DRY $31 –V

Greywacke Marlborough Pinot Gris (★★★★★)
The lovely 2009 vintage (★★★★★) debut from Kevin Judd is a single-vineyard, Brancott Valley wine, hand-picked and fermented in a 50:50 split of tanks and old French barriques; all of the wine was then barrel-aged for four months. Fleshy and generous, it is very ripely scented, with peach, pear and spice flavours, showing lovely delicacy and richness. A medium-dry style (8.5 grams/litre of residual sugar), youthful and highly refined, it's well worth cellaring to 2012+.

MED/DRY $29 V+

Grove Mill Marlborough Pinot Gris ★★★★
Grove Mill is a key pioneer of Pinot Gris in Marlborough, since 1994 producing a richly flavoured style with abundant sweetness. The 2008 vintage (★★★☆), partly French oak-fermented, is a distinctly medium style (29 grams/litre of residual sugar) with a lower level of alcohol than usual (12.5 per cent, compared to the customary 13.5 per cent). It's a scented, medium-bodied wine with very good depth of vibrant peach, pear and spice flavours.

Vintage	08	07	06
WR	7	7	6
Drink	10-12	P	P

MED $24 AV

Gunn Estate Pinot Gris ★★☆
From Sacred Hill, the 2009 vintage (★★★) is a blend of Australian and New Zealand wines. It's a medium-bodied style (12.5 per cent alcohol), not highly scented, with solid depth of fresh peach, pear and slight spice flavours and a smooth, dry (3.9 grams/litre of residual sugar) finish.

DRY $18 –V

Hans Herzog Marlborough Pinot Gris ★★★★☆
Grown on the north side of the Wairau Valley, the 2009 vintage (★★★★) was hand-picked and mostly tank-fermented; 20 per cent of the blend was fermented and matured for a year in French oak puncheons. Faintly pink, it is sturdy and bone-dry, with ripe, peachy, spicy flavours, concentrated and complex. It's a 'serious' style of Pinot Gris, in a distinctive, food-friendly style.

Vintage	09	08
WR	7	7
Drink	10-15	10-14

DRY $39 –V

Harwood Hall Marlborough Pinot Gris (★★★★)
From winemakers Bill ('Digger') Hennessy and Corey Hall, the debut 2008 vintage (★★★★) was grown at Renwick and mostly handled in tanks; 15 per cent of the blend was barrel-fermented with indigenous yeasts. It's a scented, weighty wine with excellent texture and depth of peachy, spicy flavours and a dry finish (3 grams/litre of residual sugar). Good value.

DRY $20 V+

Hawkshead Central Otago Pinot Gris ★★★★
Estate-grown and hand-picked at Gibbston, the 2009 vintage (★★★★☆) is a full-bodied, invitingly scented wine with very youthful peach, pear and lychee flavours, deliciously vibrant and rich, and a dryish, gently spicy, long finish.

MED/DRY $26 –V

Hay Maker Gisborne Pinot Gris (★★☆)

From Mud House, the 2008 vintage (★★☆) was grown at Patutahi, tank-fermented and briefly lees-aged. It's a medium-dry style (6 grams/litre of residual sugar), with a light bouquet, peachy, faintly honeyed flavours, showing solid depth, and crisper acidity than most Pinot Gris.

MED/DRY $17 –V

Hell or Highwater Central Otago Pinot Gris (★★☆)

Grown in the Highwater Vineyard, on the Tarras–Cromwell Road, the pale 2009 vintage (★★☆) is mouthfilling, with fresh flavours of pears and citrus fruits, moderate depth and an off-dry finish. Pleasant, easy drinking.

MED/DRY $18 –V

Huia Marlborough Pinot Gris ★★★★

The 2008 vintage (★★★★) was grown at Wairau Valley sites and fermented in tanks (70 per cent) and old French oak casks (30 per cent). It's a dryish style (5 grams/litre of residual sugar), mouthfilling and fresh, with very good depth of ripe stone-fruit flavours, showing some complexity, and a slightly oily richness.

Vintage	08	07
WR	6	6
Drink	10-19	10-11

MED/DRY $28 –V

Huntaway Reserve Gisborne Pinot Gris ★★★

The 2008 vintage (★★★) from Pernod Ricard NZ was blended with Gewürztraminer (6 per cent) and aged on its light yeast lees in tanks and large oak cuves. It's a medium to full-bodied style with good vigour, a sliver of sweetness (6 grams/litre of residual sugar) and pleasing depth of pear, lemon and spice flavours. The 2009 (★★★☆) is fleshy, with very good depth of slightly sweet pear and spice flavours, a touch of complexity and a well-rounded finish.

Vintage	08	07	06
WR	5	6	6
Drink	P	P	P

MED/DRY $23 –V

Hyperion Phoebe Matakana Pinot Gris ★★☆

Estate-grown north of Auckland, the 2009 vintage (★★★) was fermented in old barrels. Still youthful, it is medium-bodied, with lemon, pear and spice flavours, showing good depth, fractional sweetness (6 grams/litre of residual sugar) and fresh, appetising acidity keeping things lively.

Vintage	09
WR	6
Drink	10-15

MED/DRY $28 –V

Incognito Pinot Gris (★★★)

The 2009 vintage (★★★) from Gibbston Highgate was estate-grown and hand-picked at Gibbston, in Central Otago, tank-fermented, briefly lees-aged and made in an off-dry (9 grams/litre of residual sugar) style. Medium-bodied, it is fresh, citrusy and slightly appley, with plenty of flavour.

MED/DRY $20 –V

Isabel Marlborough Pinot Gris ★★★☆

Freshly scented and full-bodied, the 2009 vintage (★★★★☆) is a dryish wine with good depth of vibrant pear, lychee and spice flavours. Still youthful, with lively acidity, it should be at its best 2011+.

Vintage	09
WR	7
Drink	09-14

MED/DRY $25 –V

Johanneshof Marlborough Pinot Gris Medium ★★★☆

The 2008 vintage (★★★★☆) is a gently sweet style, faintly pink, mouthfilling and smooth, with good depth of stone-fruit and spice flavours, ripe and soft.

Vintage	08	07	06	05	04
WR	5	7	5	6	7
Drink	10-13	P	P	P	P

MED $27 –V

Johanneshof Marlborough Pinot Gris Trocken/Dry ★★★☆

The pale pink 2008 vintage (★★★☆) has a peachy, spicy bouquet, leading into a dryish wine with good depth of ripe stone-fruit and spice flavours and a rounded finish.

Vintage	08	07	06
WR	4	6	5
Drink	10-12	10-11	P

MED/DRY $27 –V

Johner Estate Wairarapa Pinot Gris ★★★☆

Grown at Gladstone, the 2009 vintage (★★★★) is clearly the best yet. It's an elegant, rich wine, mouthfilling, with fresh acid spine and slightly sweet, peachy, spicy flavours, showing good concentration and harmony.

MED/DRY $22 AV

Julicher Martinborough Pinot Gris (★★★☆)

The pale pink 2009 vintage (★★★☆) was hand-picked at Te Muna (but not estate-grown), and 25 per cent of the blend was fermented in old French oak casks. It's an easy-drinking style, peachy and slightly spicy, with a hint of strawberries, some complexity and a smooth, dryish (5.6 grams/litre of residual sugar) finish.

MED/DRY $20 AV

Jurassic Ridge Pinot Grigio ★★★
Grown at Church Bay, on Waiheke Island, and tank-fermented, the 2009 vintage (★★★) is a distinctive style. Pale pink/orange, it is a medium-bodied wine (11.8 per cent alcohol), with spicy, slightly earthy aromas and strawberryish, spicy flavours, refreshingly crisp and dry.

Vintage	09	08
WR	7	6
Drink	10-11	P

DRY $29 –V

Kaimira Estate Brightwater Pinot Gris ★★★☆
Estate-grown in Nelson and handled without oak, the 2009 vintage (★★★★) is one of the best yet. Richly scented, it is fleshy and mouthfilling, in an Alsace style with very fresh, vibrant flavours of ripe peaches, lychees and spices, showing good harmony and richness, and a finely textured, dry (4.5 grams/litre of residual sugar) finish.

Vintage	09
WR	6
Drink	10-14

DRY $20 AV

Kaituna Valley Canterbury Summerhill Vineyard Pinot Gris ★★★
Grown at Tai Tapu, on Banks Peninsula, the 2008 vintage (★★★) has a slightly honeyed bouquet, with crisp, slightly sweet (10 grams/litre of residual sugar) pear, lime and spice flavours, showing good depth. The 2009 (★★★) is mouthfilling, with a slightly creamy texture and pear, apple and peach flavours showing some richness.

MED/DRY $24 –V

Kaituna Valley Marlborough The Awatere Vineyard Pinot Gris ★★★★
Grown in the Awatere Valley, the 2008 vintage (★★★★) is scented and mouthfilling, with good concentration of citrus-fruit, pear and spice flavours, a splash of sweetness (12 grams/litre of residual sugar) and lively acidity.

Vintage	08
WR	5
Drink	P

MED/DRY $24 AV

Kawarau Estate Central Otago Pinot Gris ★★★☆
Certified organic, the 2008 vintage (★★★) was hand-picked at Pisa Flats, in the Cromwell Basin, fermented with indigenous yeasts and lees-aged in tanks. It's a creamy-smooth wine with mouthfilling body, solid depth of peachy, slightly spicy flavours and a slightly off-dry (4.9 grams/litre of residual sugar) finish.

Vintage	08	07
WR	6	5
Drink	10-11	P

DRY $25 –V

Kim Crawford New Zealand Pinot Gris ★★★

From 'selected vineyards across New Zealand', the 2008 vintage (★★☆) from Constellation NZ is a medium to full-bodied wine with solid depth of peachy, slightly honeyed flavour, fresh acidity and a slightly sweet finish. Ready.

MED/DRY $23 –V

Koura Bay Sharkstooth Marlborough Pinot Gris ★★★☆

Typically, a fragrant Awatere Valley wine with good body and depth of flavour. The 2009 vintage (★★★☆) is fresh-scented, mouthfilling and vibrantly fruity, with peach, pear and spice flavours, a sliver of sweetness and lively acidity.

Vintage	09	08	07	06
WR	6	5	7	6
Drink	10-12	10-11	P	P

MED/DRY $22 AV

Kumeu River Pinot Gris ★★★★

This consistently attractive wine is grown at Kumeu, in West Auckland, matured on its yeast lees, but not oak-matured. Made in a medium-dry style, it is typically floral and weighty, with a slightly oily texture, finely balanced acidity and peach, pear and spice aromas and flavours, vibrant and rich. The 2009 (★★★☆) is medium-bodied (12.5 per cent alcohol), with very good depth of citrusy, slightly minerally flavours, a touch of complexity and a finely poised, dry finish. It lacks the power and richness of a top vintage, but is a fresh, tightly structured wine with some potential.

Vintage	09	08	07	06
WR	7	7	7	7
Drink	10-13	10-12	10-11	P

MED/DRY $27 –V

Lake Chalice Eyrie Vineyard Marlborough Pinot Gris ★★★☆

From grapes grown mostly in the Eyrie Vineyard, in the Waihopai Valley, blended with fruit from two other sites in the central Wairau Valley, the 2009 vintage (★★★★) is a mouthfilling, vibrantly fruity wine. Made in an off-dry style, it has pear, lychee and spice flavours, showing excellent delicacy and purity.

MED/DRY $20 AV

Lake Hayes Central Otago Pinot Gris ★★★☆

From Amisfield, the 2009 vintage (★★★☆) was grown alongside the cellar door at Lake Hayes and at another site in Gibbston, and lees-aged in tanks. Fresh, crisp and vibrantly fruity, it has very good depth of peachy, limey, slightly spicy flavours, slightly sweet (7.5 grams/litre of residual sugar), tight and youthful.

Vintage	09	08	07
WR	5	6	5
Drink	10-12	P	P

MED/DRY $25 –V

Latitude 41 Pinot Gris ★★★
From Spencer Hill, the 2008 vintage (★★★) is a South Island regional blend, given some exposure to new French oak. It offers plenty of vibrant, appley, slightly minerally and toasty flavour, with an off-dry (7 grams/litre of residual sugar) finish.

MED/DRY $20 –V

Lawson's Dry Hills Marlborough Pinot Gris ★★★★☆
The outstanding 2009 vintage (★★★★★) was grown at two sites, harvested at 23.5 to 24.2 brix, and 25 per cent of the blend was fermented with indigenous yeasts in seasoned French oak casks; the rest was handled in tanks. It's a highly scented wine, finely balanced and rich, with good weight and strong, slightly sweet (8.3 grams/litre of residual sugar) citrus-fruit, pear, ginger and spice flavours. Fleshy and soft, with very pure varietal characters, good harmony and a touch of complexity, it's already delicious.

Vintage	09	08	07	06
WR	7	5	7	6
Drink	10-11	P	P	P

MED/DRY $26 AV

Lawson's Dry Hills The Pioneer Marlborough Pinot Gris (★★★★☆)
The debut 2009 vintage (★★★★☆) was harvested in the Waihopai Valley at 23.5 to 25.4 brix, with some botrytis in the late-picked fruit. Tank-fermented, it's a youthful, very harmonious wine with fresh pear and spice aromas and flavours, showing good richness, a sliver of sweetness (12.6 grams/litre of residual sugar) and impressive depth and harmony. Best drinking 2012+.

MED/DRY $32 –V

Lime Rock Central Hawke's Bay Pinot Gris ★★★☆
The 2008 vintage (★★★☆) was grown at Waipawa, hand-picked and fermented and lees-aged in three-year-old French oak barriques. It's a mouthfilling wine with ripe, peachy, citrusy, slightly spicy flavours, a subtle oak influence, fresh acidity, good depth and a smooth, dry finish.

DRY $25 –V

Lobster Reef Marlborough Pinot Gris (★★★☆)
From Cape Campbell, the 2009 vintage (★★★☆) is full-bodied and finely balanced, with crisp, gently sweet flavours of ripe citrus fruits, pears and spices, showing very good freshness and depth.

MED/DRY $19 V+

Locharburn Central Otago Pinot Gris ★★★☆
Grown at Lowburn and harvested at 24 to 25 brix, the 2009 vintage (★★★☆) was mostly handled in tanks, but 20 per cent was fermented in seasoned French oak puncheons. It's a fresh, lively wine with a floral bouquet, crisp peach, lemon and apple flavours, a touch of complexity and a dryish (5 grams/litre of residual sugar) finish.

Vintage	09	08
WR	6	6
Drink	10-12	10-11

MED/DRY $25 –V

Lonestone Marlborough Pinot Gris (★★★☆)

From wine distributors Bennett & Deller, the bargain-priced 2008 vintage (★★★☆) was grown in the Waihopai Valley. A basically dry style (4 grams/litre of residual sugar), it is mouthfilling, peachy, slightly spicy and honeyed, with very good balance and flavour depth.

`DRY $16 V+`

Longbush Pinot Gris (★★★)

The 'bird series' 2008 vintage (★★★) was grown in Gisborne and made in a slightly sweet (12 grams/litre of residual sugar) style. It's a slightly honeyed wine, fruity and forward, with plenty of peachy, slightly spicy flavour.

Vintage	08
WR	6
Drink	10-12

`MED/DRY $18 AV`

Longridge Hawke's Bay Pinot Gris (★★★)

The 2009 vintage (★★★) from Pernod Ricard NZ is a medium-bodied wine with refreshing pear and spice flavours, good varietal character and a finely balanced, smooth, dry finish.

`DRY $18 AV`

Mahi Ward Farm Marlborough Pinot Gris (★★★★)

From a single vineyard at Ward, the elegant 2009 vintage (★★★★) was hand-picked and fermented with indigenous yeasts in French oak barriques. Still very youthful, it's a mouthfilling dry wine, citrusy, slightly spicy, toasty and creamy, with fresh acidity and good complexity. Best drinking mid-2011+.

`DRY $30 -V`

Maimai Creek Hawke's Bay Pinot Gris ★★★☆

Priced sharply and enjoyable from the start, the 2009 vintage (★★★☆) is full-bodied (14 per cent alcohol), with ripe, pear and spice aromas and flavours, showing good varietal character, a slightly oily texture and very good depth.

`MED/DRY $20 AV`

Main Divide Pinot Gris ★★★★

From Pegasus Bay, this is a top buy. The debut 2009 vintage (★★★★) is fleshy and slightly sweet, with mouthfilling body and soft, ripe stone-fruit and spice flavours, showing good concentration. The 2010 (★★★★), grown at Waipara and partly barrel-fermented, is full-bodied, crisp and concentrated, with excellent depth of fresh pear, lychee and spice flavours, showing good immediacy.

Vintage	10	09
WR	6	7
Drink	10-14	10-13

`MED/DRY $20 V+`

Main Divide Pokiri Reserve Late Picked Waipara Valley Pinot Gris – see Sweet White Wines

Man O' War Ponui Island Pinot Gris ★★★☆

From a smaller island near the eastern coast of Waiheke, in Auckland, the 2009 vintage (★★★★) was mostly handled in tanks, but 20 per cent was fermented in new barrels. It's a skilfully crafted wine, mouthfilling, with fresh, ripe peach, citrus-fruit and spice flavours, a subtle seasoning of oak, a touch of sweetness (9 grams/litre of residual sugar), and very good depth.

Vintage	09
WR	6
Drink	11-12

MED/DRY $23 –V

Manu Marlborough Pinot Gris (★★★☆)

From Steve Bird, the 2009 vintage (★★★☆) is a ripely scented, dry wine (3 grams/litre of residual sugar), with mouthfilling body, a slightly oily texture and very good depth of peachy, gently spiced flavours.

DRY $20 AV

Maori Point Central Otago Pinot Gris ★★★☆

Grown at Tarras, north of Lake Dunstan, the 2009 vintage (★★★☆) is a crisp, dry, minerally wine with lemony, slightly spicy flavours, showing good freshness, vigour and length. It's a Pinot Grigio style, worth cellaring.

Vintage	09	08	07
WR	6	6	6
Drink	10-14	10-12	P

DRY $23 –V

Margrain Martinborough Pinot Gris ★★★☆

The 2009 vintage (★★★☆) is a full-bodied (14.5 per cent alcohol), bone-dry wine with lemon, peach and spice flavours, crisp and strong. Made in a more austere style than most, it's a good food wine.

Vintage	09	08	07	06	05
WR	6	7	7	7	6
Drink	10-15	10-16	10-13	10-12	10-11

DRY $28 –V

Marsden Bay of Islands Pinot Gris ★★★

In favourable seasons, this Kerikeri, Bay of Islands winery produces an impressive Pinot Gris. The 2009 (★★★) was made principally from Pinot Gris (90 per cent), but includes 5 per cent Flora and 5 per cent Chardonnay. It's a full-bodied wine with fresh, ripe stone-fruit, pear and spice flavours, balanced for smooth, easy drinking (9 grams/litre of residual sugar).

Vintage	09	08
WR	5	5
Drink	10-12	P

MED/DRY $27 –V

Martinborough Vineyard Pinot Gris ★★★★★

This powerful, concentrated wine is one of the finest Pinot Gris in the country. It is hand-picked and fermented with a high percentage of indigenous yeasts, and lees-aged, partly in seasoned French oak casks (50 per cent in 2008), in a bid to produce a 'Burgundian style with complexity, texture and weight'. The outstanding 2008 vintage (★★★★★) was harvested at 23.4 to 24.7 brix. It's a mouthfilling wine (14.5 per cent alcohol), with lovely, vibrant peach, pear and spice fruit characters shining through, a subtle oak influence, and notable complexity and harmony. Already delicious, it's a drink-now or cellaring proposition.

Vintage	08	07	06
WR	7	6	6
Drink	10-13	10-12	10-11

DRY $45 AV

Matakana Estate Matakana Pinot Gris ★★★☆

Estate-grown north of Auckland, the ripe, smooth 2008 vintage (★★★☆) was 20 per cent barrel-fermented and made in a dry style. It's a finely balanced, slightly Chardonnay-like wine with very good depth of peachy, citrusy, slightly toasty flavour, showing good complexity and roundness.

DRY $27 –V

Matawhero Gisborne Pinot Gris (★★★)

Balanced for easy drinking, the debut 2009 vintage (★★★) is a single-vineyard wine, medium-bodied, with a sliver of sweetness (6 grams/litre of residual sugar) amid its ripe, slightly buttery flavours of lychees, ginger and spice, which show good depth.

MED/DRY $30 –V

Matua Valley Gisborne Pinot Gris (★★)

The 2010 vintage (★★) is a pleasant, light quaffer, with pear and peach flavours, slightly sweet and soft.

MED/DRY $12 AV

Matua Valley Matua Road Pinot Gris (★★☆)

The 2009 vintage (★★☆), not identified by region, is an easy-drinking style, medium to full-bodied, with decent depth of peachy, spicy flavour and a smooth, well-rounded finish. Priced sharply.

MED/DRY $12 V+

Matua Valley New Zealand Pinot Gris (★★☆)

The 2008 vintage (★★☆) is part of the company's 'Regional Series', but is not labelled by region (apparently the grapes were grown in Marlborough). It's a medium-bodied wine with pleasant, lemony, slightly spicy and honeyed flavours and a crisp, dry (3 grams/litre of residual sugar) finish.

DRY $15 AV

Maude Central Otago Pinot Gris ★★★

The 2010 vintage (★★★☆) was grown at Bannockburn and the family-owned Mount Maude Vineyard, at Wanaka. Fresh, vibrant and smooth, it's a slightly minerally wine with lemon, pear and spice flavours, threaded with crisp acidity, a sliver of sweetness and good immediacy.

MED/DRY $22 –V

Maven Marlborough Pinot Gris ★★★

Enjoyable now, the 2008 vintage (★★★) was fermented partly with indigenous yeasts in seasoned French oak barriques. Mouthfilling and smooth, it has citrusy, slightly peachy and spicy, faintly honeyed flavours.

MED/DRY $22 –V

Michael Ramon Matakana Pinot Gris ★★★

Grown on the Tawharanui Peninsula and fully barrel-aged, the 2009 vintage (★★★) is mouthfilling, with ripe fruit flavours of stone-fruit and pear, a slightly creamy texture and biscuity oak characters adding complexity.

MED/DRY $30 –V

Mills Reef Reserve Hawke's Bay Pinot Gris (★★★)

The 2009 vintage (★★★) is an easy-drinking style, fermented and lees-aged for three months in seasoned oak casks. It's a dry style (3 grams/litre of residual sugar) with mouthfilling body, peachy, slightly spicy flavours and a very smooth finish.

DRY $25 –V

Misha's Vineyard Dress Circle Central Otago Pinot Gris ★★★★

The 2009 vintage (★★★★) was hand-picked at Bendigo at 25 brix and mostly handled in tanks; 31 per cent of the blend was fermented with indigenous yeasts in seasoned oak barrels. It's a sturdy wine (14.8 per cent alcohol), with youthful lychee, pear and spice flavours, vibrant and finely poised, a touch of complexity, fresh acidity and a dryish (5 grams/litre of residual sugar) finish. It shows very good weight, depth and harmony, but needs time; open 2011+.

Vintage	09	08
WR	7	7
Drink	10-12	10-11

MED/DRY $26 –V

Mission Hawke's Bay Pinot Gris ★★★

The Mission has long been a standard-bearer for Pinot Gris. The 2009 vintage (★★★) is full-bodied and fresh, with satisfying depth of peachy, slightly spicy flavour and a finely balanced, bone-dry finish.

DRY $18 AV

Mission Reserve Hawke's Bay Pinot Gris (★★☆)

The 2009 vintage (★★☆) was estate-grown at Taradale, hand-picked and barrel-fermented with indigenous yeasts. It's a creamy-soft wine, slightly sweet (9 grams/litre of residual sugar), with pear and lychee flavours showing some richness, but also a slight lack of fragrance and finesse.

Vintage	09	MED/DRY $25 –V
WR	4	
Drink	10-15	

Mission Vineyard Selection Ohiti Road Pinot Gris ★★★

The 2009 vintage (★★★☆), grown organically in Hawke's Bay, is mouthfilling and smooth, with a slightly oily texture and good depth of peach and lychee flavours.

DRY $18 AV

Moana Park Vineyard Selection Pinot Gris (★★★)

Grown in the Dartmoor Valley, in Hawke's Bay, the 2008 vintage (★★★) has ripe, peachy, slightly gingery flavours and a slightly sweet, crisp finish. Medium-bodied, it's bargain-priced.

Vintage	08	MED/DRY $15 V+
WR	6	
Drink	10-11	

Momo Marlborough Pinot Gris ★★★☆

From Seresin, the 2009 vintage (★★★☆) was hand-harvested at two sites, tank-fermented with indigenous yeasts and matured in a 50:50 split of tanks and old French oak barriques. It's a powerful, robust wine, slightly Chardonnay-like, with strong stone-fruit and spice flavours, a sliver of sweetness (7 grams/litre of residual sugar) and plenty of drink-young appeal.

Vintage	09	MED/DRY $23 –V
WR	6	
Drink	10-13	

Moncellier Marlborough Pinot Gris (★★★★)

From winemaker Greg Rowdon and Bill Spence (co-founder of Matua Valley), the debut 2008 vintage (★★★★) is a single-vineyard wine, grown on the banks of the Wairau River and lees-aged for three months. A dry style (3.9 grams/litre of residual sugar), it is mouthfilling and creamy, with stone-fruit and spice flavours, a hint of apricot, and good texture and richness.

Vintage 09

		MED/DRY $25 AV
WR	6	
Drink	10-14	

Monkey Bay Gisborne Pinot Gris ★★☆

From Constellation NZ, the 2008 vintage (★★☆) is a light style of Pinot Gris with fresh pear and spice aromas and flavours. It's a pleasant, all-purpose wine with a slightly sweet finish.

MED/DRY $16 AV

Montana Living Land Series Waipara Pinot Gris (★★★☆)

The floral, full-bodied 2009 vintage (★★★☆) was handled entirely in tanks and made in a medium-dry style (8 grams/litre of residual sugar). Ripely scented, it is fresh and smooth, with a slightly oily texture and peach, pear and spice flavours, showing good depth.

MED/DRY $20 AV

Montana North Island Pinot Gris ★★★

(The 2009 vintage is labelled Brancott Estate – see that entry.) Balanced for easy drinking, the 2008 vintage (★★★) of this regional blend was mostly grown in Gisborne and a small amount of Gewürztraminer was added, 'enhancing the aromatics and flavour'. Mouthfilling and smooth, it has ripe, peachy, spicy flavours, with a sliver of sweetness (6.5 grams/litre of residual sugar), moderate acidity and good depth.

MED/DRY $18 AV

Montana Reserve Hawke's Bay Pinot Gris ★★★☆

The 2008 vintage (★★★☆) was grown mostly at Matapiro, an elevated, inland district, and matured on its yeast lees in tanks for three months. It's a full-bodied, fresh and lively wine, finely textured, with very good depth of citrusy, slightly appley flavours, a touch of sweetness (6.5 grams/litre of residual sugar) and balanced acidity. The easy-drinking 2009 (★★★☆) is fleshy and smooth, with fresh acidity and good depth of lively pear and spice flavours.

MED/DRY $24 –V

Morepork Northland Pinot Gris (★★★)

The 2009 vintage (★★★) is from a vineyard named after its two pigs. It's a very easy-drinking style, gently sweet, with peachy, citrusy, slightly spicy flavours, vibrant and smooth.

Vintage	09	08
WR	5	3
Drink	10-11	P

MED/DRY $32 –V

Morepork Northland Rosemary's Reserve Pinot Gris (★★★★)

The 2010 vintage (★★★★) was grown in the Morepork Vineyard, at Kerikeri. Showing lots of personality, it's a full-bodied, concentrated wine, dryish (7 grams/litre of residual sugar), peachy, spicy and slightly gingery.

Vintage	10
WR	7
Drink	10-12

MED/DRY $25 AV

Morton Estate Private Reserve Hawke's Bay Pinot Gris (★★★★)

Still on sale, the 2007 vintage (★★★★) has strong stone-fruit and spice flavours, showing considerable complexity, and substantial body. It's a dry wine, drinking well now.

Vintage	07
WR	7
Drink	P

DRY $23 AV

Morton Estate Private Reserve Marlborough Pinot Gris (★★★)

From first-crop vines in the Awatere Valley, the 2007 vintage (★★★) is mouthfilling, fresh and rounded, with slightly sweet peach, pear and spice flavours, showing good depth, and lively acidity.

MED/DRY $23 –V

Morton Estate White Label Hawke's Bay Pinot Gris ★★★☆

Grown at the company's inland Kinross Vineyard, the 2008 vintage (★★★☆) is scented, with mouthfilling body and good depth of fresh, citrusy, slightly spicy flavours. The 2009 (★★★☆) is fleshy, with strong, peachy, slightly honeyed flavours and a distinctly spicy finish.

Vintage	09	08	07	06
WR	6	6	6	7
Drink	10-12	10-12	P	P

DRY $19 V+

Mount Dottrel Central Otago Pinot Gris ★★★★

The 2009 vintage (★★★★) from Mitre Rocks is an attractively scented, dry wine (3 grams/litre of residual sugar), with fresh, pure lychee, pear and spice flavours. Grown at Bendigo and Gibbston, and 15 per cent barrel-fermented, it shows excellent vibrancy, delicacy and depth.

Vintage	09	08
WR	6	6
Drink	10-12	10-11

DRY $23 AV

Mount Fishtail Marlborough Pinot Gris (★★★☆)

From Konrad, the 2009 vintage (★★★☆) is a fleshy, very fresh and vibrant wine with substantial body (14.5 per cent alcohol), lots of peachy, spicy flavour and a slightly sweet (7.8 grams/litre of residual sugar), rounded finish.

MED/DRY $20 AV

Mount Riley Marlborough Pinot Gris ★★★☆

The 2009 vintage (★★★★) is one of the best yet. Mostly handled in tanks but 5 per cent barrel-fermented, it's a medium-dry style, floral, fresh and sweet-fruited, with excellent texture and depth of pear and spice flavours. A good buy.

Vintage	08	07	06
WR	6	6	6
Drink	10-11	P	P

MED/DRY $18 V+

Mount Vernon Marlborough Pinot Gris (★★★★)

From Lawson's Dry Hills, the bargain-priced 2008 vintage (★★★★) is a mouthfilling, finely textured wine with good depth and purity of peach, pear and spice flavours, sweet-fruit characters, crisp acidity and a floral bouquet.

MED/DRY $20 V+

Mt Beautiful Cheviot Hills Pinot Gris (★★★★☆)

From first-crop vines and 30 per cent barrel-fermented, the 2009 vintage (★★★★☆) of this North Canterbury wine was picked at 26 brix. It's a powerful, fleshy, almost dry wine (5 grams/litre of residual sugar) with stone-fruit and spice flavours, weighty and rounded, and excellent complexity and depth.

MED/DRY $24 V+

Mt Difficulty Central Otago Pinot Gris ★★★★

Grown at five sites at Bannockburn, the 2009 vintage (★★★★☆) was hand-picked, tank-fermented and lees-aged for four months, with weekly stirring. It's a mouthfilling (14 per cent alcohol), vibrantly fruity, appetisingly crisp wine with excellent depth of lychee, pear and peach flavours, made in a drier style than most (4.3 grams/litre of residual sugar), yet still very harmonious.

DRY $25 AV

Mt Difficulty Roaring Meg Central Otago Pinot Gris ★★★☆

The 2009 vintage (★★★☆) is a gently sweet style (9 grams/litre of residual sugar), fresh and vibrant, with crisp acidity, pure varietal flavours of pears and spices, and good delicacy and depth.

MED/DRY $20 AV

Mt Difficulty Single Vineyard Mansons Farm Pinot Gris ★★★★

Late-picked at Bannockburn, in Central Otago, this is a medium style, harbouring about 25 grams per litre of residual sugar. It is typically ripely scented and sturdy, with lush, peachy and spicy flavours in a weighty, rich, Alsace style.

MED $35 –V

Mt Hector Wairarapa Pinot Gris (★★★☆)

From Matahiwi, the 2010 vintage (★★★☆) is good value. Already drinking well, it has pear-like aromas and flavours, a hint of spices and a gentle splash of sweetness in a vibrantly fresh, attractive style.

MED/DRY $15 V+

Mt Rosa Central Otago Pinot Gris ★★★☆

The 2008 vintage (★★★☆) is a scented wine, grown at Gibbston, with mouthfilling body, good depth of peachy, spicy flavours, a touch of complexity and a dry finish. The very easy-drinking 2009 (★★★☆) is fleshy, with slight sweetness and ripe, citrusy, slightly appley flavours, showing good depth.

MED/DRY $26 –V

Mud House South Island Pinot Gris (★★★)

Enjoyable young, the 2009 vintage (★★★) is clearly varietal, with fresh, peachy, slightly spicy flavours, slightly honeyed and smooth.

MED/DRY $19 AV

Pinot Gris 195

Murdoch James Wairarapa Pinot Gris ★★★☆

From grapes hand-picked at Martinborough and Masterton, the 2008 vintage (★★★☆) is mouthfilling (13.5 per cent alcohol), with crisp, citrusy, appley, slightly spicy flavours, showing cool-climate freshness and vigour, and a dryish (5.4 grams/litre of residual sugar) finish. The 2009 (★★★☆) is fresh and vibrantly fruity, with strong, peachy, slightly limey and honeyed flavours, a splash of sweetness and appetising acidity. It should come together well during 2011.

MED/DRY $20 AV

Nautilus Marlborough Pinot Gris ★★★☆

The 2009 vintage (★★★★) is one of the best yet. Harvested by hand in the Awatere Valley (mostly) and made with a subtle oak influence (15 per cent fermented in old French barrels), it's an off-dry style (5.5 grams/litre of residual sugar). Mouthfilling and fleshy, it has strong, ripe flavours of stone-fruit, spices and ginger, showing good complexity and richness, and a well-rounded finish.

Vintage	09	08	07	06
WR	7	6	7	6
Drink	10-13	10-12	10-12	P

MED/DRY $29 –V

Ned, The, Waihopai River Marlborough Pinot Gris ★★★☆

A single-vineyard wine, grown in the Waihopai Valley, the 2009 vintage (★★★☆) was mostly handled in tanks; 10 per cent of the blend was barrel-fermented. It's a finely balanced wine, full-bodied, with stone-fruit, pear and spice flavours, showing a touch of complexity, fractional sweetness (6 grams/litre of residual sugar) and fresh acidity keeping things lively.

MED/DRY $17 V+

Neudorf Maggie's Block Nelson Pinot Gris ★★★★

The 2009 vintage (★★★★) is a single-vineyard wine, grown at Brightwater, on the Waimea Plains. It was hand-picked and mostly lees-aged in tanks; 20 per cent of the blend was French oak-fermented. Still very youthful, it's a finely poised, medium-dry style (7.3 grams/litre of residual sugar), full-bodied and attractively scented, with vibrant peach, pear and spice flavours, woven with fresh acidity, and excellent depth.

Vintage	09	08	07
WR	6	5	5
Drink	10-14	10-13	10-12

MED/DRY $24 AV

Neudorf Moutere Pinot Gris ★★★★☆

Tasted in 2010, the 2001 vintage is now in full stride, with lovely, rich, citrusy, slightly honeyed flavours. The 2009 vintage (★★★★☆) is a single-vineyard wine, hand-picked at 22.6 to 23.8 brix, and fermented in tanks and old French barrels. Made in a medium-dry style (14 grams/litre of residual sugar), it is mouthfilling, with rich stone-fruit and spice flavours, a hint of biscuity oak, gentle acidity and a well-rounded finish. An Alsace style with considerable complexity, it's still developing; open mid-2011+.

Vintage	09	08	07	06	05	04
WR	7	6	7	6	7	5
Drink	10-18	10-17	10-17	10-16	10-15	P

DRY $28 AV

Nevis Bluff Central Otago Pinot Gris ★★★★

A consistently enjoyable wine. The 2007 vintage (★★★★) was hand-picked at over 24 brix in the Cromwell Basin and at Gibbston, tank-fermented and lees-aged for nine months. It's a full-bodied wine (14 per cent alcohol), fresh and vibrant, with ripe peach and slight apricot flavours, balanced acidity and a long, dry (2 grams/litre of residual sugar) finish. The 2008 (★★★☆) is fresh and mouthfilling, with lemony, slightly spicy and peachy flavours, and a fully dry, creamy-smooth finish.

Vintage	08	07
WR	5	6
Drink	10-14	10-14

DRY $33 –V

Nikau Point Marlborough Pinot Gris (★★☆)

From Morton Estate, the 2008 vintage (★★☆) is full-bodied and slightly honeyed, with lemony, slightly spicy flavours, showing decent depth. It's showing some development; drink now.

Vintage	08
WR	6
Drink	10-11

DRY $15 AV

Oak Hill Matakana Pinot Gris (★★★☆)

The 2008 vintage (★★★☆) is a fully dry style with impressive weight, strong, ripe fruit flavours and a slightly oily texture. An obvious oak influence gives it a slightly Chardonnay-like feel, but the wine is fleshy and rich.

DRY $39 –V

Odyssey Marlborough Pinot Gris ★★★☆

Estate-grown in the Odyssey Vineyard, in the Brancott Valley, the 2009 vintage (★★★★) was hand-picked, tank-fermented and then matured on its yeast lees, with no stirring, in old French oak casks. It's a distinctive style, full-bodied, with ripe stone-fruit and spice flavours, gently seasoned with biscuity oak, fresh acidity, good complexity and a dry (3.8 grams/litre of residual sugar) finish. Worth cellaring.

Vintage	09	08
WR	6	6
Drink	10-14	10-12

DRY $25 –V

Ohau Gravels Pinot Gris (★★★★)

From Ohau, north of the Kapiti Coast, in Horowhenua, the 2009 vintage (★★★★) is an excellent debut. Harvested from first-crop vines and handled without oak, it is fleshy, rich and rounded, with gentle sweetness (10.8 grams/litre of residual sugar) and ripe, peachy flavours, deliciously vibrant and strong.

MED/DRY $23 AV

Old Coach Road Nelson Pinot Gris ★★★

From Seifried, the 2009 (★★★) is a freshly scented, full-bodied wine, harvested at 23.6 brix, mostly in the Redwood Valley. It offers satisfying depth of pear and spice flavours, with a sliver of sweetness balanced by lively acidity. The 2010 vintage (★★☆) is fruity and smooth, with moderate depth of dryish (4 grams/litre of residual sugar), lemon and spice flavours, balanced for easy drinking.

DRY $17 AV

Olssen's Tom Logan Central Otago Pinot Gris (★★★)

The debut 2009 vintage (★★★☆) was estate-grown at Bannockburn, hand-picked at 23 brix and fermented in a tank and a single old French oak barrel. It's a full-bodied wine with gently sweet (9.7 grams/litre of residual sugar) pear, lemon and spice flavours, a slightly creamy texture, and some complexity and richness.

MED/DRY $29 –V

Omaha Bay Vineyard Matakana Pinot Gris ★★★☆

Fermented in seasoned oak barrels, the 2008 vintage (★★★☆) has very good depth and complexity in a dry, mouthfilling style, peachy, spicy and faintly oaked, with a well-rounded finish.

Vintage	08	07	06
WR	6	6	5
Drink	10-13	10-12	10-11

DRY $30 –V

Omaka Springs Marlborough Pinot Gris ★★★

Grown in the Omaka Valley, the 2009 vintage (★★★) is a slightly sweet (16 grams/litre of residual sugar) style, mouthfilling, with peach, pear and spice flavours, balanced for easy drinking, and a creamy-smooth texture.

Vintage	09	08
WR	7	6
Drink	10-12	10-13

MED $19 AV

Omihi Road Waipara Pinot Gris ★★★★

From Torlesse, the 2009 vintage (★★★★★) is an enticingly scented, powerful wine, fermented and lees-aged for four months in barriques. Fleshy, with ripe peach and spice flavours, it is fresh and concentrated, with a splash of sweetness (16 grams/litre of residual sugar), a rich, oily texture and lovely depth and harmony.

Vintage	09	08
WR	7	6
Drink	12-15	10-12

MED $25 AV

Omori Estate Lake Taupo Pinot Gris (★★★☆)

Grown on the south-west shores of the lake, hand-picked and lees-aged in tanks, the 2008 vintage (★★★☆) is ripely scented, with peachy, faintly spicy and honeyed flavours, showing good depth. It's an easy-drinking wine, finely textured and lingering.

DRY $25 –V

One Tree Otago Pinot Gris (★★★★)

A great buy, the 2008 vintage (★★★★) is from Capricorn Wine Estates, a division of Craggy Range. Partly oak-aged, it's a mouthfilling wine, fresh-scented and vibrantly fruity, with strong, peachy, citrusy, slightly spicy flavours, a sliver of sweetness (8.5 grams/litre of residual sugar), fresh underlying acidity – and loads of drink-young charm.

MED/DRY $16 V+

Opawa Marlborough Pinot Gris ★★★☆

The 2009 vintage (★★★☆) was made in a 'lighter, crisper' style (think Pinot Grigio) than its Nautilus Estate stablemate (an Alsace style). Hand-picked in the Wairau Valley and tank-fermented, it is full-bodied and dry (3 grams/litre of residual sugar), with lemony, slightly spicy flavours, showing good delicacy and depth.

DRY $22 AV

Open House Smooth Marlborough Pinot Gris (★★★)

From Wither Hills, the 2009 vintage (★★★) is a good buy. Mouthfilling and (yes) smooth, it has good body and depth of fresh, clearly varietal pear and spice flavours, with gentle sweetness giving an easy-drinking appeal.

MED/DRY $15 V+

Opihi Vineyard South Canterbury Pinot Gris ★★★☆

Grown on a north-facing slope inland from Timaru, in South Canterbury, this is typically a highly attractive wine. Hand-picked and tank-fermented, the 2009 vintage (★★★☆) is a tightly structured, distinctly cool-climate style, fresh and crisp, with dry (3 grams/litre of residual sugar), peachy flavours, woven with lively acidity, and good varietal character and depth. Worth cellaring.

DRY $24 –V

Ostler Audrey's Waitaki Valley Pinot Gris ★★★★

The 2009 vintage (★★★★) was estate-grown and mostly tank-fermented, but 20 per cent was barrel-fermented with indigenous yeasts, using large, old oak. Made in an off-dry style (8 grams/litre of residual sugar), it is fleshy and rounded, with fresh peach, pear and lychee aromas and flavours, and a slightly spicy, smooth finish. It shows very good depth and complexity; open mid-2011+.

Vintage	09	08
WR	7	6
Drink	10-14	10-13

MED/DRY $34 –V

Ostler Grower Selection Blue House Vines Waitaki Valley Pinot Gris ★★★☆

The 2009 vintage (★★★☆) is a medium-dry style (8 grams/litre of residual sugar), freshly scented and vibrantly fruity, with balanced acidity and very good depth of pear and spice flavours.

MED/DRY $30 –V

Palliser Estate Martinborough Pinot Gris ★★★☆
The easy-drinking 2009 vintage (★★★☆) is fleshy and clearly varietal, with mouthfilling body and good depth of slightly sweet pear and spice flavours, balanced by fresh, crisp acidity.

MED/DRY $24 –V

Parr & Simpson Limestone Bay Pinot Gris ★★★★
Full of personality. A single-vineyard Nelson wine from Pohara, in eastern Golden Bay, the 2009 vintage (★★★★☆) is one of the country's most distinctive Pinot Gris. Hand-picked at 23.4 brix and 35 per cent fermented and matured in seasoned French oak barriques, it's a dry wine (2.8 grams/litre of residual sugar) with a lemony, complex bouquet. The palate is very harmonious, with balanced acidity and rich citrus and stone-fruit flavours, slightly spicy and lingering. Good value.

DRY $22 V+

Pasquale Alma Mater Hakataramea Valley Pinot Gris/Riesling/Gewürztraminer (★★★☆)
Grown in South Canterbury, the 2008 vintage (★★★☆) is a highly aromatic wine with very good depth of citrusy, spicy flavour, a touch of complexity from aging in old oak casks, and a splash of sweetness (10.9 grams/litre of residual sugar) balanced by crisp acidity.

MED/DRY $27 –V

Passage Rock Waiheke Island Pinot Gris ★★★
The 2009 vintage (★★★) is a mouthfilling wine (14 per cent alcohol), easy-drinking, with soft peach, pear and slight spice flavours, fresh, vibrant and smooth.

MED/DRY $23 –V

Paulownia Pinot Gris (★★★☆)
The 2009 vintage (★★★☆), grown in the northern Wairarapa, is mouthfilling and creamy-textured, with ripe, peachy, slightly spicy flavours and a dryish (10 grams/litre of residual sugar) finish.

MED/DRY $18 V+

Peregrine Central Otago Pinot Gris ★★★☆
The 2009 vintage (★★★☆) was harvested in the Cromwell Basin at 24.4 to 24.7 brix, and fermented and lees-aged in tanks. It's a crisp, medium to full-bodied wine with good depth of citrusy, dryish (6.3 grams/litre of residual sugar) flavours.

MED/DRY $25 –V

Peter Yealands Marlborough Pinot Gris (★★★)
The 2009 vintage (★★★), estate-grown in the Awatere Valley, is scented, with fresh, vibrant peach, lemon and spice flavours and a crisp, basically dry (4 grams/litre of residual sugar) finish. Full-bodied and finely balanced, it's an attractive, drink-young style.

DRY $19 AV

Pisa Moorings Central Otago Pinot Gris (★★★☆)

The debut 2008 vintage (★★★☆) is invitingly scented, with mouthfilling body (14 per cent alcohol) and ripe, peachy, gently spicy flavours. Fresh and vibrant, with a sliver of sweetness (5 grams/litre of residual sugar), moderate acidity and a well-rounded finish, it's a full-flavoured wine, enjoyable from the start.

MED/DRY $22 AV

Poderi Crisci Pinot Grigio ★★★☆

Grown on Waiheke Island, the 2009 (★★★) was handled in a 50:50 split of tanks and seasoned French oak casks. It's a gently spicy wine, full-bodied, with ripe, peachy flavours and a crisp, bone-dry finish. The 2010 vintage (★★★★) is the best yet. Mouthfilling (14 per cent alcohol), it has concentrated, ripe citrus-fruit, peach and slight spice flavours, a slightly oily texture and excellent depth.

Vintage	01	09
WR	7	7
Drink	10-13	10-12

DRY $29 –V

Prophet's Rock Central Otago Pinot Gris ★★★★☆

Richly scented, the 2009 vintage (★★★★☆) was hand-picked at Pisa, in the Cromwell Basin, fermented with indigenous yeasts and lees-aged. Mouthfilling, very fresh and youthful, it has deep, ripe stone-fruit and spice flavours, a sliver of sweetness and a mouth-watering, crisp finish. Full of personality, it's a strong candidate for cellaring.

MED/DRY $30 –V

Pukeora Estate Pinot Gris ★★☆

(Past releases were sold under the brand San Hill.) Grown at Waipukurau, in Central Hawke's Bay, the 2009 vintage (★★☆) is a dry wine (3.5 grams/litre of residual sugar), handled entirely in tanks. It's a sturdy, high-alcohol style (14.9 per cent), straw-hued, with ripe, peachy, spicy flavours that show a slight lack of freshness and vibrancy.

Vintage	09	08
WR	6	5
Drink	10-12	P

DRY $20 –V

Quartz Reef Bendigo Central Otago Pinot Gris ★★★★

The 2009 vintage (★★★☆) was estate-grown and hand-picked at Bendigo, and fermented and lees-stirred for 10 months in tanks. Fresh and subtle, it has lemony, slightly appley and spicy flavours, showing good delicacy and balance, moderate concentration and a crisp, dry finish. Worth cellaring.

Vintage	09	08	07	06
WR	6	6	6	6
Drink	10-12	10-11	P	P

DRY $29 –V

Rabbit Ranch Central Otago Pinot Gris ★★★
Awarded five stars by 'Roger Rabbit', this wine is made by Chard Farm in a smooth, off-dry style with lychee, pear and spice flavours. It is typically fleshy and forward, in a very user-friendly style.

`MED/DRY $24 –V`

Ra Nui Marlborough Wairau Valley Pinot Gris ★★★☆
The 2009 vintage (★★★☆), hand-picked in the Cob Cottage Vineyard, near Blenheim, is mouthfilling, with very good depth of peach, pear and slight spice flavours, and a finely textured, dry finish. The 2010 (★★★☆) is full-bodied and ripely scented, with citrusy, slightly spicy and limey flavours and a dry (3 grams/litre of residual sugar) finish.

`DRY $24 –V`

Red Tussock Central Otago Pinot Gris ★★★
From Mark Mason, originally involved with Sacred Hill, the 2008 vintage (★★★) is a fresh, dryish wine with good body and depth of peachy, slightly spicy flavours.

`MED/DRY $20 –V`

Redoubt Hill Vineyard Nelson Pinot Gris ★★☆
Grown at Motueka, the 2009 vintage (★★☆) is lean, with fresh, appley flavours, crisp and slightly sweet (6.8 grams/litre of residual sugar), which lack real richness. The 2010 (★★★) is scented, with slightly sweet, pear and spice flavours, fresh acidity and good balance and vigour.

`MED/DRY $26 –V`

Renato Nelson Pinot Gris ★★★☆
Estate-grown at Kina, on the coast, hand-picked and lees-aged, the refined 2009 vintage (★★★★) is a slightly sweet style (8 grams/litre of residual sugar), scented and mouthfilling, with very good depth of peach, pear and spice flavours, showing excellent delicacy and harmony. It's a finely poised wine that should age well.

Vintage	09	08	07	06
WR	7	6	7	6
Drink	10-13	10-12	10-13	10-12

`MED/DRY $22 AV`

Ribbonwood Marlborough Pinot Gris ★★★
From Framingham, the 2009 vintage (★★★) is fresh-scented and mouthfilling, with citrusy, slightly spicy flavours and a dryish (5 grams/litre of residual sugar) finish. Smooth, easy drinking.

Vintage	09
WR	6
Drink	10-12

`MED/DRY $18 AV`

Rimu Grove Bronte Pinot Gris – see Bronte by Rimu Grove Pinot Gris

Rimu Grove Nelson Pinot Gris ★★★★☆

A consistent winner. The 2009 vintage (★★★★☆), grown in the Moutere hills, was mostly handled in tanks, but 15 per cent was lees-aged for four months in seasoned French oak barrels. It's a full-bodied, rich wine with strong pear and lychee flavours, showing good complexity, a touch of sweetness (8 grams/litre of residual sugar), moderate acidity and lovely harmony. Best drinking mid-2011+.

Vintage	09	08	07	06
WR	7	7	7	6
Drink	10-17	10-15	10-12	P

MED/DRY $29 AV

Riverby Estate Marlborough Pinot Gris ★★★

A single-vineyard wine, grown in the heart of the Wairau Valley, the 2009 vintage (★★★☆) is fleshy and soft, with mouthfilling body and a gentle splash of sweetness (10 grams/litre of residual sugar) amid its ripe peach, pear and spice flavours, which show very good depth.

MED/DRY $20 –V

River Farm Godfrey Road Marlborough Pinot Gris (★★★☆)

The 2009 vintage (★★★☆) is a single-vineyard wine, hand-picked and partly fermented with indigenous yeasts in seasoned French oak barrels. Fleshy and dry (4.8 grams/litre of residual sugar), it's a slightly Chardonnay-like wine with ripe, peachy, slightly toasty flavours, a touch of complexity and very good depth.

Vintage	09
WR	6
Drink	10-14

MED/DRY $20 AV

Road Works Waiheke Island Pinot Gris (★★★)

From Man O' War, the 2008 vintage (★★★) is not highly aromatic, but the palate is sturdy (14 per cent alcohol), with plenty of ripe, citrusy, peachy, slightly spicy flavour and a dry finish.

DRY $18 AV

Rockburn Central Otago Pinot Gris ★★★☆

Grown at Parkburn, in the Cromwell Basin, and at Gibbston, the 2010 vintage (★★★☆) was handled in tanks. An off-dry style (9.7 grams/litre of residual sugar), it is floral, full-bodied and fresh, with very good depth of lemony, peachy, spicy flavours and a smooth finish. It's already enjoyable.

Vintage	10
WR	6
Drink	10-13

MED/DRY $25 –V

Rock Ferry Central Otago Pinot Gris (★★★★)

The 2009 vintage (★★★★) is a single-vineyard wine, grown at Bendigo and mostly handled in tanks; 20 per cent of the blend was fermented with indigenous yeasts in one-year-old puncheons. Powerful (14.5 per cent alcohol), it has strong, peachy, citrusy, slightly spicy flavours, a sliver of sweetness (8 grams/litre of residual sugar), and an invitingly scented bouquet.

Vintage	09
WR	6
Drink	10-13

MED/DRY $27 –V

Ruby Bay Vineyard Pinot Gris ★★★☆

The 2009 vintage (★★★) is a single-vineyard Nelson wine, hand-picked. Gently aromatic, it's a fresh, medium-bodied wine (12.3 per cent alcohol) with pure, delicate, pear-like flavours and an off-dry (5 grams/litre of residual sugar) finish.

Vintage	09
WR	5
Drink	10-12

DRY $24 –V

Sacred Hill Halo Marlborough Pinot Gris (★★★★)

The 2009 vintage (★★★★) is a single-vineyard, Waihopai Valley wine with excellent weight and depth of peach, apricot and spice flavours. Mouthfilling, ripe and rounded, with a touch of sweetness, it has gentle acidity and good harmony. Ready to roll.

MED/DRY $26 –V

Sacred Hill Marlborough Vineyards Pinot Gris ★★★☆

Estate-grown in the Waihopai Valley, the 2009 vintage (★★★☆) is a dry wine (1.9 grams/litre of residual sugar), mouthfilling, with vibrant, citrusy, peachy, slightly spicy flavours, woven with fresh acidity, and very good poise and depth.

DRY $21 AV

Saddleback Central Otago Pinot Gris (★★★☆)

From Peregrine, the 2008 vintage (★★★☆) is a fleshy, gently sweet style (9.6 grams/litre of residual sugar), with mouthfilling body and very good depth of lemon and pear flavours, balanced for easy drinking.

MED/DRY $20 AV

Saint Clair Godfrey's Creek Reserve Pinot Gris ★★★☆

The 2008 vintage (★★★☆) was grown at two sites, principally the Godfrey's Creek Vineyard, at the mouth of the Brancott Valley, and mostly tank-fermented, with some handling in old French oak barrels. An off-dry style (5.5 grams/litre of residual sugar), it is a generous, mouthfilling wine, ripely flavoured, with a touch of complexity and a rounded finish.

Vintage	08	07	06
WR	6	6	6
Drink	10-11	P	P

MED/DRY $25 –V

Saint Clair Marlborough Pinot Gris ★★★☆

The 2008 vintage (★★★☆) was partly fermented with indigenous yeasts in old oak barrels and made in a dry style (4 grams/litre of residual sugar). It has mouthfilling body and finely balanced peach, pear and spice flavours, fresh, vibrant and smooth.

Vintage	08
WR	6
Drink	P

DRY $21 AV

Saint Clair Vicar's Choice Marlborough Pinot Gris ★★☆

The easy-drinking 2008 vintage (★★☆) is medium-bodied, with slightly sweet (7.7 grams/litre of residual sugar) lychee and spice flavours, showing solid depth.

Vintage	08
WR	6
Drink	P

MED/DRY $19 –V

Saints Gisborne Pinot Gris ★★★

From Pernod Ricard NZ, the 2009 vintage (★★★) is lemon-scented, with fresh, citrusy flavours, crisp and lively.

MED/DRY $18 AV

Sanctuary Marlborough Pinot Gris ★★☆

From Grove Mill, the 2008 vintage (★★☆) is fresh and vibrantly fruity, with moderate flavour depth and a sliver of sweetness (6 grams/litre of residual sugar) giving it a smooth, easy-drinking appeal.

Vintage	09	08
WR	7	5
Drink	10-11	P

MED/DRY $15 AV

Scott Base Central Otago Pinot Gris (★★★☆)

From Allan Scott, the 2009 vintage (★★★☆) is a dryish style (5 grams/litre of residual sugar), ripely scented and mouthfilling, with crisp stone-fruit, pear and spice flavours, fresh and vibrant.

MED/DRY $29 –V

Sears Road Pinot Gris (★★)

From Stirling Vines, producers of Maimai Creek, the 2009 vintage (★★) is a Hawke's Bay wine. A full-bodied, lemony, slightly gingery wine with a crisp finish, it's a solid quaffer.

DRY $12 AV

Secret Stone Marlborough Pinot Gris (★★★☆)

From Matua Valley, the 2009 vintage (★★★☆) is ripely scented and mouthfilling, with very good depth of slightly sweet pear, spice and stone-fruit flavours, a slightly oily texture, and good delicacy and harmony.

MED/DRY $20 AV

Seifried Nelson Pinot Gris ★★★☆

Grown mostly in the Redwood Valley, where the vines are up to 26 years old, the 2009 vintage (★★★☆) is a full-bodied wine with lively acidity and a sliver of sweetness amid its peachy, spicy, slightly gingery flavours, which show very good depth. The very youthful 2010 (★★★) is medium-bodied, with citrusy, slightly lemony and appley flavours, fresh, smooth and slightly sweet (11 grams/litre of residual sugar).

Vintage	10	09	08	07	06
WR	6	6	6	6	6
Drink	10-12	10-11	P	P	P

MED/DRY $21 AV

Selaks Winemaker's Favourite Hawke's Bay Pinot Gris ★★★☆

The 2009 vintage (★★★☆) is mouthfilling, with good depth of clearly varietal, peachy flavours, a slightly oily texture and a lingering, rounded finish.

MED/DRY $21 AV

Seresin Marlborough Pinot Gris ★★★★

One of the region's most distinctive Pinot Gris. The 2008 vintage (★★★★) was hand-picked at 25 brix in the Home Vineyard and the hillside Raupo Creek Vineyard, fermented with indigenous yeasts, and lees-aged for six months in seasoned French oak barriques. It's a powerful, peachy, spicy, basically dry wine (4.8 grams/litre of residual sugar) with substantial body (14.5 per cent alcohol) and excellent flavour depth.

Vintage	08	07	06	05	04
WR	7	7	7	6	6
Drink	10-15	10-13	P	P	P

DRY $30 –V

Seresin Raupo Marlborough Pinot Gris (★★★★★)

Just 394 bottles were produced of the outstanding 2008 vintage (★★★★★). Hand-picked in the Raupo Creek Vineyard, it was fermented with indigenous yeasts and matured for 15 months in seasoned French oak barrels. Powerful and complex, it has deep pear, lychee and spice flavours, layered with toasty and creamy notes, in an unusually weighty and complex style. Slightly sweet (18 grams/litre of residual sugar), with a rich, lasting finish, it's a wine of real personality.

Vintage	08
WR	7
Drink	10-15

MED $50 AV

Shaky Bridge Central Otago Pinot Gris ★★★

The 2009 vintage (★★★) was estate-grown and hand-picked at Alexandra and made in a dryish (6 grams/litre of residual sugar) style. It's a fresh, crisp wine with some 'funky' notes and decent depth of citrusy, spicy flavours.

MED/DRY $25 –V

Shaky Bridge Pioneer Series Central Otago Pinot Gris (★★★)

The 2008 vintage (★★★) was grown at Alexandra. It's a fresh, full-bodied wine, slightly sweet, with peach, lychee and spice flavours, vibrant and crisp. Enjoyable now.

MED/DRY $19 AV

Sherwood Estate Waipara Pinot Gris (★★★★)

The 2008 vintage (★★★★) is scented, with vibrant peach, pear and spice flavours, showing good richness, fresh acidity and a lingering finish.

MED/DRY $20 V+

Shingle Peak Reserve Marlborough Pinot Gris ★★★☆

The 2008 vintage (★★★☆) is mouthfilling and fleshy, with strong, ripe pear and spice flavours and a slightly sweet finish.

MED/DRY $20 AV

Sileni Cellar Selection Hawke's Bay Pinot Gris ★★★

The 2010 vintage (★★★) was mostly tank-fermented and lees-aged, with a small portion of barrel fermentation. Medium-bodied, with fresh pear and spice aromas and flavours, it's a dry style (3.8 grams/litre of residual sugar), enjoyable young, with good varietal character and harmony.

Vintage	10
WR	6
Drink	10-14

DRY $20 –V

Soho Marlborough Pinot Gris ★★★☆

The 2009 vintage (★★★☆) is moderately concentrated, with ripe, peachy, slightly spicy flavours, a hint of apricot, and good freshness and balance (7 grams/litre of residual sugar). The 2010 offers 'unadulterated flavours' – with no definition. It's a full-bodied, slightly creamy wine with off-dry, pear and spice, slightly gingery flavours, and lots of drink-young appeal.

MED/DRY $26 –V

Soljans Kumeu Pinot Gris ★★★☆

Grown in West Auckland, the 2009 vintage (★★★) is medium-bodied, with fresh, vibrant flavours and a smooth finish. The mouthfilling 2010 (★★★☆) shows clear-cut varietal characters, with good weight, ripe, slightly sweet flavours (10 grams/litre of residual sugar) and even a hint of apricot.

MED/DRY $20 AV

Southbank Estate East Coast Pinot Gris ★★★

The 2008 vintage (★★★) offers peach, pear and spice flavours, with a crisp, dry finish (2 grams/litre of residual sugar).

Vintage	08	07
WR	6	7
Drink	P	P

DRY $20 –V

Southern Cross Hawke's Bay Pinot Gris (★★☆)

From One Tree Hill Vineyards, a division of Morton Estate, the 2008 vintage (★★☆) is mouthfilling, with a scented, slightly honeyed bouquet and peachy, slightly spicy and honeyed flavours. A decent quaffer, priced right.

Vintage	08
WR	6
Drink	10-11

DRY $13 V+

Spinyback Nelson Pinot Gris ★★★☆

From Waimea Estate, the 2009 vintage (★★★☆) was harvested on the Waimea Plains at 22 to 24 brix, tank-fermented and lees-stirred. Full-bodied (14 per cent alcohol), it has crisp, slightly sweet (5.8 grams/litre of residual sugar) flavours of peaches and spices, showing good depth.

Vintage	09	08	07
WR	7	7	6
Drink	10-12	10-11	P

MED/DRY $18 V+

Spy Valley Envoy Marlborough Pinot Gris ★★★★☆

The 2009 vintage (★★★★☆) was estate-grown in the Waihopai Valley and fermented and lees-aged in large German oak ovals and old French barriques. It's a fleshy, soft wine with soaring alcohol (14.8 per cent) and very ripe, stone-fruit and spice flavours, showing some oak complexity. Still developing, it's a beautifully harmonious wine, finely textured and rich, with a very rounded finish.

Vintage	09	08	07	06
WR	7	6	6	6
Drink	10-14	10-12	10-12	10-11

MED $29 AV

Spy Valley Marlborough Pinot Gris ★★★★

The 2009 vintage (★★★★) was harvested at 23 to 27.1 brix and partly fermented in old oak casks. Beautifully scented, it's a ripely flavoured wine, peachy, spicy and slightly sweet, with very good weight and richness. Also partly barrel-fermented, the mouthfilling 2010 (★★★☆) is a medium-dry style (10.5 grams/litre of residual sugar), with lemony, peachy, moderately concentrated flavours, showing good varietal character and harmony.

Vintage	10	09	08	07	06
WR	6	7	6	6	7
Drink	10-13	10-12	10-11	P	P

MED/DRY $23 AV

Staete Landt Marlborough Pinot Gris ★★★★☆

This single-vineyard wine is hand-harvested at Rapaura and fermented and matured on its yeast lees in old French oak puncheons. It is typically weighty and concentrated, with a slightly nutty complexity. The 2009 vintage (★★★★☆) is bone-dry – unusual for Pinot Gris. Full-bodied, fresh and finely poised, with gentle acidity, it has vibrant stone-fruit and spice flavours, ripe and rich, carrying the dry style perfectly.

Vintage	09	08	07
WR	7	7	6
Drink	10-17	10-13	10-12

DRY $29 AV

Stafford Lane Nelson Pinot Gris ★★☆

The 2009 vintage (★★) is light-bodied, with restrained, lemony, spicy flavours and a slightly sweet (8.3 grams/litre of residual sugar) finish.

MED/DRY $19 –V

Starborough Marlborough Pinot Gris ★★★★

Priced attractively, the 2010 vintage (★★★★) is a blend of Wairau Valley (65 per cent) and Awatere Valley (35 per cent) fruit, mostly handled in tanks, but 15 per cent of the blend was fermented and aged in old oak barrels. Skilfully crafted, it is vibrantly fruity, with fresh, pure, delicate flavours of lychees and spice, a hint of lime and a dryish (6 grams/litre of residual sugar), finely poised finish.

Vintage	10
WR	6
Drink	10-13

MED/DRY $19 V+

Stone Bridge Gisborne Pinot Gris (★★★)

Estate-grown and picked from first-crop vines, the 2008 vintage (★★★) is freshly scented and medium-bodied, with vibrant pear and spice flavours and a slightly sweet (7.8 grams/litre of residual sugar), crisp finish.

MED/DRY $22 –V

Stoneleigh Marlborough Pinot Gris ★★★☆

Maturing well, the 2008 vintage (★★★★) from Pernod Ricard NZ is floral, mouthfilling and rich, with crisp, slightly sweet flavours showing excellent purity, delicacy and harmony. Tasted in its infancy, the 2010 (★★★☆) is promising – highly scented, with fresh pear and spice flavours, strong and smooth. Best drinking mid-2011+.

MED/DRY $23 –V

Stoneleigh Rapaura Series Marlborough Pinot Gris ★★★★☆

Richer than its Stoneleigh stablemate (above), this wine is released extremely early – the 2010 vintage (★★★★☆) was on sale within three months of the harvest. Picked at 23 to 24 brix, and aged on its yeast lees in tanks, it's a richly scented, beautifully ripe-tasting wine with concentrated stone-fruit and spice flavours and a slightly sweet, soft, harmonious finish. Delicious from the start.

MED/DRY $27 AV

Takatu Matakana Pinot Gris ★★★★☆

Grown on a north-facing hillside above Matakana, this is a sophisticated wine, fermented and lees-aged in old French oak puncheons. As usual, the 2009 vintage (★★★★) was made in a bone-dry style. Ripely scented, it is citrusy, peachy and spicy, with very good body and depth, and the subtle seasoning of oak adds complexity. Fresh and tightly structured, it's a more 'serious' style of Pinot Gris than most and an ideal food wine.

Vintage	10	09	08	07
WR	7	5	7	7
Drink	10-15	10-12	10-12	P

DRY $33 –V

Tasman Bay New Zealand Pinot Gris ★★★

The 2007 vintage (★★★) from Spencer Hill is an easy-drinking blend of Nelson and Marlborough grapes, briefly oak-aged. It's a medium to full-bodied style with citrus-fruit and pear aromas, and citrusy, faintly honeyed, smooth flavours. The 2008 (★★★) is scented, slightly sweet and crisp, offering very easy drinking.

MED/DRY $19 AV

Tatty Bogler Otago Pinot Gris ★★★★

From Forrest, the 2009 vintage (★★★★) was grown at Bannockburn, in the Cromwell Basin, and the Waitaki Valley (hence the 'Otago' statement of origin on the label, rather than 'Central Otago'). Tasted soon after bottling, it's a powerful, rounded wine, 10 per cent barrel-fermented, with mouthfilling body and strong lychee, pear and spice flavours, finely textured and rounded (7 grams/litre of residual sugar).

Vintage	09	08
WR	6	6
Drink	10-15	P

MED/DRY $29 –V

Te Henga The Westie Premium Marlborough Pinot Gris (★★★☆)

Produced by Babich for the West Auckland licensing trusts, the 2008 vintage (★★★☆) is fresh-scented, with very good body and depth of ripe, peachy, faintly honeyed flavours. A generous wine, it offers fine value.

MED/DRY $16 V+

Te Kairanga Swing Bridge Gisborne Pinot Gris (★★★☆)

The 2008 vintage (★★★☆) is a crisp, vibrantly fruity wine with pear and spice flavours showing good delicacy, a slightly oily texture and a dry (3 grams/litre of residual sugar) finish.

Vintage	08
WR	6
Drink	10-12

DRY $21 AV

Te Mania Nelson Pinot Gris ★★★☆

The 2009 vintage (★★★☆) was hand-picked and mostly tank-fermented; 5 per cent was matured in old casks. Aromatic, it's a mouthfilling wine with a slightly oily texture and dryish stone-fruit, pear and spice flavours, showing very good depth.

Vintage	09	08	07
WR	6	5	6
Drink	10-12	P	P

MED/DRY $22 AV

Te Mara Central Otago Pinot Gris ★★★★☆

The 2009 vintage (★★★★) was grown in the Cromwell Basin and handled in tanks. Richly scented, it's a fleshy, ripe-tasting wine, peachy and spicy, with a hint of honey, slight sweetness balanced by fresh, lively acidity, and very good depth and harmony. It should mature well.

MED/DRY $26 AV

Terrace Edge Waipara Valley Pinot Gris ★★★★☆
Consistently great value. The 2009 vintage (★★★★☆) was hand-picked at 25 brix and fermented with indigenous yeasts in seasoned oak barrels. A fleshy, rich wine in the classic Alsace mould, it is weighty, with concentrated, ripe flavours of peach, nectarine and spice, good texture and a medium-dry (14 grams/litre of residual sugar), softly seductive finish.

MED/DRY $21 V+

Terrace Heights Estate Marlborough Pinot Gris ★★★☆
Hand-picked and tank-fermented, the 2009 vintage (★★★☆) is weighty, with fresh, peachy, slightly sweet flavours, buttery notes and a creamy-smooth texture. The 2010 (★★★☆) is fleshy and fruity, with slightly sweet (7.5 grams/litre of residual sugar) peach, pear and spice flavours, finely balanced for easy drinking.

Vintage	10	09
WR	6	6
Drink	11-13	10-12

MED/DRY $20 AV

Terrain East Coast Pinot Gris (★★★)
Sold at New World and PAK'nSAVE (it's a Foodstuffs brand), the 2008 vintage (★★★) is a fresh, medium to full-bodied wine with good varietal character and a hint of sweetness amid its peach, pear and spice flavours, which linger to a smooth finish.

MED/DRY $13 V+

Terravin Marlborough Pinot Gris ★★★★
The 2008 vintage (★★★★) was estate-grown in the Omaka Valley, hand-picked, fermented with indigenous yeasts and lees-aged in old French oak barrels. Fleshy and complex, it is not highly aromatic but weighty, with rich, ripe peach, pear and spice flavours, good mouthfeel, texture and harmony, and a rounded, dryish finish (6 grams/litre of residual sugar). The 2009 (★★☆) is disappointing for this label. Mouthfilling and dry, with pear and spice flavours and a hint of oak, it shows considerable complexity, but also a slight loss of freshness and vibrancy.

MED/DRY $29 –V

Thornbury Waipara Pinot Gris ★★★☆
The 2009 vintage (★★★★) from Villa Maria is a full-bodied, dryish style with fresh, strongly varietal flavours of peaches, pears and spices, showing good richness and harmony. The 2010 (★★★★) was mostly handled in tanks; 5 per cent was fermented in old oak puncheons. It's an off-dry style (5.5 grams/litre of residual sugar), finely scented, with vibrant pear and spice flavours, showing excellent freshness, depth and immediacy.

Vintage	10	09
WR	5	7
Drink	10-11	10-12

MED/DRY $21 AV

Three Miners Central Otago Pinot Gris (★★★)

The 2009 vintage (★★★) is a lightly scented, medium-bodied wine with citrusy, appley flavours and a dry (3.5 grams/litre of residual sugar) finish.

DRY $19 AV

Tiki Waipara Pinot Gris (★★★☆)

The debut 2010 vintage (★★★☆) is a single-vineyard wine with fresh, lemony, appley aromas and flavours. Medium-bodied, with hints of lychees and spices, a slightly oily texture and gentle sweetness, it's a vibrantly fruity, smooth wine, offering very easy drinking.

MED/DRY $28 –V

Tinpot Hut Marlborough Pinot Gris ★★★★

The 2009 vintage (★★★★☆) was grown in the Awatere and Wairau valleys. Attractively scented, it is mouthfilling and vibrantly fruity, with strong, slightly sweet peach, pear and spice flavours, showing excellent ripeness, harmony and richness.

MED/DRY $21 V+

Ti Point Marlborough Pinot Gris ★★★★

The 2009 (★★★★) is a floral, single-vineyard wine, grown in the Waihopai Valley. An off-dry style (5.2 grams/litre of residual sugar), it has ripe peach, pear and spice flavours, showing excellent delicacy and richness, and a finely balanced finish. The 2010 vintage (★★★★) is scented and weighty, with rich, peachy, citrusy flavours, fresh acidity and a bone-dry finish. An ideal 'food' wine, it should develop well.

DRY $22 V+

Tohu Nelson Pinot Gris ★★★☆

The 2009 vintage (★★★★) is the best yet. Grown in the Whenua Matua Vineyard and partly barrel-fermented, it is ripely scented, weighty and rounded, with strong stone-fruit, spice and pear flavours, a touch of complexity and a dry (2.8 grams/litre of residual sugar), finely balanced finish. Fine value.

DRY $19 V+

Toi Toi Brookdale Vineyard Reserve Pinot Gris (★★★☆)

The debut 2009 vintage (★★★☆) was hand-picked from first-crop vines in the Omaka Valley. A dryish style (5.9 grams/litre of residual sugar), it is aromatic, with a minerally streak and fresh pear and spice flavours, showing good purity and depth.

MED/DRY $23 –V

Torea Marlborough Pinot Gris (★★★★)

From Fairhall Downs, the 2009 vintage (★★★★) was mostly handled in tanks, but 23 per cent was oak-aged. It's a full-bodied wine, weighty and rich, with a slightly oily texture and strong peachy, spicy flavours. An off-dry style (7 grams/litre of residual sugar), it offers fine value.

MED/DRY $20 V+

Torlesse Waipara Pinot Gris ★★★★

The 2009 vintage (★★★★☆) is scented, mouthfilling and finely poised, with vibrant lychee and spice flavours showing lovely purity, richness and roundness. Made in a medium style (16 grams/litre of residual sugar), it's a good buy.

Vintage	09
WR	6
Drink	12-15

MED $20 V+

Torrent Bay Nelson Pinot Gris ★★☆

From Anchorage, the 2009 vintage (★★★) is a medium-bodied wine with vibrant, crisp flavours of lemons, apples and spices and a splash of sweetness (8.3 grams/litre of residual sugar). It's a fresh, easy-drinking wine, priced right.

MED/DRY $16 AV

Tranquil Valley Matakana Pinot Gris (★★☆)

From Huasheng Wines, linked to Matakana Estate, the 2008 vintage (★★☆) is an easy-drinking wine, citrusy, peachy and slightly honeyed, with moderate depth and a smooth finish.

MED/DRY $25 –V

Tresillian Pinot Gris (★★★☆)

Estate-grown at West Melton, the 2008 vintage (★★★☆) is a medium-bodied Canterbury wine (12.5 per cent alcohol) with good depth of citrusy, peachy flavour, fresh acidity to balance its slight sweetness (5 grams/litre of residual sugar) and a lingering finish.

MED/DRY $25 –V

Trinity Hill [Black Label] Hawke's Bay Pinot Gris ★★★★

The 2008 vintage (★★★★) was grown in the Gimblett Gravels (46 per cent), at Haumoana (37 per cent) and at Mangaorapa Station, in Central Hawke's Bay (17 per cent). Hand-picked, tank-fermented and lees-aged, it's a dry wine (3 grams/litre of residual sugar), rich and full-bodied. It shows excellent balance and depth, with a lifted fragrance of pears and spices.

Vintage	08	07	06
WR	6	5	5
Drink	P	P	P

DRY $34 –V

Trinity Hill [White Label] Hawke's Bay Pinot Gris ★★★☆

The 2008 vintage (★★★☆), which includes 10 per cent Viognier, was grown at four sites, tank-fermented and lees-aged for four months. It's a full-bodied, flavoursome wine, ripe, peachy and slightly spicy, with a rounded, dry finish. The 2009 (★★★☆) is mouthfilling and soft, with citrusy, peachy flavours, fresh and pure, very good varietal character and depth, and a dry (3 grams/litre of residual sugar) finish.

DRY $20 AV

Triplebank Awatere Valley Marlborough Pinot Gris ★★★★

Pernod Ricard NZ's wine is typically aromatic and flavour-packed. The 2009 vintage (★★★★☆) is floral and gently sweet, with a slightly oily texture and lush, strongly varietal, stone-fruit and spice flavours, finely balanced and youthful.

MED/DRY $24 AV

Trout Valley Nelson Pinot Gris (★★★)

From Kahurangi Estate, the 2008 vintage (★★★) is a scented, slightly Riesling-like wine with good depth of vibrant lemon, apple and spice flavours, slightly sweet and fresh.

MED/DRY $17 AV

Tupari Marlborough Pinot Gris (★★★★☆)

The debut 2009 vintage (★★★★☆) is a single-vineyard wine, grown in the Awatere Valley. Harvested at 24 brix, it is beautifully scented, with mouthfilling body, fresh, pure, peachy, spicy flavours, a slightly oily texture and a well-rounded (7.5 grams/litre of residual sugar), very harmonious finish.

MED/DRY $29 AV

Turanga Creek New Zealand Pinot Gris ★★★☆

Grown at Whitford, in South Auckland, the debut 2008 vintage (★★★☆) is an attractively scented, medium-bodied wine with ripe peach, citrus-fruit and spice flavours, showing very good depth. The skilfully crafted 2009 (★★★★) is even better. Fleshy, ripe and rounded, it has peach, pear and spice flavours, showing very good freshness and concentration, and a dry finish (2.5 grams/litre of residual sugar).

DRY $24 –V

Tussock Nelson Pinot Gris ★★★☆

From Woollaston Estates, the 2009 vintage (★★★) is a dry style (3 grams/litre of residual sugar), fleshy and slightly buttery, with ripe, peachy, rounded flavours.

DRY $18 V+

Two Rivers of Marlborough Pinot Gris ★★★★

The weighty, finely textured and harmonious 2009 vintage (★★★★☆) was hand-picked and partly (12 per cent) barrel-fermented. It shows real power through the palate, with strong, ripe, delicate flavours of peaches, pears and spice, and a slightly oily richness.

MED/DRY $24 AV

Two Sisters Central Otago Pinot Gris (★★★★)

Hand-picked at Lowburn, the 2008 vintage (★★★★) was barrel-fermented with indigenous yeasts. It's a mouthfilling, gently sweet style, softly textured, with good concentration of peachy, spicy flavour and excellent complexity and harmony, in an Alsace style.

MED $30 –V

Two Tracks Marlborough Pinot Gris ★★★

From Wither Hills, the 2009 vintage (★★★☆) is very fresh and lively, with pure, ripe peach and spice flavours, vibrant, slightly sweet and finely poised.

MED/DRY $17 AV

Urlar Gladstone Pinot Gris (★★★☆)

The creamy, toasty 2008 vintage (★★★☆) was grown near Masterton, in the Wairarapa, and barrel-fermented. Slightly Chardonnay-like, with mouthfilling body and good complexity, it's a well-rounded wine, developing well.

DRY $28 –V

Van Asch Central Otago Pinot Gris (★★★☆)

Fleshy and full-bodied, the 2008 vintage (★★★☆) is an attractively scented, Alsace-style wine with slightly sweet pear and spice flavours, showing some complexity and very good depth.

MED/DRY $35 –V

Vavasour Awatere Valley Pinot Gris ★★★★

The 2009 vintage (★★★★) was grown in Marlborough's Awatere Valley and mostly handled in tanks, but 10 per cent was fermented in seasoned French oak barriques. Weighty, it is woven with fresh acidity, offering vibrant, pure flavours of citrus fruits, lychees and pears, slightly sweet and concentrated. Well worth cellaring.

Vintage	09	08
WR	6	5
Drink	10-13	10-12

MED/DRY $26 –V

Vidal East Coast Pinot Gris ★★★☆

The 2009 vintage (★★★☆) is a blend of Hawke's Bay, Marlborough and Gisborne grapes. It's an off-dry style (5 grams/litre of residual sugar), vibrantly fruity and finely balanced, with fresh, delicate pear and spice flavours that linger well.

Vintage	09	08
WR	6	6
Drink	10-11	P

MED/DRY $19 V+

Villa Maria Cellar Selection Marlborough Pinot Gris ★★★★

The 2009 vintage (★★★★) is full-bodied, with pear, lychee and spice flavours showing excellent depth, texture and harmony. The 2010 (★★★★), mostly hand-picked in the Awatere Valley, is a basically dry style (4.9 grams/litre of residual sugar) with rich pear and spice flavours and mouthfilling body. It's a well-rounded wine, already delicious.

Vintage	10	09
WR	6	7
Drink	10-14	10-13

DRY $23 AV

Villa Maria Private Bin East Coast Pinot Gris ★★★☆

The 2010 vintage (★★★☆) was grown in Gisborne (46 per cent), Hawke's Bay (24 per cent), Marlborough (22 per cent) and Waipara (8 per cent). It's a mouthfilling wine with ripe, peachy, gently spicy flavours, showing very good depth, and a basically dry (4.5 grams/litre of residual sugar) finish.

Vintage	10	09	08
WR	6	6	6
Drink	10-12	10-11	P

DRY $20 AV

Villa Maria Single Vineyard Seddon Pinot Gris ★★★★★

One of the country's top Pinot Gris, this Awatere Valley, Marlborough wine is typically sturdy, beautifully scented and intense. The 2009 vintage (★★★★☆) was mostly tank-fermented and lees-aged for six months, but 10 per cent was fermented in seasoned French oak barriques. Still unfolding, it's a finely textured wine with substantial body, rich, ripe stone-fruit and spice flavours and a dryish (6 grams/litre of residual sugar) finish.

Vintage	10	09	08	07	06
WR	7	7	7	7	6
Drink	10-15	10-15	10-14	10-13	10-11

MED/DRY $32 AV

Waimea Bolitho SV Pinot Gris ★★★☆

The 2009 vintage (★★★☆) was estate-grown on the Waimea Plains in Nelson and hand-picked. A gently sweet style (22 grams/litre of residual sugar), it is weighty, with generous, ripe peachy flavours, hints of pears and spices, gentle acidity and good harmony.

Vintage	09	08	07	06	05
WR	6	NM	7	7	6
Drink	10-13	NM	10-12	10-11	P

MED $25 –V

Waimea Nelson Pinot Gris ★★★★

From one vintage to the next, this is one of the best-value Pinot Gris in the country. The 2009 vintage (★★★★★), hand-picked at 24 brix, is a powerful, Alsace style, fleshy and ripely scented, with a slightly oily texture and deep stone-fruit and spice flavours. Deliciously full-bodied, it's a medium-dry wine (9.6 grams/litre of residual sugar), soft and rich.

Vintage	09	08	07	06
WR	6	7	7	6
Drink	10-13	10-12	10-11	P

MED/DRY $22 V+

Waipara Hills Soul of the South Waipara Pinot Gris (★★★☆)

Grown in the Pilgrim and Glasnevin vineyards, the 2008 vintage (★★★☆) is a slightly sweet wine with fresh, pure citrus-fruit, pear and spice flavours, crisp and lingering.

MED/DRY $25 –V

Waipara Hills Southern Cross Selection Waipara Pinot Gris (★★★★)

From the Glasnevin Vineyard, adjacent to the winery, the 2008 vintage (★★★★) is a fresh, full-bodied wine, finely textured, with impressively concentrated citrus-fruit, pear and spice flavours.

MED/DRY $29 –V

Wairau River Marlborough Pinot Gris ★★★☆

The refreshing 2009 vintage (★★★☆) has good depth of lemon, apple and pear flavours, slightly sweet and crisp, finely textured and lingering. The 2010 (★★★☆) was mostly handled in tanks, but 15 per cent was French oak-aged. Ripely scented, it is full-bodied, with peach, lemon and spice flavours, showing very good depth, gentle acidity and a well-rounded (7.5 grams/litre of residual sugar) finish. It's already drinking well.

Vintage	10	09	08
WR	6	6	4
Drink	10-13	10-12	P

MED/DRY $25 –V

Waitaki Braids Waitaki Valley Pinot Gris (★★★★)

The 2008 vintage (★★★★) was hand-picked in the Otago Station Vineyard and handled in tanks, with no use of oak. Mouthfilling (14 per cent alcohol), it's a rich wine with tight, citrusy, slightly minerally flavours that build well across the palate to a tight, dry finish (2.5 grams/litre of residual sugar).

DRY $45 –V

Weeping Sands Waiheke Island Pinot Gris (★★★☆)

The debut 2010 vintage (★★★☆) was hand-picked in the Edbrooke Vineyard and made in an off-dry (5 grams/litre of residual sugar) style. Floral, with pear and spice aromas, it is mouthfilling, with very good depth of fresh, vibrant, citrusy, slightly appley and spicy flavours.

Vintage	10
WR	7
Drink	10-14

MED/DRY $26 –V

West Brook Waimauku Pinot Gris (★★★)

The debut 2009 vintage (★★★) was estate-grown in West Auckland. It's a medium-bodied wine with fresh, vibrant pear, spice and apple flavours, a splash of sweetness (9 grams/litre of residual sugar), and easy-drinking charm.

MED/DRY $22 –V

Whitecliff Pinot Gris (★★)

A blend of Australian and New Zealand wines, the 2009 vintage (★★) is lightly scented, with moderate depth of pear, apple and spice flavours and a smooth finish. An easy-drinking quaffer.

MED/DRY $18 –V

White Gold Single Vineyard Marlborough Pinot Gris (★★★)

From Gibson Bridge, the 2009 vintage (★★★), hand-picked at Renwick, is the result of 'fastidious viticulture and low groping'. Faintly pink, it is full-bodied and fleshy, with a touch of hardness amid its strong, ripe, peachy, spicy flavours.

MED/DRY $15 V+

Whitehaven Marlborough Pinot Gris ★★★☆

Mouthfilling, with fresh pear, lychee and spice flavours, gentle sweetness (7 grams/litre of residual sugar) and a slightly oily texture, the 2009 vintage (★★★☆) is a very easy-drinking style with good depth.

Vintage	09	08	07	06
WR	7	6	6	7
Drink	10-12	P	P	P

MED/DRY $20 AV

Whitestone Waipara Pinot Gris ★★☆

The 2008 vintage (★★★☆) is medium to full-bodied, with very good depth of peach, pear and spice flavours. Slightly honeyed, with a gentle splash of sweetness, it's an easy-drinking style with good personality. However, the slightly creamy 2009 (★★) lacks a bit of freshness and vibrancy.

MED/DRY $20 –V

Wild Earth Central Otago Pinot Gris ★★★★

Estate-grown at Bannockburn, the 2008 vintage (★★★★☆) was hand-harvested and mostly handled in tanks, but 20 per cent of the blend was fermented in French oak barrels. Very fresh and pure, it's a full-bodied style with incisive, slightly sweet (11 grams/litre of residual sugar) pear and spice flavours, showing lovely balance and immediacy.

MED/DRY $27 –V

Wild Rock Otago Pinot Gris (★★★☆)

Sold only in supermarkets, the easy-drinking 2008 vintage (★★★☆) is from a subsidiary of Craggy Range. Full-bodied, it is slightly sweet, with peachy, spicy flavours showing good freshness and vibrancy, a slightly creamy texture and a well-rounded finish.

MED/DRY $19 V+

Wild Rock Sur Lie Otago Pinot Gris (★★★★)

From a Craggy Range subsidiary, the instantly attractive 2009 vintage (★★★★) was grown in the Waitaki Valley and Bendigo. Mostly handled in tanks, but 5 per cent French oak-matured, it is fleshy and creamy, deliciously scented and smooth, with slight sweetness (5.2 grams/litre of residual sugar) and ripe, stone-fruit flavours, showing good richness and harmony.

Vintage	09	08
WR	7	6
Drink	10-13	10-11

MED/DRY $20 V+

Wild South Marlborough Pinot Gris ★★★☆
From Sacred Hill and grown in the Waihopai Valley, the 2009 vintage (★★★★) is instantly likeable. Attractively scented, it is mouthfilling and smooth, with a touch of sweetness (7.3 grams/litre of residual sugar) amid its fresh peach, pear and spice flavours, and excellent balance and depth.

MED/DRY $19 V+

Wither Hills Wairau Valley Marlborough Pinot Gris ★★★☆
Scented and mouthfilling, the 2010 vintage (★★★★) is a very finely poised wine, full-bodied, with strong, ripe pear, spice and peach flavours, a sliver of sweetness, and excellent harmony and richness.

Vintage	10
WR	6
Drink	10-13

MED/DRY $20 AV

Wooing Tree Central Otago Pinot Gris (★★★☆)
The 2008 vintage (★★★☆) was grown in the Cromwell Basin, hand-picked and barrel-fermented. Fleshy and rounded, it's a creamy-textured wine with good depth of fresh, dryish, peachy, slightly toasty flavours, maturing well.

MED/DRY $28 –V

Woollaston Nelson Pinot Gris ★★★☆
The 2009 vintage (★★★☆) is a fresh, off-dry style (6 grams/litre of residual sugar) with ripe stone-fruit flavours and a hint of spices. Tightly structured, it has balanced acidity and very good delicacy and depth.

MED/DRY $20 AV

Yealands Estate Marlborough Pinot Gris ★★★☆
Estate-grown in the Awatere Valley, the youthful 2009 vintage (★★★☆) is mouthfilling, with strong, lemony flavours, hints of pears and spices, and a basically dry (4 grams/litre of residual sugar), crisp finish. Worth cellaring.

DRY $24 –V

Yealands Marlborough Pinot Gris ★★★
Estate-grown at Seaview, in the Awatere Valley, the 2009 vintage (★★★) is a very easy-drinking style with fresh, ripe, peachy flavours, a gentle splash of sweetness and good acid spine.

MED/DRY $19 AV

Riesling

Riesling isn't yet one of New Zealand's great successes in overseas markets – the 107,889 cases shipped in the year to June 2010 accounted for less than 0.7 per cent of our total wine exports. Many New Zealand wine lovers also ignore this country's Rieslings.

Scentedness and intense lemon/lime flavours enlivened by fresh, appetising acidity are the hallmarks of the top New Zealand Rieslings. Around the world, Riesling has traditionally been regarded as Chardonnay's great rival in the white-wine quality stakes, well ahead of Sauvignon Blanc. So why are wine lovers here slow to appreciate Riesling's lofty stature?

Riesling is usually made in a slightly sweet style, to balance the grape's natural high acidity, but this obvious touch of sweetness runs counter to the fashion for 'dry' wines. And fine Riesling demands time (at the very least, a couple of years) to unfold its full potential; drunk in its infancy, as it so often is, it lacks the toasty, minerally, honeyed richness that is the real glory of Riesling.

After recently being overhauled by Pinot Gris, Riesling ranks as New Zealand's fourth most extensively planted white-wine variety. Between 2007 and 2011, its total area of bearing vines is expanding slowly, from 868 to 993 hectares.

The great grape of Germany, Riesling is a classic cool-climate variety, particularly well suited to the cooler growing temperatures and lower humidity of the South Island. Its stronghold is Marlborough, where 45 per cent of the vines are clustered, but the grape is also extensively planted in Nelson, Canterbury and Otago.

Riesling styles vary markedly around the world. Most Marlborough wines are medium to full-bodied (12 to 13.5 per cent alcohol), with just a touch of sweetness. However, a new breed of Riesling has emerged in the past five years – lighter (only 7.5 to 10 per cent alcohol) and markedly sweeter. These refreshingly light, sweet Rieslings offer a more vivid contrast in style to New Zealand's other major white wines, and are much closer in style to the classic German model.

Abbey Cellars Hawke's Bay Riesling ★★★☆

Estate-grown and hand-picked in The Triangle, the 2009 vintage (★★★☆) is floral and medium-bodied, with limey, slightly toasty flavours showing a touch of sweetness (10 grams/litre of residual sugar). Crisp and lively, with very good balance and depth, it's already enjoyable.

MED/DRY $18 V+

Akarua Central Otago Riesling (★★★★)

Estate-grown at Bannockburn, the 2010 vintage (★★★★) was picked from first-crop vines. Medium-bodied, with very fresh, harmonious, gently sweet flavours (12 grams/litre of residual sugar), it is citrusy, appley and slightly spicy, with excellent delicacy and depth.

MED/DRY $25 AV

Alana Estate Martinborough Riesling ★★★★

The 2008 vintage (★★★★) is ripely scented, with crisp grapefruit, lime and passionfruit flavours in a medium-dry style (7 grams/litre of residual sugar), showing good intensity and cellar potential.

Vintage	09	08	07
WR	6	6	7
Drink	15-20	14-20	10-15

MED/DRY $30 –V

Alexia Martinborough Riesling (★★★☆)

From Jane Cooper, winemaker at Matahiwi, the 2008 vintage (★★★☆) is tangy and slightly minerally, with good depth of lemon/lime flavours and a gently sweet, crisp finish.

MED/DRY $20 AV

Allan Scott Marlborough Riesling ★★★☆

A typically attractive wine, grown in the heart of the Wairau Valley. The 2009 vintage (★★★☆) is mouthfilling, with very good depth of citrusy, grapefruit-like flavours and a minerally streak. Made in a medium-dry style (10 grams/litre of residual sugar), it's already drinking well.

Vintage	09
WR	6
Drink	10-19

MED/DRY $18 V+

Allan Scott Moorlands Marlborough Riesling ★★★★☆

A basically dry style (harbouring only 4 grams/litre of residual sugar), the 2009 vintage (★★★★☆) is from vines around 30 years old, adjacent to the winery. Tank-fermented and matured for six months in old oak barrels, it is rich and finely poised, with concentrated grapefruit and slight honey flavours, a very subtle seasoning of oak and good acid spine. It's a distinctive, rewarding wine; drink now or cellar.

Vintage	09	08
WR	6	6
Drink	10-13	10-19

DRY $26 AV

Amisfield Dry Riesling ★★★★

Estate-grown in the Cromwell Basin of Central Otago, the 2009 vintage (★★★★☆) was hand-picked and fermented to a medium-dry style (7 grams/litre of residual sugar). It's an intense wine, lemony and limey, with lovely vibrancy, delicacy and harmony, and a zingy, long finish. It's already approachable, but should be at its best 2012+.

Vintage	10	09	08	07	06
WR	6	6	6	5	5
Drink	10-18	10-17	10-12	10-12	10-11

MED/DRY $30 –V

Amisfield Lowburn Terrace Riesling – see Sweet White Wines

Anchorage Classic Nelson Riesling (★★★★)

Drinking well now, the light yellow/green 2007 vintage (★★★★) is a medium style (18 grams/litre of residual sugar) with excellent vigour and intensity. It's a very harmonious wine, with minerally, slightly toasty aromas and flavours, showing bottle-aged complexity. Great value.

MED $16 V+

Anchorage Nelson Riesling ★★★

The 2008 vintage (★★☆) is a light wine (8.5 per cent alcohol), with abundant sweetness (20 grams/litre of residual sugar) and moderate depth of crisp, lemony, appley flavours. Still on sale in 2010, the 2007 (★★★★) is a dryish style (9.5 grams/litre of residual sugar) with crisp, citrusy, limey flavours, a minerally streak and a lingering finish. It's maturing very gracefully.

Vintage	08	07	06
WR	6	6	4
Drink	10-13	10-12	10-12

MED $16 V+

Ant Moore Nelson Riesling (★★★)

Grown and hand-picked at Upper Moutere, the 2009 vintage (★★★) is tight and youthful, lemony and appley, in a crisp, minerally style with a dryish finish. Worth cellaring.

MED/DRY $22 –V

Artisan Landmark Vineyard Marlborough Riesling ★★★

Ready to roll, the 2008 vintage (★★★) is a pale yellow, medium-dry wine (11 grams/litre of residual sugar), with a slightly honeyed bouquet and grapefruit, peach and spice flavours, showing some toasty, bottle-aged development.

MED/DRY $18 AV

Astrolabe Discovery Marlborough Riesling (★★★☆)

Priced sharply, the 2008 vintage (★★★☆) is a lemony, lively wine, grown at Grovetown. It has a floral bouquet, with citrusy, slightly toasty flavours, showing good vigour and depth.

MED/DRY $16 V+

Astrolabe Experience Marlborough Riesling (★★★★)

Estate-grown at Astrolabe Farm, Grovetown, in the lower Wairau Valley, the 2009 vintage (★★★★) was stop-fermented with 9 per cent alcohol and abundant sweetness (50 grams/litre of residual sugar). Light and lively, it has fresh, intense, lemony, appley flavours, with a hint of sherbet, appetising acidity and instant appeal. Drink now or cellar.

Vintage	09
WR	6
Drink	10-14

MED $25 AV

Astrolabe Voyage Marlborough Dry Riesling ★★★★

The 2009 vintage (★★★★) is a single-vineyard, Waihopai Valley wine. It's a racy, medium-bodied wine, dryish (7.5 grams/litre of residual sugar), with citrusy, appley, limey flavours showing good freshness, purity and intensity.

Vintage	09	08
WR	6	6
Drink	12-13	10-13

MED/DRY $22 V+

Auburn Lowburn Riesling (★★★★☆)

Light, lively and lingering, the youthful 2009 vintage (★★★★☆) is a rare Central Otago wine – only 760 bottles were produced. Harvested from 16-year-old vines and made in a low-alcohol (9 per cent), medium style (31 grams/litre of residual sugar), it is very tightly structured, with pure, mouth-wateringly crisp lemon and apple flavours, showing excellent vigour and intensity. It's still a baby; open 2012+.

Vintage	09
WR	6
Drink	11-18

MED $30 –V

Auburn Twilight Riesling (★★★★☆)

From mature vines at Lowburn, in Central Otago, the 2009 vintage (★★★★☆) has a slightly honeyed bouquet and flavours. Rare – only 242 bottles were made – it is peachy and rounded, in a low-alcohol (10 per cent) style, enriched but not dominated by botrytis. Showing impressive delicacy and depth, it's already delicious.

Vintage	09
WR	6
Drink	11-14

MED $30 –V

Aurora Vineyard, The, Bendigo Riesling ★★★★

From Bendigo, in Central Otago, the 2008 vintage (★★★) was estate-grown and hand-picked at 23 brix. The bouquet is restrained, but the palate is better – lemony, tight and crisp, with good depth and a slightly sweet (10 grams/litre of residual sugar) finish.

Vintage	08	07
WR	6	6
Drink	10-13	10-12

MED/DRY $24 AV

Aurum Central Otago Riesling ★★★★

Estate-grown at Lowburn, in the Cromwell Basin, the 2008 vintage (★★★★) is a mouth-wateringly crisp, cool-climate style with a lemony, slightly toasty bouquet. Lively with a distinctly minerally streak, it has good intensity of vibrant, slightly sweet (7.9 grams/litre of residual sugar), lemon/lime flavours and a tangy, lingering finish.

Vintage	08	07
WR	6	6
Drink	10-15	10-15

MED/DRY $20 V+

Babich Marlborough Riesling Dry ★★★☆

Typically, a well-crafted wine with good drinkability. Grown in the Wairau and Waihopai valleys, the 2008 vintage (★★★) is lemony and slightly minerally, with some early, toasty development showing. Crisp and dryish, it's for drinking now onwards.

MED/DRY $20 AV

Bald Hills Last Light Riesling ★★★★
Hand-picked from a 1-hectare plot at Bannockburn, in Central Otago, the 2008 vintage (★★★☆) is a full-bodied style (14 per cent alcohol) with strong, fresh, lemony scents and good depth of citrusy, peachy, slightly spicy flavour. Slightly sweet and crisp, it's likely to mature well.

Vintage	09	08	07	06
WR	6	6	6	6
Drink	10-12	11-14	10-13	10-12

MED/DRY $23 AV

Bannock Brae Goldfields Dry Riesling ★★☆
This Central Otago wine 'exhibits the characteristics of a bygone age'. The 2008 vintage (★★☆) was grown at Bannockburn and fully barrel-fermented, with lees-stirring and partial malolactic fermentation. It's a more 'oxidative', less vibrantly fruity wine than most, lemony, dryish (6 grams/litre of residual sugar) and mellow.

Vintage	08
WR	6
Drink	10-15

MED/DRY $24 –V

Bascand Waipara Riesling ★★☆
The easy-drinking 2009 vintage (★★☆) is light-bodied, with decent depth of lemony, appley flavours, a splash of sweetness (18 grams/litre of residual sugar) and a fresh, smooth finish.

MED $17 –V

Beach House Hawke's Bay Riesling ★★★★
A single-vineyard Hawke's Bay wine, grown near the sea at Te Awanga, the 2008 vintage (★★★★) is light and lively, with a fresh, appley, minerally bouquet, good acid spine and strong, lemony, slightly sweet flavours (8 grams/litre of residual sugar).

Vintage	08
WR	6
Drink	10-25

MED/DRY $17 V+

Bishops Head Reserve Riesling (★★★)
The 2007 vintage (★★★) was grown at Waipara and 25 per cent barrel-fermented. It's an off-dry style (8.6 grams/litre of residual sugar) with strong, crisp, lemony, slightly spicy flavours, seasoned with nutty oak.

MED/DRY $23 –V

Bishops Head Waipara Riesling ★★★☆
Maturing gracefully, the 2008 vintage (★★★☆) is a medium style (20 grams/litre of residual sugar), 10 per cent barrel-aged, with balanced acidity and strong, lemony flavours, developing good harmony.

MED $19 V+

Black Barn Vineyards Single Vineyard Riesling (★★★☆)

Bright, light yellow, with a slightly honeyed, toasty bouquet, the 2007 vintage (★★★☆) is a fleshy, rounded Hawke's Bay wine, estate-grown and hand-picked at Havelock North. Slightly sweet (10 grams/litre of residual sugar), with bottle-aged complexity, it's drinking well now.

MED/DRY $25 –V

Black Estate Omihi Waipara Riesling ★★★

Hand-picked at Waipara but not estate-grown, the 2009 vintage (★★★★) is slightly honeyed. It has strong, vibrant flavours of lemons, apples and honey, woven with fresh acidity, and excellent harmony and richness. Already delicious, it's a drink-now or cellaring proposition.

MED $22 AV

Blackenbrook Vineyard Nelson Riesling ★★★★☆

Very youthful, tight and racy, the 2009 vintage (★★★★☆) was estate-grown and hand-picked. A medium style (15 grams/litre of residual sugar), it has strong peach, lemon and lime flavours, threaded with lively acidity. Vibrantly fruity, with a minerally streak, it shows excellent intensity and obvious cellaring potential.

Vintage	09	08	07
WR	7	7	7
Drink	10-12	10-11	P

MED $23 V+

Bladen Marlborough Riesling ★★★☆

Fresh and lively, the 2009 vintage (★★★☆) is a single-vineyard wine, made in a dryish style (5.5 grams/litre of residual sugar). Full-bodied, it is lemony, slightly appley and spicy, with good balance and depth.

Vintage	09
WR	7
Drink	10-13

MED/DRY $20 AV

Boreham Wood Single Vineyard Marlborough Riesling (★★★★)

The vivacious, light 2008 vintage (10 per cent alcohol) was hand-harvested in the Awatere Valley from first-crop vines. Lemony, minerally scents lead into a gently sweet style (30 grams/litre of residual sugar) with rich, citrusy, faintly honeyed flavours, threaded with appetising acidity. Finely balanced and lingering.

Vintage	09	08
WR	7	7
Drink	10-14	10-13

MED $24 AV

Borthwick Vineyard Paddy Borthwick Wairarapa Riesling ★★★★

Estate-grown at Gladstone, the 2009 vintage (★★★★) is a tight, youthful wine, made in an off-dry style (6 grams/litre of residual sugar). It shows good vigour, intensity and balance, with penetrating peach, lemon and lime flavours and a long, minerally finish.

MED/DRY $23 AV

Boulders Martinborough Prosecco Style Riesling (★★★☆)

Made by Allan Johnson, the 2009 vintage (★★★☆) has 'subtle effervescence'. Light and crisp, with low alcohol (9 per cent) and slightly sweet, green-apple and lime flavours, it's a very fresh and lively, slightly *spritzig* wine, that makes a very stimulating thirst quencher.

MED/DRY $20 AV

Boulders Martinborough Riesling (★★★)

Grown on the Martinborough Terraces, the 2009 vintage (★★★) is a medium-bodied wine with fresh, lemony, appley flavours, lively acidity and an off-dry finish, finely balanced for easy drinking.

MED/DRY $20 –V

Bouldevines Marlborough Riesling ★★★☆

Grown on the south side of the Wairau Valley, the 2009 vintage (★★★☆) is a single-vineyard wine, fresh, crisp and medium-bodied, with ripe, lemony, appley, slightly spicy flavours and an unusually dry (2.5 grams/litre of residual sugar), yet finely balanced, finish. It shows very good delicacy and length; open mid-2011+.

DRY $20 AV

Brancott Estate Reserve Waipara Riesling – see Montana Reserve Waipara Riesling

Brightside Brightwater Riesling ★★★

From Kaimira Estate, the 2009 vintage (★★★) is a medium style (15 grams/litre of residual sugar) with strong, citrusy flavours, balanced for easy drinking. Crisp, with a vague hint of honey, it's drinking well now and priced sharply.

Vintage	09	08
WR	6	5
Drink	10-14	10-12

MED $16 V+

Brightwater Vineyards Nelson Riesling ★★★★

Estate-grown and hand-picked on the Waimea Plains, this wine is always full of personality. The 2009 vintage (★★★★) is a distinctly medium style. A mouthfilling, vibrantly fruity wine with strong citrusy, limey flavours, a hint of passionfruit and appetising acidity, it's well balanced for easy drinking. The 2010 (★★★★) is an elegant, very youthful wine, medium-dry (11 grams/litre of residual sugar), with citrusy, slightly spicy flavours, fresh, pure and finely poised. It should flourish with bottle-age.

Vintage	10	09	08	07	06
WR	5	5	5	6	6
Drink	11-15	10-12	10-11	P	P

MED/DRY $20 V+

Brookfields Ohiti Estate Riesling ★★★☆

Grown at Ohiti, inland from Fernhill, the 2008 vintage (★★★☆) is a slightly sweet (11 grams/litre of residual sugar) Hawke's Bay wine, medium-bodied, lemony and slightly minerally, with good harmony and drink-young appeal.

Vintage	08
WR	7
Drink	10-13

MED/DRY $20 AV

Camshorn Waipara Classic Riesling ★★★★

The 2009 vintage (★★★★☆) from Pernod Ricard NZ is richly scented and finely poised, in a medium style with excellent depth of tightly structured, citrusy, peachy flavours, ripe, rounded and lingering.

MED $27 –V

Camshorn Waipara Dry Riesling ★★★★

The 2007 vintage (★★★★) from Pernod Ricard NZ is a classic dry style (4.5 grams/litre of residual sugar), with rich, ripe grapefruit and peach flavours and a rounded finish. It's maturing very gracefully, with toasty, bottle-aged notes adding complexity.

Vintage	07	06	05
WR	6	6	6
Drink	10-12	P	P

DRY $27 –V

Carrick Central Otago Dry Riesling ★★★★

Grown at Bannockburn and fermented with indigenous yeasts, the 2009 vintage (★★★★) is tightly structured, with vibrant, citrusy, slightly spicy flavours, showing good intensity, and a fractionally off-dry (4.1 grams/litre of residual sugar), appetisingly crisp finish. An elegant, very youthful, minerally wine, it's worth cellaring.

DRY $22 V+

Carrick Central Otago Riesling ★★★★

Consistently classy and good value. Grown at Bannockburn, the 2009 vintage (★★★★☆) is a medium style (25 grams/litre of residual sugar), poised and punchy, with a full-bloomed bouquet and concentrated grapefruit and apple flavours. Very youthful, vibrant, minerally and tangy, with racy acidity, it has a long life ahead.

Vintage	09	08	07	06
WR	6	6	6	6
Drink	10-15	10-14	10-14	10-12

MED $22 V+

Carrick Josephine Central Otago Riesling ★★★★★

The 2009 vintage (★★★★) was grown in the Lot 8 Vineyard, on the Cairnmuir Terraces at Bannockburn, hand-picked and stop-fermented in a low-alcohol (9 per cent), medium-sweet style (48 grams/litre of residual sugar). Very tight and racy, it's a light-bodied wine (9 per cent alcohol), youthful, with an array of lemon, apple, lime and sherbet flavours, showing excellent intensity and poise.

MED $26 V+

Charles Wiffen Marlborough Riesling ★★★☆

The 2009 vintage (★★★☆) is slightly sweet and crisp, with apple and slight passionfruit flavours, showing good depth.

MED/DRY $19 V+

Clark Estate Single Vineyard Awatere Valley Riesling (★★★★☆)

The lovely 2009 vintage (★★★★☆) is a light, low-alcohol style (10 per cent) with abundant sweetness (50 grams/litre of residual sugar). Hand-picked from young vines, it is attractively scented, with a fresh, poised palate, distinctly Mosel-like, showing ripe, citrusy flavours, very delicate and harmonious. It's already delicious.

MED $26 AV

Clayridge Marlborough Wild Riesling ★★★☆

Grown in the Escaroth Vineyard, high in Taylors Pass, and in the Omaka Valley, the 2008 vintage (★★★☆) was fermented with indigenous yeasts in tanks. Light-bodied (11.5 per cent), it's a distinctly medium style (22 grams/litre of residual sugar) with ripe grapefruit-like flavours, showing a hint of botrytis, and some toasty development and complexity.

Vintage	08	07
WR	6	5
Drink	10-18	10-17

MED $24 –V

Clos St William Waipara Riesling (★★★☆)

The 2009 vintage (★★★☆) was estate-grown and harvested from first-crop vines. Tank-fermented, it is crisp and lively, in a medium style (15 grams/litre of residual sugar) with citrusy, appley flavours showing very good depth.

MED $20 AV

Cloudy Bay Riesling ★★★★☆

Released at over four years old, the 2006 vintage (★★★★☆) was grown in Marlborough, fermented with indigenous yeasts and matured for six months in old French oak barrels. Still youthful in colour, it is medium to full-bodied, with penetrating grapefruit and spice flavours, a minerally streak, a sliver of sweetness (8 grams/litre of residual sugar) and good acid spine. Drink now or cellar.

MED/DRY $30 –V

Coney Ragtime Riesling ★★★☆

This characterful Martinborough wine is made in a medium-dry style. The 2009 vintage (★★★☆) is tight and youthful, with strong, citrusy, slightly honeyed flavours. It's a gently sweet style (14 grams/litre of residual sugar) with hints of passionfruit and marmalade and good acid spine.

Vintage	08	07	06
WR	7	5	6
Drink	10-11	P	P

MED/DRY $20 AV

Coney Rallentando Riesling ★★★☆

This Martinborough wine is a drier style than its stablemate (above). The 2008 vintage (★★★★) is already highly expressive. Mouthfilling, with good weight and concentrated grapefruit and slight passionfruit flavours, it is slightly minerally, with a rich finish.

DRY $20 AV

Coopers Creek Marlborough Riesling ★★★

The 2008 vintage (★★★) is full-bodied, fleshy, citrusy and spicy, with hints of honey. It's drinking well now. The slightly lighter 2009 (★★★), a medium-dry style (8.3 grams/litre of residual sugar), is fresh, vibrant and youthful, with lemony, appley flavours, showing good depth.

Vintage	09	08
WR	6	5
Drink	10-14	10-13

MED/DRY $17 AV

Coopers Creek SV Mister Phebus Marlborough Riesling (★★★★)

The 2009 vintage (★★★★) has a floral, slightly musky bouquet, leading into a peachy, limey wine, full-flavoured, gently sweet (12 grams/litre of residual sugar) and spicy, with excellent delicacy, harmony and intensity.

Vintage	09
WR	7
Drink	10-16

MED/DRY $20 V+

Corbans Homestead Waipara Riesling (★★★)

The 2009 vintage (★★★) flowed from Pernod Ricard NZ's vineyards in North Canterbury. Balanced for easy drinking, it has passionfruit and citrus-fruit flavours, showing good depth, and a slightly sweet, crisp finish.

MED/DRY $17 AV

Corbans White Label Johannisberg Riesling ★★☆

Some past vintages have been trans-Tasman blends, but the 2008 (★★☆) from Pernod Ricard NZ was made entirely from New Zealand grapes. It's a lemon-scented, gently sweet wine with light, fresh, citrusy flavours, a hint of honey and crisp acidity. Good value.

MED $9 V+

Crab Farm Hawke's Bay Riesling (★★★★)

The rich 2008 vintage (★★★★) offers top value. Crisp and gently sweet (14 grams/litre of residual sugar), it has good intensity of citrusy, limey, faintly honeyed flavour.

Vintage	08
WR	7
Drink	10-12

MED/DRY $17 V+

Craggy Range Fletcher Family Vineyard Riesling ★★★☆

Past vintages have matured well. The 2010 (★★★☆), grown in Marlborough's Wairau Valley, is light and lively, with fresh, youthful lemon, apple and spice flavours, gentle sweetness (10 grams/litre of residual sugar), a minerally thread, and good depth and harmony. Open 2012+.

Vintage	10	09	08	07	06
WR	7	7	6	6	7
Drink	10-21	10-16	10-15	10-12	10-14

MED/DRY $23 –V

Craggy Range Glasnevin Gravels Vineyard Waipara Riesling ★★★★
Like its predecessors, the 2008 vintage (★★★★) was modelled on the slender but intensely flavoured Rieslings of the Mosel. It has low alcohol (10 per cent), with penetrating, lemony, appley flavours, sweetish, slightly minerally and long.

Vintage	09	08
WR	6	7
Drink	10-16	10-13

MED $23 AV

Craggy Range Otago Station Vineyard Riesling (★★★★)
Grown in the Waitaki Valley, North Otago, the 2008 vintage (★★★★) offers pure, vibrant lemon/lime flavours, crisp, gently sweet (23 grams/litre of residual sugar) and slightly minerally.

Vintage	08
WR	6
Drink	10-15

MED/DRY $35 –V

Craggy Range Te Muna Road Vineyard Riesling ★★★☆
Hand-picked in Martinborough, the 2008 vintage (★★★★) was cool-fermented to a medium-dry style and lees-aged for four months. Invitingly scented, it has good intensity of fresh lemon, apple and lime flavours, tight, finely balanced and appetisingly crisp. The 2009 vintage (★★☆) was fermented with indigenous yeasts and matured for four months in seasoned oak puncheons. A light, slightly spicy wine, it did not shine in a recent blind tasting, but with Riesling, discernible oak influence often throws the cat among the pigeons.

Vintage	08	07	06	05
WR	6	6	7	6
Drink	10-15	10-12	10-13	P

MED/DRY $26 –V

Crater Rim, The, Dr Kohl's Waipara Riesling – see Sweet White Wines

Crater Rim, The, Waipara Riesling ★★★☆
The 2009 vintage (★★★★) is a medium-sweet style (45 grams/litre of residual sugar), grown on the valley floor and tank-fermented. Light (only 9.5 per cent alcohol) and vivacious, it has good intensity of lemon and apple flavours, crisp and slightly minerally, with excellent depth and harmony. It's already delicious.

MED $21 AV

Crossroads Marlborough Riesling (★★★)
The 2008 vintage (★★★) is crisp, light and lively, with tight, lemony, appley flavours, slightly sweet (10.3 grams/litre of residual sugar), and showing good delicacy and freshness.

MED/DRY $20 –V

Culley Marlborough Riesling ★★★
The 2008 vintage (★★☆) has appley aromas leading into a light, slightly sweet wine with appetising acidity and moderate depth.

MED/DRY $19 AV

d'Akaroa Dry Riesling (★★★)
Grown at French Farm Bay, on Banks Peninsula, in Canterbury, the 2008 vintage (★★★) is scented, with tight, very lemony flavours, woven with fresh acidity, and a dryish (6 grams/litre of residual sugar) finish.

MED/DRY $20 –V

Dancing Water Kamaka Riesling (★★★☆)
Grown at Waipara, the 2008 vintage (★★★☆) is a light-bodied style (10 per cent alcohol) with very good depth of lemony, limey, gently sweet (28 grams/litre of residual sugar) flavour, fresh and crisp.

MED $28 –V

Darjon North Canterbury Riesling (★★★☆)
The 2009 (★★★☆) is Darjon's first Riesling in a medium style – past vintages were drier. Harvested at Swannanoa at 18 to 22 brix, it is fresh, floral and light in body (11 per cent alcohol), with gentle sweetness (20 grams/litre of residual sugar) and crisp, lively, lemony flavours. Well worth cellaring.

MED $20 AV

Desert Heart Central Otago Riesling ★★★☆
The 2009 vintage (★★★☆) was hand-harvested at Bannockburn. An off-dry, minerally style, it has strong, fresh lemon, apple and lime flavours and firm acidity. It's a slightly austere wine, but shows good delicacy and length.

Vintage	09	08	07	06
WR	6	6	5	4
Drink	10-16	10-15	10-16	10-11

MED/DRY $24 –V

Discovery Point Marlborough Dry Riesling (★★★★★)
From wine distributor Bennett & Deller, the 2008 vintage (★★★★★) is a great buy. A single-vineyard wine, grown at Omaka, it is a virtually dry style (5 grams/litre of residual sugar), invitingly scented, with medium body (12.5 per cent alcohol), good acid spine and fresh, searching, lemony, limey flavours, very finely textured and lingering. Perfectly poised for current enjoyment, it's a distinctive, satisfyingly dry wine – and exactly the style that could turn Kiwis onto Riesling.

Vintage	08
WR	6
Drink	11-13

MED/DRY $22 V+

Divine Daughter, The, Riesling ★★★☆

From The Old Glenmark Vicarage, at Waipara, the 2008 vintage (★★★☆) is light-bodied and tangy, with slightly sweet lemon/apple flavours, showing good depth. It's a finely poised wine, slightly minerally and refreshing, with cellaring potential.

Vintage	08	07
WR	7	7
Drink	10-11	P

MED $23 –V

Doctors', The, Marlborough Riesling ★★★★☆

From Forrest Estate, this deliberately low-alcohol style is like biting into a fresh, crunchy Granny Smith apple. The 2010 vintage (★★★★☆) is deliciously light (8.5 per cent alcohol) and lively, with plentiful sweetness (42 grams/litre of residual sugar) and fresh, strong lemon and lime flavours, showing lovely delicacy and poise. (Most vintages break into full stride at about two years old.)

Vintage	10
WR	6
Drink	11-20

MED $22 V+

Domain Road Vineyard Central Otago Riesling ★★★★

Grown at Bannockburn, the 2009 vintage (★★★★) is unfolding well. A full-bodied style with concentrated lemon/lime flavours, a gentle splash of sweetness (13.5 grams/litre of residual sugar) and racy acidity, it has citrus-fruit and slight passionfruit flavours, showing excellent intensity and vibrancy.

Vintage	09	08
WR	6	6
Drink	10-15	10-14

MED/DRY $22 V+

Domain Road Vineyard Duffer's Creek Riesling (★★★★☆)

Grown at Bannockburn, in Central Otago, the debut 2010 vintage (★★★★☆) is full of potential. A classy wine, it is medium-bodied, with pure, delicate lemon, lime and spice flavours, slightly sweet (12.5 grams/litre of residual sugar) and minerally, and a poised, lingering finish.

Vintage	10
WR	6
Drink	11-16

MED/DRY $24 V+

Domain Road Vineyard The Water Race Dry Riesling (★★★★)

The debut 2010 vintage (★★★★) was grown at Bannockburn, in Central Otago. Tightly structured, it is dryish (7 grams/litre of residual sugar), with good weight and depth of grapefruit, spice and apple flavours, balanced acidity and obvious potential. Open 2012+.

Vintage	10
WR	6
Drink	11-16

MED/DRY $24 AV

Drylands Marlborough Dry Riesling ★★★★

From Constellation NZ, this wine has a low profile, but is typically lemon-scented, with strong, citrusy flavours and a floral bouquet. At three to four years old, it offers rich, toasty, minerally flavours in a classic dry Riesling style.

DRY $22 V+

Dry River Craighall Vineyard Riesling ★★★★★

Founder Neil McCallum believes that, in quality terms, Riesling is at least the equal of Pinot Noir in Martinborough. His Craighall Riesling, one of the finest in the country, is a wine of exceptional purity, delicacy and depth, with a proven ability to flourish in the cellar for many years: 'It's not smart to drink them at less than five years old,' says McCallum. The grapes are sourced from a small block (0.8 hectare) of vines, mostly 20 to 25 years old, in the Craighall Vineyard, with yields limited to an average of 6 tonnes per hectare, and the wine is stop-fermented just short of dryness. The 2010 vintage (★★★★★) is designated 'Amaranth' – especially recommended for cellaring. Fresh, immaculate and intense, it has lemony scents and flavours, crisp, delicate and racy. Still a baby, it is highly concentrated, finely poised, dryish and long. Open 2012+.

Vintage	10	09	08	07	06	05	04
WR	7	6	7	7	7	6	6
Drink	12-18	11-16	10-15	10-14	10-12	P	P

MED/DRY $44 AV

Esk Valley Marlborough Riesling (★★★★)

The 2009 (★★★★) is the winery's first Marlborough Riesling – past vintages were grown in Hawke's Bay. Hand-picked in the Wairau and Awatere valleys, it's a medium-dry style (6.7 grams/litre of residual sugar), lemon-scented, with tight, immaculate flavours of lemons and limes, finely poised and worth cellaring. Tasted prior to bottling (and so not rated), the 2010 is punchy and lemony, very fresh, crisp, dry (4.5 grams/litre of residual sugar) and long.

Vintage	10	09
WR	6	6
Drink	11-15	10-14

MED/DRY $24 AV

Fallen Angel Marlborough Riesling ★★★☆

The 2009 vintage (★★★☆) from Stonyridge Vineyard is a medium-bodied style, crisp and slightly sweet (9 grams/litre of residual sugar), with strong, lemony, appley flavours, showing good freshness, delicacy and harmony. The 2010 (★★★☆) is sweeter (18 grams/litre of residual sugar), with fresh, strong, citrusy, limey, slightly spicy flavours, tight and racy.

Vintage	10
WR	7
Drink	10-18

MED $25 –V

Felton Road Block 1 Riesling – see Sweet White Wines

Felton Road Dry Riesling ★★★★☆

Based on low-yielding vines in schisty soils at Bannockburn, in Central Otago, this wine is hand-picked and fermented with indigenous yeasts. The 2009 vintage (★★★★★) is full of personality. Mouthfilling (13 per cent alcohol), with concentrated, vibrant lemon/lime flavours, slightly spicy and minerally, it is dry but not austere, and crying out for cellaring.

Vintage	09	08	07	06	05	04
WR	6	6	7	6	6	6
Drink	10-19	10-18	10-17	10-16	10-15	10-14

DRY $26 AV

Felton Road Riesling ★★★★★

Estate-grown on mature vines at Bannockburn, in Central Otago, this is a gently sweet wine with deep flavours cut with fresh acidity. It offers more drink-young appeal than its Dry Riesling stablemate, but invites long-term cellaring. Tank-fermented mostly with indigenous yeasts, it is bottled with 20 to 50 grams per litre of residual sugar. The 2009 vintage (★★★★★) is finely balanced and racy, with lovely lightness (10 per cent alcohol), vivacity and intensity of lemon/lime flavours, gently sweet, crisp and harmonious. It's already quite expressive.

Vintage	09	08	07	06	05	04
WR	6	6	7	6	6	6
Drink	10-29	10-23	10-22	10-16	10-15	10-14

MED $26 V+

Fiddler's Green Waipara Classic Riesling ★★★★

The fresh, zingy 2008 vintage (★★★★) is light-bodied and vibrantly fruity, in a distinctly medium style with lemony, appley flavours showing good intensity. The 2009 (★★★☆) is vibrant and smooth, with light body (10.5 per cent alcohol), a splash of sweetness (20 grams/litre of residual sugar), and youthful, lemony, appley flavours that linger well. Worth cellaring.

Vintage	09	08
WR	6	6
Drink	10-16	10-13

MED $20 V+

Fiddler's Green Waipara Dry Riesling (★★★★)

Crisp, tight and lively, the 2008 vintage (★★★★) has good intensity of lemon, lime and passionfruit flavours and a hint of honey. It's a basically dry style (5 grams/litre of residual sugar), finely balanced.

Vintage	08
WR	6
Drink	10-15

MED/DRY $23 AV

Five Flax East Coast Riesling ★★★

The 2008 vintage (★★★) from Pernod Ricard NZ is not labelled by region. It's an easy-drinking style with fresh, crisp, citrus-fruit and passionfruit flavours, slightly sweet and crisp. A good buy on special at around $11.

MED/DRY $15 V+

Forrest Collection Riesling – see John Forrest Collection Riesling

Forrest Marlborough Riesling ★★★☆
John Forrest believes Riesling will one day be Marlborough's greatest wine, and his own wine is helping the cause. The 2009 vintage (★★★★) is attractively scented, in a vibrant, gently sweet style (14 grams/litre of residual sugar) with very good depth of crisp, lemony, appley flavours, balanced for easy drinking.

Vintage	09	08	07
WR	7	6	7
Drink	10-20	10-12	10-15

MED/DRY $20 AV

Forrest The Doctors' Riesling – see Doctors', The, Riesling

Forrest The Valleys Brancott Riesling ★★★★☆
Described by John Forrest as 'an Alsace style', the 2008 vintage (★★★★☆) is rich, with gently sweet (12 grams/litre of residual sugar), ripe citrus and peach flavours, showing impressive concentration and harmony.

Vintage	08	07
WR	7	7
Drink	11-20	11-20

MED/DRY $25 V+

Forrest The Valleys Wairau Dry Riesling ★★★★
The 2008 vintage (★★★★) is a low-alcohol wine (10.5 per cent), tight and dry (3 grams/litre of residual sugar), with pure, lemony, slightly minerally flavours, finely poised and not austere. The 2009 (★★★★☆) is full-bodied (13 per cent alcohol) and minerally, with a sliver of sweetness (5 grams/litre of residual sugar) and strong, delicate lemon, apple and lime flavours, slightly spicy, tight, minerally and long. It should cellar well, but is already highly expressive.

Vintage	09	08	07
WR	6	5	6
Drink	11-20	10-20	10-20

MED/DRY $30 –V

Forrest The Valleys Wairau Library Release Dry Riesling (★★★★★)
On sale in 2010, the 2001 vintage (★★★★★) was first released as Forrest Estate Dry Riesling. It has a beautifully scented, rich fragrance, leading into a dry (2 grams/litre of residual sugar), citrusy, slightly toasty palate, not at all austere. A great example of the benefits of cellaring.

DRY $30 AV

Foxes Island Marlborough Riesling ★★★★☆
The 2008 vintage (★★★★) is a rich, ripe style, estate-grown, hand-picked at 22 brix in the Old Ford Road Vineyard, in the Awatere Valley, and lees-aged for three months. Full-bodied and finely balanced, it's a scented wine with concentrated, peachy, slightly limey flavours, gentle sweetness (5.8 grams/litre of residual sugar), and fresh, lively acidity. (The 2009 vintage is lower-priced at $22.)

MED/DRY $34 –V

Framingham Classic Riesling ★★★★★

Top vintages of this Marlborough wine are strikingly aromatic, richly flavoured and zesty. The 2009 (★★★★☆) is tight and crisp, with good intensity of citrusy, limey flavour, gentle sweetness (18 grams/litre of residual sugar) and appetising acidity. Poised and youthful, it's full of promise, but needs another two years; open 2012+.

Vintage	09	08	07	06	05	04
WR	7	6	7	7	7	7
Drink	10-16	10-15	10-13	10-11	P	P

MED $23 V+

Framingham Dry Riesling ★★★★☆

The 2004 vintage (★★★★☆) is a classic, slow-maturing dry style (5 grams/litre of residual sugar) from Marlborough. It has a toasty, very minerally bouquet and grapefruit, lime and spice flavours, tense and slightly austere. The 2005 vintage (★★★★) has lemony, appley, toasty aromas and flavours, developing good fragrance and complexity.

Vintage	04
WR	7
Drink	10-13+

MED/DRY $28 AV

Framingham F Series Old Vine Riesling (★★★★☆)

From estate-grown vines, planted at Renwick, in Marlborough, nearly 30 years ago, the debut 2009 vintage (★★★★☆) was hand-picked and fermented with indigenous yeasts, mostly in tanks; 20 per cent was barrel-fermented. Medium-bodied, it has concentrated grapefruit and lemon flavours, in a dryish style (9 grams/litre of residual sugar) with excellent depth and harmony. Drink now or cellar.

Vintage	09
WR	6
Drink	10-15

MED/DRY $40 –V

Fromm Riesling Dry ★★★★☆

Typically, a beautifully poised, delicate Marlborough wine with citrusy, minerally flavours and a zingy, lasting finish. The 2008 vintage (★★★★☆) is a fractionally off-dry style with highly concentrated, ripe, appley and spicy flavours, tangy, minerally and sustained. A refined, finely balanced wine, it's already approachable, but should be long-lived.

Vintage	09	08	07	06	05	04
WR	6	6	6	7	6	7
Drink	10-15	10-14	10-13	10-14	10-11	10-12

DRY $24 V+

Gibbston Valley Central Otago Riesling ★★★★

The 2008 (★★★★) has good acid spine and citrusy, appley flavours, slightly minerally, tense and lively. The 2010 vintage (★★★★), estate-grown and hand-harvested at Bendigo, is lemon-scented, with lemon, lime and passionfruit flavours, fractionally sweet (8 grams/litre of residual sugar), strong and tangy.

Vintage	10
WR	7
Drink	10-20

MED/DRY $25 AV

Gibbston Valley Le Fou The Expressionist Series Riesling ★★★★☆

Estate-grown at Bendigo, in Central Otago, the 2009 vintage (★★★★) has abundant sweetness (29 grams/litre of residual sugar), balanced by mouth-watering acidity. Light (9.5 per cent alcohol) and racy, it is finely poised, with lemony, appley flavours, showing some complexity, and is likely to be long-lived. Open 2012+.

Vintage	09	08	07
WR	6	7	7
Drink	11-20	10-20	10-18

MED $35 –V

Giesen Marlborough/Canterbury Riesling ★★★

The 2008 vintage (★★★) is light-bodied, with satisfying depth of fresh, lemony flavours, gentle sweetness (20 grams/litre of residual sugar) and lively acidity. It's well balanced for easy, early drinking.

MED $17 AV

Glasnevin Classic Riesling (★★★★)

From Fiddler's Green, the 2008 vintage (★★★★) was fermented with indigenous yeasts and lees-aged in tanks. It's a medium-sweet style (43 grams/litre of residual sugar), light (9.5 per cent alcohol) and lively, with good intensity of lemony, appley flavours, showing excellent delicacy and poise. Drink now or cellar.

Vintage	08
WR	6
Drink	10-14

MED $24 AV

Goldridge Estate Marlborough Riesling ★★☆

The 2009 vintage (★★☆) is a single-vineyard wine, fresh, youthful and lively, with lemon/lime flavours woven with appetising acidity, a sliver of sweetness and good depth.

MED/DRY $16 AV

Greenhough Apple Valley Nelson Riesling ★★★★☆

Grown in a coastal vineyard at Mapua and made in a low-alcohol, medium style, the 2010 vintage (★★★★☆) is light (10 per cent alcohol) and sweetish (35 grams/litre of residual sugar), with vivacious lemon, lime and apple flavours, very fresh, intense and tasty. A lovely summer sipper, it's also full of potential.

Vintage	10	09	08	07
WR	6	6	6	6
Drink	10-16	10-15	10-14	10-13

MED $22 V+

Greenhough Hope Vineyard Riesling ★★★★☆

This Nelson wine is hand-picked from vines planted in 1979. The 2009 vintage (★★★★★) is very intense and racy, in a medium-dry style (14 grams/litre of residual sugar). Beautifully poised, with concentrated, citrusy, limey, slightly spicy flavours, a minerally streak and loads of personality, it should be long-lived.

Vintage	09	08	07	06
WR	7	7	7	6
Drink	10-15	10-13	10-12	10-11

MED/DRY $22 V+

Greystone Waipara Dry Riesling ★★★☆

The 2009 vintage (★★★★) is an off-dry style (6 grams/litre of residual sugar), invitingly scented, with good weight and intensity of ripe peach, passionfruit and spice flavours, fresh and already drinking well.

Vintage	09
WR	6
Drink	10-16

MED/DRY $26 –V

Greystone Waipara Riesling ★★★★

Estate-grown and hand-harvested, the 2009 vintage (★★★★) is a medium style (33 grams/litre of residual sugar) with excellent depth of lemony, appley flavour, balanced for easy drinking. Floral and focused, with appetising acidity, it should unfold well.

Vintage	10	09	08	07
WR	7	6	6	5
Drink	10-18	10-16	10-12	10-11

MED $24 AV

Greywacke Marlborough Riesling (★★★★☆)

From Kevin Judd, the debut 2009 vintage (★★★★☆) is an immaculate, single-vineyard wine, grown at Fairhall, hand-picked, and fermented in tanks and seasoned French oak barriques. Vivacious, it is medium-bodied and appetisingly crisp, with rich, gently sweet (20 grams/litre of residual sugar) flavours, lemony and spicy, showing excellent complexity, harmony and length.

MED $29 AV

Grove Mill Grand Reserve Seventeen Valley Vineyard Marlborough Riesling (★★★★★)

The debut 2009 vintage (★★★★★) is beautifully scented, with intense grapefruit and lime flavours, enlivened with fresh acidity, a slightly honeyed richness, and a long, harmonious finish. It's already delicious.

MED/DRY $26 V+

Grove Mill Marlborough Riesling ★★★☆

Typically a finely balanced wine with strong fruit flavours, a distinct splash of sweetness (14 grams/litre of residual sugar in 2008) and appetising acidity. The 2008 vintage (★★★☆) is attractively scented and light (11.5 per cent alcohol), with pure, delicate flavours of lemons, apples and limes.

Vintage	08	07	06	05	04
WR	6	7	7	6	7
Drink	10-14	10-14	10-13	P	10-12

MED/DRY $18 V+

Hans Herzog Marlborough Riesling (★★★★)

The 2009 vintage (★★★★) was partly handled in tanks, but 50 per cent was matured for nine months in seasoned French oak puncheons. It's a mouthfilling (13.5 per cent alcohol), fleshy wine with very ripe, citrusy flavours, in a dryish style (less than 6 grams/litre of residual sugar), showing excellent harmony and richness.

Vintage	09
WR	7
Drink	10-15

MED/DRY $44 –V

Hawkshead Central Otago Riesling ★★★★

Grown at Bendigo, the 2009 vintage (★★★★☆) is instantly attractive. Hand-picked at 22.8 brix, it is very finely scented, with vibrant, lemony, appley flavours, a minerally thread, and excellent freshness, delicacy and intensity. A medium-dry style (9.5 grams/litre of residual sugar), it's already drinking well.

MED/DRY $22 V+

Hay Maker Waipara Riesling ★★★☆

Estate-grown by Mud House, the 2008 vintage (★★★☆) is a light-bodied (11 per cent alcohol), medium style (23 grams/litre of residual sugar), instantly appealing, with lots of citrusy, slightly spicy flavour.

MED $17 V+

Hell or Highwater Central Otago Riesling (★★★☆)

From the Highwater Vineyard, on the Tarras–Cromwell Road, the 2009 vintage (★★★☆) is crisp and vibrant, with lemony, appley, gently sweet flavours, showing good balance, depth and immediacy.

MED/DRY $20 AV

Highfield Marlborough Riesling ★★★★

This is a consistently rewarding wine, priced sharply. Still youthful, the 2009 (★★★★☆) is poised and lively, with low alcohol and strong lemon/lime flavours, gently sweet, crisp and rich. The 2010 vintage (★★★★) is also light (11 per cent alcohol) and vivacious, with lemon/lime flavours, a hint of apricots, plentiful sweetness (32 grams/litre of residual sugar) and excellent intensity.

Vintage	09	08	07	06	05	04
WR	6	5	6	6	NM	5
DRINK	10-11	10-11	P	P	NM	P

MED $19 V+

Hudson RPM Martinborough Riesling ★★☆

Grown south of Martinborough, the 2008 vintage (★★★) is fresh and gently sweet, with mouthfilling body and decent depth of lemony, appley flavours.

MED/DRY $22 –V

Hudson Wharekaka Martinborough Dry Riesling (★★★)
The 2008 vintage (★★★) is a full-bodied style (13 per cent alcohol), with citrusy, slightly minerally flavours, basically dry, showing a touch of complexity and some development.

DRY $22 –V

Huia Marlborough Riesling ★★★☆
Zingy and lively, the 2008 vintage (★★★☆) is a fresh, medium-bodied wine (12.5 per cent alcohol) with minimal sweetness (5 grams/litre of residual sugar), balanced acidity, and very good harmony and depth.

Vintage	08
WR	6
Drink	10-19

MED/DRY $28 –V

Hunter's Marlborough Riesling ★★★★
This wine is consistently good – and good value. The 2009 vintage (★★★★☆) was picked at 21 brix in the Wairau Valley. Lemon-scented, it is a full-bodied, dryish style (5 grams/litre of residual sugar) with very rich, citrusy flavours, good acid backbone and a long, finely poised finish. Very fresh, lively and punchy, it should mature well.

Vintage	09	08	07	06	05	04
WR	6	6	6	6	6	5
Drink	10-14	10-12	10-11	P	P	P

MED/DRY $20 V+

Hurunui River Riesling ★★★☆
Grown north-west of Waipara, at Hawarden, in North Canterbury, the 2008 vintage (★★★★) is delicious now, with rich, gently sweet, citrusy, limey flavours, good acid spine, a hint of marmalade adding richness, and bottle-aged complexity. The 2009 (★★★) is youthful, with lemony, appley flavours, slightly peachy and well-balanced, and a crisp, dryish finish.

MED/DRY $20 AV

Isabel Marlborough Dry Riesling ★★★☆
The 2007 vintage (★★★☆) was estate-grown and fermented almost to full dryness (4 grams/litre of residual sugar). It has good body and carries the dry style well, with strong, fresh flavours, rounded for Riesling.

Vintage	08	07
WR	6	6
Drink	10-17	10-14

DRY $20 AV

Jack's Canyon Waipara Classic Riesling (★★★☆)
From Waipara Springs, the 2009 vintage (★★★☆) is an attractively scented, medium-bodied wine with fresh, gently sweet, lemon/apple flavours, lively and strong. It's drinking well now.

MED/DRY $15 V+

John Forrest Collection Riesling ★★★★★

The 2006 vintage (★★★★★) is very intense and refined. Grown at two sites in the Brancott and Wairau valleys, it was picked from low-yielding vines (4 to 6.7 tonnes per hectare) and stop-fermented in a medium-dry style (12 grams/litre of residual sugar). Finely structured, with great delicacy, it has a scented, floral bouquet and fresh, pure lemon/apple flavours, slightly minerally, intense and harmonious. Tasted in mid-2010, it's drinking superbly, building great complexity and length.

Vintage	06
WR	6
Drink	10-20

MED/DRY $50 –V

Johner Estate Wairarapa Riesling ★★★☆

The 2009 vintage (★★★★) is a refined wine, fresh and vibrantly fruity, with ripe, citrusy, faintly honeyed flavours, good acid spine, a gentle splash of sweetness, and excellent harmony. It's already delicious. The 2010 (★★★☆) is finely poised for easy drinking. Fresh and very youthful, it's a medium-bodied wine with citrusy flavours, hints of passionfruit and spices, and an off-dry finish.

MED/DRY $16 V+

Kaimira Estate Brightwater Riesling ★★★★

This wine typically ages well. The 2009 vintage (★★★★) is fleshy and ripe, full-bodied and dryish (7.6 grams/litre of residual sugar), with fresh grapefruit-like flavours, a hint of spice, lively acidity, and impressive depth and harmony.

Vintage	09	08	07	06	05
WR	6	7	5	6	5
Drink	10-15	10-13	10-12	10-11	P

MED/DRY $20 V+

Kingsmill Tippet's Race Riesling ★★★★

The 2008 vintage (★★★★) is a single-vineyard Central Otago wine, hand-picked at Bendigo. It's a tightly structured, dryish style (6 grams/litre of residual sugar), full-bodied and still youthful, with crisp, citrusy, appley, slightly minerally flavours, showing good intensity and vigour. The 2009 (★★★★) is mouthfilling (13 per cent alcohol), with citrusy, appley, slightly spicy flavours, showing excellent depth and balance, a sliver of sweetness and obvious potential. Open mid-2011+.

MED/DRY $25 AV

Konrad Marlborough Riesling ★★★☆

Estate-grown in the Waihopai Valley, the 2009 vintage (★★☆) was made in a medium-dry style (6.6 grams/litre of residual sugar). Finely balanced, it has fresh, vibrant flavours, lemony, appley and limey, and very good harmony and depth.

Vintage	09	08	07	06	05	04
WR	5	4	4	6	6	5
Drink	10-15	10-12	10-11	10-11	P	P

MED/DRY $18 V+

Kurow Village Waitaki Valley Riesling (★★★☆)

The 2008 vintage (★★★☆) is a light to medium-bodied wine, attractively scented, with citrusy, gently sweet flavours (16.7 grams/litre of residual sugar), slightly minerally and crisp. Drink now or cellar.

MED $20 AV

Lake Chalice Falcon Vineyard Marlborough Riesling ★★★☆

Grown in the company's Falcon Vineyard at Rapaura, the 2009 vintage (★★★☆) is a medium style (27 grams/litre of residual sugar), light-bodied (10.5 per cent alcohol), with fresh, strong grapefruit, apple and lemon flavours, showing good varietal character, and a smooth finish. Enjoyable from the start.

MED $20 AV

Lawson's Dry Hills Marlborough Riesling ★★★★

Here's a chance to buy a dry style of Riesling with some bottle development. Grown in the Waihopai Valley, the 2007 vintage (★★★★) is bright, light lemon/green, with a slightly toasty fragrance, a minerally streak and lemon, lime and toast flavours showing good complexity.

Vintage	08	07	06	05	04
WR	7	6	7	6	6
Drink	10-12	P	P	P	P

MED/DRY $20 V+

Leaning Rock Central Otago Riesling (★★★☆)

Estate-grown at Alexandra, the 2008 vintage (★★★☆) is crisp, with very good depth of grapefruit, slight peach and marmalade flavours. Gently sweet, with toasty, bottle-aged notes starting to emerge, it's a drink-now or cellaring proposition.

MED/DRY $25 –V

Leaning Rock Omen Central Otago Late Harvest Riesling (★★★☆)

Estate-grown at Alexandra and harvested in early June with a 'hint' of botrytis, the 2006 vintage (★★★☆) is a scented, light to medium-bodied wine. It offers very good depth of citrusy, slightly limey flavour, plentiful sweetness (36 grams/litre of residual sugar), a hint of marmalade, and some bottle-aged complexity. It's drinking well now.

MED $20 (375ML) AV

Locharburn Central Otago Riesling (★★★★)

Grown in the Cromwell Basin, the 2010 vintage (★★★★) was hand-picked and briefly lees-aged in tanks. Showing obvious potential, it's a medium-dry style (11 grams/litre of residual sugar), very fresh and crisp, with lemon, apple and slight spice flavours that build well across the palate. Very racy and youthful, with good poise, delicacy and intensity, it's a stylish wine, best opened 2012+.

Vintage	10
WR	6
Drink	10-13

MED/DRY $20 V+

Loopline Riesling (★★★★)

Grown at Opaki, near Masterton, in the northern Wairarapa, the 2009 vintage (★★★★) has a scented, lemony bouquet. Medium-bodied, it is fresh, citrusy and limey, with a touch of sweetness, appetising acidity, and excellent delicacy and length.

MED/DRY $21 V+

Maimai Creek Hawke's Bay Riesling ★★★

The 2009 vintage (★★☆) is medium-bodied, with crisp, ripe flavours, showing some early development, and a hint of sweetness. Best drinking 2010–11.

MED/DRY $20 –V

Main Divide Waipara Valley Riesling ★★★★

From Pegasus Bay, this is a bargain. The 2009 vintage (★★★★) is scented, fresh and poised, with strong lemon, lime and nectarine flavours, a splash of sweetness (30 grams/litre of residual sugar) and good acid spine. Deliberately made in a slightly *spritzig* style (to accentuate freshness), it has good vigour and intensity.

Vintage	09	08	07
WR	7	7	7
Drink	10-17	10-15	10-15

MED $20 V+

Marble Point Hanmer Springs Riesling Classic – see Sweet White Wines

Marble Point Hanmer Springs Riesling Dry ★★★★

The 2008 vintage (★★★★), grown in North Canterbury, is a Germanic style – scented, finely balanced and distinctly lemony, with excellent varietal character, purity and depth. Made in an off-dry style, it's a drink-now or cellaring proposition. The 2009 (★★★★) is weighty and fleshy, with strong, lemony flavours, moderate acidity and a dryish (5 grams/litre of residual sugar), finely balanced finish.

Vintage	09	08
WR	6	6
Drink	12-15	11-13

MED/DRY $21 V+

Margrain Proprietors Selection Riesling ★★★☆

Tightly structured and minerally, the 2009 vintage (★★★★), grown in Martinborough, is medium-bodied, with a splash of sweetness (12 grams/litre of residual sugar) and citrusy, slightly peachy flavours, showing good intensity. Lively, with firm acid spine, it has good aging potential.

Vintage	09	08
WR	6	6
Drink	10-16	10-17

MED/DRY $24 –V

Margrain River's Edge Martinborough Riesling (★★★☆)

Already enjoyable, the 2009 vintage (★★★☆) is a medium style (20 grams/litre of residual sugar) with fresh, ripe, peachy, slightly spicy flavours, showing very good depth, and lively acidity. Drink now or cellar.

Vintage	09
WR	6
Drink	10-13

`MED $20 AV`

Martinborough Vineyard Bruno Riesling – see Sweet White Wines

Martinborough Vineyard Jackson Block Riesling ★★★★

The 2009 vintage (★★★★), from 19-year-old vines in the Jackson Vineyard, near the winery, was hand-picked, with no botrytis influence. Daringly dry (4 grams/litre of residual sugar), it is full-bodied, with fresh, vibrant, lemon and apple flavours, crisp, racy and strong. It's well worth cellaring.

`DRY $26 –V`

Martinborough Vineyard Manu Riesling ★★★★

The 2009 vintage (★★★★) was grown in the Jackson Vineyard. A distinctly medium style (27 grams/litre of residual sugar), harvested with a gentle botrytis influence, it is fresh, with ripe lemon, apple and spice flavours, finely balanced, delicate and lingering.

`MED $26 –V`

Maude Mt Maude Family Vineyard Dry Riesling (★★★★)

Grown in the Mount Maude Vineyard, at Wanaka, the 2010 vintage (★★★★) shows obvious potential. Off-dry (7 grams/litre of residual sugar), it is fresh and full-bodied, with ripe peachy flavours, a minerally streak and good intensity.

`MED/DRY $20 V+`

Maude Mt Maude Family Vineyard Riesling – see Sweet White Wines

Mills Reef Hawke's Bay Riesling ★★★

The 2009 vintage (★★★) is a full-bodied, dry style (4 grams/litre of residual sugar), with good depth of lemony, slightly spicy flavours and a fresh, crisp finish.

`DRY $18 AV`

Millton Opou Vineyard Riesling ★★★★

Typically finely scented, with rich, lemony, often honeyed flavours, this is the country's northernmost fine-quality Riesling. Grown in Gisborne (some of the vines are over 25 years old), it is gently sweet, in a softer, less racy style than the classic Marlborough wines. The grapes, grown organically in the Opou Vineyard at Manutuke, are hand-harvested over a month at three stages of ripening, usually culminating in a final pick of botrytis-affected fruit. The 2008 vintage (★★★★) is gently floral, with citrus-fruit, apple and passionfruit flavours showing very good delicacy and depth. Light (8.5 per cent alcohol) and lively, with abundant sweetness (39 grams/litre of residual sugar), it's a drink-now or cellaring proposition.

Vintage	08	07	06	05
WR	7	5	6	6
Drink	10-14	10-12	P	P

`MED $26 –V`

Misha's Vineyard Limelight Riesling ★★★★☆

The 2009 vintage (★★★★☆) is a single-vineyard wine from Bendigo, in Central Otago. It was mostly handled in tanks, but 17 per cent was fermented with indigenous yeasts in old French oak casks. A medium style (26 grams/litre of residual sugar), it is finely scented and beautifully balanced, with good intensity of fresh lemon/lime flavours, a touch of complexity, and great drink-young appeal.

Vintage	09	08
WR	7	6
Drink	10-15	10-13

MED $26 AV

Misha's Vineyard Lyric Riesling (★★★★☆)

The off-dry (9 grams/litre of residual sugar) 2009 vintage (★★★★☆) was estate-grown at Bendigo, in Central Otago, and mostly tank-fermented; 18 per cent was fermented with indigenous yeasts in seasoned French oak casks. Very crisp, vibrant and youthful, it has excellent intensity of citrusy, limey flavours, with some peach and passionfruit notes, and very good harmony and length. Worth cellaring.

MED/DRY $26 AV

Mission Hawke's Bay Riesling ★★★☆

Mission's Rieslings offer good value. The 2010 vintage (★★★☆) is floral, fresh and lively, in a low-alcohol (10 per cent), distinctly medium style (19 grams/litre of residual sugar). Vibrantly fruity, with lemon and green-apple flavours, it shows good vigour and depth.

MED $17 V+

Momo Marlborough Riesling ★★★

From Seresin, the 2008 vintage (★★★) has a scented, lemony bouquet and gently sweet (12 grams/litre of residual sugar), citrusy flavours, balanced for easy drinking and showing good depth.

Vintage	08
WR	5
Drink	10-13

MED/DRY $19 AV

Mondillo Central Otago Riesling ★★★☆

Estate-grown at Bendigo, the 2009 vintage (★★★★) is medium-bodied, with excellent intensity of citrusy, slightly limey flavours, slightly sweet and youthful. Tightly structured, with firm acid spine, a hint of honey and a long, tight finish, it's well worth cellaring.

Vintage	09	08	07
WR	7	6	6
Drink	10-15	10-14	10-13

MED/DRY $25 –V

Montana Reserve Waipara Riesling ★★★☆

The easy-drinking, finely poised 2008 vintage (★★★) is a lemony, medium-bodied wine with a splash of sweetness (11.5 grams/litre of residual sugar), fresh, lively acidity and good but not great depth.

MED/DRY $24 –V

Montana South Island Riesling ★★★☆

This good-value wine has evolved from the long-popular Montana Marlborough Riesling, no longer produced. A blend of Waipara (mostly) and Marlborough grapes, the 2008 vintage (★★★☆) is intensely varietal, with very good depth of citrusy flavour, slightly sweet (13 grams/litre of residual sugar) and mouth-wateringly crisp.

MED/DRY $18 V+

Morton Estate Stone Creek Marlborough Riesling ★★★☆

Still on sale, the 2007 vintage (★★★) is a mouthfilling (14 per cent alcohol) wine with ripe, citrusy, peachy flavours and a slightly sweet, rounded finish. It's enjoyable now.

Vintage	07	06
WR	6	6
Drink	10-17	10-12

MED/DRY $21 AV

Morton Estate White Label Marlborough Riesling ★★☆

The 2007 vintage (★★☆) is slightly honeyed, with mouthfilling body (13.5 per cent alcohol) and peachy, slightly spicy flavours, showing some development. Ready; no rush.

Vintage	07	06
WR	6	6
Drink	10-16	10-12

DRY $18 –V

Mount Edward Central Otago Riesling ★★★★

The 2007 vintage (★★★★) is a single-vineyard wine from Lowburn, in the Cromwell Basin. It is finely textured and slightly sweet, with strong, citrusy flavours and a lingering finish. A tightly structured wine, it should mature well.

Vintage	07	06
WR	6	6
Drink	10-14	10-13

MED/DRY $25 AV

Mt Beautiful North Canterbury Riesling ★★★★

Grown at Cheviot, north of Waipara, the 2008 vintage (★★★★) is fleshy, mouthfilling and ripe, with excellent depth of medium-dry (11 grams/litre of residual sugar), grapefruit-like flavours and good texture and harmony. It's drinking well now.

MED/DRY $24 AV

Mt Difficulty Dry Riesling ★★★☆

Grown at Bannockburn, in Central Otago, this is a wine for purists – steely and austere in its youth, but rewarding (almost demanding) time. The 2008 vintage (★★★☆) carries the dry style well. Light and lively, it is lemony, slightly spicy and minerally, with good depth and immediacy.

DRY $25 –V

Mt Difficulty Target Gully Riesling ★★★★

Grown in the Target Gully Vineyard at Bannockburn, in Central Otago, the 2009 vintage (★★★★) is highly scented, with good intensity of lemon, apple and lime flavours, a distinct splash of sweetness (40 grams/litre of residual sugar) and fresh, tangy acidity. It's deliciously light and lively.

MED $25 AV

Mt Rosa Central Otago Riesling ★★★☆

Grown at Gibbston, the 2007 vintage (★★★★) is full of personality. A full-bodied, medium-dry style (8 grams/litre of residual sugar) with generous, citrusy, slightly earthy and spicy flavours and distinct overtones of Alsace, it offers great drinkability. The 2009 (★★★) is attractively scented, with satisfying depth of lemony, appley flavour, slightly sweet and crisp.

MED/DRY $22 AV

Muddy Water Dry Riesling ★★★★☆

The 2009 vintage (★★★★★) was hand-harvested at Waipara, hand-sorted to eliminate botrytis and fermented with indigenous yeasts to near dryness (5.4 grams/litre of residual sugar). Light lemon/green, it is medium to full-bodied, with highly concentrated, citrusy, limey flavours, very tight and finely poised, and a crisp, lasting finish. As a prospect for cellaring, it's all there.

Vintage	09	08
WR	7	7
Drink	10-20	10-15

MED/DRY $29 AV

Muddy Water Growers' Series James Hardwick Waipara Riesling ★★★★★

The 2009 vintage (★★★★☆) was hand-picked and fermented with indigenous yeasts. It's a rich, medium-dry style (12 grams/litre of residual sugar) with concentrated grapefruit and spice flavours, a hint of marmalade, minerally notes, good complexity and a crisp, long finish. Well worth cellaring.

Vintage	09	08
WR	7	6
Drink	10-19	10-18

MED/DRY $25 V+

Muddy Water Growers' Series Lough Vineyard Riesling (★★★★)

Grown at Waipara, the debut 2008 vintage (★★★★) was hand-picked and stop-fermented in a medium style (27 grams/litre of residual sugar). Ripely scented, with a hint of botrytis, it is mouthfilling (13 per cent alcohol) and ripe, with good complexity of citrusy, spicy, peachy, slightly honeyed flavours, well-rounded and generous. It's already delicious.

MED $18 V+

Muddy Water Riesling Unplugged – see Sweet White Wines

Muddy Water Waipara Riesling Reloaded (★★★★☆)

The distinctive 2009 vintage (★★★★☆) was fermented and matured on its yeast lees for eight months in old French oak puncheons. An unusually dry style (2.4 grams/litre of residual sugar), it is still very youthful, but carries the dry style well, with concentrated, ripe grapefruit and slight peach flavours, showing good complexity. Tight and minerally, crisp and long, it's full of promise; open 2012+.

Vintage	09
WR	7
Drink	10-22

DRY $35 –V

Mud House Waipara Riesling ★★★★

Estate-grown in The Mound Vineyard, the 2009 vintage (★★★★) is a fleshy, medium-dry style (11 grams/litre of residual sugar), with fresh, ripe, citrusy, limey flavours, hints of apricot and mandarin, and good acid spine. Best drinking mid-2011+.

MED/DRY $20 V+

Murdoch James Blue Rock Martinborough Riesling ★★★

The 2008 vintage (★★★) is a slightly sweet style (7.9 grams/litre of residual sugar), citrusy and crisp, with good varietal character and vigour and some toasty, bottle-aged notes emerging.

Vintage	08	07	06
WR	6	4	5
Drink	10-14	10-13	10-12

MED/DRY $20 –V

Neudorf Moutere Riesling ★★★★★

A copybook cool-climate style with excellent intensity, estate-grown at Upper Moutere. The 2009 vintage (★★★★★) was hand-picked in the Beuke Block, on a hill overlooking the Home Vineyard, and mostly lees-aged in tanks; 6 per cent was fermented with indigenous yeasts in an old barrel. It is light (9.2 per cent alcohol) and vivacious, with abundant sweetness (54 grams/litre of residual sugar) balanced by mouth-watering acidity, and lovely poise and intensity of citrusy, limey, slightly spicy flavours. It needs time; the 2005 vintage is superb now.

Vintage	09	08	07	06	05	04	03	02
WR	7	6	6	7	7	NM	6	5
Drink	10-18	10-17	10-17	10-16	10-15	NM	10-12	P

MED $28 V+

Northburn Station Central Otago Riesling ★★★☆

Grown at Northburn, on the eastern side of Lake Dunstan, the 2009 vintage (★★★☆) is a good, everyday-drinking style with fresh, citrusy aromas and flavours, a gentle splash of sweetness (14 grams/litre of residual sugar), a minerally streak and a crisp, finely balanced finish.

Vintage	09	08	07
WR	6	5	5
Drink	10-14	10-13	10-12

MED/DRY $22 AV

Northburn Station Jeweller's Shop Central Otago Riesling (★★☆)

A sweetish style (45 grams/litre of residual sugar), the 2009 vintage (★★☆) is light in body (10.5 per cent alcohol), with plenty of lemony flavour, but less floral than its stablemate (above).

MED $24 –V

Ohinemuri Estate Gisborne Riesling ★★★

Waikato winemaker Horst Hillerich usually, although not always, draws his Riesling grapes from Gisborne. The 2008 vintage (★★★), grown at Patutahi and briefly oak-matured, is citrusy, slightly honeyed and flavoursome, with a touch of sweetness (10 grams/litre of residual sugar) and a well-rounded finish. It's an easy-drinking style, enjoyable now.

Vintage	08	07
WR	6	5
Drink	09-12	09-12

MED/DRY $20 –V

Old Coach Road Nelson Riesling ★★★☆

Skilfully crafted for easy drinking, the 2009 vintage (★★★☆) from Seifried is a medium-dry style (14 grams/litre of residual sugar), very fresh and vibrant, with plenty of lemony, appley flavour, a hint of passionfruit, and good acidity to balance its appealing splash of sweetness. The 2010 (★★★) is a crisp, medium-bodied wine with moderately concentrated lemon/lime flavours, slightly sweet, fresh and lively.

Vintage	10	09	08
WR	6	6	7
Drink	10-15	10-14	10-12

MED/DRY $17 V+

Olssen's Annieburn Riesling (★★★★★)

The debut 2009 vintage (★★★★★) is a medium style, vibrant, light (10.5 per cent alcohol) and very intense, with fresh, searching, citrusy, appley, slightly peachy flavours, threaded with mouth-wateringly crisp acidity. Finely poised, it's already highly expressive, but should also reward cellaring.

Vintage	10	09
WR	7	7
Drink	10-18	10-17

MED $29 V+

Olssen's Central Otago Riesling Dry (★★★)

The 2009 vintage (★★★) was estate-grown at Bannockburn. Hand-picked at 23.4 brix and lees-aged in tanks, it's an off-dry style (6.5 grams/litre of residual sugar), with lemony, appley aromas and flavours, fresh and crisp, but is less concentrated than its stablemate (above).

MED/DRY $29 –V

Omihi Road Waipara Riesling ★★★★

From Torlesse, this is typically a scented, vibrant North Canterbury wine with pure, ripe, lemon/lime flavours, showing excellent delicacy and depth. (The 2007 is a medium-dry style, with 8 grams/litre of residual sugar.)

Vintage 07
WR 6
Drink 12-19

MED/DRY $20 V+

Opihi Vineyard South Canterbury Riesling ★★★☆

Estate-grown and hand-picked, the 2009 vintage (★★★☆) is light and lively, with strong, crisp lemon, apple and lime flavours and a slightly sweet (7.5 grams/litre of residual sugar), tightly structured finish. Still youthful, it's worth cellaring.

MED/DRY $22 AV

Orinoco Vineyards Nelson Riesling ★★★☆

The skilfully made, very harmonious 2008 vintage (★★★★) is a medium-dry style (12 grams/litre of residual sugar), with low alcohol (10.5 per cent) but plenty of body. Immediately appealing, it is fresh and crisp, with strong lemon, lime and slight passionfruit flavours, intense and tangy.

MED $19 V+

Ostler Blue House Vines Waitaki Valley Riesling ★★★☆

From the Blue House Vineyard, in Grants Road, the 2009 vintage (★★★☆) is a tightly structured young wine, with gentle sweetness (9 grams/litre of residual sugar) and very good depth of lemony, appley flavours, slightly minerally and spicy. It's well worth cellaring; open 2012+.

MED/DRY $27 –V

Palliser Estate Martinborough Riesling ★★★★

In top vintages, this is a beautifully scented wine with intense, slightly sweet flavours and a racy finish. Grown on the Martinborough Terrace, it typically matures well. The 2008 (★★★★) is an instantly appealing, medium-bodied wine with fresh, strong lemon and lime flavours, slightly sweet and crisp, a hint of passionfruit, and excellent depth and harmony. Already delicious, it's a great buy.

MED/DRY $16 V+

Paritua Central Otago Riesling ★★★

The 2008 vintage (★★★) from this Hawke's Bay-based producer is light-bodied (11.5 per cent alcohol) and lemony, with crisp, slightly sweet (12 grams/litre of residual sugar) flavours, fresh, lively and balanced for easy drinking.

Vintage 08
WR 6
Drink 10-16

MED/DRY $28 –V

Pegasus Bay Aria Late Harvest Riesling – see Sweet White Wines

Pegasus Bay Bel Canto Riesling Dry ★★★★

The 2008 vintage was the first Riesling Dry to be labelled Bel Canto ('Beautiful Singing'). Late-harvested at Waipara from mature vines and produced with some influence from noble rot and indigenous yeasts, but not barrel-aged, the 2009 (★★★★★) is a rich, dryish (8 grams/litre of residual sugar), powerful wine (14 per cent alcohol), with notably intense, citrusy flavours. Lemon-scented, with a hint of honey, it is complex, slightly spicy and minerally, with good acid spine and a lasting, basically dry finish. It shows great individuality and poise; open 2012+.

Vintage	09	08	07
WR	7	7	7
Drink	10-14	10-12	P

MED/DRY $32 –V

Pegasus Bay Riesling ★★★★★

This is classy stuff. Estate-grown at Waipara, in North Canterbury, it is richly fragrant and thrillingly intense, with flavours of citrus fruits and honey, complex and luscious. Based on mature vines and stop-fermented in a distinctly medium style, it breaks into full stride at two or three years old and most vintages keep well for a decade. The 2009 vintage (★★★★★) is bright, light yellow/green, with a musky perfume. Mouthfilling, it has concentrated grapefruit, spice and slight honey flavours, with a splash of sweetness (26 grams/litre of residual sugar), fresh, appetising acidity and lovely balance and richness, but is still very youthful; open mid-2011+.

Vintage	09	08	07	06	05	04	03	02
WR	7	7	7	6	6	7	6	6
Drink	10-20	10-19	10-18	10-16	10-16	10-15	10-14	10-12

MED $28 V+

Peregrine Central Otago Dry Riesling ★★★★

Grown in the Cromwell Basin, the fresh, tightly structured 2008 vintage (★★★★★) is unfolding well. Minerally and dryish (5.9 grams/litre of residual sugar), it has intense, lemony, slightly spicy flavours, showing excellent vigour and richness.

MED/DRY $22 V+

Peregrine Rastasburn Riesling ★★★★

Hand-picked in the Cromwell Basin, this Central Otago wine is typically slightly sweet, with a scented bouquet and excellent depth, delicacy and harmony. Made in a medium style, it matures gracefully for at least five years, acquiring a complex, toasty, honeyed richness.

MED $22 V+

Peter Yealands Marlborough Riesling (★★★)

The tautly structured 2009 vintage (★★★) was estate-grown at Seaview, in the Awatere Valley. Fresh and crisp, it has strong lemon/lime flavours, with a distinct splash of sweetness (14 grams/litre of residual sugar), balanced by firm, steely acidity. Best drinking 2011+.

MED/DRY $19 AV

Picnic by Two Paddocks Central Otago Riesling (★★★☆)

The 2009 vintage (★★★☆) is a very enjoyable, drink-young style. Medium-bodied, it is lemony, slightly sweet (14 grams/litre of residual sugar) and crisp, with good freshness, balance and vivacity.

MED/DRY $22 AV

Pond Paddock Harvest Moon Riesling ★★★

The 2007 vintage (★★★) was grown in Te Muna Road, Martinborough and harvested at 17.5 brix. It's a tightly structured wine, light to medium-bodied (11.5 per cent alcohol), with a splash of sweetness (13 grams/litre of residual sugar) and fresh, crisp, green-apple flavours.

MED/DRY $20 –V

Prophet's Rock Central Otago Dry Riesling ★★★★

The 2008 vintage (★★★★) was hand-harvested at Pisa, fermented with indigenous yeasts and lees-aged. Building up well with bottle-age, it is a medium-bodied, dryish, intensely varietal wine with strong, citrusy, slightly appley and spicy flavours, a minerally streak and a long, racy finish. It should be long-lived.

MED/DRY $30 –V

Pyramid Valley Vineyards Growers Collection Lebecca Vineyard Marlborough Riesling (★★★★)

The 2007 vintage (★★★★) was hand-picked at Rapaura, fermented with indigenous yeasts and lees-aged for eight months. It's a light (11 per cent alcohol), medium style (34 grams/litre of residual sugar) with strong, ripe citrusy flavours, finely balanced for current enjoyment.

MED $27 –V

Pyramid Valley Vineyards Growers Collection Riverbrook Vineyard Marlborough Riesling (★★★☆)

Grown in the Brancott Valley, the 2007 vintage (★★★☆) was hand-picked (15 per cent of the fruit was late-harvested, with noble rot) and fermented with indigenous yeasts. It's a medium style (20 grams/litre of residual sugar) with concentrated, lemony, slightly honeyed flavours.

MED $27 –V

Pyramid Valley Vineyards Growers Collection Rose Vineyard Marlborough Riesling (★★★☆)

Hand-picked at Rapaura, the 2007 vintage (★★★☆) was fermented with indigenous yeasts in tanks and old oak casks. Mouthfilling and dryish (9 grams/litre of residual sugar), it's a fleshy, very individual wine, not highly scented, but generous, ripe and well-rounded.

MED/DRY $27 –V

Redoubt Hill Vineyard Nelson Riesling ★★★★

Fleshy and ripe, the 2008 vintage (★★★★) is a single-vineyard wine, grown at Motueka and fermented to dryness (3 grams/litre of residual sugar). It's a classy wine, ripely scented, with good body and depth of citrusy, minerally flavours, showing excellent delicacy and concentration. Dry but not austere, finely poised, tight and immaculate, it should mature well. The 2010 (★★★★) is full of promise. Lemony, limey and minerally, it shows good intensity, with excellent freshness, vigour and length. Open mid-2011+.

Vintage	08	DRY $29 –V
WR	6	
Drink	10-12	

Ribbonwood Marlborough Riesling ★★★

Balanced for easy drinking, the 2010 vintage (★★★) is medium-bodied, with fresh, lemony scents and a splash of sweetness (9 grams/litre of residual sugar) amid its citrusy, slightly spicy flavours. (From Framingham.)

Vintage	10	MED/DRY $18 AV
WR	5	
Drink	10-13	

Richmond Plains Nelson Riesling (★★★★)

The 2009 vintage (★★★★) is fresh and vibrant, with good intensity of lemony, limey flavour, slightly sweet (8 grams/litre of residual sugar) and crisp. It's a very harmonious wine, likely to age well.

Vintage	09	MED/DRY $20 V+
WR	6	
Drink	10-14	

Rimu Grove Nelson Riesling (★★★★☆)

The debut 2009 vintage (★★★★☆) was grown on the Waimea Plains and in Moutere clay gravels, hand-picked, and tank-fermented with some use of indigenous yeasts. Rich and finely balanced, it's a medium style (25 grams/litre of residual sugar) with lemon, apple and grapefruit flavours, showing excellent poise, delicacy and depth. Minerally and slightly spicy, it's already delicious.

Vintage	09	MED $29 AV
WR	7	
Drink	10-17	

Rippon Jeunesse Young Vines Riesling ★★★★

The 2009 vintage (★★★★) was estate-grown at Lake Wanaka, in Central Otago. A tightly structured, medium-dry style, it has vibrant grapefruit and lime flavours, showing excellent vigour and intensity, good acid spine and a distinct minerality. It's already very expressive and enjoyable.

MED/DRY $25 AV

Rippon Riesling ★★★★★

This single-vineyard, Lake Wanaka, Central Otago wine is a distinctly cool-climate style, steely, long-lived and penetratingly flavoured. Based on mature vines, the 2009 vintage (★★★★★) was fermented with indigenous yeasts and given extended lees-aging. Full of personality, it's a Mosel-like wine, medium-bodied (11 per cent alcohol), with poised, incisive lemon and apple flavours, woven with mouth-watering acidity, a sliver of sweetness and a very long finish.

Vintage	09	08	07	06	05	04
WR	7	7	7	6	7	6
Drink	10-18	10-17	10-17	10-16	10-15	P

MED/DRY $32 AV

Riverby Estate Marlborough Riesling ★★★

The 2009 vintage (★★★) is a dry style with fresh lemon, apple and lime flavours, crisp and minerally. A tight, youthful wine, it should reward cellaring; open mid-2011+.

DRY $20 –V

Riverby Estate Sali's Block Marlborough Riesling ★★★☆

Balanced for easy drinking, the 2009 vintage (★★★☆) is a medium style (20 grams/litre of residual sugar) with satisfying depth of fresh, lively lemon, apple and lime flavours, crisp acidity and good harmony. Drink now or cellar.

MED $20 AV

Rockburn Central Otago Parkburn Riesling ★★★☆

Estate-grown in the Cromwell Basin, the 2008 vintage (★★★☆) has crisp, lemony, limey flavours, slightly sweet (15 grams/litre of residual sugar) and tangy. Worth cellaring.

Vintage	09	08	07	06
WR	5	5	7	6
Drink	11-20	10-15	10-15	10-13

MED $24 –V

Ruby Bay Vineyard Nelson Riesling ★★★

The 2009 vintage (★★★) is a Nelson wine, estate-grown, hand-picked and lees-aged. It's a light-bodied style with good varietal character and depth of lemony, appley, slightly spicy flavours and a dry (4.5 grams/litre of residual sugar) finish.

Vintage	09
WR	4
Drink	10-12

DRY $24 –V

Saddleback Central Otago Riesling (★★★☆)

From Peregrine, the 2008 vintage (★★★☆) offers fine value. It's a medium-bodied style (12 per cent alcohol) with fresh, vibrant, citrusy, slightly spicy flavours and a hint of apricot, balanced for easy drinking.

MED/DRY $18 V+

Saint Clair Marlborough Riesling ★★★☆

This is typically an attractive wine, grown in the Dog Point area, on the south side of the Wairau Valley. The 2008 vintage (★★★) is a medium-bodied, slightly sweet style (8 grams/litre of residual sugar), lightly floral, with satisfying depth of citrusy, appley flavours threaded with fresh acidity.

Vintage	08	07	06
WR	6	6	6
Drink	10-11	10-11	P

MED/DRY $21 AV

Saint Clair Pioneer Block 9 Big John Riesling ★★★★

Grown in the lower Brancott Valley, Marlborough, the 2008 vintage (★★★★) is a punchy, single-vineyard wine with moderate alcohol (10 per cent) and plentiful sweetness (48 grams/litre of residual sugar). Light-bodied, with strong lemon/apple aromas and flavours and fresh, racy acidity, it's enjoyable from the start.

Vintage	08	07
WR	7	7
Drink	10-13	10-12

MED $25 AV

Saint Clair Vicar's Choice Marlborough Riesling ★★★

The 2008 vintage (★★☆) is a slightly honeyed, medium-bodied wine, crisp and slightly sweet (7 grams/litre of residual sugar), with a distinct touch of botrytis. It's best drunk young.

Vintage	08	07	06
WR	6	6	6
Drink	10-11	P	P

MED/DRY $19 AV

Scott Base Central Otago Riesling (★★★★)

From mature vines grown at Cromwell, the 2009 vintage (★★★★) is a single-vineyard wine, handled in tanks. Medium-bodied, it shows good sugar/acid balance (13 grams/litre of residual sugar), with a crisp, minerally streak and strong, ripe citrusy aromas and flavours. (From Allan Scott.)

Vintage	09
WR	6
Drink	10-19

MED/DRY $26 –V

Seifried Nelson Riesling ★★★☆

Seifried is a key pioneer of Riesling in New Zealand. From Redwood Valley vines up to 26 years old and younger vines at Brightwater, the 2009 vintage (★★★☆) is full-bodied, with very good depth of lemon/lime flavours, fresh and crisp, in a finely poised, slightly sweet style. The 2010 (★★★☆) is medium to full-bodied, with fresh, lemony, limey flavours, appetising acidity, a splash of sweetness (12 grams/litre of residual sugar) and very good depth and harmony.

Vintage	10	09	08
WR	6	6	6
Drink	10-15	10-14	10-12

MED/DRY $19 V+

Seresin Memento Riesling ★★★★

Harvested by hand from mature vines in the Home Vineyard at Renwick, in Marlborough, this is a medium-sweet style. The 2009 vintage (★★★★), certified BioGro, is light (10 per cent alcohol), with good intensity of fresh lemon/lime flavours, a minerally streak, and a racy, crisp, finely poised (38 grams/litre of residual sugar) finish. It should mature well.

Vintage	09	08
WR	7	5
Drink	10-18	10-18

MED $28 –V

Shaky Bridge Central Otago Riesling ★★★☆

Estate-grown and hand-picked at Alexandra, the 2009 vintage (★★★☆) is a dryish style (5 grams/litre of residual sugar), lemony, slightly spicy and flavoursome, with fresh acidity and good harmony. Drink now onwards.

Vintage	09
WR	6
Drink	11-13

MED/DRY $20 AV

Shipwreck Bay Riesling (★★★)

From Okahu Estate, the 2008 vintage (★★★) is a Marlborough wine, full-bodied (13.5 per cent alcohol) and citrusy, with hints of passionfruit and spice, and a slightly sweet, crisp finish. It's ready for drinking.

MED/DRY $18 AV

Sileni Cellar Selection Hawke's Bay Riesling ★★★

The 2008 vintage (★★★) is enjoyable now. A dryish style (5.4 grams/litre of residual sugar), it has ripe citrus and tropical-fruit flavours, crisp and slightly toasty.

Vintage	08	07	06
WR	5	6	5
Drink	10-12	10-12	P

MED/DRY $20 –V

Sileni The Don Hawke's Bay Riesling ★★★★

One of the region's finest Rieslings yet, the 2007 (★★★★☆) is a single-vineyard wine, grown close to the winery in The Triangle. Hand-picked, tank-fermented and lees-aged, it's an off-dry style, finely balanced, with intense lemon/lime aromas and flavours, racy and long. There is no 2008. The 2009 vintage (★★★☆) is almost dry (6.3 grams/litre of residual sugar), with tight, lemony, appley flavours, slightly honeyed, crisp and strong.

Vintage	09	08	07
WR	5	NM	7
Drink	11-16	NM	10-14

MED/DRY $25 AV

Soma Nelson Riesling ★★★★

The great-value 2007 vintage (★★★★) was 'made in the Alsace style of natural stabilisation over time, approximately one year, until bottling'. Grown at Mapua and on the Waimea Plains, it is lemon-scented, with gently sweet (15 grams/litre of residual sugar) grapefruit and lime flavours that show lovely purity, poise and length. It's delicious now.

Vintage	07	06	05
WR	7	6	6
Drink	10-17	10-13	10-12

MED $17 V+

Southern Lighthouse Nelson Sauvignon Blanc (★★☆)

From Anchorage, the 2009 vintage (★★☆) is an easy-drinking style, medium-bodied, with moderate depth of crisp, citrusy, limey flavours.

DRY $17 –V

Spinyback Nelson Riesling ★★★☆

Good value from Waimea Estate. The 2008 vintage (★★★☆) has citrusy, appley, limey flavours, vibrant and strong, and a splash of sweetness (13.7 grams/litre of residual sugar) balanced by zesty acidity. The 2009 (★★★) is crisp and lively, with lemony flavours, hints of passionfruit and spice, slight sweetness and satisfying depth.

MED/DRY $14 V+

Spring Creek Estate Marlborough Riesling ★★★☆

Grown at Rapaura, the 2009 vintage (★★★) is freshly scented and off-dry (6.3 grams/litre of residual sugar), with mouthfilling body and plenty of lemony, limey, slightly spicy flavour.

Vintage	09
WR	5
Drink	10-12

MED/DRY $15 V+

Spy Valley Envoy Dry Marlborough Riesling (★★★★)

Already drinking well, the 2008 vintage (★★★★) was hand-picked and fermented and aged for seven months in a large oak oval. It shows good concentration and complexity, with fresh, strong grapefruit and lime flavours, and a faintly honeyed, dryish (7.2 grams/litre of residual sugar) finish. Drink now or cellar.

Vintage	08
WR	7
Drink	10-14

MED/DRY $30 –V

Spy Valley Envoy Marlborough Riesling – see Sweet White Wines

Spy Valley Marlborough Riesling ★★★★

The 2009 vintage (★★★☆) is an off-dry style (12 grams/litre of residual sugar) with citrus and tropical-fruit flavours showing some spicy, slightly honeyed notes and very good depth.

Vintage	10	09	08	07	06
WR	6	6	6	7	6
Drink	10-14	10-14	10-12	10-11	P

MED $23 AV

Staete Landt Marlborough Riesling Dry ★★★★

The 2009 vintage (★★★★) was estate-grown at Rapaura, hand-picked, fermented in old French oak puncheons and then cask-aged for a further six months. Dry (less than 3 grams/litre of residual sugar), full-bodied and finely textured, with a bare hint of oak amid its strong, ripe, grapefruit-like flavours, which show good complexity, it's a distinctive wine, worth cellaring.

Vintage	09	08
WR	7	7
Drink	10-17	10-14

MED/DRY $29 –V

Stafford Lane Estate Riesling ★★★

The 2009 vintage (★★) is an off-dry Nelson wine, light, crisp, lemony and appley, but it lacks flavour depth.

MED/DRY $18 AV

Stoneleigh Marlborough Riesling ★★★★

Deliciously fragrant in its youth, this is typically a refined wine from Pernod Ricard NZ with good body, incisive flavours and a crisp, long finish. The 2009 vintage (★★★★) is fresh and elegant, with finely balanced, gently sweet lemon, apple and passionfruit flavours, showing excellent ripeness, delicacy and depth.

Vintage	09	08
WR	6	5
Drink	10-12	P

MED/DRY $23 AV

Summerhouse Marlborough Dry Riesling ★★★☆

Estate-grown and hand-picked, the 2010 vintage (★★★★) is fully dry (only 2 grams/litre of residual sugar) but still finely balanced, with mouthfilling body and vibrant, ripe, citrusy, spicy flavours, showing a hint of passionfruit. Still very fresh and youthful, it should mature well; open 2012+.

DRY $27 –V

Te Kairanga East Plain Martinborough Riesling ★★★★

A consistently good wine, priced right. The 2008 vintage (★★★★) is floral, vibrant and rich, with lemony, limey, slightly minerally flavours, a touch of sweetness (7.8 grams/litre of residual sugar) and lively acidity. Drink now or cellar. (The 2009 is called Te Kairanga Estate Riesling.)

Vintage	09	08	07	06
WR	6	7	7	7
Drink	10-19	10-15	10-14	10-12

MED/DRY $21 V+

Te Mania Nelson Riesling ★★★★
A bargain. Full of youthful vigour, the 2009 vintage (★★★★) is attractively scented. Fresh, punchy and woven with crisp acidity, it's a slightly sweet style with citrusy flavours, hints of passionfruit and spice, and excellent delicacy and depth.

Vintage	09
WR	6
Drink	10-14

MED/DRY $19 V+

Te Mara Central Otago Riesling (★★★☆)
Launched from the 2009 vintage (★★★☆), this single-vineyard wine is grown in the Cromwell Basin. Floral, it's medium-bodied, with fresh, vibrant lemon and apple flavours, a touch of sweetness (6.8 grams/litre of residual sugar), firm acid spine and good length. It should age well.

MED/DRY $26 –V

Terrace Edge Waipara Valley Riesling ★★★★
Fine value. The aromatic, zingy 2009 vintage (★★★★) was hand-picked and fermented with indigenous yeasts. Fleshy and crisp, it's a medium style (17 grams/litre of residual sugar), with strong lemon and lime flavours, finely balanced and youthful.

MED $19 V+

Terrain Marlborough Riesling (★★☆)
Sold in New World supermarkets, the 2007 vintage (★★☆) is an easy-drinking wine with lemony, slightly honeyed flavours and a gently sweet, rounded finish. Ready.

MED $13 V+

Thornbury Waipara Riesling (★★★☆)
From Villa Maria, the 2008 vintage (★★★☆) is medium-bodied (12 per cent alcohol), with ripe, citrusy, slightly spicy flavours, showing good depth, and a gentle splash of sweetness (8 grams/litre of residual sugar). Tasted prior to bottling (and so not rated), the 2009 looked promising, with tight, vibrant, lemony, crisp flavour, showing good intensity.

MED/DRY $21 AV

Three Paddles Martinborough Riesling ★★★☆
From Nga Waka, the 2009 vintage (★★★★) is very fresh and vibrant, with strong, citrusy, limey flavours, a hint of apricot, and a distinct splash of sweetness. It's a very harmonious wine, delicious young.

MED $18 V+

Timara Riesling ★★☆
The 2007 vintage (★★) from Pernod Ricard NZ is a regional blend with moderate depth of citrusy, slightly peachy flavours, woven with fresh acidity. It's a slightly sweet wine, offering plain, easy drinking.

MED/DRY $12 V+

Tohu Marlborough Riesling ★★★★
Hand-picked in the Waihopai Valley, the 2009 vintage (★★★★) is a fresh, vibrant, medium-dry style (10.8 grams/litre of residual sugar), showing good intensity of lemony, limey, slightly minerally flavour. Finely balanced, with excellent delicacy and length, it offers good value.

MED/DRY $19 V+

Toi Toi Marlborough Riesling (★★★★)
Tightly structured and very youthful, the 2009 vintage (★★★★) has strong lemon and lime flavours and a mouth-watering, crisp finish. Dryish (5.6 grams/litre of residual sugar), it's a high-acid style, elegant and minerally.

MED/DRY $21 V+

Torlesse Waipara Riesling ★★★☆
The 2009 vintage (★★★☆) is a good drink-young style, medium-bodied, with faintly honeyed, citrusy, slightly peachy flavours, a gentle splash of sweetness (16 grams/litre of residual sugar) and fresh acidity.

Vintage	09	08
WR	6	7
Drink	12-19	10-15

MED $18 V+

Tresillian Dry Riesling (★★★★)
Picked from first-crop Canterbury vines, the 2008 vintage (★★★★) has a Germanic lightness and intensity, with strong, pure, lemony flavours, slightly sweet (10 grams/litre of residual sugar), very lively and harmonious.

MED/DRY $20 V+

Tresillian Riesling (★★★☆)
From Swannanoa, in Canterbury, the 2008 vintage (★★★☆) is light (9.2 per cent alcohol), lemony and appley, with gently sweet (22 grams/litre of residual sugar), finely balanced flavours.

MED $20 AV

Two Rivers Marlborough Juliet Riesling (★★★★)
Youthful, very fresh and tight, the 2009 vintage (★★★★) is a single-vineyard wine, showing good intensity of vibrant, lemony flavours. Medium-bodied, it's a strongly varietal wine, best cellared to mid-2011+.

MED/DRY $22 V+

Two Rivers Marlborough Wairau Selection Riesling ★★★☆
Hand-picked and lees-aged for 11 months, the 2008 vintage (★★★☆) is a finely balanced wine with very good depth. Medium-bodied, it has a minerally streak through its lemony, appley flavours and a dryish, harmonious finish.

MED/DRY $22 AV

Two Sisters Central Otago Riesling ★★★★☆

From a steep, north-facing slope at Lowburn, in the Cromwell Basin, the 2008 vintage (★★★★☆) was hand-picked, fermented with indigenous yeasts, and made in a medium style. Very fresh, punchy and zingy, it has intense, pure, lemony flavours, vibrant and racy, in a classic cellaring style.

MED $27 AV

Urlar Gladstone Riesling (★★★★)

Hand-picked in the northern Wairarapa and tank-fermented, the 2008 vintage (★★★★) has mouthfilling body (13 per cent alcohol) and very fresh, punchy and vibrant lemon/lime flavours, with hints of passionfruit and apricot. It's a medium-dry style with finely balanced acidity and good intensity.

MED/DRY $22 V+

Valli Old Vine Central Otago Riesling ★★★★★

The 2009 vintage (★★★★★) was harvested at 23.2 brix from low-cropping (3.5 tonnes/hectare) vines planted at Black Ridge, in Alexandra, in 1980. Pale lemon/green, it is very richly scented, with mouthfilling body, highly concentrated, citrusy, peachy flavours and firm acidity. Fully dry but not austere, it's an authoritative wine, already delicious and well worth discovering.

Vintage	09	08
WR	7	7
Drink	10-20	10-19

DRY $28 V+

Vidal Marlborough Riesling ★★★★

The 2009 vintage (★★★★), grown in the Wairau (mostly) and Awatere valleys, is lemon-scented, with lemony, slightly spicy flavours, gently sweet (8 grams/litre of residual sugar), vibrant and crisp, with very good depth.

Vintage	10	09	08	07	06
WR	6	7	7	7	7
Drink	10-15	10-15	10-13	10-12	P

MED/DRY $21 V+

Villa Maria Cellar Selection Marlborough Riesling ★★★★

The 2008 vintage (★★★★) has a slightly toasty fragrance. Limey and citrusy, it shows good purity, richness and length, with some development showing. Tasted prior to bottling (and so not rated), the 2010 is fleshy and ripe, with a sliver of sweetness (8 grams/litre of residual sugar) and excellent weight and harmony.

Vintage	10	09
WR	6	7
Drink	10-16	10-17

MED/DRY $24 AV

Villa Maria Private Bin Marlborough Riesling ★★★☆

The 2010 vintage, tasted prior to bottling (and so not rated), is a medium-dry style (8.5 grams/litre of residual sugar). Highly scented, with a slightly musky perfume, it has pure, delicate, citrusy flavours, very finely balanced.

Vintage	10	09
WR	6	7
Drink	10-16	10-14

MED/DRY $21 AV

Villa Maria Reserve Marlborough Dry Riesling (★★★★★)

The 2009 vintage (★★★★★) was grown in the Awatere Valley, hand-picked, partly barrel-fermented, and lees-aged for four months. It's a highly refined wine, beautifully scented, with intense, lemony flavours, appetising acidity, and lovely balance (9 grams/litre of residual sugar) and length.

Vintage	09
WR	7
Drink	10-17

MED/DRY $27 V+

Villa Maria Single Vineyard Fletcher Vineyard Marlborough Riesling (★★★★☆)

Hand-picked in the middle of the Wairau Valley, the 2008 vintage (★★★★☆) was stop-fermented in a medium style (28 grams/litre of residual sugar) with low alcohol (9.5 per cent). It shows excellent intensity of lemon and apple flavours, with gentle sweetness balanced by lively acidity and a long, slightly minerally finish.

Vintage	08
WR	7
Drink	10-20

MED $26 AV

Voss Estate Riesling ★★★☆

The 2008 vintage (★★★) is a medium-bodied wine from Martinborough with dryish (7 grams/litre of residual sugar), lemony flavours, fresh and finely balanced. There is no 2009.

Vintage	09	08	07	06
WR	NM	6	NM	5
Drink	NM	10-18	NM	10-12

MED/DRY $20 AV

Vynfields Classic Riesling ★★★★☆

Certified organic, the 2009 vintage (★★★★★) of this Martinborough wine is a fleshy, medium style (40 grams/litre of residual sugar). Full-bodied, with rich, peachy, slightly spicy and honeyed flavours, a hint of marmalade, and powerful personality, it is notably concentrated and harmonious, and already delicious.

MED $29 AV

Waimea Bolitho SV Nelson Riesling ★★★★

The 2006 vintage (★★★★) is a lemony, slightly toasty wine with elegant, complex flavours. The 2007 (★★★★) is a medium style (25 grams/litre of residual sugar), with excellent depth of ripe citrusy flavours and good harmony. It's delicious now. The 2008 vintage (★★★★) is clearly botrytis-influenced, with rich, gently honeyed flavours, ripe and peachy, showing good complexity and harmony.

Vintage	08	07	06	05
WR	7	7	7	7
Drink	10-18	10-17	10-16	10-15

MED/DRY $22 V+

Waimea Classic Riesling ★★★★☆

This luscious Nelson wine is balanced for easy drinking, consistently impressive – and great value. The 2008 vintage (★★★★★) is a very generous wine with rich lemon/lime flavours, abundant sweetness (21.8 grams/litre of residual sugar) and lively acidity. Refined and concentrated, it's a lovely mouthful.

Vintage	09	08	07	06
WR	7	7	7	7
Drink	10-17	10-16	10-17	10-13

MED $18 V+

Waimea Dry Riesling ★★★★

Grown on the Waimea Plains of Nelson, the 2006 vintage (★★★☆) is a tightly structured wine, dry (3.7 grams/litre of residual sugar), with a minerally streak and lemony, appley flavours that linger well.

Vintage	06	05	04
WR	7	5	6
Drink	10-16	P	P

MED/DRY $18 V+

Waipara Hills Soul of the South Waipara Riesling (★★★★☆)

The 2009 vintage (★★★★☆), estate-grown, is highly scented, with fresh, pure lemon/lime flavours and a gentle splash of sweetness (14 grams/litre of residual sugar). Poised and youthful, it's an immaculate, punchy wine, well worth cellaring.

MED/DRY $21 V+

Waipara Springs Dry Riesling (★★★☆)

The 2009 vintage (★★★☆) is mouthfilling and dryish (6 grams/litre of residual sugar), with a honeyed bouquet. Fleshy, with ripe, grapefruit-like flavours, it is slightly spicy, with a minerally streak and plenty of drink-young appeal.

MED/DRY $19 V+

Waipara Springs Premo Dry Riesling ★★★★

The 2009 vintage (★★★☆) was mostly handled in tanks, but 30 per cent was fermented in old barrels. It's a fully dry style (3.5 grams/litre of residual sugar) with a slightly honeyed bouquet, mouthfilling body (14 per cent alcohol) and lemony, spicy flavours, showing a touch of complexity and good depth.

DRY $22 V+

Waipara Springs Premo Waipara Riesling (★★★★☆)

Here's a chance to buy a bottle-aged Riesling. The 2006 vintage (★★★★☆) is a medium style (29 grams/litre of residual sugar), matured for eight weeks in old oak casks. Still fairly youthful, it is racy, with good acid spine and complexity and concentrated lemon/lime flavours. It should be very long-lived.

MED $22 V+

Waipara Springs Riesling ★★★☆

The 2009 vintage (★★★★) is scented, with fresh, intense, citrusy, limey, gently sweet flavours (28 grams/litre of residual sugar), showing considerable complexity, finely balanced acidity and good harmony.

MED $19 V+

Waipipi Wairarapa Riesling ★★★

A medium style with a slightly honeyed bouquet, the 2009 vintage (★★★☆) has strong lemon, apple and passionfruit flavours, with a hint of botrytis and good acid spine.

MED $25 –V

Wairau River Marlborough Riesling ★★★☆

The 2008 (★★★☆) is a medium-dry style with good depth of lemon/lime flavours, tight and crisp. The 2009 vintage (★★★☆), 10 per cent barrel-aged, is tight and crisp, with lemony, appley flavours, a splash of sweetness (11.5 grams/litre of residual sugar) and a slightly spicy, lingering finish.

Vintage	09	08
WR	6	4
Drink	10-12	P

MED/DRY $20 AV

Wairau River Summer Riesling ★★★☆

'Sup with frivolous frivolity' urges the back label on the 2009 vintage (★★★☆), grown in Marlborough. Light (9.5 per cent alcohol) and sweetish, it is tense and youthful, with good depth of flavour, appley and tangy. The 2010 (★★★) is similar – light, lemony, appley and slightly spicy, with ample sweetness (36 grams/litre of residual sugar) balanced by zesty acidity. Worth cellaring.

Vintage	09
WR	5
Drink	09-10

MED $20 AV

Weka River Waipara Valley Riesling ★★★★

The 2008 vintage (★★★★) is an elegant, concentrated, single-vineyard wine with good acid spine. Made in a medium style (28 grams/litre of residual sugar), it has strong lemon and slight nectarine flavours, finely balanced and tightly structured.

MED $22 V+

West Brook Marlborough Riesling ★★★★

The 2009 vintage (★★★★) is attractive from the start. Showing good vigour and intensity, it has strong, ripe lemon, lime and passionfruit flavours, gently sweet, crisp, finely balanced and lingering. Drink now or cellar.

MED/DRY $20 V+

Whitehaven Marlborough Riesling ★★★

Full-bodied, the 2009 vintage (★★★) has dryish (5 grams/litre of residual sugar), lemony, slightly spicy flavours, showing decent depth and good delicacy and harmony. It should mature well.

Vintage	10	09
WR	6	7
Drink	10-15	10-14

MED/DRY $20 –V

Wild Earth Central Otago Riesling ★★★★

The finely poised 2008 vintage (★★★★☆) was fermented in 'a single, small tank'. Rich and tightly structured, with intensely varietal, ripe, lemon and peach flavours, it has good acid spine and a slightly sweet (14 grams/litre of residual sugar), minerally, lingering finish.

MED $27 –V

Wild South Marlborough Riesling ★★★☆

Scented and finely poised, the 2009 vintage (★★★★) from Sacred Hill is a single-vineyard wine, grown in the Awatere Valley. A basically dry style (4.3 grams/litre of residual sugar), it is medium-bodied, with strong lemon, lime and slight passionfruit flavours, showing good delicacy and freshness, and a long, tight but not austere finish. Fine value.

DRY $19 V+

Wither Hills Single Vineyard Kerseley Riesling (★★★☆)

The debut 2009 vintage (★★★☆) is a floral, finely balanced Marlborough wine with fresh citrus and stone-fruit flavours and a dryish, crisp finish.

MED/DRY $20 AV

Wither Hills Single Vineyard Rarangi Riesling (★★★)

Grown in Marlborough, the 2009 vintage (★★★) is lemony, appley and crisp, in a dryish style with refreshing acidity. It needs time; open mid-2011+.

MED/DRY $20 –V

Woollaston Nelson Riesling ★★★★

The 2009 vintage (★★★★), hand-picked on the Waimea Plains and at Upper Moutere, shows excellent potential. Mouthfilling, it has strong citrusy, limey flavours, showing very good delicacy and purity, a sliver of sweetness (8.5 grams/litre of residual sugar) and a fresh, crisp, long finish.

MED/DRY $19 V+

Yealands Estate Marlborough Riesling ★★★☆

The 2009 vintage (★★★★) is a single-vineyard Awatere Valley wine, estate-grown, hand-picked and handled entirely in tanks. Tight, youthful and vibrant, it has dryish, lemony, appley flavours that linger well. Medium-bodied, it shows excellent delicacy, poise and depth.

MED/DRY $24 –V

Yealands Marlborough Riesling (★★★)

The 2008 vintage (★★★) is an easy-drinking style, grown in the Awatere Valley. It has fresh, citrusy flavours, with a hint of passionfruit, a distinct splash of sweetness (13 grams/litre of residual sugar), and good delicacy and depth.

MED/DRY $18 AV

Sauvignon Blanc

Sauvignon Blanc is New Zealand's key calling card in the wine markets of the world. At the 2009 International Wine and Spirit Competition, in London, the trophy for champion Sauvignon Blanc was awarded to Villa Maria Cellar Selection Marlborough Sauvignon Blanc 2009. In *Winestate*'s 2009 Wine of the Year Awards, in Australia, the top five places in the Sauvignon Blanc category all went to Marlborough wines.

The rise to international stardom of New Zealand Sauvignon Blanc was remarkably swift. Government Viticulturist Romeo Bragato imported the first Sauvignon Blanc vines from Italy in 1906, but it was not until 1974 that Matua Valley marketed New Zealand's first varietal Sauvignon Blanc. Montana established its first Sauvignon Blanc vines in Marlborough in 1975, allowing Sauvignon Blanc to get into full commercial swing in the early 1980s. In the year to June 2010, 82 per cent by volume of all New Zealand's wine exports were based on Sauvignon Blanc.

Sauvignon Blanc is by far New Zealand's most extensively planted variety, in 2011 comprising well over 50 per cent of the bearing national vineyard. Over 85 per cent of all vines are concentrated in Marlborough, with further significant plantings in Hawke's Bay, Nelson, Wairarapa and Waipara. Between 2005 and 2011, the area of bearing Sauvignon Blanc vines will more than double, from 7277 hectares to 16,758 hectares.

The flavour of New Zealand Sauvignon Blanc varies according to fruit ripeness. At the herbaceous, under-ripe end of the spectrum, vegetal and fresh-cut-grass aromas hold sway; riper wines show capsicum, gooseberry and melon-like characters; very ripe fruit displays tropical-fruit flavours.

Intensely herbaceous Sauvignon Blancs are not hard to make in the viticulturally cool climate of the South Island and the lower North Island (Wairarapa). 'The challenge faced by New Zealand winemakers is to keep those herbaceous characters in check,' says Kevin Judd, of Greywacke Vineyards, formerly chief winemaker at Cloudy Bay. 'It would be foolish to suggest that these herbaceous notes detract from the wines; in fact I am sure that this fresh edge and intense varietal aroma are the reasons for its recent international popularity. The better of these wines have these herbaceous characters in context and in balance with the more tropical-fruit characters associated with riper fruit.'

There are two key styles of Sauvignon Blanc produced in New Zealand. Wines handled entirely in stainless steel tanks – by far the most common – place their accent squarely on their fresh, direct fruit flavours. Alternatively, many top labels are handled principally in tanks, but five to 10 per cent of the blend is barrel-fermented, adding a touch of complexity without subduing the wine's fresh, punchy fruit aromas and flavours.

Another major style difference is regionally based: the crisp, incisively flavoured wines of Marlborough contrast with the softer, less pungently herbaceous Hawke's Bay style. These are wines to drink young (traditionally within 18 months of the vintage) while they are irresistibly fresh, aromatic and tangy, although the oak-matured, more complex wines sometimes found in Hawke's Bay (currently an endangered species, despite their quality) can mature well for several years.

The recent swing from corks to screwcaps has also boosted the longevity of the wines. Rather than running out of steam, many are now highly enjoyable at two years old.

---

3 Stones Marlborough Sauvignon Blanc ★★★

From Ager Sectus (owner of The Crossings, Crossroads and Southbank brands), the 2009 vintage (★★★☆) is balanced for easy drinking. Mouthfilling, fresh and lively, it has good depth of ripely herbaceous, melon and green-capsicum flavours, and a tangy, smooth finish.

DRY $20 –V

12,000 Miles Sauvignon Blanc ★★★☆
From Gladstone Vineyard, the 2009 vintage (★★★☆) is a full-bodied Wairarapa wine with very good depth of ripe tropical-fruit flavours and a fresh, smooth finish.

DRY $17 V+

Alexia Wairarapa Sauvignon Blanc ★★★☆
From Jane Cooper, winemaker at Matahiwi, the 2010 vintage (★★★★) is ripely scented and smooth, with passionfruit and lime flavours, showing excellent freshness, delicacy and depth. It's already delicious.

DRY $18 V+

Allan Scott Marlborough Sauvignon Blanc ★★★☆
The Scotts aim for a 'ripe tropical-fruit' Sauvignon – a style typical of the Rapaura area of the Wairau Valley, where most of the company's vineyards are clustered. The 2010 vintage (★★★★) is freshly scented and bone-dry, with ripe sweet-fruit flavours of melons and capsicums. It's a mouthfilling wine, crisp and racy, with excellent delicacy and purity.

Vintage	10	09	08
WR	6	10-12	6
Drink	10-12	10-11	P

DRY $18 V+

Allan Scott Millstone Marlborough Sauvignon Blanc ★★★
From a company-owned vineyard certified as in 'conversion to organic', the 2009 vintage (★★★) is $10 cheaper than its 2008 predecessor. A medium-bodied (11 per cent alcohol), dry wine (5 per cent oak-aged), it is crisp and dry, with tight, minerally characters, showing some potential.

Vintage	09	08
WR	6	6
Drink	10-13	10-12

DRY $20 –V

Allan Scott Moorlands Marlborough Sauvignon Blanc ★★★★
Based on vines planted in 1980 next to the winery at Rapaura, the 2009 vintage (★★★★) was tank-fermented and matured for 10 months in old oak barrels, with regular lees-stirring. It's a bone-dry style, tightly structured and mouthfilling, with fresh, ripe tropical-fruit flavours and leesy, nutty notes adding complexity. Crisp and youthful, it's well worth cellaring.

Vintage	09	08
WR	6	6
Drink	10-13	10-12

DRY $26 –V

Alpha Domus The Pilot Hawke's Bay Sauvignon Blanc ★★★
The 2009 vintage (★★★) is a typical regional style with mouthfilling body and plenty of fresh, ripe passionfruit/lime flavour, crisp, dry and lively.

Vintage	09	08
WR	6	6
Drink	10-13	10-12

DRY $19 AV

Alpine Valley Wairau Valley Marlborough Sauvignon Blanc (★★★☆)

The debut 2010 vintage (★★★☆) from Tiki is fresh, mouthfilling and rounded, with ripe tropical-fruit flavours, showing good depth. It's already drinking well.

MED/DRY $20 AV

Amisfield Central Otago Sauvignon Blanc ★★★★

The 2010 vintage (★★★★) was estate-grown at Lowburn and mostly handled in tanks, but 5 per cent of the blend was fermented in old French oak barriques. It's a stylish wine, full-bodied, with good intensity of fresh melon, grapefruit and spice flavours, a touch of complexity and a sliver of sweetness (4 grams/litre of residual sugar) to balance its fresh, appetising acidity.

Vintage	10	09	08	07
WR	6	5	5	6
Drink	10-12	10-11	P	P

DRY $25 AV

Anchorage Nelson Sauvignon Blanc ★★★★

Estate-grown at Motueka, in Nelson, this wine has shown strong form in recent vintages. The 2009 (★★★★) is a crisp, zingy, single-vineyard wine with concentrated fruit flavours of melon, passionfruit and citrus fruits, some grassy, herbal notes, and an off-dry (6.5 grams/litre of residual sugar), long finish.

MED/DRY $18 V+

Anchorage Winemakers Release Sauvignon Blanc (★★★)

The 2009 vintage (★★★) is partly oak-aged. Mouthfilling, fresh and crisp, it's still very youthful, with melon, lime and nut flavours and an off-dry (6.5 grams/litre of residual sugar) finish.

MED/DRY $18 AV

Ara Composite Marlborough Sauvignon Blanc ★★★★

From Winegrowers of Ara, the 2009 vintage (★★★★) is weighty and dry, in an understated style, minerally, sweet-fruited and finely textured. It has fresh, incisive melon and lime flavours and a slightly spicy, lingering finish.

Vintage	09	08
WR	6	6
Drink	11-12	P

DRY $22 V+

Ara Marlborough Sauvignon Blanc (★★★☆)

Sold in restaurants, the 2009 vintage (★★★☆) was estate-grown in the lower Waihopai Valley and lees-aged for four months. It's a tight, dry, minerally wine with fresh, ripe tropical-fruit and herbaceous flavours, crisp and punchy.

DRY $18 V+

Ara Pathway Marlborough Sauvignon Blanc ★★★☆

The sharply priced 2009 vintage (★★★☆) is aromatic and punchy, with ripely herbaceous flavours, good body and a rounded, dry finish.

Vintage	09
WR	6
Drink	10-11

DRY $16 V+

Ara Resolute Marlborough Sauvignon Blanc ★★★★☆

Grown in the heart of the Winegrowers of Ara Vineyard, in the lower Waihopai Valley, this wine is tank-fermented and given lengthy lees-aging. The 2009 vintage (★★★★) is tightly structured, with ripe sweet-fruit flavours of melons and limes, showing good vigour and intensity. Crisp, minerally and dry, it's a cellaring style; open mid-2011+.

Vintage	09
WR	7
Drink	11-12

DRY $28 AV

Arrow Rock Nelson Sauvignon Blanc (★★★☆)

Offering great value, the 2009 vintage (★★★☆) is a single-vineyard Brightwater wine, fresh, vibrant and woven with appetising acidity. Its gooseberry/lime flavours show very good purity, delicacy and depth.

DRY $15 V+

Artisan The Sands Block Marlborough Sauvignon Blanc ★★★★

Always good value, this single-vineyard wine is grown at the eastern (cooler) end of the Wairau Valley. The 2010 vintage (★★★★) is mouthfilling, with good intensity of tropical-fruit flavours, very fresh and vibrant, a sliver of sweetness (4 grams/litre of residual sugar) and crisp acidity. Delicious, easy drinking.

DRY $19 V+

Ash Ridge Hawke's Bay Barrel Fermented Sauvignon Blanc (★★★☆)

Grown in The Triangle, the 2009 vintage (★★★☆) is a single-vineyard wine, fermented (partly with indigenous yeasts) in old oak barrels. Ripely scented, with vibrant tropical-fruit characters to the fore, it is medium-bodied (12 per cent alcohol), with very good depth of flavour, showing some complexity, and a finely balanced, dry finish. A good food wine.

Vintage	09
WR	5
Drink	10-14

DRY $23 –V

Ashwell Sauvignon Blanc ★★★☆

This Martinborough wine is typically good, with mouthfilling body and ripely herbaceous flavours, fresh and strong. The 2009 vintage (★★★☆) is ripely scented and full-bodied, with good depth of passionfruit and lime flavours and a smooth, dry finish.

Vintage	10	09	08	07
WR	5	6	6	7
Drink	10-11	P	P	P

DRY $19 V+

Askerne Hawke's Bay Sauvignon Blanc ★★★☆

This small Havelock North winery makes a good, often excellent Sauvignon. The 2010 vintage (★★★☆) was mostly handled in tanks, but 3 per cent of the blend was barrel-fermented. Made in a bone-dry style, it is mouthfilling, crisp and slightly spicy, with tropical-fruit flavours showing good vigour and depth

Vintage	10	09	08	07	06
WR	6	6	6	6	6
Drink	10-12	10-11	P	P	P

DRY $16 V+

Aspire Hawke's Bay Sauvignon Blanc ★★★

From Matariki, the 2008 vintage (★★★) is a typical regional style, grown in the Gimblett Gravels. Mouthfilling, it has good depth of fresh tropical-fruit and gooseberry flavours, ripe and rounded (4 grams/litre of residual sugar).

Vintage	08
WR	5
Drink	P

DRY $20 –V

Astrolabe Discovery Awatere Sauvignon Blanc ★★★★

The 2009 vintage (★★★★☆) is a rich wine with strong personality. In the classic, nettley, intensely herbaceous Awatere Valley mould, it is highly aromatic and brims with passionfruit and green-capsicum flavours, crisp and lingering.

Vintage	09	08	07
WR	7	6	6
Drink	10-13	10-12	P

DRY $24 AV

Astrolabe Discovery Kekerengu Sauvignon Blanc ★★★★

Grown on a limestone site at Kekerengu, half-way between Blenheim and Kaikoura, the 2009 vintage (★★★★) is a weighty, dry, slightly minerally wine with fresh, well-ripened citrus and stone-fruit flavours, showing excellent depth, good acid spine, and a persistent finish.

Vintage	09	08
WR	7	6
Drink	10-13	10-12

DRY $26 –V

Astrolabe Experience Taihoa Sauvignon Blanc (★★★★)

The 2009 vintage (★★★★) was hand-picked at Kekerengu, half-way between Blenheim and Kaikoura, barrel-fermented with indigenous yeasts and lees-aged for 10 months in oak. Full-bodied, it is very fresh and vibrant, with melon and lime flavours, a nettley streak, a very subtle oak influence and a lingering, faintly nutty finish. Showing good complexity, it's worth cellaring.

Vintage	09
WR	6
Drink	10-12

DRY $37 –V

Astrolabe Voyage Marlborough Sauvignon Blanc ★★★★★

This label has acquired cult status. Grown at several sites in the Awatere, Waihopai and Wairau valleys, the highly drinkable 2009 vintage (★★★★) has slightly 'sweaty' aromas and a hint of 'tomato stalk'. Weighty and ripe, it is softly textured, with crisp passionfruit and gooseberry flavours, some nettley notes, excellent depth and a rounded finish.

Vintage	09	08	07	06
WR	6	6	6	6
Drink	10-13	10-12	P	P

DRY $21 V+

Ata Rangi Martinborough Sauvignon Blanc ★★★★☆

A consistently attractive wine, with ripe tropical-fruit rather than grassy, herbaceous flavours. The 2009 (★★★★☆) was mostly handled in tanks, but a small portion of the blend was fermented and lees-aged in seasoned oak barrels. Weighty, with a touch of complexity, it has rich, ripe melon, lime and passionfruit flavours, showing excellent intensity, and a finely balanced, long finish.

Vintage	09	08	07	06
WR	6	7	6	6
Drink	10-12	10-11	P	P

DRY $24 V+

Auntsfield Long Cow Sauvignon Blanc ★★★★☆

Grown and hand-harvested near the Long Cow paddock on the south side of the Wairau Valley, where Marlborough's first wines were made in the 1870s, the 2009 vintage (★★★★☆) was 15 per cent fermented and lees-aged in seasoned French oak barriques. Fleshy and rounded, mouthfilling and crisp, it's a very fresh and vibrant wine with ripe sweet-fruit delights and strong melon/lime flavours.

Vintage	09	08	07	06
WR	7	7	7	5
Drink	10-11	P	P	P

DRY $22 V+

Auntsfield Reserve Marlborough Sauvignon Blanc (★★★★★)

Delicious now, the 2007 vintage (★★★★★) was barrel-fermented and lees-aged for 10 months in oak. A weighty wine with youthful colour and a fresh, complex bouquet, suggestive of indigenous yeasts and oak, it is very concentrated and silky-textured, in a distinctly non-herbaceous style with super-ripe fruit flavours, complexity and great individuality.

DRY $34 AV

Awatere River Marlborough Sauvignon Blanc (★★★★)

The label on the 2008 vintage (★★★★) doesn't say categorically that this wine was grown in the Awatere Valley, but its fresh, strong, nettley aromas are certainly typical of the sub-region. Mouthfilling, vibrant and zingy, it's a full-bodied wine with gooseberry and green-capsicum flavours, showing excellent delicacy and depth.

`DRY $22 V+`

Babich Black Label Marlborough Sauvignon Blanc ★★★★☆

Sold principally in restaurants, this is a consistently impressive wine. The 2010 vintage (★★★★☆) was mostly handled in tanks, but a small part of the blend was fermented in seasoned oak casks. Fleshy and sweet-fruited, with some 'sweaty armpit' aromas, it is weighty and rich, with deep, ripe passionfruit/lime flavours and a long, well-rounded finish.

`DRY $23 V+`

Babich Individual Vineyards Cowslip Valley Marlborough Sauvignon Blanc ★★★★☆

Estate-grown in the Waihopai Valley, the 2010 vintage (★★★★★) has real power through the palate. Weighty and fleshy, with generous tropical-fruit flavours, it is also fresh, crisp and minerally, with lovely body, vibrancy and texture and a finely poised, dry, long finish.

`DRY $25 V+`

Babich Individual Vineyards Headwaters Organic Block Marlborough Sauvignon Blanc (★★★☆)

Certified organic, the 2010 vintage (★★★☆) is a subtle, dry wine, grown in the Wairau Valley. Medium-bodied, it is tight and crisp, with fresh, ripe flavours of peach, citrus fruits and limes that linger well. One for the cellar.

`DRY $25 –V`

Babich Lone Tree Hawke's Bay Sauvignon Blanc ★★★

Grown in Hawke's Bay, the 2008 vintage (★★☆) is still fresh and lively, with crisp apple and tropical-fruit flavours.

`DRY $16 V+`

Babich Marlborough Sauvignon Blanc ★★★★

Joe Babich favours 'a fuller, riper, softer style of Sauvignon Blanc. It's not a jump out of the glass style, but the wines develop well.' The latest releases reflect a rising input of grapes from the company's Cowslip Valley Vineyard in the Waihopai Valley, which gives less herbaceous fruit characters than its other Marlborough vineyards. The 2010 vintage (★★★★) is weighty and dry (4 grams/litre of residual sugar), fleshy and sweet-fruited, with rich tropical-fruit flavours, moderate acidity and a well-rounded finish. Delicious from the start.

`DRY $20 V+`

Babich Winemakers Reserve Marlborough Sauvignon Blanc ★★★★

A good example of gently wooded Marlborough Sauvignon Blanc, with very ripe flavours and great drinkability. Grown in the Waihopai and Awatere valleys, it is mostly handled in tanks, but

10 per cent is fermented and lees-aged in French oak barriques. The 2009 (★★★★☆) is punchy and highly aromatic, in a far more nettley, herbal style than past vintages. Fleshy and rich, with a very subtle seasoning of oak adding complexity, it's drinking well now.

DRY $25 AV

Barking Hedge Marlborough Sauvignon Blanc (★★★☆)

From Crighton Estate, in the Wairau Valley, the 2009 vintage (★★★☆) is mouthfilling and crisp, with strong gooseberry/lime flavours and good acid spine. It's a fresh, lively wine, offering good value.

DRY $18 V+

Bascand Marlborough Sauvignon Blanc (★★★☆)

A strongly herbaceous style, the 2009 vintage (★★★☆) was estate-grown at Rapaura, in the Wairau Valley. Aromatic and lively, with very good body and depth of melon and green-capsicum flavours, crisp and finely balanced, it's bargain-priced.

DRY $17 V+

Bel Echo by Clos Henri Marlborough Sauvignon Blanc ★★★☆

From Clos Henri, the 2009 vintage (★★★☆) was hand-picked, tank-fermented and matured on its yeast lees for 10 months. Full-bodied, fresh and dry, it has citrusy, limey flavours, showing good depth, vigour and personality.

Vintage	09	08	07	06
WR	6	7	5	6
Drink	10-14	10-13	P	P

DRY $22 AV

Bellbird Spring Block Eight Waipara Sauvignon Blanc (★★★★)

Hand-picked, and fermented and lees-aged in old oak barrels, the 2009 vintage (★★★★) is mouthfilling, fresh and vibrant, with a subtle oak influence. Ripely herbaceous, it has excellent vigour, depth and harmony, with considerable complexity and a rich, smooth (5 grams/litre of residual sugar) finish.

MED/DRY $32 –V

Belmonte Marlborough Sauvignon Blanc ★★★☆

From a company with family links to John Forrest, the 2009 vintage (★★★) is vibrantly fruity, in a fresh, medium-bodied style with good depth of smooth, ripe tropical-fruit flavours, finely balanced for easy drinking.

DRY $17 V+

Bensen Block Marlborough Sauvignon Blanc ★★★

From Pernod Ricard NZ, the 2008 vintage (★★★) is a very easy-drinking style, full-bodied, with ripe tropical-fruit flavours and a soft, well-rounded finish. The 2010, tasted just before bottling (and so not rated), looked very promising – ripely scented, with strong, crisp melon/lime flavours, fresh and lingering.

DRY $17 AV

Big Sky Te Muna Road Martinborough Sauvignon Blanc (★★★)

Weighty, with ripe, melon and lime flavours and gentle acidity, the 2008 vintage (★★★) is a subtle, dry style with a smooth finish.

DRY $22 –V

Bird Marlborough Sauvignon Blanc ★★★☆

Estate-grown in the Old Schoolhouse Vineyard, in the Omaka Valley, the 2008 vintage (★★★☆) is crisp and tight, with freshly herbaceous aromas. Full-bodied, it has dry melon, capsicum and lime flavours, showing very good depth.

Vintage	08	07	06
WR	6	5	4
Drink	10-11	P	P

DRY $20 AV

Black Barn Vineyards Barrel Ferment Sauvignon Blanc (★★★☆)

Still on sale in 2010, the 2007 vintage (★★★☆) was grown in Hawke's Bay, hand-picked and fermented and lees-aged for 10 months in French oak barrels (20 per cent new). A full-bodied wine, it is maturing well, with tropical-fruit flavours, showing very good depth and complexity, and a slightly buttery, dry finish.

Vintage	07
WR	6
Drink	10-11

DRY $30 –V

Black Barn Vineyards Hawke's Bay Sauvignon Blanc ★★★☆

Crisp and dry, the 2008 vintage (★★★☆) has ripe tropical-fruit flavours to the fore, with a slight herbal undercurrent. It's a fresh, lively wine with a touch of bottle-aged complexity.

DRY $20 AV

Black Barn Vineyards Hawke's Bay Tuki Tuki Valley Sauvignon Blanc (★★★☆)

Handled in tanks, with some use of indigenous yeasts, the easy-drinking 2009 vintage (★★★☆) is mouthfilling and smooth, with fresh, ripe tropical-fruit flavours, showing very good delicacy and depth.

DRY $22 AV

Black Cottage Marlborough Sauvignon Blanc (★★★★)

From Two Rivers, the 2010 vintage (★★★★) is a blend of Awatere Valley (70 per cent) and Wairau Valley fruit. An attractive medley of fresh tropical-fruit and greener, herbaceous flavours, it is aromatic and punchy, with good vigour and intensity and a crisp, racy finish.

DRY $18 V+

Blackenbrook Vineyard Nelson Sauvignon Blanc ★★★★

Grown in the Tasman district, harvested by hand at 23.5 brix and lees-aged in tanks, the 2010 vintage (★★★★) is a basically dry style (4.5 grams/litre of residual sugar). Mouthfilling and sweet-fruited, it is punchy, limey and slightly minerally, showing good freshness and liveliness and a crisp, long finish.

Vintage	10	09	08
WR	7	6	6
Drink	10-11	P	P

DRY $22 V+

Bladen Marlborough Sauvignon Blanc ★★★☆

The 2009 (★★★★) is a top vintage. The bouquet is freshly herbaceous; the palate is intensely varietal, with fresh, lively passionfruit, lime and capsicum flavours, crisp, dry and punchy.

Vintage	09
WR	6
Drink	10-11

DRY $20 AV

Blind River Marlborough Sauvignon Blanc ★★★★

The 2009 vintage (★★★★) was estate-grown in the Awatere Valley and mostly handled in tanks; 7.5 per cent was fermented in seasoned oak barriques. Intensely aromatic, it's a richly varietal wine with excellent concentration of melon and green-capsicum flavours, crisp and tight-knit.

DRY $25 AV

Boreham Wood Jane's Awatere Valley Marlborough Sauvignon Blanc (★★☆)

The 2008 vintage (★★☆) is a single-vineyard wine, tank-fermented and lees-aged for five months. Fresh, fruity and smooth, it's a light, easy-drinking dry wine, not concentrated, but priced right.

Vintage	09	08
WR	7	6
Drink	10-11	P

DRY $15 AV

Boreham Wood Marlborough Sauvignon Blanc ★★★

This single-vineyard wine is grown in the Awatere Valley. The 2009 vintage (★★★) is fresh and crisp, in a medium-bodied style with plenty of citrusy, limey flavour.

Vintage	09	08	07	06
WR	7	6	7	6
Drink	10-12	P	P	P

DRY $15 V+

Borthwick Vineyard Wairarapa Sauvignon Blanc ★★★★

The 2009 vintage (★★★★☆) is a deliciously fresh and punchy wine from Gladstone, 25 per cent barrel-fermented (in old oak). It is weighty and concentrated, with rich, ripe sweet-fruit flavours, a herbal undercurrent and a crisp, bone-dry finish.

DRY $23 AV

Boulder Bank Road Marlborough Sauvignon Blanc ★★★☆

From Vernon Family Estate, this wine is estate-grown at a coastal site on Vernon Station, above the Wairau Lagoons. The 2009 (★★★☆) has grassy, nettley aromas leading into a fresh and lively wine with herbaceous flavours and a crisp, dry finish. The 2010 vintage (★★★☆) is freshly aromatic and full-bodied, with tropical-fruit and green-capsicum flavours, vibrant and strong. Fine value.

DRY $17 V+

Bouldevines Granite Garden Reserve Sauvignon Blanc (★★★☆)

The youthful 2009 vintage (★★★☆) is a fleshy, ripe and rounded wine, grown in a rocky seam on a small ridge on the south side of the Wairau Valley. Mouthfilling, it has tropical-fruit flavours, moderate acidity and a dry finish, with very good texture and depth.

DRY $25 –V

Bouldevines Marlborough Sauvignon Blanc ★★★☆

The 2009 vintage (★★★★) is fleshy and mouthfilling, with good concentration of ripe citrus-fruit, melon and herb flavours and a balanced, dry finish. It's a classy, subtle wine with excellent weight, delicacy and length.

DRY $20 AV

Boundary Vineyards Rapaura Road Marlborough Sauvignon Blanc ★★★☆

From Pernod Ricard NZ, this is typically a very ripe and rounded style with distinctly tropical-fruit flavours, smooth and strong. The 2009 (★★★☆) is fleshy, with ripe passionfruit-like flavours, offering smooth, satisfying drinking. The 2010, tasted before bottling (and so not rated), showed good weight, with ripe tropical-fruit and capsicum flavours, well-rounded and lingering.

DRY $20 AV

Brams Run Marlborough Sauvignon Blanc (★★★★)

The 2009 vintage (★★★☆) is a fresh, crisp wine, gently aromatic, with strong, vibrant tropical-fruit and herbaceous flavours, showing good balance and drink-young appeal.

DRY $20 V+

Brancott Estate 'B' Brancott Marlborough Sauvignon Blanc – see Montana

Brancott Estate Living Land Series Marlborough Sauvignon Blanc – see Montana

Brancott Estate Reserve Marlborough Sauvignon Blanc ★★★★

Up to and including the 2009 vintage, this wine was branded 'Montana'. It is designed to highlight the fresh, herbaceous style of Sauvignon Blanc Pernod Ricard NZ achieves on the south side of the Wairau Valley, compared to its more tropical fruit-flavoured Stoneleigh Sauvignon Blanc, grown on the north side of the valley. The 2009 (★★★★) has mouthfilling body and fresh, tight gooseberry and capsicum flavours. Finely textured, it's a classic regional style, dry and long. The 2010 (★★★★), the first to carry the Brancott Estate brand, looked excellent in its infancy – weighty and dry, fleshy and ripe, with strong tropical-fruit and herbaceous flavours.

Vintage	10	09	08	07
WR	7	7	6	6
Drink	10-13	10-12	10-11	P

DRY $24 AV

Breakers Bay Nelson Sauvignon Blanc (★★★☆)

From Anchorage, the 2009 vintage (★★★☆) is a good buy. Fresh and nettley, it is aromatic and lively, with good varietal character and drink-young appeal.

`DRY $12 V+`

Brightside Brightwater Sauvignon Blanc ★★☆

The 2009 vintage (★★☆) from Kaimira is the first to be labelled 'Brightwater', rather than 'Nelson'. Priced right, it's a medium-bodied wine with clearly varietal, freshly herbaceous aromas and flavours, showing solid depth, and a smooth (5 grams/litre of residual sugar) finish.

`MED/DRY $15 AV`

Brightwater Vineyards Lord Rutherford Sauvignon Blanc ★★★★☆

Grown in Nelson, the 2010 vintage (★★★★☆) is fleshy, vibrant and concentrated, with ripe tropical-fruit flavours and real power through the palate. A deliciously sweet-fruited wine, it is generous, dry (3 grams/litre of residual sugar), lively and long.

Vintage	10
WR	6
Drink	11-13

`DRY $25 AV`

Brightwater Vineyards Nelson Sauvignon Blanc ★★★★

Grown on the Waimea Plains, this is a consistently enjoyable, ripely flavoured wine, fresh and punchy. The 2010 vintage (★★★★) is dry (4 grams/litre of residual sugar), with mouthfilling body and strong tropical-fruit flavours, very crisp, lively, fresh and punchy.

Vintage	10
WR	6
Drink	10-12

`DRY $20 V+`

Brookfields Ohiti Estate Hawke's Bay Sauvignon Blanc ★★★

The 2009 vintage (★★★) is mouthfilling and smooth, with good depth of vibrant tropical-fruit flavours, and a sliver of sweetness (5 grams/litre of residual sugar) balanced by fresh, crisp acidity.

Vintage	09	08
WR	7	7
Drink	10-12	P

`MED/DRY $19 AV`

Burnt Spur Martinborough Sauvignon Blanc ★★★

The 2009 vintage (★★★) is an easy-drinking, single-vineyard wine from Martinborough Vineyard. Weighty and rounded, it has satisfying depth of ripe melon and lime flavours.

`DRY $17 AV`

Cable Bay Marlborough Sauvignon Blanc ★★★★

This Waiheke Island-based producer wants a wine with 'restraint and textural interest, to enjoy with food'. The 2010 vintage (★★★★) was grown in the Omaka Valley and mostly handled in tanks, with a touch of barrel fermentation. Weighty, sweet-fruited and dry, it has crisp, ripe tropical-fruit flavours, showing a touch of complexity, and excellent richness.

Vintage	10
WR	7
Drink	10-12

DRY $20 V+

Camshorn Waipara Sauvignon Blanc ★★★☆

The 2008 vintage (★★★☆) from Pernod Ricard NZ is medium-bodied, with fresh, crisp tropical-fruit and herbaceous flavours, a slightly minerally streak, and good length. The 2010 (★★★☆) is fleshy, with fresh tropical-fruit flavours, ripe and rounded.

DRY $27 –V

Cape Campbell Marlborough Sauvignon Blanc ★★★☆

The 2009 vintage (★★★★) was grown at Blind River, south of the Awatere River, and in the Wairau Valley. Fresh and lively, it's a dry style (2.5 grams/litre of residual sugar), with good intensity of tropical-fruit and herbaceous flavours and a mouth-wateringly crisp finish.

DRY $19 V+

Carrick Central Otago Sauvignon Blanc ★★★☆

Grown at Bannockburn, this wine is mostly handled in tanks, but partly oak-aged. The 2010 vintage (★★★☆) was hand-picked and 30 per cent barrel-fermented. Punchy and crisp, it is dry (3.6 grams/litre of residual sugar) and aromatic, with slightly nettley, melon/lime flavours and a touch of complexity.

DRY $20 AV

Castaway Bay Marlborough Sauvignon Blanc (★★☆)

From Maven, the 2008 vintage (★★☆) was estate-grown in the Wairau Valley. It's a pleasant but plain wine with a restrained bouquet, ripe passionfruit, pear and lime flavours, and a smooth finish.

DRY $15 AV

Catalina Sounds Marlborough Sauvignon Blanc ★★★★☆

The 2010 vintage (★★★★☆) was mostly handled in tanks, with extended lees-aging, but 7 per cent of the blend was barrel-fermented. Fresh, aromatic and punchy, it is full-bodied, with a touch of complexity and fresh, dry (2.6 grams/litre of residual sugar) gooseberry, grapefruit and lime flavours, showing excellent purity, vigour and length.

DRY $24 V+

Cathedral Cove Marlborough Sauvignon Blanc (★★☆)

From One Tree Hill Vineyards, a division of Morton Estate, the 2009 vintage (★★☆) offers very good value. Medium to full-bodied, it is fresh and crisp, with decent depth of gooseberry and lime flavours.

DRY $8 V+

Chard Farm Swiftburn New Zealand Sauvignon Blanc (★★☆)

Labelled 'a classic cool-climate South Island style', the 2008 vintage (★★☆) is a fleshy, very easy-drinking style with ripe melon-like flavours and a slightly honeyed, rounded finish.

DRY $21 –V

Charles Wiffen Marlborough Sauvignon Blanc ★★★

The 2009 vintage (★★★) is fresh and crisp, with gooseberry and lime flavours, slightly minerally and showing good depth.

DRY $20 –V

Cheeky Little Sav ★★☆

From Babich, the 2009 vintage (★★☆) is a Marlborough wine, full-bodied and smooth, with decent depth of ripe tropical-fruit flavours. It's an easy-drinking style, priced sharply.

DRY $10 V+

Church Road Cuve Series Sauvignon Blanc (★★★★☆)

The 2009 vintage (★★★★★) is a superb Hawke's Bay wine. Fleshy and rich, it was estate-grown in the Redstone Vineyard, in The Triangle, hand-harvested, and fermented and lees-aged in French oak barriques (30 per cent new). Powerful, with highly concentrated tropical-fruit flavours and notable complexity and harmony, it's highly reminiscent of a fine white Bordeaux.

DRY $29 AV

Church Road Hawke's Bay Sauvignon Blanc ★★★★☆

Aiming for a wine that is 'more refined and softer than a typical New Zealand Sauvignon Blanc, with restrained varietal characters', the 2009 vintage (★★★★) was based mostly (87 per cent) on aromatic fruit from Pernod Ricard NZ's elevated Matapiro site (300 metres above sea level), blended with grapes from a warmer site at Havelock North. Partly barrel-fermented (13 per cent), it has slightly sweaty aromas leading into a mouthfilling wine, fresh and crisp, with sweet-fruit delights and ripe tropical-fruit flavours, dry and generous.

Vintage	09	08	07
WR	7	7	7
Drink	10-12	10-11	P

DRY $27 AV

Churton Marlborough Sauvignon Blanc ★★★★☆

This small producer aims for a style that 'combines the renowned flavour and aromatic intensity of Marlborough fruit with the finesse and complexity of fine European wines'. The 2009 vintage (★★★★☆) was mostly (70 per cent) estate-grown on an elevated site in the Waihopai Valley, and 10 per cent of the blend was barrel-fermented (in seasoned French oak puncheons). Fleshy, ripely scented and sweet-fruited, it is rich and rounded, with tropical-fruit flavours, showing excellent concentration, delicacy and complexity, and a bone-dry finish.

Vintage	09	08	07	06	05
WR	7	6	7	6	5
Drink	10-16	10-14	10-15	10-12	10-14

DRY $26 AV

Cicada Marlborough Sauvignon Blanc (★★☆)

The 2009 vintage (★★☆), grown at Rapaura, is a medium to full-bodied wine with solid depth of ripely herbaceous flavours, crisp and dry.

DRY $18 –V

C.J. Pask Roy's Hill Sauvignon Blanc ★★☆

Winemaker Kate Radburnd aims for 'an easy-drinking style with its emphasis on tropical-fruit flavours and a tangy lift'. Grown in Hawke's Bay, the 2009 vintage (★★☆) is medium-bodied, with smooth tropical-fruit flavours and an underlying crispness.

DRY $15 AV

Clark Estate Single Vineyard Awatere Valley Marlborough Sauvignon Blanc ★★☆

From the owners of Boreham Wood, the 2009 vintage (★★☆) is medium-bodied, with fresh, crisp flavours of melons and limes and a smooth, dry finish.

Vintage	09	08
WR	7	6
Drink	10-12	P

DRY $18 –V

Claylaur Family Estate Marlborough Sauvignon Blanc (★★★)

The 2009 vintage (★★★) was grown at two sites, in the Omaka Valley and central Wairau Valley. Lees-aged for three months, it is smooth, full-bodied and fresh, with crisp, basically dry (4.5 grams/litre of residual sugar) melon/lime flavours, balanced for easy drinking.

DRY $18 AV

Clayfork Vineyard Waihopai Ridge Marlborough Sauvignon Blanc (★★★★)

From Endeavour (owner of Catalina Sounds, Crowded House and Nanny Goat), the 2009 vintage (★★★★) is a single-vineyard wine, 15 per cent barrel-fermented. Mouthfilling, it is very fresh and vibrant, with ripe melon/lime flavours in a quietly classy, minerally style with sweet-fruit characters, a subtle oak influence and tight structure. Best drinking mid-2011+.

DRY $28 –V

Clayridge Marlborough Sauvignon Blanc ★★★★

The 2008 vintage (★★★★), 13 per cent barrel-fermented, is ripely scented and mouthfilling, with generous, distinctly tropical-fruit flavours, showing good texture and richness, and a dry finish (2.1 grams/litre of residual sugar).

Vintage	08
WR	6
Drink	P

DRY $21 V+

Clearview Estate Te Awanga Sauvignon Blanc ★★★☆

Grown near the coast in Hawke's Bay and handled entirely in tanks, the 2008 vintage (★★★☆) is crisp and dry, with ripe tropical-fruit flavours, showing good freshness, vigour and depth.

Vintage	09
WR	6
Drink	10-11

DRY $17 V+

Clearview Reserve Hawke's Bay Sauvignon Blanc ★★★★

The 2009 vintage (★★★★☆) was grown at Te Awanga, hand-picked and fermented and matured for 11 months in seasoned French oak barriques. Crisp and dry, it's an impressively rich wine, still very youthful, with ripe tropical-fruit flavours, integrated nutty oak, and excellent poise, vigour and intensity.

Vintage	09	08	07	06
WR	7	6	7	6
Drink	11-15	10-14	10-11	P

DRY $23 AV

Clifford Bay Marlborough Sauvignon Blanc ★★★★★

This is an impressive wine, bargain-priced. The 2010 vintage (★★★★☆) doesn't mention the Awatere Valley on its front or back labels (unlike past releases), but it still tastes of the Awatere. Weighty, it is refined and immaculate, with intense, pure gooseberry and lime flavours, a minerally thread and a smooth yet racy finish.

Vintage	09	08
WR	6	6
Drink	10-11	10-11

DRY $18 V+

Clos Henri Marlborough Sauvignon Blanc ★★★★★

The Clos Henri Vineyard near Renwick is owned by Henri Bourgeois, a leading, family-owned producer in the Loire Valley, which feels this wine expresses 'a unique terroir ... and French winemaking approach'. A sophisticated and distinctive Sauvignon Blanc, in top years it's a joy to drink. The 2009 vintage (★★★★) was hand-picked and mostly fermented and matured for 10 months on its yeast lees in tanks; 10 per cent was barrel-fermented. Full-bodied, with strong, ripe tropical-fruit flavours, it is tightly structured and bone-dry, with hints of pineapple and spices in a distinctive style, still unfolding.

Vintage	09	08	07	06	05
WR	6	7	5	6	6
Drink	10-15	10-13	10-11	10-12	10-11

DRY $29 V+

Clos Marguerite Marlborough Sauvignon Blanc ★★★★

Estate-grown in the Awatere Valley, the 2009 vintage (★★★★) was handled without oak, but given lengthy aging on its yeast lees in tanks. Highly aromatic, with a hint of nettles, it is weighty and ripely herbaceous, with good vigour and concentration, a mineral streak and a long finish.

DRY $26 –V

Cloudy Bay Sauvignon Blanc ★★★★★
New Zealand's most internationally acclaimed wine is sought after from Sydney to New York and London. Its irresistibly aromatic and zesty style and intense flavours stem from 'the fruit characters that are in the grapes when they arrive at the winery'. It is sourced from company-owned and several long-term contract growers' vineyards in the Rapaura, Fairhall, Renwick and Brancott districts of the Wairau Valley. The juice is mostly cool-fermented in stainless steel tanks and aged for up to two months on its yeast lees before bottling. The outstanding 2010 vintage (★★★★★) is $5 cheaper than the 2009. Finely scented, with pure melon/lime characters and a touch of barrel-aged complexity (4 per cent of the blend was handled in old oak casks), it's an authoritative style with beautifully ripe fruit flavours that retain zestiness, building to a dry, lasting finish. An authoritative wine, more subtle and sophisticated, less 'in your face' than some of its competitors, with excellent body, complexity and texture, it's the sort of Sauvignon that draws you back for a second glass … and a third.

Vintage	10	09	08	07	06
WR	7	7	5	6	7
Drink	10-12	10-11	P	10-11	10-12

DRY $30 AV

Cloudy Bay Te Koko – see Branded and Other White Wines

Coal Pit Central Otago Sauvignon Blanc ★★★☆
Estate-grown at Gibbston, the 2009 vintage (★★★☆) has a freshly herbaceous bouquet leading into a crisp, medium-bodied wine with strong, vibrant, citrusy, limey flavours, fresh and frisky.

Vintage	09	08
WR	5	7
Drink	10-12	10-11

DRY $25 –V

Cockle Bay Marlborough Sauvignon Blanc (★★☆)
Sold cheaply in supermarkets, the 2008 vintage (★★☆) was grown in the Wairau and Awatere valleys. Fresh, crisp and lively, with gooseberry and capsicum flavours, showing decent depth, it offers great value.

MED/DRY $7 V+

Cooks Beach Vineyard Sauvignon Blanc (★★☆)
Grown and hand-picked on the Coromandel Peninsula, the 2009 vintage (★★☆) is crisp and dry, with a restrained bouquet but fresh, lively, citrusy, limey flavours. It's maturing very solidly.

DRY $20 –V

Coopers Creek Marlborough Sauvignon Blanc ★★★
The 2009 vintage (★★★) is a medium-bodied style, balanced for easy drinking, with ripely herbaceous aromas and fresh, crisp and lively flavours.

Vintage	09	08	07
WR	6	6	6
Drink	10-11	P	P

DRY $19 AV

Coopers Creek Reserve Marlborough Sauvignon Blanc ★★★★☆

The 2008 vintage (★★★★☆) was grown at two sites – mostly a mature vineyard in the Brancott Valley, which contributed 'richness and texture', supplemented by a young vineyard in the Awatere Valley, which added 'high notes'. Rich, vibrant and crisp, it's a highly refined wine with melon, capsicum and lime flavours, very pure, fresh and long.

Vintage	08
WR	7
Drink	P

DRY $23 V+

Coopers Creek SV Awatere Marlborough Sauvignon Blanc (★★★☆)

The debut 2008 vintage (★★★☆) is a single-vineyard wine, grown at Blind River, in the Awatere Valley. The bouquet is nettley; the palate is fresh, with moderately intense, grassy, gooseberryish flavours, vibrant and crisp.

Vintage	08
WR	6
Drink	P

DRY $20 AV

Coopers Creek SV Dillons Point Marlborough Sauvignon Blanc ★★★★

Harvested from first-crop vines at Dillons Point – between Blenheim and the Cloudy Bay coast – the 2009 vintage (★★★★) is aromatic, with fresh tropical-fruit and herbaceous flavours, youthful, vibrant and punchy.

Vintage	09	08	07
WR	7	6	6
Drink	10-11	P	P

MED/DRY $20 V+

Corazon Single Vineyard Sauvignon Blanc ★★★☆

Grown in Marlborough, in the lower Wairau Valley, and fermented in tanks (85 per cent) and seasoned oak barrels, the 2009 vintage (★★★☆) is fresh and sweet-fruited, with tangy, ripe melon/lime flavours, showing a touch of complexity, good vigour and depth.

DRY $18 V+

Corbans Cottage Block Hawke's Bay Sauvignon Blanc ★★★★

The 2009 vintage (★★★★) was grown by Pernod Ricard NZ at Matapiro, 40 kilometres inland. Fleshy and smooth, it has strong, ripe stone-fruit, lime and spice flavours, a subtle oak influence and good complexity and roundness.

DRY $32 –V

Corbans Homestead Hawke's Bay Sauvignon Blanc ★★★

From Pernod Ricard NZ, this is typically a fresh, fruity wine with ripe passionfruit and lime flavours showing good depth and a smooth finish. The 2008 vintage (★★★) is ripely scented, in a medium to full-bodied style with fresh, vibrant tropical-fruit flavours, balanced for easy drinking.

Vintage	08	07
WR	6	6
Drink	P	P

DRY $17 AV

Corbans Private Bin Hawke's Bay Sauvignon Blanc ★★★☆

The 2008 vintage (★★★★) was grown inland, at the company-owned vineyard at Matapiro. It offers good intensity of ripe tropical-fruit flavours, with a touch of complexity, lively acidity and a fresh, dry finish.

DRY $24 –V

Cottage Block Sauvignon Blanc –
see Corbans Cottage Block Hawke's Bay Sauvignon Blanc

Couper's Shed Hawke's Bay Sauvignon Blanc (★★★☆)

The debut 2010 vintage (★★★☆) from Pernod Ricard NZ is attractively scented, with strong, ripely herbaceous flavours, fresh, crisp and lively.

DRY $20 AV

Crab Farm Hawke's Bay Sauvignon Blanc ★★★

The 2008 vintage (★★★) is a very easy-drinking style, full-bodied and fresh, with ripe passionfruit-like, non-herbaceous flavours, showing good depth.

Vintage	08
WR	7
Drink	P

DRY $17 AV

Craggy Range Avery Vineyard Marlborough Sauvignon Blanc ★★★★

Grown at a slightly cooler site in the Wairau Valley than its Old Renwick Vineyard stablemate (below), the 2010 vintage (★★★★) is weighty, with ripe stone-fruit and lime flavours, showing excellent texture and concentration. It's a bone-dry style, generous and slightly minerally, with a long finish.

Vintage	10	09	08	07	06
WR	7	6	7	6	6
Drink	10-13	10-12	P	P	P

DRY $20 V+

Craggy Range Old Renwick Vineyard Sauvignon Blanc ★★★★

From mature vines in the heart of the Wairau Valley, the 2010 vintage (★★★★) has a fresh, lifted, limey bouquet. Mouthfilling and crisp, with an array of apple, grapefruit and lime flavours, it is sweet-fruited and dry, with a mineral undertow and poised, tight finish. Not 'showy', it's a serious wine for drinking over the next several years; open mid-2011+.

Vintage	10	09	08	07	06
WR	7	7	7	5	7
Drink	10-13	10-12	P	P	P

DRY $20 V+

Craggy Range Te Muna Road Vineyard Martinborough Sauvignon Blanc ★★★★

Grown a few kilometres south of Martinborough township, this wine is mostly fermented and lees-aged in tanks, but partly fermented with indigenous yeasts in seasoned oak barrels. The

2009 vintage (★★★★), 12 per cent barrel-fermented, is a sophisticated wine, full-bodied, with ripe melon/lime flavours, lees-aging notes adding complexity and a crisp, dry finish.

Vintage	10	09	08	07
WR	6	7	7	7
Drink	10-13	10-13	10-11	P

DRY $23 AV

Crater Rim, The, Waipara Sauvignon Blanc ★★★★

The 2009 vintage (★★★★☆) was grown on the valley floor and tank-fermented. Fresh and full-bodied, it has generous, ripe passionfruit and lime flavours that build well across the palate, a minerally streak and a finely textured, long, dry finish. Delicious now, it's a wine with strong personality.

DRY $25 AV

Crawford Farm Marlborough Sauvignon Blanc ★★★★

From Constellation NZ, the 2008 vintage (★★★☆) is a freshly herbaceous style with strong gooseberry/lime flavours. Mouthfilling and dry, it has crisp, slightly nettley characters, showing very good depth.

DRY $23 AV

Croft Sauvignon Blanc (★★★☆)

Grown in Martinborough and mostly handled in tanks (5 per cent was aged in old oak casks), the 2008 vintage (★★★☆) is a fresh, melon and lime-flavoured wine, ripe and smooth, with very good balance and depth.

Vintage	08
WR	5
Drink	P

DRY $20 AV

Croney Three Ton Marlborough Sauvignon Blanc (★★★★)

Offering great value, the 2008 vintage (★★★★) was hand-picked in the Wairau Valley and a 'very small' portion was barrel-fermented; the rest was handled in tanks. Fresh, ripe-fruit aromas lead into a mouthfilling wine with tropical-fruit flavours, showing a touch of complexity, good concentration and plenty of personality.

DRY $15 V+

Crossings, The, Marlborough Sauvignon Blanc ★★★☆

The 2009 vintage (★★★★) was estate-grown in the Awatere Valley and mostly handled in tanks; 2 per cent of the blend was barrel-fermented. It shows good weight and purity, with fresh, delicate, moderately concentrated melon/lime flavours and a smooth (4.5 grams/litre of residual sugar) finish.

DRY $20 AV

Crossroads Marlborough Sauvignon Blanc ★★★

The 2009 vintage (★★☆) is a medium-bodied, dry wine with restrained, citrusy, limey flavours, pleasant and smooth.

Vintage	08
WR	6
Drink	P

DRY $20 –V

Crowded House Marlborough Sauvignon Blanc ★★★☆

A good buy. The 2010 vintage (★★★☆) is punchy, with melon, lime and green-capsicum flavours, fresh and delicate, and a lingering, dry (2.9 grams/litre of residual sugar) finish.

DRY $18 V+

Curio Castles Vineyard Awatere Valley Marlborough Sauvignon Blanc (★★★★)

From Mud House and sold mainly in restaurants, the debut 2008 vintage (★★★★) has strong 'tomato stalk' aromas, typical of the Awatere. Mouthfilling and smooth, it's a 'full-on' style with penetrating gooseberry, herb and slight spice flavours, a sliver of sweetness (7 grams/litre of residual sugar) adding smoothness, and good harmony.

MED/DRY $26 –V

Curio Gane's Vineyard Wairau Valley Marlborough Sauvignon Blanc (★★★☆)

The debut 2008 vintage (★★★☆) from Mud House is aimed at the restaurant trade. It's a full-bodied style with lively tropical-fruit flavours showing very good depth and a crisp, dry finish.

DRY $26 –V

Daisy Rock Marlborough Sauvignon Blanc ★★★

From Maven, the 2008 vintage (★★★) is a crisp, fairly herbaceous style, with gooseberry and green-capsicum flavours to the fore, some tropical-fruit notes and satisfying depth.

DRY $17 AV

Dancing Water Awatere Valley Sauvignon Blanc ★★★☆

The 2008 vintage (★★★) is a single-vineyard wine, crisp and lively, with ripe tropical-fruit and greener, nettley aromas and flavours.

DRY $20 AV

Darling, The, Barrel Marlborough Sauvignon Blanc (★★★★)

Certified organic, the debut 2010 vintage (★★★★) is a single-vineyard, Wairau Valley wine, handled in old oak casks. It's mouthfilling, with ripe melon, lime and capsicum flavours, showing good complexity, a subtle seasoning of oak, fresh acidity, and a rounded, dry finish. Best drinking mid-2011+.

Vintage	10
WR	7
Drink	10-14

DRY $28 –V

Darling, The, Marlborough Sauvignon Blanc (★★★★)

The 2009 vintage (★★★★) was grown at two sites in the Wairau Valley, under conversion to BioGro status, and mostly handled in tanks; 15 per cent was fermented with indigenous yeasts in old oak casks. Mouthfilling, with a touch of complexity, it is crisp and concentrated, with strong tropical-fruit flavours, woven with fresh, lively acidity, and a dry finish.

Vintage	09
WR	6
Drink	10-12

DRY $23 AV

Darling, The, Moscato Inspired Sauvignon Blanc (★★★☆)

The distinctive 2010 vintage (★★★☆) should really be in the Sweet White Wines section of the *Guide*, since it harbours 55 grams per litre of residual sugar. Grown in a Marlborough vineyard under conversion to BioGro status, it's a low-alcohol style (9.5 per cent), crisp, lively and refreshing, with ripe tropical-fruit flavours and some 'funky', indigenous yeast notes in the bouquet. Very easy drinking.

Vintage	10
WR	5
Drink	10-12

SW $24 –V

Dashwood Marlborough Sauvignon Blanc ★★★☆

Vavasour's drink-young, unwooded Sauvignon Blanc is typically great value. The 2009 vintage (★★★☆) is a fresh, vibrant, finely balanced blend of Awatere Valley (70 per cent) and Wairau Valley (30 per cent) grapes. Strongly varietal, it has very good delicacy and depth of melon, lime and green-capsicum flavours.

Vintage	09	08
WR	6	6
Drink	10-11	P

DRY $17 V+

Day Break Gisborne Sauvignon Blanc (★★★☆)

Unusually punchy for a Gisborne savvy, the 2009 vintage (★★★☆) was made by Nick Nobilo for Day Break Wines and on sale by May 2009. Freshly aromatic, it is crisp, tangy and ripely herbaceous, with strong passionfruit and lime flavours, balanced for early drinking.

DRY $19 V+

Delegat's Marlborough Sauvignon Blanc ★★★☆

Winemaker Michael Ivicevich aims for 'a tropical fruit-flavoured style, a bit broader and softer than some'. The 2009 vintage (★★★★) is crisp and dry, with fresh, strong melon/lime flavours, woven with racy acidity. Good value.

Vintage	09	08
WR	6	6
Drink	10-13	10-12

DRY $17 V+

Delegat's Reserve Marlborough Sauvignon Blanc ★★★★

From the Awatere Valley, the 2008 vintage (★★★★) is weighty and dry, with concentrated passionfruit and lime flavours, in a slightly riper, less herbal style than most of the valley's wines.

Vintage	08
WR	6
Drink	10-13

DRY $20 V+

Discovery Point Marlborough Sauvignon Blanc ★★★★

From wine distributor Bennett & Deller, the 2009 vintage (★★★★) was grown in the Wairau Valley and lees-aged for four months. Fully dry, it is fresh and zingy, with good intensity of ripely herbaceous flavours, substantial body and a rounded finish.

DRY $24 AV

Distant Land Hawke's Bay Sauvignon Blanc ★★★

From Lincoln, the 2009 vintage (★★★) is a very easy-drinking wine, medium-bodied, with ripe tropical-fruit flavours, fresh and vibrant, and a splash of sweetness (7.9 grams/litre of residual sugar) to add smoothness.

MED/DRY $18 AV

Distant Land Marlborough Sauvignon Blanc ★★★☆

The 2009 vintage (★★★☆) from Lincoln was grown in the Wairau Valley. A freshly herbaceous style, it's intensely varietal, with gooseberry and green-capsicum flavours, crisp and strong.

DRY $20 AV

Doctors', The, Marlborough Sauvignon Blanc (★★★☆)

From Forrest, the debut 2009 vintage (★★★☆) is a low-alcohol style (9.5 per cent), made for 'easy drinking at lunchtime'. Aromatic, it is light and lively, fresh and punchy, with gently herbaceous, limey flavours and a dryish (7 grams/litre of residual sugar), crisp finish. A good apéritif. (The 2010 vintage has 12 grams per litre of residual sugar.)

Vintage	09
WR	5
Drink	10-11

MED/DRY $22 AV

Dog Point Vineyard Marlborough Sauvignon Blanc ★★★★

This wine offers a clear style contrast to Section 94, the company's complex, barrel-aged Sauvignon Blanc (see the Branded and Other White Wines section). Hand-picked, it is lees-aged in tanks, with no exposure to oak. The 2009 vintage (★★★★) is a tight, focused style, vibrantly fruity, with mouthfilling body, very pure melon/lime flavours and a smooth (4.9 grams/litre of residual sugar), crisp finish.

DRY $25 AV

Dolbel Estate Hawke's Bay Sauvignon Blanc ★★★★

A label worth discovering. Grown at Springfield Vineyard, on the banks of the Tutaekuri River, and made by Tony Prichard, formerly of Church Road, the 2008 vintage (★★★★) is a subtle, complex, Bordeaux style, fully fermented (half with indigenous yeasts) in seasoned French oak barriques. Mouthfilling and dry, it has rich, ripe tropical-fruit flavours, slightly nutty and rounded.

Vintage	08	07	06
WR	6	6	6
Drink	10-12	10-12	10-11

DRY $22 V+

Domain Road Vineyard Central Otago Sauvignon Blanc ★★★☆

Grown at Bannockburn and 10 per cent barrel-fermented, the 2009 (★★★★) is stylish, with good richness. Mouthfilling, it is ripely scented, with dry melon/lime flavours, showing excellent delicacy and depth. The 2010 (★★★) was 30 per cent barrel-fermented. Tasted in its infancy, it was very fresh, vibrant and crisp, with fractional sweetness (4 grams/litre of residual sugar) adding smoothness, mouthfilling body and some complexity.

DRY $24 –V

Domaine Georges Michel Golden Mile Marlborough Sauvignon Blanc – see Georges Michel

Domaine Georges Michel La Reserve Marlborough Sauvignon Blanc – see Georges Michel

Drylands Marlborough Sauvignon Blanc ★★★☆
This is a consistently enjoyable wine from Constellation NZ, fermented and lees-aged in tanks. The 2009 vintage (★★★☆) is an upfront style with citrusy, nettley aromas and flavours, fresh and lively.

DRY $19 V+

Durvillea Marlborough Sauvignon Blanc ★★★☆
From Astrolabe, the 2009 vintage (★★★★) is named after a local seaweed. A top buy, it is freshly herbaceous, aromatic and vibrantly fruity, with lively acidity and good richness through the palate.

DRY $14 V+

Elephant Hill Hawke's Bay Sauvignon Blanc ★★★☆
Grown at Te Awanga, the 2009 vintage (★★★☆) has fresh, limey aromas leading into a medium-bodied wine with lively acidity, pure melon and green-capsicum flavours and a crisp, slightly minerally, dry finish.

DRY $22 AV

Elephant Hill Reserve Hawke's Bay Sauvignon Blanc (★★★☆)
The 2008 vintage (★★★☆) was estate-grown at Te Awanga and oak-aged on its yeast lees for five months. Mouthfilling, it is a tightly structured wine, clearly herbaceous, with a hint of nutty oak and a crisp, dry finish.

DRY $29 –V

Eliot Brothers Marlborough Sauvignon Blanc (★★★☆)
From an Auckland-based company, the bargain-priced 2008 vintage (★★★☆) is maturing well. Fresh and weighty, it has tropical-fruit flavours, an unobtrusive splash of sweetness (6.6 grams/litre of residual sugar), and very good liveliness and depth. Drink now.

MED/DRY $18 V+

Eradus Awatere Valley Marlborough Sauvignon Blanc ★★★★☆
The 2009 (★★★★★) is a weighty, rich, rounded wine with deep gooseberry and lime flavours, a minerally streak and the 'tomato stalk' characters typical of the Awatere. Deliciously concentrated, it's priced very sharply. The 2010 vintage (★★★★), tasted in its infancy, is mouth-watering crisp, citrusy and nettley, in a punchy, dry style with very good intensity and length.

Vintage	09
WR	6
Drink	10-11

DRY $19 V+

Esk Valley Marlborough Sauvignon Blanc ★★★★☆

This Hawke's Bay winery recently switched its Sauvignon Blanc focus to Marlborough – with immediate success. The debut 2009 vintage (★★★★★) is weighty, with punchy gooseberry/lime flavours, showing lovely vigour and intensity, racy acidity and a long, bone-dry finish. The 2010 (★★★★) was grown in the Wairau and Awatere valleys. It's an intensely aromatic wine with fresh, punchy tropical-fruit and herbaceous flavours and a crisp, dry (2.8 grams/litre of residual sugar) finish.

Vintage	10	09
WR	7	7
Drink	11-12	P

DRY $24 V+

Fairbourne Marlborough Sauvignon Blanc ★★★★☆

Grown on elevated, north-facing slopes in the Wairau Valley, the 2009 vintage (★★★★★) is a classy wine, tightly structured, with a very fresh, refined bouquet. Weighty, crisp and dry, it has searching, ripe flavours of citrus fruits and limes, showing excellent delicacy and intensity, a minerally streak, and a long, tight finish.

Vintage	09	08
WR	6	5
Drink	10-12	10-11

DRY $35 –V

Fairhall Downs Hugo Marlborough Sauvignon Blanc ★★★★☆

The 2008 vintage (★★★★☆) is a complex style, barrel-fermented with indigenous yeasts and French oak-matured for 10 months. Mouthfilling, it is sweet-fruited, with strong, ripe tropical-fruit flavours, a distinct suggestion of toasty oak, and lively acidity.

DRY $30 –V

Fairhall Downs Single Vineyard Marlborough Sauvignon Blanc ★★★★

Grown at the head of the Brancott Valley, the 2009 vintage (★★★★) is scented, vibrant and punchy, with classic gooseberry, passionfruit and lime flavours, pure, crisp and dry. Fine value.

DRY $20 V+

Fairmont Estate Sauvignon Blanc ★★☆

The 2008 vintage (★★) from this Wairarapa producer is a simple quaffer, light and plain.

DRY $15 AV

Fallen Angel Marlborough Sauvignon Blanc ★★★★

From Stonyridge Vineyard, on Waiheke Island, the 2010 vintage (★★★★) is mouthfilling and lively, with ripe tropical-fruit characters, a herbal undercurrent, and loads of crisp, dry (3.9 grams/litre of residual sugar) flavour.

Vintage	10
WR	7
Drink	10-12

DRY $28 –V

Farmers Market Growers Mark Marlborough Sauvignon Blanc (★★★☆)

The 2009 vintage (★★★☆) is a scented, freshly herbaceous wine with good depth of citrus fruit, lime and green-capsicum flavours, finely textured, dry and lingering.

DRY $25 –V

Farmers Market Marlborough Sauvignon Blanc (★★★☆)

The 2009 vintage (★★★☆) is fleshy and generous, with ripe passionfruit and lime flavours, showing very good depth, and a rounded finish.

DRY $20 AV

Farmgate Hawke's Bay Sauvignon Blanc ★★★☆

From Ngatarawa, the 2009 vintage (★★★☆) is a full-bodied style with good depth of vibrant, ripe tropical-fruit flavours and a refreshingly crisp, dry finish.

DRY $22 AV

Fiddler's Green Waipara Sauvignon Blanc ★★★★

A distinctly cool-climate style, typically with excellent vibrancy and depth. Estate-grown and tank-fermented, the 2009 vintage (★★★★) is fresh and lively, with ripely herbaceous flavours, showing very good vigour and intensity, and an appetisingly crisp, bone-dry finish.

Vintage	09
WR	6
Drink	10-11

DRY $20 V+

Fisherman's Bite Marlborough Sauvignon Blanc (★★★)

From Vernon Family Estate, the 2010 vintage (★★★) is a great buy. Nettley aromas lead into a full-bodied, basically dry wine (4.8 grams/litre of residual sugar) with good depth of gooseberry and green-capsicum flavours, fresh and racy.

DRY $13 V+

Five Flax Sauvignon Blanc ★★☆

From Pernod Ricard NZ, the 2008 vintage (★★☆) is clearly herbaceous, in a medium-bodied style with decent depth of gooseberry and herb flavours, and a smooth finish.

Vintage	08
WR	5
Drink	P

DRY $15 AV

Forrest Marlborough Sauvignon Blanc ★★★☆

This aromatic, vibrantly fruity wine has recently become noticeably drier, while retaining good drinkability. The 2009 vintage (★★★★), grown in the central Wairau Valley, is tight and elegant, with mouthfilling body, ripe passionfruit and lime flavours, fresh and delicate, a slightly minerally streak and a dry (3 grams/litre of residual sugar) finish.

Vintage	09	08
WR	6	5
Drink	10-15	10-15

DRY $22 AV

Forrest The Valleys Awatere Marlborough Sauvignon Blanc ★★★★☆

The 2010 vintage (★★★★☆) is a classic Awatere style – racy, with intense, 'tomato stalk' aromas leading into a full-bodied palate with incisive, ripely herbaceous flavours, crisp, dryish (6 grams/litre of residual sugar), tangy and lingering.

Vintage	10
WR	6
Drink	10-11

MED/DRY $22 V+

Forrest The Valleys Wairau Sauvignon Blanc ★★★★☆

(Previously labelled as James Randall.) The 2009 vintage (★★★★☆) is weighty, fleshy, finely textured and rich, with very ripe passionfruit/lime flavours, showing excellent delicacy and depth. Softer and drier (3 grams/litre of residual sugar) than its Awatere Valley stablemate (above), it's still tight and youthful, with good potential.

Vintage	09
WR	6
Drink	11-15

DRY $35 –V

Fox Junior Marlborough Sauvignon Blanc (★★★)

From Foxes Island, the 2008 vintage (★★★) is a clearly herbaceous wine with melon, lime and capsicum flavours, fresh and smooth.

DRY $20 –V

Foxes Island Marlborough Sauvignon Blanc ★★★★

The 2008 vintage (★★★★) was hand-picked at 23.5 brix, fermented in tanks (mostly) and new French oak barriques, and lees-aged for three months. Mouthfilling and punchy, with ripe tropical-fruit flavours showing good immediacy and drive, it is fleshy and slightly minerally, with excellent depth.

Vintage	09	08
WR	6	6
Drink	10-13	P

DRY $25 AV

Framingham F Series Marlborough Sauvignon Blanc (★★★★★)

The powerful 2008 vintage (★★★★★) was hand-picked, fermented with indigenous yeasts in a 2:1 mix of old oak barrels and stainless steel 'barrels', and 50 per cent of the blend went through a softening malolactic fermentation. Rich, ripe and rounded, with barrel-ferment complexity and some slightly 'funky' notes, it's a non-herbaceous style, concentrated and complex, with gentle acidity and a bone-dry, finely textured finish. Full of personality, it's maturing well.

Vintage	08
WR	6
Drink	10-12

DRY $35 AV

Framingham Marlborough Sauvignon Blanc ★★★★☆

Already delicious, the punchy, finely poised 2010 (★★★★★) is a top vintage. Grown at six sites in the Wairau Valley, it was mostly handled in tanks, but – for the first time – 5 per cent of the blend was barrel-fermented. Weighty, fleshy and rounded, with concentrated, peachy, limey, faintly nutty flavours, it has lovely depth and harmony. Showing good complexity, with a dry (3.5 grams/litre of residual sugar), lasting finish, it delivers top value.

Vintage	10		DRY $22 V+
WR	6		
Drink	10-12		

Frizzell Sauvignon Blanc (★★★★)

Still on sale in 2010, the 2008 vintage (★★★★) warns: 'Please Note: May Contain Traces of Summer.' Grown in the Wairau Valley, Marlborough, and lees-aged over winter, it has a punchy, lifted, herbaceous bouquet. Full-bodied, it has a basket of fruit flavours, with a minerally streak, and very good richness, delicacy and length.

Vintage	08		DRY $22 V+
WR	5		
Drink	10-12		

Full Circle Marlborough Sauvignon Blanc (★★)

From Yealands, the 2009 vintage (★★), packaged in a plastic bottle, is recommended for consumption 'before 13/05/2011'. It's a pale, medium-bodied, pungently herbaceous wine with green capsicum-like flavours. If you like very crisp and grassy Sauvignon Blanc, this is for you.

DRY $16 –V

Gem Marlborough Sauvignon Blanc (★★★★)

Still on sale, the 2006 vintage (★★★★) is maturing well. Tank-fermented with indigenous yeasts, it is youthful in colour, weighty, fleshy and rich, with ripe non-herbaceous fruit flavours. Minerally and lively, with a bone-dry finish, it's developing surprising complexity with bottle-age. Drink now.

Vintage	07	06	DRY $25 AV
WR	6	6	
Drink	10-17	10-16	

Georges Michel Golden Mile Marlborough Sauvignon Blanc ★★★

Grown in the Rapaura ('golden mile') district of the Wairau Valley, the easy-drinking 2009 vintage (★★★) is mouthfilling, ripe and rounded, with tropical-fruit flavours, gentle acidity and a smooth, dryish (5.5 grams/litre of residual sugar) finish.

MED/DRY $17 AV

Georges Michel La Reserve Marlborough Sauvignon Blanc ★★★☆

The 2009 vintage (★★★☆) is a tight, youthful wine, hand-harvested and fermented and matured for eight months in seasoned French oak barrels. Ripely scented, with subtle oak, it is medium to full-bodied, with very good depth of tropical-fruit flavours, crisp and bone-dry.

Vintage	09	DRY $22 AV
WR	6	
Drink	10-15	

Georges Michel Marlborough Sauvignon Blanc (★★★★)

Drier than its Golden Mile stablemate (above), the 2009 vintage (★★★★) is a tight, poised and punchy wine with fresh, crisp tropical-fruit and herbaceous flavours, showing very good depth. Aromatic, slightly nettley, lively and minerally, it's drinking well now.

DRY $16 V+

Giesen Marlborough Sauvignon Blanc ★★★

The largest-volume wine from Giesen has a low profile in New Zealand, but enjoys major export success. It is typically light and lively, with tangy acidity and good depth of fresh melon, capsicum and lime flavours. The 2009 vintage (★★★) has crisp, ripe tropical-fruit and herbaceous flavours, fresh and dry.

DRY $17 AV

Giesen Marlborough Sauvignon Blanc The August (★★★★★)

The outstanding 2009 vintage (★★★★★) is named after the Giesen brothers' grandfather, August (pronounced 'ow-goost') Giesen. Hand-picked at three sites in the Wairau Valley and fermented with indigenous yeasts in seasoned French oak casks, it has a commanding presence. Very fleshy and ripe, it is mouthfilling, sweet-fruited and highly concentrated, with good acid spine and obvious cellaring potential.

DRY $34 AV

Giesen Marlborough Sauvignon Blanc The Brothers ★★★★☆

Tightly structured, dry and concentrated, the 2009 vintage (★★★★☆) is a classic regional style, grown at four sites in the Wairau Valley. The bouquet is punchy and ripely herbaceous; the palate is weighty and concentrated, with a minerally streak and strong passionfruit/lime flavours, showing excellent delicacy and length.

DRY $27 AV

Gladstone Vineyard Sauvignon Blanc ★★★☆

The 2009 vintage (★★★★) was harvested in the northern Wairarapa and mostly handled in tanks; 5 per cent of the blend was fermented and matured in French oak barrels. Ripely scented, it is mouthfilling and crisp, with fresh, ripe passionfruit, pineapple and lime flavours, showing good vigour and richness, and a finely balanced, lingering, dry finish.

DRY $23 –V

Gladstone Vineyard Sophie's Choice [Sauvignon Blanc] (★★★★☆)

The debut 2009 vintage (★★★★☆) is based on 24-year-old vines in the northern Wairarapa. Fermented and matured for 10 months in French oak barrels, it's still youthful. Weighty, complex and creamy-textured, it is fleshy, with concentrated, ripe tropical-fruit flavours seasoned with toasty oak and a finely textured, rounded finish. Drink 2011–12.

DRY $35 –V

Glazebrook Marlborough Sauvignon Blanc ★★★

Grown at three sites in the Wairau Valley, the 2008 vintage (★★★) from Ngatarawa is fleshy and ripe, with passionfruit and lime flavours showing good balance and depth, and a dry (2.8 grams/litre of residual sugar) finish.

Vintage	08	07	06
WR	6	6	5
Drink	10-11	P	P

DRY $20 –V

Golden Hills Estate Nelson Sauvignon Blanc (★★★★)

The tightly structured, single-vineyard 2009 vintage (★★★★) was partly barrel-fermented. Weighty and youthful, it is ripely flavoured, with a subtle seasoning of oak, strong tropical-fruit flavours and good acid spine.

DRY $20 V+

Goldridge Marlborough Sauvignon Blanc ★★☆

The 2009 vintage (★★☆) was grown in the Wairau and Awatere valleys. It's clearly herbaceous, with fresh, crisp gooseberry and green-capsicum flavours, a sliver of sweetness (7.2 grams/litre of residual sugar) and solid depth.

MED/DRY $16 AV

Goldridge Premium Reserve Marlborough Sauvignon Blanc ★★★

The 2009 vintage (★★★☆) is fresh and crisp, with strong melon, lime and green-capsicum flavours and a dry (3.4 grams/litre of residual sugar) finish. Grown in the Wairau and Awatere valleys, and showing some richness, it's one of the best wines yet under this label.

DRY $19 AV

Goldwater Wairau Valley Sauvignon Blanc ★★★★

The 2009 vintage (★★★★) is a rich, ripe style with a hint of 'sweaty armpit', good weight and strong melon and capsicum flavours. The 2010 (★★★★★) is a beauty. Mouthfilling, it is tight, dry and rich, with generous tropical-fruit flavours, showing lovely ripeness and delicacy, and firm acid spine. Very intense, it's already delicious.

Vintage	10	09
WR	6	6
Drink	10-12	10-11

DRY $22 V+

Grass Cove Marlborough Sauvignon Blanc (★★★☆)

From an Auckland-based company, the 2008 vintage (★★★☆) is fresh, crisp, citrusy and limey, with good body, flavour depth and vigour, and a tight, dry (3.9 grams/litre of residual sugar) finish.

DRY $17 V+

Greenhough Nelson Sauvignon Blanc ★★★★★

Andrew Greenhough aims for a 'rich Sauvignon Blanc style with ripe, creamy mouthfeel' – and hits the target with ease. Grown at three sites at Hope, the 2009 vintage (★★★★) was mostly handled in tanks, but 4 per cent of the blend was fermented with indigenous yeasts in new oak casks. It's a finely poised, gently herbaceous wine with strong melon, peach and capsicum flavours, vibrant and crisp. The 2010 (★★★★★) has slightly 'sweaty' aromas, leading into a classy, authoritative wine. Very mouthfilling, it is sweet-fruited, with ripe tropical-fruit flavours, showing lovely delicacy and richness, finely balanced acidity, and a long, slightly spicy, dry finish.

Vintage	10	09	08	07	06
WR	7	7	7	7	6
Drink	11-14	10-13	10-12	10-11	P

DRY $20 V+

Greyrock Marlborough Sauvignon Blanc (★★☆)

From Sileni, the 2008 vintage (★★☆) is a slightly sweet style with crisp melon and lime flavours, showing decent depth.

MED/DRY $14 AV

Greystone Waipara Sauvignon Blanc ★★★★

The 2009 vintage (★★★★) was 4 per cent fermented in French oak barrels and made in a fully dry style. Ripely scented, it has good weight, fresh, delicate melon and herb flavours, a minerally streak and good intensity. (The 2010 was 33 per cent barrel-fermented.)

Vintage	10
WR	6
Drink	10-13

DRY $23 AV

Greywacke Marlborough Sauvignon Blanc (★★★★☆)

The debut 2009 vintage (★★★★☆) from Kevin Judd, formerly managing director of Cloudy Bay, was grown at various sites in the Brancott Valley and on the Wairau Plains. Partly barrel-fermented, it is mouthfilling, with punchy, ripe stone-fruit and lime flavours, finely textured, crisp and lingering. It's a tightly structured, elegant wine that should unfold well during 2010.

DRY $26 AV

Grove Mill Grand Reserve Seventeen Valley Vineyard Marlborough Sauvignon Blanc (★★★★☆)

Tight, elegant and still very fresh and youthful, the 2009 vintage (★★★★☆) is a partly barrel-fermented style with concentrated, ripe melon/lime flavours, a subtle twist of oak and a lingering, crisp, dry finish. Best drinking mid-2011+.

DRY $26 AV

Grove Mill Marlborough Sauvignon Blanc ★★★★

At its best, this is a powerful wine, with excellent drinkability, although it no longer has the high profile of a decade ago. The grapes are drawn from vineyards (both company-owned and growers') scattered across the Wairau Valley, but mostly in the Rapaura and Renwick districts.

The wine is fermented and lees-aged for three to four months in tanks, and a portion goes through malolactic fermentation, to improve the blend's complexity and texture. Most vintages mature well for several years. It is typically mouthfilling and punchy, with rich, ripe tropical-fruit flavours to the fore, a herbal undercurrent, and a finely balanced, dry, long finish.

DRY $18 V+

Gunn Estate Sauvignon Blanc (★★☆)

A New Zealand wine from 'East Coast' regions, the 2009 vintage (★★☆) is vibrantly fruity, with a sliver of sweetness (5.9 grams/litre of residual sugar) and fresh, tangy acidity. It's a solid wine with tropical-fruit and apple flavours, balanced for easy drinking.

MED/DRY $18 –V

Hans Herzog Marlborough Sauvignon Blanc Sur Lie ★★★★☆

Far outside the mainstream regional style, the 2009 vintage (★★★★★) was estate-grown on the north side of the Wairau Valley, hand-picked at 23.5 to 24.4 brix, fermented with indigenous yeasts in French oak puncheons and barriques, oak-matured for a year, and given a full, softening malolactic fermentation. A lovely example of fully oak-aged Sauvignon Blanc, it is weighty, very ripe, creamy-textured and dry, with highly concentrated tropical-fruit flavours gently seasoned with oak, and a rich, rounded finish.

Vintage	09	08
WR	7	7
Drink	10-18	10-17

DRY $44 –V

Harwood Hall Marlborough Sauvignon Blanc (★★★★)

The 2009 vintage (★★★★) was grown mostly at Dillons Point, in the lower Wairau Valley. Ripely scented, it is full-bodied and dry, with fresh, lively melon and green-capsicum flavours, showing very good depth, and a well-rounded finish.

Vintage	10	09
WR	5	5
Drink	11-13	10-12

DRY $19 V+

Hawkshead Marlborough Sauvignon Blanc (★★★☆)

Hand-picked high in the Wairau Valley, 260 metres above sea level, the 2009 vintage (★★★☆) is attractively scented, with mouthfilling body and vibrant passionfruit/lime flavours, fresh, ripe and smooth.

DRY $20 AV

Hay Maker Marlborough Sauvignon Blanc ★★★☆

From Mud House, the 2008 vintage (★★★☆) is freshly aromatic and fleshy, with strong gooseberry and lime flavours, moderate acidity and a dry finish (2.9 grams/litre of residual sugar). Good value.

DRY $17 V+

Heart of Stone Marlborough Sauvignon Blanc ★★★☆

From Forrest Estate, the 2009 vintage (★★★☆) is punchy, with melon, capsicum and slight 'tomato stalk' characters, showing good vigour, delicacy and depth. Fine value.

`DRY $17 V+`

Highfield Marlborough Sauvignon Blanc ★★★★★

Typically a very classy wine – scented and harmonious, with rich, limey fruit flavours and excellent depth. The 2009 vintage (★★★★★) was mostly handled in tanks and given extended lees contact, but 2 per cent of the blend was oak-aged. It shows lovely freshness, balance, delicacy and intensity, with sweet-fruit delights, a complex array of fruit flavours, woven with lively acidity, and a very long finish. In its infancy, the 2010 (★★★★★) also looked very classy. Weighty, it has deep, very pure and delicate flavours of melons and limes, slightly nettley, crisp, minerally and long.

Vintage	10	09	08	07
WR	7	6	4	6
Drink	10-12	10-11	P	P

`DRY $24 V+`

Himmelsfeld Vineyard Moutere Sauvignon Blanc ★★★☆

The 2008 vintage (★★★☆) is weighty, with gooseberry/lime flavours, good vigour and a crisp, dry finish. The 2007 vintage (★★★★) is a fleshy, generous, powerful wine (14 per cent alcohol) with concentrated tropical-fruit flavours and a well-rounded finish.

`DRY $30 –V`

Homer Marlborough Sauvignon Blanc ★★★

From Odyssey, the 2009 vintage (★★★) was grown in the Brancott Valley. It's a drink-young style, fruity and smooth, ripe and rounded, with good body and depth of tropical-fruit flavours. Priced right.

Vintage	09	08
WR	5	5
Drink	10-11	P

`DRY $16 V+`

Hudson Mokopuna Sauvignon Blanc ★★★

Grown near Martinborough, the 2009 vintage (★★★☆) is a single-vineyard wine, made with a small percentage of barrel fermentation. It's a full-bodied wine, showing very good depth of ripe tropical-fruit flavours and a dry finish.

`DRY $21 –V`

Huia Marlborough Sauvignon Blanc ★★★☆

Grown at six sites in the Wairau Valley, the 2008 vintage (★★★☆) is full-bodied and smooth, with ripe melon, lime and capsicum flavours. It's a tight, slightly minerally wine with a crisp, dry finish.

Vintage	08
WR	6
Drink	10-11

`DRY $22 AV`

Huntaway Reserve Marlborough Sauvignon Blanc ★★★★
Grown on heavy, clay soils in the lower Wairau Valley, the 2010 vintage (★★★★) is fleshy, concentrated and rounded, with mouthfilling body and fresh, very ripe flavours, slightly spicy and rich.

DRY $24 AV

Hunter's Kaho Roa Marlborough Sauvignon Blanc ★★★★
Based on Hunter's ripest, least-herbaceous grapes, this wine is grown in stony vineyards along Rapaura Road, on the relatively warm, north side of the Wairau Valley. Part of the blend is handled entirely in stainless steel tanks; another is tank-fermented but barrel-aged; and the third is fermented and lees-aged for eight to nine months in new French oak barriques. It typically matures well for up to five years. The 2008 vintage (★★★★) is delicious now. Ripely scented, it has attractive, passionfruit-like flavours, showing excellent depth, delicacy and dryness, gentle acidity and a lingering finish.

Vintage	08	07
WR	5	5
Drink	11-13	10-12

DRY $23 AV

Hunter's Marlborough Sauvignon Blanc ★★★★
Hunter's fame rests on the consistent excellence of this fully dry wine, which exhibits the intense aromas of ripe cool-climate grapes, uncluttered by any oak handling. The style goal is 'a strong expression of Marlborough fruit – a bell-clear wine with a mix of tropical and searing gooseberry characters'. The grapes are sourced from numerous sites in the Wairau Valley, and to retain their fresh, vibrant characters, they are processed very quickly, with protective anaerobic techniques and minimal handling. The wine is usually at its best between one and two years old. The intensely varietal 2009 vintage (★★★★) is very fresh, vibrant and punchy, with strong, ripely herbaceous flavours, good acid spine and a dry, lingering finish.

Vintage	09	08
WR	6	5
Drink	10-13	10-12

DRY $20 V+

Hurunui River Sauvignon Blanc ★★☆
Grown in North Canterbury, the 2009 vintage (★★☆) is a mouthfilling wine, fleshy and slightly creamy-textured, with crisp pear and spice flavours. I prefer the barrel-fermented 2008 (★★★), with its strong, gooseberryish, slightly toasty flavours, which show some complexity.

DRY $20 –V

Instinct Marlborough Sauvignon Blanc (★★★)
From C.J. Pask, based in Hawke's Bay, the debut 2008 vintage (★★★☆) is ripely scented, with crisp passionfruit/lime flavours, fresh and lively.

DRY $17 AV

Invivo Marlborough Sauvignon Blanc ★★★☆

From an Auckland-based company, the 2009 vintage (★★★☆) is medium-bodied (12.5 per cent alcohol), with fresh, pure melon and lime flavours, crisp and very finely balanced.

Vintage	10	
WR	5	
Drink	10-12	

DRY $20 AV

Isabel Marlborough Sauvignon Blanc ★★★

Grown in the Isabel Estate Vineyard near Renwick, in the heart of the Wairau Valley, and other sites in the Wairau and Omaka valleys, a decade ago this was a stunning wine, but its quality later slipped. The 2009 vintage (★★★★☆) is by far the best for several years. Fresh, dry and mouthfilling, it's a punchy, ripe, slightly minerally and crisp wine with good weight and intensity and a tight, lingering finish.

Vintage	09	
WR	7	
Drink	10-14	

DRY $25 –V

Jacks Canyon Waipara Sauvignon Blanc (★★★)

Enjoyable young, the 2010 vintage (★★★) is a fresh, crisply herbaceous style with melon and lime flavours, lively and smooth.

DRY $17 AV

Jackson Estate Grey Ghost Sauvignon Blanc ★★★★☆

Far outside the commercial mainstream, the 2009 vintage (★★★★★) was hand-harvested in Marlborough and fermented in tanks and seasoned French oak barriques. Delicious now, but still developing, it is very weighty and concentrated, with beautifully ripe melon, lime and passionfruit flavours, a slightly nutty, spicy complexity and a fresh, dry, lasting finish.

Vintage	09	08	07	06
WR	7	5	7	6
Drink	10-20	10-14	10-15	P

DRY $29 AV

Jackson Estate Stich Marlborough Sauvignon Blanc ★★★★★

Grown at a dozen sites in the Wairau Valley and its southern offshoots, this is typically a lush, ripe and rounded wine with concentration and huge drinkability. It has excellent aging ability, and the latest vintages are consistently outstanding. The 2010 (★★★★★) is another winner. A sophisticated wine, it is mouthfilling, rich, vibrant and sweet-fruited, with grapefruit, lime and slight spice flavours, woven with fresh acidity, and lovely harmony and length.

Vintage	10	09	
WR	6	7	
Drink	10-15	10-12	

DRY $22 V+

Johanneshof Marlborough Sauvignon Blanc ★★★☆

The 2009 vintage (★★★★) from this small producer is medium to full-bodied, with ripe passionfruit and lime flavours, showing very good depth, and a smooth finish.

Vintage	09	08	07	06
WR	5	4	4	4
Drink	10-11	P	P	P

MED/DRY $25 –V

Johner Estate Sur Lie Gladstone Sauvignon Blanc ★★★☆

The 2009 vintage (★★★☆) is an easy-drinking style, full-bodied, with ripe tropical-fruit flavours, fresh acidity and good depth. It's enjoyable now.

DRY $21 AV

Johner Estate Wairarapa Sauvignon Blanc ★★★★

The 2009 vintage (★★★★☆) is opening out well, with strong personality. A ripe, distinctly North Island style, it also shows cool-climate vivacity. Mouthfilling and crisp, it has excellent freshness and intensity of tropical-fruit flavours. The 2010 (★★★★) is full-bodied and punchy, with vibrant, racy tropical-fruit and herbaceous flavours, crisp and concentrated.

DRY $21 V+

Jules Taylor Marlborough Sauvignon Blanc ★★★★☆

The 2009 (★★★★☆) was grown in the Awatere and Wairau valleys. Richly scented, with a hint of 'sweaty armpit', it is concentrated and immaculate, with rich, vibrant melon/lime flavours, a minerally streak and a finely textured, long finish. The 2010 vintage (★★★★☆) is punchy and vibrantly fruity, with pure, penetrating tropical-fruit and herbaceous flavours, showing excellent freshness, delicacy and length.

Vintage	10	09
WR	7	6
Drink	10-13	10-12

DRY $22 V+

Julicher Martinborough Sauvignon Blanc ★★★★

The 2008 vintage (★★★★) was estate-grown, hand-picked and mostly handled in tanks, with a small percentage of barrel fermentation. It's a stylish, instantly likeable wine, vibrantly fruity, with fresh, concentrated, ripely herbaceous flavours, a touch of complexity, crisp acidity and a lingering, fully dry finish. Fine value.

Vintage	08	07
WR	5	6
Drink	P	P

DRY $19 V+

Jumper, The, Marlborough Sauvignon Blanc ★★★

Priced sharply, the 2009 vintage (★★★), grown in the Wairau Valley, is a fresh, crisp, clearly varietal wine with pineapple, melon and green-capsicum flavours, showing good depth.

DRY $16 V+

Kaimira Estate Brightwater Sauvignon Blanc ★★★

The 2009 vintage (★★★), partly (10 per cent) barrel-fermented, is a fresh, medium-bodied wine, with plenty of ripely herbaceous tropical-fruit and green-capsicum flavours and a dry (3.4 grams/litre of residual sugar) finish.

DRY $19 AV

Kaituna Valley Marlborough Awatere Vineyards Sauvignon Blanc ★★★☆

Grown at three sites in the Awatere Valley, the 2008 (★★☆) is a disappointing vintage for this normally rewarding label. Ripely flavoured, with a sliver of sweetness (5 grams/litre of residual sugar), it shows a slight lack of freshness and vibrancy.

Vintage	08
WR	7
Drink	P

MED/DRY $19 V+

Kakapo Marlborough Sauvignon Blanc ★★★★

This distributor's label (SANZ Global) is consistently good – and good value. The 2008 vintage (★★★★) is fleshy, ripe and punchy, with tropical-fruit and herbaceous flavours, showing excellent freshness, balance and depth.

DRY $19 V+

Karamea Marlborough Sauvignon Blanc (★★★☆)

Maturing well, the 2008 vintage (★★★☆) has a freshly herbaceous bouquet, leading into a mouthfilling wine with very good depth of melon and green-capsicum flavours.

DRY $20 AV

Kawarau Estate Central Otago Sauvignon Blanc ★★☆

Grown organically, the 2008 vintage (★★☆) is a single-vineyard wine, hand-picked at Pisa and lees-aged in tanks. It's a crisp, citrusy and limey wine, fresh and lively, with decent flavour depth and a slightly sweet (7.2 grams/litre of residual sugar) finish.

MED/DRY $23 –V

Kemblefield The Vista Sauvignon Blanc (★★★)

The 2008 vintage (★★★☆) of this unoaked wine, estate-grown at Mangatahi, in Hawke's Bay, has ripely herbaceous aromas. It's a vibrantly fruity wine with strong gooseberry and lime flavours, a hint of passionfruit, and a refreshingly crisp finish.

DRY $17 AV

Kennedy Point Marlborough Sauvignon Blanc ★★★

The 2009 vintage (★★★) from this Waiheke Island producer was grown in the Wairau Valley. It's a mouthfilling, fleshy, ripe tropical-fruit-flavoured wine with a hint of pineapples and a dry, rounded finish. Ready.

DRY $19 AV

Kerr Farm Vineyard Kumeu Sauvignon Blanc ★★☆

Estate-grown in West Auckland, the 2009 vintage (★★★) is a good example of the northern style. Full-bodied and dry, it has ripe tropical-fruit flavours, fresh and lively, showing good depth.

`DRY $20 –V`

Kim Crawford Marlborough Sauvignon Blanc ★★★☆

This is typically a very fresh and punchy style from Constellation NZ. The 2008 vintage (★★★☆), a 'pot-pourri' of Marlborough, was blended from grapes from 65 sites and produced in hundreds of thousands of cases. It offers strong, ripe melon/capsicum flavours, crisp acidity and a dry finish (3.7 grams/litre of residual sugar).

`DRY $23 –V`

Kim Crawford SP Flowers Marlborough Sauvignon Blanc ★★★★

This top-end label from Constellation NZ is sourced from various vineyards. A generous wine with a strong presence, the 2008 vintage (★★★★) has concentrated tropical-fruit and herbaceous flavours, crisp and dry.

`DRY $33 –V`

Kim Crawford SP Spitfire Marlborough Sauvignon Blanc ★★★★☆

The 2008 vintage (★★★★) is ripely scented and weighty, in a tropical fruit-flavoured style with a hint of herbs and good concentration. Why is it called 'Spitfire'? The grapes were grown on the site of an old airbase.

`DRY $33 –V`

Kina Beach Vineyard Estuary Block Sauvignon Blanc ★★★★

Grown at a coastal Nelson site, the easy-drinking 2010 vintage (★★★★) is already delicious. Freshly scented, poised and punchy, it is lively, with melon/lime flavours showing very good delicacy and depth, and a well-rounded (5 grams/litre of residual sugar) finish.

Vintage	10	09	08
WR	6	7	6
Drink	10-12	10-11	P

`MED/DRY $20 V+`

Kina Cliffs Nelson Sauvignon Blanc ★★★☆

From a vineyard overlooking Tasman Bay, the 2010 vintage (★★★☆) has slightly nettley aromas and flavours. Crisp and lively, it is very fresh, with a lingering finish. The 2009 (★★★☆) is mouthfilling, with ripe passionfruit, citrus-fruit and lime flavours, showing good ripeness, depth and harmony.

Vintage	10	09
WR	5	6
Drink	10-12	10-11

`DRY $20 AV`

Konrad Marlborough Sauvignon Blanc ★★★☆

The 2009 vintage (★★★☆), estate-grown in the Wairau and Waihopai valleys, was mostly handled in tanks; 3 per cent was barrel-fermented. Fresh and lively, it's a medium-bodied wine with ripe tropical-fruit flavours, a touch of complexity and a well-rounded, dry (2.9 grams/litre of residual sugar) finish.

Vintage	09	08	07
WR	5	4	4
Drink	10-11	10-11	10

DRY $18 V+

Koura Bay Awatere Valley Sauvignon Blanc ★★★☆

The 2009 vintage (★★★☆), estate-grown, is aromatic and punchy, with strong, clearly herbaceous flavours of gooseberries and capsicums, fresh and crisp.

Vintage	09	08
WR	7	5
Drink	10-12	P

DRY $19 V+

Kumeu River Sauvignon Blanc ★★★★

The 2009 vintage (★★★★), grown in Marlborough, is drinking well now. Mouthfilling, with a slightly 'funky' bouquet, reflecting the use of indigenous yeasts, and ripe tropical-fruit rather than herbaceous flavours, it shows good weight and concentration, with a crisp, fully dry finish.

DRY $22 V+

Kumeu River Village Sauvignon Blanc ★★★

Grown in Marlborough, the 2009 vintage (★★★) has 'funky', indigenous yeast aromas, leading into a lively, dry and flavoursome wine with ripe citrus-fruit, lime and spice characters, showing good individuality. It's ready to roll.

DRY $18 AV

Lake Chalice Marlborough Sauvignon Blanc ★★★★

The 2008 vintage (★★★☆) was grown at seven sites in the Wairau and Awatere valleys. Opening out well, it is mouthfilling, with very good depth of fresh, zingy gooseberry, melon and capsicum flavours, with a basically dry (4 grams/litre of residual sugar), crisply herbaceous finish.

Vintage	08
WR	6
Drink	P

DRY $20 V+

Lake Chalice The Raptor Marlborough Sauvignon Blanc ★★★★

Less than 2 per cent of the winery's Sauvignon Blanc grapes go into this top label. The 2008 (★★★★☆) has lifted, 'tomato stalk' aromas, leading into a mouthfilling, intense and zingy wine with an array of fruit flavours – melon, lime and passionfruit. It shows appetising acidity, with a long finish.

Vintage	08
WR	6
Drink	P

DRY $27 –V

La Strada Marlborough Sauvignon Blanc (★★★★)

After 16 vintages, the Fromm winery, renowned for Pinot Noir, finally made its first Sauvignon Blanc in 2008 (★★★★). Partly fermented in old French oak barrels and made in a bone-dry style, it's a fleshy, subtle wine with ripe melon/lime flavours, a touch of complexity and a smooth, finely balanced, lingering finish.

Vintage	09	08
WR	6	6
Drink	10-14	10-12

DRY $23 AV

Latitude 41 New Zealand Sauvignon Blanc ★★★☆

From Spencer Hill, the 2008 vintage (★★★☆) is a blend of Nelson and Marlborough grapes. It has mouthfilling body, with ripe, gooseberryish, slightly toasty flavours, a touch of complexity, and a well-rounded finish.

DRY $20 AV

Lawson's Dry Hills Marlborough Sauvignon Blanc ★★★★★

Consistently among the region's best Sauvignon Blancs, this is a stylish wine, vibrantly fruity, intense and finely structured. The grapes are grown at several sites (seven in 2009) in the Wairau (mostly) and Waihopai valleys. To add a subtle extra dimension, 4 to 8 per cent of the blend is fermented with indigenous and cultured yeasts in seasoned French oak barriques, and encouraged to undergo malolactic fermentation. The wine typically has great impact in its youth, but also has a proven ability to age well, acquiring toasty, minerally complexities. The 2009 vintage (★★★★☆) is a dry style (2.6 grams/litre of residual sugar) with slightly 'funky' aromas, good weight, strong, ripe tropical-fruit and herb flavours, a touch of complexity and a long, slightly minerally finish.

Vintage	09	08	07	06
WR	7	6	6	7
Drink	P	P	P	P

DRY $21 V+

Lawson's Dry Hills The Pioneer Marlborough Sauvignon Blanc (★★★★★)

The 2009 vintage (★★★★★) was grown in two vineyards near the winery, in the lower Wairau Valley, and mostly handled in tanks, with a small portion of barrel fermentation. The bouquet is very fresh and lifted, with ripe-fruit aromas and hints of 'sweaty armpit' and oak; the palate is crisp, concentrated and dry, with passionfruit, capsicum and spice flavours, showing excellent intensity and vigour. Best drinking 2011–12.

DRY $29 V+

Lime Rock Sauvignon Blanc ★★★☆

Grown at 240 metres above sea level, the 2008 vintage (★★★★) is a single-vineyard wine, hand-picked, tank-fermented and briefly lees-aged. One of the finest wines yet from Central Hawke's Bay, it has a fresh, punchy bouquet and a weighty palate with an array of grapefruit, herbal and mineral flavours, fresh, crisp, dry and long.

DRY $24 –V

Little Black Shag Sauvignon Blanc (★★☆)

From Anchorage, in Nelson, the 2009 vintage (★★☆) is a pleasant, easy-drinking wine with ripe, citrusy, limey flavours, showing decent depth. Priced sharply.

DRY $12 V+

Lobster Reef Marlborough Sauvignon Blanc ★★★☆

From Cape Campbell, the 2009 vintage (★★★★) was grown in the Wairau and Awatere valleys. Mouthfilling and vibrant, it has an array of ripe tropical-fruit and greener, herbaceous flavours, fresh and strong, with a smooth yet fully dry (2 grams/litre of residual sugar) finish. Great value.

DRY $15 V+

Locharburn Central Otago Sauvignon Blanc (★★★☆)

The 2010 vintage (★★★☆) was hand-harvested at 24 brix and mostly handled in tanks; 20 per cent of the blend was barrel-fermented, but not oak-aged. A full-bodied wine, woven with fresh acidity, it is vibrant and ripely flavoured, with good mouthfeel and texture and a touch of complexity.

Vintage	10
WR	6
Drink	10-12

DRY $23 –V

Longbush Marlborough Sauvignon Blanc (★★☆)

From a Gisborne-based producer, the 2008 vintage (★★☆) has herbaceous, gooseberry and green-capsicum flavours, with a dry, rounded finish. Priced sharply.

Vintage	08
WR	6
Drink	10-11

DRY $13 V+

Longridge Hawke's Bay Sauvignon Blanc ★★★

From Pernod Ricard NZ, the 2008 (★★★) is medium-bodied, with ripely herbaceous flavours, showing good balance and depth. The 2010 vintage was tasted before bottling, so is not rated, but it looked promising, with fresh, punchy melon/lime flavours, ripe and rounded.

DRY $18 AV

Loopline Sauvignon Blanc (★★★☆)

Grown at Opaki, in the northern Wairarapa, the 2009 vintage (★★★☆) is still youthful, with fresh tropical-fruit flavours, a slightly creamy texture and a finely balanced, dry finish.

DRY $21 AV

Lynfer Estate Wairarapa Sauvignon Blanc ★★★☆

Grown at Gladstone, this single-vineyard wine offers good value. The 2010 vintage (★★★☆) is full-bodied and dry, with fresh, ripe passionfruit and lime flavours, cut with lively acidity.

DRY $17 V+

Mahi Ballot Block Marlborough Sauvignon Blanc ★★★★☆

From a slightly elevated, relatively cool site in the Brancott Valley, the stylish 2009 vintage (★★★★☆) was hand-picked, barrel-fermented with indigenous yeasts and oak-aged for 10 months. Crisp and bone-dry, it's still youthful, with vibrant peach, pineapple and lime flavours, a very subtle seasoning of oak and good acid spine. It shows excellent purity and intensity, in a tight, minerally, fruit-focused style, built to last.

Vintage	09	08
WR	6	6
Drink	10-15	10-14

DRY $27 AV

Mahi Boundary Farm Sauvignon Blanc ★★★★☆

Grown on the lower slopes of the Wither Hills, at an early-ripening site, the 2009 vintage (★★★★) was hand-picked, fermented with indigenous yeasts and lees-aged for nearly a year in French oak barriques. It's a robust wine (14.5 per cent alcohol), fleshy, ripe, complex and dry, with stone-fruit and spice flavours, a hint of toasty oak, fresh acidity and good complexity. A powerful wine, it's well worth cellaring.

Vintage	09	08	07
WR	6	6	6
Drink	10-14	10-12	10-12

DRY $27 AV

Mahi Marlborough Sauvignon Blanc ★★★★

Drinking well now, the 2009 vintage (★★★★) was grown at several sites and mostly handled in tanks; 6 per cent of the final blend (the ripest, hand-picked fruit) was barrel-fermented. Weighty, with strong, ripe tropical-fruit flavours, it shows good concentration and complexity, with a fully dry, finely textured finish. Fine value.

Vintage	09	08	07
WR	6	6	6
Drink	10-13	P	P

DRY $20 V+

Mahi The Alias Marlborough Sauvignon Blanc (★★★★☆)

The 2008 vintage (★★★★☆) was made entirely from Sauvignon Blanc grapes, but it's not intended to be an intensely 'varietal' wine. Grown at Renwick, it was fermented with indigenous yeasts, initially in tanks, then transferred into seasoned French oak barrels, where it completed its fermentation and matured for 10 months. Fleshy and generous, it is sweet-fruited and finely textured, with very ripe fig, spice and subtle oak flavours, showing excellent complexity, and a dry, rounded finish.

Vintage	08
WR	6
Drink	10-13

DRY $27 AV

Maimai Creek Hawke's Bay Sauvignon Blanc ★★★

A good buy. The 2009 vintage (★★★) is fruity and flavoursome, in a ripe style with fresh, lively acidity and a smooth finish. The 2008 (★★★) is enjoyable now, with good depth of ripe tropical-fruit flavours and a touch of bottle-aged complexity.

DRY $15 V+

Main Divide Sauvignon Blanc ★★★☆

From Pegasus Bay. The 2009 vintage (★★★☆), not identified on the label by region, was grown in Marlborough. It's a mouthfilling wine, fleshy and sweet-fruited, with very good flavour depth and a smooth, dry finish.

Vintage	08	07	06
WR	6	6	6
Drink	10-12	10	P

DRY $20 AV

Man O' War Waiheke Island Sauvignon Blanc ★★★☆

Grown at the eastern end of the island, the 2009 vintage (★★★) was handled entirely in tanks. It's a medium-bodied wine, crisp and lively, with ripe, citrusy, limey flavours, showing good depth.

Vintage	09	08	07
WR	6	6	6
Drink	10-11	P	P

DRY $23 –V

Mansion House Bay Marlborough Sauvignon Blanc (★★★★)

From Whitehaven, the 2008 vintage (★★★★) is a fresh, vibrantly fruity wine with good body and delicious, punchy gooseberry/lime flavours threaded with lively acidity.

Vintage	08
WR	6
Drink	10-11

DRY $19 V+

Manu Marlborough Sauvignon Blanc ★★★

From Steve Bird, the 2009 vintage (★★★) is a full-bodied, dry wine, grown in the Wairau Valley. Fresh, with good balance and depth of ripe passionfruit and lime flavours, it's priced sharply.

DRY $15 V+

Map Maker Marlborough Sauvignon Blanc ★★★☆

A 'negociant' label from Staete Landt, based on vineyards in the Rapaura district and 10 per cent barrel-fermented, the 2009 vintage (★★★☆) is a crisp, fully dry style. Fresh and ripely herbaceous, with an aromatic bouquet, it shows a touch of complexity and very good depth.

Vintage	09
WR	6
Drink	10-12

DRY $19 V+

Marble Point Hanmer Springs Sauvignon Blanc (★★★★)

Grown in North Canterbury, the 2009 vintage (★★★★) was handled without oak. Vibrant, crisp and dry, it shows good intensity of fresh, ripe melon and lime flavours, a minerally streak and a long, slightly flinty finish. It's a 'serious' style of Sauvignon Blanc, not pungently varietal, but full of interest.

DRY $21 V+

Margrain Martinborough Sauvignon Blanc ★★★☆

The 2008 vintage (★★★☆) is a fresh-scented, strongly varietal, briskly herbaceous wine, slightly sweet (6.2 grams/litre of residual sugar), with very good depth of melon and green-capsicum flavours, crisp, tangy and balanced for easy drinking.

Vintage	09
WR	6
Drink	10-12

MED/DRY $24 –V

Marisco The King's Favour Marlborough Sauvignon Blanc (★★★★☆)

The classy 2009 vintage (★★★★☆) was estate-grown in the Waihopai Valley. Weighty and dry (2.7 grams/litre of residual sugar), it is vibrant and sweet-fruited, with incisive melon, capsicum and lime flavours, finely poised, crisp, slightly minerally and long.

DRY $23 V+

Marsden Marlborough Sauvignon Blanc ★★★

The 2009 vintage (★★★) from this Northland-based producer is a herbaceous style with punchy gooseberry and green-capsicum flavours. Ready.

DRY $25 –V

Martinborough Vineyard Sauvignon Blanc ★★★★

The 2009 vintage (★★★★) was hand-picked in Martinborough and mostly handled in tanks; 15 per cent of the blend was barrel-fermented. It's a full-bodied wine with fresh, dry, tropical-fruit flavours, a subtle seasoning of oak adding complexity, very good depth and a slightly creamy, rounded finish.

Vintage	09	08	07	06
WR	7	7	7	7
Drink	10-12	10-11	P	P

DRY $26 –V

Martinborough Vineyard Te Tera Sauvignon Blanc ★★★

The 2009 vintage (★★★) was hand-picked and lees-aged in tanks for four months. It's a fleshy, rounded wine with ripe melon/lime flavours, crisp and lively, with good depth.

Vintage	09	08	07	06
WR	6	6	6	6
Drink	10-12	10-11	P	P

DRY $22 –V

Massey Dacta Marlborough Sauvignon Blanc ★★★

From Glover Family Vineyards, the 2009 vintage (★★★☆) offers fine value. Fresh and finely balanced, it has vibrant tropical-fruit and gentle herbaceous flavours, moderately concentrated, ripe and smooth.

DRY $15 V+

Matahiwi Estate Holly Wairarapa Sauvignon Blanc ★★★☆

The 2009 vintage (★★★☆) was grown at Opaki, near Masterton, and mostly fermented with indigenous yeasts in seasoned oak barrels. Crisp and dry, it is mouthfilling, with fresh, ripe tropical-fruit flavours, a seasoning of nutty oak, and good depth. Best drinking 2011.

Vintage	08
WR	5
Drink	10-11

DRY $25 –V

Matahiwi Estate Wairarapa Sauvignon Blanc ★★★☆

The 2010 (★★★★) is ripely scented and fleshy, vibrant and sweet-fruited, with mouthfilling body, fresh, concentrated flavour and a rounded finish. A top vintage, it's already delicious.

Vintage	10	09	08
WR	7	5	7
Drink	10-11	P	P

DRY $19 V+

Matakana Estate Marlborough Sauvignon Blanc ★★★☆

The 2009 vintage (★★★☆) was mostly handled in tanks, but a small portion (10 per cent) of barrel fermentation and lees-aging adds a touch of complexity. Fresh, crisp and dry, it has strong, lively melon and green-capsicum flavours.

DRY $22 AV

Matariki Aspire Hawke's Bay Sauvignon Blanc – see Aspire Hawke's Bay Sauvignon Blanc

Matariki Hawke's Bay Sauvignon Blanc ★★★☆

The 2008 vintage (★★★☆) was grown in the Gimblett Gravels, tank-fermented and lees-aged for six weeks. It's a subtle, refined wine with mouthfilling body, very good depth of ripe sweet-fruit flavours of citrus fruits and limes, and an appetisingly crisp, dry finish.

Vintage	08
WR	5
Drink	10-12

DRY $22 AV

Matawara by Secret Stone Sauvignon Blanc (★★★)

Still on sale in 2010 and aging solidly, the 2007 vintage (★★★) from Matua Valley is not identified by region, but tastes like a North Island style, with ripe tropical-fruit flavours to the fore. Medium-bodied, it is non-herbaceous, with a hint of pineapple, balanced acidity and good depth. Ready.

DRY $18 AV

Matawhero Gisborne Sauvignon Blanc (★★★)

The historic Matawhero brand has recently been revived by the Searle family, owners of Brunton Road. The 2009 vintage (★★★) was grown at Makaraka, near Matawhero. A medium-bodied wine (11.5 per cent alcohol), very fresh and vibrant, it is smooth (4.8 grams/litre of residual sugar), with ripe citrus and tropical-fruit flavours and an appetisingly crisp finish.

DRY $30 –V

Matua Valley Hawke's Bay Sauvignon Blanc ★★★

Consistently good and bargain-priced. The 2009 vintage (★★★) is fresh, ripe and rounded, with satisfying depth of tropical-fruit flavours and a dry, finely balanced finish.

DRY $17 AV

Matua Valley Marlborough Sauvignon Blanc (★★★)

Balanced for easy drinking, the 2010 vintage (★★★) is mouthfilling, ripe and smooth, with good depth of fresh tropical-fruit flavours, some distinctly herbaceous notes, and lively acidity.

DRY $17 AV

Matua Valley Matua Road Sauvignon Blanc (★★☆)

Grown in New Zealand, although not identified by region, the 2008 vintage (★★☆) is an easy-drinking wine with decent depth of ripe tropical-fruit rather than herbaceous flavours and a smooth finish. Fine value.

DRY $10 V+

Matua Valley Paretai Marlborough Sauvignon Blanc ★★★★☆

The winery's flagship Sauvignon Blanc is sometimes but not always sourced from the company-controlled Northbank Vineyard, an inland site on the north bank of the Wairau River. The 2009 vintage (★★★★★) was grown in the Awatere Valley, tank-fermented and lees-aged. Punchy and dry (2 grams/litre of residual sugar), it has excellent weight and richness of ripe gooseberry/lime flavours, in a fleshy, concentrated style with a minerally streak and a lasting finish.

DRY $25 V+

Matua Valley Reserve Release Marlborough Sauvignon Blanc ★★★☆

The 2010 vintage (★★★☆) is full-bodied, dry and crisp, with punchy tropical-fruit and herbaceous flavours, showing very good depth and vigour.

DRY $20 AV

Matua Valley Shingle Peak Marlborough Sauvignon Blanc – see Shingle Peak

Maude Marlborough Sauvignon Blanc ★★★☆

Grown in the Wairau Valley, the 2009 vintage (★★★☆) is mouthfilling and fleshy, with good depth of tropical-fruit and herbaceous flavours, a sliver of sweetness (5 grams/litre of residual sugar) and lively acidity.

MED/DRY $18 V+

Maven Marlborough Sauvignon Blanc ★★★☆

The 2009 vintage (★★★☆) was estate-grown on the northern side of the Wairau Valley. Crisp, with a touch of complexity from some use of seasoned French oak casks, it has moderately concentrated passionfruit and lime flavours, showing good freshness and vigour.

DRY $18 V+

McNaught & Walker White Ash Bluff Marlborough Sauvignon Blanc ★★★★☆

This rare wine is grown in the heart of the Awatere Valley, 'before it rises into the frost barrier', where the vines are tended by Richard Bowling, the valley's most experienced viticulturist. The 2010 vintage (★★★★★) is superb. A strikingly rich, ripe wine, without any of the 'tomato stalk' characters usually associated with the valley, it is mouthfilling and sweet-fruited, with concentrated tropical-fruit flavours and a minerally undercurrent. It builds across the palate to a finely textured, lasting finish. The 2009 (★★★★) is slightly less memorable, but still impressive, with good weight, ripe tropical flavours, a minerally undertow and lingering finish.

DRY $24 V+

Metis Hawke's Bay Sauvignon Blanc ★★★★

From a joint venture between Trinity Hill and Loire producer Pascal Jolivet, this wine has set out to pioneer a new style of Hawke's Bay Sauvignon Blanc – tight, long-lived and unoaked. Weighty and dry, sweet-fruited, minerally and concentrated, the 2009 vintage (★★★★☆) is a very age-worthy wine, with ripe, rounded flavours, finely textured and lingering. Open mid-2011+.

DRY $30 –V

Michelle Richardson Marlborough Sauvignon Blanc ★★★★

The 2009 vintage (★★★★) was grown at Renwick, in the central Wairau Valley, and partly (20 per cent) fermented with indigenous yeasts in old oak casks. A medium-bodied style, it is very fresh and vibrant, with dry (3 grams/litre of residual sugar), citrusy, limey flavours, showing excellent ripeness, delicacy and depth.

DRY $23 AV

Mill Road New Zealand Sauvignon Blanc ★★☆

The non-vintage wine (★★☆) on sale in late 2010 is fresh and strongly herbaceous, with crisp, lively, grassy flavours.

DRY $13 V+

Mills Reef Reserve Hawke's Bay Sauvignon Blanc ★★★★

The 2008 (★★★★), grown in 'cooler, coastal vineyards', is a freshly mouthfilling wine with ripe tropical-fruit flavours woven with crisp acidity and a dry, lingering finish.

DRY $23 AV

Mills Reef Sauvignon Blanc ★★★
The lower-tier Sauvignon Blanc from Mills Reef used to be a Hawke's Bay regional wine, but the 2008 vintage (★★★) is a blend of Hawke's Bay and Marlborough grapes. Ripely scented, it is smooth and flavoursome, with tropical-fruit characters to the fore and a crisp, dry finish.

DRY $17 AV

Misha's Vineyard The Scarlet Sauvignon Blanc (★★★☆)
Grown at Bendigo, in Central Otago, the 2009 vintage (★★★☆) was hand-picked at 24.4 brix and mostly handled in tanks; 21 per cent of the blend was fermented with indigenous yeasts in seasoned oak barrels. It's a full-bodied wine with vibrant gooseberry, pear and spice flavours, woven with fresh, strong acidity, a sliver of sweetness (5 grams/litre of residual sugar) and strong personality.

MED/DRY $26 –V

Mission Hawke's Bay Sauvignon Blanc ★★★
The 2009 vintage (★★★☆) is a good buy. Scented, with fresh, ripe passionfruit and lime flavours and a well-rounded finish, it's an easy-drinking, bone-dry style, showing good depth.

DRY $17 AV

Mission Reserve Sauvignon Blanc ★★★☆
The 2009 vintage (★★★★) has the word 'Reserve' only on the back label. Grown at two sites in Hawke's Bay (80 per cent Ohiti and 20 per cent Mangatahi), it was fermented and lees-aged in French oak barriques. Mouthfilling and dry, with ripe tropical-fruit and slightly nutty flavours, showing very good depth and complexity, it's a fresh, tightly structured wine, likely to open out well.

Vintage	09	08	07
WR	5	4	6
Drink	10-15	10-12	P

DRY $24 –V

Mission Vineyard Selection Sauvignon Blanc ★★★★
The generous 2009 vintage (★★★★), grown in Ohiti Road, is a mouthfilling, bone-dry style with ripe tropical-fruit flavours, woven with fresh acidity, slightly leesy notes and a creamy texture. Tight, youthful and elegant, it has good potential.

DRY $18 V+

Moana Park Vineyard Selection Cover Point Sauvignon Blanc ★★★
Grown in the Dartmoor Valley, Hawke's Bay, the 2009 vintage (★★☆) is full-bodied, dry and rounded, with tropical-fruit flavours, showing decent depth.

DRY $20 –V

Momo Marlborough Sauvignon Blanc ★★★☆

From Seresin, the 2009 vintage (★★★☆) is an organically certified wine, hand-picked at two sites. Mouthfilling, it's a dry wine with well-ripened tropical-fruit rather than herbaceous flavours, showing very good depth.

Vintage 09
WR 7
Drink 10-12

DRY $20 AV

Moncellier Marlborough Sauvignon Blanc (★★★★)

The debut 2008 vintage (★★★★) was grown in the Awatere and Omaka valleys. Freshly herbaceous, with good intensity, it is crisp and dry, with pure melon and capsicum flavours, vibrant, dry and long.

Vintage 09
WR 5
Drink 10-12

DRY $24 AV

Monkey Bay Hawke's Bay Sauvignon Blanc/Pinot Gris (★★☆)

The debut 2010 vintage (★★☆) is a lively blend of Sauvignon Blanc (80 per cent) and Pinot Gris (20 per cent). Fresh, citrusy and limey, with hints of passionfruit and spices, it's an off-dry style, offering very easy drinking.

MED/DRY $16 AV

Monkey Bay Marlborough Sauvignon Blanc ★★★

From Constellation NZ, this wine is a roaring success in the US (reflecting its effective promotion, style and modest price). It is typically gently sweet, fresh and vibrant, with medium body, ripe-fruit flavours of melons and limes, and lots of drink-young charm. The 2009 vintage (★★★) is crisp and herbaceous, in a lively, refreshing style with good harmony and depth.

MED/DRY $15 V+

Monowai Crownthorpe Sauvignon Blanc ★★★★

Estate-grown at a cool, elevated, inland site in Hawke's Bay, the 2008 vintage (★★★★) was handled entirely in tanks. Medium-bodied, with slightly 'sweaty', ripe-fruit aromas, it has concentrated tropical-fruit flavours, with fresh acidity and a lingering, off-dry (6 grams/litre of residual sugar) finish. Priced sharply.

MED/DRY $18 V+

Montana 'B' Brancott Marlborough Sauvignon Blanc ★★★★★

Promoted as 'our finest expression of Marlborough's most famous variety', Pernod Ricard NZ's wine lives up to its billing. 'Palate weight, concentration and longevity' are the goals. It has traditionally been grown in the company's sweeping Brancott Estate Vineyard, on the south, slightly cooler side of the Wairau Valley, and a small portion of the blend is fermented and lees-aged in French oak barriques and cuves, to add 'some toast and spice as well as palate richness'. It matures well for several years, developing nutty, minerally, toasty flavours in the best vintages; fresh asparagus notes in others. Delicious now, the 2009 vintage (★★★★★) is ripely scented and fleshy, with rich passionfruit and lime flavours, good acid spine and a dry, rounded, lasting finish. (The 2010 vintage, to be branded as Brancott Estate, was tasted just before bottling – and so not rated. It's a typically rich, ripe style with some 'sweaty armpit' notes and vibrant, concentrated tropical-fruit flavours.)

DRY $34 AV

Montana Living Land Series Marlborough Sauvignon Blanc (★★★☆)
From vines at Omaka being converted to organic production, the debut 2009 vintage (★★★☆) is full-bodied and ripely herbal, fresh and punchy, with tropical-fruit and capsicum flavours, balanced for easy drinking. (The 2010 vintage, to be branded as Brancott Estate, was tasted before bottling – and so is not rated. It looked good – sweet-fruited and lively, with strong, ripe melon/lime flavours and a tight finish.)

DRY $20 AV

Montana Marlborough Sauvignon Blanc ★★★☆
This famous, bargain-priced label rests its case on the flavour explosion of slow-ripened Marlborough fruit – a breathtaking style of Sauvignon Blanc which this wine, more than any other, has introduced to wine lovers in key markets around the world. Recent vintages are less lush, more pungently herbaceous than some other Marlborough labels; 'this is the style we can sell locally and the UK wants,' reports Pernod Ricard NZ. Production is now running at about one million cases per year. It is mostly grown in the Wairau Valley; since 2008 the inclusion of Awatere Valley fruit has given 'a more herbal note, vibrancy and aromatic lift'. Punchy and fresh, with good vigour and depth, it's highly enjoyable in its youth. The 2009 vintage (★★★★) is a real standout, with a freshly herbaceous bouquet leading into a crisp, lively palate, offering pure melon, herb and capsicum flavours that linger well. The 2010 (★★★☆) is a medium-bodied (12.5 per cent alcohol) style, ripely scented, with very good vibrancy and depth of melon, lime and capsicum flavours, fresh and finely balanced (3.9 grams/litre of residual sugar) for early drinking.

Vintage	10	09	08	07
WR	7	7	6	6
Drink	10-11	P	P	P

DRY $18 V+

Montana Reserve Marlborough Sauvignon Blanc ★★★★
This label is designed to highlight the fresh, herbaceous style of Sauvignon Blanc Pernod Ricard NZ achieves on the south side of the Wairau Valley, compared to its more tropical fruit-flavoured Stoneleigh Sauvignon Blanc, grown on the north side of the valley. The 2009 vintage (★★★★) has mouthfilling body and fresh, tight gooseberry and capsicum flavours. Finely textured, it's a classic regional style, dry (2.5 grams/litre of residual sugar) and long. (The 2010 vintage is branded as Brancott Estate – see that entry.)

Vintage	10	09	08	07
WR	7	7	6	6
Drink	10-13	10-12	10-11	P

DRY $24 AV

Montana Showcase Series Awatere Marlborough Sauvignon Blanc (★★★★☆)

Full of drink-young appeal, the 2009 vintage (★★★★☆) is an upfront style with the 'tomato stalk' aromas typical of the sub-region. Weighty and concentrated, it is crisp and ripely herbaceous, with an array of fruit flavours, fresh, pure and minerally.

DRY $24 V+

Montana Terroir Conders Forest Marlborough Sauvignon Blanc ★★★★

Grown in the relatively warm Rapaura district, on the northern side of the Wairau Valley, and lees-aged in tanks, the 2008 vintage (★★★★) is punchy, with smooth, ripe tropical-fruit flavours, showing excellent delicacy and length.

Vintage	08	07
WR	6	6
Drink	P	P

DRY $24 AV

Montana Terroir Festival Block Marlborough Sauvignon Blanc ★★★★

From Pernod Ricard NZ, this wine is grown on the relatively cool, southern side of the Wairau Valley. The 2008 vintage (★★★★) is punchy, with intensely varietal, clearly herbaceous flavours, crisp, dry and lingering.

Vintage	08	07
WR	6	7
Drink	P	P

DRY $24 AV

Montana Terroir Rail Bridge Marlborough Sauvignon Blanc ★★★★☆

Grown in the Awatere Valley, the 2008 vintage (★★★★☆) is intensely varietal and herbaceous, with the classic 'tomato stalk' aromas and flavours of the sub-region, and excellent body, texture and depth.

Vintage	08	07
WR	6	6
Drink	P	P

DRY $24 V+

Morton Estate Black Label Awatere Sauvignon Blanc (★★★★)

The classy 2009 vintage (★★★★) was estate-grown in the upper Awatere Valley and mostly handled in tanks; 30 per cent of the blend was oak-aged for several months. Fresh and full-bodied, it is rich and lively, with citrusy, grassy, slightly nutty flavours, a minerally streak, and a dry finish.

Vintage	09
WR	7
Drink	10-14

DRY $26 –V

Morton Estate Black Label Marlborough Sauvignon Blanc (★★★☆)

Estate-grown in the upper Awatere Valley, the 2009 vintage (★★★☆) is fresh and direct, in a strongly herbaceous style with some riper passionfruit and lime characters. Full-bodied and rounded, it's drinking well now.

DRY $26 –V

Morton Estate Private Reserve Marlborough Sauvignon Blanc (★★★☆)

Estate-grown in the upper Awatere Valley, the 2009 vintage (★★★☆) is punchy, with fresh tropical-fruit and herbaceous flavours, crisp and lively, and a smooth finish.

Vintage	09
WR	7
Drink	10-12

DRY $21 AV

Morton Estate Stone Creek Marlborough Sauvignon Blanc ★★★

The 2009 vintage (★★★☆) was estate-grown in the upper Awatere Valley. Mouthfilling and lively, it is full-flavoured, with clearly herbaceous flavours, fresh, crisp, and finely balanced for easy drinking.

Vintage	09
WR	7
Drink	P

DRY $20 –V

Morton Estate White Label Hawke's Bay Sauvignon Blanc ★★★☆

The 2009 vintage (★★★) is an easy-drinking style, ripely scented, with satisfying depth of tropical-fruit flavours, crisp and lively, and a well-rounded finish.

Vintage	09	08
WR	6	5
Drink	10-11	P

MED/DRY $16 V+

Morton Estate White Label Marlborough Sauvignon Blanc ★★★

The 2009 vintage (★★★), grown in the Awatere and Wairau valleys, is crisp and lively, with attractive melon and green-capsicum flavours.

Vintage	10	09
WR	6	7
Drink	10-12	10-11

DRY $18 AV

Mountain Road Taranaki Sauvignon Blanc ★★★

Grown at Brixton, just north of New Plymouth, the 2009 vintage (★★★☆) is from vines planted in 2004. From a record crop, 143 cases were produced. Made with some use of barrel fermentation and lees-stirring, it's a medium-bodied wine with very good vigour and depth of ripe passionfruit and lime flavours, a hint of toasty oak and fresh, tangy acidity. Well worth discovering.

MED/DRY $24 –V

Mount Fishtail Marlborough Sauvignon Blanc ★★☆

From Konrad and Co, the ripely scented 2009 vintage (★★★) was grown in the Wairau and Waihopai valleys. It's a fresh, medium-bodied wine with melon, gooseberry and lime flavours, showing good depth, and a crisp, dry finish. Good value.

Vintage	10	09
WR	5	3
Drink	10-12	10-11

DRY $15 AV

Mount Nelson Marlborough Sauvignon Blanc ★★★★

Mount Nelson is owned by Tenuta Di Biserno, itself controlled by members of the famous Tuscan wine family, Antinori. The company owns a vineyard on the south side of the Wairau Valley, from which most of the grapes are drawn. The aim is to make 'a classic Marlborough Sauvignon Blanc, with stronger emphasis on texture and length'. Crisp and dry, this is typically a full-bodied wine with very good depth of melon/lime flavours and a slightly minerally, lingering finish. Quietly classy.

DRY $21 V+

Mount Riley Limited Release Marlborough Sauvignon Blanc (★★★★)

Offering fine value, the 2009 vintage (★★★★) is a rich, ripe style with mouthfilling body and excellent depth of passionfruit and lime flavours.

DRY $20 V+

Mount Riley Marlborough Sauvignon Blanc ★★★★

Notably fresh and full-bodied, with ripely herbaceous flavours, deep, dry and lasting, the 2008 (★★★★★) shared the Best White Wine Buy of the Year award in the 2009 *Guide*. The 2009 vintage (★★★★) is another bargain – mouthfilling, with fresh gooseberry/lime flavours showing excellent depth and a crisp, dry (3 grams/litre of residual sugar) finish.

Vintage	09	08	07
WR	6	6	6
Drink	P	P	P

DRY $18 V+

Mount Riley Seventeen Valley Sauvignon Blanc ★★★★

Built to last, the 2009 vintage (★★★★) is a tightly structured, single-vineyard wine, hand-picked in the Wairau Valley and fermented with indigenous yeasts in seasoned French oak barrels. Fresh, full-bodied and youthful, it is finely textured, slightly creamy and toasty, with sweet-fruit delights, tropical-fruit flavours and gentle acidity.

Vintage	09
WR	6
Drink	10-12

DRY $22 V+

Mount Vernon Marlborough Sauvignon Blanc (★★☆)

From Lawson's Dry Hills, the 2008 vintage (★★☆) was blended with Sémillon (10 per cent). It's a smooth, ripe-tasting wine with melon and capsicum flavours, showing moderate depth.

DRY $18 –V

Mt Beautiful Cheviot Hills North Canterbury Sauvignon Blanc ★★★★

From a new sub-region, north of Waipara, the 2009 vintage (★★★★☆) is rich and racy. Concentrated and vibrantly fruity, with appetising acidity, it has ripe tropical-fruit flavours, showing a slightly oily richness, and a dry, lingering finish.

DRY $22 V+

Mt Campbell Nelson Sauvignon Blanc ★★★

From Anchorage, the 2009 vintage (★★★☆) is priced sharply. Fresh and lively, it is full-bodied and finely balanced, with ripely herbaceous flavours, showing good vigour and length.

DRY $15 V+

Mt Difficulty Central Otago Sauvignon Blanc ★★★☆

Grown at Bannockburn, the 2009 vintage (★★★★) was hand-picked, tank-fermented and matured for four months on its yeast lees, with weekly stirring. Weighty and fully dry, but not austere, it has crisp, ripe tropical-fruit flavours to the fore and a touch of lees-aged complexity. Showing excellent body, vigour and richness, it's one of the best Central Otago Sauvignon Blancs I've tasted.

Vintage	09	08
WR	7	6
Drink	10-13	10-12

DRY $25 –V

Mt Hector Wairarapa Sauvignon Blanc (★★☆)

From Matahiwi, the 2008 vintage (★★☆) is a medium-bodied, green-edged wine with fresh, crisp, capsicum-like flavours, showing solid depth. Good value.

Vintage	08
WR	5
Drink	P

DRY $13 V+

Mt Rosa Sauvignon Blanc ★★☆

The 2009 vintage, grown at Gibbston, in Central Otago, was bottle-shocked when tasted, so is not rated. Crisp and basically dry (4 grams/litre of residual sugar), it looked promising, with lively gooseberry/lime, slightly minerally flavours.

DRY $22 –V

Mud House Marlborough Sauvignon Blanc ★★★★

This is typically a strongly herbaceous style, offering a style contrast to its riper-tasting stablemate under the Waipara Hills Marlborough Sauvignon Blanc label. The 2010 vintage (★★★★☆), grown in the Wairau, Awatere and Ure valleys, is very stylish for such a large-volume wine. Garden-fresh, nettley aromas lead into a crisp, vibrantly fruity, finely poised palate with incisive but not aggressive flavours, a herbal undercurrent and a dry (3.5 grams/litre of residual sugar), lingering finish.

Vintage	10
WR	7
Drink	10-12

DRY $20 V+

Mud House Swan Marlborough Sauvignon Blanc (★★★★☆)

The 2008 vintage (★★★★☆) is slightly 'sweaty', with excellent intensity of melon/capsicum flavours, very fresh, vibrant and crisp.

DRY $25 V+

Muddy Water Growers Series Waipara Sauvignon Blanc ★★★★

Hand-harvested at two sites at Waipara, the 2009 vintage (★★★★☆) was fermented with indigenous yeasts. Two-thirds of the blend was fermented and lees-aged for six months in old barrels; the rest was handled in tanks. It's a tightly structured, concentrated wine with punchy, ripe passionfruit/lime flavours, gently seasoned with toasty oak, fresh, balanced acidity and a basically dry (4.6 grams/litre of residual sugar) finish. It's a complex style, worth cellaring.

Vintage	09
WR	7
Drink	10-14

DRY $29 –V

Murdoch James Wairarapa Sauvignon Blanc ★★☆

The 2008 vintage (★★☆) was grown at Martinborough and Masterton. It's a medium-bodied wine with appley, limey flavours and a sliver of sweetness (5.1 grams/litre of residual sugar) balanced by crisp, lively acidity.

Vintage	08
WR	5
Drink	P

MED/DRY $20 –V

Murray's Barn Marlborough Sauvignon Blanc ★★★

From Terrace Heights, the 2010 vintage (★★☆) is a solid quaffer, priced sharply. It's crisp and dry, with moderate depth of tropical-fruit and green-apple flavours.

Vintage	10
WR	5
Drink	11-12

DRY $11 V+

Murray's Road Marlborough Sauvignon Blanc (★★★★☆)

The immaculate 2009 vintage (★★★★☆) is a single-vineyard wine, grown at Spring Creek, in the lower Wairau Valley. Very fresh and vibrant, with concentrated, ripe tropical-fruit flavours, woven with crisp acidity, and a dry, sustained finish, it's a fine debut.

Vintage	09
WR	7
Drink	10-11

DRY $25 V+

Nautilus Marlborough Sauvignon Blanc ★★★★☆

Released a year after the harvest, this is typically a richly fragrant wine with mouthfilling body and a surge of ripe passionfruit and lime-like flavours, enlivened by fresh acidity. Oak plays no part in the wine, but it is briefly matured on its yeast lees. The finely poised 2009 vintage

(★★★★★) was grown at several sites, some estate-owned, in the Wairau and Awatere valleys. Scented and sweet-fruited, it has excellent vibrancy and concentration, with intense, very pure melon and green-capsicum flavours and a crisp, dry (2.4 grams/litre of residual sugar), lasting finish.

Vintage	09	08	07	06
WR	7	6	7	6
Drink	10-12	P	P	P

DRY $25 V+

Navrina Cove Marlborough Sauvignon Blanc (★★★☆)

From Two Rivers, the 2009 vintage (★★★☆) is fresh and slightly minerally, with very good delicacy and depth of gooseberry, 'tomato stalk' and lime flavours.

DRY $20 AV

Ned, The, Waihopai River Marlborough Sauvignon Blanc ★★★☆

The 2009 vintage (★★★★) is a single-vineyard wine, tight and punchy, with excellent vigour and depth of passionfruit and lime flavours. Minerally and crisp, it's a finely balanced wine, priced sharply.

DRY $18 V+

Nest, The, Marlborough Sauvignon Blanc (★★★☆)

From Lake Chalice, the debut 2008 vintage (★★★☆) is mouthfilling, with very good depth of fresh tropical-fruit flavours and a rounded finish.

DRY $20 AV

Neudorf Nelson Sauvignon Blanc ★★★★☆

Looking for a Sauvignon Blanc 'with texture, that is complex and satisfying', Neudorf grew the grapes for the 2009 vintage (★★★★☆) at Brightwater, on the Waimea Plains. Partly (12 per cent) fermented in old oak barrels, and bottle-aged prior to its release, it is a dry style (1.7 grams/litre of residual sugar), full-bodied, punchy and crisp, with ripe, concentrated tropical-fruit flavours, deliciously fresh and vibrant.

Vintage	09	08	07	06	05
WR	6	5	6	6	5
Drink	10-12	10-11	10-12	P	P

DRY $22 V+

Ngatarawa Silks Marlborough Sauvignon Blanc ★★★

Light and smooth, the 2008 vintage (★★★) has decent depth of citrusy, limey flavours, gentle acidity and a dry finish.

Vintage	08	07	06
WR	6	6	5
Drink	10-11	P	P

DRY $20 –V

Ngatarawa Stables Sauvignon Blanc ★★★

Grown in Hawke's Bay and Marlborough, the 2008 vintage (★★☆) is a solid, medium to full-bodied wine with ripe tropical-fruit flavours, ready now.

DRY $18 AV

Vintage	08	07	06
WR	6	6	5
Drink	10-11	P	P

Nga Waka Martinborough Sauvignon Blanc ★★★★★

Substantial in body, with concentrated, ripe, bone-dry flavours, this is a cool-climate style of Sauvignon Blanc, highly aromatic and zingy. The grapes are grown in the Home Block, on the Martinborough Terrace, planted in 1988, and the Top Block, a few kilometres away in the low hills between Martinborough and Te Muna, established in 1996. The vinification, 'very straightforward', with no use of oak, yields a wine that typically peaks at four to six years old, when it is rich, toasty, minerally and complex. The 2009 vintage (★★★★☆) is tight, crisp and dry, with good intensity of melon/lime flavours, punchy, vibrant, minerally and lingering. Best drinking 2011+.

DRY $25 V+

Vintage	09	08
WR	7	7
Drink	10+	10+

Nikau Point Hawke's Bay Sauvignon Blanc ★★☆

From One Tree Hill Vineyards (owned by Morton Estate), the 2009 vintage (★★☆) is a crisp, medium-bodied wine with melon/lime flavours, light and lively.

DRY $15 AV

Vintage	09	08
WR	6	5
Drink	10-11	P

Nikau Point Marlborough Reserve Sauvignon Blanc ★★★☆

This is Morton Estate's 'most minerally, acidic and grassy' Sauvignon Blanc. The 2009 vintage (★★★☆) is fresh and punchy, with vibrant melon and green-capsicum flavours, showing good balance and depth.

DRY $18 V+

Vintage	09	08
WR	7	6
Drink	10-11	P

Nikau Point Marlborough Sauvignon Blanc (★★☆)

The 2009 vintage (★★☆) from Morton Estate is a medium-bodied wine, freshly herbaceous, with gooseberry and lime flavours, showing solid depth.

DRY $15 AV

Vintage	09
WR	6
Drink	10-11

Nobilo Icon Marlborough Sauvignon Blanc ★★★★

A consistently impressive wine from Constellation NZ. The 2009 vintage (★★★★☆) is richly scented, with 'tomato stalk' aromas. Weighty and concentrated, it has fresh acid spine and vibrant melon, gooseberry, lime and capsicum flavours, penetrating, racy and long.

DRY $24 AV

Nobilo Regional Collection Marlborough Sauvignon Blanc ★★★

A riper style from Constellation NZ than its more herbaceous stablemate under the Selaks Premium Selection label, this wine recently topped the Sauvignon Blanc sales charts in the US. It typically has fresh gooseberry/lime flavours and a crisp, slightly off-dry finish. Balanced for easy drinking, the lightly scented 2009 vintage (★★★) is a medium-bodied wine with lively, citrusy, limey flavours, a hint of grassiness, and a crisp, smooth (5 grams/litre of residual sugar) finish.

MED/DRY $17 AV

Northfield Frog Rock Vineyard Waipara Valley Sauvignon Blanc/Sémillon (★★★☆)

Still youthful, the 2008 vintage (★★★☆) is fresh, limey, slightly grassy and nettley, with good body, delicacy and depth, a minerally streak and a dry, flinty finish. Worth cellaring.

DRY $19 V+

Odyssey Marlborough Sauvignon Blanc ★★★☆

Estate-grown in the Brancott Valley, the 2009 vintage (★★★☆) is medium-bodied (12.5 per cent alcohol), with crisp, ripe tropical-fruit flavours in a non-herbaceous style, balanced for easy drinking. It's maturing well.

Vintage	09	08
WR	6	6
Drink	10-11	P

DRY $19 V+

Ohau Gravels Sauvignon Blanc (★★★★☆)

Grown at Ohau, just north of the Kapiti Coast, in Horowhenua, the 2009 vintage (★★★★☆) is a highly auspicious debut. Hand-picked from first-crop vines, it was mostly handled in tanks; 5 per cent of the blend was fermented with indigenous yeasts in old oak barrels. Fresh, 'tomato stalk' aromas (reminiscent of the classic Awatere Valley style) lead into a weighty wine with concentrated gooseberry, lime and capsicum flavours, a touch of complexity, lively acidity, and excellent delicacy and richness. Fine value.

DRY $21 V+

Ohinemuri Estate Wairau Valley Marlborough Sauvignon Blanc ★★★

The 2008 vintage (★★★) was matured on its yeast lees for three months and 10 per cent barrel-fermented. It's a mouthfilling wine with strong gooseberry, melon and capsicum flavours, slight asparagus notes emerging with bottle-age, and a dry finish. (The 2010 vintage was 27 per cent barrel-fermented.)

Vintage	08	07
WR	6	6
Drink	10	10

DRY $24 –V

Old Coach Road Nelson Sauvignon Blanc ★★★

Seifried Estate's lower-tier Sauvignon. The 2009 vintage (★★★) was estate-grown, inland at Brightwater and on the coast, at Rabbit Island. An enjoyably fresh, crisp and lively wine, it is tangy, with melon and green-capsicum flavours, in a clearly herbaceous style with lots of youthful vigour. The 2010 (★★★) is mouthfilling, very fresh and crisp, with good depth of lively gooseberry and lime flavours, dry and tangy.

Vintage	10
WR	6
Drink	10-12

DRY $17 AV

Olsen's Central Otago Sauvignon Blanc ★★☆

Estate-grown at Bannockburn, the 2009 vintage (★★☆) is a smooth wine (6.6 grams/litre of residual sugar), partly barrel-fermented. Appley and woven with crisp acidity, it offers fresh, easy drinking.

Vintage	10
WR	6
Drink	11-15

MED/DRY $25 –V

Omaka Springs Marlborough Sauvignon Blanc ★★★

This wine has fresh, direct, grassy aromas in a traditional style of Marlborough Sauvignon Blanc, zesty and strongly herbaceous. The 2009 vintage (★★★), which includes 9 per cent Sémillon, is crisp and dry (2.9 grams/litre of residual sugar), in a medium-bodied style with fresh melon, lime and green-capsicum flavours.

Vintage	10	09	08
WR	6	6	6
Drink	10-13	10-12	10-11

DRY $18 AV

Omihi Road Waipara Sauvignon Blanc ★★★★

Barrel-fermented and lees-aged for four months, the 2009 vintage (★★★★) from Torlesse has substantial body, sweet-fruit delights and excellent depth and delicacy of ripe melon, lime and pear flavours. It's still youthful, with a subtle oak influence adding complexity and a well-rounded finish.

Vintage	09
WR	6
Drink	12-15

DRY $20 V+

One Tree Marlborough Sauvignon Blanc ★★★

Made by Capricorn, a division of Craggy Range, for sale in restaurants and supermarkets (New World, PAK'nSAVE), this is typically an aromatic wine with good depth of freshly herbaceous flavours, lively and balanced for easy drinking. Ready now, the 2009 vintage (★★★) is fleshy, with tropical-fruit flavours, a herbal undercurrent and a dry, rounded finish. Fine value.

Vintage	09	08
WR	7	6
Drink	P	P

DRY $15 V+

Opawa Marlborough Sauvignon Blanc (★★★★)

From Nautilus, the 2010 vintage (★★★★) is already delicious. Handled mostly in tanks, with a touch of barrel fermentation (5 per cent), it is mouthfilling and vibrant, with fresh, ripe passionfruit and lime flavours, a touch of complexity, and a finely textured, smooth finish.

DRY $22 V+

Open House Smooth Marlborough Sauvignon Blanc ★★★

Created 'especially with women in mind', the 2009 vintage (★★★) was produced at Wither Hills. Offering good value, it is medium-bodied, fresh and crisp, with tropical-fruit and herbaceous flavours, balanced for easy drinking.

MED/DRY $15 V+

Orinoco Nelson Sauvignon Blanc ★★★☆

Grown on the Waimea Plains, the 2008 vintage (★★★) is a crisp, full-flavoured wine with ripe tropical-fruit characters to the fore, a herbal undercurrent and firm acid spine.

DRY $19 V+

O:TU Marlborough Sauvignon Blanc ★★★★

From Otuwhero Estates, in the Awatere Valley, the 2009 vintage (★★★★) is a freshly aromatic, weighty wine with strong melon, lime and gooseberry flavours, a minerally streak, and good purity and length.

DRY $20 V+

O:TU Single Vineyard Marlborough Sauvignon Blanc ★★★★☆

From the company's original Otuwhero Vineyard in the Awatere Valley, the 2009 vintage (★★★★☆) is weighty, with pure, penetrating melon/lime flavours, showing excellent delicacy and depth, and a long, tangy finish.

DRY $25 V+

Overstone Marlborough Sauvignon Blanc (★★☆)

From Sileni, the 2008 vintage (★★☆) is a medium-bodied style, fresh and smooth, with tropical-fruit and herbaceous flavours, showing decent depth.

DRY $14 V+

Oyster Bay Marlborough Sauvignon Blanc ★★★★

Oyster Bay is a Delegat's brand, reserved principally for Marlborough wines and enjoying huge success in international markets, especially Australia. Handled entirely in stainless steel tanks, this wine is grown at dozens of vineyards around the Wairau and Awatere valleys and made in a dry style with tropical-fruit and herbaceous flavours, crisp and punchy. The 2009 (★★★★☆) is a top vintage. Weighty and intense, it has a lovely array of fresh, dry melon, lime, passionfruit and green-capsicum flavours. Fine value.

Vintage	09	08	07
WR	6	5	6
Drink	10-13	10-11	10-11

DRY $20 V+

Palliser Estate Martinborough Sauvignon Blanc ★★★★★

At its best, this is a wholly seductive wine, one of the greatest Sauvignon Blancs in the country. A distinctly cool-climate style, it offers an exquisite harmony of crisp acidity, mouthfilling body and fresh, penetrating fruit characters. The grapes are mostly estate-grown, but are also purchased from growers on the Martinborough Terrace and a few kilometres away, at Te Muna. The fruit gives the intensity of flavour – there's no blending with Sémillon, no barrel fermentation, no oak-aging. The 2009 vintage (★★★★★) is a mouthfilling, vibrantly fruity wine with intense, ripe passionfruit-like flavours. It has excellent weight and texture, with moderate acidity and a finely balanced, sustained finish. Great value.

DRY $22 V+

Partington Upper Moutere Sauvignon Blanc (★★☆)

The 2009 vintage, certified BioGro, was hand-picked and barrel-aged. The bouquet is restrained; the palate is medium-bodied and limey, with some leesy complexity. Pale and youthful, with some 'funky' notes, it's still settling down; open mid-2011+.

Vintage	09	08
WR	5	4
Drink	10-15	10-12

MED/DRY $24 –V

Passage Rock Waiheke Island Sauvignon Blanc ★★★

The 2009 vintage (★★★) was estate-grown at Te Matuku Bay. It's a fleshy, mouthfilling (14 per cent alcohol), well-rounded wine, sweet-fruited, with ripe, citrusy, appley flavours, creamy-textured, in a typical northern style.

DRY $23 –V

Paua Marlborough Sauvignon Blanc (★★★☆)

From Highfield Estate, the 2009 vintage (★★★☆) is weighty and ripely scented, with fresh acidity and very good balance and depth of citrusy, slightly nettley flavours.

DRY $20 AV

Peak Marlborough Sauvignon Blanc (★★)

The 2008 vintage (★★) is a simple, slightly honeyed wine with fresh acidity and a clear botrytis influence. Drink up.

DRY $14 –V

Pebble Row Marlborough Sauvignon Blanc (★★★☆)

From Clifford Bay, the punchy 2010 vintage (★★★☆) has slightly nettley aromas leading into a mouthfilling wine with fresh, vibrant melon/lime flavours, showing very good vigour and depth. Fine value.

DRY $15 V+

Pegasus Bay Sauvignon/Sémillon ★★★★☆

At its best, this Waipara, North Canterbury wine is lush, concentrated and complex, with loads of personality. The 2008 vintage (★★★★☆) is a slightly minerally and nutty blend of Sauvignon Blanc (70 per cent) and Sémillon (30 per cent), fermented with indigenous yeasts and lees-aged for nine months in a mix of stainless steel tanks, large oak vats and old barriques. Weighty and sweet-fruited, it has ripe flavours of citrus fruits, gooseberries and lime, appetising acidity and impressive vigour, complexity and length.

Vintage	08	07
WR	7	6
Drink	10-15	10-13

DRY $28 AV

Pencarrow Sauvignon Blanc ★★★☆

Pencarrow is the second-tier label of Palliser Estate, but this is typically a satisfying wine in its own right, bargain-priced. The 2009 vintage (★★★☆) is a blend of Martinborough (80 per cent) and Marlborough (20 per cent) grapes. A crisp, buoyant, tightly structured wine with very good body and depth of fresh tropical-fruit and herbal flavours, it offers great value.

DRY $15 V+

Penny Lane Marlborough Sauvignon Blanc ★★☆

From Morton Estate, the 2009 vintage (★★★) has a freshly herbaceous bouquet and lively, nettley flavours, strong and smooth. Priced sharply.

Vintage	09	08
WR	6	5
Drink	10-11	P

MED/DRY $15 AV

People's, The Sauvignon Blanc (★★★☆)

Within weeks of its launch by Constellation NZ at $23, the 2010 vintage (★★★☆) could be bought for closer to $15. Grown in the Awatere Valley, it has fresh, grassy aromas and strong, herbaceous flavours, in a very upfront style with lots of youthful impact.

DRY $23 –V

Peregrine Central Otago Sauvignon Blanc ★★★☆

The aromatic, clearly herbaceous 2009 vintage (★★★★) was grown at Gibbston and Cromwell. It has excellent vigour, impact and length of fresh, citrusy, limey, minerally flavours.

DRY $22 AV

Peter Yealands Marlborough Sauvignon Blanc (★★★☆)

The label on the 2009 vintage (★★★☆) makes no mention of the Awatere Valley – but it sure smells of it, with the lifted, 'tomato stalk' aromas typical of the sub-region. An intensely herbaceous style, it is vibrant, with punchy gooseberry and green-capsicum flavours, crisp and lively.

DRY $19 V+

Petit Clos by Clos Henri Marlborough Sauvignon Blanc ★★★☆

From young, estate-grown vines, the 2009 vintage (★★★☆) was harvested in the Wairau Valley and lees-aged for eight months. It's a mouthfilling, ripely flavoured wine with fresh, vibrant tropical-fruit characters to the fore, very good depth and a dry, rounded finish.

DRY $19 V+

Pruner's Reward, The, Waipara Sauvignon Blanc (★★★☆)

From Bellbird Spring, the 2009 vintage (★★★☆) was estate-grown and handled without oak. It's a full-bodied, ripely herbaceous wine with tropical-fruit and herbaceous flavours, dry and showing very good depth.

DRY $20 AV

Ra Nui Marlborough Wairau Valley Sauvignon Blanc ★★★★

The 2010 vintage (★★★★) was mostly handled in tanks (5 per cent of the blend was barrel-fermented and aged). Enjoyable from the start, it has strong, ripe passionfruit and lime flavours, showing excellent freshness and vigour, and a crisp, fully dry finish.

DRY $21 V+

Rapaura Springs Marlborough Sauvignon Blanc ★★★

The 2009 vintage (★★☆) is full-bodied, with ripe tropical-fruit flavours, showing moderate depth.

DRY $15 V+

Redoubt Hill Vineyard Nelson Sauvignon Blanc ★★★☆

From 'probably the steepest vineyard in Nelson', the 2010 vintage (★★★☆) was grown at Motueka, hand-picked and handled entirely in tanks. A crisp, medium-bodied wine, it is tight and youthful, with ripe melon, herb and slight spice flavours, minerally and lingering. Worth cellaring.

DRY $23 –V

Redwood Pass by Vavasour Marlborough Sauvignon Blanc ★★★★

The 2010 vintage (★★★☆) is fresh, crisp and lively, with good depth of gooseberry and lime flavours and a dry finish. A good buy.

Vintage	10	09
WR	7	6
Drink	10-12	10-11

MED/DRY $17 V+

Renato Nelson Sauvignon Blanc ★★★★

The 2009 (★★★★) is medium-bodied, crisp and punchy, with tropical-fruit and herbaceous flavours, showing excellent balance, vigour and intensity. The 2010 vintage (★★★★) was 15 per cent barrel-aged. Instantly appealing, it's a generous wine with fresh, vibrant passionfruit and lime flavours, woven with racy acidity.

Vintage	10	09	08	07
WR	6	7	5	6
Drink	11-13	10-12	10-11	10-11

DRY $19 V+

Ribbonwood Marlborough Sauvignon Blanc (★★★☆)

From Framingham, the 2008 vintage (★★★☆) is an aromatic, freshly herbaceous wine with passionfruit and green-capsicum flavours, crisp and lively, a smooth finish and very good depth.

DRY $18 V+

Richmond Plains Nelson Sauvignon Blanc ★★★☆

Grown organically and certified by BioGro, the 2009 vintage (★★★☆) is a lively, medium-bodied wine with fresh, grassy aromas leading into a tangy wine with plenty of crisp, limey flavour.

Vintage	09	08	07
WR	6	6	7
Drink	10-11	P	P

DRY $20 AV

Richmond Plains Whakatu Sauvignon Blanc (★★★★)

The 2009 vintage (★★★), certified organic, has strong, herbaceous aromas leading into a concentrated, lively wine with crisp, dry, lasting flavours.

DRY $20 V+

Riverby Estate Marlborough Sauvignon Blanc ★★★☆

A single-vineyard wine, grown in the heart of the Wairau Valley, the 2009 vintage (★★★) is a fleshy wine, ripe and rounded, with moderate acidity, good depth of tropical-fruit flavours, and an easy-drinking appeal.

DRY $19 V+

River Farm Ben Morven Marlborough Sauvignon Blanc ★★★

The 2009 vintage (★★☆) was sourced from the Ben Morven Vineyard, on the south side of the Wairau Valley, and 5 per cent barrel-fermented. It's a full-bodied, slightly appley wine with decent flavour depth and a smooth, dry finish.

Vintage	09	08
WR	6	5
Drink	10-12	10-11

DRY $20 –V

River Farm Saint Maur Marlborough Sauvignon Blanc ★★★★☆

A rich and complex style, the weighty, dry 2009 vintage (★★★★★) was hand-harvested at just under 23 brix in the Saint Maur Vineyard on the south side of the Wairau Valley and fermented with indigenous yeasts in seasoned French oak. Fleshy, with very ripe, distinctly tropical-fruit flavours and balanced acidity, it has excellent richness and complexity, coupled with great drinkability.

Vintage	09	08
WR	6	6
Drink	10-13	10-12

DRY $29 AV

Road Works Waiheke Island Sauvignon Blanc (★★★)

From Man O' War, the 2008 vintage (★★★) is mouthfilling and dry, with good depth of ripe tropical-fruit flavours, threaded with fresh, firm acidity.

DRY $19 AV

Rochfort Rees Awatere Valley Marlborough Sauvignon Blanc (★★★★)

From an Auckland-based company, the 2008 vintage (★★★★) is a blend of Awatere Valley (95 per cent) and Wairau Valley grapes. Fresh, brisk and clearly herbaceous, with tropical-fruit flavours too, it's a lively wine with good intensity and immediacy.

DRY $20 V+

Rockburn Central Otago Sauvignon Blanc ★★★

The 2009 vintage (★★★) was grown in the Cromwell Basin and at Gibbston, and 58 per cent barrel-fermented (French, one year old). Mouthfilling, crisp and grassy, it has good body and plenty of flinty, green-edged, slightly nutty flavour.

Vintage	09	08
WR	5	7
Drink	10-12	10-14

DRY $24 –V

Rock Ferry Marlborough Sauvignon Blanc ★★★☆

The 2009 vintage (★★★★), certified BioGro, was hand-picked in The Corners Vineyard, in the Wairau Valley, and 70 per cent of the blend was barrel-fermented with indigenous yeasts; the rest was handled in tanks. Mouthfilling and smooth, it has good complexity, in a fleshy, rounded style with tropical-fruit flavours, showing excellent delicacy, harmony and richness.

DRY $27 –V

Rongopai Marlborough Sauvignon Blanc ★★★

From Babich, the 2009 vintage (★★★) is a mid-weight style, citrusy and herbaceous, with decent depth of flavour, fresh and lively. Fine value.

DRY $12 V+

Rua Whenua Hawke's Bay Reserve Sauvignon Blanc (★★★☆)

Still on sale in 2010, the highly distinctive 2006 vintage (★★★☆) was estate-grown at Te Awanga and harvested from 24-year-old vines at an average of 26 brix, 'with a fair amount of dry botrytis'. It is tight, very crisp, concentrated and minerally, in a dry, slightly austere style, proving to be long-lived.

DRY $19 V+

Ruby Bay Vineyard Sauvignon Blanc ★★★

The 2009 vintage (★★★) is a single-vineyard Nelson wine. It's a medium-bodied style (11.5 per cent alcohol), with fresh, ripe gooseberry and lime flavours, appetisingly crisp and dry.

Vintage	09
WR	5
Drink	10-12

DRY $20 –V

Sacred Hill Halo Marlborough Sauvignon Blanc (★★★★)

The tight, intensely flavoured 2009 vintage (★★★★) was estate-grown in the Waihopai Valley. Ripely scented, it has vibrant tropical-fruit flavours to the fore, a herbal undercurrent, lively acidity and a lingering finish.

DRY $26 –V

Sacred Hill Marlborough Sauvignon Blanc ★★★☆

Unfolding well, the 2009 vintage (★★★★) has a fresh, lifted bouquet, mingling tropical-fruit and herbaceous notes. It's an intensely varietal wine, showing good body, balance and intensity.

DRY $21 AV

Sacred Hill Sauvage Sauvignon Blanc ★★★★

One of the country's most expensive Sauvignon Blancs, at its best this is an impressively rich, complex example of the widely underrated, barrel-matured Hawke's Bay Sauvignon Blanc style. The 2008 (★★★★) was hand-picked in the Dartmoor Valley, barrel-fermented with indigenous yeasts and French oak-aged for 10 months. Weighty and tightly structured, it's a fully dry (3 grams/litre of residual sugar), mouth-wateringly crisp wine with strong pineappley, slightly nutty flavours, woven with tense acidity, and obvious cellaring potential.

DRY $33 –V

Saint Clair Marlborough Sauvignon Blanc ★★★★☆

This label has shown fine form lately and is a top buy. Grown mostly in the lower and central Wairau Valley, it is handled entirely in tanks. The 2010 vintage (★★★★☆) is pungently aromatic, very fresh and vibrant, with an array of passionfruit, lime and green-capsicum flavours, crisp, lively and concentrated. It's a high-impact style, already delicious.

Vintage	10	09	08
WR	7	7	7
Drink	10-12	10-11	P

DRY $21 V+

Saint Clair Pioneer Block 1 Foundation Marlborough Sauvignon Blanc ★★★★☆

This single-vineyard Marlborough wine is grown east of Blenheim, in the lower Wairau Valley, at a site formerly the source of the Wairau Reserve Sauvignon Blanc. The 2009 vintage (★★★★★) is finely scented and weighty, with tropical-fruit and gently herbaceous flavours, strikingly fresh, pure, intense and racy.

Vintage	09	08	07
WR	7	7	7
Drink	P	P	P

DRY $25 V+

Saint Clair Pioneer Block 2 Swamp Block Marlborough Sauvignon Blanc ★★★★

Sourced from a vineyard with a 'cooler climate', close to the coast at Dillons Point, in the lower Wairau Valley of Marlborough, the 2010 vintage (★★★★) is mouthfilling and vibrantly fruity, with good intensity of fresh, pure melon, lime and passionfruit flavours, crisp and long.

Vintage	10	09
WR	7	7
Drink	10-11	P

DRY $25 AV

Saint Clair Pioneer Block 3 43 Degrees Marlborough Sauvignon Blanc ★★★★☆

This Marlborough wine is grown in the lower Wairau Valley, at a site with rows 'running at an unusual angle of 43 degrees north-east to south-west', which gives 'a slightly more herbaceous Sauvignon Blanc'. The 2010 vintage (★★★★☆) is mouthfilling and sweet-fruited, with fresh, vibrant gooseberry and lime flavours, slightly spicy, very rich and harmonious.

Vintage	10	09	08
WR	7	7	7
Drink	10-11	P	P

DRY $25 V+

Saint Clair Pioneer Block 6 Oh! Block Marlborough Sauvignon Blanc ★★★★☆

Grown in fertile, silty soils in the lower Rapaura district of Marlborough's Wairau Valley, the 2009 vintage (★★★★) has lifted, freshly herbaceous aromas and vibrant flavours of melons, capsicums and limes, crisp and strong. If you like a 'full-on' style of Sauvignon Blanc, try this.

Vintage	09	08	07
WR	7	7	7
Drink	P	P	P

DRY $25 V+

Saint Clair Pioneer Block 11 Cell Block Marlborough Sauvignon Blanc ★★★★☆

From a relatively cool site at Dillons Point, east of Blenheim, the 2010 vintage (★★★★☆) is full-bodied, very fresh and vibrant, with deep, delicate passionfruit, pear and lime flavours, showing excellent texture and length.

Vintage	10
WR	7
Drink	10-11

DRY $25 V+

Saint Clair Pioneer Block 18 Snap Block Marlborough Sauvignon Blanc ★★★☆

Grown east of Blenheim, in the lower Wairau Valley, the 2010 vintage (★★★☆) is an easy-drinking style, full-bodied, ripe and rounded, with fresh, strong, citrusy, limey flavours.

Vintage	10	09
WR	7	7
Drink	10-11	P

DRY $25 –V

Saint Clair Pioneer Block 19 Bird Block Marlborough Sauvignon Blanc ★★★★

Grown north of Blenheim, in the lower Rapaura district of the Wairau Valley, the 2010 vintage (★★★★) is still very youthful. Full-bodied, it is ripe and rounded, with fresh melon, capsicum and lime flavours, showing excellent delicacy and length. Open mid-2011+.

Vintage	10	09
WR	7	7
Drink	10-11	P

DRY $25 AV

Saint Clair Pioneer Block 20 Cash Block Marlborough Sauvignon Blanc (★★★★)

Grown close to the sea, at a relatively cool site east of Blenheim, the 2009 vintage (★★★★) is a 'full-on' style, with a blast of herbaceous aromas and penetrating gooseberry and green-capsicum flavours, crisp and long.

Vintage	09
WR	7
Drink	P

DRY $25 AV

Saint Clair Pioneer Block 21 Bell Block Marlborough Sauvignon Blanc (★★★★)

Grown east of Blenheim, close to the sea in the lower Wairau Valley, the 2010 vintage (★★★★) is a briskly herbaceous style, with nettley aromas and flavours. Very fresh and racy, it shows good intensity, with a crisp, dry finish.

DRY $25 AV

Saint Clair Vicar's Choice Marlborough Sauvignon Blanc ★★★☆

Vicars, like many of us, will gladly worship a bargain – and this easy-drinking wine delivers the goods. The 2010 vintage (★★★☆) is smooth, with very good depth of vibrant passionfruit/lime flavours, a herbal undercurrent and instant appeal.

Vintage	09	08	07
WR	7	6	6
Drink	10	P	P

DRY $19 V+

Saint Clair Wairau Reserve Marlborough Sauvignon Blanc ★★★★★

The 2001 and subsequent vintages have been exceptional, in a super-charged, deliciously ripe and concentrated style, lush and rounded, that has enjoyed glowing success on the show circuit, here and overseas. The vineyards vary from vintage to vintage, but all are at the cooler, lower end of the Wairau Valley. The wine is handled entirely in stainless steel tanks and drinks best in its first couple of years, while still fresh, zingy and exuberantly fruity. The 2009 vintage (★★★★★) is very weighty and sweet-fruited, with rich passionfruit and lime flavours, tight, crisp, dry (2.9 grams/litre of residual sugar) and long. The 2010 (★★★★★) has ripe 'sweaty armpit' aromas. Mouthfilling, with vibrant melon, passionfruit and lime flavours, possessing an almost oily richness, it has lovely purity, delicacy and flow, fresh acidity and a long, finely poised finish. It's not the region's most complex Sauvignon Blanc, but in terms of sheer pungency, it's a star.

Vintage	10	09	08	07
WR	7	7	7	7
Drink	10-11	P	P	P

DRY $33 AV

Saints Hawke's Bay Sauvignon Blanc (★★★☆)

Tasted prior to bottling (and so not rated), the 2010 vintage has fresh ripe-fruit aromas and lively tropical-fruit flavours, fresh, crisp and dry.

DRY $20 AV

Sanctuary Marlborough Sauvignon Blanc ★★★

Grove Mill's lower-tier label. The 2008 vintage (★★☆) is a fresh, medium-bodied wine with solid depth of melon, gooseberry and lime flavours, and a basically dry (4 grams/litre of residual sugar), crisp finish.

Vintage	09	08
WR	7	6
Drink	P	P

DRY $18 AV

Satellite Marlborough Sauvignon Blanc (★★★)

From Spy Valley, the 2008 vintage (★★★) is fresh and lively, with punchy melon and green-capsicum flavours in a strongly herbaceous style, crisp and dry.

DRY $17 AV

Savée Sea Marlborough Sauvignon Blanc (★★★)

The 2008 vintage (★★★) is a ripely scented, full-bodied and fresh blend of Wairau Valley (70 per cent) and Awatere Valley grapes. It has tropical-fruit flavours, with a hint of lime and a crisp, lively finish. Good value.

DRY $13 V+

Sea Level Awatere Marlborough Sauvignon Blanc ★★★☆

The 2010 vintage (★★★☆) offers good value. A single-vineyard wine, it is ripely scented, with vibrant melon and green-capsicum flavours, showing very good freshness, delicacy and depth. It's finely balanced for easy drinking.

DRY $18 V+

Sears Road Hawke's Bay Sauvignon Blanc ★★☆

'Best enjoyed barefoot on a sunny deck', the 2009 vintage (★★☆) is a pleasant quaffer, fresh, light, crisp and smooth. A bargain.

DRY $10 V+

Secret Stone Marlborough Sauvignon Blanc ★★★★

From Matua Valley, the 2009 vintage (★★★★) was 'passionately created'. Full-bodied, it shows good intensity, with crisp, vibrant passionfruit and lime flavours, finely balanced and dry. It's drinking well now.

DRY $20 V+

Seifried Nelson Sauvignon Blanc ★★★★

Typically a good buy. The 2009 vintage (★★★★), mostly grown in the Cornfield Vineyard, adjacent to the winery, has slightly 'sweaty' aromas leading into a punchy wine with vibrant gooseberry and lime flavours, showing good fruit sweetness, and a fully dry, mouth-wateringly crisp finish. The 2010 (★★★☆) is fresh, mouthfilling and smooth, with very good depth of ripe tropical-fruit flavours and a crisp, fully dry finish.

Vintage	10	09
WR	6	6
Drink	10-12	10-11

DRY $19 V+

Seifried Winemakers Collection Nelson Sauvignon Blanc ★★★★☆

From a new, inland vineyard on the Waimea Plains, the 2009 (★★★★) is mouthfilling and punchy, with fresh, lively, ripely herbaceous gooseberry/lime flavours and a long, dry (1.7 grams/litre of residual sugar) finish. The 2010 vintage (★★★★★) has 'sweaty armpit' aromas, fresh and lifted. Very rich and racy, it is crisp, dry and slightly minerally, with ripe sweet-fruit characters and searching passionfruit and green-capsicum flavours, showing excellent vigour and length.

Vintage	10	09	08
WR	6	6	7
Drink	10-12	10-11	P

DRY $23 V+

Selaks Premium Selection Hawke's Bay Sauvignon Blanc/Pinot Gris (★★★)

The 2010 vintage (★★★) is not a Sauvignon Gris – a variety in its own right – but a blend of two grapes, Sauvignon Blanc and Pinot Gris. Sauvignon Blanc (70 per cent) has the upper hand here, in a mouthfilling dry wine with fresh acidity and good depth of ripe tropical-fruit flavours.

DRY $17 AV

Selaks Premium Selection Marlborough Sauvignon Blanc ★★★

The 2009 vintage (★★★) from Constellation NZ is freshly herbaceous, in a traditional style with lively green-capsicum-like flavours and a smooth finish.

DRY $17 AV

Selaks Winemakers Favourite Marlborough Sauvignon Blanc ★★★★

From Constellation NZ, the 'full-on' 2009 vintage (★★★★) is a pungent, nettley style, at the greener end of the flavour spectrum, grown predominantly in the Awatere Valley. It has strong gooseberry, lime and green-capsicum flavours, with a minerally streak and a long, finely balanced finish.

DRY $21 V+

Sentinel Vineyard Marlborough Sauvignon Blanc ★★★☆

A single-vineyard, Brancott Valley wine, the 2008 vintage (★★★☆) is medium-bodied, fresh, crisp, dry and lively, with good intensity of ripe gooseberry and lime flavours.

DRY $28 –V

Seresin Marama Sauvignon Blanc ★★★★☆

This complex style of Sauvignon Blanc is hand-picked from the oldest vines in the estate vineyard at Renwick, in Marlborough, fermented with indigenous yeasts in French oak barriques (25 per cent new in 2007) and wood-matured for well over a year. The 2007 vintage (★★★★★) has a scented, ripely herbal, complex bouquet. Sturdy (14.5 per cent alcohol) and rich, it's a very powerful, sweet-fruited wine with highly concentrated stone-fruit flavours, slightly nutty, dry and long.

Vintage	07
WR	7
Drink	10-15

DRY $40 –V

Seresin Marlborough Sauvignon Blanc ★★★★★

This is one of the region's most sophisticated, subtle and satisfying Sauvignons. It's also one of the most important, given its widespread international distribution and BioGro status. The grapes are grown in the original estate vineyard near Renwick, and in the company's two younger vineyards – Tatou, further inland, and Raupo Creek, on an elevated slope in the Omaka Valley. The wine (which includes 5 to 9 per cent Sémillon) is mostly fermented in tanks (80 per cent with indigenous yeasts in 2008), but 15 per cent of the blend is fermented and lees-aged in seasoned French oak casks. The 2009 vintage (★★★★★) is an authoritative wine, rich and complex. Weighty and sweet-fruited, it has deep, ripe tropical-fruit flavours, a subtle seasoning of oak and a dry (3 grams/litre of residual sugar), rounded, lasting finish. Outstanding.

Vintage	09	08	07
WR	7	6	7
Drink	10-15	10-15	10-12

DRY $27 V+

Seresin Reserve Marlborough Sauvignon Blanc ★★★★★

Grown organically, the 2008 vintage (★★★★★) was hand-picked from 18-year-old vines in the Home Vineyard at Renwick, 'pruned to less than half their normal crop'. Fermented with indigenous yeasts in a 50/50 split of tanks and seasoned French oak barriques, it's a beauty – very ripely scented, with notable body, delicacy and depth. Fresh and vibrant, with passionfruit, pear and spice flavours, it is complex and finely textured, with great personality.

Vintage	08	07
WR	6	7
Drink	10-18	10-18

DRY $50 AV

Seven Terraces Marlborough Sauvignon Blanc ★★★☆

From Foxes Island, the 2008 vintage (★★★) was tank-fermented and lees-aged for three months. Mouthfilling, it has good depth of ripe grapefruit and lime flavours, fresh and vibrant, and a smooth finish.

DRY $22 AV

Shepherds Ridge Vineyard Marlborough Sauvignon Blanc ★★★☆

From Wither Hills, the 2009 vintage (★★★☆) is a fresh, medium to full-bodied wine with crisp, lively gooseberry and lime flavours, showing very good delicacy and depth.

Vintage	09	08
WR	6	6
Drink	10-11	P

DRY $20 AV

Shingle Peak Marlborough Sauvignon Blanc ★★★☆

From Matua Valley, the 2009 (★★★☆) is punchy, with clearly herbaceous gooseberry and lime flavours, fresh, vibrant and strong, and an appetisingly crisp, dry finish. The 2010 vintage (★★★☆) is fresh and lively, with strong, vibrant tropical-fruit and herbaceous flavours, crisp and dry. As usual, it's a good buy.

DRY $16 V+

Shingle Peak Reserve Release Marlborough Sauvignon Blanc ★★★☆

The 2010 vintage (★★★★) is weighty and sweet-fruited, with excellent depth of fresh, pure passionfruit and lime flavours, good acid spine, and a lingering finish.

DRY $20 AV

Shipwreck Bay Sauvignon Blanc (★★☆)

From Okahu Estate, the 2008 vintage (★★☆) is an easy-drinking Marlborough wine, medium-bodied, with gooseberry/lime flavours showing decent depth and a smooth finish.

DRY $18 –V

Sileni Benchmark Block Two Omaka Slopes Marlborough Sauvignon Blanc (★★★★)

From two north-facing hillside vineyards, the 2008 vintage (★★★★) is a highly aromatic, fleshy wine with pure, ripe flavours of passionfruit, melon and capsicum, fresh acidity and a long, dry finish.

DRY $25 AV

Sileni Benchmark Block Three Thirteen Rows Marlborough Sauvignon Blanc (★★★☆)

The 2008 vintage (★★★☆) is a single-vineyard wine, grown on the floor of the Wairau Valley, in a band of shingly soil that gives early-ripening fruit. It's a medium to full-bodied, well-rounded wine with very good depth of ripe, gently herbaceous flavours, fresh acidity and a smooth finish.

DRY $25 –V

Sileni Benchmark Block Trinity Vines Marlborough Sauvignon Blanc (★★★☆)

A single-vineyard, Awatere Valley wine, grown at Blind River, the 2009 vintage (★★★☆) is medium-bodied, with tight melon, lime and green-capsicum flavours, showing fresh acidity and very good depth.

Vintage	09
WR	5
Drink	10-12

DRY $25 –V

Sileni Benchmark Block Woolshed Marlborough Sauvignon Blanc (★★★★☆)

Harvested from first-crop vines on Benmorven Station, the 2009 vintage (★★★★☆) has a pungent, lifted, ripely herbaceous bouquet. Mouthfilling, it is very fresh and vibrant, with pure passionfruit and lime flavours, rich, dry and rounded.

Vintage	09
WR	4
Drink	10-12

DRY $25 V+

Sileni Cellar Selection Marlborough Sauvignon Blanc ★★★☆

The 2009 vintage (★★★★) is the best yet. Highly aromatic, it is a medium-bodied style with fresh tropical-fruit and herbaceous flavours, finely balanced and deliciously vibrant and punchy. Showing lots of drink-young charm, the 2010 (★★★☆) has fresh, strong passionfruit and lime flavours and a crisp, dry, finely balanced finish.

Vintage	10	09	08	07
WR	6	6	5	6
Drink	10-11	P	P	P

DRY $20 AV

Sileni The Cape Hawke's Bay Sauvignon Blanc ★★★★

The 2009 vintage (★★★★) is mouthfilling, with strong tropical-fruit flavours, hints of pears and spices, lively acidity, and good freshness and length. It's a top example of the regional style.

Vintage	09
WR	6
Drink	10-12

DRY $25 AV

Sileni The Straits Marlborough Sauvignon Blanc ★★★★☆

The 2009 vintage (★★★★☆) is very aromatic, crisp and punchy, with excellent weight and intensity of fresh gooseberry, lime and capsicum flavours.

Vintage	09	08	07
WR	7	5	6
Drink	10-11	P	P

DRY $25 V+

Sisters, The, Single Vineyard Marlborough Sauvignon Blanc ★★★
Grown in the Awatere Valley, the 2009 vintage (★★★) is a freshly herbaceous style with good depth of gooseberry and green-capsicum flavours, threaded with crisp, flinty acidity.

DRY $17 AV

Sliding Hill Marlborough Sauvignon Blanc (★★★★)
From Kesbury Estate, the 2008 vintage (★★★★) is mouthfilling and dry, with ripe tropical-fruit flavours showing excellent freshness and depth.

DRY $19 V+

Soho Marlborough Sauvignon Blanc ★★★☆
From an Auckland-based company, the 2010 vintage (★★★☆) is lively, with freshly herbaceous, slightly nettley aromas, mouthfilling body and good depth of crisp passionfruit and lime flavours.

DRY $22 AV

Soho White Marlborough Sauvignon Blanc (★★★★)
The fine-value 2010 vintage (★★★★) was grown in the Brancott and Awatere valleys. It has fresh, strong, nettley aromas, leading into a full-bodied wine with strong gooseberry, melon, lime and capsicum flavours, crisp, punchy and dry.

DRY $18 V+

Soljans Marlborough Sauvignon Blanc ★★☆
The 2009 vintage (★★☆) is a single-vineyard wine, medium-bodied, with moderate depth of gooseberry and lime flavours and a dry (4 grams/litre of residual sugar), crisp finish.

DRY $20 –V

Southbank Estate Marlborough Sauvignon Blanc ★★★☆
The 2009 vintage (★★★★) is a quietly satisfying wine with fresh, ripe passionfruit and lime flavours, showing excellent delicacy, vigour and length.

Vintage	08	07
WR	6	7
Drink	P	10

DRY $20 AV

Southern Cross Marlborough Sauvignon Blanc ★★☆
From One Tree Hill Vineyards, a division of Morton Estate, the 2010 vintage (★★★☆) is fresh, crisp and lively, in a herbaceous, nettley style with decent depth. Priced right.

Vintage	10
WR	6
Drink	10-12

DRY $13 V+

Southern Lighthouse Nelson Sauvignon Blanc (★★★)

From Anchorage, the 2009 vintage (★★★) is priced sharply. A crisp, dry wine, it has strong flavours of melons, apples and limes, fresh and lively.

DRY $13 V+

Spinyback Nelson Sauvignon Blanc ★★★★

From Waimea Estates, this is a great buy. The 2009 vintage (★★★★) is a generous, dry wine (4 grams/litre of residual sugar), with excellent depth of ripe passionfruit, citrus and spice flavours. Finely textured, it has fresh, lively acidity and a long finish.

Vintage	10	09	08
WR	7	6	7
Drink	10-11	P	P

DRY $15 V+

Sprig Marlborough Sauvignon Blanc (★★★)

From Bouldevines, the vibrantly fruity 2009 vintage (★★★) is mouthfilling, with moderate acidity and good depth of fresh, ripe tropical-fruit flavours, offering smooth, easy drinking.

DRY $17 AV

Spring Creek Estate Marlborough Sauvignon Blanc ★★★

Priced sharply, the 2009 vintage (★★★) was grown at Rapaura, in the Wairau Valley. It's a fleshy wine with fresh, ripe pineapple and passionfruit flavours, woven with fresh acidity, and a dry finish.

Vintage	09
WR	5
Drink	11-12

DRY $15 V+

Spring Creek Estate Seismic Marlborough Sauvignon Blanc (★★★☆)

The 2009 vintage (★★★☆) is a fleshy, ripe, gently herbaceous style with slightly 'sweaty' aromas and very good depth of passionfruit and lime flavours.

DRY $20 AV

Spy Valley Envoy Marlborough Sauvignon Blanc (★★★☆)

Estate-grown in the Waihopai Valley, the 2009 vintage (★★★☆) was hand-picked from the oldest vines at 24.2 to 25.2 brix. Fermented and lees-aged for a year in French oak barrels, it is very tight, dry and flinty, with ripe, non-herbaceous flavours of peach and grapefruit, subtle oak and a steely finish. Austere in its youth, it's worth cellaring.

Vintage	09
WR	6
Drink	10-15

DRY $30 –V

Spy Valley Marlborough Sauvignon Blanc ★★★★

Always a good buy. The 2010 vintage (★★★★) was harvested at 22 to 24.9 brix and tank-fermented. It's a mouthfilling, punchy wine with very fresh, concentrated flavours of passionfruit, grapefruit and lime, slightly spicy, crisp and long.

Vintage	10	09	08	07
WR	6	6	6	6
Drink	11-12	10-11	P	P

DRY $20 V+

Squawking Magpie Reserve Marlborough Sauvignon Blanc ★★★

The 2009 vintage (★★★) is fresh and crisp, in a clearly herbaceous style with melon and green-capsicum flavours, woven with lively acidity.

DRY $20 –V

Staete Landt Marlborough Sauvignon Blanc ★★★★★

Ripely scented, rich and zingy, this single-vineyard wine is grown at Rapaura and mostly handled in tanks, with some fermentation and lees-aging in seasoned French oak casks (20 per cent in 2009). The 2009 vintage (★★★★★) is very subtle and satisfying. Bone-dry, it is fleshy, with rich, ripe tropical-fruit flavours, crisp and lively, and excellent drive, immediacy and punch.

Vintage	09	08	07	06
WR	6	7	6	6
Drink	10-17	10-13	10-12	P

DRY $23 V+

Stafford Lane Estate Nelson Sauvignon Blanc ★★☆

Grown on the Waimea Plains, the 2009 vintage (★★☆) is light and crisp, with moderate depth of citrusy, limey, appley flavours, fresh and tangy. Priced right.

DRY $15 AV

Stanley Estates Marlborough Sauvignon Blanc (★★★★)

The 2009 vintage (★★★★) is a single-vineyard, Awatere Valley wine. A vividly herbal expression of Sauvignon Blanc, it is very aromatic, with mouthfilling body and incisive melon and green-capsicum flavours, fresh, crisp and lasting.

Vintage	10	09
WR	6	5
Drink	11-12	10-11

DRY $23 AV

Starborough Marlborough Sauvignon Blanc ★★★★

A consistently good buy. The 2010 vintage (★★★★) is based on estate-grown grapes, from the Awatere Valley (60 per cent) and Wairau Valley (40 per cent), and was mostly handled in tanks; 7 per cent of the blend was barrel-fermented. Freshly herbaceous and highly aromatic, it has a clear, pure Awatere Valley influence, but also shows some riper, Wairau Valley notes. Very fresh and vibrant, it's a finely balanced wine with a dry (4 grams/litre of residual sugar) finish.

Vintage	10
WR	5
Drink	10-12

DRY $19 V+

Stoneburn Marlborough Sauvignon Blanc (★★★)

From Hunter's, the 2009 vintage (★★★) is lively and full-bodied, with good depth of fresh, ripe melon and capsicum flavours and a rounded, dry finish. Fine value.

Vintage	09
WR	5
Drink	10-11

DRY $15 V+

Stonecroft Sauvignon Blanc ★★★☆

This Hawke's Bay winery uprooted its own Sauvignon Blanc vines after the 2001 vintage, but now sources grapes from Te Mata Estate's Woodthorpe Vineyard, in the Dartmoor Valley. The 2009 vintage (★★★☆) is ripely scented and smooth, with fresh melon/lime flavours, showing good depth. The 2010 (★★★), made with a small portion of barrel fermentation, has fresh, ripe tropical-fruit flavours, offering smooth, easy drinking.

DRY $21 AV

Stoneleigh Marlborough Sauvignon Blanc ★★★★

From Pernod Ricard NZ, this consistently good wine flows from the stony and relatively warm Rapaura district of the Wairau Valley, which produces a ripe style of Sauvignon Blanc, yet retains good acidity and vigour. Over 300,000 cases are produced. The 2009 (★★★★) is mouthfilling, with strong, pure flavours of passionfruit, melon and lime, showing excellent freshness, delicacy and depth. The 2010 vintage (★★★★) is weighty and rounded, with fresh, rich tropical-fruit flavours and a finely textured, dry (3.5 grams/litre of residual sugar) finish.

Vintage	10	09	08
WR	7	7	6
Drink	10-11	P	P

DRY $23 AV

Stoneleigh Vineyards Rapaura Series Marlborough Sauvignon Blanc ★★★★☆

This richly flavoured wine is grown in the warm, shingly soils of the Rapaura district and lees-aged for two months, with regular stirring. The 2009 (★★★★☆) is full-bodied, with a strong surge of fresh, ripe tropical-fruit flavours, pure, dry and lingering. The 2010 vintage (★★★★☆) was on the market by July 2010. Richly scented, it is a medium-bodied wine, sweet-fruited, with intense, ripe non-herbaceous flavours, slightly minerally, dry, rounded and long.

Vintage	10	09	08	07
WR	7	7	6	7
Drink	10-11	P	P	P

DRY $27 AV

Stone Paddock Hawke's Bay Sauvignon Blanc ★★★

From Paritua Vineyards, the 2008 vintage (★★★) was mostly handled in tanks, but 10 per cent of the blend was fermented and matured for two months in seasoned French oak casks. It's a medium-bodied wine with ripe tropical-fruit flavours, fresh, crisp, slightly spicy and dry.

Vintage	08
WR	6
Drink	10-12

DRY $20 –V

Stonewall Marlborough Sauvignon Blanc ★★☆
The 2009 vintage (★★☆) is a solid, no-fuss wine from Forrest, medium-bodied, with citrusy, appley, limey flavours, crisp and dry.

DRY $17 –V

Stop Banks Marlborough Sauvignon Blanc (★★★★)
The 2008 vintage (★★★★) is worth buying, with a freshly herbaceous bouquet leading into a mouthfilling, punchy, intensely varietal wine with good intensity of gooseberry/lime flavours.

DRY $18 V+

Sugar Loaf Marlborough Sauvignon Blanc ★★★★
Grown in the Wairau and Awatere valleys, the 2009 vintage (★★★★) is a fleshy, ripe tropical-fruit-flavoured style. Fresh and refined, it shows excellent delicacy, purity and depth.

DRY $17 V+

Summerhouse Marlborough Sauvignon Blanc ★★★★☆
This single-vineyard, Wairau Valley wine is consistently impressive, and the especially intense 2010 vintage (★★★★★) is outstanding. Richly scented, it is mouthfilling and sweet-fruited, with concentrated, ripe passionfruit and lime flavours, very fresh and vibrant, and a racy, bone-dry, long finish.

DRY $22 V+

Takutai Sauvignon Blanc ★★
From Waimea Estates, in Nelson, the 2008 vintage (★★) is a solid but plain wine with crisp, citrusy, green-edged flavours.

DRY $15 –V

Tasman Bay New Zealand Sauvignon Blanc ★★★
The 2008 vintage (★★★) is a fresh, vibrantly fruity blend of Nelson and Marlborough fruit, oak-aged for three months. It's a ripely herbaceous style, clearly varietal, with plenty of flavour and a smooth, well-balanced finish.

DRY $19 AV

Te Awa Sauvignon Blanc ★★★★
'A wine for the table, not the bar', the 2009 vintage (★★★★☆) is an excellent example of the Hawke's Bay regional style, ripely scented, weighty and fully dry. A finely structured wine (it includes 5 per cent Sémillon), likely to age gracefully, it has sweet-fruit delights, with concentrated melon/lime flavours, and a subtle seasoning of oak (15 per cent of the blend was barrel-fermented) adding complexity.

DRY $27 –V

Te Kairanga Martinborough Sauvignon Blanc ★★★☆

The 2008 vintage (★★★☆) is a mouthfilling, fleshy wine with strong, ripe flavours that linger well. Entirely estate-grown, it is finely balanced, with good acidity and a dry finish. (The 2009 is labelled Te Kairanga Martinborough Estate Sauvignon Blanc. There is also a Regional Selection Sauvignon Blanc 2009, blended from Marlborough and Martinborough grapes.)

Vintage	09	08	07
WR	7	6	6
Drink	10-13	10-12	10-11

DRY $21 AV

Te Mania Nelson Sauvignon Blanc ★★★☆

Typically a good wine – fresh and full-flavoured, with tropical-fruit characters, some nettley notes and lively, balanced acidity.

Vintage	09	08	07
WR	6	5	6
Drink	10-11	P	P

DRY $19 V+

Te Mania Reserve Nelson Sauvignon Blanc ★★★☆

Packed with flavour, the characterful 2008 vintage (★★★★) was tank-fermented, then matured in a 50/50 split of tanks and seasoned oak barrels. Clearly herbaceous, it is fleshy and rich, with strong gooseberry, herb, fig and spice flavours, a slightly nutty twist and considerable complexity.

Vintage	08	07
WR	6	6
Drink	10-12	10-11

DRY $25 –V

Te Mata Cape Crest Sauvignon Blanc ★★★★★

This oak-aged Hawke's Bay label is impressive for its ripely herbal, complex, sustained flavours. Most of the grapes come from the company's relatively warm Bullnose Vineyard, inland from Hastings (the rest is grown at Woodthorpe, in the Dartmoor Valley), and the blend includes small proportions of Sémillon (to add longevity) and Sauvignon Gris (which contributes weight and mouthfeel). The wine is fully fermented and lees-aged for eight months in French oak barriques (33 per cent new). In a vertical tasting, the two to four-year-old wines look best – still fresh, but very harmonious. The 2009 (★★★★★) is fleshy and dry, with rich tropical-fruit flavours, hints of figs and spices, and finely integrated oak. Fragrant, complex and concentrated, it's a top vintage.

Vintage	09	08	07	06	05	04
WR	7	7	7	7	7	7
Drink	10-14	10-12	10-12	10-11	P	P

DRY $28 V+

Te Mata Estate Woodthorpe Vineyard Sauvignon Blanc ★★★★

Estate-grown at an inland site in the Dartmoor Valley of Hawke's Bay, the 2009 vintage (★★★★☆) was handled entirely in tanks. Highly aromatic, it is weighty, with punchy, ripe tropical-fruit flavours, crisp and zesty, a slightly minerally streak and a long, dry finish. Notably fresh, vibrant and intense, it's a top buy. The 2010 (★★★★) is mouthfilling, tight and very youthful, with fresh, zingy melon/lime flavours, crisp, dry and lingering. Best drinking mid-2011+.

Vintage	10	09	08	07	06
WR	7	7	7	7	7
Drink	10-12	10-11	P	P	P

DRY $19 V+

Terrace Heights Estate Marlborough Sauvignon Blanc ★★★☆

The 2010 vintage (★★★☆) is full-bodied and fresh, with very good depth of ripe melon, passionfruit, herb and spice flavours, and a dry (3 grams/litre of residual sugar), finely balanced finish.

Vintage	10
WR	5
Drink	11-12

DRY $19 V+

Terrain Marlborough Sauvignon Blanc ★★☆

Sold in supermarkets, the 2009 vintage (★★☆) is a distinctly ripe style with hints of pineapples and a dry finish. Smooth, easy, no-fuss drinking.

DRY $12 V+

Terravin Marlborough Sauvignon Blanc ★★★★

Drinking well now, the 2009 vintage (★★★★) was mostly handled in tanks; 9 per cent of the blend was barrel-fermented. Weighty and vibrantly fruity, it has rich tropical-fruit flavours, sweet-fruited and crisp, with a touch of complexity and a finely balanced, dry finish.

DRY $24 AV

Terravin Single Vineyard Marlborough Sauvignon Blanc (★★★★☆)

Hand-harvested on the south side of the Wairau Valley, the 2009 vintage (★★★★☆) is a classy wine, mostly handled in tanks; one-third of the blend was fermented and matured for five months in seasoned French oak. Still developing, weighty and tightly structured, it is ripely scented and flavoured, with excellent intensity, a very subtle seasoning of nutty oak and a rich, dry finish.

DRY $29 AV

Thornbury Marlborough Sauvignon Blanc ★★★★☆

The 2010 vintage (★★★★★) from Villa Maria is striking in its infancy. Grown in the Awatere and Wairau valleys, it is intensely aromatic, weighty, sweet-fruited and dry, with a lovely array of fresh, pure fruit flavours – passionfruit, lime and grapefruit – and a sustained, slightly minerally, racy finish. A top buy.

Vintage	10	09	08
WR	7	7	6
Drink	10-11	10-11	P

DRY $22 V+

Three Stones Marlborough Sauvignon Blanc –
see 3 Stones Marlborough Sauvignon Blanc (at the start of this section)

Three Paddles Martinborough Sauvignon Blanc ★★★★

A top buy. From Nga Waka, the 2009 vintage (★★★★) is crisp and dry, with vibrant melon, lime and passionfruit flavours showing excellent freshness, delicacy and depth. Fleshy and finely balanced, it's already delicious.

Vintage	09	08
WR	7	7
Drink	10+	P

DRY $18 V+

Tiki Single Vineyard Marlborough Sauvignon Blanc (★★★★)

Grown in the Wairau Valley, the 2009 vintage (★★★★) is a finely textured wine from McKean Estates, fresh and full-bodied, with excellent delicacy and depth of ripe gooseberry and lime flavours and a well-rounded finish.

DRY $25 AV

Tiki Single Vineyard Waipara Sauvignon Blanc (★★★★)

A high-impact style, the 2010 vintage (★★★★) has slightly 'sweaty' aromas and crisp, penetrating passionfruit and lime flavours, very fresh and racy.

DRY $28 –V

Tiki Single Vineyard Wairau Alpine Valley Sauvignon Blanc (★★★★★)

The intense, immaculate 2010 vintage (★★★★★) is notably aromatic, vibrant and punchy, with ripe tropical-fruit flavours, a herbal undercurrent and a long, minerally, dry (3.6 grams/litre of residual sugar) finish. Mouth-wateringly fresh, crisp and intense, it's already delicious.

DRY $28 V+

Tiki Wairau Alpine Valley Sauvignon Blanc (★★★☆)

The easy-drinking 2010 vintage (★★★☆) is mouthfilling, with fresh, ripe tropical-fruit flavours, showing very good depth, and a smooth (5 grams/litre of residual sugar), rounded finish.

MED/DRY $20 AV

Timara Sauvignon Blanc (★★★)

From Pernod Ricard NZ, the 2008 vintage (★★★) is not labelled by region, but was made from New Zealand grapes. Fresh, crisp, lively and smooth, with punchy tropical-fruit flavours, it offers top value.

DRY $12 V+

Tinpot Hut Marlborough Sauvignon Blanc ★★★★☆

Mostly estate-grown at Blind River, in the Awatere Valley, the 2009 vintage (★★★★★) is a richly scented wine with 'tomato stalk' aromas and concentrated tropical-fruit and herbal flavours. Crisp, lively and finely poised, with a minerally streak, it shows real intensity through the palate.

DRY $21 V+

Ti Point Marlborough Sauvignon Blanc ★★★★

Fresh, vibrant and punchy, the 2009 vintage (★★★☆) is a medium-bodied, appetisingly crisp wine. It's a ripe tropical fruit-flavoured style with a sliver of sweetness (4.5 grams/litre of residual sugar) to balance its appetising acidity, and very good liveliness and length.

DRY $21 V+

Tohu Marlborough Sauvignon Blanc ★★★★☆

This is a consistently excellent wine and the 2009 vintage (★★★★☆) offers outstanding value. A single-vineyard wine, grown in the Awatere Valley, it is weighty and sweet-fruited, with strong, ripe passionfruit-like flavours to the fore, some of the herbaceous, 'tomato stalk' notes typical of the valley, excellent concentration and a crisp, dry (3 grams/litre of residual sugar), racy finish.

DRY $19 V+

Tohu Mugwi Marlborough Sauvignon Blanc ★★★★

Named after a Blenheim kaumatua, the 2008 vintage (★★★☆) has pungent aromatics, with a soft, rounded, clearly herbaceous palate, showing good but not great depth.

DRY $23 AV

Toi Toi Marlborough Reserve Sauvignon Blanc (★★★★)

The 2009 vintage (★★★★) has slightly 'sweaty' aromas leading into a sweet-fruited wine, full-bodied, rich and rounded, with grapefruit, passionfruit and lime flavours, finishing crisp and long.

DRY $23 AV

Torea Marlborough Sauvignon Blanc (★★★★)

From Fairhall Downs, the 2009 vintage (★★★★) is full-bodied and dry, with fresh, vibrant, ripely herbaceous flavours, finely balanced, crisp, pure and lingering. A top buy.

DRY $19 V+

Torlesse Waipara Sauvignon Blanc ★★★☆

The 2009 vintage (★★★☆) is aromatic and sweet-fruited, with lively, gooseberryish, tangy flavours showing very good depth and a smooth (5 grams/litre of residual sugar) finish.

Vintage	09	08
WR	5	5
Drink	10-15	P

MED/DRY $18 V+

Torrent Bay Nelson Sauvignon Blanc ★★★

From Anchorage Wines, at Motueka, the 2009 vintage (★★★) is citrusy and limey, with a sliver of sweetness (4.5 grams/litre of residual sugar) amid its fresh, tangy flavours, which show good depth.

DRY $17 AV

Tranquil Valley Marlborough Sauvignon Blanc ★★☆
From Huasheng Wines, based at Matakana, the 2008 vintage (★★☆) is a dry wine with moderate depth of melon and green-capsicum flavours, crisp and lively.

DRY $20 –V

Tranquillity Bay Nelson Sauvignon Blanc (★★☆)
From Anchorage, the sharply priced 2009 vintage (★★☆) is an easy-drinking style, medium-bodied, with fresh, citrusy, ripely herbaceous flavours and a smooth finish.

DRY $12 V+

Trinity Hill Hawke's Bay Sauvignon Blanc ★★★★
This 'Sancerre-like' wine is one of the region's finest, mid-priced Sauvignon Blancs. The 2009 vintage (★★★☆), grown in several vineyards, coastal and inland, was harvested at 17.6 to 24.5 brix and tank-fermented to near dryness (3.5 grams/litre of residual sugar). Ripely scented, it is vibrant, crisp and full-bodied, with tropical-fruit flavours showing good freshness and immediacy. The 2010 (★★★★☆) is a cracker. Fresh and ripely scented, it offers an array of fruit flavours at the ripe end of the spectrum, enlivened by fresh acidity. Sweet-fruited, slightly minerally and long, it has excellent poise, depth and drive.

MED/DRY $20 V+

Triplebank Awatere Valley Marlborough Sauvignon Blanc ★★★★
From Pernod Ricard NZ, the 2009 vintage (★★★★) is mouthfilling, with vibrant, ripely herbaceous flavours, slightly nettley, minerally and fully dry (1.7 grams/litre of residual sugar). The 2010 (★★★★) is weighty, with an attractive mingling of tropical-fruit and herbaceous notes, crisp, slightly minerally and long.

Vintage	09	08	07
WR	7	6	6
Drink	P	P	P

DRY $24 AV

Tupari Marlborough Sauvignon Blanc ★★★★★
Grown in the upper Awatere Valley, the 2009 vintage (★★★★) is a single-vineyard wine, made by Glenn Thomas, formerly of Vavasour. Handled in tanks and matured on its yeast lees for six months, with weekly stirring (to give 'creaminess on the palate'), it is mouthfilling, rich and ripe, yet also minerally and racy, with concentrated passionfruit and lime flavours that build to a zingy, dry (3.9 grams/litre of residual sugar), lasting finish. Classy stuff.

DRY $29 V+

Turning Point New Style Sauvignon Blanc (★★★)
From Spencer Hill, the 2008 vintage (★★★) is a blend of Marlborough and Nelson grapes, based mostly on Sauvignon Blanc, supplemented by five other 'aromatic' varieties, accounting for 15 per cent of the blend. The bouquet is clearly herbaceous, with fresh gooseberry and green-capsicum flavours, some peachy and spicy notes, a hint of toasty oak, and a crisp, dry finish.

DRY $16 V+

Tussock Nelson Sauvignon Blanc ★★★

From Woollaston, the 2010 vintage (★★★) is a crisp, medium-bodied wine with strongly varietal melon, lime and herb flavours, slightly nettley and dry.

DRY $17 AV

Twin Islands Marlborough Sauvignon Blanc ★★★

Negociants' wine offers very easy drinking. The 2010 vintage (★★★☆) has fresh, ripe melon and lime flavours, showing good depth, delicacy and liveliness, and a smooth finish.

DRY $19 AV

Two Rivers of Marlborough Convergence Sauvignon Blanc ★★★★☆

The 2009 (★★★★☆) is a classy, intense blend of equal parts of Awatere Valley and Wairau Valley grapes, 5 per cent barrel-fermented. A fruit bowl of tropical-fruit and herbaceous flavours, showing excellent freshness, depth and harmony, it is rich, finely balanced and lingering. The 2010 vintage (★★★★★) is even more impressive. Lees-aged for four months, it is mouthfilling, beautifully vibrant, poised and concentrated, with sweet-fruit delights, a touch of complexity and deep passionfruit, gooseberry and lime flavours.

DRY $22 V+

Two Tails Marlborough Sauvignon Blanc ★★★☆

From Fairbourne, the 2009 vintage (★★★☆) was grown in the Wairau Valley. Fresh and vibrant, it is medium-bodied and sweet-fruited, with very good depth and delicacy of melon and lime flavours.

DRY $18 V+

Two Tracks Marlborough Sauvignon Blanc ★★★

From Wither Hills, the 2009 vintage (★★★) is a crisp, vibrant, ripely herbaceous style, showing good freshness, delicacy and depth.

DRY $17 AV

Unison Hawke's Bay Sauvignon Blanc (★★★☆)

The 2010 vintage (★★★☆) was hand-picked and fermented in a mix of tanks and barrels. Mouthfilling and dry, it's a ripely flavoured wine with tropical-fruit characters, hints of spice and toasty oak, and a crisp finish. Showing some complexity, it's still coming together; open mid-2011+.

DRY $20 AV

Urlar Gladstone Sauvignon Blanc ★★★★

Fermented in tanks (mostly) and seasoned oak barrels, the 2009 vintage (★★★★) is a rich, mouthfilling, gently oaked style with a creamy texture and concentrated, ripe tropical-fruit flavours. Powerful, vibrantly fruity and finely balanced, it's worth cellaring.

DRY $22 AV

Vavasour Awatere Valley Sauvignon Blanc ★★★★★

A consistently classy wine. The 2010 vintage (★★★★★) is a classic Awatere style, weighty, vibrant and racy. Intensely aromatic, it has pure melon and green-capsicum flavours, slightly nettley, with a dry, lasting finish.

Vintage	10	09
WR	7	6
Drink	10-12	10-11

DRY $21 V+

Vavasour Claudia's Vineyard Awatere Valley Sauvignon Blanc (★★★★)

The 2007 vintage (★★★★) was hand-harvested and fermented with indigenous yeasts in old French oak casks, with lengthy lees-aging. It's a finely textured wine with good weight and strong, ripe tropical-fruit flavours, showing some toasty complexity.

DRY $40 –V

Vidal AJ Organic Hawke's Bay Sauvignon Blanc (★★★)

Certified BioGro, the 2009 vintage (★★★) was estate-grown in the Joseph Soler Vineyard and tank-fermented, with some lees-aging. It's a quietly satisfying wine, not intensely aromatic, but mouthfilling, with crisp, dry tropical-fruit flavours and a touch of complexity.

DRY $16 V+

Vidal Marlborough Sauvignon Blanc ★★★★

The 2009 vintage (★★★★) is a mouthfilling wine with strong melon and green-capsicum flavours, fresh, ripe and smooth. Finely balanced, with appetising acidity and slight minerally touches, it shows excellent delicacy, purity and length.

Vintage	10	09	08	07
WR	7	7	6	7
Drink	10-12	10-11	P	P

DRY $20 V+

Villa Maria Cellar Selection Marlborough Sauvignon Blanc ★★★★☆

An intensely flavoured wine, typically of a very high standard. Grown in the Wairau and Awatere valleys and tank-fermented, the 2009 (★★★★☆) is freshly aromatic and zingy, with vibrant, ripe melon and lime flavours, showing excellent delicacy and concentration, and a long, dry finish. The 2010 vintage (★★★★☆), matured on its yeast lees for several months, is weighty, with concentrated, ripe tropical-fruit flavours, deliciously crisp and dry (2.5 grams/litre of residual sugar).

Vintage	10	09	08	07
WR	7	7	6	7
Drink	10-12	10-11	P	P

DRY $24 V+

Villa Maria Private Bin Marlborough Sauvignon Blanc ★★★★☆

This large-volume label offers impressive quality and consistently great value. The 2010 vintage (★★★★☆) was grown in the Wairau and Awatere valleys and made in a dry style (3.5 grams/litre of residual sugar). Offering wonderful value at its average price on 'special' of $11.99, it is fleshy, ripe and finely textured, yet also very fresh and zingy, with sweet-fruit delights and rich melon, lime and capsicum flavours, crisp, lingering, and already quite open and expressive.

Vintage	10	09	08	07
WR	6	7	6	7
Drink	10-12	10-11	P	P

DRY $21 V+

Villa Maria Reserve Clifford Bay Sauvignon Blanc ★★★★★

Grown in the Awatere Valley (although the label refers only to 'Clifford Bay', into which the Awatere River empties), this is an exceptional Marlborough wine. Seddon Vineyards and the Taylors Pass Vineyard – both managed but not owned by Villa Maria – are the key sources of fruit. Handled entirely in stainless steel tanks and aged on its light yeast lees for two months, the wine typically exhibits the leap-out-of-the-glass fragrance and zingy, explosive flavour of Marlborough Sauvignon Blanc at its inimitable best. The 2009 (★★★★★) is a classic sub-regional style, with intense, 'tomato stalk' aromas. Rich and vibrantly fruity, it has intense melon, lime and capsicum flavours, and a long, bone-dry, racy finish. The 2010 vintage (★★★★★) is another lovely wine – weighty, rich and zingy, with intense, pure gooseberry/lime flavours and a long, dry (2.5 grams/litre of residual sugar) finish.

Vintage	10	09	08	07	06
WR	7	7	6	7	7
Drink	10-12	10-11	P	P	P

DRY $27 V+

Villa Maria Reserve Wairau Valley Sauvignon Blanc ★★★★★

An authoritative wine, it is typically ripe and zingy, with impressive weight and length of flavour, and tends to be fuller in body, less herbaceous and rounder than its Clifford Bay stablemate (above). The contributing vineyards vary from vintage to vintage, but Peter and Deborah Jackson's warm, stony vineyard in the heart of the valley has long been a key source of grapes, and sometimes a small part of the blend is barrel-fermented, to enhance its complexity and texture. The 2009 vintage (★★★★★) is highly scented, with slight 'armpit' aromas and fresh, finely poised passionfruit, melon and lime flavours that build across the palate to a long, dry finish. It's very refined and vivacious. The 2010 (★★★★★) is mouthfilling, deliciously rich and rounded, with concentrated, ripe tropical-fruit flavours, a hint of 'sweaty armpit' and a finely textured, long, dry (3 grams/litre of residual sugar) finish.

Vintage	10	09	08	07
WR	7	7	7	7
Drink	10-12	10-11	P	P

DRY $27 V+

Villa Maria Single Vineyard Graham Marlborough Sauvignon Blanc ★★★★

Grown in the Awatere Valley, near the coast, the 2009 vintage was tasted prior to bottling (and so not rated). It looked highly promising, with nettley aromas and crisp, dry gooseberry and lime flavours, fresh, strong and zingy. The 2010 (also tasted before bottling) has strong, 'tomato stalk' aromas and flavours, very crisp and zingy, incisive and long.

Vintage	10	09
WR	7	7
Drink	10-12	10-11

DRY $27 –V

Villa Maria Single Vineyard Southern Clays Marlborough Sauvignon Blanc ★★★★

(The 2008 vintage was called 'Single Vineyard Maxwell'.) Grown in the foothills on the south side of the Wairau Valley, the 2009, tasted prior to bottling (and so not rated), is a bone-dry wine with strong, ripe tropical-fruit flavours, threaded with mouth-watering acidity. The 2010 vintage, also tasted before bottling, is very ripely scented and zingy, with incisive passionfruit and lime flavours and a deliciously long and dry (2.3 grams/litre of residual sugar) finish.

Vintage	10
WR	7
Drink	10-12

DRY $27 –V

Villa Maria Single Vineyard Taylors Pass Marlborough Sauvignon Blanc ★★★★★

Taylors Pass vineyard lies 100 metres above sea level in the Awatere Valley. The 2009 (★★★★★), lees-aged for three months, is a classic example of the sub-regional style. Very vibrant and punchy, it is minerally and herbal, with intense capsicum and 'tomato stalk' aromas and a long, dry, racy finish. The 2010 vintage (★★★★★) is also highly impressive – weighty, with fresh, rich tropical-fruit and herbaceous flavours, deliciously vibrant, dry (2.5 grams/litre of residual sugar) and lasting.

Vintage	10	09
WR	7	7
Drink	10-12	10-11

DRY $27 V+

Waimea Barrel Fermented Nelson Sauvignon Blanc (★★★★)

The full-bodied 2008 vintage (★★★★) was grown on the Waimea Plains and fermented and matured for four months in seasoned oak barrels. A fleshy, ripely flavoured wine, nutty, dry, slightly creamy and rounded, it's maturing well.

Vintage	08
WR	6
Drink	10-13

DRY $22 V+

Waimea Bolitho SV Nelson Sauvignon Blanc ★★★☆

'SV' means Signature Vineyard. Weighty, with ripe tropical-fruit flavours, some cut-grass notes and a dry, mouth-wateringly crisp finish, the 2008 vintage (★★★☆) is fresh, lively and zingy.

Vintage	08
WR	6
Drink	10-11

DRY $22 AV

Waimea Nelson Sauvignon Blanc ★★★★

A good buy. The 2009 vintage (★★★☆), estate-grown on the Waimea Plains, is medium-bodied, with strong, slightly grassy flavours, very fresh, lively, crisp and finely balanced (4.6 grams/litre of residual sugar).

Vintage	10	09	08
WR	7	6	7
Drink	10-12	10-12	10-11

DRY $18 V+

Waipara Hills Soul of the South Marlborough Sauvignon Blanc (★★★★★)

A wine of strong presence, the 2009 vintage (★★★★★) was grown in the Awatere and Wairau valleys. Weighty and rich, it is generous and very finely balanced, with strong, ripe tropical-fruit flavours, good acid spine, and a lingering finish. It's delicious now.

DRY $21 V+

Waipara Hills Southern Cross Selection Waipara Sauvignon Blanc (★★★☆)

The 2008 vintage (★★★☆) is fresh and vibrantly fruity, with ripely herbaceous flavours, showing very good depth and vigour.

DRY $30 –V

Waipara Springs Waipara Sauvignon Blanc ★★★☆

The 2009 vintage (★★★) is mouthfilling, with fresh, ripe grapefruit and lime flavours and a fully dry finish.

DRY $19 V+

Waipara West Sauvignon Blanc ★★★☆

The 2008 vintage (★★★☆) is a fresh, vibrant wine with strong, crisp limey flavours, flinty, dry and lingering.

DRY $20 AV

Waipipi Wairarapa Sauvignon Blanc ★★☆

The 2009 vintage (★★☆) was grown near Masterton and made with some use of indigenous yeasts and barrel fermentation. It's a solid, moderately varietal wine with fresh, crisp pear and lime flavours.

Vintage	09
WR	5
Drink	P

DRY $25 –V

Wairau River Marlborough Sauvignon Blanc ★★★☆

The 2009 vintage (★★★★) is full-bodied, with good intensity of melon and green-capsicum flavours, fresh, vibrant and zingy. The 2010 (★★★☆) is freshly herbaceous and dry (4 grams/litre of residual sugar), with vibrant, pure melon and green-capsicum flavours, showing good depth.

Vintage	10	09	08
WR	6	6	5
Drink	10-11	P	P

DRY $20 AV

Wairau River Reserve Marlborough Sauvignon Blanc ★★★★

The 2009 (★★★★) is a single-vineyard wine, grown alongside the Opawa River and made in a slightly off-dry style. It's a classy, weighty wine with strong, fresh tropical-fruit flavours, rich, ripe and rounded. The 2010 vintage (★★★★) is fresh and dry (2.7 grams/litre of residual sugar), weighty and punchy, with concentrated pineapple and lime flavours, a herbal undercurrent, and a finely textured, long finish.

Vintage	09
WR	6
Drink	10-12

DRY $30 –V

Walnut Block Collectables Marlborough Sauvignon Blanc ★★★☆

The 2009 vintage (★★★☆) is a fresh, vibrantly fruity wine with strong, ripe tropical-fruit flavours showing very good vigour, ripeness and depth, and a crisp, dry finish.

DRY $18 V+

Walnut Block Marlborough Sauvignon Blanc ★★★★

The 2009 vintage (★★★★) is a single-vineyard, hand-harvested Wairau Valley wine. Most of the blend was handled in tanks, but 25 per cent was fermented with indigenous yeasts in old French barriques. Mouthfilling and crisp, it's a fully dry style with strong tropical-fruit flavours, a very subtle seasoning of oak, and excellent vibrancy, delicacy and depth.

DRY $22 V+

Weka River Waipara Valley Sauvignon Blanc (★★★★)

From a single vineyard, 'approximately two rugby fields in size', the 2008 vintage (★★★★) is dry and minerally, with citrusy, limey flavours that linger well. A distinctive wine, it is tightly structured and should mature well.

DRY $20 V+

West Brook Marlborough Sauvignon Blanc ★★★☆

The 2009 vintage (★★★☆), 10 per cent barrel-fermented, is fresh and crisp, with lively acidity and vibrant gooseberry, lime and herb flavours showing very good depth.

DRY $20 AV

Whalesback Marlborough Sauvignon Blanc ★★★

From Koura Bay, the 2008 vintage (★★★) has good depth of tropical-fruit and herbaceous flavours, threaded with fresh, lively acidity.

Vintage	09	08
WR	6	6
Drink	10-11	P

DRY $16 V+

Whitecaps Marlborough Sauvignon Blanc (★★☆)

From Whitehaven, the 2008 vintage (★★☆) doesn't set the world on fire – but it's a top buy at $10. Fresh and crisp, it has citrusy and appley flavours, only moderately varietal. A good drink-young quaffer.

DRY $10 V+

Whitecliff Sauvignon Blanc (★★★)

The lively 2009 vintage (★★★) is a New Zealand wine, not labelled by region. Fresh, crisp and smooth, with good depth of ripe tropical-fruit and herbal flavours, it has plenty of youthful impact.

MED/DRY $18 AV

Whitehaven Greg Marlborough Sauvignon Blanc ★★★★★

Dedicated to the memory of founder Greg White, the 2009 (★★★★★) is a super-charged wine, grown in the Awatere Valley. It has notably rich gooseberry, melon and lime flavours, showing excellent purity, delicacy and length. The 2010 vintage (★★★★★) was grown in the Awatere and Ure valleys. Mouthfilling and smooth, it shows lovely balance, delicacy and depth of tropical-fruit and herbaceous flavours, in a highly concentrated style with a basically dry (4.5 grams/litre of residual sugar) finish, balanced by racy acidity.

Vintage	10	09
WR	7	7
Drink	10-12	10-11

DRY $25 V+

Whitehaven Marlborough Sauvignon Blanc ★★★★★

Whitehaven adopts a low profile in New Zealand, but this consistently impressive wine is a big seller in the US, where it is distributed by one of its shareholders, global wine giant E & J Gallo. The grapes are grown at dozens of sites in the Wairau and Awatere valleys, and the wine is handled entirely in tanks. At its best within two years, it offers beautifully fresh, deep and delicate flavours of passionfruit and limes, pure and smooth. The 2010 vintage (★★★★☆) has a lifted, nettley, aromatic bouquet. Crisp and punchy, it has intense, fresh melon, gooseberry and lime flavours, with a minerally streak and a dry (3.5 grams/litre of residual sugar), racy finish.

Vintage	10	09
WR	7	7
Drink	10-12	10-11

DRY $20 V+

Whitestone Waipara Sauvignon Blanc ★★★☆

The 2009 vintage (★★★☆), a single-vineyard wine, is an attractively ripe and rounded style with good flavour depth and harmony. It's balanced for fresh, easy drinking.

DRY $20 AV

Wild Rock Elevation Marlborough Sauvignon Blanc ★★★☆

Full-bodied, crisp and dry, this wine is designed to accentuate 'floral' and 'stone-fruit' characters, by blending Sauvignon Blanc with small portions of Riesling and Viognier. Delicious from the start, the 2010 vintage (★★★★) is weighty, with an array of tropical-fruit, peach and spice flavours, very fresh and vibrant, excellent mouthfeel, and a finely textured, dry (2.5 grams/litre of residual sugar) finish.

Vintage	10	09	08
WR	7	6	6
Drink	10-13	10-11	10

DRY $19 V+

Wild Rock Marlborough Sauvignon Blanc (★★★☆)

Sold only in supermarkets, the 2008 vintage (★★★☆) is aromatic, with fresh, vibrant tropical-fruit and capsicum flavours, crisp and strong.

DRY $19 V+

Wild Rock The Infamous Goose Marlborough Sauvignon Blanc ★★★

From Wild Rock, a division of Craggy Range, the 2010 vintage (★★★☆) is punchy and vibrant, with crisp, dry melon and lime flavours, showing good freshness, vigour and depth.

Vintage	10	09	08
WR	7	6	7
Drink	10-13	10-11	10

DRY $19 AV

Wild South Marlborough Sauvignon Blanc ★★★☆

From Sacred Hill, the 2009 vintage (★★★★) is very fresh and lively, with strong passionfruit and lime flavours, appetisingly crisp and dry (1.8 grams/litre of residual sugar). It's a finely balanced wine, priced sharply.

DRY $19 V+

William Thomas Marlborough Sauvignon Blanc ★★★★

(A brand owned by Fromm.) The 2008 vintage (★★★★) was grown at the base of the Brancott Valley and a small portion was matured in old barrels. It's a crisp, medium-bodied wine, dry, with sweet-fruit characters and very good depth of fresh, ripe melon/lime flavours.

Vintage	09	08	07
WR	6	6	6
Drink	10-13	10-12	10-11

DRY $20 V+

Wingspan Sauvignon Blanc ★★★☆

From Woollaston, the 2010 vintage (★★★) is a Nelson wine with fresh, crisp and punchy flavours of melons, capsicums and limes, showing good balance and depth. Fine value.

DRY $13 V+

Wither Hills Single Vineyard Rarangi Sauvignon Blanc ★★★★★
Grown at Rarangi, on the Wairau Valley coast, this is a striking wine. The 2009 vintage (★★★★★) is a full-on style, clearly herbaceous, weighty and rich, with intense, pure gooseberry/lime aromas and flavours, racy and long.

Vintage	09	08	07
WR	7	7	7
Drink	10-13	P	P

DRY $25 V+

Wither Hills Wairau Valley Marlborough Sauvignon Blanc ★★★☆
This huge-selling wine is sourced mostly from company-owned vineyards, planted since 1993 in the Wairau Valley. Oak plays no part in the recipe: 'The vines are old enough to offer weight, texture and length,' says winemaker Ben Glover, who matures part of the final blend on yeast lees, to add palate weight, but avoids lees-stirring. The 2010 vintage (★★★☆) has an aromatic, slightly nettley bouquet. The palate is fresh and herbaceous, in a medium to full-bodied style with gooseberry and lime flavours, smooth and lingering.

Vintage	10	09	08
WR	6	5	6
Drink	10-12	10-11	P

DRY $20 AV

Woollaston Nelson Sauvignon Blanc ★★★
The 2009 (★★★) is medium-bodied (12.5 per cent alcohol), with tropical-fruit and gentle herbaceous flavours, finely balanced and crisp. The 2010 vintage (★★★☆) is punchy, vibrantly fruity and crisp, with fresh, tight, ripely herbaceous flavours, a dryish finish (5 grams/litre of residual sugar) and good, youthful impact.

MED/DRY $18 AV

Woven Stone Ohau Sauvignon Blanc (★★★★)
Offering fine value, the 2009 vintage (★★★★) is from first-crop vines at Ohau, north of the Kapiti Coast, in Horowhenua. The bouquet is intensely aromatic and ripely herbaceous; the palate crisp, lively and dry, with good concentration of passionfruit, lime and green-capsicum flavours, intensely varietal and zingy.

DRY $17 V+

Yealands Estate Marlborough Sauvignon Blanc ★★★★
Estate-grown at Seaview, in the lower Awatere Valley, the 2009 vintage (★★★★☆) has a pungent, aromatic bouquet, incisive gooseberry/lime flavours, very crisp, vibrant and punchy, and a long, dry finish. (Note – there is also a lower-priced wine, not labelled 'Estate'.)

DRY $24 AV

Sauvignon Gris

Pernod Ricard NZ has launched New Zealand's first bottlings of an old French variety, Sauvignon Gris. Also known as Sauvignon Rosé – due to its pink skin – Sauvignon Gris typically produces less aromatic, but more substantial, wines than Sauvignon Blanc.

Sauvignon Gris is not a blend of Sauvignon Blanc and Pinot Gris, or a crossing, but a variety in its own right. In Bordeaux, Sauvignon Gris is commonly used as a minority partner in dry white blends dominated by Sauvignon Blanc, but in Chile producers are bottling and exporting it as a varietal wine. In Marlborough, it has proved to be fairly disease-resistant, ripening in the middle of the Sauvignon Blanc harvest.

Montana Reserve Marlborough Sauvignon Gris (★★★★)

The debut 2009 vintage (★★★★) was grown in the Wairau and Awatere valleys and handled without oak. It shows good weight (nearly 14 per cent alcohol), with richness from lees-aging and crisp, dryish (5.2 grams/litre of residual sugar) flavours of citrus fruits, limes and nectarines, lively and lingering.

MED/DRY $24 AV

Montana Showcase Series Marlborough Sauvignon Gris (★★★★)

The 2009 vintage (★★★★) smells and tastes like a ripe Sauvignon Blanc, or even Sémillon. Weighty and smooth, with peach/melon flavours and hints of herbs, spices and limes, it has a touch of complexity and an off-dry (5 grams/litre of residual sugar), lengthy finish.

MED/DRY $24 AV

Sémillon

You'd never guess it from the tiny selection of labels on the shelves, but Sémillon is New Zealand's seventh most widely planted white wine variety – just behind Viognier. The few winemakers who 20 years ago played around with Sémillon could hardly give it away, so aggressively stemmy and spiky was its flavour. Now, there is a new breed of riper, richer, rounder Sémillons emerging – and they are ten times more enjoyable to drink.

The Sémillon variety is beset by a similar problem to Chenin Blanc. Despite being the foundation of outstanding white wines in Bordeaux and Australia, Sémillon is out of fashion in the rest of the world, and in New Zealand its potential is still largely untapped. The area of bearing Sémillon vines has contracted markedly between 2007 and 2011, from 230 to 182 hectares.

Sémillon is highly prized in Bordeaux, where as one of the two key varieties both in dry wines, most notably white Graves, and the inimitable sweet Sauternes, its high levels of alcohol and extract are perfect foils for Sauvignon Blanc's verdant aroma and tartness. With its propensity to rot 'nobly', Sémillon forms about 80 per cent of a classic Sauternes.

Cooler climates like those of New Zealand's South Island, however, bring out a grassy-green character in Sémillon which, coupled with its higher acidity in these regions, can give the variety strikingly Sauvignon-like characteristics.

Grown principally in Marlborough (42 per cent of the country's plantings), Gisborne (33 per cent) and Hawke's Bay (21 per cent), Sémillon is mostly used in New Zealand not as a varietal wine but as a minor (and anonymous) partner in wines labelled Sauvignon Blanc, contributing complexity and aging potential. By curbing the variety's natural tendency to grow vigorously and crop bountifully, winemakers are now overcoming the aggressive cut-grass characters that in the past plagued the majority of New Zealand's unblended Sémillons. The spread of clones capable of giving riper fruit characters (notably BVRC-14 from the Barossa Valley) has also contributed to quality advances.

Askerne Hawke's Bay Sémillon ★★☆

Estate-grown near Havelock North, the 2009 vintage (★★☆) was matured in tanks (67 per cent) and old oak casks (33 per cent). It has tropical-fruit and slight nut flavours, crisp and fully dry, but lacks real charm.

Vintage	09
WR	6
Drink	10-12

DRY $16 AV

Clearview Hawke's Bay Sémillon ★★★★

The 'gloriously oaky' 2009 vintage (★★★☆) was hand-picked at Te Awanga and fermented with indigenous yeasts in new American and one-year-old French oak barriques. An easy-drinking style with some complexity, it is mouthfilling, with good depth of fresh, ripe, tropical-fruit flavours, strongly seasoned with toasty oak, and an off-dry (6 grams/litre of residual sugar) finish. Well worth cellaring.

Vintage	09	08
WR	7	6
Drink	10-20	10-18

MED/DRY $25 AV

Kaimira Estate Brightwater Sémillon ★★★

Grown in Nelson, the 2009 vintage (★★★) is a medium to full-bodied, fully dry wine with fresh, smooth, citrusy, slightly spicy and herbal flavours, showing a touch of complexity. Worth cellaring.

Vintage	09	08	07
WR	6	6	5
Drink	10-16	10-15	10-12

DRY $20 –V

Verdelho

Verdelho, a Portuguese variety traditionally grown on the island of Madeira, preserves its acidity well in hot regions, yielding enjoyably full-bodied, lively, lemony table wines in Australia. It is still extremely rare in New Zealand, with only 2 hectares of bearing Verdelho vines in 2011, mostly in Hawke's Bay.

Esk Valley Hawke's Bay Verdelho ★★★★

Hand-picked and 50 per cent barrel-fermented with indigenous yeasts, the 2009 vintage (★★★★) is a full-bodied wine with excellent freshness and depth of ripe pear, spice and apricot flavours, dryish (6 grams/litre of residual sugar), crisp and finely balanced. The 2010 (★★★★), 60 per cent barrel-fermented (in old oak), is tightly structured and elegant, with mouthfilling body (14 per cent alcohol), fresh, vibrant flavours, showing good intensity, and a basically dry (4 grams/litre of residual sugar) finish.

Vintage	10	09	08	07
WR	6	7	7	7
Drink	11-12	10-11	P	P

MED/DRY $24 AV

Villa Maria Single Vineyard Ihumatao Vineyard Auckland Verdelho (★★★★☆)

The debut 2008 vintage (★★★★☆) is classy. Estate-grown at Mangere, in South Auckland, it was partly (55 per cent) fermented with indigenous yeasts in two-year-old French oak barriques; the rest was handled in tanks. Sturdy (14.5 per cent alcohol), it has excellent delicacy and depth of tropical-fruit flavours, a subtle seasoning of oak, balanced acidity and a dry, finely poised, long finish. Tasted prior to bottling (and so not rated), the 2010 vintage is a powerful, fleshy wine with strong tropical-fruit and spice flavours.

Vintage	08
WR	7
Drink	10-12

DRY $26 AV

Viognier

Viognier is a classic grape of the Rhône Valley, in France, where it is renowned for its exotically perfumed, substantial, peach and apricot-flavoured dry whites. A delicious alternative to Chardonnay, Viognier (pronounced *Vee-yon-yay*) is an internationally modish variety, popping up with increasing frequency in shops and restaurants here.

Viognier accounts for only 0.6 per cent of the national vineyard, but the area of bearing vines is expanding steadily, from 15 hectares in 2002 to 189 hectares in 2011. Over 70 per cent of the vines are clustered in Gisborne and Hawke's Bay, with further significant plantings in Marlborough (15 per cent) and Auckland (6 per cent).

As in the Rhône, Viognier's flowering and fruit set have been highly variable here. The deeply coloured grapes go through bud-burst, flowering and *veraison* (the start of the final stage of ripening) slightly behind Chardonnay and are harvested about the same time as Pinot Noir.

The wine is often fermented in seasoned oak barrels, yielding scented, substantial, richly alcoholic wines with gentle acidity and subtle flavours. If you enjoy mouthfilling, softly textured, dry or dryish white wines, but feel like a change from Chardonnay and Pinot Gris, try Viognier. You won't be disappointed.

Alpha Domus The Wingwalker Hawke's Bay Viognier ★★★★

The 2009 vintage (★★★☆), fermented and aged for over a year in French and European oak casks, is a smooth, off-dry (5 grams/litre of residual sugar) style. The bouquet is slightly oaky; the palate is peachy, slightly buttery and toasty. It lacks some of the floral charm of Viognier, but shows a Chardonnay-like richness.

Vintage	09
WR	6
Drink	10-14

MED/DRY $23 AV

Anchorage Nelson Viognier ★★☆

The 2009 vintage (★★☆) is a light, easy-drinking style with lemony, appley flavours, some creamy notes and a dry (4.4 grams/litre of residual sugar) finish.

DRY $19 –V

Ascension The Apogee Matakana Viognier ★★★☆

The 2008 vintage (★★★) was hand-picked at 24 brix and mostly tank-fermented; 20 per cent of the blend was fermented in seasoned French oak barriques. It's a fleshy wine, peachy and slightly toasty, with a tight, dry finish.

MED/DRY $30 –V

Askerne Hawke's Bay Viognier (★★★☆)

The debut 2010 vintage (★★★☆) was mostly (66 per cent) barrel-fermented. It's a bone-dry style, fresh and full-bodied (14.5 per cent alcohol), with youthful pear, lemon and spice flavours, showing good ripeness and complexity, some creamy notes, good mouthfeel and a well-rounded finish.

Vintage	10
WR	5
Drink	10-12

DRY $20 AV

Babich Hawke's Bay Viognier ★★★

The 2007 vintage (★★★) was fermented and lees-aged in a mix of tanks (70 per cent) and old French oak casks. It's a full-bodied wine with attractive, citrusy, slightly appley flavours and a crisp, dry finish. The 2008 (★★★) is an enjoyable, drink-young style – mouthfilling, fruity, lemony, slightly spicy and crisp.

DRY $20 –V

Brookfields Milestone Viognier ★★★☆

Grown in Hawke's Bay and fermented in a 50:50 split of tanks and barrels, the 2010 vintage (★★★☆) is full-bodied (14.5 per cent alcohol) and creamy-textured, with melon, grapefruit and spice flavours, showing some leesy complexity, and a soft, dry finish.

DRY $19 V+

Bushmere Estate Gisborne Viognier ★★★☆

The 2009 vintage (★★★☆) was hand-picked at 25 brix and the fermentation was finished in seasoned French oak barriques. Still coming together, but showing good potential, it's a robust (14.5 per cent alcohol), fleshy, creamy wine with plenty of peachy, toasty flavour and a dry (3 grams/litre of residual sugar) finish.

DRY $25 –V

Butterfish Bay Northland Viognier (★★★★)

Grown in the Far North on Paewhenua Island – a small peninsula reaching into Mangonui Harbour – the 2009 vintage (★★★★) is an impressive debut. Robust (14.5 per cent alcohol), it is fresh and vibrant, with a deliciously soft, slightly oily texture, ripe citrus-fruit, pear and spice flavours, and a rounded, fully dry finish.

Vintage	09
WR	6
Drink	10-11

DRY $28 –V

Cable Bay Waiheke Island Viognier (★★★★☆)

Seductively soft, the debut 2009 vintage (★★★★☆) was hand-picked and matured in tanks and seasoned French oak casks. It's a floral, weighty wine (14.5 per cent alcohol), fresh and vibrant, with sweet-fruit delights and very generous, peachy, slightly spicy flavours, dry, rich and rounded.

Vintage	10	09
WR	7	7
Drink	10-15	10-14

DRY $33 –V

Church Road Reserve Hawke's Bay Viognier ★★★★☆

The 2007 vintage (★★★★☆) was hand-picked in Pernod Ricard NZ's Redstone Vineyard and fermented in seasoned French oak barriques. Weighty, with high alcohol and peach, grapefruit and apricot flavours, it is creamy-textured and rich. The 2009 (★★★★☆) is fleshy and concentrated, with mouthfilling body, an oily texture and concentrated, ripe-fruit flavours, deliciously peachy, creamy and rounded.

DRY $37 –V

Clayridge Marlborough Viognier (★★★☆)

The 2008 vintage (★★★☆) is a single-vineyard wine, 30 per cent barrel-fermented. It shows very good body and depth, in a cool-climate, relatively crisp style with ripe, citrusy, spicy flavours, a slightly oily texture and a dryish (7 grams/litre of residual sugar) finish.

MED/DRY $24 –V

Clos de Ste Anne Viognier Les Arbres ★★★★★

An organic Gisborne wine of arresting richness and complexity. The 2007 vintage (★★★★★) from Millton was hill-grown, hand-picked and fermented with indigenous yeasts in large, 600-litre barrels. Weighty and complex, with a hint of honey and a slightly oily texture, it has deep, beautifully ripe flavours of stone-fruit and spice and a subtle seasoning of oak.

Vintage	07	06	05
WR	7	6	7
Drink	10-12	P	P

DRY $54 AV

Coopers Creek Gisborne Viognier ★★★☆

The easy-drinking 2008 (★★★) is mouthfilling, with peach, pear and spice flavours and a rounded finish. The 2009 vintage (★★★☆) is sturdy (14 per cent alcohol) and basically dry (3.9 grams/litre of residual sugar), with a slightly creamy texture and ripe, peachy, slightly spicy and nutty flavours.

Vintage	09	08	07
WR	5	5	6
Drink	10-12	P	P

DRY $17 V+

Coopers Creek SV Chalk Ridge Hawke's Bay Viognier ★★★★

Mouthfilling, dry and vibrantly fruity, the 2009 vintage (★★★★) is a barrel-fermented style with concentrated, peachy, slightly spicy flavours, a subtle oak influence, and a rich, dry (3 grams/litre of residual sugar) finish.

Vintage	09	08	07
WR	6	6	5
Drink	10-12	P	P

DRY $20 V+

Craggy Range Gimblett Gravels Vineyard Viognier ★★★★★

The softly seductive 2009 vintage (★★★★★) is a fully dry wine, hand-picked at 24 brix and fermented and matured for six months in seasoned French oak barriques. Already delicious, it's a very generous, sturdy and enticingly floral wine, with the subtle oak influence adding complexity without overpowering its concentrated, ripe peach, pear and spice varietal flavours.

Vintage	09	08
WR	6	6
Drink	10-13	10-12

DRY $38 AV

Cypress Terraces Hawke's Bay Viognier ★★★★

From a steep, terraced site at Roy's Hill, the 2008 vintage (★★★★) is a powerful (14.5 per cent alcohol) dry wine, barrel-fermented. It's a creamy-textured wine with a subtle oak influence, concentrated, ripe, peachy, slightly spicy flavours, an oily texture and a rich, rounded finish.

Vintage	08	07
WR	6	5
Drink	10-12	10-11

DRY $30 –V

Dry River Martinborough Viognier ★★★★☆

Estate-grown, the 2010 vintage (★★★★★) is highly seductive in its infancy. Richly scented, with a late-harvest feel, it shows lovely weight, ripeness and delicacy, with deep, vibrant stone-fruit flavours, gentle acidity, a slightly oily texture, and exceptional richness and harmony.

Vintage	10	09	08
WR	7	7	7
Drink	11-15	10-14	10-13

MED/DRY $45 –V

Elephant Hill Hawke's Bay Viognier ★★★☆

Grown at Te Awanga, the 2009 vintage (★★★☆) is fleshy and rounded, with stone-fruit and spice flavours, gentle acidity, and good texture and depth.

DRY $28 –V

Framingham F Series Marlborough Viognier (★★★★)

From estate-grown, first-crop vines, the 2009 vintage (★★★★) was handled without oak, but lees-aged for 11 months in tanks. Full-bodied, it has concentrated, citrusy, distinctly peachy flavours, showing good mouthfeel and texture, a gentle splash of sweetness (7 grams/litre of residual sugar), and strong drink-young appeal.

Vintage	09
WR	6
Drink	10-12

MED/DRY $25 (500 ML) –V

Georges Michel La Reserve Marlborough Viognier (★★★★)

A highly promising debut, the 2009 vintage (★★★★) is a finely balanced, vibrantly fruity wine, hand-picked from young vines and fermented and matured for eight months in French oak barrels (partly new). It's a powerful (14.5 per cent alcohol), fleshy wine, dry and rounded, with ripe, citrusy, peachy flavours, hints of apricot and spice, and a gentle oak influence.

Vintage	09
WR	6
Drink	10-15

DRY $25 AV

Gladstone Vineyard Viognier ★★★★

The 2009 vintage (★★★★☆) was grown in the northern Wairarapa and fermented and matured in an even split of tanks and old French oak barrels. It's a mouthfilling, finely textured wine with good varietal character, sweet-fruit delights, rich, ripe citrus and tropical-fruit flavours and a fully dry finish.

Vintage	09
WR	4
Drink	10-13

DRY $29 –V

Glazebrook Regional Reserve Hawke's Bay Viognier ★★★

From Ngatarawa, the 2008 vintage (★★★☆) is mouthfilling, with complexity from full barrel fermentation (French, one-third new). It has moderately concentrated stone-fruit and spice flavours, with a creamy texture, and a rounded, dry finish. The 2009 (★★★) is similar – not rich, but showing good weight and texture.

Vintage	08
WR	6
Drink	10-11

DRY $27 –V

Hans Herzog Marlborough Viognier ★★★★☆

The 2009 vintage (★★★★☆) was hand-picked from 14-year-old vines and fermented and lees-aged for a year in French oak puncheons. Pale straw, it is full-bodied and rounded, with peachy, spicy aromas and flavours, showing good complexity and harmony. Fragrant and sweet-fruited, it is dry and rich.

Vintage	09	08
WR	7	7
Drink	10-15	10-14

DRY $44 –V

Harwood Hall Marlborough Viognier (★★★☆)

Enjoyable young, the 2009 vintage (★★★☆) was fermented with indigenous yeasts and lees-aged for eight months in barriques. Scented and smooth, it's a fruit-driven style with slight sweetness (7 grams/litre of residual sugar) and very good body and depth of vibrant, peachy flavour.

Vintage	09
WR	6
Drink	10-15

MED/DRY $24 –V

Hawkes Ridge Viognier (★★★☆)

From Hawke's Bay, the 2009 vintage (★★★☆) is a fleshy, generous, slightly Chardonnay-like wine with peachy, slightly appley and buttery flavours, a creamy texture and very good complexity and depth.

DRY $29 –V

Joseph Ryan Viognier (★★★☆)

Grown in the northern Wairarapa, the 2008 vintage (★★★☆) is mouthfilling and creamy, with ripe, citrusy flavours, fresh and strong, and a rounded finish.

MED/DRY $28 –V

Kim Crawford SP Moteo Vineyard Hawke's Bay Viognier (★★★★)
Attractively scented, the 2008 vintage (★★★★) is full-bodied, with rich, dry flavours of peaches and melons. French oak-aged, it's a vibrant, fruit-driven style with good immediacy.

DRY $33 –V

Matawhero Gisborne Viognier (★★★)
The debut 2009 vintage (★★★) is a medium-bodied wine, grown at Patutahi. A slightly sweet style (8 grams/litre of residual sugar), with drink-young appeal, it has a gently floral bouquet and decent depth of citrus-fruit, apple and pear flavours.

MED/DRY $30 –V

Matua Valley Innovator Hawke's Bay Viognier (★★★)
The 2007 vintage (★★★) was mostly handled in tanks, but 20 per cent of the blend was fermented and matured for six months in old French oak casks. It's a fully dry style with mouthfilling body and lemon, pear, apple and spice flavours, showing some complexity, but lacks real richness and roundness.

DRY $25 –V

Millton Clos de Ste Anne Viognier Les Arbres – see Clos de Ste Anne Viognier Les Arbres

Millton Riverpoint Vineyard Gisborne Viognier ★★★★☆
Floral and fleshy, the 2009 vintage (★★★★★) is intensely aromatic, with ripe-fruit characters of apricots and musk, excellent flavour concentration, a sliver of sweetness and a deliciously oily, creamy texture.

Vintage	09	08	07
WR	7	6	7
Drink	10-11	P	P

MED/DRY $28 AV

Mission Reserve Hawke's Bay Viognier ★★★☆
The 2008 vintage (★★★☆) is a single-vineyard wine, fermented and matured in French oak casks (10 per cent new). Medium-bodied, with peachy, faintly buttery and toasty flavours and a dry, finely balanced finish, it is floral, with a hint of apricots.

Vintage	09
WR	5
Drink	10-13

DRY $24 –V

Moana Park Vineyard Tribute Viognier ★★★☆
Grown in the Gimblett Gravels of Hawke's Bay, hand-picked at 24.6 brix and matured in seasoned French oak barriques, the 2009 vintage (★★★☆) is fleshy and creamy, with a slightly oily texture, strong, citrusy flavours and a dry finish.

DRY $26 –V

Montana Showcase Series Gisborne Viognier (★★★★)

Partly barrel-fermented with indigenous yeasts, the 2008 vintage (★★★★) is a finely scented, mouthfilling wine with rich peach, citrus-fruit and pear flavours, a hint of honey and a slightly sweet (6 grams/litre of residual sugar), rounded finish.

MED/DRY $24 AV

Morton Estate White Label Hawke's Bay Viognier ★★★☆

The 2009 vintage (★★★☆) is a full-bodied (14 per cent alcohol), fruity wine with ripe stone-fruit and spice flavours, showing good depth, and a soft, well-rounded finish.

Vintage	09
WR	7
Drink	10-12

DRY $19 V+

Morton Estate White Label Private Reserve Hawke's Bay Viognier ★★★☆

Weighty and fleshy, the 2007 vintage (★★★★) has peachy, spicy, faintly honeyed flavours showing good intensity. The 2009 (★★★) is aromatic, with hints of apricots, mouthfilling body, good depth of ripe, peachy flavours and a rounded finish.

Vintage	09
WR	7
Drink	10-12

DRY $23 –V

Mudbrick Vineyard Reserve Viognier (★★★★)

Grown on Waiheke Island and fermented in a 50:50 split of tanks and oak barrels, the 2009 vintage (★★★★) is a weighty, fruit-driven style with a subtle oak influence and fresh, strong citrus and stone-fruit flavours.

DRY $36 –V

Obsidian Waiheke Island Viognier ★★★★

Likely to age well, the 2009 vintage (★★★★) is a partly barrel-fermented wine, full-bodied, with stone-fruit and spice flavours, subtle oak and a dry, creamy-smooth finish. Showing good complexity and concentration, it's still unfolding; open 2011+.

Vintage	09	08	07
WR	6	7	6
Drink	10-15	10-11	P

DRY $33 –V

Passage Rock Viognier ★★★★

Grown on Waiheke Island, the barrel-fermented 2008 vintage (★★★★) is powerful, rich and oily, with concentrated, stone-fruit flavours, fresh, ripe and slightly creamy. The 2009 (★★★★), partly barrel-fermented, is rich and ripe, with strong, peachy flavours, showing good complexity.

DRY $30 –V

Rock Ferry Central Otago Viognier (★★★)

The 2008 vintage (★★★) was hand-picked at Bendigo and mostly handled in tanks, but 15 per cent was fermented with indigenous yeasts in old oak barrels. Tightly structured, it's a mouthfilling, medium-dry style with peachy, citrusy, slightly toasty flavours. Lively acidity gives a crisper finish than most Viogniers from further north.

MED/DRY $34 –V

Salvare Hawke's Bay Viognier (★★★)

The 2008 vintage (★★★) was grown in the Dartmoor Valley and matured for six months in very old oak casks. It is vibrant and mouthfilling, with dry, citrusy, slightly spicy flavours.

DRY $25 –V

Selaks Winemaker's Favourite Hawke's Bay Viognier ★★★★

The 2009 vintage (★★★★) from Constellation NZ is a seductively soft, strapping wine (15 per cent alcohol), grown at Haumoana and handled without oak. It has fresh stone-fruit and spice flavours, very ripe-tasting, with a slightly oily richness and dry finish.

DRY $21 V+

Staete Landt Marlborough Viognier ★★★★

Estate-grown at Rapaura, the 2009 vintage (★★★★☆) was hand-harvested, and fermented and lees-aged for six months in seasoned French oak puncheons. It is very full-bodied (14.5 per cent alcohol), with slight sweetness (9.7 grams/litre of residual sugar), gentle acidity, a subtle seasoning of oak, and rich, beautifully ripe, peachy, slightly spicy flavours.

Vintage	09	08	07
WR	6	6	5
Drink	10-15	10-13	10-12

MED/DRY $48 –V

Stone Bridge Gisborne Viognier ★★★☆

The 2009 vintage (★★★★) was estate-grown and matured in seasoned French oak casks. Richly scented and vibrantly fruity, with good concentration of ripe peach and apricot flavours, it is fresh and fully dry. The 2008 (★★★) is an easy-drinking style, fleshy, soft and peachy, with good depth and a dry, rounded finish.

DRY $22 AV

Te Mata Zara Viognier ★★★★☆

This estate-grown wine is from Woodthorpe Terraces, on the south side of the Dartmoor Valley in Hawke's Bay. Hand-picked, it is mostly (80 per cent in 2009) fermented and lees-aged for eight months in seasoned French oak barriques. The 2009 vintage (★★★★★) is fragrant, with aromas of pears, cream and nuts. Full-bodied, rich and soft, it is already drinking well, with peach and slight apricot flavours, a creamy texture, and lovely ripeness and concentration.

Vintage	09	08	07	06	05	04
WR	7	7	7	7	7	7
Drink	10-13	10-12	10-12	10-11	P	P

DRY $28 AV

Terrace Heights Estate Marlborough Viognier ★★★

The 2010 vintage (★★★), handled without oak, is full-bodied, fresh and smooth, with a sliver of sweetness (7 grams/litre of residual sugar) and lively peach, lemon and slight apricot flavours.

Vintage	10
WR	5
Drink	11-13

MED/DRY $22 –V

Ti Point Gisborne Viognier (★★★☆)

The 2009 vintage (★★★☆) is a fruit-driven style, harvested at 24 brix and 20 per cent barrel-fermented. It's a mouthfilling wine with peachy, citrusy, slightly spicy flavours, a touch of oak and a fresh, crisp, bone-dry finish.

DRY $21 AV

Trinity Hill Gimblett Gravels Hawke's Bay Viognier ★★★★★

An emerging star. Peachy, slightly nutty and full-flavoured, the 2008 vintage (★★★★) was hand-picked and fermented in a mix of tanks and seasoned French oak barrels. It's a complex, fully dry wine with an oily texture and impressive harmony.

Vintage	08	07	06
WR	5	6	6
Drink	10-12	10-12	10-11

DRY $35 AV

Trinity Hill Hawke's Bay Viognier ★★★☆

The 2008 vintage (★★★☆) is ripely scented and fruity, with very good body and depth of peachy, faintly honeyed flavour and a well-rounded, dry (4 grams/litre of residual sugar) finish.

DRY $20 AV

Turanga Creek New Zealand Viognier (★★★)

Estate-grown at Whitford, in South Auckland, the 2009 vintage (★★★) is weighty (14.5 per cent alcohol), ripe and soft, with good depth of stone-fruit and spice flavours and a hint of honey. It's drinking well now.

DRY $26 –V

Vidal East Coast Viognier ★★★★

A good, well-priced introduction to Viognier. The 2009 vintage (★★★☆) is a blend of Gisborne (59 per cent), Hawke's Bay and Marlborough grapes, partly handled in tanks, but 60 per cent of the blend was fermented and lees-aged for four months in seasoned French oak barriques. A bone-dry style, it's full-bodied (14.5 per cent alcohol), with gentle acidity, a touch of complexity and good depth of pear and spice flavours, fresh and well-rounded. There is no 2010.

Vintage	10	09	08	07
WR	NM	6	7	7
Drink	NM	10-11	P	P

DRY $20 V+

Vidal Reserve Hawke's Bay Viognier (★★★★☆)

Grown mostly in the Gimblett Gravels (84 per cent), supplemented by fruit from the Tuki Tuki Valley, the 2007 vintage (★★★★☆) was fermented and lees-aged for six months in seasoned French oak barriques. Maturing well, it's a sturdy, fully dry wine with rich stone-fruit and spice flavours, slightly nutty, complex and rounded.

Vintage	08	07
WR	NM	6
Drink	NM	10-11

DRY $30 –V

Villa Maria Cellar Selection Hawke's Bay Viognier ★★★★☆

The 2010 vintage (★★★★☆) was hand-picked and partly handled in tanks, but 85 per cent of the blend was fermented in French oak barriques (15 per cent new). It's a fleshy (14.5 per cent alcohol), rich wine with a fresh, fragrant bouquet of peaches and apricots. Creamy-textured, with concentrated stone-fruit flavours, a hint of spices and a fully dry (1.6 grams/litre of residual sugar) finish, it offers great value.

Vintage	10	09
WR	7	7
Drink	11-14	10-14

DRY $24 V+

Villa Maria Private Bin East Coast Viognier ★★★☆

The 2009 vintage (★★★☆) is a blend of Hawke's Bay and Gisborne fruit (including 5 per cent Verdelho), fermented in tanks (30 per cent) and French oak barriques (10 per cent new). It's a fragrant, peachy, creamy-textured dry wine, drinking well now. The 2010 (★★★★) was mostly handled in tanks; 20 per cent of the blend was fermented in seasoned oak barrels. Full-bodied (14.5 per cent alcohol), it is floral and finely textured, with strong, vibrantly fruity, peachy, slightly spicy flavours and a dry (2 grams/litre of residual sugar), well-rounded finish. Fine value.

Vintage	10	09	08
WR	7	6	6
Drink	10-13	10-12	10-11

DRY $21 AV

Villa Maria Single Vineyard Omahu Gravels Vineyard Hawke's Bay Viognier ★★★★★

The classy, rich 2009 vintage (★★★★★) was fermented – mostly with indigenous yeasts – and lees-aged for nine months in French oak barriques (35 per cent new). It's a very fleshy, powerful wine (14.5 per cent alcohol), with highly concentrated stone-fruit flavours, creamy and complex.

Vintage	09	08	07	06
WR	7	7	7	6
Drink	10-14	10-14	10-12	10-12

DRY $32 AV

Waimea Nelson Viognier ★★★★

The 2009 vintage (★★★★☆) is one of the South Island's finest Viogniers yet. Fleshy, with substantial body, it has strong, ripe peach and apricot flavours, slightly oily and spicy, and a creamy, well-rounded finish.

Vintage	09	08	07	06
WR	7	7	6	5
Drink	10-13	10-12	P	P

DRY $24 AV

Wairau River Reserve Marlborough Viognier (★★★★)

The 2010 vintage (★★★★) was estate-grown on the banks of the Wairau River and mostly handled in tanks; 10 per cent was matured in seasoned French oak barriques. Floral, full-bodied, fresh and lively, it is finely textured, with peachy, slightly spicy flavours, hints of pears, oranges and honey, and a smooth (7.8 grams/litre of residual sugar) finish. Delicious from the start.

MED/DRY $30 –V

Waitapu Estate Reef Point Viognier/Chardonnay (★★★☆)

Grown at Ahipara, in Northland, the 2009 vintage (★★★☆) is a mouthfilling, creamy-smooth blend of Viognier (75 per cent) and oak-aged Chardonnay (25 per cent). It shows good concentration of ripe tropical-fruit flavours, slightly buttery, nutty and honeyed.

DRY $22 AV

Yealands Estate Marlborough Viognier (★★★)

The fresh, vibrant 2008 vintage (★★★) is an Awatere Valley wine with mouthfilling body, good depth of citrusy, peachy, slightly spicy flavours and a dry (4 grams/litre of residual sugar) finish. Handled without oak and balanced for easy drinking, it's a promising debut.

DRY $23 –V

Würzer

A German crossing of Gewürztraminer and Müller-Thurgau, Würzer is extremely rare in New Zealand, with 1 hectare of bearing vines in 2011. Seifried has 'a few rows' at its Redwood Valley Vineyard, in Nelson.

Seifried Nelson Würzer ★★★★

Grown in the Redwood Valley, the 2009 vintage (★★★☆) is very undemanding, with pear, spice and slight apricot flavours, a splash of sweetness and enough acidity to keep things lively. The 2010 (★★★★) is a fleshy, medium style (16 grams/litre of residual sugar), floral and weighty (14.5 per cent alcohol), with strong pear, apricot and spice flavours.

Vintage	10	09	08
WR	6	6	6
Drink	10-12	10-11	10-11

MED $19 V+

Sweet White Wines

New Zealand's sweet white wines (often called dessert wines) are not taking the world by storm, accounting for just 0.02 per cent of our wine exports. Yet, around the country, winemakers work hard to produce some ravishingly beautiful, honey-sweet white wines that are worth discovering and can certainly hold their own internationally.

New Zealand's most luscious, concentrated and honeyish sweet whites are made from grapes which have been shrivelled and dehydrated on the vines by 'noble rot', the dry form of the *Botrytis cinerea* mould. Misty mornings, followed by clear, fine days with light winds and low humidity, are ideal conditions for the spread of noble rot, but in New Zealand this favourable interplay of weather factors occurs irregularly.

Some enjoyable but rarely exciting dessert wines (often labelled Ice Wine) are made by the freeze-concentration method, whereby a proportion of the natural water content in the grape juice is frozen out, leaving a sweet, concentrated juice to be fermented.

Marlborough has so far yielded a majority of the finest sweet whites. Most of the other wine regions, however – except Auckland (too wet) and Central Otago (usually too dry and cool) – can also point to the successful production of botrytised sweet whites in favourable vintages.

Riesling has been the foundation of the majority of New Zealand's most opulent sweet whites, but Sauvignon Blanc, Sémillon, Gewürztraminer, Pinot Gris, Müller-Thurgau, Chenin Blanc, Viognier and Chardonnay have all yielded fine dessert styles. With their high levels of extract and firm acidity, most of these wines mature well for two to three years, although few are very long-lived.

Abbey Cellars Mary Noble Riesling (★★★)

Estate-grown in The Triangle district of Hawke's Bay, the 2009 vintage (★★★) was hand-picked at 30.5 brix and matured for six months in seasoned French oak casks. Mouthfilling, it is citrusy, slightly appley and spicy, with moderate sweetness (59 grams/litre of residual sugar), lively acidity and good drink-young appeal.

SW $23 (375ML) –V

Alana Estate Martinborough L'Apéritif ★★★★

The 2008 vintage (★★★★) is a perfumed, musky Riesling with concentrated, citrusy, limey flavours and a sweet (100 grams/litre of residual sugar), crisp finish. It's a lovely, late-harvest style, designed as an apéritif rather than a dessert wine.

Vintage	08
WR	6
Drink	10-18

SW $35 (375ML) –V

Allan Scott Late Harvest Marlborough Sauvignon Blanc (★★★★☆)

The golden 2008 vintage (★★★★☆) is a rich, complex style, hand-picked and fermented and matured for six months in old French oak barriques. Mouthfilling (although only 9 per cent alcohol), with a fragrant, honeyed bouquet, it has an oily texture and lovely depth of sweet (230 grams/litre of residual sugar), very ripe tropical-fruit flavours, enriched by noble rot.

SW $29 (375ML) V+

Alluviale Anobli (★★★★★)

The light gold, Sauternes-style 2008 vintage (★★★★★) was made from botrytised Sauvignon Blanc grapes, harvested at Mangatahi, in Hawke's Bay, at 52 brix. French oak-aged, with a beautiful, richly honeyed fragrance, it is a flawless wine, concentrated and sweet (270 grams/litre of residual sugar), with an oily texture and lovely ripeness, richness and roundness.

SW $40 (375ML) AV

Alluviale Mangatahi Hawke's Bay Tardif (★★★☆)

Ensconced in a full-sized bottle, the 2010 vintage (★★★☆) was picked at Mangatahi, in Hawke's Bay, in early June. Made from late-harvested (35 brix), raisined but not botrytised grapes, it's ripely scented, mouthfilling, sweet (65 grams/litre of residual sugar) and soft, with fresh, gentle peach, pear and spice flavours. Already enjoyable, it's recommended by the producer as an apéritif.

SW $27 V+

Alpha Domus AD Noble Selection ★★★★★

The golden 2009 vintage (★★★★★) is a richly botrytised blend of Sémillon and Sauvignon Blanc, fermented and matured for eight months in French oak barrels (60 per cent new). It's a gloriously lush, decadent wine, very honeyed, sweet (280 grams/litre of residual sugar), concentrated and oily, while retaining good freshness and harmony.

Vintage	09
WR	6
Drink	10-15

SW $49 (375ML) AV

Alpha Domus The Pilot Leonarda Late Harvest Sémillon ★★★☆

Already delicious, the youthful 2009 vintage (★★★☆) is mouthfilling and slightly honeyed, with strong, ripe fruit flavours and plentiful sweetness (134 grams/litre of residual sugar). Fermented in an even split of tanks and seasoned French oak barrels, it's a gentle Sauternes style from Hawke's Bay.

Vintage	09	08	07
WR	6	6	6
Drink	10-14	10-11	10-11

SW $19 (375ML) V+

Amisfield Lowburn Terrace Central Otago Riesling ★★★★★

Estate-grown in the Cromwell Basin, the classy 2009 vintage (★★★★★) was harvested early (at 21 brix) and stop-fermented with low alcohol (18.8 per cent) and plentiful sweetness (51 grams/litre of residual sugar), balanced by racy acidity. The bouquet is intense, minerally and complex; the palate is highly concentrated, with deep lemon, apple and spice flavours, fresh, gently sweet, racy and long. Very classy.

SW $35 V+

Amisfield Noble Sauvignon Blanc (★★★★☆)

Hand-picked at 39.9 brix on 8 July, then fermented and matured for over a year in new French oak casks, the 2008 vintage (★★★★☆) is a pale gold Central Otago wine, powerful (14.5 per cent alcohol) and highly fragrant. Made in a classic Sauternes style, it has very deep, fresh, ripe and pure flavours, with plentiful sweetness, lively acidity and excellent complexity from the lengthy oak aging.

SW $45 (375ML) –V

Anchorage Noble Nelson Chardonnay (★★★★)

Pale gold, the 2009 vintage (★★★★) is already delicious. The bouquet is fresh and honeyed; the palate concentrated, with flavours of peaches, nectarines and apricots, enriched by botrytis, and a sweet (165 grams/litre of residual sugar), smooth finish.

SW $26 (375ML) AV

Artisan Late Harvest Marlborough Riesling (★★★☆)

Ready for drinking, the 2008 vintage (★★★☆) is golden, with a botrytised, honeyed bouquet and sweet (90 grams/litre of residual sugar), ripe flavours of peaches and apricots, showing very good depth.

SW $19 (375ML) V+

Askerne Late Harvest Sémillon ★★☆

The golden, treacly 2008 vintage (★★☆) was harvested in Hawke's Bay at 36 brix. It has strong, sweet (160 grams/litre of residual sugar) flavours of peaches, apricots and honey, but lacks a bit of freshness.

SW $20 (375ML) –V

Askerne Noble Sémillon ★★★★

At its best, this is a ravishing Hawke's Bay beauty in the mould of classic Sauternes. The 2007 vintage (★★★★) was fermented in French oak barrels (25 per cent new). Deep amber, it's an oily, treacly wine with highly concentrated flavours of honey and apricots, soaring sweetness (350 grams/litre of residual sugar) and a powerful botrytis influence. Drink now.

Vintage	07	06	05	04
WR	5	6	6	7
Drink	10-14	10-12	10-11	P

SW $30 (375ML) –V

Ata Rangi Kahu Botrytis Riesling ★★★★

Grown in the Kahu Vineyard, neighbouring the Ata Rangi winery in Martinborough, the 2009 vintage (★★★★) is a late-harvest style with a gentle botrytis influence. Light yellow/green, it's already delicious, with fresh acidity and rich, sweet, citrusy, slightly spicy and honeyed flavours.

Vintage	09	08
WR	6	6
Drink	10-13	10-12

SW $32 (375 ML) –V

Aurora Vineyard, The, Late Harvest Riesling (★★★☆)

Light and lively, the bargain-priced 2008 vintage (★★★☆) is a Central Otago wine with plentiful sweetness (95–100 grams/litre of residual sugar). Picked in early May, 'due to a lack of space in the fermenters for normal Riesling', it is scented, with a citrusy, slightly honeyed fragrance and fresh, lemony flavours showing very good delicacy and purity.

SW $17 (375ML) V+

Aurum Pinot Gris 18 Carat (★★★★)

Estate-grown at Lowburn, in Central Otago, the 2009 vintage (★★★★) was made only from bunches with at least a 50 per cent 'noble rot' infection and not oak-aged. Pale straw, it is already delicious, with good weight, abundant sweetness (170 grams/litre of residual sugar) and strong, pure, pear and spice flavours, faintly honeyed, very smooth and harmonious.

Vintage 09
WR 6
Drink 10-20

SW $32 (375ML) –V

Aurum Pinot Gris 24 Carat (★★★★☆)

Sweeter and more youthful than its stablemate (above), the 2008 vintage (★★★★☆) was made from botrytised grapes, estate-grown at Lowburn, in Central Otago. Barrel-fermented, it's a gently honeyed wine with fresh, vibrant pear and lychee flavours, sweet (220 grams/litre of residual sugar) and rich. Best drinking 2011+.

Vintage 09
WR 7
Drink 10-20

SW $55 (375ML) –V

Beach House Noble Sauvignon Blanc (★★★★)

The 2009 vintage (★★★★) was harvested in Hawke's Bay at 28 to 40 brix, with a 70 per cent botrytis infection. The fragrant, strongly honeyed bouquet leads into a concentrated, luscious, finely textured wine, although not highly complex, with rich, sweet, marmalade-like flavours and a rounded finish.

SW $28 (375ML) AV

Brookfields Indulgence ★★★☆

Delicious now, the 2007 vintage (★★★☆) is a botrytis-affected Sauvignon Blanc, grown in Hawke's Bay. Attractively scented, it's a medium-bodied style (10 per cent alcohol) with ripe late-harvest fruit flavours to the fore, very non-herbaceous and sweet, and a smooth finish. The 2008 (★★★☆) is similar – a late-harvest style, with fresh, ripe fruit flavours, gently honeyed and delicious young.

Vintage 08
WR 7
Drink 10-13

SW $25 (375ML) –V

Charles Wiffen Late Harvest Riesling (★★★☆)

Grown in Marlborough, the pale gold 2007 vintage (★★★☆) has a honeyed bouquet and a crisp, sweet palate (120 grams/litre of residual sugar), with strong, citrusy, honeyed, slightly limey flavours and firm acid spine. Ready.

SW $35 (500ML) AV

Church Road Reserve Noble Viognier ★★★★★

The 2008 vintage (★★★★★) is classy. Hand-picked from 'raisined and botrytised' grapes in the company's Redstone Vineyard, in Hawke's Bay, it's a beautifully scented, deliciously soft wine with a subtle oak influence and lush, ripe stone-fruit, pear and spice flavours, slightly oily, concentrated, sweet and complex. The 2009 (★★★★★) is another winner. Already impossible to resist, it is very rich and soft, with sweet stone-fruit, spice and honey flavours, showing lovely depth, complexity and harmony.

SW $36 (375 ML) AV

Clearview Noble Harvest Chardonnay ★★★★☆

From hand-picked, botrytised Chardonnay grapes, left on the vines to raisin, the 2007 vintage (★★★★) of this Hawke's Bay wine is light green/gold, with rich, peachy, honey-sweet flavours (130 grams/litre of residual sugar). Barrel-fermented, it has hints of tea and spice, and good complexity. Drink now or cellar.

Vintage	07	06	05	04
WR	7	6	NM	6
Drink	10-12	P	P	P

SW $65 (375 ML) –V

Cloudy Bay Late Harvest Riesling ★★★★★

Cloudy Bay only makes this Marlborough wine about every second year, on average, but it's usually worth waiting for. The 2005 vintage (★★★★★) was matured for six months in old oak barrels. Pale gold, it is highly scented, poised and rich, with citrusy, peachy, slightly spicy and honeyed flavours, considerable sweetness (128 grams/litre of residual sugar), a minerally streak and good, bottle-aged complexity. Full of personality, it's lovely now.

Vintage	05	04	03	02	01	00
WR	6	6	NM	6	NM	6
Drink	10-11	P	NM	P	NM	P

SW $30 (375ML) V+

Coopers Creek Reserve Marlborough Late Harvest Riesling ★★★★

Still on sale, the 2004 vintage (★★★★) is pale gold, with a mature, honeyed bouquet. Rich, with abundant sweetness and concentrated, citrusy, peachy, honeyish flavours, it's near or at its peak. The 2009 (★★★★) was made from heavily botrytised grapes, grown at the mouth of the Omaka Valley. It's a youthful, finely poised wine, light (8.5 per cent alcohol), with rich, ripe, lemony, honeyed flavours, a hint of sherbet, plentiful sweetness (200 grams/litre of residual sugar) and good potential. Priced sharply.

Vintage	09
WR	7
Drink	10-16

SW $23 (375ML) V+

Corbans Cottage Block Hawke's Bay Cut Cane Pinot Gris (★★★★★)

The enticingly scented 2008 vintage (★★★★★) was hand-picked at 34 to 38 brix at Matapiro, fermented in stainless steel barrels and lees-aged for 10 months. The grapes, shrivelled but not botrytis-affected, have yielded a lovely late-harvest style, weighty and rounded, with ripe stone-fruit and spice flavours showing notable delicacy and depth, plentiful sweetness (130 grams/litre of residual sugar), gentle acidity and a long finish.

SW $32 (375ML) V+

Crater Rim, The, Dr Kohl's Waipara Riesling (★★★★)

The stylish 2008 vintage (★★★★) is a light (8.5 per cent alcohol), sweet wine (90 grams/litre of residual sugar), fermented with indigenous yeasts and matured on its yeast lees for 14 months. Pale lemon/green, it is rich and soft, with vibrant, lemony flavours, showing good delicacy, concentration and harmony. It's already delicious.

SW $30 V+

Crater Rim, The, From the Ashes Late Harvest Waipara Pinot Gris (★★★★)

The 2008 vintage (★★★★) is a sweet but not super-sweet wine (72 grams/litre of residual sugar), fermented in tanks (70 per cent) and seasoned oak casks. Straw-hued, it's already drinking well, with soft, concentrated flavours of peaches, pears and spices, showing some oak complexity, and a slightly oily, honeyed richness.

SW $23 (375ML) V+

Doctors', The, Noble Chenin Blanc (★★★★★)

From Forrest Estate, in Marlborough, the 2008 vintage (★★★★★) is a gorgeous sweet wine (220 grams/litre of residual sugar) with a richly honeyed fragrance. Concentrated, with an oily texture, it has beautifully ripe peach and apricot flavours, enriched but not swamped by noble rot, good acid spine and lovely freshness and harmony. Drink now or cellar.

Vintage	08
WR	6
Drink	10-20

SW $30 (375 ML) V+

Dry River Bunch Selection Martinborough Gewürztraminer (★★★★★)

Estate-grown in the Lovat Vineyard, the 2009 vintage (★★★★★) was picked at over 30 brix. Delicious from the start, it is full-bodied (although 10 per cent alcohol), citrusy, peachy, spicy and slightly honeyed, with notable richness and harmony. Showing advanced ripeness, it's a lovely late-harvest style.

SW $60 AV

Dry River Late Harvest Riesling ★★★★★

Dry River produces beautiful botrytised sweet wines in Martinborough – sometimes light and fragile, sometimes high in alcohol and very powerful – from a range of varieties, but for founder Neil McCallum, Riesling is the queen of dessert wines. Grown in the Craighall Vineyard, 500 metres from the winery, the grapes are hand-selected over a one-month period, extending into late May. The pale yellow 2009 vintage (★★★★★) is richly scented. Already delicious, it has concentrated lemon/lime flavours, sweet and crisp, a gentle, marmalade-like, botrytis influence, and lovely freshness, balance and richness. Drink now or cellar.

SW $56 AV

Fallen Angel Sweet FA (★★★☆)

The 2009 vintage (★★★☆) from Stonyridge is a sweet, late-harvest Riesling from Marlborough. Fresh and light, it has vibrant pear, lemon and apple flavours, gentle acidity, and very good delicacy and depth.

SW $36 (375ML) –V

Farmgate Noble Harvest Riesling (★★★★★)

Lovely now, the 2007 vintage (★★★★★) from Ngatarawa was hand-picked in Hawke's Bay and stop-fermented with 10 per cent alcohol and 279 grams per litre of residual sugar. Golden, it's a strongly botrytised style with an oily texture and fresh, concentrated peach, apricot and honey flavours, showing beautiful poise and richness.

Vintage	07
WR	7
Drink	10-11

SW $40 (375ML) AV

Felton Road Block 1 Riesling ★★★★☆

Grown on a 'steeper slope' which yields 'riper fruit' without noble rot, this Bannockburn, Central Otago wine is made in a style 'similar to a late-harvest, Mosel spätlese', says winemaker Blair Walter. The 2009 vintage (★★★★★) is deliciously light (9.5 per cent alcohol) and lively, with very incisive lemon/lime flavours, minerally and racy. Approachable now, it should flourish with cellaring.

Vintage	09	08	07	06
WR	7	6	7	6
Drink	10-29	10-28	10-27	10-26

SW $34 V+

Forrest Estate Botrytised Riesling ★★★★★

Since 2001, this Marlborough beauty has been outstanding. Luscious, ripe and oily, the 2008 vintage (★★★★☆) is very honeyed, with a powerful botrytis influence and sweet, concentrated, apricot-like flavours. The 2009 (★★★★★) is golden and richly scented, with mouthfilling body, sweet (180 grams/litre of residual sugar) flavours of apricots and honey, an oily richness, good acid spine, and lovely poise and length.

Vintage	09	08	07	06	05	04
WR	5	6	6	6	4	6
Drink	10-15	10-20	10-12	10-12	P	P

SW $35 (375ML) AV

Forrest Late Harvest Gewürztraminer (★★★☆)

The scented 2007 vintage (★★★☆), grown in Marlborough, is a sweet wine (90 grams/litre of residual sugar) with pear, lemon, apple and spice flavours, showing some richness. There's an intriguing back label reference to 'hokey pokey ice cream' characters – and it's true. Ready; no rush.

Vintage	07
WR	4
Drink	10-11

SW $20 (375ML) AV

Forrest Late Harvest Riesling ★★★☆

The 2007 vintage (★★★), grown in Marlborough, is light in body (9.5 per cent alcohol) and gently sweet (70 grams/litre of residual sugar), with pure, ripe, lemon/lime flavours and a floral bouquet.

Vintage	07
WR	4
Drink	09-11

SW $20 (375 ML) AV

Framingham Estate F Series Gewürztraminer VT (★★★★★)

The 2009 vintage (★★★★★) was made from dehydrated Marlborough grapes, harvested at 34 brix with just a touch of botrytis (5 per cent). Fermented with indigenous yeasts in old oak barrels, it's a low-alcohol style (8.5 per cent), golden, with a gingery fragrance and lovely richness of sweet (180 grams/litre of residual sugar), citrusy, spicy flavours, layered, complex and well-rounded.

Vintage	09
WR	7
Drink	10-12

SW $40 (500 ML) V+

Framingham F Series Riesling Auslese (★★★★☆)

The 2009 vintage (★★★★☆) was harvested early at 19 brix, with a 30–40 per cent botrytis infection, to protect the rest of the crop during a spell of bad weather. The grapes were initially discarded on the ground, but then salvaged and made into wine. Fermented in an even split of tanks and old oak casks, it's light (7.5 per cent alcohol) and sweet (140 grams/litre of residual sugar), with a honeyed bouquet, firm acid spine, and intense, lemony, slightly honeyed flavours, showing a hint of sherbet. Drink now or cellar.

Vintage	09
WR	7
Drink	10-12

SW $40 (500 ML) –V

Framingham Gewürztraminer SGN (★★★★☆)

Estate-grown in Marlborough, the 2008 vintage (★★★★☆) is pale gold, with a distinctly spicy, exotically perfumed bouquet. Light (8 per cent alcohol), sweet and rich, it has concentrated, spicy, honeyed flavours, showing a lovely harmony of fruit and botrytis.

SW $40 (375 ML) –V

Framingham Noble Riesling ★★★★☆

From two blocks of vines approaching 30 years old on the estate in Marlborough, the 2009 vintage (★★★★★) is still a baby, with obvious potential, but it's already delicious. Finely scented, it is fresh, ripe, citrusy and gently honeyed, with low alcohol (7.5 per cent), an oily texture, advanced sweetness (195 grams/litre of residual sugar), and lovely harmony and richness.

Vintage	09	08	07	06	05	04
WR	7	6	6	7	6	7
Drink	10-14	10-13	10-12	10-11	P	P

SW $40 (375 ML) –V

Framingham Select Riesling ★★★★☆

The 2009 vintage (★★★★★), estate-grown in Marlborough and late-picked by hand, was inspired by the German spätlese style. It's a beauty. Light (8.5 per cent alcohol), it is ravishingly scented, with lovely depth of citrusy, appley, limey flavour, gentle sweetness (72 grams/litre of residual sugar), and lovely poise and minerality. Already delicious, it shows a Mosel-like fragility and intensity.

Vintage	09	08	07	06	05	04
WR	7	6	7	6	6	7
Drink	10-17	10-17	10-14	10-12	10-12	P

SW $31 V+

Fromm Gewürztraminer Late Harvest ★★★★

The 2008 vintage (★★★★) is the Marlborough winery's second late-harvest Gewürztraminer. Drinking well from the start, it's a medium-bodied wine (12 per cent alcohol), soft and peachy, slightly spicy and gingery, with excellent delicacy and complexity.

Vintage	09	08	07	06	05
WR	6	6	6	6	6
Drink	10-15	10-14	10-13	10-12	10-11

SW $24 (375ML) V+

Fromm Riesling Spätlese ★★★★☆

This vivacious Marlborough wine is made from the ripest, hand-harvested grapes with no botrytis infection, in an intense, low-alcohol style with plentiful sweetness and incisive, lemony, limey, minerally flavours. The 2008 vintage (★★★★★) is one of the lowest-alcohol (7 per cent) New Zealand wines I've ever encountered – but it's definitely a wine! Offering lovely richness of fresh, lemony, appley, spicy flavour, it's finely poised, sweet, minerally and racy. Drink now or cellar.

Vintage	09	08	07	06	05	04
WR	7	6	6	7	6	6
Drink	10-19	10-16	10-15	10-16	10-15	10-14

SW $28 V+

Gibbston Valley Late Harvest Riesling ★★★☆

The 2010 vintage (★★★★) was grown in the Red Shed Vineyard at Bendigo, in Central Otago. It's a light (7 per cent alcohol) wine with lovely ripe flavours of lemons and apples, a hint of sherbet, good intensity and a rounded finish. Already delicious.

Vintage	08
WR	7
Drink	12-20

SW $26 (375ML) –V

Gibbston Valley Noble Riesling (★★★★)

The 2008 vintage (★★★★) was grown at Bendigo, in the Mondillo Vineyard. Mouthfilling (12.5 per cent alcohol), it is rich, peachy and honeyed, with plentiful sweetness (120 grams/litre of residual sugar) and good acid spine.

Vintage	08
WR	7
Drink	12-20

SW $40 (375ML) –V

Gibson Bridge Marlborough Sweet 16 (★★★★)

The gently botrytised 2009 vintage (★★★★) was late-harvested from 16 rows of Pinot Gris vines in mid-July. It has a scented bouquet of stone-fruit and honey, leading into a soft, sweet palate with peach, spice, apricot and honey flavours, rich and rounded. It's already delicious.

SW $35 (375ML) –V

Giesen Canterbury Riesling The Brothers (★★★★★)

From the Giesens' last season at Burnham, the original vineyard south of Christchurch, the 2005 vintage (★★★★★) is light (7.5 per cent alcohol) and sweet (97 grams/litre of residual sugar), very elegant and lively, with lemony, limey, slightly peachy flavours, showing lovely delicacy and richness. Drink now.

SW $34 V+

Glazebrook Regional Reserve Noble Harvest Riesling ★★★★★

From Ngatarawa, this Hawke's Bay wine is typically richly botrytised and honey-sweet, concentrated and treacly, in top vintages dripping with honey, apricot and raisin flavours. The luscious 2009 (★★★★) is golden, with concentrated lemon/lime flavours and a strong botrytis influence, adding apricot and honey notes.

SW $32 (375ML) V+

🍇🍇

Gravitas Hugo's Delight Late Harvest Riesling ★★★☆

The 2007 vintage (★★★★) was picked in Marlborough at 34 brix and stop-fermented with 150 grams per litre of residual sugar. Golden, with a strongly botrytised bouquet, it is rich, peachy and honeyed, with crisp acidity keeping things lively.

SW $25 (375ML) –V

Gravitas Marlborough Noble Riesling (★★★★)

The 2007 vintage (★★★★) was harvested at 33 brix, when 60 per cent of the berries were shrivelled and 30 per cent were nobly rotten. It's a strongly botrytised wine, golden, with a honeyed bouquet and intense, citrusy, peachy flavours, sweet (150 grams/litre of residual sugar) and crisp, with an oily richness.

Vintage	07
WR	6
Drink	10-12

SW $27 (375ML) AV

Greystone Waipara Late Harvest Riesling (★★★★☆)

The debut 2009 vintage (★★★★☆) is light (9 per cent alcohol) and sweet (102 grams/litre of residual sugar), with strong, ripe, lemony, slightly spicy flavours, gentle acidity and a well-rounded finish. A very harmonious wine with lovely delicacy and purity, and a vague hint of honey, it's already delicious.

SW $34 V+

Greywacke Marlborough Late Harvest Gewürztraminer (★★★★☆)

The debut 2009 vintage (★★★★☆) is a single-vineyard wine, hand-picked in the Brancott Valley, tank-fermented and lees-aged for four months in old barrels. Bright, light lemon/green, it is youthful, sweet (90 grams/litre of residual sugar) and rich, with concentrated, ripe peach, lychee and spice flavours, showing lovely vibrancy, delicacy and harmony. Worth cellaring.

SW $36 (375ML) –V

Hudson Late Harvest Martinborough Riesling (★★★★)

The gently botrytised 2009 vintage (★★★★), ensconced in a full bottle, has vibrant, citrusy, slightly sweet and honeyed flavours, showing good acid spine and intensity.

SW $44 AV

Johanneshof Gewürztraminer Vendange Tardive (★★★★☆)

The 2009 vintage (★★★★☆), grown in Marlborough, is rich and ripe, sweet but not super-sweet, with concentrated lychee and spice flavours, slightly gingery and honeyed, and impressive freshness and concentration. It should be long-lived.

Vintage	09
WR	6
Drink	10-15

SW $29 (375ML) V+

Johanneshof Noble Late Harvest Riesling ★★★★☆

The 2007 vintage (★★★★★), made from fully botrytised grapes, is golden, oily and complex, with citrusy, richly honeyed flavours, a hint of apricots, and lovely poise and intensity.

Vintage	08	07	06
WR	6	6	6
Drink	10-17	10-16	10-15

SW $40 (375ML) –V

Johner Estate Wairarapa Noble Pinot Noir ★★★

Estate-grown at Gladstone, the 2009 vintage (★★★☆) is a distinctive dessert wine, straw-coloured, with a hint of amber. Rich and oily, with apricot and honey flavours, sweet and crisp, it's already drinking well.

SW $22 (375ML) –V

Johner Estate Wairarapa Noble Sauvignon Blanc (★★★☆)

Estate-grown at Gladstone, the 2009 vintage (★★★☆) is vibrant, sweet and peachy, with firm acidity and a hint of honey. (There is also a strawberryish, slightly spicy, sweet and crisp Noble Syrah 2008 [★★★☆], well worth trying.)

SW $22 (375ML) AV

John Forrest Collection Noble Riesling ★★★★★

The 2006 vintage (★★★★★) was grown in the Brancott Valley, Marlborough. Gorgeous now, it is golden, rich and sweet (220 grams/litre of residual sugar), with a very honeyed and complex bouquet and concentrated stone-fruit and marmalade flavours.

Vintage	06	05
WR	6	6
Drink	10-15	10-15

SW $50 (375ML) AV

Kirkpatrick Estate Winery Patutahi Late Harvest Chardonnay (★★★☆)

Grown in Gisborne and oak-aged for 10 months, the 2007 vintage (★★★☆) is bright, light lemon/green, with concentrated, peachy, sweet flavours (220 grams/litre of residual sugar) and an oily richness.

Vintage	07
WR	5
Drink	10-12

SW $25 (375ML) –V

Konrad Bunch Selection Marlborough Riesling ★★★★

The 2009 vintage (★★★★) was estate-grown in the Waihopai Valley and stop-fermented with low alcohol (8.5 per cent) and gentle sweetness (57 grams/litre of residual sugar). Tightly structured and youthful, with good acid spine, it is vibrant, lemony and appley, with a minerally streak and obvious potential.

Vintage	09	08
WR	6	5
Drink	10-18	10-19

SW $25 V+

Konrad Sigrun Noble Two ★★★★
Showing a Sauternes-style richness, the 2008 vintage (★★★★☆) of this estate-grown, Waihopai Valley beauty is a blend of 58 per cent tank-fermented Riesling and 42 per cent barrel-fermented Sauvignon Blanc, hand-picked between early May and mid-June at an average of 45 brix. Pale gold, it is weighty and luscious, with impressively concentrated, honey-sweet flavours, showing lovely harmony and depth.

Vintage	08	07
WR	6	5
Drink	10-18	10-17

SW $25 (375ML) AV

Lincoln Ice Wine ★★★
The 2009 vintage (★★★) is a freeze-concentrated Riesling, light (10 per cent alcohol) and lively, with ripe, citrusy, limey, spicy flavours, sweet, crisp and already drinking well.

SW $20 (375ML) –V

Main Divide Pokiri Reserve Late Picked Waipara Valley Pinot Gris (★★★★★)
From Pegasus Bay, the 2009 vintage (★★★★★) was harvested at 28 brix, 'long after the leaves had gone', when the grapes had dehydrated and shrivelled. Sweet but not super-sweet (70 grams/litre of residual sugar), it is fragrant, beautifully ripe and rounded, with concentrated stone-fruit and spice flavours, hints of ginger and honey, and great poise and personality. Great value.

Vintage	09
WR	7
Drink	10-17

SW $25 V+

Marble Point Hanmer Springs Riesling Classic ★★★☆
'A low alcohol style, for the mother-in-law', the 2009 vintage (★★★☆) was harvested at 19.4 brix in North Canterbury. Light (8.5 per cent alcohol) and lively, it is crisp, lemony and appley, with gentle sweetness (80 grams/litre of residual sugar) and very good flavour depth. Worth cellaring.

Vintage	09
WR	6
Drink	12-15

SW $21 V+

Margrain Botrytis Selection Chenin Blanc ★★★★☆
The 2008 vintage (★★★★★) is a rare Martinborough beauty, picked from 25-year-old vines in early June and stop-fermented at 240 grams per litre of residual sugar. Light gold, with an enticing, honeyed fragrance and concentrated, ripe flavours of citrus fruits and honey, it is notably pure and vibrant, with good acid spine, and should be long-lived.

Vintage	09	08
WR	7	7
Drink	10-19	10-19

SW $38 (375 ML) –V

Margrain Botrytis Selection Sauvignon Blanc (★★★★☆)

Harvested from a neighbouring vineyard in Martinborough at 46.8 brix, the 2008 vintage (★★★★☆) is a golden, Sauternes-style wine, with a richly honeyed bouquet. It's a highly concentrated wine, super-sweet (286 grams/litre of residual sugar), with stone-fruit and honey flavours that retain firm acidity. Delicious drinking now onwards.

Vintage	09	08
WR	7	7
Drink	10-19	10-19

SW $28 (375ML) V+

Martinborough Vineyard Bruno Riesling (★★★★)

Hand-harvested from 19-year-old vines in the Jackson Block, the 2009 vintage (★★★★) is a sweet (55 grams/litre of residual sugar) but not super-sweet wine, fresh, ripe and citrusy, balanced for good, easy, early drinking. Lemon and limey, with appetising acidity, it's already delicious.

SW $26 V+

Matua Valley Shingle Peak Reserve Botrytis Riesling (★★★★)

From an early June harvest of botrytised grapes, the 2007 vintage (★★★★) is a rich, oily, single-vineyard Marlborough wine with strong, citrusy, slightly spicy, honeyed flavours. It's a very elegant wine with a rich but not overwhelming botrytis influence.

Vintage	07
WR	6
Drink	10-13

SW $25 (375ML) AV

Maude Mt Maude Family Vineyard Off-Dry Riesling (★★★★)

Grown at Wanaka, in Central Otago, the 2010 vintage (★★★★) is light-bodied (9 per cent alcohol), with vibrant, citrusy, appley flavours, gently sweet (65 grams/litre of residual sugar) and mouth-wateringly crisp. Finely balanced, very fresh and racy, it should flourish with cellaring.

SW $20 V+

Millton Clos Samuel Viognier Special Bunch Selection (★★★★★)

The hedonistic 2007 vintage (★★★★★) was grown biodynamically in Gisborne. Golden, it is lush and sweet (250 grams/litre of residual sugar), with super-rich flavours of peaches, apricots and honey, showing good complexity. Very oily and concentrated, with underlying acidity, it's delicious now but also worth cellaring.

Vintage	07
WR	7
Drink	10-15

SW $43 (375ML) AV

Millton Muskats @ Dawn – see the Muscat section

Mission Ice Wine (★★☆)

Enjoyable now, the 2008 vintage (★★☆) is a Hawke's Bay wine, made by the freeze-concentration method. Light gold, it's a low-alcohol style (10 per cent) with peachy, honeyed flavours, smooth and sweet.

SW $18 (375ML) –V

Morton Estate Black Label Late Harvest Sémillon (★★★☆)

Still on sale, the 2006 vintage (★★★★) was grown in Hawke's Bay and oak-aged. Amber-hued, with a bouquet of honey and tea, it's a strongly botrytised wine, with apricot and honey flavours, firm acidity and very good depth. Ready.

Vintage	06
WR	6
Drink	10-12

SW $35 (375ML) –V

Muddy Water Sugar Daddy Riesling (★★★★★)

'Controlled decadence', I jotted down after tasting the 2008 vintage (★★★★★) of the Waipara winery's first 'fully botrytised' sweet wine. Hand-picked at 47 brix and fermented with indigenous yeasts for over 10 months, it has just 6.6 per cent alcohol. Pale gold/slight amber, with a richly honeyed bouquet and intense, apricot-like flavours, it has a powerful botrytis influence and enough acidity to balance its advanced level of sweetness (306 grams/litre of residual sugar). Already delicious, it should be long-lived.

Vintage	08
WR	7
Drink	10-25

SW $50 (375ML) AV

Muddy Water Riesling Unplugged ★★★★

The 2008 vintage (★★★★), part of the 'Growers' Series', was hand-harvested in Waipara at 28 to 32 brix. Based solely on 'clusters infected with noble rot', it was tank-fermented with indigenous yeasts and lees-aged for seven months. It's a sweet (73 grams/litre of residual sugar) but not cloying wine, with rich grapefruit, lime and honey flavours, balanced acidity and strong drink-young appeal. The 2009 (★★★★☆), estate-grown, was made from hand-picked, botrytis-infected bunches. Rich and honeyed, it is sweet (77 grams/litre of residual sugar) and crisp, with slight apricot and marmalade notes, a minerally streak and good complexity.

Vintage	09	08
WR	7	6
Drink	10-19	10-17

SW $29 V+

Ngatarawa Alwyn Winemaker's Reserve Noble Harvest Riesling ★★★★★

'Botrytis plays a huge part in this wine,' says Hawke's Bay winemaker Alwyn Corban. The 2006 vintage (★★★★★) was hand-harvested at 44 brix and fermented and matured for five months in French oak barriques (one and two years old). A golden, abundantly sweet wine (220 grams/

litre of residual sugar), with beautifully ripe pear, spice and honey flavours, enriched but not overwhelmed by botrytis, it's the most finely balanced, exquisite wine yet under this label.

Vintage	07	06	05
WR	NM	7	NM
Drink	NM	10-11	NM

SW $60 (375ML) –V

Ngatarawa Glazebrook Noble Harvest Riesling – see Glazebrook Regional Reserve Noble Harvest Riesling

Ngatarawa Stables Late Harvest (★★★☆)

This Hawke's Bay wine is called 'a fruit style' by winemaker Alwyn Corban, meaning it doesn't possess the qualities of a fully botrytised wine. The 2009 vintage (★★★☆) is a blend of Gewürztraminer (87 per cent) and Riesling (13 per cent). Full-bodied (13.5 per cent alcohol), it's a gently sweet wine (60 grams/litre of residual sugar) with generous, peachy, citrusy, slightly spicy flavours and a slightly honeyed bouquet. Drink now or cellar.

Vintage	09
WR	6
Drink	10-14

SW $17 (375ML) V+

Palliser Estate Noble Riesling (★★★★)

The 2008 vintage (★★★★), grown in Martinborough, is a late-harvest style with lemony, appley, slightly honeyed aromas and flavours, abundant sweetness (111 grams/litre of residual sugar) and gentle acidity. It's a light wine, fresh and elegant, with aging potential.

SW $24 (375ML) V+

Paritua Dinah Noble Harvest Sémillon (★★★☆)

Grown in Hawke's Bay, barrel-fermented and oak-aged for five months, the 2008 vintage (★★★★) is a weighty, Sauternes-style wine, rich and honeyed. Sweet (184 grams/litre of residual sugar), with ripe fruit flavours enriched by noble rot, it has an oily texture and considerable complexity.

Vintage	08
WR	5
Drink	09-20

SW $37 (375ML) –V

Paulownia Noble Sauvignon Blanc (★★★☆)

The 2009 vintage (★★★☆), grown at Gladstone, in the northern Wairarapa, has honeyed aromas and flavours, with sweet, vibrantly fruity, pear-like flavours woven with fresh acidity.

SW $18 (375ML) V+

Pegasus Bay Aria Late Harvest Riesling ★★★★★

The 2008 vintage (★★★★★) is a classy, very elegant Waipara wine, made from ripe bunches in which at least a third of the berries were nobly rotten. It has a floral, gently honeyed bouquet and fresh, pure, late-harvest fruit flavours, showing excellent richness. Finely focused, with a luscious sweetness (100 grams/litre of residual sugar) coupled with mouth-watering acidity, it's a beauty.

Vintage	08	07	06	05	04	03	02
WR	7	7	7	NM	6	NM	5
Drink	10-20	10-18	10-15	NM	10-14	NM	10-15

SW $37 V+

Pegasus Bay Encore Noble Riesling ★★★★☆

Still a baby, the 2008 vintage (★★★★★) is a Waipara beauty, made from botrytised bunches, late-harvested at 32 brix. Light lemon/green, it is fresh, sweet (124 grams/litre of residual sugar), concentrated and citrusy, with a gentle overlay of honey, an oily richness and lovely poise and length.

Vintage	08	07
WR	6	5
Drink	10-20	10-19

SW $37 (375ML) –V

Pegasus Bay Finale Noble Sémillon (★★★★☆)

The deliciously rich, honey-sweet 2007 vintage (★★★★☆) was harvested at Waipara during late autumn and early winter (with a final pick in late June), barrel-fermented and oak-aged for two years. Light gold, with a full-bloomed, honeyed bouquet, revealing a strong noble rot influence, it is full-bodied and sweet (140 grams/litre of residual sugar), with concentrated, ripe tropical-fruit and honey flavours, and mouth-watering acidity.

Vintage	07
WR	6
Drink	10-16

SW $37 (375ML) –V

Pyramid Valley Vineyards Growers Collection Hille
Vineyard Marlborough Sémillon Late Harvest (★★★★☆)

The Sauternes-style 2008 vintage (★★★★☆) was grown in the upper Brancott Valley and late-picked at 39 brix, with 90 per cent botrytis infection of the berries; the rest were ripe and desiccated. Fermented slowly – over 19 months – with indigenous yeasts in French oak hogsheads (60 per cent new), it has honey and herb scents, leading into a full-bodied, fresh wine, sweet (100 grams/litre of residual sugar), oily and rich, with vibrant, citrusy, slightly limey flavours showing lovely concentration.

SW $45 V+

Richmond Plains Nelson Aries (★★★★)

The first New Zealand wine made from certified biodynamic grapes, the 2008 vintage (★★★★) was grown in the same vineyard that produced the country's first certified organic Sauvignon Blanc and Pinot Noir. A late-harvest Pinot Noir, hand-picked on 1 June, 'as the moon moved through the constellation of Aries', it is very rare – only 300 bottles were produced. Delicious now, it is sweet and smooth, with plum and strawberry flavours, showing excellent harmony and depth.

SW $30 (375ML) –V

Riverby Noble Riesling ★★★★☆

From 'totally botrytised' grapes, harvested in Marlborough, the 2009 vintage (★★★★) is a low-alcohol style (9 per cent), with fresh passionfruit, spice and citrus flavours, sweet (230 grams/litre of residual sugar), rounded and luscious.

Vintage	09	08
WR	7	7
Drink	10-13	10-12

SW $25 (375 ML) V+

Rock Ferry Marlborough Select Harvest Riesling (★★★★★)

BioGro certified, the finely poised 2009 vintage (★★★★★) is a late-harvest style, grown in the Corners Vineyard, in the Wairau Valley, and fermented with indigenous yeasts in seasoned oak barrels. Highly scented, with a citrusy bouquet, it is light (9.5 per cent alcohol) and rich, with a hint of sherbet, lovely freshness and depth of lemon and apricot flavours, abundant sweetness (143 grams/litre of residual sugar), good acid spine, and real complexity. It should be long-lived.

Vintage	09
WR	5
Drink	10-12

SW $29 (375ML) V+

Rose Tree Cottage Noble Riesling ★★★★

From Constellation NZ, the 2007 vintage (★★★★) was grown at the Matador Estate in Marlborough. Golden, it's an elegant wine with citrusy, slightly honeyed flavours, sweet (150 grams/litre of residual sugar) and rich.

SW $24 (375 ML) V+

Saints Gisborne Noble Sémillon ★★★★

The 2009 vintage (★★★★) from Pernod Ricard NZ is a Sauternes style with a clear botrytis influence. Pale gold, with mouthfilling body and concentrated, tropical-fruit flavours, it is sweet, gently honeyed and smooth, with good harmony and loads of drink-young appeal.

SW $20 (375ML) V+

Seifried Winemakers Collection Sweet Agnes Riesling ★★★★

This freeze-concentrated wine is priced sharply. The 2009 (★★★★) was hand-harvested at Brightwater, in Nelson, freeze-concentrated to the equivalent of 38 brix, and then stop-fermented at 10 per cent alcohol. Sweet and mouth-wateringly crisp, it offers strong, lemony, limey, spicy flavours, fresh, pure, lively and long. The 2010 vintage (★★★★☆) is sweet (195 grams/litre of residual sugar), with rich lemon and apricot flavours, hints of sherbet and spices, and lovely concentration and poise.

Vintage	10	09
WR	7	7
Drink	10-18	10-17

SW $19 (375ML) V+

Selaks Premium Selection East Coast Ice ★★★☆

This low-priced, freeze-concentrated wine is popular in supermarkets. The 2007 vintage (★★★), blended from Gewürztraminer (51 per cent) and Riesling (49 per cent), is light-bodied, with enjoyable but straightforward, lemony, slightly spicy flavours, sweet (141 grams/litre of residual sugar) and fresh.

SW $17 (375ML) V+

Seresin Late Harvest Marlborough Riesling (★★★★☆)

Released recently, the 2005 vintage (★★★★☆) was hand-picked in the Home Vineyard in late May, with 'minimal' botrytis. Still youthful in colour, it is invitingly scented, with beautifully ripe, lemony, limey flavours, overlaid with a toasty, bottle-aged complexity. A sweetish (68 grams/litre of residual sugar) wine, developing real personality, it's drinking well now.

Vintage	05
WR	5
Drink	10-15

SW $27 (375ML) V+

Sileni Estate Selection Late Harvest Sémillon ★★★☆

The 2009 (★★★★) is a top vintage. A gently sweet style (96 grams/litre of residual sugar) from Hawke's Bay, it is full-bodied, with concentrated, ripe citrus-fruit, pear and spice flavours. Handled entirely in tanks, it shows good richness and cellaring potential.

SW $21 (375 ML) AV

Sileni Exceptional Vintage Pourriture Noble ★★★★☆

The 2009 vintage (★★★★☆) is a Sauternes-style wine, full-bodied and honeyed, made from Sémillon grapes harvested in Hawke's Bay at 38 brix. Rich and finely balanced, it has ripe stone-fruit, spice and slight honey flavours, sweet and concentrated.

SW $32 (375ML) AV

Soljans Estate Late Harvest Marlborough Riesling (★★★)

Light and lemony, the 2009 vintage (★★★) is fresh, citrusy and gently spicy, with abundant sweetness (85 grams/litre of residual sugar) and a smooth finish. It's a very easy-drinking style, for enjoying now or cellaring.

Vintage	09
WR	6
Drink	10-20

SW $20 (375ML) –V

Spy Valley Envoy Marlborough Riesling ★★★★★

Already delicious, the 2008 vintage (★★★★★) was hand-picked from mature vines at 22.7 brix and partly barrel-fermented. Beautifully scented, it is light (9 per cent alcohol) and gently sweet (79 grams/litre of residual sugar). Finely poised, in a very Germanic style, it shows lovely delicacy and intensity of lemony, limey flavours, a minerally streak, fresh acidity and great harmony, complexity and length.

Vintage	09	08
WR	7	7
Drink	11-18	10-16

SW $30 (375ML) V+

Spy Valley Marlborough Noble Chardonnay ★★★★
The 2009 vintage (★★★☆) was late-harvested at 31 brix and barrel-fermented. Sweet (120 grams/litre of residual sugar), ripe and smooth, it is peachy, slightly spicy and honeyed, with a touch of complexity and drink-young charm.

Vintage	09
WR	6
Drink	10-13

SW $23 (375ML) V+

Spy Valley Marlborough Noble Riesling ★★★★
The attractively scented 2008 vintage (★★★★) was hand-picked at 36.6 brix, tank-fermented and matured for three months in small oak barrels. Delicious from the start, it has a citrusy, gently honeyed bouquet, generous depth of ripe, citrusy, honeyed flavours, hints of lime and marmalade, and a sweet, smooth finish.

SW $23 (375 ML) V+

Spy Valley Marlborough Noble Sauvignon Blanc ★★★☆
The 2009 vintage (★★★☆) was late-harvested at 31 brix, and fermented and matured for three months in old French oak barrels. Balanced for easy, early drinking, it's a medium-bodied, sweet wine (120 grams/litre of residual sugar), with ripe tropical-fruit flavours, slightly spicy and well-rounded.

Vintage	09
WR	7
Drink	10-13

SW $23 (375ML) AV

Staete Landt Marlborough Riesling Auslese ★★★☆
Estate-grown and hand-picked at Rapaura, the 2008 vintage (★★★★) stop-fermented of its own accord with 8.5 per cent alcohol, leaving 67 grams per litre of residual sugar. Matured for five months in old oak casks, it is ripely flavoured, lemony, appley and spicy, with a lovely interplay of sweetness and crispness and good intensity.

Vintage	08	07
WR	7	5
Drink	10-15	10-15

SW $32 V+

Stone Paddock Isabella Late Harvest Sémillon ★★★★
From Paritua Vineyards, in Hawke's Bay, the 2008 vintage (★★★★) was hand-picked at 36–38 brix, blended with Sauvignon Blanc (10 per cent) and partly barrel-fermented. Pale gold, it's a Sauternes-style dessert wine, rich, peachy and honeyed, with plentiful sweetness (158 grams/litre of residual sugar), a slightly oily texture, and good concentration.

Vintage	08
WR	5
Drink	10-15

SW $25 (375ML) AV

Te Awa Noble Chardonnay (★★★★)

The 2009 vintage (★★★★) was harvested at 42.3 brix in Hawke's Bay. Pale gold, it's a honey-sweet beauty, very fresh and lively, with rich, ripe, citrusy flavours, a gentle botrytis influence, and excellent balance of sweetness (250 grams/litre of residual sugar) and acidity.

SW $30 (375ML) –V

Te Mania Nelson Koha Ice Wine ★★★☆

From hand-picked Riesling grapes, freeze-concentrated in tanks, the 2009 vintage (★★★★) is a low-alcohol style (8.5 per cent), lemony and sweet (120 grams/litre of residual sugar), with good sugar/acid balance and lovely lightness, delicacy and harmony. It's well worth cellaring.

Vintage	09
WR	5
Drink	10-14

SW $25 (375ML) –V

Torlesse Waipara Sticky Riesling (★★★☆)

The golden, concentrated 2008 vintage (★★★☆) was harvested in late June with noble rot. It has rich apricot and honey flavours, showing some development, and plentiful sweetness (160 grams/litre of residual sugar).

Vintage	08
WR	6
Drink	12-15

SW $25 (375ML) –V

Trinity Hill Gimblett Gravels Hawke's Bay Noble Viognier ★★★★☆

The 2008 vintage (★★★★★) was made from hand-picked, botrytised grapes and partly barrel-fermented. Hard to resist, it is lush, sweet, rich and soft, with mouthfilling body, lovely, ripe stone-fruit flavours and a highly perfumed bouquet. The 2009 (★★★★) was handled in tanks and old French oak barrels. Unabashedly sweet (200 grams/litre of residual sugar), it has concentrated peach and apricot flavours, an oily texture, and good complexity and richness.

Vintage	09	08	07	06	05
WR	5	6	6	4	6
Drink	10-17	10-17	10-15	P	10-12

SW $35 (375ML) –V

Turanga Creek New Zealand Late Harvest Viognier (★★★)

Grown at Whitford, in South Auckland, the 2008 vintage (★★★) isn't quite sweet enough (43 grams/litre of residual sugar) to qualify for the Sweet White Wines chapter, but it's reviewed here due to its Late Harvest designation and small bottle. Drinking well now, it's a peachy, medium-sweet wine, with soft acidity and gentle stone-fruit flavours.

SW $35 (375ML) –V

TW Grower's Selection Botrytis Viognier ★★★★

Gold/amber, with tea and honey aromas, the 2008 vintage (★★★☆) shows considerable early development. Rich, oily and sweet, with strong apricot and honey flavours, it's probably at its best now.

SW $32 (375ML) –V

Urlar Noble Riesling (★★★★)

Grown at Gladstone, in the northern Wairarapa, the 2009 vintage (★★★★) has concentrated flavours of citrus fruits, spices, marmalade and honey, and a sweet, lingering finish.

SW $28 (375ML) AV

Villa Maria Reserve Noble Riesling ★★★★★

One of New Zealand's top sweet wines on the show circuit. It is typically stunningly perfumed, weighty and oily, with intense, very sweet honey/citrus flavours and a lush, long finish. The grapes are grown mainly in the Fletcher Vineyard, in the centre of Marlborough's Wairau Plains, where trees create a 'humidity crib' around the vines and sprinklers along the vines' fruit zone create ideal conditions for the spread of noble rot. The 2007 vintage (★★★★★) is outstanding. Deep yellow, with a richly honeyed bouquet, it is very refined and youthful, with concentrated, citrusy, honeyed flavours, enriched but not overpowered by botrytis, and lovely balance of sweetness and acidity.

Vintage	07
WR	7
Drink	10-18

SW $50 (375ML) AV

Waimea Bolitho SV Noble Chardonnay ★★★★☆

Still on sale, the 2006 vintage (★★★★☆) is a richly botrytised Nelson wine, hand-picked at 44.7 brix and barrel-fermented. Golden, with abundant sweetness (217 grams/litre of residual sugar), it has excellent depth and complexity of honey and toast flavours, fresh acidity and a long finish.

Vintage	06
WR	6
Drink	10-11

SW $30 (375ML) AV

Waimea Bolitho SV Noble Riesling ★★★★☆

The gold/amber, very rich and treacly 2004 vintage (★★★★☆) was estate-grown in the Annabrook Vineyard, in Nelson, harvested in mid-June at 50 brix and aged in seasoned French oak casks. Highly concentrated, with low alcohol (7.5 per cent) and a soaring level of sweetness (310 grams/litre of residual sugar), it has softening, toffee and marmalade flavours, ready now. The 2005 (★★★★), harvested at 44.4 brix, is a deep amber, treacly wine with sweet (200 grams/litre of residual sugar) apricot, tea and honey flavours, showing some maturity.

Vintage	04	03
WR	7	7
Drink	10-14	10-13

SW $30 (375ML) AV

Waimea Late Harvest Riesling ★★★★

Still on sale, the 2006 vintage (★★★★) is an absolute steal. A Nelson wine made from fully botrytised grapes, hand-picked at 32 brix, it is intense, citrusy and gently honeyed, in a sweet (84 grams/litre of residual sugar) but not super-sweet style with a creamy, oily richness.

Vintage	06
WR	6
Drink	10-11

SW $14 (375ML) V+

Waipara Downs Late Harvest Riesling (★★☆)

The pale gold 2008 vintage (★★☆) was fermented with indigenous yeasts in seasoned French oak puncheons. It's a citrusy, sweet, honeyed wine, showing some early development and probably best drunk young.

SW $22 (375ML) –V

Wooing Tree Tickled Pink (★★★★)

The distinctive, instantly appealing 2010 vintage (★★★★) was made from Pinot Noir grapes, late-harvested in the Cromwell Basin, Central Otago, and fermented in old oak barrels. Bright pink, with floral, berryish scents, it is light (9.5 per cent alcohol) and lively, with rich plum and red-berry flavours, slightly spicy and peachy, and a gently sweet (100 grams/litre of residual sugar), smooth finish.

SW $35 (375ML) –V

Sparkling Wines

Fizz, bubbly, *méthode traditionnelle*, sparkling – whatever name you call it by (the word Champagne is reserved for the wines of that most famous of all wine regions), wine with bubbles in it is universally adored.

How good are Kiwi bubblies? Good enough for the local industry to ship 193,000 cases of bubbly in the year to June 2010 – but that was down from 284,000 cases in 2005. In the past year, sparkling wine accounted for 1.2 per cent of New Zealand's wine exports.

The selection of New Zealand sparklings is not wide. Most small wineries find the production of bottle-fermented sparkling wine too time-consuming and costly, and the domestic demand for premium bubbly is limited. The vast majority of purchases are under $15.

New Zealand's sparkling wines can be divided into two key classes. The bottom end of the market is dominated by extremely sweet, simple wines which acquire their bubbles by simply having carbon dioxide pumped into them. Upon pouring, the bubbles race out of the glass.

At the middle and top end of the market are the much drier, bottle-fermented, *méthode traditionnelle* (formerly *méthode Champenoise*, until the French got upset) labels, in which the wine undergoes its secondary, bubble-creating fermentation not in a tank but in the bottle, as in Champagne itself. Ultimately, the quality of any fine sparkling wine is a reflection both of the standard of its base wine and of its later period of maturation in the bottle in contact with its yeast lees. Only bottle-fermented sparkling wines possess the additional flavour richness and complexity derived from extended lees-aging.

Pinot Noir and Chardonnay, both varieties of key importance in Champagne, are also the foundation of New Zealand's top sparkling wines. Pinot Meunier, also extensively planted in Champagne, is still rare here, with 19 hectares planted.

Two-thirds of the grapes for the country's most popular bubbly, Lindauer, are grown in Gisborne, where grape yields are high (necessary for such a low-priced wine) and the fruit is harvested early to retain the desired high levels of acidity. However, Marlborough, with its cool nights preserving the grapes' fresh natural acidity, has emerged as the country's premier region for bottle-fermented sparkling wines (8 per cent of the region's Pinot Noir is cultivated specifically for sparkling – rather than red – wine).

The vast majority of sparkling wines are ready to drink when marketed and need no extra maturation. A short spell in the cellar, however, can benefit the very best bottle-fermented sparklings.

Allan Scott Blanc de Blancs Marlborough Brut NV ★★★★

This refreshing Marlborough bubbly is based entirely on Chardonnay. The batch on sale in 2010 (★★★★) was disgorged after two years on its yeast lees. Pale straw, it is lemony, yeasty and smooth, with excellent delicacy and complexity, and a finely balanced, dryish (5 grams/litre of residual sugar) finish.

MED/DRY $28 AV

Allan Scott Cecilia Marlborough Brut NV (★★★★)

The batch on sale in 2010 (★★★★) is a good buy. Blended from Pinot Noir and Chardonnay disgorged after 18 months' maturation on yeast lees, it is vivacious, fresh, citrusy and slightly nutty, with good complexity and intensity.

MED/DRY $24 V+

Allan Scott Les Joues Rouges Reserve Brut NV ★★★☆

Based entirely on Pinot Noir, grown in Marlborough, the batch on sale in 2010 (★★★☆) is pale pink, with strawberryish flavours, a hint of oranges, a gentle, yeasty influence and a crisp, dryish finish.

MED/DRY $24 AV

Allan Scott Marlborough Sparkling Sauvignon Blanc [Vintage] (★★★★)

The debut 2009 vintage (★★★★), bottle-fermented, is New Zealand's best Sauvignon Blanc bubbly to date. A bone-dry style, it is ripely scented, crisp and lively, with delicious passionfruit and lime flavours, slightly yeasty and tangy, and greater complexity than you'd expect in such a young wine.

DRY $22 V+

Allan Scott Marlborough Sparkling Sauvignon Blanc NV (★★★☆)

The non-vintage batch on sale in late 2010 (★★★☆) was made mostly from 2010 fruit, with some 2009 material included. Fresh, crisp and dry, with tropical-fruit flavours, it is gently yeasty, with good vigour and depth.

DRY $20 AV

Aquila Sparkling Wine ★★☆

This low-priced bubbly is fresh and fruity, with a sweetish finish. Within Pernod Ricard NZ's range of sparklings, in terms of sweetness Aquila (which has 50 grams/litre of residual sugar) sits between the medium Lindauer Sec and the unabashedly sweet Bernadino Spumante. The non-vintage wine I tasted in mid-2009 (★★☆) was perfumed and light, with simple, lemony, appley flavours, fresh, lively and smooth.

SW $10 AV

Arcadia NV Brut ★★★☆

This bottle-fermented bubbly is produced by Amisfield in Central Otago from Pinot Noir and Chardonnay. The non-vintage wine I tasted in mid-2009 (★★★☆) was pale straw, with a hint of pink, peachy, strawberryish, yeasty flavours, showing good complexity, and a slightly buttery, softening finish.

MED/DRY $30 –V

Bernadino Spumante ★★★

What great value! Pernod Ricard NZ's popular Asti-style wine is an uncomplicated style, based on Muscat grapes grown in Gisborne. A slightly higher-alcohol wine (9.5 per cent) than most true Asti Spumantes (which average around 7.5 per cent) and less ravishingly perfumed, it's still delicious, with grapey flavours and distinct sweetness (75 grams/litre of residual sugar). The non-vintage wine I tasted in mid-2009 (★★★) was finely balanced, with fresh, vibrant flavours of lemons and oranges and a sweet, crisp finish.

SW $8 V+

Brancott Estate Brut Cuvée Reserve (★★★☆)

The pale straw, non-vintage wine on sale in late 2010 (★★★☆) is a blend of Chardonnay and Pinot Noir, grown in 'East Coast vineyards'. Vibrantly fruity and smooth, it is gently yeasty, with citrusy, slightly creamy flavours, a hint of cashews, and good freshness, harmony and immediacy.

MED/DRY $22 AV

Brancott Estate Reserve Sparkling Pinot Noir (★★★)

Launched in late 2010, this non-vintage wine was made from Waipara and Marlborough grapes. Full-coloured, it is a sparkling red wine with fresh berry and plum aromas and flavours, a hint of dark chocolate, and a gently sweet, crisp finish.

MED $24 –V

Brancott Estate Reserve Sparkling Sauvignon Blanc (★★★☆)

The non-vintage wine launched in late 2010 is a richer style than Lindauer Sauvignon, with a touch of Pinot Gris. It is a vivacious wine with strong, ripe melon and lime flavours, crisp, slightly sweet and smooth.

MED/DRY $24 AV

Chardon Medium Sparkling White Wine ★★

Frothy and simple, the non-vintage wine on sale in 2009 (★★) from Pernod Ricard NZ was pale and very light (only 5.8 per cent alcohol), offering pleasant, lemony, appley flavours, sweet and crisp.

MED $8 –V

Corbans Verde – see Verde

Cuvée No. 1 ★★★★

This is a non-vintage blanc de blancs style, based entirely on Marlborough Chardonnay. Made by Daniel Le Brun (in his family company) and matured for 18 months on its yeast lees, the wine I tasted in late 2009 (★★★★) was stylish, with refined, citrusy, appley, yeasty flavours, showing excellent delicacy, and a crisp, dryish (6 grams/litre of residual sugar), tight-knit finish.

MED/DRY $35 –V

Cuvée No. 1 [Rosé] (★★★★)

Just labelled as Cuvée No. 1, but made in a rosé style, the non-vintage wine (★★★★) I tasted in late 2009 was made from Marlborough Pinot Noir, matured on its yeast lees for 20 months. Pink/orange, with strawberryish, yeasty, dryish flavours (6 grams/litre of residual sugar), it shows very good delicacy, crispness and length.

MED/DRY $47 –V

Cuvée Number Eight ★★★

An 'apéritif style' from Daniel Le Brun's family company, this is a non-vintage blend of Marlborough Pinot Noir and Chardonnay. The batch on the market in late 2009 (★★★★), disgorged after 10 months on its yeast lees, was one of the best yet – pale straw, creamy and smooth, with strong, yeasty flavours showing good complexity and harmony.

MED/DRY $30 –V

Cuvée Remy (★★★★☆)

The 2007 vintage (★★★★☆) from No. 1 Family Estate is a tribute to Daniel and Adele Le Brun's son, Remy. Made from Marlborough Pinot Noir (80 per cent) and Chardonnay (20 per cent), disgorged after two years on its yeast lees, it is pale straw, with generous, citrusy, biscuity flavours, showing good freshness, yeasty, bready notes, and excellent vigour, complexity and length.

MED/DRY $55 –V

Daniel Le Brun Brut NV ★★★★

After buying Cellier Le Brun, Mahi sold the Daniel Le Brun brand to Lion Nathan, but the brand now has a much lower profile than in the past. A Marlborough blend of Pinot Noir (60 per cent), Chardonnay (30 per cent) and Pinot Meunier (10 per cent), it is typically rich and toasty, in a high-flavoured style, crisp and yeasty, with good vigour and freshness.

MED/DRY $29 AV

Deutz Marlborough Cuvée Blanc de Blancs ★★★★★

New Zealand's most awarded bubbly on the show circuit. This Chardonnay-predominant blend is hand-harvested on the south side of the Wairau Valley, mostly at Renwick Estate, and matured for three to five years on its yeast lees. It is typically a very classy wine with delicate, piercing, lemony, appley flavours, well-integrated yeastiness and a slightly creamy finish. The 2007 vintage (★★★★★) has a lemony, biscuity fragrance. It has citrus-fruit, yeast and cashew nut flavours, showing lovely freshness, depth, delicacy and harmony, that float effortlessly across the palate to a crisp, racy finish.

MED/DRY $40 AV

Deutz Marlborough Cuvée Brut NV ★★★★★

The marriage of Pernod Ricard NZ's fruit at Marlborough with the Champagne house of Deutz's 150 years of experience created an instant winner. Bottled-fermented and matured on its yeast lees for two to three years, this non-vintage wine has evolved over the past decade into a less overtly fruity, more delicate and flinty style. The Pinot Noir grapes are drawn principally from Kaituna Estate, on the north side of the Wairau Valley; the Chardonnay comes mostly from Renwick Estate, in the middle of the valley. Before being bottled, the base wine is lees-aged for up to three months and given a full malolactic fermentation. Reserve wines, a year or two older than the rest, are added to each batch, contributing consistency and complexity to the final blend. The wine I tasted in 2010 (★★★★☆) was lean, intense and racy, with incisive, lemony, slightly appley flavours, showing plenty of yeast-derived complexity. (The average retail price in supermarkets is currently $22.50.)

MED/DRY $35 AV

Deutz Marlborough Cuvée Rosé NV ★★★★☆

The wine (★★★★☆) on the market in 2010 – made predominantly from Pinot Noir – is pale pink, very fresh and finely balanced, with smooth, strawberry and spice flavours, showing yeast-derived complexity and lovely lightness and vivacity.

MED/DRY $37 –V

Deutz Prestige Marlborough Cuvée (★★★★★)

The debut 2005 vintage (★★★★★) is a classy, Chardonnay-based style, blended with 35 per cent Pinot Noir. Disgorged after three and a half years on its yeast lees, it is rich and highly refined, citrusy, yeasty and crisp, with excellent intensity on the palate and a fresh, aromatic bouquet, toasty, yeasty and complex. The 2006 (★★★★★) is also distinguished – weighty, with a powerful surge of rich, citrusy, yeasty flavours, showing excellent freshness, complexity and roundness.

MED/DRY $37 AV

Doctors', The, Bubbles for Beth (★★★☆)

The 2005 vintage (★★★☆) from Forrest is a sparkling red, made from Marlborough Syrah and Malbec and bottle-fermented. Full-coloured, it is berryish and gently yeasty, with a hint of dark chocolate and a smooth, lively finish. Worth trying.

MED/DRY $35 –V

Doctors', The, Remedy Marlborough Méthode Traditionnelle (★★★☆)

Made by Forrest, the 2005 vintage (★★★☆) is a bottle-fermented Marlborough sparkling, based on Pinot Noir and Chardonnay. Light, crisp and elegant, with gentle yeastiness, it's a delicate, slightly nutty wine, showing good freshness and vigour.

MED/DRY $35 –V

Dolbel Estate Méthode Traditionnelle (★★★★)

Full of personality, the 2006 vintage (★★★★) is a rich, ripe style from Hawke's Bay, made from equal portions of Chardonnay and Pinot Noir, fermented in old French barriques and disgorged after two years on its yeast lees. Pale straw, it has strong, peachy, very toasty and nutty flavours and a long, dry, yeasty finish.

MED/DRY $30 –V

Elstree Marlborough Cuvée Brut ★★★★

The 2006 vintage (★★★★☆) from Highfield is a blend of hand-picked Pinot Noir and Chardonnay, partly barrel-fermented and disgorged after three years on its yeast lees. Pale straw, with a very yeasty, rich fragrance, it is tight and elegant, with strong, crisp, lemony, toasty flavours, showing excellent vigour, complexity and richness.

Vintage	06	05	04
WR	6	6	5
Drink	10-12	10-11	P

MED/DRY $37 –V

Fallen Angel Marlborough Méthode Traditionnelle NV Brut (★★★☆)

From Stonyridge, the non-vintage wine on sale in 2010 (★★★☆) is crisp and lively, with citrusy, limey, dryish flavours, showing some yeasty, slightly earthy notes that reminded me of Spanish cava.

MED/DRY $40 –V

Forrest Estate Bubbles for Brigid ★★★★

Bottled with a crown seal, rather than a cork, the 2005 vintage (★★★★) is a bottle-fermented Marlborough blend of Pinot Noir and Chardonnay. Pale straw, with an eruption of tiny bubbles, it is elegant and light, lemony and biscuity, with good yeast-derived complexity and a tight-knit, unusually dry (3 grams/litre of residual sugar) but very harmonious finish.

Vintage	05
WR	6
Drink	10-11

DRY $30 AV

Frizzell Méthode Traditionnelle Brut NV (★★★★)

The non-vintage wine on sale in 2010 (★★★★) is a Hawke's Bay wine with crisp, lemony, limey flavours, yeasty and toasty, and excellent complexity, vigour and length.

MED/DRY $32 –V

Fusion Sparkling Muscat – see Soljans Fusion Sparkling Muscat

Georges Michel Marlborough Méthode Traditionnelle NV (★★★)

The wine on sale in 2010 is a blanc de blancs made from unexpected varieties – Sémillon (70 per cent) and Sauvignon Blanc (30 per cent), harvested in 2009. Briefly lees-aged, it is pale yellow, crisp, fruity and lively, although not complex, with dryish, tropical-fruit flavours, in a stimulating apéritif style.

MED/DRY $20 –V

Hinchco Sparkling Merlot Rosé (★★)

From Matakana, the 2008 vintage (★★) is rust-coloured, crisp and dryish, with strawberry and spice flavours that lack a bit of freshness and charm.

MED/DRY $25 –V

Huia Marlborough Brut ★★★☆

The 2004 vintage (★★★★), a blend of Chardonnay (55 per cent), Pinot Noir (41 per cent) and Pinot Meunier (4 per cent), was fermented in old barrels prior to its secondary fermentation in the bottle, and disgorged after several years on its yeast lees. Straw-coloured, with a toasty, yeasty bouquet, it's a rich style with lively, nutty, yeasty, smooth flavours, showing good complexity. Delicious now.

MED/DRY $39 –V

Hunter's Miru Miru NV ★★★☆

'Miru Miru' means bubbles. A stimulating apéritif, this wine is disgorged a year earlier than its Reserve stablemate (below), has a lower Pinot Noir content and a crisper finish. A vivacious blend of Chardonnay, Pinot Noir and Pinot Meunier, the wine on sale in 2010 (★★★★) shows good richness, with intense, distinctly citrusy, slightly nutty flavours and a lingering finish.

MED/DRY $23 AV

Hunter's Miru Miru Reserve ★★★★

This has long been one of Marlborough's finest sparklings, full and lively, with loads of citrusy, yeasty, nutty flavour and a creamy, long finish. It is matured on its yeast lees for an average of three and a half years. The 2006 vintage (★★★★) is a blend of Chardonnay (55 per cent), Pinot Noir (41 per cent) and Pinot Meunier (4 per cent). Straw-hued, it is crisp, toasty and yeasty, in a high-flavoured style with excellent vigour, richness and harmony.

MED/DRY $27 AV

Italiano Bianco Spumante (★★★)

From Pernod Ricard NZ, this non-vintage bubbly typically offers great value. Muscat-scented, it is light and lively, sweet and soft, with a steady stream of bubbles, good freshness and vivacity, and lots of charm. Easy to underestimate!

SW $9 V+

Johanneshof Emmi ★★★★

The non-vintage wine (★★★★) I tasted in 2009 was a Marlborough blend of Pinot Noir and Chardonnay, disgorged after 'several' years on its yeast lees. Bright, light yellow/green, it showed excellent vigour and freshness, with strong, crisp, nutty flavours, dryish, lemony and long.

MED/DRY $35 –V

Joseph Ryan Méthode Traditionnelle (★★☆)

Grown in the northern Wairarapa, the 2008 vintage (★★☆) is straw-hued, with crisp, strawberryish, toasty flavours, showing some complexity and richness, but lacks fragrance.

MED/DRY $36 –V

Kaimira June Nelson Méthode Traditionnelle (★★★☆)

The non-vintage wine on sale in 2010 (★★★☆) is pale straw, lemony and lively, with fresh, crisp, gently yeasty flavours, showing some complexity, good delicacy and a fully dry finish.

DRY $29 –V

Lake Chalice Cracklin' Savie NV (★★★)

Closed with a crown seal and not vintage-dated, the wine on the market in 2010 (★★★) is a gently *spritzig* Marlborough Sauvignon Blanc. Full-bodied and fresh, it has ripe passionfruit, pineapple and lime flavours and a crisp, dryish finish.

MED/DRY $20 –V

La Michelle ★★★★

From Margrain, the classy 2007 vintage (★★★★☆) is a 2:1 blend of Martinborough Pinot Noir and Chardonnay, lees-aged for two and a half years. Full of personality, it is very smooth, yet unusually dry (4 grams/litre of residual sugar), with rich, lemony, appley flavours, very biscuity and yeasty, and a crisp, harmonious finish.

Vintage	07
WR	7
Drink	10-15

MED/DRY $38 –V

Lindauer Brut NV ★★★☆

Given its very good quality, ultra-low price (the current average in supermarkets is $10) and huge volumes (batch variation is inevitable), this non-vintage bubbly from Pernod Ricard NZ is a miracle of modern winemaking. It is blended from Pinot Noir and Chardonnay, grown in Gisborne and Hawke's Bay, and matured for a year on its yeast lees. Fractionally sweet (12 grams/litre of residual sugar), it generally shows good vigour and depth in a refined style, crisp and finely balanced, with lively, lemony, slightly nutty and yeasty flavours. The wine I tasted at Pernod Ricard NZ in August 2010 (★★★★) was highly fragrant, with strong, slightly sweet, yeasty flavours, showing impressive richness and complexity.

MED/DRY $16 V+

Lindauer Fraise ★★☆

Pronounced 'Frez', the strawberry-flavoured Lindauer is 'aimed at the RTD [ready-mixed drinks] market', according to a major wine retailer. Made 'with an added touch of natural strawberry', the non-vintage wine on sale in 2009 (★★☆) was bright pink, with flavours that are very smooth and – well – strawberryish, in a fresh, light and lively, simple style with gentle sweetness. It's unlikely to appeal to regular wine drinkers, but we are obviously not the target market.

MED $16 –V

Lindauer Rosé ★★★

Pernod Ricard NZ's bottle-fermented rosé is blended from Chardonnay and Pinot Noir, grown in Gisborne and Hawke's Bay. It is typically pink, with strawberryish, moderately yeasty aromas and flavours, fresh and lively, and a crisp, gently sweet (16 grams/litre of residual sugar) finish.

MED $16 AV

Lindauer Sauvignon ★★★

The only Lindauer-branded bubbly that is not bottle-fermented, this is a *spritzig* (gently sparkling) blend of Marlborough Sauvignon Blanc (85 per cent), Chardonnay (14 per cent) and Pinot Noir (1 per cent). It's an easy summer sipper – refreshing, with lively, limey flavours and a slightly sweet (16 grams/litre of residual sugar), appetisingly crisp finish. The wine I tasted in August 2010 (★★★) was just like a sparkling Sauvignon Blanc – light, crisp, simple and herbaceous, with good freshness and vivacity.

MED $15 AV

Lindauer Sec ★★★

The medium version of Pernod Ricard NZ's best-seller is twice as sweet (24 grams/litre of residual sugar) as its Brut stablemate (which has 12 grams/litre). A bottle-fermented blend of Chardonnay and Pinot Noir, grown in Gisborne and Hawke's Bay, it is typically fresh and vivacious, with moderately yeasty flavours and a crisp, gently sweet finish.

MED $16 AV

Lindauer Special Reserve Blanc de Blancs ★★★☆

This non-vintage wine, based entirely on Chardonnay grown in Gisborne (mostly) and Hawke's Bay, is disgorged after two years on its yeast lees. It's a deliciously well-balanced wine, lemony and nutty, with gentle yeast autolysis characters and a slightly creamy, dryish (12 grams/litre of residual sugar) finish. The wine I tasted in August 2010 (★★★☆) was pale and lemon-scented, with lemon, apple and lime flavours, lightly yeasty and crisp, showing good vivacity.

MED/DRY $21 AV

Lindauer Special Reserve Brut Cuvée ★★★☆

Pernod Ricard NZ's immensely drinkable bubbly is a non-vintage blend of Pinot Noir (60 per cent) and Chardonnay (40 per cent), grown in Gisborne and Hawke's Bay, and matured on its yeast lees for two years. Tasted in August 2010 (★★★★), it is pale pink, with strawberryish, yeasty aromas and flavours, very crisp, dryish (12 grams/litre of residual sugar) and lively. (The average price in supermarkets is $12.80.)

MED/DRY $20 AV

Mahana Méthode Traditionnelle Brut NV (★★★☆)

From Woollaston Estates, the wine on the market in 2010 (★★★☆) is a Nelson sparkling, blended from equal amounts of Chardonnay and Pinot Noir, grown at Upper Moutere, and disgorged after two years on its yeast lees. Faintly pink, it has good freshness, vigour and complexity, with strawberry, biscuit and yeast flavours and a crisp, fully dry finish.

DRY $24 AV

Matua Valley ★★☆

When launched in 2006, this non-vintage wine was a Gisborne blend of Chardonnay (90 per cent) and Muscat, crisp, simple and lively. The wine I tasted in late 2009 (★★☆) tasted like Chardonnay with gentle bubbles, fresh acidity and a slight butteriness.

MED $16 –V

Matua Valley Sparkling Chardonnay (★★☆)

Launched in late 2010, this non-vintage wine (★★☆) was grown in Gisborne. Crisp and lively, with fresh, lemony, appley flavours, it is light and simple, slightly sweet and frothy, with easy-drinking appeal.

MED $15 –V

Matua Valley Sparkling Pinot Gris (★★☆)

The non-vintage wine launched in late 2010 (★★☆) was grown in Gisborne. Fresh and lively, it's a simple but enjoyable wine, lemony, slightly sweet and crisp.

MED $15 –V

Matua Valley Sparkling Sauvignon Blanc (★★★)

Easy to enjoy, the wine launched in late 2010 (★★★) is bouncy and cheerful, with fresh pineapple and lime flavours, crisp, off-dry, lively and zesty.

MED/DRY $15 AV

Mimi (★★★☆)

From Morton Estate, the non-vintage wine on the market in 2010 (★★★☆) is a distinctly medium style (22 grams/litre of residual sugar), appetisingly crisp and vibrant, with citrusy, gently yeasty flavours, showing very good freshness and immediacy. Fine value.

MED $15 V+

Montana Reserve Chardonnay/Pinot Noir Brut Cuvée NV ★★★★

This deliciously easy-drinking wine was the first-ever bottle-fermented bubbly under the Montana label when it was launched in 2006. Unexpectedly stylish (for the price), it is based mostly on Gisborne Chardonnay, with 30 per cent Pinot Noir (mostly from Hawke's Bay), and disgorged after a year of lees-aging in the bottle. It is typically crisp and lively, with elegant fruit flavours, biscuity, nutty, yeasty notes adding complexity, and a dryish (12 grams/litre of residual sugar), lingering finish.

MED/DRY $22 V+

Montana Reserve Chardonnay/Pinot Noir Brut Cuvée NV Rosé ★★★☆

This bottle-fermented sparkling is typically pale pink, with considerable elegance and complexity. Crisp and lively, with strawberryish, yeasty flavours, showing good delicacy, it's a vivacious, dryish wine, priced right.

MED/DRY $22 AV

Morton Black Label Méthode Traditionnelle ★★★★

Still on sale, the 2002 vintage (★★★★), grown mostly at the Riverview Vineyard in Hawke's Bay, is a blend of Pinot Meunier (62 per cent), Pinot Noir (33 per cent) and Chardonnay (5 per cent). Disgorged after over five years on its yeast lees, it is pale straw, with complex, very biscuity and nutty flavours, crisp and dry.

Vintage	02
WR	7
Drink	10-12

MED/DRY $35 –V

Morton Blanc de Blancs ★★★★

Still on the market, the 2000 vintage (★★★★) was made solely from Chardonnay, grown in Hawke's Bay and Marlborough, and disgorged after seven years on its yeast lees. The bouquet is very yeasty; the palate is crisp, citrusy and bready, with good vigour and intensity and a long, nutty, dryish finish.

Vintage	00
WR	6
Drink	10-12

MED/DRY $28 AV

Morton IQ3 (★★★★)

'IQ3' stands for 'improving quietly for three years'. A blend of Chardonnay, Pinot Noir and Pinot Meunier, grown in Hawke's Bay and Marlborough, it started life as Morton Premium Brut, then spent three years on its yeast lees. Pale straw, it is an elegant wine, lemony, appley, nutty and yeasty, with excellent freshness, vigour and crispness.

MED/DRY $25 AV

Morton Premium Brut ★★★☆

This has long been popular as an easy-drinking, creamy-smooth, bottle-fermented bubbly. Blended from Pinot Noir, Chardonnay and Pinot Meunier, grown in Marlborough and Hawke's Bay, and given a full, softening malolactic fermentation, it is disgorged on demand after a minimum of 18 months on its yeast lees, and includes base wine from earlier vintages. It typically shows some elegance and lovely harmony, with crisp, citrusy, appley flavours, very fresh, delicate and lively, and a moderately yeasty finish. The sample I tasted in mid to late 2009 (★★★☆) was fresh, crisp and vigorous, with citrusy, gently yeasty flavours.

MED/DRY $21 AV

Morton Reserve Sec ★★★☆

This pale straw, non-vintage wine is a bottle-fermented blend of Chardonnay, Pinot Noir and Pinot Meunier, grown in Hawke's Bay and disgorged after a minimum of 18 months on its yeast lees. The wine I tasted in mid to late 2009 (★★★☆) was a slightly sweet style with lively, lemony, appley, crisp flavours, a hint of cashew nuts, and good vivacity.

MED/DRY $20 AV

Mount Riley Savée Sparkling Sauvignon Blanc ★★★☆

This Marlborough bubbly is bottle-fermented but made to retain its fresh, tangy varietal characters. The 2009 vintage (★★★☆) is crisp, with tropical-fruit flavours to the fore, some yeasty, creamy notes, and an easy, slightly sweet finish.

MED/DRY $21 AV

Nautilus Cuvée Marlborough ★★★★★

Recent releases of this non-vintage, bottle-fermented sparkling have generally revealed an intensity and refinement that positions the label among the finest in the country. A blend of Pinot Noir (75 per cent) and Chardonnay (25 per cent), it is blended with older, reserve stocks held in old oak barriques and disgorged after a minimum of three years' aging on its yeast lees. Lean and crisp, piercing and long, it's a beautifully tight, vivacious and refined wine, its Marlborough fruit characters enriched with intense, bready aromas and flavours. The wine I tasted in mid to late 2010 (★★★★★) was richly fragrant, slightly citrusy, toasty, nutty and rich, in a very crisp and vivacious style. Intense and yeasty, with a long finish, it has real immediacy.

MED/DRY $39 AV

No. 1 Family Estate Cuvée 10 ★★★★

Celebrating the first decade of Daniel and Adele Le Brun's No. 1 Family Estate, this wine varies in terms of its varietal blend. The current release (★★★☆), based on Chardonnay (65 per cent), Pinot Meunier (20 per cent) and Pinot Noir (15 per cent), was disgorged after four years on its yeast lees. It's a rich, biscuity, slightly buttery wine with loads of flavour and considerable complexity, but less charm and finesse than you'd expect at its high price.

MED/DRY $49 –V

Nobilo Méthode Traditionnelle ★★★☆

The classy 2005 vintage (★★★★) from Constellation NZ is a bottle-fermented blend based on Pinot Noir (46 per cent) and Chardonnay (43 per cent), plus 11 per cent Pinot Meunier. The bouquet is stylish, fresh and slightly nutty; the palate is lean and lively, with good vigour and delicacy and lemony, nutty, yeasty flavours that linger well.

MED/DRY $23 AV

Palliser Estate Martinborough Méthode Traditionnelle ★★★★

This is Martinborough's finest sparkling (although few have been produced). The 2006 vintage (★★★★), made from Pinot Noir and Chardonnay, has a fragrant, complex bouquet, yeasty and biscuity. Richly flavoured, it is fresh, citrusy and toasty, with excellent liveliness and length.

MED/DRY $34 –V

Pelorus ★★★★★

Cloudy Bay's bottle-fermented sparkling is typically a powerful wine, creamy, nutty and full-flavoured. A blend of Pinot Noir and Chardonnay – with always a higher proportion of Pinot Noir – it is given its primary alcoholic fermentation (partly with indigenous yeasts) in a mixture of stainless steel tanks, large oak vats and French oak barriques, followed by malolactic fermentation and lengthy lees-aging of the base wines prior to blending, and once bottled it is matured for three years on its yeast lees before it is disgorged. The pale straw 2006 vintage (★★★★★) is rich, nutty, lively and dry, in a slightly more elegant, less bold and buttery style than some past releases. It's still notably rich, but shows greater delicacy and finesse, with a yeasty, crisp, long finish.

MED/DRY $45 AV

Pelorus NV ★★★★☆

Cloudy Bay's non-vintage Marlborough bubbly is a Chardonnay-dominant style, with 20 per cent Pinot Noir, matured for at least two years on its yeast lees (a year less than for the vintage). It is made in a more fruit-driven style than the vintage, but still refined. The batch on sale in 2010 (★★★★☆) is pale straw, with a very fresh and inviting, citrusy, yeasty bouquet. Vivacious, with incisive, lemony, biscuity, gently yeasty flavours, it is crisp, elegant and refreshing.

MED/DRY $33 AV

Quartz Reef Méthode Traditionnelle NV ★★★★☆

This increasingly Champagne-like, non-vintage bubbly is from a Central Otago company. The batches vary in varietal composition, but the latest release (★★★★★) in 2010 is a blend of Pinot Noir (76 per cent) and Chardonnay (24 per cent), grown at Bendigo. Pale, very lively and racy, with yeasty, nutty flavours, intense, tight-knit and lasting, it is beautifully poised, rich and harmonious. The best NV yet from Quartz Reef.

MED/DRY $30 AV

Quartz Reef Méthode Traditionnelle Rosé (★★★★)

The non-vintage wine (★★★★) released in 2010 is a blend of Pinot Noir (89 per cent) and Chardonnay (11 per cent), grown at Bendigo, in Central Otago. Pink/pale red, it is crisp and vivacious, with strawberryish, slightly spicy and yeasty flavours, showing good intensity, and a dryish finish.

MED/DRY $35 –V

Quartz Reef Méthode Traditionnelle [Vintage] ★★★★★

The 2000–2002 vintages were all outstanding, showing great vigour and complexity in a distinctly Champagne-like style, intense and highly refined. The 2006 vintage (★★★★★) is the first since 2002. A blend of Chardonnay (97 per cent) and Pinot Noir (3 per cent), grown at Bendigo, in Central Otago, it was disgorged after maturing for three years and nine months on its yeast lees. A very elegant, tight-knit wine, it is rich, lemony, yeasty and lively, with a long, crisp, nutty finish.

MED/DRY $40 AV

Riverstone Bubbles (★★☆)

This non-vintage sparkling from Villa Maria is made mostly from Chardonnay. The wine tasted in early 2010 (★★☆) is simple but attractive, with fresh, vibrant, peachy flavours, a sliver of sweetness and a crisp, lively finish.

MED/DRY $13 AV

Rock Ferry Marlborough Blanc de Blancs (★★★☆)

Still very lively, the fragrant 2005 vintage (★★★☆) was made entirely from Chardonnay, grown in The Corners Vineyard, in the Wairau Valley. Bottle-fermented, it is citrusy and limey, gently nutty and yeasty, with a crisp, dryish finish. It's drinking well now.

Vintage	05
WR	6
Drink	10-11

MED/DRY $42 –V

Selaks Winemaker's Favourite Méthode Traditionnelle (★★★★)

The stylish 2006 vintage (★★★★) is a Marlborough blend of Pinot Noir (78 per cent) and Chardonnay (22 per cent). Disgorged after two years on its yeast lees, it is pale straw, very fresh and lively, with tight, citrusy, slightly nutty flavours, showing good delicacy and immediacy.

MED/DRY $25 AV

Shingle Peak Marlborough Sauvignon Blanc (★★★)

From Matua Valley, this non-vintage wine has exactly the same name as its non-sparkling stablemate – but it's a bubbly. Crisp and lively, it is ripely herbaceous, with tropical-fruit flavours and a gentle splash of sweetness in a very easy-drinking, vivacious style.

MED/DRY $20 –V

Sileni Cellar Selection Sparkling Brut (★★★)

Light and lively, the non-vintage wine (★★★) released in 2010 is made from Hawke's Bay Chardonnay. Fermented in tanks, it was matured briefly on its yeast lees, then bottled, without secondary bottle fermentation. It offers fresh lemon/apple flavours, crisp and refreshing, with a touch of nutty, yeasty complexity.

MED/DRY $20 –V

Sileni Cellar Selection Sparkling Rosé (★★★)

The non-vintage wine (★★★) released in 2010 is a vivacious Hawke's Bay bubbly, based principally on Merlot and not bottle-fermented. Pink/pale red, with crisp raspberry and strawberry flavours, it is slightly yeasty, gently sweet and smooth.

MED/DRY $20 –V

Sileni Cellar Selection Sparkling Sauvignon Blanc (★★★)

Launched in 2010, this non-vintage bubbly (★★★) was made from Hawke's Bay grapes, cool-fermented in tanks and bottled young. Slightly sweet and appetisingly crisp, with fresh, ripe fruit flavours, it's an uncomplicated but lively, enjoyable style that makes a stimulating apéritif.

MED/DRY $20 –V

Soljans Fusion Sparkling Muscat ★★★★

Soljans produces this delicious bubbly from Muscat grapes grown in Gisborne. It is fresh and vivacious, perfumed and sweetly seductive (80 grams/litre of residual sugar), with low alcohol (8 per cent), a steady stream of bubbles and rich, lemony, appley flavours, ripe and smooth. An excellent Asti Spumante copy, it's full of easy-drinking charm and bargain-priced.

SW $16 V+

Soljans Fusion Sparkling Rosé (★★★☆)

The light red, non-vintage wine on sale in 2010 (★★★☆) is a Gisborne blend of Pinotage (75 per cent) and Muscat (25 per cent). Lively, with berryish aromas and flavours, it is gently sweet (53 grams/litre of residual sugar), crisp and vibrantly fruity, with great drinkability.

SW $19 V+

Soljans Legacy Méthode Traditionnelle ★★★★

The 2006 vintage (★★★★) is a blend of Pinot Noir and Chardonnay, grown in Marlborough. It's a stylish wine, rich, lively and mouth-wateringly crisp, with peachy, nutty notes and good, yeast-derived complexity.

MED/DRY $32 –V

Spy Valley Echelon Marlborough Méthode Traditionnelle ★★★☆

The 2007 vintage (★★★★) is a blend of Pinot Noir (59 per cent) and Chardonnay (41 per cent). The base wine was fermented and aged for a year in old oak casks, and after its secondary fermentation in the bottle, the wine matured for 18 months on its yeast lees, prior to disgorging. Faintly pink, it's a very distinctive wine, strawberryish, yeasty and richly flavoured, with a slightly creamy texture and an unusually dry (3 grams/litre of residual sugar), long, smooth finish.

DRY $29 –V

Summerhouse Marlborough Blanc de Blancs (★★★★)

Made from estate-grown Chardonnay and lees-aged for two years, this non-vintage wine (★★★★) is attractively scented, lively and crisp, with citrusy, nutty and yeasty flavours, showing good complexity and intensity, and a dryish finish.

MED/DRY $32 –V

Te Hana Sparkling Reserve Cuvée (★★★☆)

The non-vintage wine (★★★☆) from Wither Hills, launched in 2010, is a blend of Chardonnay and Pinot Noir, grown in Gisborne. Pale, with lemony, appley aromas and flavours, it is crisp and dryish, with a gentle yeast influence adding some bready, nutty complexity, and good freshness and vigour.

MED/DRY $18 V+

Trinity Hill 'H' Blanc de Blancs NV (★★★☆)

This elegant, non-vintage wine is made from Hawke's Bay Chardonnay. Following eight months' lees-aging of the base wine in tanks, it was bottle-fermented, then disgorged after the relatively short period of 10 months on its yeast lees. The batch on sale in 2010 (★★★☆) is moderately yeasty and complex, with strong, crisp, citrusy flavours, very lively and refreshing.

MED/DRY $29 –V

Twin Islands Chardonnay/Pinot Noir Brut NV ★★★★

'A great bottle to be seen with in some of the classiest bars and restaurants', Nautilus's lower-priced bubbly sold for $17 a few years ago, then vanished for a while, until its relaunch in late 2009. The price is now $25, but it's worth it. Very fresh, delicate and lively, it's a refined Marlborough wine, lemony and slightly nutty, that floats very smoothly across the palate.

MED/DRY $25 AV

Verde NV ★★★☆

Popular as 'a wedding wine, upmarket from Lindauer', this Hawke's Bay sparkling from Pernod Ricard NZ is based on Chardonnay (60 per cent) and Pinot Noir (to provide a style contrast to the Pinot Noir-dominant Lindauer Special Reserve Brut Cuvée). Matured on its yeast lees for 18 months, it is typically very lively, with lemony, slightly sweet (12 grams/litre of residual sugar) flavours showing good, yeast-derived complexity.

MED/DRY $21 AV

Villa Maria Méthode Traditionnelle NV (★★★★)

Launched in 2009, this is a rich, mature style, based on 68 per cent Pinot Noir (grown in Hawke's Bay and Auckland) and 32 per cent Chardonnay (Marlborough), with base wines dating back to 2003. Disgorged after three years on its yeast lees (and closed with a crown seal, rather than a cork), it's pale yellow, citrusy, yeasty and nutty, with a crisp, almost bone-dry finish (3.5 grams/litre of residual sugar), and excellent complexity and harmony.

DRY $35 –V

Waipara Hills Marlborough Cuvée (★★☆)

The non-vintage wine (★★☆) on sale in 2010 was made from Sauvignon Blanc – as the first sip will tell you. It offers fresh tropical-fruit and herbaceous flavours in a simple but crisp and lively style, offering pleasant, easy drinking.

MED/DRY $21 –V

Waipara Hills Waipara Southern Cuvée (★★★)

Riesling – rather than the more common Chardonnay and Pinot Noir – is the basis of this non-vintage bubbly. It is vibrantly fruity and fresh, although not complex, with plenty of lemony, appley flavour, slightly sweet (19 grams/litre of residual sugar) and crisp.

MED $21 –V

Waipipi Chenin Blanc Brut Méthode Traditionnelle ★★★★

Disgorged from its yeast lees in mid-2009, the 2007 vintage (★★★★) was made from Chenin Blanc grapes, grown at Opaki, north of Masterton, in the Wairarapa. Very fresh and lively, it is light (11 per cent alcohol), with strong, lemony, appley and nutty, gently sweet flavours, fresh, vivacious and racy, with good yeast-derived complexity. Well worth discovering.

Vintage	07	06	05
WR	6	6	6
Drink	10-15	10-13	P

MED/DRY $33 –V

White Cloud Sparkling (★★☆)

A blend of New Zealand and Australian wines, the non-vintage bottling (★★☆) on the market in 2010 is a crisp, medium style with fresh, gently sweet, citrusy aromas and flavours and a distinct hint of pineapple. Lively, easy drinking.

MED $10 AV

Rosé Wines

The number of rosé labels on the market has exploded recently, as drinkers discover that rosé is not an inherently inferior lolly water, but a worthwhile and delicious wine style in its own right. New Zealand rosé is even finding offshore markets (62,111 cases shipped in the year to June 2010, a steep rise from 905 cases in 2003) and collecting overseas awards.

In Europe many pink or copper-coloured wines, such as the rosés of Provence, Anjou and Tavel, are produced from red-wine varieties. (Dark-skinned grapes are even used to make white wines: Champagne, heavily based on Pinot Meunier and Pinot Noir, is a classic case.) To make a rosé, after the grapes are crushed, the time the juice spends in contact with its skins is crucial; the longer the contact, the greater the diffusion of colour, tannin and flavour from the skins into the juice.

'Saignée' (bled) is a French term that is seen occasionally on rosé labels. A technique designed to produce a pink wine or a more concentrated red wine – or both – it involves running off or 'bleeding' free-run juice from crushed, dark-skinned grapes after a brief, pre-ferment maceration on skins. An alternative is to commence the fermentation as for a red wine, then after 12 or 24 hours, when its colour starts to deepen, drain part of the juice for rosé production and vinify the rest as a red wine.

Pinot Noir and Merlot are the grape varieties most commonly used in New Zealand to produce rosé wines. Regional differences are emerging. South Island and Wairarapa rosés, usually made from Pinot Noir, are typically fresh, slightly sweet and crisp, while those from the middle and upper North Island – Hawke's Bay, Gisborne and Auckland – tend to be Merlot-based, fuller-bodied and drier.

These are typically charming, 'now-or-never' wines, peaking in their first six to 18 months with seductive strawberry/raspberry-like fruit flavours. Freshness is the essence of the wines' appeal.

Ake Ake Vineyard Rosé (★★★★)

A good buy. Grown at Kerikeri, in Northland, the 2010 vintage (★★★★) was made mostly from Chambourcin, with some Merlot and Cabernet Franc. Bright, light red in hue, it is mouthfilling (14.5 per cent alcohol), ripe and rounded, with fresh cherry, red-berry and spice flavours, showing excellent delicacy, vibrancy and richness, and a bone-dry but balanced finish.

Vintage	10
WR	6
Drink	10-11

DRY $18 V+

Alexia Hawke's Bay Rosé ★★★☆

The 2009 vintage (★★★) is pale red, with mouthfilling body, fresh, gentle berry and spice flavours and a slightly sweet, smooth finish. Drink now.

MED/DRY $18 V+

Alpha Domus The Pilot Hawke's Bay Rosé (★★☆)

Pink, with a slight orange tint, the 2009 vintage (★★☆) is smooth, with strawberry, spice and herb flavours showing some development. Ready.

Vintage	09
WR	5
Drink	10-12

DRY $20 –V

Amisfield Saignée Rosé ★★★★
Made from Pinot Noir, estate-grown in the Cromwell Basin and tank-fermented. The 2010 vintage (★★★★☆) of this Central Otago wine is a beauty. Bright pink, it is invitingly scented, with buoyant strawberry and spice flavours, showing lovely delicacy, harmony and depth. Hard to resist.

Vintage	10	09	08
WR	6	5	6
Drink	10-12	10-11	10-12

DRY $25 AV

Artisan Oratia Rosé (★★☆)
Grown in West Auckland, the 2009 vintage (★★☆) was made mostly from Syrah, with a small portion of Gamay Noir. Showing some development, it's a dry style (4 grams/litre of residual sugar), with slightly herbal, strawberry and spice flavours. Ready.

DRY $19 –V

Ascension The Rosarian Matakana Rosé ★★★
Pink-hued and lively, this has typically been a Merlot-based rosé – with smaller portions of such grapes as Malbec, Pinotage and Cabernet Franc – fresh and vibrant, with crisp, strawberryish, spicy flavours.

MED/DRY $24 –V

Askerne Hawke's Bay Rosé ★★★
The 2010 vintage (★★★) is a full-bodied Hawke's Bay wine (13.5 per cent alcohol) with pink/pale red colour. Fresh and lively, it has strawberry and spice flavours, with a sliver of sweetness (5 grams/litre of residual sugar) and lots of drink-young appeal.

Vintage	10	09
WR	6	6
Drink	10-11	P

MED/DRY $16 V+

Ata Rangi Summer Rosé ★★★☆
The 2009 vintage (★★★☆) is a blend of Merlot (mostly) and Cabernet Sauvignon, grown in Martinborough and Hawke's Bay. Pale red, it is full-bodied, with satisfying depth of berryish, slightly spicy flavours and a finely balanced, dry finish.

DRY $18 V+

Awaroa Waiheke Island Rosé (★★)
The 2009 vintage (★★) was estate-grown and hand-picked. A pink/red blend of Syrah (70 per cent) and Cabernet Sauvignon (30 per cent), it is medium-bodied, with smooth, berry and herb flavours, showing a slight lack of freshness and vibrancy.

DRY $18 –V

Bannock Brae Cathy's Rosé ★★★☆

Named after the partnership's 'better-looking half' and still available, the 2008 vintage (★★★☆) was made from estate-grown, Central Otago Pinot Noir. Bright pink/red, it is still fresh, with red-berry and spice flavours, showing good depth, and a slightly sweet (7 grams/litre of residual sugar), rounded finish.

Vintage	08	MED/DRY $24 –V
WR	6	
Drink	10-12	

Bascand Waipara Rosé (★★★)

The pale pink/slight orange 2009 vintage (★★★) was made from Pinot Noir. Still fresh, it's a full-bodied, medium-dry wine (12 grams/litre of residual sugar), with balanced acidity and smooth, red-berry and strawberry flavours. A very easy-drinking style.

MED/DRY $17 AV

Butterfish Bay Northland Paewhenua Rose (★★★☆)

Grown on a peninsula extending into Mangonui Harbour, the 2009 vintage (★★★☆) is a good debut. Pink/pale red, with red-berry aromas, it's a medium-bodied wine, vibrantly fruity, with plenty of slightly sweet (7 grams/litre of residual sugar), plummy flavour.

MED/DRY $19 V+

Cable Bay Waiheke Island Rosé ★★★★

Waiheke Island is producing excellent rosés, such as the 2010 vintage (★★★★) from Cable Bay. Made from Merlot and Malbec grapes, grown at Church Bay, it is pink/red and full-bodied, with smooth, raspberry and spice flavours, showing very good depth and texture. It's a 'serious' style of rosé, designed to accompany food.

Vintage	10	DRY $20 V+
WR	7	
Drink	10-12	

Cambridge Road Arohanui Martinborough Pinot Syrah Rosé (★★★★☆)

The classy 2009 vintage (★★★★☆) is a blend of Pinot Noir (72 per cent) and Syrah (28 per cent). Pale pink, it is weighty, with concentrated strawberry and spice flavours and a bone-dry finish. A 'serious' style of rosé, it's full of personality.

Vintage	09	DRY $28 AV
WR	6	
Drink	10-12	

Cambridge Road Papillon Martinborough Rosé (★★★★)

The 2009 vintage (★★★★) is a single-vineyard blend of Pinot Noir (76 per cent) and Syrah (24 per cent), made in an off-dry (5.3 grams/litre of residual sugar) style. Light pink/red, it is strawberryish and smooth, with excellent freshness, texture and depth. Delicious now.

Vintage	09	MED/DRY $22 V+
WR	5	
Drink	10-11	

Clearview Estate Black Reef Blush ★★★★

A top buy. Delicious in its youth, the 2009 vintage (★★★★) is a full-bodied wine, grown at Te Awanga, in Hawke's Bay. Based on the French hybrid, Chambourcin, it is bright pink/pale red, with a floral bouquet and strong red-berry and plum flavours, refreshingly crisp and dry (3 grams/litre of residual sugar).

Vintage	09	08	07
WR	7	6	6
Drink	10-11	P	P

DRY $17 V+

Coal Pit Central Otago Rosé (★★★)

Estate-grown at Gibbston, the 2009 vintage (★★★) was made from Pinot Noir. Pale red, it has fresh, berryish aromas, mouthfilling body and good depth of berryish, slightly spicy and herbal flavour, crisp and lively.

Vintage	09
WR	7
Drink	10-11

MED/ DRY $20 –V

Coopers Creek Huapai Rosé ★★★☆

Enjoyable from the start, the 2010 vintage (★★★☆) is an estate-grown blend of Malbec and Merlot. Pink/pale red, it is full-bodied, fresh, berryish, plummy and smooth, in a dryish style (5 grams/litre of residual sugar) with lots of drink-young charm.

MED/DRY $17 V+

Desert Heart Saignée Rosé ★★★☆

Pale pink, the vivacious 2009 vintage (★★★★) was made from Pinot Noir, grown at Bannockburn, in Central Otago, and aged for six months in seasoned French oak barrels. Showing good freshness and delicacy, it has strawberry, spice and slight apricot flavours, dry, very lively and lingering.

DRY $23 –V

Dolbel Estate Hawke's Bay Rosé (★★★☆)

Made from Merlot and briefly oak-aged, the pale pink 2008 vintage (★★★☆) is a dry style, designed for the table rather than as an apéritif. Mouthfilling, with gentle strawberry and spice flavours, it shows greater complexity than most rosés.

DRY $20 AV

Domaine Georges Michel Summer Folly Rosé Pinot Noir ★★☆

Grown in Marlborough, the 2009 vintage (★★★) has a bright, light red colour, with berry and spice aromas and flavours, fresh, lively and smooth.

DRY $15 AV

Domain Road Central Otago Pinot Noir Rosé ★★★★

Full of drink-young charm, the 2009 vintage (★★★★) is scented and pink, with fresh, lively raspberry, strawberry and spice flavours, dryish, finely balanced and lingering. The 2010 (★★★★), partly barrel-fermented, has an inviting, bright pink hue and a floral, scented bouquet. Mouthfilling, it has fresh, delicate strawberry and spice flavours, a hint of peaches and a dry (3 grams/litre of residual sugar) finish.

DRY $24 AV

Drumsara Central Otago Pinot Rosé (★★★☆)

Grown at Alexandra, the 2009 vintage (★★★☆) is bright pink, with fresh, berryish, slightly spicy flavours, showing good delicacy and depth. It's a fully dry style, crisp and appetising.

DRY $25 –V

Elephant Hill Rosé (★★★☆)

Made from Central Otago Pinot Noir, the 2009 vintage (★★★☆) is bright pink, floral and fresh, with attractive, strawberryish flavours, showing good delicacy and depth. Vibrantly fruity and soft, it's a drink-young charmer.

MED/DRY $20 AV

Esk Valley Merlot/Malbec Rosé ★★★★★

This has been clearly New Zealand's best rosé over the past decade, with several trophies to prove it. There is no 2009. The 2010 vintage (★★★★) is a Hawke's Bay blend of Merlot (94 per cent) and Malbec (6 per cent). Handled without oak, it's a mouthfilling, dry wine (4 grams/litre of residual sugar) with attractive, bright pink colour and fresh, ripe berryish scents. Fleshy and generous, it has smooth, berryish, plummy, slightly spicy flavours, lively and refreshing.

Vintage	10	09	08	07
WR	7	NM	6	6
Drink	11-12	NM	P	P

DRY $24 V+

Fossil Ridge Rosé ★★★

Pale pink, the easy-drinking 2009 vintage (★★★) is a hand-picked, single-vineyard Nelson Pinot Noir, gently sweet (10 grams/litre of residual sugar), with strawberryish, slightly spicy flavours, fresh and smooth.

MED/DRY $20 –V

Framingham F-Series Montepulciano Rosato (★★★★)

Bright pink, the instantly attractive 2010 vintage (★★★★) was made from Montepulciano grapes, grown in Marlborough. It's a vivacious wine, off-dry (5 grams/litre of residual sugar), with vibrant, delicate flavours of raspberries and strawberries, showing lovely freshness and harmony.

Vintage	10
WR	6
Drink	10-12

MED/DRY $25 AV

Gibbston Valley Blanc de Pinot Noir ★★★☆

This Central Otago wine 'will make truck drivers weep for the agonising beauty of the world'. The 2009 vintage (★★★☆) is bright pink/pale red, mouthfilling and fresh, with vibrantly plummy, spicy flavours, crisp and slightly sweet. A good summer thirst-quencher.

MED/DRY $28 –V

Gibson Bridge Marlborough Pinot Rosé (★★★)

Pale pink, with a hint of orange, the 2009 vintage (★★★) is based on Pinot Gris, with a dash of Pinot Noir. Fruity and smooth (4.7 grams/litre of residual sugar), it has strawberry, peach and spice flavours, dryish, fresh and lively.

DRY $22 –V

Gillman Matakana Clairet (★★★☆)

The 2009 vintage (★★★☆) is closer to a light red than a rosé. Made from Cabernet Franc and Merlot, it was matured for a year in oak casks (50 per cent new). Pale red in hue, it is berryish and spicy, developed and smooth, with considerable complexity, gentle tannins, and an enjoyable mellowness. Drink now.

Vintage	09
WR	6
Drink	11-19

DRY $45 –V

Gladstone Vineyard Rosé ★★★

Grown in the northern Wairarapa, the 2009 vintage (★★★) is pink/pale red, with strawberry and spice aromas and flavours, a hint of herbs, and a fresh, smooth (4 grams/litre of residual sugar) finish.

DRY $22 –V

Greystone Waipara Rosé Pinot Noir (★★★☆)

Full of drink-young appeal, the 2009 vintage (★★★☆) is bright pink/red, mouthfilling and smooth, with berryish, slightly spicy flavours, showing good depth. It's an easy-drinking, slightly sweet style (14 grams/litre of residual sugar).

MED/DRY $19 V+

Hincho Matakana Merlot Rosé (★★)

Created 'to enhance the foods of a Matakana long lunch', the 2008 vintage (★★) is an off-dry style with slightly developed colour and simple berry, spice and herb flavours.

MED/DRY $20 –V

Hitchen Road Rosé ★★★☆

Estate-grown at Pokeno, in North Waikato, the salmon-pink 2010 vintage (★★★☆) was made from hand-picked Pinotage. Full-bodied (14.5 per cent alcohol), it has gentle, berryish flavours, fresh, lively, ripe and rounded, with a dry finish. Fine value.

Vintage	10	09
WR	7	7
Drink	10-12	10-12

DRY $15 V+

Huia Marlborough Rosé (★★★)

Grown in the Brancott Valley, the 2009 vintage (★★★) is a blend of Merlot and Malbec. Pale pink, it's a dryish style (5.5 grams/litre of residual sugar), mouthfilling, berryish, slightly savoury and spicy.

Vintage	09
WR	7
Drink	10-12

MED/DRY $23 –V

Hunter's Marlborough Rosé ★★★☆

Enjoyable summer sipping, the 2009 vintage (★★★☆) is bright, pale red, very fresh and smooth, with red-berry and plum flavours, showing good depth, and a finely balanced, off-dry (8 grams/litre of residual sugar) finish.

Vintage	09
WR	4
Drink	10-11

MED/DRY $15 V+

Johner Estate Wairarapa Pinot Noir Rosé ★★★☆

The pale pink 2009 vintage (★★★☆) has substantial body, strawberry, spice and apricot flavours, showing good delicacy and harmony, and a dryish finish. The 2010 (★★★☆) is similar – pale pink, crisp and dryish, with strawberry and spice flavours, very fresh and lively.

MED/DRY $18 V+

Judge Rock Central Otago Rosé (★★★★)

Already delicious, the 2010 vintage (★★★★) was made from Pinot Noir, grown at Alexandra and fermented in seasoned oak barriques. Bright, pale pink, it is mouthfilling and vivacious, with strawberry and spice flavours, showing greater complexity than most rosés, a sliver of sweetness, and excellent freshness and harmony.

MED/DRY $20 V+

Jules Taylor Gisborne Rosé ★★★☆

Not identified by region, the charming 2009 vintage (★★★★) from this Marlborough-based producer is a very pretty wine, slightly sweet, smooth and delicious from the start. The 2010 (★★★☆), labelled as of Gisborne origin, is bright pink/pale red, floral, fresh and smooth, with vibrant raspberry, strawberry and spice flavours, offering very easy drinking.

Vintage	10	09
WR	7	5
Drink	10-13	10-12

MED/DRY $22 AV

Julicher Rosé (★★★)

The floral, fresh 2008 vintage (★★★) is a Martinborough wine, based entirely on Pinot Noir. Strawberryish, spicy and smooth, it has a hint of sweetness and plenty of drink-young charm.

MED/DRY $20 –V

Jurassic Ridge Waiheke Island Syrah Rosé (★★★★★)

The bright pink/red 2009 vintage (★★★★★) is fleshy, dry and rich, with sweet-fruit characters and strong, vibrant, berry and spice flavours. Hand-picked at Church Bay, it's a serious yet charming wine, already delicious.

DRY $29 V+

Kerr Farm Vineyard Bella Rosa (★★★)

Estate-grown in West Auckland, the 2009 vintage (★★★) was made from Pinotage. Light pink, it is fruity and very smooth, with gentle strawberry, spice and herb flavours. It's a very easy-drinking wine, with an obvious splash of sweetness.

MED/DRY $20 –V

Kina Beach Vineyard Nelson Merlot Rosé ★★★

The 2010 vintage (★★★) includes 15 per cent Cabernet Franc. Bright pink, it's a medium-bodied, smooth wine with plum, spice and slight herb flavours, showing good depth, and a rounded (8 grams/litre of residual sugar) finish.

Vintage	10	09	08
WR	6	6	6
Drink	10-12	10-11	P

MED/DRY $20 –V

Kirkpatrick Estate Patutahi Gisborne Wild Rosé (★★★☆)

The 2009 vintage (★★★☆) is pink/slight orange, with mouthfilling body and a splash of sweetness (7 grams/litre of residual sugar). Strawberry and spice-flavoured, it is buoyantly fruity, with very good delicacy and depth.

Vintage	09
WR	5
Drink	10-11

MED/DRY $18 V+

Kumeu River Village Pinot Rosé (★★☆)

The 2009 vintage (★★☆) was made from Pinot Noir grown at Kumeu, in West Auckland. Pink/pale red, with earthy aromas, it is light to medium-bodied, with strawberry and spice flavours, gentle tannins and a dry finish.

DRY $18 –V

La Strada Marlborough Rosé (★★★☆)

Produced by the Fromm winery, the 2009 vintage (★★★☆) is a bone-dry blend of Merlot (80 per cent) and Pinot Noir (20 per cent). Pale pink, it is mouthfilling, fresh and berryish, with finely balanced acidity and very good depth.

DRY $20 AV

Lawson's Dry Hills Pinot Rosé ★★★

Floral, with pink/pale red colour, the 2009 vintage (★★★) of this Marlborough wine is fresh and medium-bodied, with lively red-berry and plum flavours, a sliver of sweetness and a refreshingly crisp finish.

Vintage	09	08	07
WR	7	6	7
Drink	P	P	P

MED/DRY $20 –V

Locharburn Central Otago Pinot Rosé ★★★☆

Grown at Lowburn, the 2009 vintage (★★★☆) was made from Pinot Noir, hand-picked at 24–25 brix, and 15 per cent of the blend was fermented in a seasoned French oak puncheon. Pink-hued, it offers smooth, easy drinking (7 grams/litre of residual sugar), with vibrant strawberry and spice aromas and flavours, a hint of apricots and mouthfilling body.

Vintage	09	08
WR	6	5
Drink	10-11	P

MED/DRY $23 –V

Lochiel Estate Mangawhai Rosé (★★★☆)

The attractive 2009 vintage (★★★☆) was made from Merlot, grown in Northland. Bright pink/light red, with fresh, berryish scents, it is full-bodied, with vibrant raspberry and spice flavours, buoyantly fruity, crisp and dryish.

MED/DRY $20 AV

Lowburn Ferry Central Otago Pinot Rosé (★★★★)

Delicious from the start, the 2009 vintage (★★★★) is a vibrantly fruity, crisp, dry style (3 grams/litre of residual sugar), bright pink, with mouthfilling body (14 per cent alcohol) and fresh, strong berry and spice flavours, showing excellent delicacy and immediacy.

DRY $24 AV

Mahurangi River Pretty in Pink Merlot Rosé (★★★)

Launched from the 2010 vintage (★★★), this is a medium style (20 grams/litre of residual sugar). From Merlot grapes, estate-grown at Matakana, it is bright pink, with plenty of fresh, crisp, berryish, spicy, slightly peachy flavour and an easy-drinking charm.

MED $24 –V

Maimai Creek Hawke's Bay Rosé ★★★

Full-bodied and smooth, the easy-drinking 2009 vintage (★★★) is bright, light red, with plenty of berryish, spicy flavour and a rounded finish. Ready.

DRY $18 AV

Man O' War Waiheke Island Rosé (★★★★)

Almost a light red style, the 2009 vintage (★★★★) was made from Merlot and bottled with 'a pleasant spritz of carbon dioxide'. Mouthfilling, it has deep berry and spice flavours, a hint of herbs and a smooth finish. Weighty, fresh, ripe and rounded, it's an instantly appealing wine. Drink now.

DRY $25 AV

Maori Point Central Otago Pinot Noir Rosé (★★★☆)

Grown at Tarras, the pink/orange 2008 vintage (★★★☆) is a mouthfilling, dryish style (5.5 grams/litre of residual sugar) with strong, smooth berry and spice flavours, hints of apricots and peaches, and a lingering finish. Ready.

Vintage	08
WR	6
Drink	10-12

MED/DRY $19 V+

Margrain Pinot Rosé ★★★☆

The 2008 vintage (★★★☆), grown in Martinborough, is bright pink/light red, with good depth and delicacy of berry, plum and spice flavours, crisp, slightly sweet (11.8 grams/litre of residual sugar) and lively.

Vintage	09
WR	6
Drink	P

MED/DRY $24 –V

Marsden Bay of Islands Rosé ★★★

From Merlot grapes grown in Northland, the 2010 vintage (★★★☆) is balanced for easy drinking, with a gentle splash of sweetness (7 grams/litre of residual sugar). Pink/pale red, it is medium-bodied, fresh, lively and smooth, with very good depth of plum, red-berry and spice flavours, vibrant and refreshing.

MED/DRY $18 AV

Martinborough Vineyard Rosé ★★★☆

Made from Pinot Noir, the 2009 vintage (★★★☆) is floral, vibrantly fruity and berryish, with bright, light red colour, loads of charm and a deliciously smooth, off-dry (8 grams/litre of residual sugar) finish.

MED/DRY $20 (375ML) –V

Matahiwi Hawke's Bay Rosé (★★)

The 2009 vintage (★★) is pale red, berryish and smooth, but lacks the freshness and vibrancy to rate higher.

Vintage	09
WR	5
Drink	P

MED/DRY $19 –V

Matua Valley Matua Road Rosé (★★★)

Enjoyable from the start, the 2009 vintage (★★★) is bright pink/light red, with berryish aromas and flavours, a sliver of sweetness and good harmony. It's a fresh, very easy-drinking style, priced right.

MED/DRY $12 V+

Matua Valley North Island Rosé ★★★

Designed to go 'with a bit of shade from the sun, a book and the cricket on the radio', the 2009 vintage (★★★☆) was made in a gently sweet style (6 grams/litre of residual sugar). Bright pink/red, with fresh, raspberryish aromas, it's a full-bodied wine with strong red-berry and plum flavours, very smooth and harmonious.

MED/DRY $15 V+

Millton Te Arai Vineyard Merlot Rosé ★★★★

Enjoyed during summer in 'bars, cafés and back gardens all around the country', this very easy-drinking wine is grown in Gisborne and made in an off-dry style. Bright pink/red, it is typically vibrantly fruity, with ripe berry, plum and spice flavours, refreshing acidity and a floral bouquet.

MED $21 V+

Miro Vineyard Rosé ★★★

Grown at Onetangi, on Waiheke Island, the 2009 vintage (★★★) is a blend of Merlot and Cabernet Franc. Pale pink, it is medium-bodied, with fresh, ripe, berryish, peachy flavours and a fully dry finish.

DRY $22 –V

Mission Hawke's Bay Rosé ★★☆

The 2009 vintage (★★★) is pink/slight orange, with high alcohol (14.5 per cent) and generous, berryish, spicy flavours, dry and smooth. (The 2010 is again a fully dry style.)

DRY $17 –V

Montana East Coast Rosé ★★★

This easy-drinking wine from Pernod Ricard NZ is medium-bodied, with Merlot as the key variety, blended with such grapes as Pinotage, Pinot Noir and Cabernet Franc. The 2008 vintage (★★★) is crisp, with raspberry and spice flavours, slightly sweet and smooth.

MED/DRY $18 AV

Morton Estate Musetta Hawke's Bay Rosé ★★★☆

The 2009 vintage (★★★) was made from Malbec. Light red, it is freshly aromatic, with vibrant flavours of red berries, smooth and lingering.

Vintage	09
WR	6
Drink	10-11

DRY $18 V+

Mount Dottrel Central Otago Saignée Rosé ★★★★

The charming 2009 vintage (★★★★), made from Pinot Noir, was estate-grown, hand-picked and partly (20 per cent) fermented in seasoned French oak barriques. Bright pink, it is weighty (14 per cent alcohol) and fleshy, with vibrant flavours of strawberries and spices, showing excellent depth and harmony, a touch of complexity, and a dry (4 grams/litre of residual sugar) finish.

Vintage	09	08
WR	6	7
Drink	10-11	P

DRY $23 AV

Mt Rosa Rosé ★★☆

The 2009 vintage (★★☆) is a Central Otago wine, bright pink, with fresh, smooth berry, plum and herb flavours, a slightly earthy streak and a crisp, dry finish (4 grams/litre of residual sugar).

DRY $22 –V

Muddy Water Growers' Series Waipara Rosé ★★★★

The 2010 vintage (★★★★) is a great buy. Made from Pinot Noir, it is bright pink/pale red, with a floral bouquet, strong, vibrant raspberry and spice flavours, and a crisp, finely balanced, dry (4 grams/litre of residual sugar) finish.

Vintage	10	09
WR	6	7
Drink	10-12	10-11

DRY $15 V+

Nikau Point Hawke's Bay Rosé (★★☆)

From Morton Estate, the 2009 vintage (★★☆) is a very easy-drinking style with bright, light red colour and fresh red-berry, plum and herb flavours, slightly sweet and smooth.

MED/DRY $16 AV

Northburn Station Central Otago Rosé (★★★)

Made from Pinot Noir grown in the Cromwell Basin, the 2010 vintage (★★★) has bright red colour, deep for a rosé. Fresh, berryish aromas lead into a crisp, plummy, berryish wine with plenty of flavour and an off-dry, crisp finish.

MED/DRY $23 –V

Northfield Waipara Valley Rosé (★★★)

From Pinot Noir grown in the Home Creek Vineyard, the 2009 vintage (★★★) is bright pink, with plenty of strawberryish, smooth flavour, woven with fresh acidity. It's still very lively; drink this summer.

MED/DRY $19 AV

Oak Hill Matakana Merlot Rosé (★★)

Now a bit past its best, the 2008 vintage (★★) was blended with a small portion of Pinot Gris and made in a bone-dry style. The colour is slightly developed; the flavours are plummy and spicy, but starting to lose freshness and charm.

DRY $18 –V

Odyssey Marlborough Rosé ★★★☆

Made from estate-grown Pinot Noir, the thirst-quenching 2009 vintage (★★★☆) is bright pink/pale red, with good body and depth of berryish flavours, fresh and vibrant, and a crisp, dry finish.

DRY $19 V+

Olssen's Summer Dreaming Pinot Noir Rosé ★★★☆

Estate-grown at Bannockburn, in Central Otago, the 2009 vintage (★★★★) was hand-picked at 24 brix and partly barrel-fermented. An enticing, bright pink, it shows good freshness and vibrancy, with delicate strawberry and spice flavours, a splash of sweetness (7.7 grams/litre of residual sugar) and a refreshingly crisp finish.

MED/DRY $25 –V

Omaha Bay Vineyard Matakana Rosé (★★★★)

Made from Syrah, the 2009 vintage (★★★★) has an inviting, bright pink colour. It's a very attractive wine, softly mouthfilling, very fresh and delicate, with an array of plum, spice and strawberry flavours, showing lovely harmony.

Vintage	09
WR	6
Drink	10-12

MED/DRY $20 V+

Passage Rock Waiheke Island Rosé ★★★☆

The 2009 vintage (★★★☆) is a blend of Malbec, Merlot and Syrah. 'Best consumed within 24 hours of purchase', it is pink/red, fleshy and smooth, with good depth of berry, plum and spice flavours, fresh, slightly sweet, and finely balanced for easy, summer drinking.

MED/DRY $22 AV

Paulownia Rosé (★★☆)

Grown in the northern Wairarapa, the 2009 vintage (★★☆) is light and smooth, with gentle, strawberryish flavours, offering very easy drinking.

MED/DRY $15 AV

Peacock Sky Rosé (★★★)

The 2009 vintage (★★★) is a Waiheke Island blend of estate-grown Cabernet Sauvignon, Cabernet Franc, Malbec and Merlot. It's an off-dry style, fresh and vibrant, with red-berry and spice flavours, and a very smooth finish.

MED/DRY $25 –V

Poderi Crisci Rosé (★★☆)

The 2009 vintage (★★☆) was grown on Waiheke Island and made from Merlot. Pale pink, it has ripe, berryish, spicy, slightly peachy flavours, showing decent depth, and a fully dry finish.

Vintage	09
WR	5
Drink	10-11

DRY $20 –V

Poverty Bay Riverpoint Rosé (★★★★★)

Delicious from the start, the 2009 vintage (★★★★★) was made from vines planted in 1985 by Matawhero at Bridge Estate Vineyard, in Gisborne. A blend of Merlot and Malbec, it is pink/pale red, mouthfilling and smooth, with ripe strawberry and spice flavours, showing lovely richness and harmony. Fleshy and rounded, it has greater body and flavour depth than the vast majority of New Zealand rosés, yet retains freshness and charm.

MED/DRY $20 V+

Richmond Plains Nelson Blanc de Noir ★★★

Made from hand-picked Pinot Noir, the 2009 vintage (★★★) is faintly pink, but more of a white wine than a rosé. Showing good personality, it is medium-bodied, with peachy, slightly spicy flavours, slightly sweet, refreshingly crisp and lively.

MED/DRY $20 –V

Rockburn Stolen Kiss ★★★☆

The refreshing 2010 vintage (★★★) showcases 'the sweetly frivolous and fruity side of Central Otago Pinot Noir'. Bright, light pink, with gentle strawberry, peach and spice flavours, it offers smooth, easy drinking, with a slightly sweet, appetisingly crisp finish.

MED/DRY $20 AV

Selaks Premium Selection Rosé ★★☆

Still on sale, the 2008 vintage (★★☆), grown in Gisborne, is pale red/slight orange. It's a slightly sweet wine, berryish and green-edged.

MED/DRY $18 –V

Shaky Bridge Pinot Noir Rosé (★★★)

The 2009 vintage (★★★), grown in Central Otago, was made in an off-dry (8 grams/litre of residual sugar) style. Bright pink, it is full-bodied, with good depth of strawberry and spice flavours, ripe and smooth.

MED/DRY $16 V+

Sileni Cellar Selection Hawke's Bay Cabernet Franc Rosé ★★★☆

The 2009 vintage (★★★☆) is a dryish style (5.8 grams/litre of residual sugar). Pink/pale red, with strawberryish, spicy aromas, it is fresh and lively, with good body and roundness, and greater character and depth than many rosés.

Vintage	09	08	07
WR	5	6	6
Drink	10-12	P	P

MED/DRY $20 AV

Soho Hawke's Bay Rosé ★★★

The 2009 vintage (★★★) is bright pink/light red, with strawberry and spice flavours, fresh, lively and balanced for easy drinking.

MED/DRY $21 –V

Soho Waiheke Island Rosé ★★★☆

The 2010 vintage (★★★★) is pink/pale red, with mouthfilling body, sweet-fruit delights and very good depth of fresh, ripe berry and plum flavours. It's a buoyantly fruity wine, delicious young.

MED/DRY $22 AV

Southbank Estate Marlborough Sauvignon Pink ★★★

It's not labelled as a rosé, but the 2009 vintage (★★★) looks and tastes like one. Pale pink – following the addition of a splash of red – it has gentle strawberry and spice flavours, showing good freshness and liveliness, and a dry (3.5 grams/litre of residual sugar), crisp finish.

DRY $20 –V

Stonecroft Hawke's Bay Rosé (★★★☆)

The debut 2010 vintage (★★★☆) is a blend of Cabernet Sauvignon and Syrah. Bright pink, it's a good food wine, fully dry, with ripe red-berry and spice flavours, a hint of peaches, and good freshness and vivacity.

DRY $21 AV

Stoneleigh Marlborough Pinot Noir Rosé ★★★

Grown in the Wairau Valley, the pretty 2009 vintage (★★★) is a fresh, off-dry style with smooth strawberry and spice flavours, showing an easy-drinking charm.

MED/DRY $21 –V

Stone Paddock Jolie Rosé (★★★)

The 2009 vintage (★★★) is a fresh Hawke's Bay rosé, blended from Merlot (90 per cent) and Malbec (10 per cent). Pale red, it has good body and depth of red-berry flavours, vibrant and crisp.

MED/DRY $20 –V

Takatu Poppies Rosé (★★★☆)

Grown at Matakana, the 2009 vintage (★★★☆) is a single-vineyard blend of Merlot and Cabernet Franc. Matured in seasoned French oak casks, it's a bone-dry style with full, pink colour. Mouthfilling, with ripe strawberry and spice flavours, it shows good complexity, with plenty of personality.

Vintage	10	09
WR	7	7
Drink	10-13	10-12

DRY $25 –V

Tarras Vineyards Florian Pinot Noir Rosé (★★★☆)

A dry style, the 2008 vintage (★★★☆) is a bright pink, mouthfilling Central Otago wine, fully barrel-fermented. It's a full-bodied wine, with plenty of plummy, spicy flavour and a creamy-smooth finish.

Vintage	08
WR	7
Drink	10-12

DRY $28 –V

Tarras Vineyards Rosé (★★★☆)

The bright pink 2008 vintage (★★★☆) is a Central Otago wine, made from Pinot Noir and 20 per cent barrel-fermented. It shows very good body and depth of fresh berry/spice flavours and a crisp, dry finish.

DRY $20 AV

Tatty Bogler Otago Pinot Noir Rosé (★★★★)

Fresh and floral, the 2010 vintage (★★★★) from Forrest has raspberryish scents and an inviting, pink/red hue. It's a deliciously fresh wine with vibrant red-berry and plum flavours, showing good immediacy, and a smooth (7 grams/litre of residual sugar) finish.

Vintage	10
WR	7
Drink	10-11

MED/DRY $25 AV

Te Henga The Westie Rosé (★★★)

From Babich, the 2008 vintage (★★★) is a blend of Merlot and Pinotage, grown in the North Island. Pale red/slight orange, it is still fresh, with ripe strawberry and spice flavours, lively, finely balanced and dry.

DRY $16 V+

Te Kairanga East Coast Rosé (★★★)

Still on sale, the 2008 vintage (★★★) is pink/pale red, with satisfying body, good depth of strawberry and spice flavours and a smooth, dryish finish.

MED/DRY $17 AV

Te Mania Nelson Pinot Noir Rosé ★★★

Bright pink, the 2009 vintage (★★★☆) has mouthfilling body and fresh, finely balanced strawberry and spice flavours, crisp, lively, dryish and strong.

MED/DRY $19 AV

Te Whau Rosé of Merlot ★★★★☆

Grown on Waiheke Island, the 2009 vintage (★★★★) is rare – only 290 bottles were made. Barrel-fermented with indigenous yeasts, it's a fully dry style, pale pink, mouthfilling and smooth, with strawberry and apricot flavours, a very subtle oak influence and excellent complexity and concentration.

DRY $35 –V

Ti Point Matakana Coast Rosé (★★★☆)

Estate-grown at Leigh, near Matakana, the 2010 vintage (★★★☆) was made from early-picked Merlot grapes. Bright pink, it's a 'serious', food-friendly style, unusually dry (2.3 grams/litre of residual sugar) for a rosé, with very good depth of berryish, slightly spicy flavour, fresh and lively.

DRY $22 AV

Torlesse Rosé (★★☆)

The non-vintage bottling on sale in 2010 (★★☆) is not identified by region, but was made from Pinot Noir. Pink/pale red, it is medium-bodied and berryish, with hints of herbs and spices, and a slightly sweet, crisp finish.

MED/DRY $15 AV

Trinity Hill Hawke's Bay Rosé ★★★☆

The 2010 vintage (★★★☆) blends Cabernet Franc (47 per cent) with Pinot Noir, Merlot, Tempranillo, Cabernet Sauvignon and Syrah. Bright pink, it is attractively scented, fresh, berryish and lively, with very good depth and vivacity and a smooth, dry (4 grams/litre of residual sugar) finish.

DRY $20 AV

Tussock Nelson Pinot Noir Rosé ★★☆

From Woollaston, the 2009 vintage (★★★) is pale pink, light and lively, with gently sweet strawberry and spice flavours, a hint of apricots and mouth-watering acidity.

MED $15 AV

Unison Hawke's Bay Rosé ★★★★

This is a 'serious', dry style. The 2009 vintage (★★★★) was made from Merlot, Syrah and Cabernet Sauvignon. Pale red, it is full-bodied and buoyantly fruity, with fresh, strong flavours of plums and spice. The 2010 (★★★★), pink/pale red, is a medium-bodied wine, slightly earthy and savoury, with dry flavours of raspberries, strawberries and spices. A good 'food' wine.

DRY $20 V+

Villa Maria Private Bin East Coast Rosé ★★★☆

A pale pink blend of Hawke's Bay, Gisborne and Marlborough grapes, the 2010 vintage (★★★☆) is crisp and dry (4.5 grams/litre of residual sugar), with refreshing strawberry, spice and slight peach flavours, showing very good depth.

Vintage	10
WR	5
Drink	10-11

DRY $21 AV

Vynfields Martinborough Pinot Rosé ★★★★

The pale pink 2009 vintage (★★★★), grown organically, offers fresh strawberry, peach and spice aromas and flavours. Smooth and slightly sweet, it has mouthfilling body, excellent depth and strong personality.

MED/DRY $26 –V

Waimea Pinot Rosé ★★★☆

The charming 2009 vintage (★★★☆), made from Nelson Pinot Noir, was partly (17 per cent) fermented in one-year-old American oak barrels; the rest was handled in tanks. Bright, light pink, it is fruity, plummy and slightly spicy, with fresh acidity and a slightly sweet (7.5 grams/litre of residual sugar) finish.

Vintage	10	09	08
WR	7	7	6
Drink	10-11	P	P

MED/DRY $18 V+

Weeping Sands Waiheke Island Rosé ★★★☆

The rosés from Obsidian Vineyard are always full of interest. The 2010 vintage (★★★☆) is an off-dry (5 grams/litre of residual sugar) style, Merlot-based. Salmon-pink, with some earthy notes on the nose and palate, it has a touch of complexity and very good depth of strawberry and spice flavours.

MED/DRY $24 –V

Wild Rock Vin Gris Hawke's Bay Rosé ★★★☆

The 2009 vintage (★★★) from Wild Rock (a division of Craggy Range) is a bright pink blend of Merlot (95 per cent), Malbec and Syrah. Fresh, mouthfilling and smooth, it has strawberry and spice flavours, a gentle splash of sweetness (6 grams/litre of residual sugar) and lively acidity.

Vintage	09	08
WR	6	6
Drink	10-11	10-11

MED/DRY $19 V+

Wooing Tree Rosé ★★★★

The 2010 vintage (★★★★) was made from estate-grown Pinot Noir, hand-harvested in the Cromwell Basin, Central Otago, and 20 per cent fermented in seasoned French oak casks. Pale pink, it is mouthfilling, with fresh, strong strawberry, spice and peach flavours and a slightly creamy texture. Delicious from the start.

MED/DRY $23 AV

Red Wines

Branded and Other Red Wines

Most New Zealand red wines carry a varietal label, such as Pinot Noir, Syrah, Merlot or Cabernet Sauvignon (or blends of the last two). Those not labelled prominently by their principal grape varieties – often prestigious wines such as Tom, Esk Valley The Terraces, Mills Reef Elspeth One or Unison Selection – can be found here.

Although not varietally labelled, these wines are mostly of high quality and sometimes outstanding.

Alluviale ★★★★★

A great buy. The 2008 vintage (★★★★★), blended from Merlot (55 per cent), Cabernet Sauvignon (25 per cent) and Cabernet Franc (20 per cent), was grown at two sites in the heart of the Gimblett Gravels, Hawke's Bay, and matured for 16 months in French oak barriques (90 per cent new). Densely coloured, it is finely fragrant, very rich and flowing, in a full-bodied style (14.5 per cent alcohol) with concentrated blackcurrant, plum and spice flavours, seasoned with nutty oak, and ripe, supple tannins. Coupling power and elegance, it is already delicious.

DRY $30 V+

Alpha Domus AD The Aviator ★★★★☆

The 2007 vintage (★★★★☆), the first since 2002, is $15 cheaper. Grown at Maraekakaho, in The Triangle, it is a blend of Cabernet Sauvignon (36 per cent), Cabernet Franc (27 per cent), Merlot (23 per cent) and Malbec (14 per cent), matured for 17 months in French oak barriques (75 per cent new). Deep and still youthful in colour, it is scented and supple, with rich blackcurrant and nut flavours, hints of dark chocolate and olives, and impressive depth and complexity. An elegant, slightly herbal Bordeaux style, it is well worth cellaring to 2012+.

Vintage	07
WR	6
Drink	10-20

DRY $50 –V

Alpha Domus AD The Navigator ★★★☆

The 2005 vintage (★★★☆) is enjoyable now. A blend of Merlot (40 per cent), Cabernet Sauvignon (35 per cent), Cabernet Franc (13 per cent) and Malbec (12 per cent), it was grown at Maraekakaho, in Hawke's Bay, and matured in French (70 per cent) and American oak barriques (40 per cent new). Deeply coloured, with some development showing, it has generous, brambly flavours, with a distinct hint of herbs, and good complexity and depth. The 2007 (★★★☆) is full-coloured, very vibrant and youthful, with fresh blackcurrant-like flavours and a subtle oak influence. Best drinking mid-2011+.

DRY $25 –V

Artisan The Matriarch (★★★★)

From young Syrah vines at Oratia, in West Auckland, the 2007 vintage (★★★★) is dark and youthful in colour. Fleshy, rich and well-rounded, with gentle tannins, it has a peppery fragrance and spicy, nutty flavours, showing excellent depth and complexity. It should mature well for several years.

DRY $27 AV

Ata Rangi Célèbre ★★★★☆

Pronounced say-lebr, this is a varietal and regional blend. Robust and vibrantly fruity, it has impressive weight and depth of plummy, spicy flavour in a complex style that matures well. The excellent 2007 vintage (★★★★☆) is a blend of Merlot (40 per cent), Syrah (30 per cent) and Cabernet Sauvignon (30 per cent), grown in Hawke's Bay and Martinborough. Deeply coloured, with a fragrant, spicy bouquet, seasoned with fine-quality oak, it is sturdy and very finely textured, with fresh, concentrated flavours of plums, herbs and spices. It's already delicious.

Vintage	07	06	05	04
WR	7	7	7	6
Drink	10-19	10-18	P	P

DRY $32 AV

Babich The Patriarch ★★★★★

This is Babich's best red, regardless of the variety or vineyard, but all vintages have been grown in the company's shingly vineyards in Gimblett Road, Hawke's Bay. It is typically a dark, ripe and complex, deliciously rich red, matured for 15 to 22 months in mostly French oak barriques (30 to 35 per cent new). The 2007 vintage (★★★★★) is densely coloured, powerful and highly concentrated. A blend of Cabernet Sauvignon (49 per cent), Malbec (29 per cent) and Cabernet Franc (22 per cent), it is savoury and complex, with bold blackcurrant, spice, coffee and dark chocolate flavours, ripe, firm and long. It should be a 10-year wine, at least. The 2008 (★★★★☆) is dark and very youthful, with concentrated, ripe blackcurrant, plum and slight coffee flavours, good backbone and complexity, and the power to age. Open 2012+.

Vintage	08
WR	5
Drink	11-18

DRY $60 AV

Benfield & Delamare ★★★★★

Bill Benfield and Sue Delamare specialise in claret-style reds of exceptional quality and impressive longevity at their tiny Martinborough winery. Benfield & Delamare is typically slightly leaner than the leading Hawke's Bay reds, yet very elegant, intensely flavoured and complex. Estate-grown, it is produced from ultra-low-yielding vines (2.4 tonnes/hectare), and the wine is matured in French oak barriques (up to two-thirds new) for about 20 months. The 2006 vintage (★★★★) is a blend of Merlot (60 per cent), Cabernet Sauvignon (25 per cent) and Cabernet Franc (15 per cent). Densely coloured, with a bouquet of raspberries and pencil shavings, it is fresh and vibrant, with concentrated blackcurrant and plum flavours and a firm backbone of tannin. It's an elegant, structured wine for cellaring.

Vintage	06	05	04	03	02
WR	6	6	NM	7	6
Drink	10-25	10-20	NM	10-20	10-20

DRY $58 AV

Brick Bay Martello Rock (★★★)

Estate-grown at Matakana, the 2006 vintage (★★★) is a medium-bodied blend of Malbec (44 per cent), Cabernet Sauvignon (25 per cent), Merlot (25 per cent) and Petit Verdot (6 per cent). Matured for a year in French oak casks, it is fullish in colour, with berry, herb and plum flavours, showing some spicy, nutty complexity, and a smooth finish. It's enjoyable now.

Vintage	06
WR	6
Drink	10-14

DRY $24 –V

Brick Bay Pharos ★★★★

Brick Bay's top red (pronounced fair-ross) is named after the famous lighthouse off the coast of Alexandria. A blend of Malbec (30 per cent), Cabernet Franc (23 per cent), Cabernet Sauvignon (21.5 per cent), Merlot (21.5 per cent) and Petit Verdot (4 per cent), the 2006 vintage (★★★☆) was grown at Sandspit, near Matakana, and matured in new French oak barriques. Full but not dense in colour, it is mouthfilling and smooth, with moderately concentrated plum, spice and slight herb flavours, showing some savoury complexity.

Vintage	06	05	04	03	02
WR	6	7	7	NM	7
Drink	10-16	10-13	10-12	NM	P

DRY $32 –V

Cable Bay Vineyards Five Hills ★★★★☆

Grown at several sites on Waiheke Island, the 2008 vintage (★★★★☆) is one of the finest yet. A blend of Merlot (46 per cent), Malbec (31 per cent), Cabernet Sauvignon (17 per cent) and Cabernet Franc (6 per cent), French oak-aged for a year, it is deeply coloured, with a fragrant, spicy bouquet. Refined and concentrated, it is youthful and age-worthy, with fresh blackcurrant, red-berry and spice flavours, showing excellent ripeness and density. The 2007 (★★★★☆), sold only at the winery, is also classy, with pure, blackcurrant-like flavours, finely poised and lingering.

Vintage	08	07	06	05	04
WR	7	6	6	7	6
Drink	10-16	10-15	10-13	10-11	P

DRY $33 AV

Cheeky Little Red ★★☆

Created by Babich for supermarkets owned by Foodstuffs, the 2008 vintage (★★☆) is an easy-drinking blend, grown in Hawke's Bay. Medium-bodied, it is fresh and fruity, with plummy, spicy, slightly earthy flavours. Fine value.

DRY $10 V+

Clearview Enigma ★★★★★

This consistently distinguished Hawke's Bay red is a Merlot-based blend. Typically dark and flavour-crammed, it matures well and is matured for about 18 months in French oak barriques (predominantly new). The 2008 vintage (★★★★☆) is a powerful, concentrated blend of Merlot (75 per cent), Malbec (11 per cent) and Cabernet Franc (14 per cent). Dark and sturdy, with ripe plum and spice flavours, slight coffee notes, and excellent complexity and density, it's still very youthful.

Vintage	08	07	06	05	04
WR	7	7	6	7	7
Drink	10-18	10-18	10-15	10-14	10-15

DRY $45 AV

Clearview Old Olive Block ★★★★★

This Hawke's Bay red, based on Cabernet Sauvignon and Cabernet Franc, is grown in the estate vineyard at Te Awanga, which has a very old olive tree in the centre, and in the Gimblett Gravels. The rich 2008 vintage (★★★★★) is a dark, complex blend of 59 per cent Cabernets (Sauvignon and Franc), supplemented by Merlot (38 per cent) and Malbec (3 per cent). Matured for 17 months in predominantly new French oak barriques, it is bold and youthful in colour, with deep, blackcurrant-like flavours, ripe and supple, a hint of coffee and good complexity. Dense and savoury, it's very age-worthy.

Vintage	08	07	06	05	04	03
WR	6	7	6	7	7	5
Drink	10-17	10-17	10-14	10-14	P	P

DRY $40 AV

Clearview The Basket Press ★★★★★

The rare, high-priced 2007 vintage (★★★★★) is a Cabernet Sauvignon-based blend (75 per cent), with minor portions of Merlot, Cabernet Franc and Malbec. Matured for 30 months in new French oak barriques, it's a powerful Hawke's Bay red, dark and fleshy, with highly concentrated blackcurrant, plum, spice and nut flavours and ripe, supple tannins. Still very youthful, it's a notably stylish, complex and harmonious wine, likely to mature gracefully for a decade or longer.

Vintage	07
WR	6
Drink	10-18

DRY $145 –V

Clearview Two Pinnacles ★★★★

Estate-grown at Te Awanga, in Hawke's Bay, the 2008 vintage (★★★★) is a blend of Malbec (85 per cent) and the two Cabernets (Sauvignon and Franc), matured for 17 months in mostly French oak barriques. Deliciously rich and smooth, it's a drink-young style, fleshy, dark and purple-flushed, with mouthfilling body and strong plum, spice, coffee and sweet oak flavours, showing good complexity.

DRY $28 AV

Coopers Creek Four Daughters Hawke's Bay Red ★★★

The 2006 vintage (★★★) is a full-flavoured blend of Cabernet Franc (30 per cent), Syrah (30 per cent), Merlot (20 per cent) and Malbec (20 per cent). It's a good, gutsy quaffer, still bright in colour, with plenty of firm, plummy, spicy flavour.

Vintage	06	05
WR	6	6
Drink	10-12	10-11

DRY $17 AV

Craggy Range Aroha ★★★★★

The 2008 vintage (★★★★★) was made from Pinot Noir, estate-grown at Te Muna, just south of Martinborough, fermented with indigenous yeasts and matured for 14 months in French oak casks (37 per cent new). Deep and youthful in colour, it is silky-textured, lush and sweet-fruited, with real density and the power to age. Savoury, it's a very complete and harmonious wine, best cellared to 2012+.

Vintage	08	07
WR	7	7
Drink	11-21	10-18

DRY $100 –V

Craggy Range Le Sol ★★★★★

This super-charged Syrah has pushed the boundaries in terms of its enormous scale – and succeeded brilliantly. Grown in the Gimblett Gravels district of Hawke's Bay, it is hand-harvested when the grapes are 'supremely ripe', in several 'passes' through the vineyard, fermented with indigenous yeasts, and bottled without fining or filtering. The 2008 vintage (★★★★★), matured for 18 months in French oak barriques (47 per cent new), has dense, purple-flushed colour. Powerful and notably concentrated, it has great depth of blackcurrant, plum and black-pepper flavours, coffee and spice notes, and a firm backbone of tannin. All latent power, it should be a 10-year wine, easily.

Vintage	08	07	06	05	04	03	02
WR	7	7	6	7	7	NM	7
Drink	11-23	10-22	10-20	10-15	10-13	NM	10-12

DRY $100 AV

Craggy Range Sophia ★★★★★

A relatively forward vintage, the 2008 (★★★★★) is a Gimblett Gravels, Hawke's Bay blend of Merlot and Cabernet Franc, matured for 18 months in French oak barriques (52 per cent new). Bold and youthful in colour, it is highly fragrant, with blackcurrant, spice and coffee aromas. Mouthfilling and dense, yet supple, it is richly flavoured, with fine-grained tannins, and lovely texture and richness. Drink now or cellar.

Vintage	08	07	06	05	04	03	02	01
WR	7	7	7	7	6	6	7	6
Drink	11-23	10-27	10-26	10-20	10-15	10-13	10-12	10-11

DRY $60 AV

Craggy Range Te Kahu ★★★★☆

The great-value 2008 vintage (★★★★☆) is a Hawke's Bay red, Merlot-based (64 per cent), with smaller portions of Cabernet Franc, Cabernet Sauvignon and Malbec. Matured for 18 months in French oak barriques (half new), it is mouthfilling, generous and supple, with sweet-fruit delights, strong blackcurrant, plum, spice and coffee flavours and a finely textured, lasting finish.

Vintage	08	07	06
WR	6	7	6
Drink	11-15	10-22	10-20

DRY $23 V+

Craggy Range The Quarry ★★★★★

Already delicious, the 2008 vintage (★★★★★) of this Cabernet Sauvignon/Merlot blend was estate-grown in the Gimblett Gravels, Hawke's Bay and matured for 18 months in French oak barriques (59 per cent new). Quietly classy, it is fragrant and dark, concentrated and complex, in a more open and relaxed style than some past releases. It offers an array of blackcurrant, plum and spice flavours, slightly leathery and nutty, with ripe, balanced tannins, and notable complexity and harmony. It's already very complete, but also has a real sense of depth and potential.

Vintage	08	07	06	05	04	03	02	01
WR	7	7	7	7	6	NM	6	6
Drink	11-23	10-27	10-26	10-17	10-14	NM	10-12	10-13

DRY $60 AV

Crazy by Nature Cosmo Red (★★★☆)

The 2009 vintage (★★★☆) is a medium-bodied, buoyantly fruity Gisborne red from Millton, blended from Malbec, Merlot, Syrah and Viognier. Full-coloured, with a spicy fragrance, it is fresh, berryish and lively, with some savoury complexity and ripe, supple tannins.

DRY $20 AV

Crossroads Talisman ★★★★

A blend of several red varieties whose identities the winery delights in concealing (I see Malbec as a prime suspect), Talisman has long been estate-grown in the Origin Vineyard at Fernhill, in Hawke's Bay, but now also includes fruit from the Gimblett Gravels. The 2008 vintage (★★★★) was matured for over a year in French (principally) and American oak barriques (92 per cent new). Dark and purple-flushed, with an earthy, spicy bouquet, it is mouthfilling, vibrantly fruity and supple, with strong, ripe plum/spice flavours showing good complexity. It's a forward vintage; drink now or cellar.

Vintage	08	07	06	05
WR	6	7	NM	6
Drink	10-14	10-13	NM	P

DRY $40 –V

Destiny Bay Destinae ★★★★☆

Grown on Waiheke Island, the 2006 vintage (★★★★★) is a classy, Cabernet Sauvignon-based blend (46 per cent), with Merlot (22 per cent), Cabernet Franc (16 per cent) and Malbec (16 per cent). Harvested at 23.6 to 26.1 brix, and matured in American (60 per cent) and French oak barriques (half new), it has bright, rich colour, a fragrant, nutty bouquet, and highly concentrated, ripe berry-fruit and spice flavours. Sweet-fruited, with firm tannins and impressive complexity, it's still youthful, with the power and structure to age. The 2007 (★★★★) is a blend of Cabernet Sauvignon (35 per cent), Merlot (33 per cent), Cabernet Franc (21 per cent) and Malbec (11 per cent). Berryish, plummy, ripe and silky, but slightly less concentrated than the 2006, it's already enjoyable.

Vintage	07	06
WR	6	6
Drink	10-17	10-16

DRY $75 –V

Destiny Bay Magna Praemia ★★★★★

The very high-priced 2006 vintage (★★★★★) of this Waiheke Island producer's flagship red is a Cabernet Sauvignon-based blend (74 per cent), with smaller portions of Merlot (14 per cent), Malbec (7 per cent) and Cabernet Franc (5 per cent). Matured in a 60:40 split of French and American oak casks (new and one-year-old), it is deeply coloured, lush and silky, with gentle tannins and lovely depth, complexity, harmony and length. The 2007 (★★★★★) is also Cabernet Sauvignon-based (69 per cent). Invitingly fragrant, it has substantial body, sweet-fruit delights and deep blackcurrant and nut flavours, complex, savoury and supple. Drink now or cellar.

Vintage	06	05
WR	7	7
Drink	12-16	10-15

DRY $275 –V

Destiny Bay Mystae ★★★★☆

The 2006 vintage (★★★★) of this Waiheke Island red is a blend of Cabernet Sauvignon (57 per cent), Merlot (22 per cent), Cabernet Franc (17 per cent) and Malbec (4 per cent), matured in French and American oak barriques (60 per cent new). Vibrant and supple, with fruity, spicy flavours and a hint of dark chocolate, it shows very good concentration, complexity and length. The 2007 vintage (★★★★☆) is Cabernet Sauvignon-based (55 per cent), with Merlot (26 per cent), Cabernet Franc (11 per cent), Malbec (6 per cent) and Petit Verdot (2 per cent). Very finely textured, it has impressive depth of plum, berry, spice and herb flavours, seasoned with nutty oak, and good complexity. Already approachable, it should also cellar well.

Vintage	07	06
WR	6	6
Drink	10-17	10-16

DRY $115 –V

Esk Valley The Terraces ★★★★★

Grown on the steep, terraced, north-facing hillside flanking the winery at Bay View, Hawke's Bay, this is a strikingly bold, dark wine with bottomless depth of blackcurrant, plum and strongly spicy flavour. Malbec (43 per cent of the vines) and Merlot (35 per cent) are typically the major ingredients, supplemented by Cabernet Franc; the Malbec gives 'perfume, spice, tannin and brilliant colour'. Yields in the 1-hectare vineyard are very low, and the wine is matured for 17 to 22 months in all-new French oak barriques. En primeur (payment at a reduced price of $98, in advance of delivery) has been the best way to buy. It typically matures well, developing a beautiful fragrance and spicy, Rhône-like complexity. The 2006 vintage (★★★★★) is tightly structured and harmonious, with lovely ripeness and density of berry and spice flavours. You can drink it now, with pleasure, but it should flourish for a decade. There was no 2007 or 2008, but the 2009 vintage will be offered for sale in early 2011, at a price yet to be announced.

Vintage	09	08	07	06	05	04	03	02	01	00
WR	7	NM	NM	7	NM	7	NM	7	NM	7
Drink	11-25	NM	NM	10-18	NM	10-16	NM	10-17	NM	10-12

DRY $? V?

Gibson Bridge Trésor Rouge (★★★☆)

The rare (300 bottles only) 2009 vintage (★★★☆) is a Marlborough blend of Syrah, Merlot, Pinot Noir and Malbec. Full but not dense in colour, with fresh plum and spice flavours, it's a middleweight style with some complexity and very good depth.

DRY $65 –V

Gillman ★★★★☆

This rare Matakana red is blended from Cabernet Franc, Merlot and Malbec, and matured for two years in French oak barriques (most recently 60 per cent new). The star wine to date is the finely scented, deeply coloured 2004 vintage (★★★★★), which shows lovely concentration and complexity. It's still maturing well. The 2005 (★★★★) is full-bodied and supple, with generous blackcurrant and herb flavours. The 2006 (★★★★☆) is an elegant wine, medium to full-bodied, with youthful cassis, plum, herb and spice flavours, showing good complexity and depth. The 2007 (★★★★), not yet released, is deeply coloured, with rich, slightly herbal flavours, showing good complexity. The 2008 (★★★★★) is the finest since 2002 – dark and generous, in a bold, muscular style, fleshy, complex and likely to be long-lived. These are classy wines, full of personality.

Vintage	08	07	06	05	04
WR	7	6	6	7	7
Drink	12-22	11-19	10-18	10-17	10-18

DRY $70 –V

Gladstone Auld Alliance ★★★☆

The 'premier Bordeaux-style' from this Wairarapa winery struggles to match the quality of those from Hawke's Bay. The 2008 vintage (★★★) is a blend of Cabernet Franc (54 per cent), Merlot (27 per cent), Malbec (10 per cent) and Cabernet Sauvignon (9 per cent), barrel-aged for over a year. The colour is fullish, with a hint of development; the palate is fresh and smooth, with some savoury notes, but lacks real warmth and stuffing. Drink now.

Vintage	08
WR	5
Drink	10-15

DRY $45 –V

Goldwater Goldie ★★★★★

This Waiheke Island wine has long been one of New Zealand's top claret-style reds. For many years called Goldwater Cabernet Sauvignon & Merlot, since the 2002 vintage it has been renamed as Goldwater Goldie. The vineyard (recently extensively replanted), lies on sandy clay soils on the hillside overlooking Putiki Bay, and the vinification is based on classic Bordeaux techniques, including maturation for 14 to 18 months in French oak barriques (typically half new). The wine generally matures well for 10 to 12 years, gaining in complexity and personality. The 2005 (★★★★★) is a blend of Cabernet Sauvignon (60 per cent) and Merlot (40 per cent). A star vintage, it is dark and highly fragrant, with lovely richness of blackcurrant, plum and spice flavours. Very generous, sweet-fruited and supple, it's already a delight to drink.

Vintage	05	04	03	02	01	00	99	98
WR	7	7	NM	7	NM	7	7	7
Drink	10-15	10-12	NM	10-12	NM	P	10-11	P

DRY $55 AV

Great Red (★★☆)

A Merlot-based blend from Preston Wine Group (owner of Mills Reef), the 2008 vintage (★★☆) is a good quaffer. Grown in Hawke's Bay, it is full-coloured and gutsy, with smooth, plummy, slightly spicy flavours.

DRY $10 V+

Hay Paddock, The ★★★★☆

The debut 2006 vintage (★★★★) of this Waiheke Island red is an Onetangi blend of Syrah (88 per cent) and Petit Verdot (12 per cent). Harvested at 24 brix from young vines and matured for over a year in French oak barriques (75 per cent new), it is deeply coloured and finely textured, with an array of plum, pepper, herb and nut flavours, silky-smooth and rich. The 2007 (★★★★★) is again Syrah-based, with a splash of Petit Verdot to make it a 'slightly bigger wine'. Intensely varietal, it is very sweet-fruited and savoury, with ripe, peppery flavours, showing lovely balance and density.

Vintage	07	06
WR	6	5
Drink	10-15	10-13

DRY $68 –V

Hunter's The Chase (★★☆)

The 2008 vintage (★★☆) is a Marlborough blend of Pinot Noir and Merlot, oak-aged for over a year. Lightish in colour, it is a smooth, pleasant red, light to medium-bodied, with cherryish, slightly spicy flavours and gentle tannins. Priced right.

Vintage	08
WR	4
Drink	10-12

DRY $15 AV

Karikari Estate Toa (★★★☆)

The 2007 vintage (★★★☆), grown at Muriwhenua, in the Far North, is a blend of Cabernet Franc and Malbec. Full and fairly developed in colour, with firm blackcurrant, herb and spice flavours, it's slightly leafy, but also shows some savoury, nutty complexity.

DRY $40 –V

Karikari Estate Toa Iti (★★★☆)

Estate-grown on the Karikari Peninsula, in the Far North, the 2006 vintage (★★★☆) is a Cabernet Sauvignon-based red (44 per cent), with Merlot (30 per cent), Cabernet Franc (16 per cent), and minor portions of Malbec, Syrah and Pinotage. Full-coloured, it is flavoursome and spicy, although slightly leafy, with good complexity and a firm backbone of tannin.

DRY $29 –V

Kidnapper Cliffs Ariki ★★★★☆

A Hawke's Bay red of real substance, the 2008 vintage (★★★★★) from Te Awa is an estate-grown, Gimblett Gravels blend of Merlot (75 per cent), Cabernet Franc (20 per cent) and Cabernet Sauvignon (5 per cent). Highly concentrated, yet supple, it is deeply coloured, vibrant, silky and rich, with plum and spice flavours, hints of herbs and coffee, and a lasting finish. Notably elegant, it's a youthful wine, yet already approachable. The 2007 (★★★★☆) is still very fresh. Sturdy and complex, it has deep blackcurrant, plum and chocolate flavours, but is less finely textured than the 2008.

DRY $55 –V

Manaia George (★★★)

The 2008 vintage (★★★) is an inky, vibrant blend of Chambourcin (80 per cent) and Malbec (20 per cent), grown in Northland and American oak-aged. Berryish and fruit-packed, it's a flavoursome, upfront style offering smooth, easy drinking.

DRY $30 –V

Man O' War Ironclad ★★★★

The powerful, youthful 2008 vintage (★★★★☆), from the eastern end of Waiheke Island, is Merlot-based (52 per cent), with smaller portions of Cabernet Franc, Malbec, Petit Verdot and Cabernet Sauvignon. Matured in French and American oak casks (25 per cent new), it is deeply coloured, sturdy (14.5 per cent alcohol) and packed with blackcurrant, plum, spice and nut flavours, slightly chocolatey, ripe and long. Savoury, rich, complex and firmly structured, it's one for the cellar; open 2012+.

Vintage	08	07
WR	6	6
Drink	11-18	10-12

DRY $46 –V

Marsden Bay of Islands Cavalli ★★☆

The 2008 vintage (★★☆), grown at Kerikeri, is a blend of Chambourcin (50 per cent), Pinotage and Merlot. Full-coloured, it is plummy and slightly herbal, with some rustic notes.

DRY $22 –V

Matariki Quintology ★★★★

This Gimblett Gravels, Hawke's Bay red is a blend of five varieties, in 2005 (★★★★) Merlot (41 per cent), Cabernet Sauvignon (30 per cent), Malbec (12 per cent), Cabernet Franc (10 per cent) and Syrah (7 per cent). Matured for 17 months in French oak casks (50 per cent new), it is full-flavoured, with blackcurrant and spice notes, and savoury, nutty characters adding complexity. Showing some development, it's drinking well now.

Vintage	07	06	05	04	03	02
WR	7	NM	7	7	NM	7
Drink	11-17	NM	10-15	10-14	NM	10-12

DRY $50 –V

Messenger, The (★★★★★)

The 2008 vintage (★★★★★) from Duck Creek Wines, at Stillwater, north of Auckland city, is a memorable debut. A blend of roughly equal portions of Malbec, Cabernet Franc and Merlot, matured for two years in French oak barrels, it is dense and youthful in colour, with a highly concentrated palate. Already lovely, it has fresh, bold blackcurrant, plum and spice flavours, reflecting the upfront nature of Malbec, a silky texture, and compelling richness and complexity.

DRY $96 –V

Morton Estate The Regent of Morton ★★★

Still on sale, the 2004 vintage (★★☆) is a Merlot-based blend, with Cabernet Sauvignon and Cabernet Franc. A mouthfilling Hawke's Bay wine with full, developed colour, it is spicy and savoury, but past its best.

DRY $55 –V

Morton Estate White Label The Mercure ★★★

The 2007 vintage (★★★☆) is a Hawke's Bay, Merlot-based blend with deep, developed colour. It has blackcurrant, herb and slight nut flavours, showing good concentration, and a rounded finish. Ready.

Vintage	07	06
WR	6	6
Drink	10-15	10-15

DRY $19 AV

Mud Brick Vineyard Velvet (★★★★★)

The debut 2008 vintage (★★★★★) is a sumptuous, beautifully fragrant Waiheke Island red made from unidentified grapes – but it smells and tastes of Cabernet Sauvignon and Merlot. Sturdy and rich, with blackcurrant and plum flavours, hints of spice, liquorice and coffee, and notable concentration and complexity, it's already delicious, but should mature gracefully for many years.

DRY $105 –V

Muddy Water Deliverance Red Table Wine ★★★☆

The 2008 vintage (★★★) is a blend of Pinotage and Syrah, grown at Waipara, which did not meet the winery's standards for varietal wines. Fullish in colour, with a gamey, earthy, spicy bouquet, it has plum, herb and spice flavours, not concentrated but smooth, with drink-young appeal. The 2009 (★★★☆) is full-coloured, with a spicy, slightly rustic bouquet. Mouthfilling and firmly structured, it has plum, spice and dark chocolate flavours, showing very good depth.

Vintage	09	08
WR	6	6
Drink	10-16	10-14

DRY $15 V+

Newton Forrest Estate Cornerstone ★★★★★

Grown in the Cornerstone Vineyard, on the corner of Gimblett Road and State Highway 50 – where the first vines were planted in 1989 – this is a distinguished Hawke's Bay blend of Cabernet Sauvignon, Merlot and Malbec, matured in French (principally) and American oak barriques. The 2007 vintage (★★★★★), still purple-flushed, is finely textured, with lovely richness of vibrant plum and spice flavours, highly concentrated and built to last. Best drinking 2012+.

Vintage	07	06	05	04	03	02
WR	6	6	7	5	NM	6
Drink	11-20	10-20	15-25	10-12	NM	P

DRY $50 AV

Newton Forrest Estate Stony Corner (★★★★☆)

A bold, upfront style, the 2007 vintage (★★★★☆) is a Gimblett Gravels, Hawke's Bay blend of Cabernet Sauvignon, Merlot and Malbec, matured in French (60 per cent) and American (40 per cent) oak. Deeply coloured, with a fragrant, spicy, sweetly oaked bouquet, it is powerful, with cassis, plum and spice flavours, a hint of coffee and excellent concentration.

Vintage	07
WR	5
Drink	10-11

DRY $30 AV

Obsidian ★★★★★

The Obsidian Vineyard at Onetangi produces one of the most stylish claret-style reds on Waiheke Island. Looking set for a decade, but already approachable, the 2008 vintage (★★★★★) is based primarily on Cabernet Sauvignon (38 per cent) and Merlot (30 per cent), with smaller portions of Cabernet Franc, Petit Verdot and Malbec. Notably dark and rich, it has dense, ripe flavours of blackcurrant, plums and spices, with a hint of dark chocolate. Highly concentrated, fresh and finely textured, it's a top year, likely to be at its best 2012+.

Vintage	08	07	06	05	04	03	02	01	00
WR	7	5	NM	7	6	NM	7	NM	7
Drink	10-20	10-19	NM	10-15	10-14	NM	10-12	NM	10-12

DRY $53 AV

Olssen's Robert the Bruce ★★★☆

The 2009 vintage (★★★☆) is a Central Otago blend of Pinotage, Cabernet Sauvignon and Syrah, French and American oak-aged. Deeply coloured, it's a distinctive wine, with a fresh, peppery bouquet. Vibrantly fruity, it has plum, spice and herb flavours, showing very good depth.

Vintage	09
WR	6
Drink	10-20

DRY $29 –V

Paritua 21.12 (★★★★★)

The commanding 2007 vintage (★★★★★) was grown at 2112 (hence the name) Maraekakaho Road, in Hawke's Bay, and matured for 18 months in French oak barriques (half new). A blend of Cabernet Sauvignon (51 per cent), Merlot (28 per cent) and Cabernet Franc (21 per cent), it is dense and youthful in colour, very powerful and concentrated, with layers of blackcurrant, plum, herb, spice and nut flavours, buried tannins, and loads of cellaring potential.

Vintage	07
WR	7
Drink	10-20

DRY $50 AV

Paritua Red (★★★★)

Grown in The Triangle district, Hawke's Bay, the powerful 2007 vintage (★★★★) is a blend of Cabernet Sauvignon (54 per cent), Merlot (32 per cent), Cabernet Franc (9 per cent) and Malbec (5 per cent), French oak-matured (60 per cent new). Boldly coloured, it is concentrated, with cassis, spice, herb and nut flavours, showing considerable complexity.

Vintage	07
WR	7
Drink	10-20

DRY $37 –V

Passage Rock Sisters ★★★☆

The Waiheke Island winery's early-drinking red from 2008 (★★★☆) is a blend of Merlot (50 per cent), Syrah (30 per cent), Cabernet Franc (10 per cent) and Malbec (10 per cent). Full-coloured, with a sweet oak influence, it is youthful and vibrantly fruity, with ripe blackcurrant, plum and spice flavours, smooth and generous.

DRY $24 AV

Pegasus Bay Maestro ★★★★

The 2005 vintage (★★★★☆) is a Waipara blend of Merlot (85 per cent) and Malbec (15 per cent). Matured for two years in barriques, followed by nine months in larger barrels, it has substantial body (14.5 per cent alcohol) and rich colour, in a fragrant, highly concentrated style with blackcurrant and herb flavours, nutty, leathery notes adding complexity, and a firm foundation of tannin.

Vintage	06	05
WR	6	7
Drink	10-18	10-16

DRY $47 –V

Poderi Crisci Viburno (★★★★)

Grown on Waiheke Island, the 2008 vintage (★★★★) is a blend of Merlot (70 per cent) and Cabernet Franc (30 per cent). Already highly enjoyable, it's a weighty wine with strong, ripe, plummy, spicy flavours, showing good, savoury complexity.

DRY $39 –V

Providence – see Providence Private Reserve Merlot/Cabernet Franc/Malbec [Merlot]

Puriri Hills Estate ★★★★

The 2005 vintage (★★★★☆) of this impressive Clevedon, South Auckland red is the finest yet. A blend of Merlot (63 per cent), Cabernet Sauvignon (17 per cent) and Cabernet Franc (11 per cent), with smaller amounts of Carmenère and Malbec, it has deep, youthful colour. The bouquet is perfumed; the palate is rich and welcoming, with concentrated blackcurrant, plum, herb and spice flavours, seasoned with quality French oak, and silky tannins. It's a very refined, harmonious and supple wine, offering delicious drinking from now onwards. The 2004 (★★★★), released after the 2005, has deep, fairly mature colour. Still fresh, it's a generous wine, fleshy, savoury and complex, probably nearing its peak and delicious now.

Vintage	05	04	03	02	01
WR	7	7	6	6	5
Drink	10-20	10-15	P	P	P

DRY $36 –V

Puriri Hills Pope (★★★★★)

The very classy debut 2005 vintage (★★★★★) was named after Ivan Pope, who planted and tended the vines at this Clevedon, South Auckland vineyard. Blended from Merlot (47 per cent), Carmenère (33 per cent), Cabernet Franc (10 per cent) and Malbec (10 per cent), it has dark colour and a brambly, slightly toasty bouquet. Youthful, with obvious potential, it is rich, ripe and highly concentrated, with hints of coffee and spices, and notable power, complexity and density.

Vintage	06	05
WR	6	7
Drink	10-18	10-20

DRY $120 –V

Puriri Hills Reserve ★★★★★

A regional classic. Grown at Clevedon, in South Auckland, the 2004 vintage (★★★★★) was released in 2008 – after the 2005 (★★★★★). Deep and still fairly youthful in colour, it is deliciously harmonious, rich and silky, with vibrant blackcurrant, herb and spice flavours, nutty, savoury, generous and long. The 2006 (★★★★★), a blend of Merlot (53 per cent), Carmenère (33 per cent) and Cabernet Franc (14 per cent), was matured in French oak barrels (60 per cent new), and bottled unfined and unfiltered. Dark, rich and supple, it is lush and finely textured, with blackcurrant, spice, herb and plum flavours, showing lovely richness and roundness.

Vintage	06	05	04	03	02
WR	6	7	7	NM	6
Drink	10-20	10-20	10-20	NM	P

DRY $70 AV

Ransom Dark Summit ★★★☆

Still on sale, the 2005 vintage (★★★★), grown at Matakana, is a Cabernet Sauvignon and Carmenère-based blend, with smaller portions of Cabernet Franc, Merlot and Malbec. Barrel-aged for a year, it has deep colour, a slightly leafy bouquet and generous, brambly, plummy flavours, savoury and complex, with a strong finish. It shows good personality.

DRY $35 –V

Recession Red (★★★)

From Unison, in Hawke's Bay, the 2008 vintage (★★★) is a barrel-aged blend of Cabernet Sauvignon and Syrah, released as a one-year-old 'fun wine'. Ruby-hued, it's medium-bodied (12.5 per cent alcohol), with decent depth of fresh berry and spice flavours, slightly peppery and lightly oaked, in a supple, easy-drinking style.

DRY $15 V+

Redd Gravels ★★★★★

The 2006 vintage (★★★★★) is the third release of the top label from Blake Family Vineyard, which was sold a few years ago (the 2007 vintage was the last). Grown in Gimblett Road, Hawke's Bay, it was fermented with indigenous yeasts, and matured for 18 months in French oak barriques (92 per cent new). A blend of Merlot (84 per cent) and Cabernet Franc (16 per cent), like its predecessors it is notably generous and refined. Deep and youthful in colour, with a fragrant, ripe, spicy bouquet, it is concentrated and silky-textured, with an array of blackcurrant, plum, coffee and dark chocolate flavours, complex and deliciously rich and smooth. Drink now or cellar.

DRY $80 AV

Red Wire ★★★☆

From Mount George, owned by Paritua, the 2008 vintage (★★★) is a Hawke's Bay blend of Merlot, Malbec, Cabernet Franc and Cabernet Sauvignon, partly barrel-aged. It's a full-coloured wine, fresh and vibrantly fruity, with plenty of plummy, berryish flavour and gentle tannins, in an easy-drinking style.

Vintage	08
WR	6
Drink	10-13

DRY $15 V+

Rua Whenua Simply Red (★★★☆)

The 2006 vintage (★★★☆) is a Hawke's Bay blend of Merlot (82 per cent) and Cabernet Franc (18 per cent). Fullish in colour, it is savoury, berryish and spicy, firm and fragrant, showing good complexity. It just lacks the richness to rate more highly.

DRY $20 AV

San Hill The Benches Red ★★★

Still unfolding, the 2007 vintage (★★★☆) of this Central Hawke's Bay red from Pukeora Estate is a deeply coloured, Merlot-predominant blend, with smaller portions of Cabernet Sauvignon, Syrah and Malbec. Matured for 20 months in barriques (half new), it has a fragrant, berryish, spicy bouquet, tinged with sweet oak. Mouthfilling and vibrantly fruity, it is plummy, spicy and oaky, with some savoury complexity, very good depth and obvious cellaring potential. (Note: the 2008 vintage is not rated highly by the producer and has been sold cheaply.)

Vintage	08	07	06
WR	3	6	6
Drink	10-12	10-12	P

DRY $25 –V

Seifried Sylvia ★★☆
Named after Agnes Seifried's late mother, this Nelson red is made from an Austrian variety, Zweigelt, which the Seifrieds have pioneered here. Grown at Brightwater and French oak-aged, the 2008 vintage (★★☆) is an easy-drinking quaffer, simple and smooth.

Vintage	08
WR	5
Drink	10-14

DRY $19 –V

Soho Revolver ★★★★
The 2008 vintage (★★★★) is a Waiheke Island blend of Merlot (46 per cent), Malbec (31 per cent), Cabernet Sauvignon (17 per cent) and Cabernet Franc (6 per cent), matured in French oak casks (20 per cent new). It's a full-coloured wine, fragrant and ripe, with strong, plummy, spicy flavours, showing good concentration and complexity.

DRY $38 –V

Stonecroft Ruhanui ★★★★
The 2008 vintage is a Hawke's Bay blend of Merlot (74 per cent) and Cabernet Sauvignon (26 per cent), estate-grown in the Gimblett Gravels and French oak-matured for over 18 months. Tasted prior to bottling (and so not rated), it was full-coloured, with spice and plum flavours in an elegant, rather than heavyweight, style, ripe and savoury, with fine-grained tannins. The 2007 (★★★★) is similar – medium to full-bodied, with red-berry and spice flavours, complex and savoury, and a foundation of ripe, supple tannins.

Vintage	08
WR	5
Drink	12-17

DRY $35 –V

Stone Paddock Scarlet (★★★☆)
Estate-grown by Paritua in The Triangle district of Hawke's Bay, the 2007 vintage (★★★☆) is a fragrant blend of Merlot (37 per cent), Cabernet Sauvignon (35 per cent), Cabernet Franc (16 per cent) and Malbec (12 per cent). Barrel-aged for a year, it's a gutsy, full-coloured wine with strong blackcurrant, mint and nut flavours and firm tannins.

Vintage	07
WR	7
Drink	10-16

DRY $25 –V

Stonyridge Airfield ★★★★
Sold as 'the little brother of our flagship wine, Larose', the 2009 vintage (★★★★) is a blend of Cabernet Sauvignon (38 per cent), Malbec (27 per cent), Petit Verdot (13 per cent), Merlot (12 per cent) and Cabernet Franc (10 per cent), grown at Onetangi, on Waiheke Island, and matured in French and American oak casks (40 per cent new). Like a minor Bordeaux, it is full-coloured, with fresh, strong flavours of blackcurrants and spices, ripe and savoury, finely integrated oak and good tannin support. A stylish, medium to full-bodied red, still youthful, it should mature well; open 2012+.

Vintage	09
WR	7
Drink	11-15

DRY $45 –V

Stonyridge Faithful (★★★☆)

From a neighbouring vineyard, managed by Stonyridge, the 2009 vintage (★★★☆) is a Waiheke blend of Merlot (67 per cent), Cabernet Sauvignon (17 per cent), Malbec (12 per cent) and Cabernet Franc (4 per cent), American oak-aged. Already enjoyable, it's a middleweight style, plummy, spicy, savoury and slightly earthy, with considerable complexity and ripe, supple tannins.

Vintage	09		DRY $25 –V
WR	5		
Drink	10-14		

Stonyridge Larose ★★★★★

Typically a stunning Waiheke wine. Dark and seductively perfumed, with smashing fruit flavours, at its best it is a magnificently concentrated red that matures superbly for a decade or longer, acquiring great complexity. The vines – Cabernet Sauvignon, Merlot, Cabernet Franc, Malbec and Petit Verdot, ranging up to 28 years old – are grown in free-draining clay soils on a north-facing slope, a kilometre from the sea at Onetangi, and are very low-yielding (4 tonnes/hectare). The wine is matured for a year in French oak barriques (half new, half one-year-old), and is sold largely on an en primeur basis, whereby the customers, in return for paying for their wine about nine months in advance of its delivery, secure a substantial price reduction. The 2009 vintage (★★★★★) is a blend of Cabernet Sauvignon (52 per cent), Malbec (18 per cent), Petit Verdot (15 per cent), Merlot (10 per cent) and Cabernet Franc (5 per cent). Highly Bordeaux-like, it has dark, youthful colour, fresh, dense, brambly, spicy flavours, with hints of leather and dark chocolate, and ripe, supple tannins. Elegant, savoury and complex, it's already quite approachable, but best cellared to at least 2014.

Vintage	09	08	07	06	05	04	03	02	01	00
WR	7	7	7	7	7	7	7	7	6	7
Drink	11-21	14-25	10-17	10-17	11-22	10-17	10-14	10-15	P	10-13

DRY $190 –V

Te Awa Boundary ★★★★★

This very stylish Hawke's Bay red is a Merlot-based blend. Produced from low-yielding, mature vines in the Gimblett Gravels and matured in French oak barriques, it was made until recently by Jenny Dobson, who was once maitre d'chais at a respected Haut-Médoc cru bourgeois, Château Senejac; Ant Mackenzie, formerly of Spy Valley, is now at the helm. Subtle, multi-faceted and beautifully harmonious, it is typically more complex and savoury than most New Zealand reds. Recently released, the 2006 vintage (★★★★★) is outstanding. A densely coloured blend of Merlot (74 per cent) and Cabernet Sauvignon (21 per cent), with splashes of Cabernet Franc and Malbec, it is powerful and highly concentrated, with dense blackcurrant, spice, dark chocolate and nut flavours, substantial body and impressive complexity. A distinctly Bordeaux-like red, it should be very long-lived.

Vintage	06	05	04	03	02	01	00
WR	7	NM	7	NM	7	6	7
Drink	10-16	NM	10-14	NM	10-12	P	P

DRY $40 AV

Te Henga The Westie Vintara Red ★★☆
From Babich, the 2008 vintage (★★☆) is a North Island blend offering fresh, easy drinking. Ruby-hued, it is fruity, plummy and smooth.

DRY $13 V+

Te Mata Coleraine ★★★★★
Breed, rather than brute power, is the hallmark of Coleraine, which since its first vintage in 1982 has carved out an illustrious reputation among New Zealand's claret-style reds. Since the 2005 vintage, it is no longer labelled as a Cabernet/Merlot, but simply as Coleraine (and in some recent vintages has contained more Merlot than Cabernet Sauvignon). At its best, it is a magical Hawke's Bay wine, with a depth, complexity and subtlety on the level of a top-class Bordeaux. The grapes are grown in the Havelock North hills, in the company's warm, north-facing Buck and 1892 vineyards, and the wine is matured for 18 to 20 months in French oak barriques, predominantly new. Cabernet Sauvignon in 2008 accounted for 53 per cent of the blend, Merlot 28 per cent and Cabernet Franc 19 per cent (Malbec is definitely not in the recipe). A complete vertical tasting of Coleraine (1982 to 2006), held in mid-2008, showed that all vintages since 1989 were still drinking well and the 2004 to 2006 vintages had scaled new heights (surpassing the great trio of 1989–91). The 2008 vintage (★★★★★) is dark, with dense flavours of blackcurrants and plums, distinctly spicy, savoury and complex, and ripe, supple tannins. Already approachable, it's open and expressive in its youth, but best cellared for at least five years.

Vintage	08	07	06	05	04	03	02	01	00
WR	7	7	7	7	7	7	7	6	7
Drink	14-20	11-27	10-26	10-25	10-16	10-18	10-15	10-13	10-15

DRY $75 AV

Te Whau The Point ★★★★☆
This classy Waiheke Island red flows from a steeply sloping vineyard at Putiki Bay. The distinguished 2008 vintage (★★★★★) is a Cabernet Sauvignon-based blend (57 per cent), with Merlot (30 per cent), Cabernet Franc (10 per cent) and Malbec (3 per cent). Fermented with indigenous yeasts and matured for 18 months in French oak barriques (one-third new), it is deeply coloured, mouthfilling and sweet-fruited, with concentrated plum, spice, dark chocolate and nut flavours and good tannin backbone. Very generous and highly complex, with a long life ahead, it's a wine of great depth, structure and personality.

Vintage	08	07	06	05	04	03	02	01	00	99
WR	7	7	6	7	6	5	7	NM	7	7
Drink	13-25	12-22	10-15	10-20	10-15	P	10-15	NM	10-12	P

DRY $70 –V

Tom ★★★★★
Pernod Ricard NZ's top Hawke's Bay claret-style red honours pioneer winemaker Tom McDonald, the driving force behind New Zealand's first prestige red, McWilliam's Cabernet Sauvignon. The early vintages in the mid-1990s were Cabernet Sauvignon-predominant, but since 1998 Merlot has emerged as an equally crucial part of the recipe. Made at the Church Road winery, it is typically not a blockbuster but a wine of great finesse, savoury, complex and

more akin to a quality Bordeaux than other New World reds. I have not tasted the 2005 vintage, released in 2009 at $95 – down from $135 for the 2002 (★★★★★). The 2007 (★★★★★) is a wine of great richness, subtlety and refinement. Dense and youthful in colour, it is finely scented, with highly concentrated blackcurrant, plum, spice and slight nut flavours, beautifully ripe, deep and smooth. Elegant and finely poised, a wine of real beauty, it should flourish for 15–20 years.

Vintage	07	06	05	04	03	02	01	00	99	98
WR	7	NM	7	NM	NM	7	NM	6	NM	7
Drink	10-20	NM	10-15	NM	NM	10-12	NM	P	NM	10-15

DRY $95 AV

Trinity Hill The Gimblett ★★★★★

A great buy, from one vintage to the next. The 2008 (★★★★★) is based mainly on Cabernet Sauvignon (43 per cent) and Merlot (41 per cent), blended with Petit Verdot (7 per cent), Malbec (6 per cent) and Cabernet Franc (3 per cent). Hand-picked in the Gimblett Gravels, Hawke's Bay, and matured for over 18 months in principally French oak barrels (25 per cent new), it is dense and very age-worthy. Dark, with blackcurrant and spice flavours, notably rich, ripe and firmly structured, it's still very youthful, but finely balanced, layered and lingering.

Vintage	08	07	06	05
WR	5	6	6	6
Drink	12-18	13-18	12-18	10-14

DRY $35 V+

Trinity Hill The Trinity ★★★☆

The 2008 vintage (★★★☆) is a Gimblett Gravels, Hawke's Bay blend of Cabernet Sauvignon, Cabernet Franc, Merlot and Syrah, matured mostly in seasoned French oak barrels. Mouthfilling, fruity and supple, it has very satisfying depth of blackcurrant, plum and spice flavours, showing good complexity. Finely balanced for early drinking.

DRY $20 AV

Turanga Creek Lone Oak Blend (★★★)

From grapes grown at Clevedon, in South Auckland, the easy-drinking 2008 vintage (★★★) is a blend of Merlot, Malbec and Cabernet Franc. Fullish in colour, mouthfilling and smooth, it has berry, spice and slight herb flavours, seasoned with sweet oak, and some savoury complexity.

DRY $28 –V

Two Gates Hawke's Bay Omahu (★★★★★)

The 2007 vintage (★★★★★) is an outstanding debut. Certified organic, it is a single-vineyard, Hawke's Bay blend of Merlot (62 per cent), Cabernet Franc (29 per cent) and Cabernet Sauvignon (9 per cent), hand-picked at over 24 brix and matured for 18 months in French oak barriques (45 per cent new). Deep and bright in colour, with a beautifully scented bouquet, it is highly concentrated and silky-textured, with rich, ripe blackcurrant, plum, coffee and nut flavours, very refined and harmonious. Best drinking 2012+.

DRY $55 AV

Unison Classic Blend ★★★★☆

Based on a block of densely planted vines in the Gimblett Gravels, Hawke's Bay, this blend of Merlot, Cabernet Sauvignon and Syrah is typically dark, concentrated and firmly structured. The 2007 vintage (★★★★☆) is deeply coloured, with fresh, strong blackcurrant, plum and spice flavours, hints of coffee and nuts, and excellent depth, complexity and harmony. Savoury and refined, it's a drink-now or cellaring proposition.

Vintage	07	06	05	04	03	02	01	00
WR	7	6	6	7	NM	7	6	7
Drink	10-16	10-15	10-14	10-14	NM	10-12	P	P

DRY $28 V+

Unison Selection ★★★★★

Designed for cellaring and oak-matured longer than the above wine, this is a consistently outstanding Hawke's Bay red. The Gimblett Gravels vines, more than a decade old, are densely planted and cropped lightly. A vineyard (rather than barrel) selection of Merlot, Cabernet Sauvignon and Syrah, it is matured initially for 20 months in French and American oak barriques (half new), then (for 'harmonising') for a further five months in large Italian casks of French and Slavonian oak. The 2006 vintage (★★★★★) is dark and still youthful in colour. Delicious now, it is rich and silky-textured, with sweet-fruit delights and deep blackcurrant and plum flavours. Drink now or cellar.

Vintage	06	05	04	03	02	01	00
WR	6	6	7	NM	7	6	7
Drink	10-17	10-16	10-16	NM	10-15	10-13	10-13

DRY $50 AV

Vin Alto Celaio ★★★☆

This Clevedon, South Auckland red was blended from traditional French and Italian grape varieties, such as Merlot, Sangiovese, Cabernet Franc and Montepulciano, and given a lengthy spell in oak barrels. Still on sale, the ruby-hued 2004 (★★★☆) is plummy, vibrantly fruity, flavoursome and supple.

Vintage	04
WR	6
Drink	10-12

DRY $39 –V

Vin Alto Retico ★★★★☆

On a relatively cool, elevated site at Clevedon, in South Auckland, Enzo Bettio set out 'to make traditional Italian-style wines in New Zealand'. His most prized wine, Retico, based on air-dried, highly concentrated grapes, is Clevedon's equivalent of the prized amarones of Verona. Based on traditional French and Italian grape varieties (such as Cabernet Franc, Merlot and Montepulciano), it is barrique-aged for two years. Still on sale, the 2003 vintage (★★★★☆) is a strapping wine (15.5 per cent alcohol), with full colour and rich, spicy, raisiny flavours. A muscular, concentrated and complex wine, it is best served at the end of a meal, 'with cheese, in front of the fire'.

Vintage	03
WR	7
Drink	10-17

DRY $85 –V

Vin Alto Ritorno ★★★★
Created in the Veronese ripasso tradition, this Clevedon, South Auckland red is a blend of traditional French and Italian grape varieties (such as Merlot, Cabernet Franc and Montepulciano), fermented on the skins of the air-dried Retico grapes (above) and oak-matured for two years. Still on sale, the 2000 vintage (★★★★) is fragrant and leathery, concentrated and slightly raisiny, in a style that demands food.

Vintage	00	99
WR	7	7
Drink	P	P

DRY $59 –V

Waipipi Wairarapa Waipipi Red ★★☆
The 2008 vintage (★★☆) is a blend of Cabernet Sauvignon (55 per cent), Merlot (25 per cent) and Cabernet Franc (20 per cent), grown in the Wairarapa and matured in French and American oak casks. Fullish in colour, with a sweet oak perfume, it is plummy and smooth, in an easy-drinking, mid-weight style.

Vintage	08
WR	5
Drink	10-12

DRY $25 –V

Wishart Legend ★★★☆
The rich, mature 2005 vintage (★★★★) is a Bay View, Hawke's Bay blend of Merlot (50 per cent), Malbec, Cabernet Franc and Syrah, barrel-aged for 20 months. It has a fragrant, complex bouquet, leading into a savoury wine with deep blackcurrant, spice and coffee flavours and firm, ripe tannins. Ready.

DRY $35 –V

Cabernet Franc

New Zealand's fifth most widely planted red-wine variety – just ahead of Malbec – Cabernet Franc is probably a mutation of Cabernet Sauvignon, the much higher profile variety with which it is so often blended. Jancis Robinson's phrase, 'a sort of claret Beaujolais', aptly sums up the nature of this versatile and underrated red-wine grape.

As a minority ingredient in the recipe of many of New Zealand's top reds, Cabernet Franc lends a delicious softness and concentrated fruitiness to its blends with Cabernet Sauvignon and Merlot. However, admirers of Château Cheval Blanc, the illustrious St Émilion (which is two-thirds planted in Cabernet Franc) have long appreciated that Cabernet Franc need not always be Cabernet Sauvignon's bridesmaid, but can yield fine red wines in its own right. The supple, fruity wines of Chinon and Bourgueil, in the Loire Valley, have also proved Cabernet Franc's ability to produce highly attractive, soft, light reds.

According to the latest national vineyard survey, the bearing area of Cabernet Franc will be 161 hectares in 2011 – well below the 213 hectares in 2004. Two-thirds of the vines are clustered in Hawke's Bay. As a varietal red, Cabernet Franc is lower in tannin and acid than Cabernet Sauvignon; or as Michael Brajkovich of Kumeu River puts it: 'more approachable and easy'.

Artisan Kauri Ridge Cabernet/Merlot (★★★★)

The densely coloured 2006 vintage (★★★★) is a generous, supple West Auckland blend of Cabernet Franc (60 per cent) and Merlot (40 per cent). It offers blackcurrant, spice and green-olive flavours, showing excellent concentration.

Vintage	06
WR	5
Drink	10-12

DRY $27 AV

Ascension The Benediction Reserve Cabernet Franc (★★★☆)

Grown at Matakana, the 2007 vintage (★★★☆) is a blend of Cabernet Franc (82 per cent) and Merlot (18 per cent), matured for 14 months in French and American oak barriques (a third new). It's a medium to full-bodied wine with plum, berry, herb and spice flavours, showing very good complexity and length, firm tannins, and more than a hint of red Bordeaux.

DRY $35 –V

Beach House Hawke's Bay Cabernet Franc (★★★★☆)

Grown in The Track Vineyard, in the Gimblett Gravels, the 2007 vintage (★★★★☆) was matured for a year in French and American oak casks. Deeply coloured, with a spicy fragrance, it's full-bodied, with strong, youthful flavours of blackcurrants, plums and spices, hints of dark chocolate and sweet oak, and a rich, smooth finish. Enjoyable now, it should also be long-lived.

Vintage	07
WR	7
Drink	10-30

DRY $25 V+

Clearview Reserve Cabernet Franc ★★★★☆

The very classy and elegant 2007 vintage (★★★★★) was hand-harvested from 21-year-old vines at Te Awanga, in Hawke's Bay, blended with Merlot (7 per cent) and Cabernet Sauvignon

(2 per cent), and matured for 16 months in French oak barriques (predominantly new). Deep and youthful in colour, with a floral bouquet and rich blackcurrant, plum, herb and nut flavours, it's a complex, age-worthy, distinctly Bordeaux-like style. Drink 2012+.

Vintage	07	06
WR	7	6
Drink	10-17	10-12

DRY $40 –V

Hawk's Nest Orchard Block Matakana Cabernet Franc/Malbec ★★★☆

The 2007 vintage (★★★☆) was grown at Matakana and matured in French oak casks (40 per cent new). A blend of Cabernet Franc (62 per cent) and Malbec (38 per cent), it has full, youthful colour. Mouthfilling, it has strong plum and spice flavours, fresh, vibrant and moderately complex, with smooth tannins.

DRY $32 –V

Jurassic Ridge Cabernet Franc ★★★☆

Grown at Church Bay, on Waiheke Island, the 2007 vintage (★★★★), which includes 14 per cent Merlot, has very attractive berry, plum and spice flavours, showing good freshness, ripeness and complexity.

Vintage	08
WR	7
Drink	10-14

DRY $29 –V

Man O' War Cabernet Franc/Merlot (★★★☆)

From the eastern end of Waiheke Island, the 2007 vintage (★★★☆) is a blend of Cabernet Franc (68 per cent), Merlot (24 per cent), Cabernet Sauvignon (5 per cent) and Petit Verdot (3 per cent), matured for 10 months in French and American oak casks. Full-coloured, fresh and vibrantly fruity, with cassis, plum and spice flavours, gently seasoned with oak, it's a mouthfilling, flavoursome wine, drinking well now.

DRY $28 –V

Matakana Estate Hawke's Bay Cabernet Franc/Merlot ★★★

Deeply coloured, the 2008 vintage (★★★☆) has a bouquet of blackcurrants and herbs. Full-flavoured, it is cedary, spicy and savoury, with some development showing.

DRY $27 –V

Omaha Bay Vineyard Matakana Cabernet Franc/Malbec/Petit Verdot ★★★☆

The 2007 vintage (★★★★), the best yet, is dark, brambly, concentrated and supple, in a very generous style, maturing well. The 2008 (★★★☆) is full-coloured, with good depth of vibrant, plummy, slightly herbal flavour, seasoned with sweet oak, and a smooth finish.

Vintage	08	07	06
WR	6	7	5
Drink	10-15	10-19	10-12

DRY $40 –V

Pyramid Valley Vineyards Growers Collection
Howell Family Vineyard Hawke's Bay Cabernet Franc (★★★★★)

Powerful and densely coloured, the 2007 vintage (★★★★★) was hand-picked in The Triangle from low-cropped vines (2 tonnes/hectare), fermented with indigenous yeasts, and matured for 20 months in French oak barriques (35 per cent new). It's a highly concentrated red with ripe blackcurrant, herb and plum flavours showing excellent density, structure and cellaring potential. Best drinking 2012+.

DRY $52 AV

Sileni The Pacemaker Hawke's Bay Cabernet Franc ★★★☆

Grown in The Triangle and matured in French (85 per cent) and American oak barriques, the 2008 vintage (★★★☆) is drinking well now, with deep colour and strong blackcurrant and herb flavours, soft and attractive. It's an easy-drinking style with very satisfying weight, balance and depth.

Vintage	08
WR	7
Drink	11-16

DRY $30 –V

Te Kairanga Jack's Union Cabernet Franc/Cabernet Sauvignon ★★★☆

The 2005, 2006 and 2007 vintages of Te Kairanga's Cabernet Franc-based reds, grown in Hawke's Bay, are all on sale now. Based on different varietal proportions (and labelled accordingly), they are all of very good quality. My pick is the 2006 (★★★★), a blend of 76 per cent Cabernet Franc and 24 per cent Cabernet Sauvignon. Deeply coloured, it is rich and ripe, vibrantly fruity and concentrated, with good complexity and harmony.

Vintage	07	06	05
WR	6	6	6
Drink	10-15	10-14	10-13

DRY $22 AV

Cabernet Sauvignon and Cabernet-predominant blends

Cabernet Sauvignon has proved a tough nut to crack in New Zealand. Mid-priced models were – until recently – usually of lower quality than a comparable offering from Australia, where the relative warmth suits the late-ripening Cabernet Sauvignon variety. Yet a top New Zealand Cabernet-based red from a favourable vintage can hold its own in illustrious company, and the overall standard of today's offerings is far higher than many wine lovers realise – which makes for some great bargains.

Cabernet Sauvignon was widely planted here in the nineteenth century. The modern resurgence of interest in the great Bordeaux variety was led by Tom McDonald, the legendary Hawke's Bay winemaker, whose string of elegant (though, by today's standards, light) Cabernet Sauvignons under the McWilliam's label, from the much-acclaimed 1965 vintage to the gold-medal winning 1975, proved beyond all doubt that fine-quality red wines could be produced in New Zealand.

During the 1970s and 1980s, Cabernet Sauvignon ruled the red-wine roost in New Zealand. Since then, as winemakers – especially in the South Island, but also Hawke's Bay – searched for red-wine varieties that would ripen more fully and consistently in our relatively cool grapegrowing climate than Cabernet Sauvignon, it has been pushed out of the limelight by Merlot, Pinot Noir and Syrah. According to the latest national vineyard survey, between 2003 and 2011, the country's total area of bearing Cabernet Sauvignon vines will contract from 741 to 519 hectares. Growers with suitably warm sites have often retained faith in Cabernet Sauvignon, but others have moved on to less challenging varieties.

Three-quarters of the country's Cabernet Sauvignon vines are clustered in Hawke's Bay, and Auckland also has significant plantings. In the South Island, where only 7 per cent of the vines are planted, Cabernet-based reds have typically lacked warmth and richness. This magnificent but late-ripening variety's future in New Zealand clearly lies in the warmer vineyard sites of the north.

What is the flavour of Cabernet Sauvignon? When newly fermented a herbal character is common, intertwined with blackcurrant-like fruit aromas. New oak flavours, firm acidity and taut tannins are other hallmarks of young, fine Cabernet Sauvignon. With maturity the flavour loses its aggression and the wine develops roundness and complexity, with assorted cigar-box, minty and floral scents emerging. It is infanticide to broach a Cabernet Sauvignon-based red with any pretensions to quality at less than two years old; at about four years old the rewards of cellaring really start to flow.

Abbey Cellars Cardinal Cabernet Sauvignon ★★★

Still on sale and maturing very solidly, the 2006 vintage (★★★) was grown at Bridge Pa, in Hawke's Bay. A blend of Cabernet Sauvignon (87 per cent) with Cabernet Franc, Merlot and Malbec, it was matured for a year in new French oak casks. Medium to full-bodied, with blackcurrant, plum and slight chocolate flavours, an earthy streak and a smooth finish, it's a mellow style, ready for drinking.

DRY $30 –V

Artisan Kauri Ridge Vineyard Cabernet/Merlot – see the Cabernet Franc section

Ashwell Martinborough Cabernet Sauvignon ★★★

The 2008 vintage (★★★), matured in French oak barriques, has deep, youthful colour. It's a medium-bodied style, fruity, flavoursome and supple, with fresh acidity, and should mature solidly. The more substantial 2009 (★★★☆) is full-coloured, fruity and smooth, with ripe blackcurrant, herb and nut flavours, gentle tannins and some savoury complexity. Drink now or cellar.

Vintage	09	08
WR	6	5
Drink	10-16	10-14

DRY $26 –V

Askerne Reserve Cabernet/Merlot/Franc ★★★☆

Still on sale, the 2006 vintage (★★☆) is a blend of Cabernet Sauvignon (50 per cent), Merlot (35 per cent) and Cabernet Franc (15 per cent), matured for 20 months in French oak casks (60 per cent new). It has deep, slightly developed colour and moderately herbaceous flavours, fairly soft and mature.

DRY $30 –V

Aspire Cabernet Sauvignon/Merlot (★★★)

From Matariki, the 2006 vintage (★★★) is a Hawke's Bay red, grown in the Gimblett Gravels and barrel-aged for a year. Full-coloured, with a slightly leafy bouquet, it's a fruit-driven style with fresh berry, plum and spice flavours and a very restrained oak influence.

Vintage	06
WR	5
Drink	10-11

DRY $20 –V

Awaroa Waiheke Island Cabernet/Merlot/Malbec ★★★☆

The 2006 vintage (★★★★) was hand-picked from 'organic' vineyards and matured in French oak casks (50 per cent new). Deeply coloured, with lots of spicy French oak on the nose, it has good density of vibrant, blackcurrant-like flavours and a hint of herbs, in a savoury, firm style. The 2007 (★★★) has solid depth of plum, spice and herb flavours, showing some complexity.

Vintage	06	05	04
WR	6	7	5
Drink	10-14	10-14	P

DRY $30 –V

Babich Irongate Cabernet/Merlot/Franc ★★★★★

Grown in the Irongate Vineyard in Gimblett Road, Hawke's Bay and matured in French oak barriques (30 per cent new), this elegant, complex, firmly structured red is designed for cellaring. The 2007 vintage (★★★★★) is notably classy and refined. A blend of Cabernet Sauvignon (34 per cent), Merlot (33 per cent) and Cabernet Franc (33 per cent), it was barrel-aged for 21 months. Deeply coloured, it has pure, blackcurrant-like flavours to the fore, rich and ripe, but not heavy, in a subtle style that will appeal strongly to Bordeaux lovers. Fragrant and savoury, with plummy, spicy, slightly earthy flavours, it offers excellent complexity, harmony and depth – and great drinkability.

DRY $33 V+

Babich The Patriarch – see the Branded and Other Red Wines section

Beach House Hawke's Bay Cabernet/Malbec (★★★★)

The 2007 vintage (★★★★) is a 60:40 blend of Cabernet Sauvignon and Malbec, grown in The Track Vineyard in Mere Road, in the Gimblett Gravels, and matured for a year in French and American oak casks. Boldly coloured, it is youthful and concentrated, with fresh, vibrant blackcurrant, plum and spice flavours, tinged with sweet oak, a hint of coffee, and good tannin support. Fine value.

Vintage	07
WR	7
Drink	10-30

DRY $20 V+

Brookfields Ohiti Estate Cabernet Sauvignon ★★★☆

Hawke's Bay winemaker Peter Robertson believes that Ohiti Estate produces 'sound Cabernet Sauvignon year after year – which is a major challenge to any vineyard'. The 2007 vintage (★★★★), matured for a year in French and American oak casks, is one of the best. Dark, with the distinctive aromas of Cabernet Sauvignon and mouthfilling body, it has strong blackcurrant, plum, spice and herb flavours, showing good concentration.

Vintage	07	06
WR	7	7
Drink	10-17	10-13

DRY $19 V+

Brookfields Reserve Vintage ['Gold Label'] Cabernet/Merlot ★★★★★

Brookfields' 'gold label' red is one of the most powerful and long-lived reds in Hawke's Bay. At its best, it is a thrilling wine – robust, tannin-laden and overflowing with very rich cassis, plum and mint flavours. Since 2000, the grapes have been sourced from the Lyons family's sloping, north-facing vineyard at Bridge Pa, and the wine is matured for 18 months in French oak barriques (95 to 100 per cent new). The 2007 vintage (★★★★★) is dark and youthful in colour, with a fragrant bouquet of blackcurrants and herbs. Highly concentrated, yet supple, it has deep cassis, herb and spice flavours, in a serious, complex yet approachable style that reminded me of a good St Estèphe. Drink now or cellar.

Vintage	07	06	05	04	03	02	01	00
WR	7	7	NM	7	NM	7	NM	7
Drink	10-19	10-16	NM	10-12	NM	P	NM	10-12

DRY $55 AV

Canadoro Cabernet Sauvignon ★★★☆

The dark 2006 vintage (★★★★) of this Martinborough red should be long-lived. Matured for 18 months in French oak barriques (new and seasoned), it's a stylish, finely textured wine with highly concentrated, well-ripened blackcurrant, herb and nut flavours.

DRY $30 –V

Church Road Cabernet/Merlot – see Church Road Merlot/Cabernet

Church Road Cuve Series Hawke's Bay Cabernet Sauvignon (★★★★★)

The 2007 vintage (★★★★★) was grown at two sites – Pernod Ricard NZ's Redstone Vineyard in The Triangle and in the Gimblett Gravels – and matured for 22 months in French oak barriques (50 per cent new). A classic claret style, with deep colour and deliciously concentrated blackcurrant and spice flavours, it shows lovely fruit sweetness and varietal purity, with firm, fine-grained tannins. A top buy.

DRY $26 V+

Church Road Reserve Hawke's Bay Cabernet/Merlot ★★★★★

The dark, flavour-drenched 2007 vintage (★★★★★) shows just what Hawke's Bay can do in a favourable season with Cabernet Sauvignon-predominant reds. Hand-picked and matured for 21 months in French oak barriques, it is dense and boldly coloured, with concentrated blackcurrant, herb and nut flavours, showing good, savoury complexity, and a firm underlay of tannin. A top candidate for the cellar.

Vintage	07
WR	7
Drink	10-15

DRY $36 V+

C.J. Pask Declaration Cabernet/Merlot/Malbec ★★★★

Refined, with deep, youthful colour, the 2005 vintage (★★★★) is a Gimblett Gravels blend of Cabernet Sauvignon (48 per cent), Merlot (35 per cent) and Malbec (17 per cent), matured for 18 months in French and American oak casks. Warm, savoury and tightly structured, it offers excellent concentration of brambly, herbal, spicy flavours. The 2007 (★★★★), matured for 18 months in oak barriques (100 per cent new), is dark, with rich blackcurrant, spice and herb flavours, braced by firm tannins.

DRY $45 –V

C.J. Pask Gimblett Road Cabernet/Merlot/Malbec ★★★★

The 2007 vintage (★★★☆) is a blend of Cabernet Sauvignon (56 per cent), Merlot (27 per cent) and Malbec (17 per cent), barrel-aged for 16 to 18 months. Dark, it has concentrated plum and spice flavours, the herbal, leafy notes typical of Cabernet Sauvignon, and good structure and complexity.

DRY $20 V+

Clearview Cape Kidnappers Cabernet/Merlot ★★★☆

Grown in Hawke's Bay and matured for a year in French and American oak casks (mostly seasoned), this is typically a sturdy red with sweet-fruit characters and plenty of savoury, spicy flavour. The 2007 vintage (★★★☆) is a blend of estate-grown, hand-picked Cabernet Sauvignon (44 per cent) with Merlot (42 per cent) and Malbec (14 per cent). Made for early drinking, it's a vibrantly fruity, deeply coloured red with good depth of berryish, slightly minty flavour, a hint of sweet oak and a smooth finish.

Vintage	07
WR	7
Drink	10-14

DRY $21 AV

Coopers Creek SV Gimblett Gravels Cabernet Sauvignon (★★★)

The 2007 vintage (★★★) is a 'straight' Cabernet Sauvignon, barrel-aged for a year. Dark, it is concentrated and tannic, with ripe blackcurrant and cedar notes, showing some complexity and length, but also a slight lack of charm.

Vintage	07
WR	7
Drink	10-12

DRY $28 –V

Coopers Creek SV Gimblett Gravels Hawke's Bay Cabernet/Merlot ★★★★

The 2007 vintage (★★★★) is dark, with blackcurrant and spice flavours, hints of herbs and coffee, and a firm finish. A tightly structured blend (65 per cent Cabernet Sauvignon, 35 per cent Merlot), barrel-aged for a year, it shows good concentration and length.

Vintage	07
WR	7
Drink	10-13

DRY $28 AV

Corbans Cottage Block Hawke's Bay Cabernet/Merlot (★★★★★)

The 2007 vintage (★★★★★) is a majestic red. Matured for two years in French oak barriques (new and one-year-old), and bottled without fining or filtration, it is deeply coloured, with layers of blackcurrant, plum and spice flavours, complex and concentrated, and ripe, supple tannins. Dense and savoury, it should flourish for a decade; open 2012+.

DRY $35 V+

Corbans Homestead Hawke's Bay Cabernet Sauvignon/Merlot ★★★

From Pernod Ricard NZ, the 2008 vintage (★★★) is deeply coloured, with good body, satisfying depth of blackcurrant and herb flavours and a smooth finish.

DRY $17 AV

Cornerstone Cabernet/Merlot/Malbec –
see Newton Forrest Estate Cornerstone in the Branded and Other Red Wines section

Delegat's Hawke's Bay Cabernet/Merlot ★★★☆

The 2007 vintage (★★★☆) is dark, with generous blackcurrant, plum and spice flavours. Fruity and supple, with a gentle seasoning of oak, it shows very good ripeness, balance and depth. The 2008 (★★★) is medium-bodied, with fresh blackcurrant and herb flavours in a fruit-driven style with a touch of complexity.

Vintage	08	07	06	05
WR	7	6	6	6
Drink	10-14	10-13	10-12	10-12

DRY $17 V+

Delegat's Reserve Hawke's Bay Cabernet Sauvignon/Merlot ★★★★

Top vintages offer great value. The 2007 (★★★★) is a 50:50 blend of Cabernet Sauvignon and Merlot, grown in the Gimblett Gravels and barrel-aged for a year. Dark, with cedary, spicy oak seasoning blackberry and green-olive flavours, it shows good richness and complexity.

Vintage	07	06
WR	6	5
Drink	10-13	10-13

DRY $20 V+

Distant Land Hawke's Bay Cabernet/Merlot (★★★★)

The black label 'reserve' 2006 vintage (★★★★) is a dark, Cabernet Sauvignon-based red (71 per cent), with Merlot (20 per cent) and Cabernet Franc (9 per cent). Grown in the Gimblett Gravels and matured for 16 months in French oak barrels (half new), it's vibrant, with excellent concentration of cassis, plum and spice flavours, ripe and firm. A tightly structured wine, it should reward cellaring.

DRY $34 –V

Doubtless Cabernet Sauvignon ★★★

Estate-grown at Doubtless Bay, in Northland, the 2004 vintage (★★★) includes 5 per cent Merlot and was matured for 22 months in new French oak barriques. Maturing well, it's a full-coloured wine with good varietal character and plenty of blackcurrant-like flavour, firm and moderately complex. The 2005 (★★★) is full-coloured, with blackcurrant and spice flavours, showing some depth and complexity.

Vintage	05	04	03	02
WR	5	5	4	2
Drink	10-13	10-12	P	P

DRY $20 –V

Dunleavy Cabernet/Merlot ★★★☆

The second-tier red from Waiheke Vineyards, best known for Te Motu Cabernet/Merlot. It is typically like a minor Bordeaux – savoury and leafy, with plummy, spicy flavours, balanced for early consumption. Drinking well now, the 2006 vintage (★★★☆) is medium-bodied, with vibrant blackcurrant, herb and spice flavours, showing some savoury complexity.

DRY $45 –V

Goldwater Cabernet Sauvignon & Merlot –
see Goldwater Goldie in the Branded and Other Red Wines section

Hyperion Kronos Cabernet/Merlot/Malbec ★★★☆

Still on sale, the 2005 vintage (★★★☆) was grown at Matakana, north of Auckland. A blend of Cabernet Sauvignon (60 per cent), Merlot (30 per cent) and Malbec (10 per cent), matured for a year in French and American oak casks, it is fullish in colour, berryish, plummy, fruity and smooth, with gentle tannins.

Vintage	05	04
WR	6	6
Drink	10-15	10-14

DRY $31 –V

Hyperion The Titan Cabernet Sauvignon ★★★☆

This Matakana red is very good, but not as gigantic as 'titan' suggests. The 2007 vintage (★★★☆), matured in European and American oak casks, is full-coloured, with perfumed, sweet oak aromas. Mouthfilling and smooth, with blackcurrant, herb, olive and spice flavours tinged with sweet oak, it is savoury and complex, and drinking well now.

Vintage	07	06	05	04
WR	6	6	4	6
Drink	10-20	10-16	10-14	10-14

DRY $42 –V

Isola Estate Cabernet/Merlot (★★★★)

Grown on Waiheke Island, the 2008 vintage (★★★★) is an impressive blend of Cabernet Sauvignon (52 per cent), Merlot (42 per cent), Cabernet Franc (5 per cent) and Malbec (1 per cent). Deeply coloured, it offers fresh, youthful, generous berry and plum flavours, showing excellent concentration. Drink 2011+.

DRY $37 –V

John Forrest Collection Cabernet Sauvignon (★★★★★)

A star label on the rise. The authoritative 2005 vintage (★★★★★) is based on mature, low-cropped (4 to 5.6 tonnes/hectare) vines in the Gimblett Gravels district of Hawke's Bay, and matured in French oak barriques (one-third new). Notably concentrated, complex and well-structured, with bold colour, it is dense, warm, spicy, nutty and layered, with firm, ripe tannins and great potential. The more forward 2006 vintage (★★★★☆) is already delicious. Dark, with rich, ripe blackcurrant, plum, spice and nut flavours, it shows impressive complexity and density, with a well-rounded finish.

Vintage	06	05
WR	6	6
Drink	12-20	12-20

DRY $65 AV

Johner Estate Lyndor Wairarapa Cabernet & Merlot ★★★★

Full of personality, the 2009 vintage (★★★★) is deeply coloured, with hints of coffee and spices on the nose. Fresh, sweet-fruited and rich, it has strong blackcurrant, plum, herb and spice flavours, seasoned with nutty oak, and fairly firm tannins. Well worth cellaring.

Vintage	09	08
WR	6	6
Drink	11-20	10-17

DRY $50 –V

Johner Estate Wairarapa Cabernet/Merlot/Malbec ★★★★

The classy, deeply coloured 2009 vintage (★★★★) is rich, with concentrated plum, nut, herb and spice flavours. Showing good complexity, it's a dense, firmly structured wine, built to last; open 2012+.

Vintage	09	08	07
WR	6	6	5
Drink	11-18	12-17	10-11

DRY $39 –V

Kennedy Point Reserve Cabernet Sauvignon ★★★★

The 2005 vintage (★★★★☆) was grown on Waiheke Island, in Auckland, and blended with Merlot (12 per cent) and Cabernet Franc (3 per cent). Deeply coloured, with rich, ripe flavours of blackcurrants, herbs and spices, it's drinking beautifully now.

Vintage	05	04
WR	7	6
Drink	10-17	10-15

DRY $49 –V

Kerr Farm Kumeu Cabernet Sauvignon ★★☆

Full marks to Kerr Farm for keeping the Cabernet Sauvignon flag flying, but it's not an easy variety to succeed with in West Auckland. The 2006 vintage (★★☆) was matured for a year in French and American oak casks (30 per cent new). Fullish in colour, it has leafy aromas and flavours in a berryish, fruity style, offering smooth, easy drinking. Ready.

DRY $22 –V

Longview Estate Gumdiggers Reserve Cabernet Sauvignon (★★★)

The 2005 vintage (★★★) is a Northland red, estate-grown south of Whangarei and French oak-aged for 18 months. It's an honest, mellow red with fullish, slightly developed colour and moderately concentrated, spicy, herbal flavours.

DRY 28 –V

Man O' War Cabernet Sauvignon/Cabernet Franc/Merlot (★★★★)

Grown on Waiheke Island, the 2007 vintage (★★★★) was matured for 10 months in French and American oak casks. Full-coloured, with a fragrant, spicy bouquet, it has good concentration of blackcurrant, spice and plum flavours, finely integrated oak and firm, ripe tannins. Already highly approachable, it should mature well.

Vintage	07
WR	5
Drink	10-12

DRY $28 AV

Matariki Hawke's Bay Cabernet Sauvignon/Merlot (★★★★)

The sturdy, rich 2007 vintage (★★★★) is a blend of Cabernet Sauvignon (57 per cent), Merlot (28 per cent), Cabernet Franc (10 per cent) and Syrah (5 per cent), grown in the Gimblett Gravels, Hawke's Bay, and matured for 21 months in French oak barriques (20 per cent new). Still fresh and youthful, it is boldly coloured, with deep blackcurrant, plum, mint and spice flavours, vibrant and supple. Worth cellaring.

Vintage	07
WR	6
Drink	10-14

DRY $27 AV

Matariki Reserve Cabernet Sauvignon (★★★★★)

Showing power and elegance, the outstanding 2007 vintage (★★★★★) is a hand-picked blend of Cabernet Sauvignon (90 per cent), Merlot (5 per cent) and Cabernet Franc (5 per cent), grown in the Gimblett Gravels, Hawke's Bay, and matured for 22 months in oak casks (58 per cent new). Deeply coloured, it is fleshy and ripe, with concentrated blackcurrant, plum and spice flavours, a hint of mint, and fine-grained tannins giving a lovely texture.

Vintage	07
WR	7
Drink	10-15

DRY $40 AV

Mebus Dakins Road Wairarapa Cabernet/Merlot/Malbec (★★☆)

The 2007 vintage (★★☆) is flavoursome and spicy, with some complexity, but also lacks full ripeness, with green, leafy notes detracting.

DRY $18 –V

Mills Reef Elspeth Cabernet/Merlot ★★★★★

Grown at the company's close-planted Mere Road site in the Gimblett Gravels, this is a consistently impressive Hawke's Bay red. The 2007 vintage (★★★★★), harvested at 24 brix, is a blend of Cabernet Sauvignon (70 per cent) and Merlot (30 per cent) matured for over a year in French oak barriques (20 per cent new). It's a full-bodied, very 'complete' wine, fragrant and finely textured with rich blackcurrant, plum and spice flavours, ripe, supple tannins and a long finish. Fleshy, savoury and generous, it's already delicious.

Vintage	07	06	05	04	03	02
WR	7	7	7	7	NM	7
Drink	10-17	10-16	10-15	10-15	NM	P

DRY $40 AV

Mills Reef Elspeth Cabernet Sauvignon ★★★★★

The 2007 vintage (★★★★☆) was hand-picked in the company's Mere Road Vineyard, in the Gimblett Gravels of Hawke's Bay, fermented partly with indigenous yeasts, and matured for 16 months in French oak barrels (60 per cent new). Rich, sweet-fruited and smooth, it has very ripe blackcurrant, plum, spice and liquorice flavours, showing good density and complexity, and gentle, silky tannins.

Vintage	07	06	05	04
WR	7	7	7	7
Drink	10-18	10-17	10-16	10-15

DRY $40 AV

Mills Reef Elspeth Trust Vineyard Cabernet Sauvignon ★★★★☆

The elegant 2007 vintage (★★★★☆) is a blend of Cabernet Sauvignon (85 per cent) and Cabernet Franc (15 per cent), harvested at 24.2 brix in Mere Road, in the Gimblett Gravels of Hawke's Bay, and matured for over a year in French oak casks (60 per cent new). Fragrant and boldly coloured, with a distinct but attractive herbal element, it has rich blackcurrant, green-olive and nut flavours, and fine, supple tannins.

Vintage	07	06
WR	7	6
Drink	10-17	10-16

DRY $40 –V

Mills Reef Reserve Cabernet/Merlot ★★★★☆

The latest releases of this Hawke's Bay red have delivered fine value. The 2007 vintage (★★★★), blended from Cabernet Sauvignon (65 per cent) and Merlot (35 per cent), is dark, fragrant and full, with the lovely, blackcurrant-like flavours of ripe Cabernet Sauvignon to the fore, a subtle oak influence – six months in French (70 per cent) and American (30 per cent) casks (35 per cent new) – and the underlying structure to age.

Vintage	07	06	05	04	03	02
WR	7	7	7	7	6	7
Drink	10-12	10-11	P	P	P	P

DRY $25 V+

Miro Cabernet/Merlot/Franc/Malbec (★★★★)

The highly attractive 2008 vintage (★★★★) is a Waiheke Island blend of Cabernet Sauvignon (52 per cent), Merlot (30 per cent), Cabernet Franc (17 per cent) and Malbec (1 per cent). An elegant, youthful red, it is deeply coloured, with concentrated, plummy, spicy flavours, ripe and savoury.

DRY $45 –V

Mission Hawke's Bay Cabernet/Merlot ★★★

The 2007 vintage (★★★★) is a top buy. A blend of Cabernet Sauvignon (43 per cent), Merlot (42 per cent), Cabernet Franc (10 per cent) and Malbec (5 per cent), it is deeply coloured, with strong blackcurrant, spice and coffee flavours, brambly, ripe and supple. The 2008 (★★★) is a mouthfilling, lightly oaked style with plenty of blackcurrant, red-berry and spice flavour, fruity and smooth.

DRY $17 AV

Mission Hawke's Bay Cabernet Sauvignon ★★★

In favourable vintages, this red offers good value. The 2007 (★★★☆) includes 10 per cent Cabernet Franc and 5 per cent Malbec. Deeply coloured, it has very good depth of berry and green-olive flavours, tinged with sweet oak, and silky tannins. The 2008 (★★☆) is dark and flavoursome, but distinctly leafy, with a smooth finish.

DRY $17 AV

Mission Jewelstone Hawke's Bay Cabernet Sauvignon (★★★★☆)

The powerful, boldly coloured 2008 vintage (★★★★☆) is a blend of Cabernet Sauvignon (86 per cent) and Cabernet Franc (14 per cent), grown in the Gimblett Gravels and matured for 18 months in French oak casks (half new). Firm and youthful, it is fragrant, with ripe, sweet fruit characters, dense blackcurrant, plum and spice flavours, and powerful tannins. It's built to last; open 2013+.

Vintage	08
WR	7
Drink	12-20

DRY $38 AV

Mission Jewelstone Hawke's Bay Cabernet Sauvignon/Merlot/Cabernet Franc/Petit Verdot ★★★★☆

The 2007 vintage (★★★★☆) is a Gimblett Gravels blend of Cabernet Sauvignon (46 per cent), Merlot (31 per cent), Cabernet Franc (19 per cent) and Petit Verdot (4 per cent), matured in French oak barrels (73 per cent new). Dark, it is sweet-fruited and complex, with rich flavours of blackcurrants, spices and herbs, a hint of coffee, and firm tannins.

Vintage	07
WR	7
Drink	10-20

DRY $38 AV

Mission Reserve Gimblett Gravels Cabernet Sauvignon (★★★☆)

The 2008 vintage (★★★☆) of this Hawke's Bay red was grown in the Gimblett Gravels and matured in French oak casks (30 per cent new). Densely coloured, with a strong seasoning of nutty oak, it has cassis, plum, spice and herb flavours, with a firm tannin grip. An impressively concentrated red, but with a slight lack of roundness and charm in its youth, it could well reward cellaring; open 2012+.

Vintage	08
WR	7
Drink	11-20

DRY $24 AV

Mission Reserve Hawke's Bay Cabernet/Merlot ★★★★

Blended from four grape varieties – mostly Cabernet Sauvignon (49 per cent), Merlot (40 per cent) and Cabernet Franc (9 per cent) – with a splash of Petit Verdot, the 2007 vintage (★★★★) was grown in the Gimblett Gravels and matured in French oak casks (20 per cent new). Deep and youthful in colour, it is mouthfilling, with concentrated blackcurrant, plum, spice and nut flavours, and supple tannins. Already enjoyable, it should cellar well.

Vintage	07	06
WR	7	5
Drink	10-16	10-12

DRY $24 V+

Mission Reserve Hawke's Bay Cabernet Sauvignon ★★★☆

Grown at Moteo and in the Gimblett Gravels, and matured for over a year in French oak barriques (20 per cent new), the 2007 vintage (★★★☆) includes minor portions of Cabernet Franc (8 per cent) and Merlot (7 per cent). It's a generous, slightly leafy wine, concentrated and finely textured, with some coffee notes and supple tannins.

Vintage	07	06
WR	7	5
Drink	10-19	10-12

DRY $24 AV

Moana Park Vineyard Tribute Cabernet Sauvignon (★★★☆)

Deep and youthful in colour, the 2007 vintage (★★★☆) was hand-picked in the Gimblett Gravels, fermented with indigenous yeasts, and bottled unfined and unfiltered. It's a mouthfilling wine (14 per cent alcohol) with ripe berry and spice flavours, a hint of olives, and a smooth, well-rounded finish.

DRY $20 AV

Mudbrick Vineyard Cabernet Sauvignon/Merlot (★★★★)

Grown at Church Bay and Onetangi, on Waiheke Island, the 2008 vintage (★★★★) is deeply coloured and sturdy (14.2 per cent alcohol), with fresh, strong cassis, plum and spice flavours and ripe, supple tannins. Best drinking 2011+.

DRY $29 AV

Mudbrick Vineyard Cabernet
Sauvignon/Merlot/Cabernet Franc/Malbec (★★★☆)

The 2007 vintage (★★★☆) was grown on Waiheke Island. Richly coloured, it's a generous red, distinctly herbal, with very good complexity and depth. It's drinking well now.

DRY $26 –V

Newton/Forrest Cornerstone Cabernet/Merlot/Malbec
– see Newton Forrest Estate Cornerstone in the Branded and Other Red Wines section

Newton/Forrest Estate Gimblett Gravels
Hawke's Bay Cabernet Sauvignon ★★★★☆

Grown in the Cornerstone Vineyard, the 2007 vintage (★★★★☆) was matured in French (60 per cent) and American oak casks. Boldly coloured, it's a powerful wine (14.4 per cent alcohol), brambly, plummy and spicy, with hints of coffee and nuts, and firm, slightly chewy tannins.

Vintage	07	06
WR	7	7
Drink	10-15	10-12

DRY $40 –V

Ngatarawa Stables Cabernet/Merlot ★★★

Typically a sturdy Hawke's Bay red with drink-young appeal. The 2008 vintage (★★★) is full-coloured, with good depth of plum, berry and herb flavours, smooth and finely balanced for current drinking.

Vintage	08	07	06
WR	6	6	6
Drink	10-13	10-12	10-12

DRY $17 AV

Passage Rock Reserve Waiheke Island Cabernet Sauvignon/Merlot ★★★★☆

The 2008 vintage (★★★★) is a classy red, blended from Cabernet Sauvignon (80 per cent), Merlot (15 per cent) and Malbec (5 per cent), matured in 'predominantly new oak barriques'. Deep and bright in colour, it has good weight and strong blackcurrant, berry, spice and nut flavours, showing good density and complexity. Finely balanced and supple, it's well worth cellaring.

DRY $40 –V

Peacock Sky Cabernet Sauvignon (★★★☆)

The 2009 vintage (★★★☆) is a Waiheke Island red, blended from Cabernet Sauvignon (90 per cent) and Cabernet Franc (10 per cent). Matured for a year in new barrels, it is sweetly oaked, with blackcurrant and plum flavours in a smooth, easy-drinking style.

Vintage	09
WR	5
Drink	11-18

DRY $35 –V

St Jerome Matuka Cabernet Sauvignon/Merlot ★★★☆

Grown and hand-harvested on a north-facing clay slope in Henderson, West Auckland, the 1999 vintage (★★★☆) was French oak-aged for two years. Spicy, slightly herbal, nutty and savoury, with fullish, mature colour, it has good complexity and depth, and is drinking well now. (Also tasted in mid to late 2008, the 1989 vintage is nutty, leafy and mellow, while the 1993 is probably at its peak, with lots of spicy, herbal, nutty flavour, firm and deep.)

DRY $43 –V

Sacred Hill Helmsman Cabernet/Merlot ★★★★★

The 2007 vintage (★★★★★) is crying out for cellaring. A powerful Hawke's Bay blend of Cabernet Sauvignon (53 per cent), Merlot (42 per cent) and Cabernet Franc (5 per cent), it was hand-picked in the Deerstalkers Vineyard, in the Gimblett Gravels, and French oak-matured for 18 months. Dark and fleshy, with a strong surge of blackcurrant, plum and spice flavours, showing excellent complexity, and fine-grained tannins, it's a bold, youthful red with obvious, long-term potential.

Vintage	07	06
WR	7	7
Drink	10-25	10-23

DRY $65 AV

Saints Hawke's Bay Cabernet/Merlot ★★★☆

The easy-drinking 2007 vintage (★★★☆) from Pernod Ricard NZ was partly matured in French and American oak casks. Deeply coloured, it has very good depth. The 2008 (★★★☆) is dark, with strong blackcurrant and plum flavours, showing some savoury complexity, and a smooth finish.

Vintage	08	07	06
WR	5	6	5
Drink	10-12	P	P

DRY $20 AV

Seifried Nelson Cabernet/Merlot ★★☆

Typically a medium-bodied red with lightish colour and berryish, leafy flavours, offering easy drinking. The 2009 vintage (★★★) was matured for a year in French oak barriques. Fullish in colour, it is gutsy (14.5 per cent alcohol), with strong berry, plum and spice flavours.

Vintage	09	08
WR	5	7
Drink	10-16	10-15

DRY $19 –V

Te Awa Cabernet/Merlot ★★★★

Estate-grown in the Gimblett Gravels of Hawke's Bay, the 2007 vintage (★★★★☆) is a dark, youthful blend of Cabernet Sauvignon (43 per cent) and Merlot (42 per cent), with splashes of Cabernet Franc and Malbec. Sturdy, with dense blackcurrant, plum and spice flavours, showing excellent complexity, it's a classic, firmly structured, claret-style red, approachable now, but still unfolding.

DRY $30 –V

Te Kairanga Jack's Union Hawke's Bay Cabernet Sauvignon/Merlot (★★★★)

Bargain-priced, the 2005 vintage (★★★★) is a blend of Cabernet Sauvignon (68 per cent) and Merlot (32 per cent), grown in the Gimblett Gravels and oak-aged. Deeply coloured, it is full-bodied, with excellent depth of cassis, plum, herb and spice flavours, oak complexity and good tannin support. It's drinking well now.

Vintage	05
WR	6
Drink	10-12

DRY $22 V+

Te Mata Awatea Cabernets/Merlot ★★★★★

Positioned below its Coleraine stablemate in Te Mata's hierarchy of Hawke's Bay, claret-style reds, since 1995 Awatea has been grown at Havelock North and in the Bullnose Vineyard, inland from Hastings. A blend of Cabernet Sauvignon, Merlot and Cabernet Franc – with a splash of Petit Verdot since 2001 – it is matured for about 18 months in French oak barriques (partly new). Compared to Coleraine, in its youth Awatea is more seductive, more perfumed, and tastes more of sweet, ripe fruit, but is more forward and slightly less concentrated. The wine can mature gracefully for many years, but is also typically delicious at two years old. The 2008 vintage (★★★★☆) is a blend of Cabernet Sauvignon (44 per cent), Merlot (33 per cent), Cabernet Franc (16 per cent), and Petit Verdot (7 per cent). Deeply coloured, it is refined, with concentrated, ripe blackcurrant, plum, herb and dark chocolate flavours, savoury, supple and showing good complexity. Already delicious, it's a forward vintage; drink now or cellar.

Vintage	08	07	06	05	04	03	02	01	00
WR	7	7	7	7	7	6	7	6	7
Drink	10-16	10-20	10-16	10-15	10-12	10-10	P	P	P

DRY $34 V+

Te Mata Coleraine – see the Branded and Other Red Wines section

Te Mata Woodthorpe Cabernet/Merlot –
see Te Mata Woodthorpe Merlot/Cabernet in the Merlot section

Te Motu Cabernet/Merlot ★★★★

The Dunleavy family's flagship Waiheke Island red is grown at Onetangi – over the fence from Stonyridge – and matured for three winters (about 28 months) in French (mostly), American and Hungarian barrels. Compared to its neighbour, it is less ripe and opulent than Stonyridge Larose, in a more earthy, leafy and savoury style. The disappointing 2004 vintage (★★★) is green-edged, showing some savoury complexity, but also a lack of real ripeness and richness. The 2005 (★★★★☆) is markedly better. Fragrant, it is full-coloured, with rich, complex, spicy flavours, hints of herbs and leather, and a good foundation of tannin. The 2006 (★★★★) is full-bodied and savoury, with vibrant berry and spice flavours, showing good complexity, and ripe tannins. (Note: the price varies slightly from vintage to vintage.)

DRY $90 –V

Terravin J Cabernet/Merlot/Malbec – see Terravin J Merlot/Malbec/Cabernet in the Merlot section

Villa Maria Reserve Hawke's Bay Cabernet Sauvignon/Merlot ★★★★★

The densely coloured 2008 vintage (★★★★★) is a blend of Cabernet Sauvignon (70 per cent) and Merlot (30 per cent), grown in the Gimblett Gravels and matured for 20 months in French oak barriques (60 per cent new). Purple/black, it is powerful, with fine-grained tannins and highly concentrated, brambly, plummy, spicy flavours, cedary and complex, showing excellent harmony and finesse. One for the cellar.

Vintage	08	07	06	05	04
WR	6	7	7	6	7
Drink	12-18	10-22	10-19	10-20	10-14

DRY $51 AV

Weeping Sands Waiheke Cabernet/Merlot ★★★★

The second label of Obsidian is grown at Onetangi ('weeping sands'). The 2007 vintage (★★★☆) is a blend of Cabernet Sauvignon (77 per cent), Merlot (18 per cent) and minor portions of Petit Verdot, Cabernet Franc and Malbec. Fragrant, full-coloured and sturdy, it has blackcurrant, plum and spice flavours, a leafy edge, and very good complexity and depth. The 2008 (★★★★☆), matured in new French (20 per cent) and seasoned French and American oak casks, is the one to buy. Deep and youthful in colour, it is generous and likely to be long-lived. Showing real power through the palate, it has blackcurrant, spice, herb and nut flavours, and the density and structure of many much higher-priced reds. Best drinking 2012 onwards.

Vintage	08	07	06	05	04	03	02
WR	7	5	6	6	6	4	7
Drink	11-16	10-15	10-14	10-14	P	P	P

DRY $26 AV

Carmenère

Ransom, at Matakana, in 2007 released New Zealand's first Carmenère. Now virtually extinct in France, Carmenère was once widely grown in Bordeaux and still is in Chile, where, until the 1990s, it was often mistaken for Merlot. In Italy it was long thought to be Cabernet Franc.

In 1988, viticulturist Alan Clarke imported Cabernet Franc cuttings here from Italy. Planted by Robin Ransom in 1997, the grapes ripened about the same time as the rest of his Cabernet Franc, but the look of the fruit and the taste of the wine were 'totally different'. So Ransom arranged DNA testing at the University of Adelaide. The result? His Cabernet Franc vines are in fact Carmenère.

The latest national vineyard survey records just 1 hectare of Carmenère in New Zealand.

Ransom Carmenère (★★★)

Still on sale, the 2006 vintage (★★★) is a deeply coloured Matakana red with a berryish, spicy, sweetly oaked bouquet. It's a medium to full-bodied wine (12 per cent alcohol) with blackcurrant and herb flavours and fresh acidity.

DRY $28 –V

Chambourcin

Chambourcin is one of the more highly rated French hybrids, well known in Muscadet for its good disease-resistance and bold, crimson hue. Rare in New Zealand (with only 4 hectares planted), it is most often found as a varietal red in Northland.

Ake Ake Chambourcin ★★★★

New Zealand's best Chambourcin. Grown near Kerikeri, in the Bay of Islands, the 2009 vintage (★★★★) is a typically fine example of the variety. Matured for a year in seasoned American and French barrels, it is densely coloured, sweet-fruited and mouthfilling, with concentrated plum, spice and slight liquorice flavours, fresh and finely balanced. If you enjoy Malbec, try this.

Vintage	09	08
WR	6	5
Drink	10-13	10-12

DRY $24 AV

Marsden Bay of Islands Chambourcin ★★★

The 2008 vintage (★★★☆) is a generous Northland red, matured for 16 months in predominantly American oak casks. Deeply coloured, it is mouthfilling and full-flavoured, ripe, plummy and soft.

DRY $24 –V

Okahu Chambourcin ★★★☆

The 2007 vintage (★★★) is an estate-grown Northland red, aged in American and French oak casks. It is a deeply coloured wine with fresh acidity, strong, fruity, plummy flavours and the sweet, coconutty aromas of American oak.

DRY $30 –V

Dolcetto

Grown in the north of Italy, where it produces purple-flushed, fruity, supple reds, usually enjoyed young, Dolcetto is extremely rare in New Zealand, with 2 hectares of bearing vines in 2011.

Hitchen Road Dolcetto ★★★☆

Grown at Pokeno, in North Waikato, the 2009 vintage (★★★☆) was barrel-matured for 10 months. Full-coloured, it is mouthfilling, with vibrant cherry/plum flavours, showing very good depth, a subtle oak influence and fresh acidity. It shows a slight lack of optimal warmth and roundness, but is a skilfully crafted wine, priced sharply.

Vintage	09
WR	6
Drink	10-13

DRY $15 V+

Waimea Nelson Dolcetto ★★★

The 2008 vintage (★★★) is a single-vineyard red, picked at 24 brix and matured for eight months in American oak barrels (25 per cent new). Ruby-hued, it is floral and distinctly spicy, in a moderately ripe style with tight plum and spice flavours, fresh acidity, and some savoury complexity.

Vintage	08
WR	6
Drink	10-12

DRY $22 –V

Gamay Noir

Gamay Noir is single-handedly responsible for the seductively scented and soft red wines of Beaujolais. The grape is still rare in New Zealand, although the area of bearing vines will rise between 2005 and 2011 from 9 to 12 hectares. In the Omaka Springs Vineyard in Marlborough, Gamay ripened later than Cabernet Sauvignon (itself an end-of-season ripener), with higher levels of acidity than in Beaujolais, but at Te Mata's Woodthorpe Terraces Vineyard in Hawke's Bay, the crop is harvested as early as mid-March.

Te Mata Estate Woodthorpe Vineyard Gamay Noir ★★★★

The 2010 vintage (★★★☆) is a single-vineyard Hawke's Bay red, whole-bunch fermented (in the traditional Beaujolais manner) and matured for three months in seasoned French oak casks. Ruby-hued, it is floral and supple, with cherry and plum flavours, fresh and lively, and a touch of nutty complexity. It's already drinking well.

Vintage	10	09	08
WR	7	7	7
Drink	10-12	P	P

DRY $19 V+

Malbec

With a leap from 25 hectares of bearing vines in 1998 to 157 hectares in 2011, this old Bordeaux variety is starting to make its presence felt in New Zealand, where two-thirds of all plantings are clustered in Hawke's Bay. It is often used as a blending variety, adding brilliant colour and rich, sweet fruit flavours to its blends with Merlot, Cabernet Sauvignon and Cabernet Franc. Numerous unblended Malbecs have also been released recently, possessing loads of flavour and often the slight rusticity typical of the variety.

Abbey Cellars Temptation Malbec (★★★☆)

The generous 2009 vintage (★★★☆) was estate-grown and hand-picked in The Triangle district of Hawke's Bay and French oak-matured for nine months. A 'fruit bomb' style, it has bold, purple-flushed colour and loads of plummy, smooth flavour, not complex, but enjoyably soft, fresh and strong.

DRY $31 –V

Awa Valley Malbec (★★☆)

Grown in West Auckland and oak-matured for a year, the 2009 vintage (★★☆) is full-coloured and fruity, in a medium-bodied style with vibrant berry and plum flavours that show a slight lack of warmth and roundness.

DRY $19 –V

Brookfields Hawke's Bay Sun Dried Malbec (★★★★)

Labelled as 'Malbec on steroids!', the bold, flavour-crammed 2009 vintage (★★★★) was made from sun-dried grapes, which concentrates their sugars and flavours. Dark and youthful in colour, it is robust (14.5 per cent alcohol), with plum, spice and nutty oak flavours, fresh, firm and dense. Best drinking 2012+.

Vintage	09
WR	7
Drink	11-20

DRY $25 AV

C.J. Pask Declaration Malbec ★★★☆

The 2006 vintage (★★★★) was grown in Gimblett Road, Hawke's Bay, and barrel-aged. Showing the typically slightly earthy and rustic notes of Malbec, it has vibrant blackcurrant and plum flavours, showing excellent concentration.

Vintage	06
WR	5
Drink	10-15

DRY $50 –V

Coopers Creek SV Huapai Malbec The Clays ★★★★

The boldly coloured 2008 vintage (★★★★) was estate-grown in West Auckland and matured for over a year in French oak casks (50 per cent new). Fleshy and vibrantly fruity, with concentrated plum and pepper flavours, it's a more elegant wine than many Malbecs, with fine-grained tannins and some aging potential.

Vintage	08	07	06
WR	6	NM	6
Drink	10-13	NM	10-12

DRY $28 AV

Fromm Malbec Fromm Vineyard ★★★★☆

Grown in Marlborough and matured for 16–18 months in French oak casks, the 2005 vintage (★★★★☆) is a classy red. Deeply coloured, with coffee and spice aromas, it is firm and highly concentrated, with cool-climate freshness and an almost Syrah-like spiciness. Winemaker Hätsch Kalberer suggests drinking it with 'a large piece of wild venison'.

Vintage	08	07	06	05	04	03	02
WR	6	6	6	6	6	NM	6
Drink	13-23	12-22	10-18	10-17	10-16	NM	1012

DRY $45 –V

Hawkesby Waiheke Island Coastal Malbec (★★★★☆)

From Stonyridge, the densely coloured and bold 2008 vintage (★★★★☆) is a single-vineyard red, grown at Church Bay. Matured for a year in one-year-old French oak barrels, it is fresh and youthful, with highly concentrated plum, spice and liquorice flavours, good tannin backbone, and the power to be long-lived.

DRY $80 –V

Hitchen Road Malbec ★★★

The mouthfilling 2008 vintage (★★★☆) was grown at Pokeno, in North Waikato. Barrique-aged for 10 months, it is deeply coloured, with fresh, strong, vibrant, plummy flavours and gentle tannins.

DRY $17 AV

Hyperion Midas Malbec ★★★

The 2008 vintage (★★☆) of this Matakana wine was French oak-aged for a year. Vibrantly fruity, berryish and plummy, it's an easy-drinking red, but lacks the complexity and richness you'd expect in its price bracket.

Vintage	08	07
WR	7	7
Drink	10-15	10-15

DRY $36 –V

Kirkpatrick Estate Winery Patutahi Reserve Malbec (★★★★)

The impressive 2009 vintage (★★★★) was estate-grown in Gisborne and barrel-aged for a year (with 30 per cent new oak). Dark and purple-flushed, it is fresh and vibrant, with blackcurrant, plum and spice flavours, showing excellent complexity and density. It's still very youthful; open 2012+.

Vintage	09
WR	7
Drink	10-15

DRY $35 –V

Lochiel Estate Reserve Mangawhai Malbec (★★★☆)

Estate-grown in Northland, the 2008 vintage (★★★☆) was aged for a year in American oak barriques. Deeply coloured, with the confectionery aromas of Malbec, it is fresh, with very good depth of ripe berry fruit and spice flavours, seasoned with sweet oak. Worth cellaring.

DRY $25 –V

Longview Estate Milly's Malbec (★★★★)

Estate-grown in Northland, the 2006 vintage (★★★★) was harvested three days before the death of Longview's co-founder, Milly Vuletich. Matured for two years in French oak barriques, it is full-coloured and sweet-fruited, with ripe, plummy, spicy flavours, showing good complexity. A generous, well-rounded northern style, it's delicious now.

DRY $45 –V

Maximus Matakana Malbec (★★)

From Mahurangi River, the 2008 vintage (★★) was estate-grown and matured for four months in French oak barriques. Light and leafy, with developed colour, it has green-edged aromas and flavours, lacking ripeness and richness. (At the time of writing, no price had been set, but the 2008 Maximus Merlot/Malbec was sold at $10.)

DRY $? V?

Miro Malbec (★★★☆)

Grown on Waiheke Island, the 2007 vintage (★★★☆) is a blend of Malbec (88 per cent) and Cabernet Sauvignon (12 per cent). Drinking well now, it's a medium-bodied style, with good depth of vibrant, plum/spice flavours, and a well-rounded finish.

DRY $35 –V

Newton Forrest Gimblett Gravels Hawke's Bay Malbec ★★★★☆

The 2006 vintage (★★★★☆) has dense, purple-flushed colour and a fragrant bouquet of spices, dark chocolate and sweet oak. Sturdy (14 per cent alcohol), it's a full-on style for those who enjoy super-charged reds. The 2007 (★★★★☆), matured in French (80 per cent) and American (20 per cent) oak casks, is dark, with a spicy, sweetly oaked, fragrant bouquet. It's a gutsy, concentrated wine, spicy, nutty, bold and firm, with plenty of life ahead.

Vintage	07	06
WR	6	6
Drink	10-12	10-12

DRY $35 AV

Stonyridge Luna Negra Waiheke Island Hillside Malbec ★★★★★

From Stonyridge, this is a consistently bold and classy red. Grown in the company's Vina del Mar Vineyard at Onetangi, it is matured for a year in American oak barriques (50 per cent new). The 2008 vintage (★★★★★) couples full-throttle power with complexity and the structure to age. Densely coloured, it's a powerful, fruit-packed wine with layers of blackcurrant, plum, spice and coffee flavours, needing another two years to round out. The 2009 (★★★★☆) is dark and dense, with oak complexity and concentrated plum and blackcurrant flavours. Still very fresh and vibrant, it needs time; open 2012+.

Vintage	09	08	07	06
WR	7	7	7	7
Drink	11-15	10-15	10-13	10-12

DRY $80 AV

TW Gisborne Malbec (★★★☆)

Enjoyable now, the 2007 vintage (★★★☆) is a full-coloured, American oak-aged red with good depth of plum and spice flavours, sweetly wooded and smooth.

Vintage	07
WR	7
Drink	10-15

DRY $24 AV

West Brook Waimauku Estate Malbec (★★★☆)

Deeply coloured, the 2008 vintage (★★★☆) was estate-grown in West Auckland. It has a floral, berryish bouquet, with the slight medicinal notes typical of Malbec, leading into a fresh, sweet-fruited wine, plummy and smooth, with plenty of flavour and drink-young appeal.

DRY $20 AV

Marzemino

Once famous, but today rare, Marzemino is cultivated in northern Italy, where it typically yields light, plummy reds. Not recorded separately in the latest national vineyard survey, it was first planted in New Zealand in 1995. Pernod Ricard NZ made the country's first commercial Marzemino under the Church Road brand in 2005.

Church Road Cuve Series Hawke's Bay Marzemino ★★★☆

The 2007 vintage (★★★☆) is densely coloured and gutsy, with bold blackcurrant and plum flavours and a rustic streak. The 2008 (★★★☆) is very well crafted, but reveals that Marzemino is not a classy variety. Dense and inky in colour, it is weighty and fruit-packed, but simple, with moderate length.

DRY $30 –V

Merlot

Pinot Noir is New Zealand's red-wine calling card on the world stage, but our Merlots are also proving competitive. In the year to June 2010, New Zealand exported over 290,000 cases of Merlot – a steep rise from only 24,194 cases in 2003.

Interest in this most extensively cultivated red-wine grape in Bordeaux is especially strong in Hawke's Bay (although Syrah has recently become the region's hottest red-wine variety). Everywhere in Bordeaux – the world's greatest red-wine region – except in the Médoc and Graves districts, the internationally higher-profile Cabernet Sauvignon variety plays second fiddle to Merlot. The elegant, fleshy wines of Pomerol and St Émilion bear delicious testimony to Merlot's capacity to produce great, yet relatively early-maturing, reds.

In New Zealand, after initial preoccupation with the more austere and slowly evolving Cabernet Sauvignon, the rich, rounded flavours and (more practically) earlier-ripening ability of Merlot are now fully appreciated. Poor fruit set can be a major drawback with the older clones, reducing yields, but Merlot ripens ahead of Cabernet Sauvignon, a major asset in cooler wine regions, especially in vineyards with colder clay soils. Merlot grapes are typically lower in tannin and higher in sugar than Cabernet Sauvignon's; its wines are thus silkier and a shade stronger in alcohol.

Hawke's Bay has almost three-quarters of New Zealand's Merlot vines; the rest are clustered in Marlborough, Auckland and Gisborne. The country's fifth most widely planted variety (now trailing Pinot Gris), Merlot covers more than two and a half times the area of Cabernet Sauvignon. Between 2003 and 2011, the total area of bearing Merlot vines is expanding at a very moderate pace, from 1249 to 1386 hectares, but in top vintages, such as 2007, the wines offer terrific value.

Merlot's key role in New Zealand was traditionally that of a minority blending variety, bringing a soft, mouthfilling richness and floral, plummy fruitiness to its marriages with the predominant Cabernet Sauvignon. Now, with a host of straight Merlots and Merlot-predominant blends on the market, this aristocratic grape is fully recognised as a top-flight wine in its own right.

Abbey Cellars Graduate Merlot/Cabernets ★★★☆

The 2006 vintage (★★★☆) is a full-coloured Hawke's Bay blend of Merlot (72 per cent) with smaller portions of Cabernet Franc, Malbec and Cabernet Sauvignon. Estate-grown at Bridge Pa and French oak-aged for a year, it is an earthy style with good body, strong, ripe, sweet-fruit flavours of plums and spices, and a rounded finish. Showing good, bottle-aged complexity, it's ready for drinking.

DRY $30 –V

Ake Ake Northland Merlot (★★★)

Grown at Kerikeri, the 2009 vintage (★★★) was matured in tanks and seasoned American oak barriques. Perfumed, sweet oak aromas lead into a vibrant wine with ripe, plummy flavours, seasoned with sweet, coconut-like oak, and some savoury complexity. Drink mid-2011+.

Vintage	09
WR	5
Drink	10-13

DRY $20 –V

Alexander Martinborough Merlot ★★★

The 2009 vintage (★★★☆) is a single-vineyard red, matured in American and French oak barrels. Full and bright in colour, it is mouthfilling and vibrantly fruity, with generous, plummy flavours, tinged with sweet oak, and ripe, supple tannins. It's enjoyable young.

DRY $25 –V

Alexia Hawke's Bay Merlot (★★☆)

The 2007 vintage (★★☆) was harvested from young vines at Maraekakaho and partly oak-aged. It is now showing considerable development, with green, leafy notes emerging.

DRY $18 –V

Alpha Domus The Pilot Hawke's Bay Merlot/Cabernet ★★★

Enjoyable now, the full-coloured 2007 vintage (★★★☆) is a blend of Merlot, Cabernet Sauvignon, Cabernet Franc and Malbec, matured for 19 months in seasoned French (80 per cent) and American oak barriques. It's a fairly firm red with very good depth of blackcurrant, spice and dark chocolate flavours, hints of sweet oak and some savoury complexity.

Vintage	07
WR	6
Drink	10-15

DRY $20 –V

Ascension The Twelve Apostles Matakana Merlot/Malbec ★★☆

Made from 'twelve special rows of vines we call "The Twelve Apostles"', this American oak-aged blend is typically berryish, plummy and slightly herbal. The 2007 vintage (★★), which includes 20 per cent Malbec, is fullish in colour, with a leafy bouquet and crisp, green-edged flavours that lack ripeness and roundness.

DRY $24 –V

Askerne Hawke's Bay Merlot/Franc/Malbec ★★★

The 2007 vintage (★★★) is a blend of Merlot (67 per cent), Cabernet Franc (20 per cent) and Malbec (13 per cent), matured in French oak casks (22 per cent new). Estate-grown, it is deeply coloured and full-bodied, with strong plum, spice and herb flavours. It's green-edged, but also shows some complexity and generosity.

Vintage	07	06	05
WR	6	5	6
Drink	12-15	10-11	P

DRY $20 –V

Askerne Reserve Hawke's Bay Merlot ★★★☆

The 2007 vintage (★★★☆) was estate-grown near Havelock North and matured for a year in French oak casks (62 per cent new). Deep and still youthful in colour, it is fleshy, with generous blackcurrant, spice and plum flavours, seasoned with quality oak; but with bottle-age, distinctly leafy notes are emerging.

Vintage	07	06
WR	5	6
Drink	13-17	10-12

DRY $30 –V

Ataahua Waipara Merlot (★★★☆)

Estate-grown at Waipara and matured for over a year in seasoned oak casks, the 2009 vintage (★★★☆) is full-coloured, mouthfilling and smooth, with generous, distinctly plummy, moderately complex flavours. Vibrantly fruity and supple, it's a fairly rare example of good South Island Merlot, already enjoyable.

Vintage	09
WR	5
Drink	10-13

DRY $26 –V

Awaroa Stell Hawke's Bay Merlot ★★★

From a Waiheke Island-based winery, the 2007 vintage (★★★) was grown at Te Awanga and matured in seasoned French oak casks. It's a full-bodied red with berry and plum flavours, slightly spicy and nutty, and a firm backbone of tannin.

DRY $20 –V

Awa Valley Merlot (★★★☆)

A good buy, the 2009 vintage (★★★☆) was grown in West Auckland, and oak-aged for a year. Medium to full-bodied, it's a slightly Bordeaux-like red, full-coloured, with smooth plum and spice flavours, a hint of dark chocolate, and some savoury notes adding complexity.

DRY $19 V+

Awa Valley James Reserve Single Vineyard Merlot/Malbec (★★★★)

Offering great value, the 2009 vintage (★★★★) is an estate-grown, Kumeu blend of Merlot and Malbec, hand-picked and barrel-aged for a year. It's a powerful, full-coloured wine, sweet-fruited, with concentrated plum, spice, liquorice and nut flavours, firm underlying tannins and the structure to age. Open mid-2011+.

DRY $20 V+

Awa Valley Merlot/Cabernet Franc ★★☆

Grown at Kumeu, in West Auckland, the 2009 vintage (★★☆) was oak-aged for a year. Medium-bodied, it is fullish in colour, with fresh, berry and plum flavours that show a slight lack of ripeness and richness. Priced right.

DRY $15 AV

Babich Lone Tree Hawke's Bay Merlot/Cabernet ★★★

The 2007 vintage (★★★) is full-coloured, with good depth of berry, plum, herb and spice flavours and a well-rounded finish.

DRY $16 V+

Babich Winemakers Reserve Merlot ★★★☆

Grown in the Gimblett Gravels, Hawke's Bay, and matured in French oak casks, the 2008 vintage (★★★★) is deeply coloured and mouthfilling, with fresh blackcurrant, plum and spice flavours, showing excellent varietal character. Savoury and ripe, it's an elegant, Bordeaux-style red with good tannin backbone. Well worth cellaring.

Vintage	08	07	06	05	04
WR	6	7	6	7	6
Drink	10-15	10-16	10-15	10-15	10-14

DRY $27 –V

Beach House Reserve Merlot ★★★☆

Grown at The Track Vineyard in Mere Road, in the Gimblett Gravels of Hawke's Bay, the 2007 vintage (★★★☆) was matured for a year in French (25 per cent new) and seasoned American oak casks. Deep and youthful in colour, it is plummy and spicy, with ripe sweet-fruit flavours and very good depth.

Vintage	07
WR	7
Drink	10-30

DRY $25 –V

Bell Bird Bay Hawke's Bay Merlot ★★★☆

A great buy. Made at Alpha Domus, the 2008 vintage (★★★☆) is fleshy and deeply coloured, with strong, plummy, slightly herbal flavours and some oak-derived complexity.

DRY $16 V+

Bensen Block Merlot ★★★

From Pernod Ricard NZ, the 2008 vintage (★★★☆) makes no claims about region of origin. It's a spicy red with good depth of ripe-fruit flavours and some savoury complexity.

DRY $17 AV

Black Barn Hawke's Bay Merlot/Cabernet Franc/Malbec ★★★

The slightly rustic 2007 vintage (★★★) is a full-coloured blend of Merlot (42 per cent), Cabernet Franc (32 per cent), Malbec (20 per cent) and Cabernet Sauvignon (6 per cent), with plenty of blackcurrant and spice flavour and some toasty oak complexity. Ready.

DRY $28 –V

Bladen Marlborough Merlot/Malbec ★★★

The 2007 vintage (★★☆) is a blend of Merlot (75 per cent) and Malbec (25 per cent), matured in French oak casks (50 per cent new). Full and bright in colour, it is fresh and fruity, but lacks real complexity and depth.

DRY $33 –V

Brookfields Burnfoot Merlot ★★★☆

The 2009 vintage (★★★★) is the best yet. Dark and youthful in colour, it is full-bodied, with concentrated plum and spice flavours, seasoned with toasty oak, and a firm backbone of tannin.

Vintage	09	08	07
WR	7	7	7
Drink	11-19	10-16	10-14

DRY $19 V+

Brunton Road Gisborne Merlot ★★★☆

Enjoyable young, the 2008 vintage (★★★) was estate-grown at Patutahi and matured for seven months in old French and American oak barrels. It's a smooth wine with fullish colour and good depth of fresh, ripe, plum and spice flavours, showing some savoury complexity.

Vintage	08	07
WR	5	6
Drink	10-11	10-11

DRY $21 AV

Cathedral Cove Hawke's Bay Merlot/Cabernet (★★)

From One Tree Hill Vineyards (a division of Morton Estate), the non-vintage wine (★★) on the market in 2010 is a solid quaffer, with fullish colour. Medium to full-bodied, it is berryish and spicy, with a slightly herbal, firm finish.

DRY $8 V+

Charles Wiffen Marlborough Merlot ★★☆

The 2007 vintage (★★☆), French oak-aged for 10 months, is a pleasant, drink-young style with fullish colour, berryish aromas and fruity, slightly leafy flavours.

DRY $24 –V

Church Road Cuve Hawke's Bay Merlot ★★★★★

The great-value 2007 vintage (★★★★★) from Pernod Ricard NZ was grown in the Gimblett Gravels and matured for 20 months in French oak barriques. It's a powerful, richly fragrant and concentrated red with bold, bright colour and dense cassis, plum and spice flavours. A strong oak influence combines well with concentrated, sweet-fruit characters, a creamy-smooth texture and impressive length. The 2008 (★★★★☆) is deeply coloured, very generous and sweet-fruited, with concentrated plum and spice flavours, spicy oak and buried tannins. A complex wine with slight coffee and dark chocolate notes, it should be long-lived; open 2012+.

DRY $27 V+

Church Road Hawke's Bay Merlot/Cabernet Sauvignon ★★★★☆

This is typically a full-flavoured and complex, distinctly Bordeaux-like red from Pernod Ricard NZ. The 2007 vintage (★★★★☆) was grown mostly in the company's Redstone Vineyard, in The Triangle, with smaller components from the Gimblett Gravels and Havelock North. Matured for a year in French and Hungarian oak barrels (30 per cent new), it's a top buy, dark and generous, with ripe blackcurrant, plum and spice flavours, finely integrated oak and a rich, lingering finish. The 2008 (★★★★☆) is a blend of Merlot (45 per cent), Cabernet Sauvignon

(42 per cent) and Malbec (13 per cent), bottled without filtering. Dark and fragrant, it is mouthfilling and concentrated, with blackcurrant-like flavours, showing good, savoury complexity, and excellent warmth and density. It's already delicious. (On 'special' at around $15, it's a great buy.)

Vintage	08	07	06
WR	6	7	6
Drink	10-14	10-14	P

DRY $26 V+

Church Road Reserve Hawke's Bay Merlot/Cabernet Sauvignon ★★★★★

Built to last, the 2008 vintage (★★★★★) has a fragrant, spicy bouquet and dense, purple-flushed colour. Very rich, ripe and youthful, it has highly concentrated plum, spice, cassis, coffee and nut flavours, in a powerful but not heavy style, complex and firmly structured. Best drinking mid-2012+.

DRY $36 V+

C.J. Pask Declaration Merlot ★★★★

The 2006 vintage (★★★★) was grown in the Gimblett Gravels and matured for 18 months in new French and American oak barriques. Fragrant, firm and youthful, it has a smoky bouquet, with good complexity and strong, ripe flavours of berry fruits, spices, herbs and nuts. The 2007 (★★★★) is deeply coloured, concentrated and firm, savoury and nutty, with good concentration and the structure to age well. Open 2012+.

Vintage	06
WR	5
Drink	10-15

DRY $50 –V

C.J. Pask Gimblett Road Merlot ★★★☆

The 2007 vintage (★★★☆) was grown in the Gimblett Gravels, Hawke's Bay and matured in French and American oak casks. Firm and concentrated, with blackcurrant and spice flavours and hints of thyme and dried herbs, it shows some density and complexity, with firm tannins and good length. Verging on four stars.

DRY $20 AV

C.J. Pask Roy's Hill Merlot/Cabernet ★★★

Drinking well now, the full-coloured 2007 vintage (★★★) is generous and smooth, with blackcurrant, herb and slight nut flavours, ripe and rounded. Good value.

DRY $15 V+

Clearview Cape Kidnappers Merlot/Malbec ★★★☆

The 2007 vintage (★★★☆) is a Hawke's Bay blend of Merlot (76 per cent), Malbec (18 per cent) and Cabernet Franc (6 per cent), made for early drinking. Matured for a year in mostly seasoned French oak casks, it's a fruit-driven style, gutsy and smooth, with dark, purple-flushed colour and plenty of plummy, spicy flavour.

Vintage	08	07
WR	6	7
Drink	10-13	10-13

DRY $19 V+

Cliff Edge Awhitu Merlot/Cabernet Franc ★★★☆

From a vineyard originally called Garden of Dreams, on the Awhitu Peninsula, in South Auckland, the 2008 vintage (★★★★) is a blend of Merlot (70 per cent) and Cabernet Franc (30 per cent), matured for a year in French and American oak casks. It tastes like a minor Bordeaux – savoury and spicy, with good concentration, oak complexity and a firm finish. The 2009 (★★★☆) is slightly less rich and complex, but scented, vibrantly fruity and supple, with lots of drink-young charm.

DRY $28 –V

Coopers Creek Hawke's Bay Merlot ★★★☆

Coopers Creek's most popular red is typically great value. The 2009 vintage (★★★☆) was blended with Malbec (7 per cent) and oak-aged for 10 months. Full-coloured, it has good substance, with strong, vibrant plum, spice and dark chocolate flavours, a hint of sweet oak, and a firm finish.

Vintage	09	08
WR	7	NM
Drink	10-13	NM

DRY $17 V+

Corazon Vineyard Selection Merlot/Malbec (★★★☆)

The fine-value 2008 vintage (★★★☆) is a North Island blend of Merlot (65 per cent) and Malbec (35 per cent). Deeply coloured, it is fleshy, with good density of blackcurrant, herb and spice flavours, nutty and savoury. It's delicious now.

DRY $18 V+

Corbans Homestead Hawke's Bay Merlot ★★☆

The 2007 vintage (★★★) from Pernod Ricard NZ is the best yet, with a touch of complexity and plenty of smooth, plummy, spicy flavour.

DRY $17 –V

Corbans Private Bin Hawke's Bay Merlot/Cabernet Sauvignon ★★★★

Tasted prior to bottling, and so not rated, the 2007 looked excellent, with impressively dense blackcurrant, plum and spice flavours, firm, ripe tannins, and the power and structure to mature well.

DRY $24 V+

Couper's Shed Hawke's Bay Merlot/Cabernet ★★★★

A great buy from Pernod Ricard NZ. The 2009 vintage (★★★★) is deeply coloured, with strong plum, herb and dark chocolate flavours, fresh, vibrant and generous. Fruity and supple, it's a very finely textured, harmonious wine, with drink-young appeal.

DRY $23 V+

Crab Farm Pukera Merlot (★★★★)

The dark 2006 vintage (★★★★) was grown in Hawke's Bay and matured for 16 months in French oak casks (80 per cent new). Coffee and spice aromas lead into a powerful (14.5 per cent alcohol), still fresh and vibrant wine, gutsy but not heavy, with brambly, spicy flavours, a hint of liquorice, firm tannins and good concentration. Drink now or cellar.

Vintage	06
WR	6
Drink	10-11

DRY $25 AV

Craggy Range Gimblett Gravels Merlot ★★★★★

This is a top buy – superior to many higher-priced Hawke's Bay reds. The 2008 vintage (★★★★), harvested at 23.8 brix, includes Cabernet Franc (5 per cent), Cabernet Sauvignon (4 per cent) and Malbec (3 per cent), and was matured for 18 months in French oak barriques (46 per cent new). Fragrant and dark, with gentle tannins, it has deep blackcurrant, plum and spice flavours, hints of dark chocolate, herbs and nuts, and substantial body. Drink now or cellar.

Vintage	08	07	06	05	04	03
WR	6	7	6	6	6	5
Drink	11-15	10-22	10-18	10-13	10-12	P

DRY $30 V+

Crawford Farm New Zealand Merlot ★★★☆

From Constellation NZ, the 2009 vintage (★★★) is a full-coloured Hawke's Bay red. Still youthful, it is mouthfilling, fresh and vibrant, with plum, spice and slight herb flavours, showing some savoury, earthy touches, satisfying depth and a smooth finish.

DRY $21 AV

Crossroads Hawke's Bay Merlot (★★★)

The 2008 vintage (★★★) offers moderately concentrated plum and spice flavours, showing some complexity. Matured for a year in French oak casks (40 per cent new), it is medium to full-bodied, with earthy, slightly rustic notes and gentle tannins.

DRY $20 –V

Cypress Hawke's Bay Merlot ★★★☆

Estate-grown at Roy's Hill and briefly oak-aged (three months in seasoned casks), the 2009 vintage (★★★★) is dark and still very youthful, with rich, vibrant flavours of plums, blackcurrants and spices and coffee. It's a delicious, fruit-driven style, likely to be at its best from mid-2011+. The 2008 (★★★☆), barrel-aged for five months, is fresh, fruity and forward, with very good depth of plummy, spicy, smooth flavour. It's enjoyable now.

Vintage	09	08	07
WR	7	6	6
Drink	11-12	10-11	P

DRY $20 AV

Delegat's Reserve Hawke's Bay Merlot ★★★☆

The 2007 vintage (★★★☆) was grown in the Gimblett Gravels and matured for a year in new and one-year-old French oak barriques. Boldly coloured, it has strong plum/spice flavours seasoned with toasty oak, an earthy streak and firm tannins.

Vintage	07	06
WR	6	6
Drink	10-14	10-13

DRY $20 AV

Distant Land Hawke's Bay Merlot/Malbec ★★★☆

From Lincoln, the 2008 vintage (★★★☆) was matured for a year in French oak casks (30 per cent new). It's a full-coloured wine, mouthfilling, vibrantly fruity, berryish and spicy, with moderately concentrated flavours, showing some savoury complexity, and a well-rounded finish.

DRY $20 AV

Dolbel Estate Hawke's Bay Merlot/Cabernet (★★★★)

The elegant, savoury 2007 vintage (★★★★) is a blend of Merlot (70 per cent), estate-grown inland at the Springfield Vineyard, and Cabernet Sauvignon from the Gimblett Gravels. Hand-picked and matured in French oak casks (60 per cent new), it is dark, with a highly fragrant, spicy, nutty bouquet, rich blackcurrant, herb and plum flavours, and fine-grained tannins. It shows excellent texture, complexity and length.

Vintage	07
WR	6
Drink	10-15

DRY $30 –V

Elephant Hill Hawke's Bay Merlot (★★★☆)

Grown at Te Awanga, the 2009 vintage (★★★☆) is a youthful red, deeply coloured, with strong, vibrant cassis and plum flavours, ripe, firm and tightly structured. Best drinking mid-2011+.

DRY $24 AV

Esk Valley Gimblett Gravels Merlot/Cabernet Sauvignon/Malbec ★★★★

The generous 2009 vintage (★★★★) is a blend of Merlot (41 per cent), Cabernet Sauvignon (38 per cent) and Malbec (21 per cent), grown in the Gimblett Gravels and matured for a year in French oak barriques. Deeply coloured, it is mouthfilling, fresh and flowing, with strong blackcurrant and plum flavours, hints of coffee and oak, and gentle tannins. It should mature well.

Vintage	09	08	07	06	05
WR	7	6	6	7	6
Drink	11-15	10-12	10-12	10-12	P

DRY $24 V+

Esk Valley Winemakers Reserve Merlot/Cabernet Sauvignon/Malbec ★★★★★

This powerful, classy red was labelled 'Reserve', rather than 'Winemakers Reserve', up to and including the 2006 vintage (★★★★★). Dark, vibrantly fruity and bursting with ripe, sweet-tasting blackcurrant, plum and French oak flavours, it is one of Hawke's Bay's greatest wines. Grown in the company-owned Ngakirikiri Vineyard and the Cornerstone Vineyard, both in the Gimblett Gravels, it is matured for up to 20 months in French oak barriques (70 per cent new in 2007). The 2007 vintage (★★★★★), from vines then 15 to 17 years old, is a blend of Merlot (54 per cent), Cabernet Sauvignon (33 per cent) and Malbec (13 per cent). Dark and rich, it's a powerful wine with mouthfilling body (14 per cent alcohol) and deep plum and spice flavours, savoury and complex. Best drinking 2012+. (Due to frost, there is no 2008.)

Vintage	08	07	06	05	04	03	02
WR	NM	7	7	7	7	NM	7
Drink	NM	10-20	10-16	10-14	10-16	NM	10-14

DRY $60 AV

Fall Harvest Merlot (★★☆)

From Constellation NZ, the 2007 vintage (★★☆) is a decent quaffer, not identified by region. Vibrantly fruity, slightly spicy and smooth, it's a very easy-drinking style.

DRY $13 V+

Farmers Market Hawke's Bay Merlot (★★★☆)

The sturdy, deeply coloured 2009 vintage (★★★☆) was grown at Te Awanga. It's a fruit-driven style with very good depth of ripe blackcurrant and plum flavours, a hint of sweet oak and gentle tannins.

DRY $20 AV

Five Flax Merlot/Cabernet ★★☆

From Pernod Ricard NZ, the 2007 vintage (★★★) is a very easy-drinking style, plummy and soft, with plenty of flavour.

Vintage	07	06
WR	5	5
Drink	P	P

DRY $15 AV

Frizzell Hawke's Bay Merlot (★★★★)

The 2007 vintage (★★★★) is boldly coloured, mouthfilling and vibrantly fruity, with strong plum and spice flavours, and hints of coffee and liquorice. Sweet-fruited, with good concentration, it's still fresh and youthful.

Vintage	07
WR	7
Drink	10-15

DRY $25 AV

Frizzell Merlot/Malbec (★★★★)

The 2007 vintage (★★★★) is a single-vineyard Hawke's Bay red, with some Cabernet Franc in the blend, matured for 18 months in French and American oak barrels. Deeply coloured, with sweet oak aromas, it's a fruity, moderately complex wine with hints of coffee and spices, and very good ripeness and concentration. Fine value.

DRY $22 V+

Gem Hawke's Bay Merlot (★★★★☆)

The very elegant 2007 vintage (★★★★☆) is a single-vineyard red, grown in The Triangle and matured for 18 months in French oak casks (50 per cent new). Full but not dense in colour, with a fragrant, savoury, complex bouquet, it's a distinctive wine with sweet-fruit delights, strong plum and spice flavours, with leathery notes emerging, gentle tannins and lovely texture and harmony. A wine of finesse, rather than sheer power, it's delicious now.

Vintage	07
WR	7
Drink	10-16

DRY $30 AV

Glazebrook Regional Reserve Hawke's Bay Merlot/Cabernet ★★★★

The 2007 vintage (★★★★☆) from Ngatarawa winery was grown in the Gimblett Gravels (89 per cent) and The Triangle (11 per cent). A blend of Merlot (68 per cent) and Cabernet Sauvignon (32 per cent), it was matured for a year in French oak barriques (50 per cent new). Classy, powerful and firm, it is deep and youthful in colour, with concentrated blackcurrant and plum flavours, a hint of dark chocolate, chewy tannins, and excellent depth and structure. Showing good complexity, it should be long-lived.

Vintage	07	06	05	04
WR	7	6	6	6
Drink	10-16	10-15	10-12	10-11

DRY $27 AV

Goldridge Estate Hawke's Bay Merlot ★★☆

The full-coloured 2009 vintage (★★★) was matured for a year in barriques, mostly French. An ideal quaffer, it is a fresh, fruit-driven style with vibrant plum, spice and slight coffee flavours, showing good ripeness and depth.

DRY $16 AV

Goldridge Estate Premium Reserve Hawke's Bay Merlot ★★★☆

Priced sharply, the 2008 vintage (★★★★) is a single-vineyard red, grown in The Triangle. A blend of Merlot (89 per cent), Cabernet Franc (6 per cent) and Malbec (5 per cent), it was matured in mostly French oak barriques (25 per cent new). Still very fresh and lively, it is firm, concentrated and deeply coloured, with vibrant plum and spice flavours and firm tannins.

DRY $19 V+

Goldwater Esslin Waiheke Island Merlot ★★★★

This stylish but in the past far too expensive wine has recently been halved in price, from $90 to $45. Grown in the Esslin Vineyard and matured for 20 months in French oak barriques (50 per cent new), the 2005 vintage (★★★★☆) is deeply coloured, with strong, concentrated blackcurrant, plum and spice flavours, leathery, savoury and complex. Drink now onwards.

DRY $45 –V

Greyrock Hawke's Bay Merlot (★★★)

From Sileni, the 2008 vintage (★★★) is full-coloured and mouthfilling, with plenty of ripe, plummy, slightly earthy and spicy flavour. A fruit-driven style, it's enjoyable now.

DRY $17 AV

Hans Herzog Spirit of Marlborough Merlot/Cabernet Sauvignon ★★★★★

Who says you can't make outstanding claret-style reds in the South Island? Grown on the banks of the Wairau River, matured for two years in new and one-year-old French oak barriques, and then bottle-aged for several years, this is typically a densely coloured wine with a classy fragrance, substantial body and notably concentrated blackcurrant, plum, herb and spice flavours. It is blended from Merlot (principally), with smaller amounts of Cabernet Sauvignon, Cabernet Franc and Malbec, and bottled without fining or filtration. The 2002 vintage (★★★★★) is deep, with some colour development showing. It's a very harmonious, Bordeaux-like wine, savoury and complex, with cassis, herb, spice and leather notes, like a good St Estèphe. Drink now onwards.

Vintage	02	01
WR	7	7
Drink	10-21	10-20

DRY $39 V+

Hay Maker Hawke's Bay Merlot (★★★)

From Mud House, the 2007 vintage (★★★) was partly oak-aged. It's a full-coloured wine with lots of plummy, spicy flavour, soft and smooth. A good, drink-young quaffer.

DRY $17 AV

Hihi Merlot/Malbec ★★★

The 2007 vintage (★★★) is a Gisborne red, grown at Manutuke. A blend of Merlot (82 per cent), Malbec and Cabernet Franc, it was matured for 10 months in oak casks (15 per cent new). Full-coloured, it is mouthfilling, with plenty of plummy, spicy flavour, supported by firm tannins.

DRY $18 AV

Hinchco Paddock Block Matakana Merlot ★★☆

The 2008 vintage (★★☆) is pale red, in a pleasant, light style with moderate depth of plum and red-berry flavours, offering easy drinking.

DRY $20 –V

Huntaway Reserve Gisborne/Hawke's Bay Merlot/Cabernet ★★★★

The 2007 vintage (★★★★) from Pernod Ricard NZ was grown in Gisborne and Hawke's Bay and matured for a year in French oak casks (48 per cent new). Deeply coloured, with a smoky bouquet, it is ripe and concentrated, with blackcurrant, spice and dark chocolate flavours, toasty and savoury.

Vintage	07	06
WR	7	5
Drink	10-12	P

DRY $23 V+

Hyperion Zeus Matakana Merlot/Cabernet ★★☆

Estate-grown, the 2008 vintage (★★☆) was matured for a year in French and American oak casks. It's a pleasant, fruity, full-coloured red with blackcurrant, plum and herb flavours and a very smooth finish.

Vintage	08	07	06	05
WR	5	5	7	6
Drink	10-15	10-13	10-12	P

DRY $22 –V

Isola Estate Merlot/Cabernets (★★★☆)

Grown on Waiheke Island, the 2007 vintage (★★★☆) is a blend of Merlot (55 per cent), Cabernet Sauvignon (40 per cent), Cabernet Franc (4 per cent) and Malbec (1 per cent). Ruby-hued, it is fresh, fruity and firm, with good depth of plum and spice flavours, showing some complexity.

DRY $37 –V

Kawau Bay Merlot/Cabernet Franc – see Takatu Kawau Bay Merlot/Cabernet Franc

Kennedy Point Merlot ★★★★☆

The classy 2006 vintage (★★★★☆) was grown at four sites on Waiheke Island, fermented with indigenous yeasts and matured for 18 months in French oak casks. Deeply coloured, it is mouthfilling, with strong, ripe blackcurrant, plum and spice flavours, seasoned with nutty oak, in a very elegant, Bordeaux-like style with a firm backbone of tannin. Showing bottle-aged complexity, it's drinking well now.

Vintage	06
WR	7
Drink	12-18

DRY $39 AV

Kim Crawford Hawke's Bay Merlot ★★★☆

The 2007 vintage (★★★) from Constellation NZ includes 4 per cent Malbec and 3 per cent Cabernet Franc. Partly barrel-aged, it's a full-coloured, fruity and flavoursome wine with ripe plum and spice characters and gentle oak and tannins, giving an easy-drinking appeal.

DRY $22 AV

Kim Crawford Limited Release Hawke's Bay Merlot (★★★☆)

A blend of Merlot (93.5 per cent) and Malbec (6.5 per cent), the 2007 vintage (★★★☆) is medium to full-bodied, with full colour, good depth of plummy, spicy flavour and some savoury complexity. It's enjoyable now.

DRY $30 –V

Kim Crawford Regional Reserve Hawke's Bay Merlot (★★★☆)

Grown mostly in The Triangle, the 2009 vintage (★★★☆) is a full-coloured, medium-bodied red, vibrantly fruity, with very good depth of fresh plum and spice flavours, moderate complexity and gentle tannins. It's enjoyable young.

DRY $23 AV

Kim Crawford SP Corner 50 Vineyard Hawke's Bay Merlot (★★★★☆)

The sturdy, generous 2008 vintage (★★★★☆) was hand-picked and matured for 16 months in French and American oak casks. Deeply coloured, it has fresh, brambly, plummy flavours, showing excellent concentration, hints of coffee and sweet oak, good complexity, and the power to age.

DRY $33 AV

Kirkpatrick Estate Winery Merlot ★★★☆

Grown at Patutahi, in Gisborne, the 2009 vintage (★★★) was matured for nearly a year in barrels (30 per cent new). Full-coloured, with fresh plum and slight herb flavours, showing a touch of complexity, and a smooth finish, it's enjoyable young.

Vintage	09
WR	5
Drink	10-15

DRY $22 AV

Kumeu River Melba's Vineyard Merlot ★★★★

Named in honour of the family matriarch, Melba Brajkovich, the 2006 vintage (★★★★) is the first for several years (it was previously labelled as Kumeu River Melba). Based on the company's sole surviving plot of Merlot vines at Kumeu, in West Auckland, it is full-coloured, with a spicy bouquet. Vibrantly fruity and flavoursome, with strong coffee and spice characters, it's a well-structured wine, ready for drinking now onwards.

DRY $30 –V

Lake Chalice Vineyard Selection Merlot ★★☆

The 2007 vintage (★★☆) is a 3:1 blend of Hawke's Bay and Marlborough fruit. Matured in tanks and French oak casks, it is a fruit-driven style with vibrant flavours of plums, herbs and spices, fresh and smooth.

Vintage	07
WR	5
Drink	P

DRY $20 –V

Lochiel Estate Mangawhai Merlot/Malbec (★★☆)

The 2008 vintage (★★☆) was grown in Northland and oak-aged for a year. Fullish in colour, with a bouquet showing the confectionery notes of Malbec, it is fresh and fruity, in a medium-bodied style offering easy, no-fuss drinking.

DRY $20 –V

Longbush Gisborne Merlot ★★★

Bargain-priced, the 2007 vintage (★★★) is a full-coloured, fairly gutsy red with plenty of berryish, slightly spicy and earthy flavour, braced by firm tannins. An excellent quaffer.

DRY $13 V+

Longridge Hawke's Bay Merlot/Cabernet Sauvignon ★★★

The 2009 vintage (★★★) from Pernod Ricard NZ has full, purple-flushed colour. Vibrantly fruity, berryish, plummy and smooth, with hints of spices and dark chocolate, and gentle tannins, it's a flavoursome, easy-drinking red.

DRY $18 AV

Mahurangi River Winery Mostly Merlot Merlot/Cabernet Sauvignon/Malbec (★★★☆)

The 2009 vintage (★★★☆) was estate-grown, hand-picked, fermented with indigenous yeasts and matured for 14 months in French oak casks (25 per cent new). It shows good personality, with full colour and spicy, nutty flavours, showing some leathery, savoury complexity. Drink now or cellar.

DRY $35 –V

Maimai Creek Hawke's Bay Merlot ★★☆

The full-coloured 2008 vintage (★★☆) is gutsy and firm, with spicy, slightly herbal flavours. A decent quaffer.

DRY $25 –V

Maimai Creek Hawke's Bay Merlot/Malbec ★★★

The generous 2008 vintage (★★★☆) is mouthfilling, with strong, plummy, spicy flavours, hints of dark chocolate and sweet oak, and a firm finish. It's drinking well now. (The 2009 ★★☆ is a more simple, fruit-driven style, sold at around $18.)

DRY $25 –V

Main Divide Merlot/Cabernet ★★★☆

The 2008 vintage (★★★☆) from Pegasus Bay was grown in Marlborough and matured for two years in French oak barriques. Full-coloured and mouthfilling, it has good depth of plum and slight herb flavours, showing some savoury complexity, and a smooth finish. Drink now onwards.

Vintage	08	07	06	05	04
WR	5	5	6	7	6
Drink	10-14	10-13	10-13	10-12	P

DRY $20 AV

Man O' War Waiheke Island Merlot/Cabernet Franc/Malbec ★★★☆

Grown at the eastern end of the island, the 2008 vintage (★★★★) was matured in seasoned French and American oak casks. A blend of Merlot (42 per cent), Cabernet Franc (27 per cent), Malbec (19 per cent) and Cabernet Sauvignon (12 per cent), it is dark, robust and concentrated, with blackcurrant, plum and spice flavours, a hint of coffee and good complexity. A powerful, tightly structured wine with finely integrated oak, it's approachable now, but should reward cellaring.

DRY $28 –V

Matahiwi Estate Hawke's Bay Merlot ★★★

From young vines at Maraekakaho, the 2008 vintage (★★★) was harvested at 24 brix and lightly oaked. It's a good, gutsy, mouthfilling quaffer, in an exuberantly fruity style with gentle tannins and satisfying flavour depth.

Vintage	08
WR	5
Drink	10-12

DRY $19 AV

Matakana Estate Elingamite Limited Edition Merlot/Cabernet Franc (★★★★☆)

The powerful, deeply coloured 2007 vintage (★★★★☆) is a Hawke's Bay blend of Merlot (60 per cent) and Cabernet Franc (40 per cent), with vibrant blackcurrant, plum and spice flavours, well seasoned with quality oak (mostly French, all new). It's a highly concentrated, ripe-tasting wine with good complexity, a firm foundation of tannin and obvious cellaring potential.

DRY $59 –V

Matakana Estate Hawke's Bay Merlot/Cabernet Franc (★★★★)

The dark, generous 2007 vintage (★★★★) is a blend of Merlot (71 per cent) and Cabernet Franc (29 per cent), grown in The Triangle district and matured in French oak barriques (40 per cent new). Brambly and sweet-fruited, it has hints of mint chocolate and coffee and excellent depth.

DRY $29 AV

Matawara by Secret Stone Merlot (★★☆)

From Matua Valley, the 2007 vintage (★★☆) is medium-bodied, with fullish, slightly developed colour. Pleasant, with decent depth of berryish, spicy flavours and a smooth finish, it lacks real richness. Ready.

DRY $18 –V

Matawhero Gisborne Merlot (★★★☆)

The full-coloured 2009 vintage (★★★☆) was grown at Patutahi and barrel-aged. Medium to full-bodied, it has very good depth of youthful berry and spice flavours, showing a hint of dark chocolate, and some savoury complexity.

DRY $30 –V

Matua Valley Bullrush Merlot ★★★☆

The 2007 vintage (★★★☆) is a single-vineyard red, grown in The Triangle district of Hawke's Bay and matured for 18 months in French oak casks (35 per cent new). Deeply coloured, it is sturdy, with concentrated blackcurrant, plum and slight herb flavours, moderate complexity and some cellaring potential.

DRY $25 –V

Matua Valley Hawke's Bay Merlot ★★★

The 2009 vintage (★★★) is ruby-hued, fresh, fruity and smooth, with plummy, slightly spicy flavours, showing a touch of complexity. It's finely balanced for early drinking.

DRY $17 AV

Matua Valley Hawke's Bay Merlot/Cabernet ★★★

The 2009 vintage (★★☆) is full-coloured, fresh and fruity, with plum, spice and herb flavours, showing decent depth.

DRY $17 AV

Matua Valley Reserve Merlot/Cabernet (★★★)

The 2007 vintage (★★★) is a Hawke's Bay blend of Merlot (55 per cent) and Cabernet Sauvignon (45 per cent), matured for 15 months in French oak casks. Full-coloured, it is fruity and smooth, with plum/spice flavours, a gentle seasoning of oak and good depth. It's a fruit-driven, moderately complex style.

DRY $20 –V

Mill Road Hawke's Bay Merlot/Cabernet ★★

From Morton Estate, the non-vintage wine (★★☆) on sale in 2010 has fullish, slightly developed colour. Gutsy and firm, with blackcurrant, herb and spice flavours, it's a good quaffer, priced right.

DRY $14 –V

Mills Reef Elspeth Merlot ★★★☆

The 2007 vintage (★★★☆) was estate-grown in Mere Road, in the Gimblett Gravels of Hawke's Bay, and matured for 13 months in French oak barriques (34 per cent new). It is a powerful, firmly structured red with full colour and generous, spicy, plummy, nutty flavours, showing considerable complexity. However, my three tasting notes suggest there is some bottle variation.

Vintage	07	06	05	04	03	02
WR	7	7	7	7	NM	7
Drink	10-18	10-17	10-15	10-15	NM	10-14

DRY $40 –V

Mills Reef Hawke's Bay Merlot/Cabernet ★★★

The 2008 vintage (★★★) was barrel-aged for over a year. Full-coloured, with plum, spice, herb and slight coffee flavours, it is fruity and smooth, in an easy-drinking style with good depth.

DRY $18 AV

Mills Reef Reserve Hawke's Bay Merlot ★★★★

The 2008 vintage (★★★☆) was grown in the Gimblett Gravels and matured in French oak casks (55 per cent new). Full-coloured, it is mouthfilling, with a hint of coffee and very good depth of plum and spice flavours, fresh and savoury.

Vintage	08	07	06	05
WR	6	7	7	7
Drink	10-12	10-12	10-11	P

DRY $25 AV

Mills Reef Reserve Hawke's Bay Merlot/Malbec ★★★★

The 2008 vintage (★★★☆) was grown in the Gimblett Gravels and matured for a year in a 70:30 split of French and American oak barriques (58 per cent new). Deeply coloured, it has coffee and spice aromas and flavours, fresh and vibrant, with some complexity and good harmony.

Vintage	08	07	06	05
WR	6	7	6	7
Drink	10-12	10-12	10-12	10-11

DRY $25 AV

Mission Hawke's Bay Merlot ★★★

The 2009 vintage (★★★), partly oak-aged, is slightly leafy, but full-coloured, with plenty of plum, herb and spice flavour and some toasty, savoury notes adding a touch of complexity.

DRY $17 AV

Mission Reserve Gimblett Gravels Merlot ★★★★

The 2009 vintage (★★★★) was grown in Mere Road, Hawke's Bay, harvested at over 24 brix and matured in French oak casks (25 per cent new). It's a dark, powerful red (14.5 per cent alcohol), with strong, ripe blackcurrant, plum and spice flavours, a hint of dark chocolate and firm tannins. Still very youthful, it's well worth cellaring.

Vintage	09	08	07
WR	6	5	7
Drink	11-17	10-15	10-15

DRY $24 V+

Mission Vineyard Selection Ohiti Road Merlot ★★★

The 2008 vintage (★★★☆) is a single-vineyard wine, grown in Hawke's Bay and matured in seasoned French oak barrels. Full-coloured, with a spicy, slightly herbal bouquet, it has very satisfying depth of blackcurrant, plum, spice and slightly nutty oak flavours, showing good balance and complexity.

DRY $18 AV

Moana Park Vineyard Selection Merlot/Malbec ★★★

The 2009 vintage (★★★) is a Hawke's Bay blend of Merlot (80 per cent), Malbec (12 per cent) and Cabernet Sauvignon (8 per cent), grown in the Gimblett Gravels and Dartmoor Valley. French oak-aged for a year, it is dark and gutsy, with strong berry, plum and herb flavours.

DRY $22 –V

Moana Park Vineyard Tribute Gimblett Road Merlot ★★★★☆

The lush, soft 2008 vintage (★★★★★) of this Hawke's Bay wine was harvested at 26 brix, fermented with indigenous yeasts, matured for a year in French oak barriques (60 per cent new), and bottled unfined and unfiltered. Densely coloured, it is powerful (14.5 per cent alcohol) and fruit-packed, with lovely depth of plum, spice and nut flavours and a silky-smooth texture. It's delicious young.

DRY $32 AV

Monkey Bay Hawke's Bay Merlot ★★☆

The 2008 vintage (★★★) from Constellation NZ is a deeply coloured, vibrantly fruity red with plenty of berryish, plummy flavour, hints of spices and coffee adding interest, a smooth finish, and lots of drink-young appeal.

DRY $15 AV

Montana North Island Merlot/Cabernet Sauvignon ★★★

The 2009 vintage (★★★) is full-coloured, with good depth of fresh, berryish flavours, hints of spices, herbs and dark chocolate, and a smooth finish.

DRY $18 AV

Montana Reserve Hawke's Bay Merlot ★★★☆

The bargain-priced 2007 vintage (★★★★) was matured in predominantly French oak casks. It is deeply coloured, rich and silky, with deep plum, spice and slight coffee flavours, sweet-fruit delights, good complexity, and strong drink-young appeal.

DRY $24 AV

Morton Estate Black Label Hawke's Bay Merlot (★★★☆)

Ready for drinking, the 2005 vintage (★★★☆) is full-coloured, with mouthfilling body and moderately rich, plummy, spicy flavour, showing good complexity.

Vintage	05
WR	6
Drink	10-12

DRY $35 –V

Morton Estate Black Label Hawke's Bay Merlot/Cabernet (★★★)

The 2004 vintage (★★★) was grown at Bridge Pa, in the company's Tantallon Vineyard on State Highway 50, and in the Gimblett Gravels, and matured in French and American oak casks. Fullish and slightly developed in colour, it is spicy, savoury and moderately concentrated, with considerable complexity, but lacks real fruit sweetness and richness.

Vintage	04
WR	6
Drink	10-12

DRY $35 –V

Morton Estate White Label Hawke's Bay Merlot ★★☆

The 2007 vintage (★★☆) is fullish in colour, with smooth berry and spice flavours, slightly leafy and rustic. Ready.

Vintage	07
WR	6
Drink	10-12

DRY $18 –V

Mudbrick Vineyard Merlot/Cabernet Sauvignon ★★★★

Grown on Waiheke Island, the 2009 vintage (★★★★) was blended mostly from Merlot and Cabernet Sauvignon, supplemented by Malbec (10 per cent) and Cabernet Franc (10 per cent). Already drinking well, it's a savoury, medium-bodied red, with strong plum and spice flavours, showing good complexity.

DRY $30 –V

Mudbrick Vineyard Reserve Merlot/Cabernet Sauvignon ★★★★

The 2008 vintage (★★★★☆) is a Waiheke Island blend, matured in French and American oak barriques (30 per cent new). Dark, powerful and highly concentrated, with perfumed oak aromas, it has dense blackcurrant, plum, spice, nut and coffee flavours, chewy and firm.

Vintage	08
WR	7
Drink	10-18

DRY $50 –V

Mud House Hawke's Bay Merlot ★★★☆

The 2008 vintage (★★★☆) is a youthful, full-coloured red, partly barrel-matured, with some richness of plum and berry flavours, hints of chocolate and herbs and a smooth finish. It's an appealing, moderately complex style.

DRY $21 AV

Nest, The, Hawke's Bay Merlot (★★★)

From Lake Chalice, the 2008 vintage (★★★) was matured in tanks and French oak barrels. Ruby-hued, it is mouthfilling and smooth, with fresh, vibrant plum and spice flavours, showing good depth.

DRY $20 –V

Newton Forrest Estate Gimblett Gravels Hawke's Bay Merlot ★★★★☆

The 2007 vintage (★★★★☆) was grown in the Cornerstone Vineyard and matured in a 4:1 mix of French and American oak casks. Deeply coloured, with a spicy, nutty fragrance, it is sturdy (14.3 per cent alcohol), with strong, vibrant cassis, plum and spice flavours, finely integrated oak, firm underlying tannins, and the power and structure to age well.

Vintage	07
WR	6
Drink	10-15

DRY $30 AV

Ngatarawa Alwyn Merlot/Cabernet ★★★★★

Grown in Hawke's Bay, the 2007 vintage (★★★★★) is a blend of Merlot (80 per cent) and Cabernet Sauvignon (20 per cent), matured for 16 months in French oak barriques. Deeply coloured, it has sweet-fruit delights, with highly concentrated plum, blackcurrant and slight herb flavours, buried tannins, and the power and structure to flourish for a decade.

Vintage	07	06	05
WR	7	6	7
Drink	10-16	10-15	10-14

DRY $55 AV

Ngatarawa Silks Hawke's Bay Merlot ★★★☆

Priced right, the 2008 vintage (★★★☆) is a deeply coloured red, oak-aged for a year, with strong blackcurrant and plum flavours, an earthy streak and considerable complexity. Drink now or cellar.

Vintage	08	07	06	05
WR	7	6	6	6
Drink	10-12	10-11	10-11	P

DRY $20 AV

Ngatarawa Stables Hawke's Bay Merlot ★★★

An easy-drinking, mid-weight style, the 2008 vintage (★★★) has full, youthful colour and plenty of berry, plum and spice flavour, slightly earthy and smooth.

Vintage	08	07	06
WR	6	7	6
Drink	10-13	10-12	10-12

DRY $17 AV

Ngatarawa Stables Reserve Merlot (★★★★)
Tightly structured and age-worthy, the 2009 vintage (★★★★) is a fruit-driven style with deep, bright colour and youthful, concentrated flavours of plums and spices, with a hint of coffee.

DRY $22 V+

Nikau Point Hawke's Bay Merlot/Malbec ★★☆
From One Tree Hill Vineyards (a division of Morton Estate), the 2008 vintage (★★☆) is a solid quaffer – plummy, spicy and earthy, with a rustic streak and decent flavour depth.

Vintage	08
WR	5
Drink	10-12

DRY $17 –V

Nikau Point Reserve Hawke's Bay Merlot/Cabernet Franc ★★☆
From Morton Estate, the 2008 vintage (★★★) is full but not dense in colour, with plum and spice flavours, showing some nutty complexity, and a smooth finish.

Vintage	08
WR	5
Drink	10-14

DRY $18 –V

Nobilo Regional Collection Hawke's Bay Merlot ★★★
Fresh and full-coloured, the 2008 vintage (★★★) is a vibrantly fruity style with plum and spice flavours showing good depth and a smooth, rounded finish.

DRY $17 AV

Omaka Springs Marlborough Merlot ★★☆
The 2008 vintage (★★), American oak-aged for 10 months, is pale red, with berry and herb flavours, very light and smooth. Ready.

Vintage	08
WR	6
Drink	10-12

DRY $19 –V

One Tree Hawke's Bay Merlot ★★★☆
Made by Capricorn Wine Estates (a division of Craggy Range) for sale in supermarkets, the 2008 vintage (★★★) is deeply coloured, with strong spice, herb and slight coffee flavours. Fruity and smooth, it has an upfront, drink-young appeal.

DRY $15 V+

Oyster Bay Hawke's Bay Merlot ★★★☆

From Delegat's, this red accounts for a big slice of New Zealand's exports of 'Bordeaux-style' wines (Merlot or Cabernet Sauvignon). Winemaker Michael Ivicevich aims for a wine with 'sweet fruit and silky tannins. The trick is – not too much oak.' The 2008 vintage (★★★☆) is dark, with a fragrant bouquet of blackcurrants and spices. Mouthfilling, it's a substantial wine with strong blackcurrant, herb and dark chocolate flavours, supple tannins, and plenty of drink-young appeal.

Vintage	08	07	06
WR	6	7	7
Drink	10-14	10-14	10-14

DRY $20 AV

Passage Rock Reserve Waiheke Island Merlot ★★★★

The estate-grown 2008 vintage (★★★★) is a densely coloured, youthful red with highly concentrated, plummy, spicy flavours, and powerful tannins. It needs time, but shows obvious potential.

DRY $30 –V

Peacock Sky Merlot/Malbec (★★★)

Estate-grown on Waiheke Island, the 2009 vintage (★★★) was matured for nearly a year in new oak casks. It's an easy-drinking, smooth, middleweight red with satisfying depth of ripe plum and spice flavours.

Vintage	09
WR	5
Drink	11-15

DRY $30 –V

Pegasus Bay Merlot/Cabernet ★★★★

The 2006 vintage (★★★★) is a Waipara blend of Merlot, Cabernet Sauvignon, Malbec and Cabernet Franc, matured for two years in French oak casks. Deeply coloured, with a hint of development, it is mouthfilling, rich and complex, with blackcurrant, spice and herb flavours, dense and savoury, and a firm finish. Showing good muscle and tannin structure, it's a drink-now or cellaring proposition.

Vintage	06	05	04
WR	6	7	6
Drink	10-15	10-15	10-14

DRY $29 AV

Penny Lane Hawke's Bay Merlot/Cabernet ★★

From Morton Estate, the 2006 vintage (★★) is a blend of Merlot, Cabernet Sauvignon and Cabernet Franc. It has fullish, fairly developed colour and moderate depth of spicy, leafy flavour. Ready.

Vintage	06
WR	5
Drink	10-11

DRY $15 –V

Poderi Crisci Merlot ★★★

Grown on Waiheke Island, the 2008 vintage (★★★☆) is the best yet. Full-coloured, with a spicy bouquet, it is sweet-fruited, with very satisfying depth of blackcurrant, plum and spice flavours, an earthy streak and good complexity. It's quite forward; drink now onwards. The 2007 (★★★) is a mid-weight style, enjoyable now, with plummy, slightly herbal flavours, fruity and well-rounded.

Vintage	07
WR	6
Drink	10-17

DRY $29 –V

Poverty Bay Matawhero Merlot/Cabernets (★★★★)

From 'the oldest vines in the Gisborne region', the 2008 vintage (★★★★) was grown at the Bridge Estate Vineyard, planted by Matawhero in 1985. A blend of Merlot (64 per cent) with smaller portions of Cabernet Sauvignon (22 per cent), Cabernet Franc and Malbec, it was matured in French oak barriques (partly new). It's a wine of strong personality – full-coloured, ripe, brambly and spicy, with good concentration and hints of leather and chocolate. Already enjoyable and worth cellaring, it's an excellent debut.

DRY $24 V+

Providence Private Reserve Merlot/Cabernet Franc/Malbec ★★★★★

Past vintages of this Matakana red were priced around $180, including the full-coloured and fragrant, very elegant and silky-textured 2002 (★★★★★). The 2005 (★★★★★) is a top vintage, beautifully perfumed, with rich, blackcurrant-like flavours, complex and harmonious. If you are a Bordeaux fan with deep pockets, it's well worth trying.

DRY $120 –V

Rannach Merlot ★★★

Grown at Clevedon, in South Auckland, the 2008 vintage (★★★) has fullish, youthful colour. It's an easy-drinking style, medium to full-bodied, with some savoury complexity.

Vintage	08
WR	5
Drink	10-14

DRY $20 –V

Redmetal Vineyards Basket Press Merlot/Cabernet Franc ★★★☆

Grown in The Triangle, the 2007 vintage (★★★) is a blend of Merlot (90 per cent) and Cabernet Franc (10 per cent), oak-aged for over a year. Deep and bright in colour, it has good depth of red-berry, plum and spice flavours, slight leafy notes, and finely balanced tannins.

DRY $29 –V

Redmetal Vineyards Hawke's Bay Merlot/Cabernet Franc ★★★☆

The 2008 vintage (★★★☆) offers fine value. A blend of Merlot (88 per cent) and Cabernet Franc (12 per cent), oak-aged for a year, it's an easy-drinking, finely balanced wine with good body and depth of flavour, slightly spicy and earthy.

DRY $17 V+

Renato Nelson Merlot (★★☆)

Hand-picked from 10-year-old vines at Kina, on the coast, the 2009 vintage (★★☆) was matured for a year in seasoned French oak casks. Fullish in colour, it is medium-bodied, fruity and berryish, with green-edged flavours showing some savoury complexity, but also a slight lack of ripeness and roundness.

Vintage	09
WR	6
Drink	11-13

DRY $24 –V

River Farm Godfrey Road Marlborough Merlot (★★★★)

Dark and dense, the 2009 vintage (★★★★) was estate-grown, hand-harvested at 25.4 brix, fermented with indigenous yeasts and matured for nearly a year in French oak barriques. Deeply coloured, with highly concentrated, fresh blackcurrant, spice and herb flavours, it has some leafy notes, but is savoury, complex and finely structured, with excellent depth and obvious potential.

Vintage	09
WR	6
Drink	10-20

DRY $29 AV

Riverstone Merlot/Cabernet Sauvignon/Shiraz (★★★☆)

From Villa Maria, the non-vintage bottling (★★☆) on sale in 2009 was an easy-drinking blend of New Zealand, Chilean and Australian wines. Bright and fullish in colour, it's a fruity, smooth red with berry, plum and herb flavours, simple and undemanding.

DRY $12 V+

Road Works Waiheke Island Merlot/Cabernet Franc (★★★)

From Man O' War, the 2008 vintage (★★★) is a gutsy red (14.5 per cent alcohol), full-coloured, with strong, plummy, slightly herbal and earthy flavours.

DRY $18 AV

Rongopai Hawke's Bay Merlot ★★★

If you are looking for an affordable Gimblett Gravels red, try this. From Babich, the 2008 vintage (★★★) is a good quaffer, full-coloured, with fresh berry and plum flavours, gentle tannins and a smooth finish. It's a quietly satisfying, slightly savoury red, offering fine value.

DRY $15 V+

Rua Whenua Family Reserve Merlot/Cabernet Franc ★★★★

The 2007 vintage (★★★★☆) was harvested at Te Awanga, in Hawke's Bay, and matured for nearly two years in French and American oak barriques (60 per cent new). Fragrant and full-coloured, it is a blend of Merlot (60 per cent) and Cabernet Franc (40 per cent), sweet-fruited and savoury, with excellent depth of blackcurrant, plum, spice and nut flavours. A distinctive, complex wine, it's worth cellaring.

Vintage	07	06	05
WR	6	NM	7
Drink	10-17	NM	10-15

DRY $30 –V

Sacred Hill Brokenstone Merlot ★★★★★

This is an often outstanding Hawke's Bay red. Since 2002, the grapes have been sourced entirely from the Gimblett Gravels (mostly the company's joint-venture Deerstalkers Vineyard). The wine spends its first year in mostly new French oak barriques, then another several months in new and older barrels. The 2008 vintage (★★★★☆) is a blend of Merlot (90 per cent) and Cabernet Sauvignon (10 per cent). Deeply coloured, it offers strong plum and spice flavours, well-integrated, cedary French oak, and ripe, supple tannins. Finely poised, it's a stylish red, still very youthful; open 2012+.

Vintage	08	07
WR	6	7
Drink	11-15	10-15

DRY $65 AV

Sacred Hill Halo Hawke's Bay Merlot/Cabernet Sauvignon/Cabernet Franc (★★★★)

The floral, deeply coloured 2008 vintage (★★★★) was estate-grown and hand-picked in the Gimblett Gravels, and matured in French oak barriques. It's a refined red with strong, ripe blackcurrant and red-berry flavours seasoned with nutty oak, and the power and structure to age.

DRY $26 AV

Sacred Hill Hawke's Bay Merlot/Cabernet ★★★★

(Previously labelled 'Basket Press'.) The 2009 vintage (★★★☆) is a blend of Merlot (85 per cent) with minor proportions of Malbec (8 per cent) and Cabernet Sauvignon (7 per cent). A dark, purple-flushed red, it shows good density, with a restrained oak influence. Made in a boldly fruity style, it has ripe blackcurrant, plum and spice flavours, and hints of earth and dark chocolate.

Vintage	09	08
WR	7	7
Drink	10-12	10-11

DRY $21 V+

Saint Clair Marlborough Merlot ★★★

The 2008 vintage (★★★), grown in the relatively warm Rapaura district and partly barrel-aged, is a mouthfilling, finely balanced wine with cherry, plum, spice and herb flavours, showing a touch of complexity, and a smooth finish.

Vintage	08	07	06
WR	6	6	6
Drink	10-11	P	P

DRY $21 –V

Saint Clair Rapaura Reserve Marlborough Merlot ★★★☆

This is a more wood-influenced style than its 'Marlborough Merlot' stablemate (above). The 2008 vintage (★★★☆) was matured for 10 months in French oak barriques (80 per cent new). Full-coloured, it is fleshy and supple, with blackcurrant, plum and spice flavours, showing very good depth, and gentle tannins. Drink now or cellar.

Vintage	08	07	06	05	04
WR	6	6	6	6	6
Drink	10-12	10-11	10-11	10-11	P

DRY $27 –V

Merlot 499

Saint Clair Vicar's Choice Marlborough Merlot ★★☆

The 2008 vintage (★★☆) was partly barrel-aged. Ruby-hued, it is fruity and smooth, with berryish, slightly spicy flavours, in a very easy-drinking style.

Vintage	08	07
WR	6	6
Drink	10-11	P

DRY $19 –V

Saints Vineyard Selection Gisborne/Hawke's Bay Merlot/Cabernet (★★★☆)

Offering satisfying depth, the 2009 vintage (★★★☆) is full-coloured, with some savoury complexity and smooth, generous plum, spice and slight coffee flavours. Drink now or cellar.

DRY $20 AV

Salvare Hawke's Bay Merlot (★★★☆)

Grown in Gimblett Road, the 2007 vintage (★★★☆) is deeply coloured. It's a fleshy red made in a fruit-driven style, with very good depth of fresh, ripe, berryish, gently oaked flavours, and gentle tannins.

DRY $25 –V

Sears Road Merlot/Malbec (★★★)

Grown in Hawke's Bay, the 2008 vintage (★★★) is a good quaffer, priced sharply. Fruity and berryish, fresh, ripe and smooth, it's a lightly oaked style, gutsy and flavoursome.

DRY $14 V+

Selaks Founders Reserve Hawke's Bay Merlot ★★★☆

The 2006 vintage (★★★★) from Constellation NZ is a single-vineyard red, grown at Bridge Pa, in The Triangle, and matured for a year in French oak barriques (60 per cent new). Deeply coloured, with a spicy, slightly earthy bouquet, it shows good power through the palate, with concentrated, brambly, spicy flavours, complex and firm.

DRY $33 –V

Selaks Premium Selection Hawke's Bay Merlot/Cabernet ★★★

The full-coloured 2008 vintage (★★★) is a fruit-driven style with fresh, berryish aromas, vibrant blackcurrant, herb and plum flavours, showing good depth, and a smooth finish. Drink now onwards. The 2009 (★★★) is a blend of Merlot (57 per cent), Cabernet Sauvignon (40 per cent) and Malbec (3 per cent). Matured in tanks (mostly) and barrels, it is still very youthful, with mouthfilling body and vibrant, plummy, slightly herbal flavours, fresh and smooth.

DRY $18 AV

Selaks Winemaker's Favourite Hawke's Bay Merlot/Cabernet ★★★★

The 2008 vintage (★★★☆) is a blend of Merlot (56 per cent), Cabernet Sauvignon (42 per cent) and Malbec (2 per cent). Grown in Constellation NZ's Corner 50 Vineyard, and matured in French and American oak barriques (partly new), it is full-coloured, with good body and depth of plum and spice flavours, sweet-fruited and supple, and lots of drink-young appeal.

DRY $21 V+

Shipwreck Bay Merlot/Cabernet (★★)

The 2007 vintage (★★), estate-grown in Northland and oak-matured, is a ruby-hued, medium-bodied red, slightly rustic, with moderate depth of berry, plum and spice flavours.

DRY $18 –V

Sileni Cellar Selection Hawke's Bay Merlot ★★★☆

Already drinking well, the full-coloured, mouthfilling 2009 vintage (★★★☆) is fruity and smooth, with very satisfying depth of ripe, plummy, spicy flavour, gentle tannins and some savoury complexity.

Vintage	09	08	07	06
WR	5	5	6	6
Drink	10-13	10-11	10-11	P

DRY $20 AV

Sileni Exceptional Vintage Hawke's Bay Merlot (★★★★☆)

The densely coloured 2008 vintage (★★★★☆) was matured for 15 to 16 months in French oak barriques. Sturdy (14.5 per cent alcohol), it's a powerful, highly concentrated red, rich, ripe, plummy and savoury, with a fragrant, complex bouquet of coffee and spices. Already approachable, it's a finely balanced wine, well worth cellaring.

Vintage	08	07
WR	6	5
Drink	12-16	11-15

DRY $60 –V

Sileni The Plains Merlot/Cabernet Franc (★★★★)

The generous 2008 vintage (★★★★) is a single-vineyard blend of Merlot (72 per cent) and Cabernet Franc (28 per cent), grown in The Triangle and matured in French (85 per cent) and American oak barriques. Full-coloured, with concentrated, plummy, spicy flavours, it shows good complexity, and ripe, supple tannins.

Vintage	08
WR	6
Drink	12-16

DRY $30 –V

Sileni The Triangle Hawke's Bay Merlot ★★★☆

The 2008 vintage (★★★☆) is deeply coloured, fleshy and concentrated, with plum and spice flavours, savoury and complex, some leafy notes emerging and a finely balanced, rounded finish.

Vintage	08
WR	5
Drink	10-12

DRY $30 –V

Soljans Hawke's Bay Merlot/Cabernet/Malbec ★★★

An enjoyable drink-young style, the 2009 vintage (★★★) is a blend of Merlot (60 per cent), Cabernet Sauvignon (28 per cent) and Malbec (12 per cent), barrel-aged for five months. Fruity and flavoursome, it's a fresh, berryish, moderately complex red, with hints of coffee and spices and a smooth finish.

Vintage	09
WR	5
Drink	10-17

DRY $20 –V

Southern Cross Hawke's Bay Merlot/Cabernet Sauvignon (★★★)

The bargain-priced 2007 vintage (★★★) is from One Tree Hill Vineyards, a division of Morton Estate. A blend of Merlot (65 per cent), Cabernet Sauvignon (20 per cent) and Cabernet Franc (15 per cent), it is full-coloured, with a spicy bouquet. Mouthfilling, it offers plenty of plummy, spicy flavour, with a moderately firm finish.

Vintage	07
WR	6
Drink	10-12

DRY $13 V+

Spy Valley Marlborough Merlot/Malbec ★★★★

The good-value 2008 vintage (★★★★) was hand-picked at 23.8 to 25 brix, fermented with indigenous yeasts and matured for 14 months in French oak barrels (40 per cent new). It's a sturdy, deeply coloured red, fresh and smooth, with concentrated blackcurrant, plum, spice and dark chocolate flavours, showing excellent ripeness and complexity. Drink now or cellar.

Vintage	08	07	06	05	04
WR	5	7	5	6	5
Drink	10-12	10-12	P	P	P

DRY $23 V+

Squawking Magpie The Chatterer Merlot/Syrah/Malbec ★★★★

The 2007 vintage (★★★★) is a Gimblett Gravels, Hawke's Bay blend, matured in French oak barriques. Boldly coloured, it is packed with plum and spice flavours, fresh and ripe, with a hint of chocolate, and finely balanced oak and tannins.

DRY $25 AV

Stone Bridge North Slope Merlot (★★★)

Grown in Gisborne and French oak-aged, the 2007 vintage (★★★) is full-coloured, fresh and lively, with vibrant plum and spice flavours, a gentle seasoning of oak, smooth tannins and good depth.

DRY $19 AV

Stonecroft Ruhanui Merlot/Cabernet Sauvignon ★★★★

Grown in the Gimblett Gravels, the 2008 vintage (★★★★) is a blend of Merlot (74 per cent) and Cabernet Sauvignon (26 per cent), matured for over 18 months in French oak casks. Full but not dense in colour, with a fragrant, spicy bouquet, it has plummy, spicy flavours, showing good complexity. A savoury, firmly structured red, it should be at its best 2012+.

Vintage	08	07
WR	5	6
Drink	12-17	12-20

DRY $35 –V

Stoneleigh Marlborough Merlot ★★★

The 2009 vintage (★★★☆) from Pernod Ricard NZ was grown in the Wairau Valley and matured in French oak casks. It's a sturdy, deeply coloured red with plum, herb, spice and slight coffee flavours, showing very good depth, and fairly firm tannins.

DRY $22 –V

Takatu Kawau Bay Merlot/Cabernet Franc ★★★★

From a year in which the top label did not appear, the 2007 vintage (★★★★) is a quietly classy Matakana red. Full-coloured and invitingly fragrant, it has very good depth of blackcurrant, plum and spice flavours, still fresh and vibrant, and a subtle seasoning of French oak. An elegant wine with a good backbone of tannin, it should reward cellaring.

Vintage	07
WR	6
Drink	10-13

DRY $24 V+

Takatu Matakana Merlot/Cabernet Franc ★★★★☆

The silky, generous 2005 vintage (★★★★★) was a splendid debut, with savoury, earthy notes and a good foundation of tannin, in a classic Bordeaux mould. The 2008 (★★★★☆), matured in French oak casks (20 per cent new), is the first since 2005. Deep and youthful in colour, it is bold and generous, with powerful, brambly, spicy flavours and slightly chewy tannins. It's built to last; open 2012+.

Vintage	08
WR	6
Drink	10-15

DRY $39 AV

Tama Matakana Merlot/Cabernet Sauvignon/Malbec (★★★)

From the property formerly known as The Antipodean, the 2008 vintage (★★★) is a blend of Merlot (46 per cent), Cabernet Sauvignon (41 per cent) and Malbec (13 per cent), matured for 15 months in French oak barrels (half new). Fullish in colour, it's a gentle Bordeaux style, not concentrated, but berryish and slightly herbal, with some savoury complexity and a smooth finish. Ready.

Vintage	08
WR	6
Drink	10-13

DRY $26 –V

Te Awa Left Field Hawke's Bay Merlot/Malbec ★★★★

The 2007 vintage (★★★★) (labelled 'Merlot' rather than 'Merlot/Malbec') is a bold, single-vineyard Gimblett Gravels red, blended with Malbec (10 per cent) and French oak-aged for 18 months. Dark and youthful in colour, with strong, very ripe blackcurrant, plum, spice and dark chocolate flavours, it is fleshy and supple. The 2009 (★★★★) is purple-flushed, fresh and bold, with concentrated blackcurrant and spice flavours, a hint of liquorice, a subtle seasoning of oak, and loads of body and flavour.

DRY $25 AV

Te Kairanga Regional Selection Hawke's Bay Merlot/Cabernet Sauvignon/Malbec (★★★)

A good, gutsy quaffer, the 2008 vintage (★★★) is a blend of Merlot (42 per cent), Cabernet Sauvignon and Malbec, barrique-aged for seven months. Boldly coloured, it is vibrantly fruity, plummy and supple, in an upfront style with moderate complexity and a fresh, smooth finish.

DRY $19 AV

Te Kairanga Runholder Hawke's Bay Merlot/Cabernet Franc (★★★☆)

The 2008 vintage (★★★☆), grown in the Gimblett Gravels, is a blend of Merlot (70 per cent) and Cabernet Franc, strongly seasoned with new French oak. It has a spicy bouquet and fresh, strong, moderately ripe blackcurrant and plum flavours, with a tight, firm finish.

Vintage	08
WR	7
Drink	10-18

DRY $29 –V

Te Mania Three Brothers Nelson Merlot/Malbec/Cabernet Franc ★★☆

The 2008 vintage (★★☆), matured for 10 months in seasoned French and American oak casks, is full-coloured and fruity, with straightforward red-berry, plum and herbal flavours, fresh and crisp.

Vintage	08	07	06
WR	5	6	5
Drink	10-13	10-12	P

DRY $20 –V

Te Mata Estate Woodthorpe Vineyard Merlot/Cabernets ★★★★

This bargain-priced red is Te Mata's biggest seller – and deservedly so. The 2008 vintage (★★★★), estate-grown in Hawke's Bay, is a blend of Merlot, Cabernet Sauvignon and Cabernet Franc, matured for 17 months in French oak casks (new and seasoned). Full-coloured, with a fragrant, slightly spicy bouquet, it is fresh and vibrant, with generous blackcurrant and spice flavours, slightly herbal and nutty. It's finely balanced for early drinking or moderate cellaring.

Vintage	08	07	06	05
WR	7	7	7	7
Drink	10-14	10-15	10-14	10-13

DRY $19 V+

Terravin J Merlot/Malbec/Cabernet ★★★★☆

Ensconced in a magnum, the 2008 vintage (★★★★☆) proves Marlborough can produce a delicious, Bordeaux-style red. Matured for 18 months in French oak casks (50 per cent new), it is dark and purple-flushed, with a fragrant bouquet of ripe fruit and toasty oak. Rich yet elegant, it has deep blackcurrant, plum and spice flavours, supple tannins, a hint of mint, and excellent density and structure. Still very fresh and vibrant, it's a wine to enjoy over the next decade.

Vintage	08	07
WR	6	7
Drink	12-18	12-20

DRY $120 (1.5L) –V

Thornbury Gimblett Gravels Merlot ★★★★☆

From Villa Maria, the 2009 vintage (★★★★☆) is an extremely youthful Hawke's Bay red (8 per cent Malbec, 2 per cent Cabernet Sauvignon), matured in French (70 per cent) and American oak casks (25 per cent new). Fresh and deeply coloured, quite savoury and Bordeaux-like, it has rich, blackcurrant-evoking flavours to the fore, with plum, spice and slight coffee notes adding complexity. Open mid-2011+.

Vintage	09	08
WR	6	6
Drink	10-15	10-15

DRY $22 V+

Ti Point Two Merlot/Cabernet Franc ★★★★

The 2009 vintage (★★★★) is a silky-textured Auckland red with great drinkability, estate-grown at Leigh, near Matakana. A blend of Merlot (75 per cent) and Cabernet Franc (25 per cent), matured for eight months in seasoned French oak barrels, it's a classic claret style, medium to full-bodied, with very satisfying depth of blackcurrant, plum and spice flavours, slightly earthy, chocolatey notes and ripe, supple tannins. It's already delicious.

DRY $22 V+

Unison Reserve Hawke's Bay Merlot ★★★★

Estate-grown in the Gimblett Gravels and barrel-aged, the 2008 vintage (★★★★) is full and youthful in colour, with a savoury, spicy bouquet. Fresh, plummy and spicy, with hints of earth and dark chocolate, good complexity, and a long finish, it's well worth cellaring.

DRY $25 AV

Vidal Hawke's Bay Merlot/Cabernet Sauvignon ★★★★★

Always a great buy. The 2009 vintage (★★★★☆) is a blend of Merlot (68 per cent), Cabernet Sauvignon (17 per cent), Malbec (9 per cent) and Cabernet Franc (6 per cent), 60 per cent barrel-aged. It's a mouthfilling, ripe, silky-textured red with deep plum and spice flavours, complexity – and great drinkablity.

Vintage	10	09	08	07	06	05	04
WR	7	7	6	7	7	7	6
Drink	10-14	10-14	10-15	10-15	10-11	P	P

DRY $21 V+

Vidal Reserve Hawke's Bay Merlot/Cabernet Sauvignon ★★★★★

The 2007 vintage (★★★★) is a blend of Merlot (46 per cent) and Cabernet Sauvignon (46 per cent), with a splash of Malbec, matured for 20 months in French oak barriques (64 per cent new). Boldly coloured, with a strong seasoning of toasty oak, it has concentrated, plummy, berryish, slightly chocolatey flavours, showing good complexity and richness. There is no 2008.

Vintage	08	07	DRY $30 V+
WR	NM	7	
Drink	NM	10-17	

Villa Maria Cellar Selection Hawke's Bay Merlot [Organic] (★★★★)

BioGro certified, the 2009 vintage (★★★★) is a blend of Merlot (90 per cent) and Malbec (10 per cent), grown in the company's Joseph Soler Vineyard, on the edge of the Gimblett Gravels, and matured in tanks and French oak barriques (15 per cent new). Floral and supple, it is a full-coloured, very graceful red with strong, ripe, youthful, plummy flavours that flow to a finely textured finish. Still youthful, with good tannin backbone, it's well worth cellaring to 2012+.

Vintage	09	DRY $24 V+
WR	6	
Drink	11-15	

Villa Maria Cellar Selection Hawke's Bay Merlot/Cabernet Sauvignon ★★★★★

The 2000 (★★★★★) and 2002 (★★★★★) vintages offered exceptional value, winning Best Buy of the Year awards in the *Buyer's Guide*. The 2008 vintage (★★★★☆) is a blend of Merlot (64 per cent), Cabernet Sauvignon (26 per cent) and Cabernet Franc (10 per cent), grown mostly in the Gimblett Gravels and matured in French, American and Hungarian oak barriques (45 per cent new). Dark, with blackcurrant, plum and slight herb flavours, vibrant and concentrated, spice and fruit cake notes, and a firm backbone of tannin, it's worth cellaring.

Vintage	08	07	06	DRY $24 V+
WR	7	7	6	
Drink	11-15	10-15	10-14	

Villa Maria Private Bin Hawke's Bay Merlot ★★★★

The 2009 vintage (★★★★) is a blend of Merlot (87 per cent), Malbec (7 per cent), Cabernet Sauvignon (4 per cent) and Cabernet Franc (2 per cent), grown principally in the Gimblett Gravels, and matured in tanks and seasoned French and American oak casks. A youthful, concentrated red with deep, bright colour and well-ripened plum and spice flavours, it is fresh and vibrantly fruity, with some savoury notes and a rich, firm finish. Best drinking mid-2011+.

Vintage	09	08	DRY $21 V+
WR	6	6	
Drink	10-13	10-12	

Villa Maria Private Bin Hawke's Bay Merlot [Organic] (★★★★)

Certified BioGro, the 2009 vintage (★★★★) was grown in the company's Joseph Soler Vineyard, on the boundary of the Gimblett Gravels, and matured in tanks and seasoned French and American oak barriques. A blend of Merlot (91 per cent) and Malbec (9 per cent), it is full-coloured, fruity and supple, with ripe, spicy flavours, good tannin support, and excellent texture, harmony and depth. It's already delicious, but worth cellaring.

Vintage	09
WR	6
Drink	10-13

DRY $21 V+

Villa Maria Private Bin Hawke's Bay Merlot/Cabernet Sauvignon ★★★☆

The 2009 vintage (★★★★) is a blend of Merlot (58 per cent), Cabernet Sauvignon (28 per cent), Cabernet Franc (10 per cent) and Malbec (4 per cent). Matured in tanks and seasoned French and American oak barrels, it is fragrant and full-coloured, with strong, plummy, spicy flavours, showing good ripeness, hints of dark chocolate and coconut, and some complexity.

Vintage	09	08	07	06
WR	6	6	6	6
Drink	10-13	10-12	10-12	P

DRY $21 AV

Villa Maria Reserve Hawke's Bay Merlot ★★★★★

This consistently outstanding wine is grown at company-owned vineyards in the Gimblett Gravels – Ngakirikiri, Omahu Gravels and Twyford Gravels – and matured for 18 to 20 months in French (principally) and American oak barriques (40 to 80 per cent new). The 2008 vintage (★★★★★), which includes 10 per cent Cabernet Sauvignon, is arrestingly dark and dense, with layered blackcurrant, spice and slight coffee flavours. It's an extremely concentrated, notably ripe style, highly seductive in its youth, but also an obvious candidate for cellaring.

Vintage	08	07	06	05	04
WR	6	7	7	7	6
Drink	12-16	10-19	10-18	10-17	10-16

DRY $51 AV

Waimea Bolitho SV Merlot ★★★☆

Grown in Nelson, the 2008 vintage (★★★☆) is a single-vineyard red, grown on the Waimea Plains, matured in French oak casks (partly new), and bottled unfined and unfiltered. A tightly structured, deeply coloured red, it is vibrantly fruity, with strong plum and spice flavours, some herbal notes and a fresh, crisp finish.

Vintage	08
WR	7
Drink	10-11

DRY $27 –V

Waimea Nelson Merlot/Malbec ★★☆

The 2008 vintage (★★☆) is a blend of Merlot (72 per cent) and Malbec (28 per cent), grown on the coast at Kina, and on the Waimea Plains. Matured in American and French oak casks, it is medium-bodied, with plum and herb flavours that lack real ripeness and roundness.

Vintage	08	DRY $22 –V
WR	6	
Drink	10-14	

Weeping Sands Waiheke Island Merlot (★★★★)

Still very youthful, the 2009 vintage (★★★★) from Obsidian is an estate-grown red, matured in French oak casks (15 per cent new). Mouthfilling and full-coloured, with fresh, deep plum and spice flavours, a hint of coffee and oak complexity, it's a concentrated, ripe and savoury red, with good cellar potential.

Vintage	09	DRY $31 –V
WR	6	
Drink	10-18	

Whitecliff Merlot (★★☆)

The fruity, smooth 2008 vintage (★★☆) is a pleasant, undemanding blend of Australian and New Zealand wines, from Sacred Hill. Ruby-hued, it is berryish and spicy, with a soft finish.

DRY $10 V+

Wild Rock Gravel Pit Red Merlot/Malbec ★★★★

From Wild Rock Wine Company (a subsidiary of Craggy Range), the 2008 vintage (★★★★) was grown in the Gimblett Gravels, Hawke's Bay, and matured for 14 months in French oak casks (20 per cent new). Harvested at 24 brix, it's a blend of Merlot (71 per cent), Malbec (25 per cent) and Cabernet Franc (4 per cent). A top buy, it is dark, mouthfilling and concentrated, with youthful, brambly, spicy flavours, a gentle seasoning of oak and impressive density.

Vintage	08	07	DRY $20 V+
WR	7	7	
Drink	10-15	10-14	

Montepulciano

Montepulciano is widely planted across central Italy, yielding deeply coloured, ripe wines with good levels of alcohol, extract and flavour. In the Abruzzi, it is the foundation of the often superb-value Montepulciano d'Abruzzo, and in the Marches it is the key ingredient in the noble Rosso Conero.

In New Zealand, Montepulciano is a rarity and there has been confusion between the Montepulciano and Sangiovese varieties. Some wines may have been incorrectly labelled. According to the latest national vineyard survey, between 2005 and 2011 New Zealand's area of bearing Montepulciano vines will expand slightly from 6 to 10 hectares (mostly in Auckland, Hawke's Bay and Marlborough).

Beach House Hawke's Bay Montepulciano (★★★★☆)

Densely coloured, the 2007 vintage (★★★★☆) was grown in The Track Vineyard, in the Gimblett Gravels, and matured for a year in French and American oak casks. Sturdy, it has concentrated, ripe, brambly, spicy, plummy flavours and finely integrated oak, in a very rich and fruity style, with the power and structure to age.

Vintage	07
WR	7
Drink	10-30

DRY $45 –V

Black Barn Hawke's Bay Montepulciano ★★★★

The 2009 vintage (★★★★★) is a lovely marriage of power and approachability. Estate-grown at Havelock North, it is floral and rich, with substantial body (14.5 per cent alcohol) and an invitingly scented bouquet. Packed with plum, cherry, spice and chocolate flavours, it shows notable ripeness and density, with a silky texture and power right through the palate. One of New Zealand's best-ever Montepulcianos.

DRY $48 –V

Blackenbrook Vineyard Nelson Montepulciano (★★★☆)

The 2008 vintage (★★★★) is very fresh, vibrant and fruity, tasting like a good Beaujolais. Plummy and spicy, with a touch of oak-derived complexity, it is full-flavoured and well-rounded, offering good, early drinking.

Vintage	09
WR	6
Drink	10-13

DRY $27 –V

Framingham Marlborough Montepulciano ★★★☆

The 2008 vintage (★★★★), matured in French oak barriques (30 per cent new), is the best yet. Deeply coloured, it is full-bodied and smooth, with strong plum and spice flavours, a hint of fruit cake, a firm backbone of tannin and good concentration. It should age well.

Vintage	08	07	06
WR	5	6	6
Drink	10-14	10-15	10-11

DRY $28 –V

Hans Herzog Marlborough Montepulciano ★★★★★

Typically a giant of a red, overflowing with sweet, ripe fruit flavours. The 2007 vintage (★★★★☆) was fermented with indigenous yeasts, matured for two years in French oak barriques, and bottled without fining or filtration. Deep and youthful in colour, it's a strapping (14.5 per cent alcohol), highly complex wine, nutty, firm and very savoury, although the Montepulciano varietal characters are less clear-cut than in some past vintages.

Vintage	07	06	05
WR	7	7	7
Drink	10-19	10-20	10-20

DRY $64 AV

Jurassic Ridge Montepulciano (★★★★☆)

An excellent debut, the 2008 vintage (★★★★☆) is a strapping red (14.8 per cent alcohol), estate-grown at Church Bay, on Waiheke Island, and hand-picked at 25 brix from first-crop vines. Matured in French oak casks (30 per cent new), it is deeply coloured, rich and sweet-fruited, with concentrated plum, cassis and spice flavours, slightly earthy notes adding complexity, buried tannins, and a rounded finish. Well worth cellaring.

Vintage	08
WR	6
Drink	10-15

DRY $35 AV

Morton Estate Hawke's Bay Montepulciano (★★☆)

The 2007 vintage (★★☆) is a pleasant, medium-bodied style (11.5 per cent alcohol), with a hint of sweet oak and decent depth of fresh, vibrantly fruity flavour.

Vintage	07
WR	6
Drink	10-12

DRY $19 –V

Stafford Lane Estate Nelson Montepulciano (★★)

Estate-grown and hand-harvested at 22.5 brix at Appleby, the 2008 vintage (★★) was matured for 10 months in French oak barriques (30 per cent new). Light ruby, it's a light, simple red, berryish, slightly spicy and plummy, but lacks real richness and roundness.

DRY $25 –V

Trinity Hill Hawke's Bay Montepulciano ★★★★

Winery founder John Hancock doesn't believe Montepulciano has a strong future in Hawke's Bay – but still wins high accolades. The 2009 vintage (★★★★), grown in the Gimblett Gravels, was blended with some Cabernet Sauvignon and given 'minimal' exposure to oak. Made for early drinking, it hits the target with ease, offering lots of vibrant, plummy, spicy flavour, seductively fresh and smooth.

DRY $20 V+

Weeping Sands Waiheke Island Montepulciano ★★★★☆

The strapping 2009 vintage (★★★★☆) was grown by the Obsidian winery at Onetangi and matured for 10 months in French (75 per cent) and American oak casks (20 per cent new). Although robust (15 per cent alcohol), it retains freshness and vibrancy. Deeply coloured and powerful, with concentrated flavours of plums, spices and nuts, very ripe, lush and lingering, it should be long-lived.

Vintage	09	08	07	06
WR	6	7	7	6
Drink	10-18	10-18	10-15	10-12

DRY $34 AV

Pinotage

Pinotage is overshadowed by more glamorous varieties in New Zealand, with 74 hectares of bearing vines in 2011. After being passed during the past decade by Cabernet Franc, Malbec and Syrah, Pinotage now ranks as the country's seventh most extensively planted red-wine variety.

Pinotage is a cross of the great Burgundian grape, Pinot Noir, and Cinsaut, a heavy-cropping variety popular in the south of France. Cinsaut's typically 'meaty, chunky sort of flavour' (in Jancis Robinson's words) is also characteristic of Pinotage. Valued for its reasonably early-ripening and disease-resistant qualities, and good yields, its plantings are predominantly in the North Island – notably Hawke's Bay and Gisborne – with other significant pockets in Marlborough and Auckland.

A well-made Pinotage displays a slightly gamey bouquet and a smooth, berryish, peppery palate that can be reminiscent of a southern Rhône. It matures swiftly and usually peaks within two or three years of the vintage.

Ascension The Bell Ringer Matakana Pinotage (★★☆)

Lightish in colour, the 2008 vintage (★★☆) is a medium-bodied red with solid depth of plum, spice and tamarillo flavours, but lacks real ripeness and richness.

DRY $27 –V

Babich East Coast Pinotage/Cabernet ★★★

Over several decades, this honest, bargain-priced red has built up a deservedly strong following. The 2007 vintage (★★★) is full-coloured, fruity, ripe and supple, with the earthy notes typical of Pinotage and good flavour depth. Drink now.

DRY $12 V+

Hihi Gisborne Pinotage ★★★

The 2007 vintage (★★★) was harvested at 25.6 brix at Patutahi and blended with splashes of Merlot (4 per cent), Malbec (4 per cent) and Cabernet Franc (4 per cent). Barrel-aged for 10 months, it's mouthfilling and spicy, with a slightly sweet, American oak influence and firm tannins. A gutsy style, it's a good quaffer.

DRY $18 AV

Hitchen Road Pinotage ★★★

The 2009 vintage (★★☆) was estate-grown at Pokeno, in North Waikato, and harvested at 24 brix. Oak-matured for over a year, it has lightish colour. A slightly leafy wine, it's drinking solidly now, but lacks the ripeness and stuffing of the 2008 (★★★☆).

Vintage	09
WR	6
Drink	10-14

DRY $15 V+

Karikari Estate Pinotage ★★★★

Estate-grown in the Far North, the 2007 vintage (★★★★) was matured in American (mostly) and French oak barrels (30 per cent new). It's a substantial red, built to last, with firm, concentrated, spicy flavours, nutty, savoury and complex. Drink now.

Vintage	07
WR	6
Drink	11-18

DRY $40 –V

Kerr Farm Vineyard Kumeu Pinotage ★★☆

Kerr Farm's wine is to be enjoyed 'with friends on the verandah for a cruisy afternoon'. Estate-grown in West Auckland and matured in American and French oak barriques, it is typically an honest country red. The 2007 vintage (★★★) is one of the best. Fresh and vibrantly fruity, with lightish, still-youthful colour, it is berryish, slightly spicy and earthy, with gentle tannins. Drink now.

DRY $22 –V

Kidnapper Cliffs Hawke's Bay Pinotage (★★★★★)

From Te Awa (a winery with a strong track record with Pinotage), the debut 2009 vintage (★★★★★) could easily be mistaken for Syrah. Bold and bright in colour, it is vibrantly fruity, with lovely ripeness and density of plum/pepper flavours and earthy, savoury notes adding complexity. Notably rich and supple, it avoids the rusticity typical of Pinotage and is a wine of real finesse.

DRY $45 AV

Marsden Bay of Islands Pinotage ★★☆

Still on sale in 2010, the 2006 vintage (★★☆) was harvested at 25.6 brix and oak-aged for 18 months. It's a deeply coloured, gutsy (14 per cent alcohol) and spicy wine, but now slightly past its best.

Vintage	06
WR	6
Drink	10-12

DRY $24 –V

Muddy Water Waipara Pinotage ★★★★

'Not for the faint-hearted' (in the winery's words), this is typically a robust red, full of personality. The 2009 (★★★★☆) is a top vintage. Matured for over a year in French oak casks (20 per cent new), it's like a good Côtes-du-Rhône, combining power and charm. Full-coloured, mouthfilling and supple, with vibrant, sweet-fruit flavours of cherries and plums, and a hint of liquorice, it is deliciously fruity and smooth, in a graceful style with excellent complexity and depth.

Vintage	09
WR	7
Drink	10-19

DRY $39 –V

Okahu Pinotage ★★★☆

The youthful 2008 vintage (★★★☆) is a Northland red, estate-grown, hand-picked and matured in a 50/50 split of French and American oak (partly new). It's a dark, vibrantly fruity wine, medium-bodied (12.5 per cent alcohol), fresh, plummy and supple, with plenty of flavour.

DRY $30 –V

Soljans Gisborne Pinotage ★★★☆

This small West Auckland winery has a strong reputation for Pinotage. The 2008 vintage (★★★), barrel-aged for six months, is a full-coloured, medium-bodied red, vibrantly fruity, with berry and plum flavours, slightly spicy and savoury.

Vintage	08	07
WR	5	7
Drink	10-15	10-14

DRY $18 V+

Te Awa Pinotage ★★★★☆

Grown in the Gimblett Gravels, Hawke's Bay, and harvested at 23.5 to over 25 brix, the 2007 vintage (★★★★★) is one of the country's finest Pinotages yet. Densely coloured, it is brambly, plummy, earthy and spicy, in a robust style (14.5 per cent alcohol) with real complexity and a rich, rounded finish. Delicious drinking now onwards.

DRY $30 –V

Waitapu Estate Reef Point Pinotage (★★☆)

Grown at Ahipara, in Northland, and French oak-aged, the 2008 vintage (★★☆) is fruity and plummy, fresh and mouthfilling, but green-edged, with a slight lack of real ripeness and richness.

DRY $28 –V

Pinot Noir

New Zealand Pinot Noir enjoyed buoyant overseas demand in the year to June 2010, with 912,000 cases shipped – a steep rise from the 139,188 cases exported in 2003. There are now almost countless Pinot Noir labels, as producers cater for cash-strapped consumers by introducing second and third-tier labels (and others under brands you and I have never heard of). The wines are enjoying notable success in international competitions, but you need to be aware that most of the world's elite Pinot Noir producers, especially in Burgundy, do not enter.

The 2010 vintage yielded 23,655 tonnes of Pinot Noir grapes, far ahead of Merlot with 8885 tonnes and Cabernet Sauvignon with 2203 tonnes. Between 2000 and 2011, New Zealand's area of bearing Pinot Noir vines is expanding from 1126 hectares to 4803 hectares.

Pinot Noir is the princely grape variety of red Burgundy. Cheaper wines typically display light, raspberry-evoking flavours which lack the velvety riches of classic Burgundy. Great red Burgundy has substance, suppleness and a gorgeous spread of flavours: cherries, fruit cake, spice and plums.

Pinot Noir over the past decade has become New Zealand's most internationally acclaimed red-wine style. The vine is our second most commonly planted variety overall, now well ahead of Chardonnay and behind only Sauvignon Blanc. Over 40 per cent of the country's total Pinot Noir plantings are in Marlborough (where 8 per cent of the vines are grown for bottle-fermented sparkling wine), and the variety is also well established in Central Otago, Canterbury, Wairarapa, Hawke's Bay, Gisborne and Nelson.

Yet Pinot Noir is a frustrating variety to grow. Because it buds early, it is vulnerable to spring frosts; its compact bunches are also very prone to rot. One crucial advantage is that it ripens early, well ahead of Cabernet Sauvignon. Low cropping and the selection of superior clones are essential aspects of the production of fine wine.

Martinborough (initially) and Central Otago have enjoyed the highest profile for Pinot Noir over the past 20 years. As their output of Pinot Noir has expanded, average prices have fallen, reflecting the arrival of a tidal wave of 'entry-level' (drink-young) wines.

Of the other small regions, Nelson and Waipara, in North Canterbury, are also enjoying great success. Marlborough's potential for the production of outstanding – but all too often underrated – Pinot Noir, in sufficient volumes to supply the burgeoning international demand, has also been tapped.

3 Terraces Wairarapa Pinot Noir ★★☆

The 2009 vintage (★★) has lightish, slightly developed colour. Fruity and plummy, with crisp acidity, it lacks ripeness and richness.

DRY $20 –V

25 Steps Central Otago Pinot Noir ★★★☆

From a terraced site at Lowburn, the 2008 vintage (★★★) is ruby-hued, with fresh acidity, good but not great depth of cherry and plum flavours, a touch of complexity and gentle tannins.

DRY $35 –V

36 Bottles Central Otago Pinot Noir ★★★☆

Grown at Bendigo, the 2008 vintage (★★★☆) is a ruby-hued wine with a floral, scented bouquet, showing good complexity. Moderately concentrated, it has vibrant, cherryish, spicy flavours, fresh acidity and supple tannins. The 2009 (★★★☆), matured for 10 months in French oak barriques, is generous and silky, with cherry and plum flavours, showing some savoury complexity, and good harmony. Drink now or cellar.

Vintage	08
WR	6
Drink	10-13

DRY $35 –V

1769 Central Otago Pinot Noir ★★★☆

From Wild Earth, the 2009 vintage (★★★☆) is already highly enjoyable. Full-coloured, it is sweet-fruited and harmonious, with fresh cherry, plum and spice flavours, showing very good depth, supple tannins and considerable complexity.

DRY $25 AV

1912 by Lindis River Central Otago Pinot Noir (★★★)

Enjoyable now, the 2008 vintage (★★★) is ruby-hued and supple, with ripe, moderately concentrated cherry, herb and spice flavours, showing a touch of complexity.

DRY $25 –V

12,000 Miles Pinot Noir ★★★

From the Gladstone winery, in the northern Wairarapa, the easy-drinking 2009 vintage (★★☆) was partly barrel-aged. Ruby-hued, it is light, with berry, plum and herb flavours, threaded with fresh acidity, and a smooth finish.

Vintage	09
WR	5
Drink	10-15

DRY $26 –V

Akarua Central Otago Pinot Noir ★★★★☆

In the past called 'The Gullies', this is as an early-drinking style, compared to its Reserve stablemate (below), but top vintages are still outstanding. Estate-grown at Bannockburn and matured in French oak barriques (36 per cent new), the 2009 (★★★★★) is instantly attractive. Highly refined, it is full-coloured, floral and supple, with vibrant, well-ripened plum and cherry flavours, finely integrated oak, fresh acidity, and lovely harmony.

Vintage	09	NM	07	06	05
WR	7	NM	6	5	6
Drink	10-17	NM	10-15	10-12	P

DRY $40 –V

Akarua Reserve Central Otago Pinot Noir ★★★★★

(Formerly labelled as 'Cadence'.) Estate-grown at Bannockburn, the 2009 vintage (★★★★★) was picked at 25 brix from 13-year-old vines, matured in French oak barriques (36 per cent new), and bottled unfined and unfiltered. Deeply coloured, it is fleshy, generous and savoury, in a notably ripe style, highly fragrant, with substantial body and highly concentrated cherry, plum and spice flavours. Powerful and very sweet-fruited, it should blossom with cellaring.

Vintage	09	08	07	06	05
WR	7	NM	6	5	6
Drink	10-18	NM	10-17	10-15	10-11

DRY $55 AV

Alana Estate Martinborough Pinot Noir ★★★★☆

The 2007 vintage (★★★★★) is dark, silky and sustained, with rich, ripe cherry, plum and spice flavours, savoury and lingering. It's a beautifully fragrant wine, concentrated and supple.

Vintage	07	06
WR	5	7
Drink	10-12	10-16

DRY $60 –V

Alexander Dusty Road Martinborough Pinot Noir ★★★☆

The 2009 vintage (★★★☆) is a good-value single-vineyard red, partly barrel-aged, with drink-young appeal. Mouthfilling and supple, it has very good depth of cherry and plum flavours, fresh, ripe and rounded.

Vintage	09	08	07	06
WR	6	5	NM	6
Drink	10-12	10-11	NM	P

DRY $24 V+

Alexander Martinborough Pinot Noir ★★★★

The 2008 vintage (★★★★) is a floral, supple, mid-weight style, showing good complexity and already highly enjoyable. It's an elegant wine with ripe cherry, plum and spice flavours, finely integrated French oak (22 per cent new) and silky tannins.

Vintage	08	07	06	05
WR	6	NM	6	7
Drink	10-13	NM	P	P

DRY $35 AV

alex.gold Central Otago Pinot Noir ★★★★

From Alexandra Wine Company, the 2008 vintage (★★★★) has deep, cherryish flavours and a strong seasoning of French oak (40 per cent new). It's a richly coloured, savoury and complex wine with a fresh, crisp, almost peppery finish.

Vintage	07	06
WR	6	5
Drink	12-13	P

DRY $30 AV

Alexandra Wine Company Davishon Pinot Noir ★★★★

The 2007 vintage (★★★★) is a vibrant, supple red, grown at Alexandra. Full and bright in colour, with a core of sweet fruit, it has concentrated cherry and herb flavours, seasoned with French oak (40 per cent new).

Vintage	08	07	06
WR	5	6	5
Drink	12-13	12-13	10-11

DRY $35 AV

Alexia Wairarapa Pinot Noir ★★★☆

The 2008 vintage (★★★☆) is an attractive drink-young style, grown at Opaki, near Masterton, and partly barrel-aged. Full-coloured, it is fresh and vibrantly fruity, with ripe cherry and plum flavours, gently seasoned with oak.

Vintage	08
WR	6
Drink	10-13

DRY $22 V+

Allan Scott Hounds Marlborough Pinot Noir ★★★★

Allan Scott's top red label. A single-vineyard wine, fermented with indigenous yeasts and matured for over a year in French oak casks (mainly new), the 2009 vintage (★★★★☆) is mouthfilling, sweet-fruited, rich and supple. Deeply coloured, with concentrated cherry and plum flavours, seasoned with fine-quality oak, it is elegant and finely poised, offering excellent drinking from mid-2011+.

Vintage	09	08
WR	6	6
Drink	11-15	10-14

DRY $35 AV

Allan Scott Marlborough Pinot Noir ★★★☆

The 2009 vintage (★★★☆) is ruby-hued, floral, fruity and supple. Fermented with indigenous yeasts, it was matured for 10 months in French oak puncheons (25 per cent new). Cherryish, plummy and slightly spicy, with some savoury complexity, it's a very enjoyable, drink-young style.

Vintage	09	08
WR	6	6
Drink	10-14	10-12

DRY $26 AV

Amisfield Central Otago Pinot Noir ★★★★★

Estate-grown at Lowburn, in the Cromwell Basin, and matured in French oak barriques (25 per cent new), the 2008 vintage (★★★★☆) is a beautifully floral, supple red with vibrant cherry/plum flavours, seasoned with quality oak. Refined and savoury, with the muscle to age and good complexity, it's still very youthful; open mid-2011+.

Vintage	09	08	07	06	05	04	03
WR	7	7	7	6	5	6	5
Drink	12-20	11-19	10-18	10-15	10-12	P	P

DRY $40 V+

Amisfield Rocky Knoll Pinot Noir (★★★★★)

Still on sale, the debut 2006 vintage (★★★★★) was grown at Rocky Knoll, a stony terrace within the Amisfield Vineyard at Lowburn, in Central Otago. Picked at over 26 brix, it was matured for 15 months in French oak barriques (44 per cent new). Deep ruby, it's a strikingly rich, complex and harmonious wine, notably concentrated, sweet-fruited and savoury, with supple, silky tannins giving instant appeal.

Vintage	07	06
WR	7	7
Drink	12-20	11-19

DRY $95 –V

Anchorage Nelson Pinot Noir ★★☆

Grown at Motueka and maturing solidly, the 2008 vintage (★★) is a barrel-aged red, pale ruby, light and smooth, with pleasant, slightly herbal flavours, lacking real ripeness and richness.

DRY $21 –V

Anchorage Pinot Noir Moon Creek Block (★★☆)

Grown at Motueka, the 2008 vintage (★★☆) is pale, with smooth, light, slightly leafy flavours. Drink young.

DRY $19 –V

Anthem Discover Central Otago Pinot Noir ★★★

The 2007 vintage (★★★) is a ruby-hued mid-weight with fresh, tight flavours, slightly leafy and smooth.

DRY $25 –V

Ara Composite Marlborough Pinot Noir ★★★☆

From the Winegrowers of Ara Vineyard, at the entrance to the Waihopai Valley, the 2008 vintage (★★★☆) is fragrant and supple, sweet-fruited and lively, with cherry, plum and spice flavours, showing good texture and complexity. The 2009 (★★★★) was matured for 10 months in French oak casks (25 per cent new). Ruby-hued, it is strongly varietal, with cherry, plum and spice flavours, ripe and supple, good complexity, and the structure to age.

Vintage	09	08
WR	6	6
Drink	10-15	10-14

DRY $26 AV

Ara Marlborough Pinot Noir ★★★

This label is aimed at the restaurant trade. The 2009 vintage (★★★) was made from young vines and partly oak-aged. Light ruby, it is a medium-bodied red with cherry, plum and spice flavours, showing good freshness and immediacy. An enjoyable, drink-young style.

DRY $20 AV

Ara Pathway Marlborough Pinot Noir ★★★

A drink-young style, the 2008 vintage (★★★) is ruby-hued and vibrantly fruity, with fresh cherry/plum flavours, some savoury notes and a rounded finish. The 2009 (★★★) was partly handled in tanks; 40 per cent of the blend was matured for six months in French oak casks (10 per cent new). Ruby-hued and vibrantly fruity, it has cherryish, plummy flavours, a hint of herbs, some savoury complexity and gentle tannins.

DRY $21 AV

Ara Resolute Marlborough Pinot Noir ★★★☆

From Winegrowers of Ara, the 2007 vintage (★★★★) was made from vines in the heart of the Ara Vineyard, hand-picked at 23.8 brix and matured for a year in French oak casks (20 per cent new). Ruby-hued, it is graceful and savoury, medium-bodied and supple, with ripe cherry and nut flavours, showing good harmony. Attractively perfumed, it's enjoyable now. There is no 2008.

Vintage	09
WR	7
Drink	10-15

DRY $45 –V

Archangel Central Otago Pinot Noir (★★★★)

The 2008 vintage (★★★★) is a very elegant, ruby-hued, single-vineyard red, grown at Queensberry, half-way between Cromwell and Wanaka. Sweet-fruited and supple, with cherry, herb and spice flavours, it is showing some savoury complexity.

DRY $39 AV

Artisan The Best Paddock Marlborough Pinot Noir ★★☆

The 2008 vintage (★★☆) was grown in the lower Wairau Valley. It's a pleasant light style, berryish and smooth, with a touch of spicy, nutty complexity.

DRY $25 –V

Ashwell Martinborough Pinot Noir ★★★☆

Grown on the Martinborough Terraces, the 2009 vintage (★★★) was matured for a year in French oak casks. Ruby-hued, it is ripe and supple, with cherry, spice and slight herb flavours, showing good but not great depth, and moderate complexity. It's enjoyable young, with some aging potential.

Vintage	09	08
WR	6	6
Drink	10-15	10-14

DRY $30 –V

Ashwell Martinborough Reserve Pinot Noir ★★★★

The 2009 vintage (★★★☆) was matured in French oak casks (30 per cent new). Full-coloured, it is fragrant, sturdy and firm, with plum, cherry and herb flavours, showing very good depth. It's already drinking well.

Vintage	09
WR	6
Drink	10-16

DRY $34 AV

Ashwell The Quails Martinborough Pinot Noir (★★)

The fresh, medium-bodied 2008 vintage (★★) was matured in French oak barriques (33 per cent new). Full-coloured, it's a crisp wine, simple and only moderately varietal.

Vintage	08
WR	6
Drink	10-14

DRY $30 –V

Askerne Hawke's Bay Pinot Noir ★★☆

Estate-grown near Havelock North, the 2007 vintage (★★☆) was matured for 10 months in French oak barriques (35 per cent new). Light ruby, it's a floral wine with cherry, plum and herb aromas and flavours and gentle tannins.

Vintage	07	06	05	04
WR	5	6	6	5
Drink	10-13	10-11	P	P

DRY $20 –V

Aspire Pinot Noir (★★★)

From Matariki, the 2007 vintage (★★★) was grown in Hawke's Bay and lightly oaked. It's drinking well now, with fresh cherry, herb and spice flavours, showing a touch of complexity and satisfying depth.

Vintage	08	07
WR	5	6
Drink	10-12	10-11

DRY $22 AV

Astrolabe Voyage Marlborough Pinot Noir ★★★★

The 2008 vintage (★★★★) was hand-picked, fermented partly with indigenous yeasts and oak-aged for 10 months. A generous, sweet-fruited red, it is full-coloured, with cherry, plum, spice and nut flavours, showing excellent ripeness, youthful tannins and good complexity.

Vintage	08	07	06
WR	6	6	5
Drink	10-12	10-14	P

DRY $29 V+

Ata Rangi Crimson Pinot Noir ★★★★

This second-tier label is based on young vines in Martinborough and designed for early drinking – within three years of the harvest. Matured in French oak barriques, the 2008 vintage (★★★★) was hand-picked at 23 to 25.5 brix. It's an instantly appealing wine with gentle tannins and rich cherry, plum and spice flavours, showing very good ripeness, complexity and harmony.

Vintage	08	07
WR	7	6
Drink	10-12	P

DRY $32 AV

Ata Rangi Pinot Noir ★★★★★

One of the greatest of all New Zealand wines, this Martinborough red is powerfully built and concentrated, yet seductively fragrant and supple. 'Intense, opulent fruit with power beneath' is winemaker Clive Paton's goal. 'Complexity comes with time.' The grapes are drawn from numerous sites, including the estate vineyard, planted in 1980, and the vines, ranging up to 30 years old, have an average yield of only 4.5 tonnes of grapes per hectare. The wine is fermented with indigenous yeasts and maturation is for 11 months in French oak barriques, 25 to 30 per cent new. The 2008 vintage (★★★★) has deep, youthful colour. Full-bodied and flowing, it has dense plum, cherry and spice flavours, notably complex and savoury, and a silky-textured, harmonious finish. A very 'complete' wine, it's still unfolding; open 2012+.

Vintage	08	07	06	05	04	03	02
WR	7	7	7	7	6	7	6
Drink	10-20	10-19	10-11	10-13	P	P	P

DRY $65 AV

Ataahua Waipara Pinot Noir ★★★☆

The charming 2009 vintage (★★★★) is a single-vineyard red, matured for a year in seasoned French oak barrels. Already delicious, it is ruby-hued, mouthfilling and vibrantly fruity, with sweet-fruit delights and strong cherry, plum and spice flavours, gently seasoned with oak. A finely textured wine, showing good complexity, it's a drink-now or cellaring proposition.

Vintage	09
WR	6
Drink	10-13

DRY $34 –V

Auntsfield Hawk Hill Marlborough Pinot Noir ★★★★☆

Hawk Hill is the name of the elevated, north-facing slopes at Auntsfield, on the south side of the Wairau Valley. The 2008 vintage (★★★★☆), fermented with indigenous yeasts and matured in French oak barriques (40 per cent new), is a powerful yet elegant red, dark and fleshy, with deep plum, spice and slight herb flavours, earthy notes adding complexity, ripe tannins and a lasting finish. Generous, warm and well-structured, it should mature gracefully.

Vintage	08	07	06	05	04	03
WR	6	7	6	7	5	5
Drink	10-16	10-15	10-14	10-15	10-11	P

DRY $44 AV

Auntsfield Heritage Pinot Noir ★★★★☆

The 2007 vintage (★★★★☆) was estate-grown on the south side of the Wairau Valley, in Marlborough, and matured in French oak barriques (65 per cent new). Boldly coloured, with a fragrant, toasty bouquet, it is very powerful and sweet-fruited, with lush plum and spice flavours, strongly seasoned with oak, and earthy notes adding complexity. A big, ripe style, it's built for cellaring.

Vintage	07	06	05
WR	7	NM	7
Drink	10-21	NM	10-20

DRY $75 –V

Aurora Vineyard, The, Bendigo Pinot Noir ★★★★☆

The savoury, dense 2008 vintage (★★★★★) is a Central Otago red, hand-picked at 24.5 brix and oak-aged for 10 months. Deeply coloured, with deliciously concentrated plum, cherry and spice flavours, oak complexity and a fairly firm finish, it's an opulent wine with a core of sweet fruit and good supporting tannins.

Vintage	08	DRY $39 V+
WR	6	
Drink	10-14	

Aurum Central Otago Pinot Noir ★★★★

Estate-grown at Lowburn, in the Cromwell Basin, and matured for 11 months in French oak casks, the 2008 vintage (★★★★) is floral and ruby-hued, with lots of charm. Supple and vibrantly fruity, it offers ripe cherry and plum flavours, finely integrated oak and some savoury complexity. The 2009 (★★★★) has rich, youthful colour and concentrated cherry, plum and spice flavours. Still very youthful, it has fresh acidity, good complexity and the structure to mature well. Open 2012+.

Vintage	09	08	07	DRY $32 AV
WR	6	5	6	
Drink	10-16	10-15	10-12	

Aurum Madeleine Central Otago Pinot Noir (★★★★★)

Named after the winemaker's daughter, the powerful 2007 vintage (★★★★★) is a two-barrel selection, estate-grown at Lowburn and French oak-aged for 20 months. Deep and bright in colour, it's a sturdy (14.5 per cent alcohol), highly fragrant, very ripe and generous red, boldly fruity, with layers of cherry, plum, spice and nut flavours, plus hints of liquorice and chocolate. It's drinking superbly now, but should also be long-lived.

Vintage	07	DRY $85 –V
WR	7	
Drink	10-20	

Aurum Mathilde Reserve Central Otago Pinot Noir ★★★★

Estate-grown at Lowburn, in the Cromwell Basin, the 2009 vintage (★★★★☆) was matured for 14 months in French oak barriques. Full-coloured, it is refined and rich, with a strong presence. Still a baby, it is sturdy (14.5 per cent alcohol), with dense plum and spice flavours, oak complexity and the power and structure to age well. Open 2013+.

DRY $45 –V

Awa Valley Pinot Noir ★★☆

Grown at Kumeu in West Auckland, the easy-drinking 2007 vintage (★★☆) was 'hand-picked from old vines' and matured for 11 months in seasoned oak casks. Light ruby, it has moderate depth of strawberry and spice flavours, a hint of oak and gentle tannins.

Vintage	07	DRY $20 –V
WR	6	
Drink	P	

Awatere River Marlborough Block 333 Pinot Noir (★★★☆)

Grown at 333 metres above sea level in the Awatere Valley (hence the name), the 2008 vintage (★★★☆) is a floral, finely textured red, bright ruby, with vibrant cherry/plum flavours and a hint of herbs. Soft and elegant, with a subtle oak influence, it's enjoyable now.

DRY $25 AV

Babich Marlborough Pinot Noir ★★☆

The 2009 vintage (★★☆) is light and pleasant, with berry and spice flavours, gentle tannins and drink-young appeal.

DRY $20 –V

Babich Winemakers Reserve Marlborough Pinot Noir ★★★☆

The 2008 (★★★☆) is mouthfilling and supple, with cherryish, spicy, moderately complex flavours, showing very good depth. The 2009 vintage (★★★☆) was grown in the Waihopai Valley and French oak-matured. Ruby-hued, it is supple and moderately concentrated, with cherry, herb and spice flavours, and some aging potential.

Vintage	09	08	07	06	05	04
WR	7	7	7	7	7	7
Drink	10-15	10-14	10-13	10-12	10-12	P

DRY $30 –V

Bald Hills Single Vineyard Central Otago Pinot Noir ★★★★☆

Estate-grown at Bannockburn, hand-harvested and matured in French oak barriques (30 per cent new), the 2008 vintage (★★★★☆) is an elegant, poised, finely scented red, tightly structured and still very youthful. Sweet-fruited and ruby-hued, with rich cherry and plum flavours, a hint of herbs, and ripe, supple tannins, it's a complex wine, well worth cellaring.

Vintage	08	07	06	05	04
WR	6	6	6	7	6
Drink	10-19	11-17	10-16	10-15	10-15

DRY $46 –V

Bannock Brae Barrel Selection Pinot Noir ★★★★★

Top vintages of this single-vineyard Bannockburn, Central Otago red are outstanding. Showing great potential, the 2009 (★★★★★) was matured for 11 months in French oak casks, and bottled unfined and unfiltered. A powerful wine (14.3 per cent), it is richly coloured, very savoury and complex, with deep, ripe cherry and spice flavours, a hint of dark chocolate, and good tannin support. Open 2013+.

Vintage	09	08	07	06	05
WR	7	6	7	6	7
Drink	11-18	10-15	10-14	P	10-11

DRY $45 AV

Bannock Brae Goldfields Pinot Noir ★★★★☆

Estate-grown at Bannockburn, in Central Otago, and matured in French oak barriques, this is typically a very graceful, supple wine. The 2009 vintage (★★★★☆), bottled unfined and unfiltered, is one of the best. Mouthfilling and concentrated, it is still very youthful, with concentrated, vibrant plum, cherry and spice flavours and finely integrated oak. Exuberantly fruity, yet showing good complexity, it's a good buy.

Vintage	09	08	07	06	05
WR	7	6	6	6	6
Drink	11-16	10-14	10-14	P	P

DRY $30 V+

Barking Hedge Marlborough Pinot Noir (★★★☆)

From Crighton Estate, in the Wairau Valley, the 2007 vintage (★★★☆) was hand-picked, and matured for about 18 months in French oak casks. It's a generous, full-coloured red, with strong, ripe plum and spice flavours, considerable complexity and a fairly firm finish.

DRY $30 –V

Bascand Marlborough Pinot Noir ★★☆

Hand-picked in the Rapaura district and matured for a year in French oak barriques, the 2008 vintage (★★☆) is light ruby, with a hint of development. The palate is light-bodied, with smooth berry and herb flavours, offering easy, early drinking.

DRY $20 –V

Bascand Waipara Pinot Noir (★★★☆)

The 2009 vintage (★★★☆) is a great buy. Hand-picked and matured for a year in French oak barriques (30 per cent new), it is ruby-hued, with a fragrant, spicy bouquet. Generous and sweet-fruited, it has fresh, strong plum and spice flavours, with a hint of olives, and finely balanced tannins. Open mid-2011+.

DRY $19 V+

Bel Echo by Clos Henri Terroir Portrait Marlborough Pinot Noir ★★★☆

The 2008 vintage (★★★☆) was grown on the more stony, less clay-bound soils at Clos Henri. Partly French oak-aged, it is ruby-hued, with mouthfilling body and ripe cherry, plum and spice flavours, showing some savoury complexity and very good depth.

Vintage	08
WR	6
Drink	10-14

DRY $28 AV

Bellbird Spring Block Eight Pinot Noir (★★★☆)

The 2009 vintage (★★★☆) was hand-picked at Waipara and matured in seasoned oak barriques. Deeply coloured, it is buoyantly fruity, with ripe plum and spice flavours, showing some savoury complexity. Worth cellaring.

DRY $32 –V

Bell Hill Pinot Noir ★★★★★

From a 1-hectare plot of vines on a limestone slope at Waikari, inland from Waipara, in North Canterbury, this is a rare, highly distinguished red. It is typically a generous wine, powerful yet silky, with sweet cherry, plum and spice flavours, complex, very harmonious and graceful. The 2007 vintage (★★★★★) was matured in French oak barrels (70 per cent new). Very deeply coloured, it is gorgeously scented, with dense cherry and plum flavours, hints of herbs and spices, and a very refined, long finish. A wine with great presence, it is years away from maturity.

DRY $95 –V

Belmonte Marlborough Pinot Noir ★★★

From Forrest, the 2008 vintage (★★★) is light ruby, medium-bodied and supple, with ripe, cherryish, slightly spicy flavours, showing good varietal character, and a touch of complexity.

DRY $20 AV

Big Sky Martinborough Pinot Noir ★★★★

Grown in Te Muna Road and matured in French oak barriques, the 2007 vintage (★★★★) is a generous, tightly structured red with full, bright colour. It has strong cherry, plum and dried-herb flavours, with smoky oak adding complexity and a backbone of firm, ripe tannins. The 2008 (★★★★) is generous, sweet-fruited, savoury and supple, with ripe plum and spice flavours, gentle tannins, good complexity, and lots of drink-young appeal.

DRY $39 AV

Bilancia Central Otago Pinot Noir (★★★☆)

The 2008 vintage (★★★☆) from this Hawke's Bay producer was matured in French oak casks (10 per cent new). Full and youthful in colour, it is vibrantly fruity and supple, with ripe cherry, plum and spice flavours, showing very good depth. It's an elegant wine, delicious young.

DRY $28 AV

Bird Marlborough Big Barrel Pinot Noir ★★★☆

Estate-grown in the Old Schoolhouse Vineyard, in the Omaka Valley, and fermented and matured in 900-litre barrels, the 2009 vintage (★★★☆) is a full-bodied, moderately rich red with ripe cherry, plum and slight herb flavours, a gentle oak influence, and plenty of drink-young appeal.

Vintage	09	08
WR	6	5
Drink	10-13	10-12

DRY $39 –V

Bishop's Head Waipara Valley Pinot Noir ★★

From Pimlico Vineyards, the 2008 vintage (★★) is a sub-regional blend, matured for a year in French oak barrels (20 per cent new). It has light, slightly developed colour and lacks real ripeness and freshness.

DRY $28 –V

Black Barn Vineyards Hawke's Bay Pinot Noir (★★★☆)

Grown inland at Crownthorpe, the 2008 vintage (★★★☆) is full-bodied and supple, with strong, fresh cherry, plum and spice flavours. Showing good complexity, it's drinking well now, but worth cellaring.

DRY $32 –V

Black Cottage Central Otago Pinot Noir 2009 (★★★☆)

From Two Rivers, based in Marlborough, the 2009 vintage (★★★☆) is deep ruby, with strong cherry, plum and spice flavours, ripe and firm. Fresh and vibrant, with some savoury complexity, it has good aging potential.

DRY $27 AV

Black Estate Omihi Waipara Pinot Noir ★★★☆

This is a single-vineyard, North Canterbury label. The 2007 vintage (★★★☆), fermented with indigenous yeasts and barrel-aged for 10 months (30 per cent new), is deeply coloured, with vibrant cherry and herb flavours, generous and supple. It shows good concentration, but the leafy notes detract.

Vintage	07	06
WR	6	5
Drink	10-13	10-12

DRY $40 –V

Black Quail Estate Central Otago Pinot Noir ★★★☆

Grown at Cromwell, the 2008 vintage (★★★★) is ruby-hued, generous and vibrantly fruity, with ripe sweet-fruit characters and gently oaked cherry, red-berry and spice flavours, showing good complexity. Drink now or cellar.

DRY $30 –V

Black Ridge Pinot Noir ★★★☆

A decade ago, this was one of Central Otago's first consistently impressive Pinot Noirs. Grown at Alexandra, the 2007 vintage (★★★★) was hand-picked and French oak-matured. Full-coloured, sturdy and sweet-fruited, it is generous, with rich cherry and plum flavours, some savoury complexity and gentle tannins.

DRY $32 –V

Blackenbrook Vineyard Nelson Reserve Pinot Noir ★★★★

The 2009 vintage (★★★☆) was estate-grown, hand-picked at 25 brix and matured for a year in French oak barriques. Full-coloured, it is very ripely scented, fleshy, vibrant and youthful, with strong cherry, plum and spice flavours, gentle tannins, and good, savoury complexity. It's a muscular wine (14.5 per cent alcohol), yet already highly approachable.

Vintage	09
WR	7
Drink	10-13

DRY $31 AV

Bladen Marlborough Pinot Noir ★★★☆

The 2008 vintage (★★★) is a single-vineyard, Wairau Valley red, hand-picked and matured for over a year in French oak barriques. Ruby-hued, it is fruity and supple, with moderately concentrated plum, cherry and slight herb flavours, balanced for easy drinking.

Vintage 08	DRY $30 –V
WR 5	
Drink 10-11	

Blairpatrick Estate Pinot Noir (★★☆)

Grown in the northern Wairarapa, the 2008 vintage (★★☆) is mouthfilling, with some confectionery notes and ripe, smooth flavours in a very easy-drinking style.

DRY $20 –V

Bloody Bay Marlborough Pinot Noir (★★☆)

From wine distributor Federal Geo, the 2009 vintage (★★☆) is a light red with gentle strawberry and spice flavours. It lacks richness, but offers pleasant, early drinking.

DRY $17 AV

Blue Ridge Marlborough Pinot Noir ★★★☆

From West Brook, the 2007 vintage (★★★★) is deep ruby, with a scented, ripe bouquet and generous, plummy flavours. Sweet-fruited and flowing, with gentle tannins, it is generous and supple, with loads of charm.

DRY $29 AV

Boatshed Bay by Goldwater Marlborough Pinot Noir (★★☆)

The ruby-hued 2008 vintage (★★☆) is medium-bodied, with berryish aromas and fresh raspberry and spice flavours. Tight, with a hint of toasty oak, it shows a slight lack of ripeness and roundness.

Vintage 08	DRY $21 –V
WR 7	
Drink 10-12	

Borthwick Vineyard Wairarapa Pinot Noir ★★★★

Grown at Gladstone, near Masterton, and matured in French oak casks (40 per cent new), the 2008 vintage (★★★★☆) is a deeply coloured, attractively perfumed red with vibrant cherry and plum flavours, showing excellent depth, ripeness and suppleness. Showing good, savoury complexity and plenty of muscle, it should mature well.

DRY $36 AV

Bouldevines Marlborough Pinot Noir ★★★☆

A big style of Pinot Noir, the 2009 vintage (★★★★) was hand-picked at nearly 25 brix and matured for 10 months in French oak casks (20 per cent new). Powerful and deeply coloured, it has concentrated cherry, plum, herb and spice flavours. Still very youthful, it is savoury, with undeniable power and good potential; open 2012.

DRY $30 –V

Boundary Vineyards Kings Road Waipara Pinot Noir ★★★☆

The 2009 vintage (★★★★) from Pernod Ricard NZ is the best yet. Deeply coloured, it is muscular (14.5 per cent alcohol) and fleshy, with ripe cherry, plum and spice flavours, gentle tannins and a fragrant bouquet. It's already delicious.

DRY $23 V+

Bracken's Order Central Otago Pinot Noir ★★★★

Based on grapes grown at Mt Rosa, Gibbston, and matured in all-new French oak casks, the debut 2007 vintage (★★★★☆) is highly scented, spicy, savoury, rich and complex, with excellent ripeness and density. The 2008 (★★★★) is a refined, sweet-fruited wine, floral and supple, with cherry and plum flavours, spicy oak and a rounded, very harmonious finish.

DRY $35 AV

Bracken's Order Small Parcel Central Otago Pinot Noir (★★★★☆)

The 2008 vintage (★★★★☆) is beautifully floral and supple, with sweet-fruit delights and cherry and plum flavours showing a subtle oak influence, gentle tannins, and excellent delicacy and charm.

DRY $40 AV

Brams Run Marlborough Pinot Noir (★★★☆)

From Invivo, the 2008 vintage (★★★☆) is a ruby-hued, tightly structured wine with good depth of vibrant cherry, herb and spice flavours, showing some complexity. Hand-picked in the Brancott Valley and French oak-aged for 11 months, it's priced right.

DRY $24 V+

Brancott Estate 'T' Terraces Marlborough Pinot Noir ★★★★☆

(Formerly labelled Montana.) The 2008 vintage (★★★★☆), the first branded as Brancott Estate, is finely scented and mouthfilling, with good density. Ruby-hued, it is savoury, with ripe cherry, plum and spice flavours, showing excellent complexity, and a silky texture. Drink 2011–13.

DRY $41 AV

Breaksea Sound Central Otago Pinot Noir ★★★☆

From wine distributor Bennett & Deller, the 2008 vintage (★★★☆) was grown at Bannockburn and French oak-aged for a year. Ruby-hued, with fresh strawberry, herb and spice aromas, it is vibrant and supple, with a touch of complexity, good immediacy, and lots of drink-young charm.

Vintage	08	07
WR	6	6
Drink	10-13	10-13

DRY $22 V+

Brennan Gibbston Pinot Noir (★★★★)

The 2007 vintage (★★★★) is a distinctly cool-climate style from Gibbston, in Central Otago. A single-vineyard red, it was matured for 11 months in French oak barriques (55 per cent new), and bottled unfined and unfiltered. Slightly leafy, it has excellent substance and structure, with strong cherry, plum and herb flavours, showing good, spicy complexity.

DRY $43 –V

Brightside Nelson Pinot Noir ★★★

From Kaimira, the 2009 vintage (★★★☆) is a youthful wine, bright ruby, with ripe plum and spice aromas and flavours, some toasty oak complexity and good depth. Fine value.

DRY $18 V+

Brightwater Vineyards Lord Rutherford Nelson Pinot Noir (★★★☆)

The 2008 vintage (★★★☆) was estate-grown and matured for a year in seasoned French oak casks. It's a full-flavoured wine, ripe, plummy and spicy, with sweet-fruit characters and savoury oak adding complexity. Worth cellaring.

Vintage	08	07
WR	5	6
Drink	10-14	10-11

DRY $35 –V

Brightwater Vineyards Nelson Pinot Noir ★★★☆

Ruby-hued, the 2008 vintage (★★★☆) was matured for 10 months in French oak barrels. It's a flavoursome, supple wine, slightly leafy, with very satisfying depth and some nutty, savoury complexity. A good, drink-young style.

DRY $25 AV

Brodie Estate Pinot Noir (★★★★☆)

The 2008 vintage was hand-picked in Martinborough and matured for 10 months in French oak barriques. Scented, savoury and supple, it has excellent depth of cherryish, gently spicy flavours. A stylish wine with sweet-fruit delights and good complexity, it shows obvious potential.

DRY $48 –V

Bronte by Rimu Grove Nelson Pinot Noir ★★★☆

Estate-grown and hand-picked, the 2009 vintage (★★★) was matured for 11 months in French oak barriques. Ruby-hued, it is quite forward, with fresh cherry, herb and nut flavours, showing some savoury complexity.

Vintage	09	08	07	06
WR	6	6	6	6
Drink	10-17	10-16	10-15	10-12

DRY $28 AV

Burnt Spur Martinborough Pinot Noir ★★★★
This single-vineyard red is grown south of the town, on heavier soils than those found on the Martinborough Terrace. The 2008 (★★★★) is weighty, with excellent complexity and richness. The 2009 vintage (★★★☆), French oak-aged for 10 months, is sturdy and savoury, with strong plum, spice, herb and olive flavours, considerable complexity and finely balanced tannins. Drink now or cellar.

DRY $44 –V

Cable Bay Central Otago Pinot Noir (★★★☆)
The debut 2009 vintage (★★★☆) was hand-picked in the Cromwell Basin and matured in French oak barriques. Ruby-hued, it is floral, vibrantly fruity and supple, with fresh, ripe, moderately concentrated, cherryish flavours, finely textured and offering lots of drink-young appeal.

Vintage	09
WR	6
Drink	10-15

DRY $33 –V

Cable Bay Marlborough Pinot Noir ★★★☆
The 2007 (★★★★) was the best to date – deeply coloured, rich and sweet-fruited, generous and supple, with ripe plum and spice flavours, showing some savoury complexity. However, the light, fairly simple 2008 vintage (★★☆) is on a much lower level.

DRY $34 –V

Cable Station Marlborough Pinot Noir ★★☆
From Cape Campbell, the 2008 vintage (★★☆) has cherry and plum flavours, slightly earthy and light.

DRY $22 –V

Cambridge Road Noblestone Pinot Noir (★★★★)
From vines planted at Martinborough in 1986 by Murdoch James, the 2007 vintage (★★★★) was matured in French oak casks (50 per cent new). Rich and rounded, with very deep cherry, plum and herb flavours, it is slightly leafy, but shows outstanding density.

Vintage	07
WR	5
Drink	10-14

DRY $63 –V

Camshorn Waipara Pinot Noir ★★★☆
From Pernod Ricard NZ, the 2007 vintage (★★★) is deeply coloured, with spice and green-olive notes on the nose and palate, lively acidity and plenty of flavour. It shows good richness and complexity, but leafy notes detract.

Vintage	07	06
WR	5	5
Drink	10-11	P

DRY $37 –V

Cape Campbell Marlborough Pinot Noir ★★★

An enjoyable drink-young style, the 2008 vintage (★★★) is ruby-hued and medium-bodied, with ripe, cherryish, slightly spicy flavours, a gentle seasoning of oak and fresh acidity.

Vintage	08	07
WR	5	5
Drink	10-12	10-11

DRY $25 –V

Carrick Central Otago Pinot Noir ★★★★★

This Bannockburn label is a regional classic. There was no 2008 vintage, but the 2009 (★★★★☆) was matured for a year in French oak barriques (30 per cent new). Scented and supple, mouthfilling and sweet-fruited, it's a youthful wine with cherry, plum and spice flavours and gentler tannins than in some past vintages. Showing good, savoury complexity, it's an elegant wine that needs time; open mid-2011+.

Vintage	09	08	07	06	05	04	03	02
WR	7	NM	7	6	7	5	6	6
Drink	12-17	NM	10-15	10-14	10-14	10-12	10-11	P

DRY $45 AV

Carrick Crown & Cross Central Otago Pinot Noir (★★★★)

The 2008 vintage (★★★★) was grown at Bannockburn, hand-picked, fermented with indigenous yeasts, and bottled unfined and unfiltered. A softly mouthfilling red (14.5 per cent alcohol), it is ruby-hued, with strong, ripe sweet-fruit flavours of cherries and plums, and finely integrated oak. Fleshy and supple, it's a youthful wine, worth cellaring.

DRY $33 AV

Carrick Excelsior Central Otago Pinot Noir ★★★★★

From mature, estate-grown vines at Bannockburn, the 2007 vintage (★★★★★) was matured for 18 months in French oak barriques (30 per cent new). A serious yet sensuous red, it is rich and youthful in colour, bold and fruity, with dense plum, herb, spice and liquorice flavours, showing lovely fruit sweetness and concentration. It should be very long-lived; open 2012+.

DRY $85 AV

Carrick Unravelled Central Otago Pinot Noir ★★★☆

Designed to be 'easy-drinking, laidback', the 2009 vintage (★★★☆) does not claim to be estate-grown at Bannockburn. Matured for a year in French oak barriques (20 per cent new), it's a freshly scented, ruby-hued wine with good depth of smooth cherry, plum and spice flavours. A drink-young style – with style.

DRY $25 AV

Catalina Sounds Pinot Noir ★★★

The 2008 vintage (★★★) was grown in Marlborough and matured in French oak casks (20 per cent new). Ruby-hued, with a hint of development, it is medium to full-bodied, with cherry and herb flavours, showing some savoury complexity. Ready.

DRY $28 –V

Cellar 9 Waipara Pinot Noir (★★☆)

Sold in supermarkets, the 2008 vintage (★★☆) is a light style, with gentle strawberry and spice flavours, and a smooth finish. Good value.

DRY $10 V+

Central Schist Central Otago Pinot Noir (★★☆)

Enjoyable young, the 2008 vintage (★★☆) is a light style of Pinot Noir, floral and soft, with moderate depth of cherry and plum flavours.

DRY $20 –V

Charcoal Gully Sally's Pinch Pinot Noir ★★★

Grown at Pisa, in Central Otago, the ruby-hued 2008 vintage (★★★☆) has ripe sweet-fruit characters, good depth of cherry and spice flavours, light tannins and some savoury complexity.

DRY $29 –V

Chard Farm Finla Mor Pinot Noir ★★★☆

This Central Otago red typically has vibrant cherry/spice flavours, subtle oak and gentle tannins. Grown at Lowburn, in the Cromwell Basin, and matured in French oak barriques, the 2008 vintage (★★★☆) is ruby-hued and sweet-fruited, with moderately concentrated, cherryish flavours, vibrant and supple.

DRY $36 –V

Chard Farm Mata-Au Central Otago Pinot Noir (★★★★)

The debut 2009 vintage (★★★★) was grown at Lowburn and Parkburn, in the Cromwell Basin, on terraces formed by the Mata-Au (Clutha) River. Ruby-hued, it is savoury and supple, with sweet-fruit delights and finely textured, cherryish, plummy flavours that linger well. Delicious young, it should mature well.

DRY $44 –V

Chard Farm River Run Pinot Noir ★★★☆

This is an attractive, fruit-driven style. The 2009 vintage (★★★☆) was grown and hand-picked mostly at Lowburn, in the Cromwell Basin, but includes some Gibbston fruit. Ruby-hued, it is mouthfilling and sweet-fruited, with fresh, ripe cherry, plum and spice flavours and gentle tannins. Floral, with good depth, it's already drinking well.

DRY $30 –V

Charles Wiffen Marlborough Pinot Noir ★★★

The 2008 vintage (★★☆) is lightish in colour, with moderate depth of berry, spice and herb flavours, showing a slight lack of ripeness and richness, and a smooth finish.

DRY $27 –V

Charles Wiffen Reserve Marlborough Pinot Noir ★★★★

French oak-aged for 10 months, the 2007 vintage (★★★★☆) is full and bright in colour, with good warmth and complexity. Concentrated, spicy, nutty and savoury, it's a powerful, dense and slightly oaky style with cellaring potential.

DRY $35 AV

Church Road Central Otago Pinot Noir (★★★★)

Pernod Ricard NZ's decision to extend the Church Road brand – indivisibly associated with Hawke's Bay – to Central Otago, is a surprise, but in the past, Marlborough has sometimes made a key contribution to the Sauvignon Blanc. The debut 2009 vintage (★★★★) was grown mostly at Bendigo and matured for nine months in French oak casks (27 per cent new). Ruby-hued, mouthfilling and supple, it is savoury and complex, with cherry, plum, spice and nut flavours, finely textured and harmonious. It's already drinking well.

DRY $27 V+

Churton Marlborough Pinot Noir ★★★★☆

Winemaker Sam Weaver wants a 'delicate, refined' style of Pinot Noir. Estate-grown at the elevated Waihopai Slopes site, hand-picked at over 24 brix and matured for a year in French oak barriques (20 per cent new), the 2008 vintage (★★★★☆) is sturdy and sweet-fruited, with dense cherry, herb and spice flavours, a hint of dark chocolate, and good, savoury complexity. Still youthful, it should be at its best 2012+.

Vintage	08	07	06	05	04	03
WR	6	5	4	6	4	6
Drink	10-18	10-16	10-14	10-16	10-12	P

DRY $44 AV

Churton The Abyss Marlborough Pinot Noir ★★★★★

The 2008 vintage (★★★★★) was estate-grown on a steep, north-east clay slope, 200 metres above sea level in the Waihopai Valley. Hand-picked from the oldest vines, fermented with indigenous yeasts, matured in French oak casks (50 per cent new) and bottled unfiltered, it is deeply coloured, with lovely richness and harmony. It offers great depth of plum, spice, herb and liquorice flavours, in a very rich, 'complete' style, more silky and graceful than its stablemate (above).

Vintage	08
WR	7
Drink	10-20

DRY $75 AV

Clayridge Marlborough Pinot Noir ★★★☆

The 2007 vintage (★★★☆) is a full-coloured, vibrantly fruity red with a gentle oak influence, a touch of savoury complexity and gentle tannins.

Vintage	07	06
WR	5	5
Drink	10-13	10-12

DRY $29 AV

Clearview Pinot Noir Des Trois ★★★★☆

From a Hawke's Bay winery, the 2008 vintage (★★★★) is a fleshy, rich, regional blend of Central Otago, Wairarapa and Waipara grapes, barrel-aged for 15 months. Ruby-hued, it has substantial body, ripe, cherryish, spicy flavours, hints of herbs and liquorice, and a fairly firm finish. Drink now or cellar.

DRY $40 AV

Clevedon Hills Pinot Noir ★★★☆

The 2008 vintage (★★★★) was estate-grown at Clevedon, in South Auckland. An instantly likeable wine, it has bright, youthful colour and fresh strawberry and spice aromas and flavours. Generous, sweet-fruited and supple, with gentle acidity, a silky texture and good, savoury complexity, it is one of the finest Pinot Noirs yet produced in the Auckland region.

DRY $40 –V

Clos de Ste Anne Naboth's Vineyard Pinot Noir ★★★★

This Gisborne red from Millton is one of the country's northernmost quality Pinot Noirs. Grown biodynamically at the hillside Clos de Ste Anne site at Manutuke, the 2008 vintage (★★★★) is mouthfilling and supple, with ripe cherry, plum and spice flavours, showing good, savoury complexity. Softly textured, it's already drinking well.

Vintage	08	07	06	05
WR	6	7	5	6
Drink	10-13	10-13	10-12	10-12

DRY $54 –V

Clos Henri Marlborough Pinot Noir ★★★☆

From Henri Bourgeois, a top Loire Valley producer with a site near Renwick, the 2008 vintage (★★★☆) was matured for a year in French oak barriques (25 per cent new). Full-coloured, it is fresh and flavoursome, with some herbal notes, an earthy complexity and fairly firm tannins. Open mid-2011+.

Vintage	08	07
WR	6	6
Drink	10-16	10-15

DRY $42 –V

Clos Marguerite Marlborough Pinot Noir ★★★☆

This single-vineyard Awatere Valley red is hand-picked and matured for a year in French oak barriques (10 to 15 per cent new in 2008). The 2008 vintage (★★★☆) is a ruby-hued, mid-weight style, with cherry, plum and herb flavours, showing good depth and complexity, and a fairly firm finish.

DRY $33 –V

Cloudy Bay Pinot Noir ★★★★☆

This is a consistently elegant, richly varietal red. Grown on the south side of the Wairau Valley and in the Omaka Valley, the 2008 vintage (★★★★☆) was hand-picked at an average of 24.5 brix from low-yielding vines (64 tonnes/hectare), and was matured for a year in French oak barriques (50 per cent new). Softly mouthfilling, with strong cherry, plum and spice flavours, finely integrated nutty oak and ripe, supple tannins, it is enticingly scented, with a hint of herbs, good, savoury complexity and lovely flow across the palate.

Vintage	08	07	06	05
WR	5	7	6	7
Drink	11-14	10-14	10-13	10-12

DRY $58 –V

Coal Pit Tiwha Pinot Noir ★★★☆

This single-vineyard red is grown at Gibbston, in Central Otago. The 2008 vintage (★★★★) was matured in French oak casks (40 per cent new). Deeply coloured, with fragrant plum and herb aromas, it is mouthfilling and supple, with good concentration of cherry, plum, spice and green-olive flavours. Sweet-fruited and generous, it's a drink-now or cellaring proposition.

Vintage	08	07	06
WR	4	5	7
Drink	10-12	10-11	P

DRY $42 –V

Coney Pizzicato Pinot Noir ★★★☆

The 2009 vintage (★★★) of this Martinborough red was matured in French oak casks (30 per cent new). It's a drink-young style, fruity and supple, with some fruit sweetness and depth, and good varietal character, but also fairly light and forward.

Vintage	09	08
WR	5	5
Drink	11-14	10-13

DRY $30 –V

Coopers Creek Marlborough Pinot Noir ★★★

The 2009 vintage (★★★) is ruby-hued, floral and supple, with cherry, plum, spice and slight herb flavours, fresh, ripe and smooth. A good, drink-young style.

Vintage	09	08	07	06
WR	5	6	5	6
Drink	10-12	10-11	P	P

DRY $20 AV

Coopers Creek SV Gibsons Run Marlborough Pinot Noir ★★★★

The 2008 vintage (★★★★) is full-coloured and mouthfilling, with concentrated cherry and spice flavours. Sweet-fruited and savoury, with good tannin backbone, it's drinking well now, but also worth cellaring.

Vintage	08	07	06
WR	6	NM	6
Drink	10-12	NM	P

DRY $28 V+

Coopers Creek SV Razorback Central Otago Pinot Noir (★★★☆)

Floral, vibrantly fruity and supple, the 2008 vintage (★★★☆) was hand-picked and matured for a year in French oak casks (33 per cent new). It's a charming, moderately concentrated wine, with ripe sweet-fruit flavours, a subtle seasoning of oak and good harmony.

Vintage	08
WR	6
Drink	10-12

DRY $28 AV

Crab Farm Hawke's Bay Pinot Noir ★★★

The sturdy 2007 vintage (★★★) was matured for 16 months in French oak casks (50 per cent new). Full-coloured, with a spicy bouquet, it is mouthfilling (14 per cent alcohol), with strong cherry and spice flavours, firm, ripe and gutsy. It's slightly 'dry reddish', reflecting the relatively warm growing environment, but has plenty of depth and personality.

Vintage	07	DRY $25 –V
WR	7	
Drink	10-12	

Craggy Range Bannockburn Sluicings Vineyard Central Otago Pinot Noir ★★★★☆

The 2009 vintage (★★★★★) is the best yet. Hand-harvested from a vineyard on the northern side of Felton Road, it was matured for 10 months in French oak barriques (35 per cent new). Bright ruby, it is beautifully floral and supple, with rich, sweet-fruit flavours of plums, spices and dark chocolate, very fine-grained tannins and impressive complexity. Built to last, it's best opened mid-2011+.

Vintage	09	08	07	DRY $50 –V
WR	7	6	6	
Drink	10-18	10-16	10-14	

Craggy Range Calvert Vineyard Bannockburn Pinot Noir ★★★★☆

The 2008 vintage (★★★★☆) was grown in the biodynamically managed Calvert Vineyard in Felton Road, and matured for 10 months in French oak barriques (35 per cent new). Scented and supple, it's a full-coloured wine with good muscle, a core of sweet fruit, and rich plum and spice flavours. The 2009 (★★★★☆) is floral, mouthfilling and vibrantly fruity, with deliciously ripe sweet-fruit flavours, savoury and complex, and gentle tannins. Drink now onwards.

Vintage	09	08	07	DRY $50 –V
WR	7	7	6	
Drink	10-18	10-16	10-16	

Craggy Range Te Muna Road Vineyard Pinot Noir ★★★★☆

The 2008 vintage (★★★★★) of this Martinborough red was hand-harvested at over 24 brix, fermented with indigenous yeasts, and matured for 10 months in French oak barriques (33 per cent new). Deeply coloured, it is finely scented, mouthfilling and supple, with delicious cherry and plum flavours, softly textured and savoury. It's already delicious, but has the muscle and structure to age. The 2009 (★★★★★) is another winner. Sturdy and rich, with substantial body and deep, ripe cherry/plum flavours, showing excellent concentration and complexity, it's an obvious candidate for cellaring.

Vintage	09	08	07	06	05	04	DRY $40 AV
WR	7	7	7	7	7	6	
Drink	10-18	10-16	10-16	10-13	10-12	P	

Craggy Range Waitaki Valley Otago Station Vineyard Pinot Noir ★★★★

Grown in North Otago and matured for 10 months in French oak barriques (33 per cent new), the 2009 vintage (★★★★☆) is a classy young red. Deeply coloured, it is finely scented, very graceful and supple, with rich cherry and plum flavours, complex and youthful, and lovely texture and harmony. Open mid-2011+.

Vintage	09	08
WR	7	7
Drink	10-18	10-16

DRY $45 –V

Craggy Range Zebra Vineyard Central Otago Pinot Noir ★★★★

The 2008 vintage (★★★★) was grown at Bendigo, hand-picked at 24.6 brix, fermented with indigenous yeasts and matured for 10 months in French oak barriques (40 per cent new). Full-coloured, it is mouthfilling, with concentrated, very ripe cherry and plum flavours, seasoned with spicy oak, and supple tannins.

Vintage	08	07
WR	6	6
Drink	10-16	10-14

DRY $40 –V

Crater Rim, The, Bendigo Terrace Central Otago Pinot Noir ★★★★

The 2009 vintage (★★★☆) is a single-vineyard red, matured in French oak casks (partly new). Deeply coloured, it is very youthful, fresh and smooth, with moderately concentrated cherry, spice and herb flavours, showing good complexity.

DRY $31 AV

Crater Rim, The, From the Ashes Waipara Pinot Noir (★★★)

On Friday, 13 November 2009, the Crater Rim winery burnt to the ground. The 2009 vintage (★★★) has fullish colour and slightly herbal aromas. Mouthfilling, it has good depth of cherryish, spicy, green-edged flavours, showing some development and considerable complexity.

DRY $30 –V

Crater Rim, The, Waipara Pinot Noir ★★★★

The 2009 vintage (★★★★) is a single-vineyard wine, fermented with indigenous yeasts and barrel-aged. Full-coloured, with fresh, strong cherry, plum and spice flavours, savoury and complex, it's a finely textured wine. Delicious now, it's also worth cellaring.

DRY $37 AV

Crawford Farm New Zealand Pinot Noir ★★☆

From Constellation NZ, the 2008 vintage (★★☆) is a blend of Marlborough, Gisborne and Hawke's Bay grapes. Light ruby, it has pleasant strawberry and spice flavours, with a hint of toasty oak, moderate depth and a fairly firm finish.

DRY $21 –V

Croft Vineyard Martinborough Pinot Noir ★★★★
Matured in French oak casks (30 per cent new), the floral, finely balanced 2008 vintage (★★★★) is ruby-hued and supple, with strong, ripe cherry, plum and spice flavours that flow well to a long, rounded finish.

DRY $35 AV

Croney Two Ton Marlborough Pinot Noir (★★★☆)
The sturdy good-value 2008 (★★★☆) was hand-harvested from low-cropped vines (5 tonnes/hectare), and matured in French oak barriques (30 per cent new). It shows good concentration, with firm, ripe plum, spice and cherry flavours.

DRY $20 V+

Crossings, The, Marlborough Pinot Noir ★★★☆
Estate-grown in the Awatere Valley, the 2008 vintage (★★★☆) spent seven months in French oak casks (25 per cent new). Maturing well, it's an easy-drinking, vibrantly fruity red with ripe cherry and plum flavours, a subtle twist of oak and gentle tannins. Ruby-hued and supple, it's full of charm.

Vintage	08	07	06
WR	6	7	7
Drink	10-12	10-12	10-12

DRY $26 AV

Crossroads Marlborough Pinot Noir (★★★)
Priced sharply, the partly barrel-aged 2008 vintage (★★★) is ruby-hued, with ripe, plummy, spicy flavours, savoury notes adding a touch of complexity, and a smooth, finely textured finish. It's drinking well now.

DRY $20 AV

Crowded House Marlborough/Nelson/Central Otago Pinot Noir ★★★☆
The 2009 vintage (★★★☆) is more savoury and complex than you'd expect at the price. A blend of Marlborough (40 per cent), Nelson (40 per cent) and Central Otago (20 per cent) grapes, partly oak-aged, it is ruby-hued, with a fragrant bouquet of berries and spices. Mouthfilling, ripe and supple, it is flavoursome, sweet-fruited and full of drink-young charm.

DRY $22 V+

Culley Marlborough Pinot Noir ★★★
From Cable Bay, the 2008 vintage (★★☆) is ruby-hued, with moderate depth of cherry, plum and herb flavours.

DRY $20 AV

Curio Bendigo Vineyard Central Otago Pinot Noir (★★★)
From Mud House, the stylishly packaged, debut 2008 vintage (★★★) was harvested at 24.5 brix and matured in tanks (50 per cent) and French oak barriques. Ruby-hued, it's an off-dry style (5 grams/litre of residual sugar), with fresh acidity and good depth of berryish, slightly spicy flavours. Drink young.

MED/DRY $30 –V

Dancing Water Cabal Waipara Pinot Noir (★★★☆)

Barrel-aged for a year, the 2007 vintage (★★★☆) is ruby-hued, with cherryish fruit flavours, lively acidity and some spice and 'forest floor' notes adding complexity.

DRY $38 –V

Darling, The, Marlborough Pinot Noir (★★★☆)

Grown in the Wairau's southern valleys, the 2009 vintage (★★★☆) was matured in one-year-old French oak casks. Ruby-hued, it is sweet-fruited and supple, with mouthfilling body and moderately concentrated, cherryish flavours. Finely textured, with hints of herbs and nuts, and considerable complexity, it's verging on four-star quality.

Vintage	09
WR	6
Drink	10-15

DRY $32 –V

Dashwood Marlborough Pinot Noir ★★☆

The 2008 vintage (★★☆), partly French oak-aged (30 per cent), is an easy-drinking style, ruby-hued and floral, with vibrant cherry, plum and slight herb flavours, light and smooth.

Vintage	08	07
WR	5	7
Drink	10-12	10-12

DRY $22 –V

Dawn Ghost Central Otago Pinot Noir ★★★

From Drumsara, based at Alexandra, the 2008 vintage (★★★☆) is sturdy and full-coloured, with very satisfying depth of ripe plum and spice flavours, showing some savoury complexity. It's drinking well now.

DRY $25 –V

Deep Cove Central Otago Pinot Noir (★★★☆)

From Wild Earth, the 20008 vintage (★★★☆) is a blend of estate-grown, Lowburn and Bannockburn grapes, with fruit purchased from other growers. Matured for eight months in French oak barriques (33 per cent new), it is ruby-hued and floral, mouthfilling and vibrantly fruity, with cherry, plum and herb flavours, some savoury, spicy notes adding complexity and a well-rounded finish. Drink now.

DRY $32 –V

Delegat's Awatere Valley Pinot Noir (★★★★)

Deeply coloured, the 2007 vintage (★★★★) is a cherryish red with rich sweet-fruit flavours seasoned with toasty oak. It's a powerful, savoury and complex wine, with a firm foundation of tannin.

DRY $39 AV

Delegat's Reserve Marlborough Pinot Noir (★★★★)

Grown in the Awatere Valley, the 2007 vintage (★★★★) is deeply coloured, with spicy, cherryish, slightly herbal flavours, seasoned with toasty oak, showing good concentration.

Vintage	07		DRY $28 V+
WR	6		
Drink	10-12		

Delta Hatters Hill Marlborough Pinot Noir ★★★★

The top label from the vineyard – 6 kilometres inland from Renwick, at the mouth of the Waihopai Valley – the 2008 vintage (★★★★) was 90 per cent oak-aged (barriques, 40 per cent new). Rich and full-coloured, with sweet-fruit characters, it has cherry, plum and spice flavours, woven with fresh acidity, in a vibrant, youthful style, best opened 2011+.

Vintage	08	07	DRY $32 AV
WR	6	7	
Drink	10-14	10-13	

Delta Marlborough Pinot Noir ★★★☆

The 2008 vintage (★★★☆) was 90 per cent matured in barrels (20 per cent new). A good drink-young style, it is ruby-hued, floral and supple, with good depth of ripe cherry, plum and spice flavours, moderately concentrated but intensely varietal. Drink now or cellar.

Vintage	08	DRY $25 AV
WR	6	
Drink	10-13	

Desert Heart Central Otago Pinot Noir ★★★☆

Grown at Bannockburn and matured in French oak barriques, the 2008 vintage (★★★☆) is bright ruby, with ripe fruit characters, moderately concentrated berry/plum flavours and gentle tannins. Supple, with a sweet-fruit charm and restrained oak influence, it's drinking well now.

Vintage	07	06	DRY $37 –V
WR	6	6	
Drink	10-16	10-15	

Desert Heart McKenzie's Run Pinot Noir (★★★☆)

Estate-grown at Bannockburn, in Central Otago, and matured in French oak casks (30 per cent new), the ruby-hued 2008 vintage (★★★☆) is forward in its appeal, with cherry and herb flavours, showing some savoury complexity, and supple tannins. The 2009 (★★★★) is deeply coloured and fragrant, with concentrated plum, spice and slight herb flavours, savoury and complex. A firmly structured wine that needs more time, it shows good potential.

DRY $40 –V

Devil's Staircase Central Otago Pinot Noir ★★★

From Rockburn, the 2009 vintage (★★★☆) is an attractive drink-young style. Freshly scented, it is ruby-hued, with very good depth of vibrant plum, spice and herb flavours, showing some complexity.

Vintage	09	08
WR	7	6
Drink	10-12	10-11

DRY $22 AV

Distant Land Marlborough Pinot Noir ★★★

The 2008 vintage (★★★) from Lincoln was hand-picked at Spring Creek, in the Wairau Valley, and French oak-matured. It's a sturdy wine (14 per cent alcohol), with cherry, plum, spice and herb flavours, slightly nutty and firm.

DRY $25 –V

Dog Point Vineyard Marlborough Pinot Noir ★★★★★

The classy 2008 vintage (★★★★★) was hand-harvested from very low-cropped vines (under 5 tonnes/hectare), fermented with indigenous yeasts and matured for 18 months in French oak barriques (50 per cent new). Deep and youthful in colour, it's a powerful, weighty wine, sweet-fruited and supple, with dense cherry, plum and spice flavours, warm, complex and finely balanced. A lovely mouthful.

Vintage	08	07	06	05	04	03	02
WR	6	6	5	6	5	6	6
Drink	10-14	10-14	10-12	10-13	10-11	10-12	P

DRY $42 V+

Domain Road Vineyard Central Otago Pinot Noir ★★★★☆

This single-vineyard, Bannockburn red is an emerging star. Scented, sweet-fruited and supple, the 2008 vintage (★★★★☆) couples substance and charm, with warm cherry, plum and spice flavours, showing excellent concentration, texture and complexity. The 2009 (★★★★★) was fermented with indigenous yeasts and barrel-aged for 10 months. Perfumed and deeply coloured, it has lush, beautifully ripe cherry, plum and spice flavours, showing great concentration and complexity. Still very youthful, it's a powerful, densely packed wine, best cellared to 2012+.

Vintage	09	08	07
WR	7	6	6
Drink	11-17	10-16	10-15

DRY $39 V+

Domaine Georges Michel – see Georges Michel

Domaine Jaquiery Central Otago Pinot Noir ★★★

Grown at Wanaka, the 2007 vintage (★★★☆) is a weighty, firmly structured style, spicy and nutty, with good complexity. Worth cellaring. The 2006 (★★☆) is full-coloured, with cherry, plum and tamarillo flavours, showing a slight lack of ripeness, and crisp acidity.

DRY $39 –V

Drumsara Central Otago Ventifacts Block Pinot Noir ★★★★☆

Grown at Alexandra, in the Ventifacts Block (wind-shaped boulders), the 2008 vintage (★★★★☆), matured for nine months in French oak casks (30 per cent new), has a lovely, floral bouquet. Delicious now, but still developing, it's a very graceful, finely poised wine, sweet-fruited and supple, mouthfilling and savoury, in a less dense, but riper-tasting, style than the 2007 (★★★★☆).

Vintage	08	07
WR	7	7
Drink	10-13	10-12

DRY $44 AV

Dry Gully Central Otago Pinot Noir ★★★☆

Grown in the Alexandra sub-region, but no longer a single-vineyard red, the 2008 vintage (★★★☆) was matured in French oak casks (25 per cent new). Ruby-hued, it is supple, with ripe, moderately concentrated flavours of plums and spices, some savoury complexity and gentle tannins. It's drinking well now.

Vintage	08	07	06	05
WR	5	5	6	5
Drink	10-15	10-12	10-13	10-11

DRY $30 –V

Drylands Marlborough Pinot Noir ★★★

The 2008 vintage (★★★☆) from Constellation NZ is an attractive mid-weight style with ripe cherry, plum and spice flavours, vibrantly fruity and supple. Enjoyable young, it shows some complexity and good harmony.

DRY $22 AV

Dry River Pinot Noir ★★★★★

Dark and densely flavoured, this Martinborough red ranks among New Zealand's greatest Pinot Noirs. Its striking depth, says winemaker Dr Neil McCallum, comes from 'getting the grapes really ripe' and 'keeping the vines' crops below 2.5 tonnes per acre [6 tonnes/hectare]'. It is grown in three company-owned vineyards – Dry River Estate, Craighall and Lovat – on the Martinborough Terrace, and 90 per cent of the vines are over 20 years old. Matured for a year in French oak hogsheads (20 to 30 per cent new), it is a slower developing wine than other New Zealand Pinot Noirs, but matures superbly. The 2008 vintage (★★★★★) is dark and still purple-flushed. Very youthful, vibrant and supple, it is beautifully sweet-fruited and floral, with concentrated cherry and plum flavours, a spicy underlay and a long, savoury finish. A highly refined wine, it should flourish with long-term cellaring.

Vintage	08	07	06	05	04	03	02	01	00
WR	7	7	7	7	6	7	6	7	7
Drink	10-17	10-16	10-14	10-17	10-12	10-16	P	10-12	P

DRY $82 AV

Edge, The, Martinborough Pinot Noir ★★★☆

From Escarpment, this is the winery's fourth-tier label (behind Kupe, the single-vineyard wines and the district blend). The fine-value 2008 vintage (★★★★) is a full-coloured, concentrated wine with cherry, plum and spice flavours, ripe and strong.

DRY $25 AV

Elephant Hill Central Otago Pinot Noir ★★★☆

The 2008 vintage (★★★☆) from this Hawke's Bay producer was grown at Alexandra and barrique-aged for a year. Mouthfilling and supple, it is ruby-hued, with ripe sweet-fruit characters and very good depth of vibrant, cherryish flavours, showing some complexity. The 2009 (★★★), also grown at Alexandra, was hand-picked and matured in French oak casks (40 per cent new). It's a full-bodied red with good depth of cherryish, distinctly herbal flavours.

DRY $29 AV

Eliot Brothers Marlborough Pinot Noir (★★★☆)

From an Auckland-based company, the well-made 2007 vintage (★★★☆) is savoury and supple. Full-coloured, it has ripe cherry and spice flavours, showing good varietal character and some complexity.

DRY $20 V+

Ellero Pisa Terrace Central Otago Pinot Noir (★★★)

The 2008 vintage (★★★), matured in French oak casks (25 per cent new), is cherryish and spicy, in an earthy, slightly rustic style with firm tannins.

DRY $36 –V

Escarpment Kiwa by Escarpment Martinborough Pinot Noir (★★★★★)

From vines planted in 1989, the 2008 vintage (★★★★★) is 'the biggest expression' of Pinot Noir in his range of single-vineyard reds, says winemaker Larry McKenna. Grown in the Cleland Vineyard, in Cambridge Road, it was matured in French oak barriques (30 per cent new). Deeply coloured, it is richly scented, with highly concentrated plum, spice and dark chocolate flavours, firm and lasting. It should be very long-lived.

DRY $65 AV

Escarpment Kupe by Escarpment Pinot Noir ★★★★★

This estate-grown Pinot Noir, based on closely planted vines at Te Muna, in Martinborough, is fermented in French cuves and matured in French oak barriques (50 per cent new). The 2008 vintage (★★★★☆) needs time. Still very youthful, it is warm and savoury, with concentrated cherry, plum and spice flavours and tight tannins. Open 2012+.

DRY $85 –V

Escarpment Pahi by Escarpment Pinot Noir (★★★★☆)

Based on vines then 27 years old in the McCreanor Vineyard in Princess Street, the 2008 vintage (★★★★☆) is a single-clone (10/5) wine, matured for a year in French oak casks (30 per cent new). Designed as a 'pure fruit expression', it's a very elegant red, scented and supple, with concentrated cherry and spice flavours, showing good, savoury complexity.

DRY $65 –V

Escarpment Te Rehua by Escarpment Pinot Noir ★★★★☆

Grown in the Barton Vineyard in Huangarua Road, Martinborough, where the Pinot Noir vines (of many clones) are well over 20 years old, the 2008 vintage (★★★★★) was matured for a year in French oak barriques (30 per cent new). It's a lovely, supple wine, elegant, ripe and savoury, combining power and elegance. Showing notable depth and complexity, it's already delicious, but well worth cellaring.

DRY $65 –V

Escarpment Vineyard Martinborough Pinot Noir ★★★★☆

This is the company's third-tier label, behind the single-vineyard wines and Kupe, but the 2008 vintage (★★★★☆) is impressive and enjoyable from the start. Mostly (70 per cent) estate-grown in Te Muna Road, it is scented, savoury and supple, in an elegant style with sweet-fruit delights and strong cherry and spice flavours, showing good complexity. Drink now or cellar.

Vintage	08	07	06	05	04	03
WR	7	6	7	6	5	7
Drink	10-16	10-15	10-15	10-12	P	P

DRY $45 –V

Esk Valley Marlborough Pinot Noir (★★★★)

The debut 2008 vintage (★★★★) was hand-picked in the Wairau and Awatere valleys and barrique-aged for a year. It's a sweet-fruited wine with fresh, ripe cherry and plum flavours, supple and strong.

Vintage	09	08
WR	7	6
Drink	11-15	10-11

DRY $30 AV

Eve Central Otago Pinot Noir (★★★)

From Wild Earth, the 2008 vintage (★★★) was estate-grown at Bannockburn and Pisa. Full-flavoured, it has deep ruby colour, with funky, barnyard notes adding complexity and a leafy streak.

DRY $24 AV

Fairhall Downs Single Vineyard Marlborough Pinot Noir ★★★★

Grown in the Brancott Valley, hand-picked and matured for 11 months in French oak barriques, the 2008 vintage (★★★★) is finely scented, mouthfilling, sweet-fruited and supple. A forward vintage, already delicious, it has gentle tannins and cherry/spice flavours showing good complexity.

DRY $35 AV

Fairmont Estate Block One Pinot Noir ★★★☆

Grown in the northern Wairarapa, the 2007 vintage (★★★) has deep, slightly developed colour. The bouquet is earthy, with 'forest floor' and barnyard notes, and the flavours are cherryish, spicy and slightly leafy, with good depth.

DRY $30 –V

Fall Harvest Pinot Noir (★★)

From Constellation NZ (formerly Nobilo), the 2007 vintage (★★) is a blend of French and New Zealand wines. An easy-drinking style, it's a ruby-hued, cherryish, spicy red with a soft, ultra-smooth finish.

DRY $13 AV

Fallen Angel Central Otago Pinot Noir ★★★★

The 2008 vintage (★★★★) from Stonyridge Vineyard – far better known for Waiheke Island claret-style reds – was blended from three sub-regions of Central Otago. Floral and supple, it is ruby-hued, with mouthfilling body and strong, ripe cherry, plum, herb and spice flavours, well seasoned with toasty oak. It shows good complexity and potential.

DRY $59 –V

Farmers Market Petite Pinot (★★★)

'Petite Pinot' is an odd name for a Beaujolais-style red, blended from Pinot Noir, grown in Marlborough, and Gisborne Merlot. Still, the blend works. Ruby-hued, the 2009 vintage (★★★) is full-bodied, fruity and supple, with smooth, cherryish, slightly spicy flavours, a hint of herbs, and gentle tannins. Drink now.

DRY $20 AV

Felton Road Block 3 Pinot Noir ★★★★★

Grown at Bannockburn, on a north-facing slope 270 metres above sea level, this is a majestic Central Otago wine, among the finest Pinot Noirs in the country. The mature vines are cultivated in a section of the vineyard where the clay content is relatively high, giving 'dried herbs and ripe fruit characters'. The wine is matured for 11 to 14 months in Burgundy oak barrels (50 to 60 per cent new), and bottled without fining or filtration. The 2008 vintage (★★★★★) is very fragrant, complex and savoury, with full, bright colour, sweet-fruit delights, deep, cherryish, spicy flavours and good tannin backbone. Best drinking 2011+.

Vintage	08	07	06	05	04	03	02	01	00
WR	7	7	6	7	7	6	7	7	7
Drink	10-20	10-18	10-17	10-18	10-12	10-11	P	P	P

DRY $69 AV

Felton Road Block 5 Pinot Noir ★★★★★

This is winemaker Blair Walter's favourite Felton Road red. Grown in a single block of the vineyard at Bannockburn, in Central Otago, the 2008 vintage (★★ ★★ ★) was matured for 11 months in French oak barriques (30 per cent new), followed by six months in seasoned oak barrels. Deeply coloured, it is mouthfilling and concentrated, with lovely depth of ripe, spicy, plummy, nutty flavours, firm yet supple. It should be long-lived; open 2011+.

Vintage	08	07	06	05	04	03	02	01	00
WR	7	7	6	7	7	7	7	7	7
Drink	10-17	10-18	10-17	10-18	10-11	P	P	P	P

DRY $69 AV

Felton Road Calvert Pinot Noir ★★★★

The deeply coloured 2008 vintage (★★★★☆) was grown in the Calvert Vineyard at Bannockburn – which neighbours and is managed by Felton Road – and matured for 14 months in French oak barriques (30 per cent new). A graceful Central Otago red, it's finely scented, with strong, youthful plum, cherry and spice flavours, woven with fresh acidity. Elegant and sweet-fruited, it needs time; open 2012+.

Vintage	08	07	06
WR	7	7	6
Drink	10-20	10-18	10-17

DRY $55 –V

Felton Road Central Otago Pinot Noir ★★★★★

The Bannockburn winery's 'standard' Pinot Noir is a distinguished wine in its own right, and the 2008 vintage (★★★★★) is another top example. Matured for 11 months in French oak casks (30 per cent new), it is very finely balanced, with deep colour and notable richness and harmony. A graceful red, already delicious, it is generous, warm and supple, with deep, ripe cherry, plum and nut flavours, savoury and complex, and good tannin support. Best drinking 2011+.

Vintage	08	07	06	05	04	03	02	01	00
WR	7	7	6	7	7	6	7	6	7
Drink	10-20	10-18	10-17	10-15	10-11	P	P	P	P

DRY $46 AV

Felton Road Cornish Point Pinot Noir (★★★★★)

From the company-owned Cornish Point Vineyard at Bannockburn (originally sold under a separate label), this is always one of my favourite Felton Road reds. The 2008 vintage (★★★★★) was matured for 14 months in French oak barriques (33 per cent new). Deep and youthful in colour, it is perfumed, mouthfilling, sweet-fruited and generous, with lovely depth of cherry, plum and spice flavours, a fine thread of acidity, and a sustained finish. It's a notably elegant wine, with the power to age.

Vintage	08
WR	7
Drink	10-20

DRY $55 AV

Fiddler's Green Waipara Pinot Noir ★★★☆

Matured for a year in French oak barriques (20 per cent new), the 2008 vintage (★★★☆) is ruby-hued, vibrantly fruity and supple, with very good depth of cherry, plum and nut flavours, showing some savoury complexity.

Vintage	08
WR	6
Drink	10-14

DRY $25 AV

Fiddler's Green Waipara Reserve Pinot Noir (★★★☆)

The 2008 vintage (★★★☆) was matured for 16 months in French oak barriques (40 per cent new). Ruby-hued and supple, it is moderately concentrated, with fresh, vibrant plum, herb and spice flavours, seasoned with spicy oak. Drink now or cellar.

Vintage	08
WR	6
Drink	10-16

DRY $30 –V

Folding Hill Bendigo Central Otago Pinot Noir (★★★★)

The youthful 2008 vintage (★★★★) was hand-picked from low-yielding vines (4 tonnes/hectare), matured in French oak barriques (35 per cent new), and bottled unfined and unfiltered. Showing the power to age well, it is sturdy and deeply coloured for Pinot Noir, with ripe sweet-fruit characters and fresh, concentrated cherry, plum and spice flavours, savoury and complex.

DRY $35 AV

Forrest Marlborough Pinot Noir ★★★

This easy-drinking wine rests its case on charm rather than power. The 2008 vintage (★★★) is fragrant and fresh, in a medium-bodied style with supple tannins and some spicy, nutty complexity.

Vintage	09	08	07
WR	5	5	6
Drink	11-15	10-14	10-15

DRY $25 –V

Forrest The Valleys Brancott Marlborough Pinot Noir (★★★☆)

The 2007 vintage (★★★☆) was hand-harvested from 25-year-old vines and matured in French oak casks (40 per cent new). A medium to full-bodied style, it is cherryish and slightly herbal, with gentle tannins, some savoury, earthy complexity and very good depth and harmony.

Vintage	07
WR	6
Drink	11-20

DRY $40 –V

Fossil Ridge Nelson Pinot Noir ★★☆

French oak-aged for a year, the 2007 vintage (★★☆) has slightly developed colour and moderate depth of cherry, plum and herb flavours, showing a slight lack of ripeness and roundness.

Vintage	07
WR	6
Drink	10-13

DRY $27 –V

Fox Junior Marlborough Pinot Noir (★★★★)

The debut 2008 vintage (★★★★) was hand-picked at 24 brix and matured for 10 months in French oak casks (10 per cent new). It's a generous wine with sweet-fruit delights, strong plum and cherry flavours, some savoury notes and a long, silky finish.

Vintage	08
WR	6
Drink	10-12

DRY $29 V+

Foxes Island Marlborough Pinot Noir ★★★☆

The 2006 vintage (★★★) lacks the class of its predecessors. Estate-grown, barrel-aged and bottled unfiltered, it shows fairly developed colour, with moderately ripe cherry, plum and spice flavours, showing some savoury complexity, and some leafy notes. Ready.

DRY $45 –V

Framingham F Series Marlborough Pinot Noir (★★★★☆)

The 2008 vintage (★★★★☆) was grown on clay soils at Fareham Lane, at the foot of the Waihopai Valley, and matured for 15 months in French oak casks (32 per cent new). A much more 'masculine' style than its stablemate (below), it is sturdy and rich, with full colour and a fragrant, plummy, spicy bouquet. Full-bodied and firm, with strong, ripe plum and spice flavours, and a good foundation of tannin, it shows excellent muscle, concentration and structure, with obvious cellaring potential.

Vintage	08
WR	6
Drink	10-14

DRY $40 AV

Framingham Marlborough Pinot Noir ★★★★

This wine is 'feminine', says winemaker Andrew Hedley, meaning it is elegant, rather than powerful. The 2009 vintage (★★★☆) was matured in French oak casks (24 per cent new). Mouthfilling and supple, it is softly seductive, with cherry, plum, spice and herb flavours. Moderately concentrated, it's already drinking well.

Vintage	09	08	07	06	05	04
WR	6	6	7	6	7	6
Drink	10-13	10-13	P	P	P	P

DRY $28 V+

Freefall Central Otago Pinot Noir ★★★☆

The 2007 vintage (★★★☆) is a fruit-driven style, grown at Bendigo and matured in mostly seasoned oak barrels. Deeply coloured, fresh, ripe and vibrant, it has good depth of cherry and plum flavours, a hint of liquorice and moderately firm tannins.

DRY $30 –V

Frizzell Pinot Noir ★★★

From a Hawke's Bay company, the 2008 vintage (★★★) was grown in Central Otago. Mouthfilling, sweet-fruited and smooth, it has good depth of plum, cherry and herb flavours, enjoyable young. The 2009 (★★★) is fresh-scented, very fruity and smooth, with generous plum and spice flavours, woven with lively acidity, and strong drink-young appeal.

Vintage	09
WR	6
Drink	10-15

DRY $25 –V

Fromm Brancott Valley Pinot Noir ★★★★☆

Still maturing, the 2007 vintage (★★★★☆) is a deeply coloured Marlborough red. Barrel-aged for over a year, with limited use of new oak, it is very generous, with concentrated, ripe, spicy, slightly nutty flavours and firm, balanced tannins. Savoury and complex, it should be long-lived.

Vintage	08	07	06	05
WR	6	6	6	6
Drink	10-16	10-15	10-14	10-13

DRY $45 –V

Fromm Clayvin Vineyard Pinot Noir ★★★★★

This Marlborough red is estate-grown at the hillside Clayvin Vineyard in the Brancott Valley, matured in French oak barriques (10–20 per cent new), and bottled without fining or filtering. It tends to be more floral and charming than its Fromm Vineyard stablemate. The 2007 (★★★★★) is a lovely wine. Deep and youthful in colour, it is very fragrant, concentrated and supple, with deep plum, spice and nut flavours, complex, finely poised and rich. Authoritative and approachable, it's still unfolding.

Vintage	08	07	06	05	04	03	02	01	00
WR	6	7	7	7	6	6	6	7	7
Drink	11-16	10-17	10-14	10-15	10-12	10-11	P	10-11	P

DRY $61 AV

Fromm Fromm Vineyard Pinot Noir ★★★★☆

Winemaker Hätsch Kalberer describes this Marlborough red as 'not a typical New World style, but the truest expression of terroir you could find'. In the Fromm Vineyard near Renwick, in the heart of the Wairau Valley, 11 clones of Pinot Noir are close-planted on a flat site with alluvial topsoils overlying layers of clay and free-draining gravels. The wine is fermented with indigenous yeasts and matured in Burgundy oak barrels (up to 10 per cent new). It needs at least four or five years to unleash its full class. The 2007 (★★★★) is deep and slightly developed in colour. A masculine red, rich and firm, it is cherryish, plummy, spicy, nutty and tautly structured, with good concentration and complexity.

Vintage	08	07	06	05	04	03	02	01	00
WR	6	7	6	7	6	6	6	7	7
Drink	12-20	11-19	10-16	10-17	10-16	10-15	10-12	10-11	P

DRY $65 –V

Fromm La Strada Pinot Noir – see La Strada Pinot Noir

Georges Michel Golden Mile Pinot Noir ★★☆

The easy-drinking 2008 vintage (★★☆), grown at Rapaura, in Marlborough, was oak-aged for nine months. Light ruby, it's a supple, mid-weight style with ripe plum and red-berry flavours, not concentrated, but enjoyable young.

Vintage	08	07
WR	5	6
Drink	10-12	10-12

DRY $25 –V

Georges Michel La Reserve Marlborough Pinot Noir ★★☆

Hand-picked in the Rapaura district and matured for over a year in French oak barriques, the 2007 vintage (★★) is lightish in colour, with a hint of development. Medium-bodied, with cherry, spice and nut flavours, it's a slightly rustic wine, lacking real richness and roundness.

Vintage	07	06	05	04	03	02
WR	5	6	6	6	6	5
Drink	10-15	10-13	10-12	P	P	P

DRY $30 –V

Georges Michel Legend Marlborough Pinot Noir (★★★)

Grown on stony soils at Rapaura, on the north side of the Wairau Valley, and barrel-aged for over a year, the 2007 vintage (★★★) is a full-coloured red with ripe cherry, plum and spice flavours, oak complexity and fairly firm tannins. It shows a slight lack of silkiness and charm, but should reward cellaring.

Vintage	07
WR	6
Drink	10-14

DRY $36 –V

Georgetown Vineyard Central Otago Pinot Noir (★★★★★)

The 2007 vintage (★★★★★) was grown in the Kawarau Gorge and bottled without fining or filtering. Dark and youthful in colour, it is fragrant, plummy, spicy and very rich. Dense and savoury, it is sweet-fruited and supple, with long-term cellaring potential.

DRY $50 AV

Gibbston Highgate Estate Soultaker Pinot Noir ★★★☆

The 2009 vintage (★★★☆), grown at Gibbston, in Central Otago, was matured in French oak barriques (40 per cent new), and bottled without filtering. Floral, with purple-flushed colour, it is vibrant, with strong cherry, plum and spice flavours, showing moderate complexity, and lots of youthful vigour. Supple and charming, it should be at its best mid-2011+.

DRY $35 –V

Gibbston Valley Central Otago Pinot Noir ★★★★☆

The 2008 vintage (★★★★☆) was estate-grown at Bendigo and matured for 11 months in French oak barriques (40 per cent new). Deeply coloured, it is rich, with concentrated cherry, plum, spice and slight herb flavours, poised, savoury and long. The 2009 (★★★★☆) is full-coloured, finely scented and generous, with mouthfilling body and concentrated cherry, plum, spice and nut flavours. Rich and ripe, complex and savoury, it's already delicious, but well worth cellaring. Best 2012+.

Vintage	09	08	07	06	05	04	03	02
WR	7	7	7	7	6	6	6	7
Drink	10-17	10-14	10-14	10-14	10-13	10-12	P	10-12

DRY $42 AV

Gibbston Valley China Terrace Central Otago Pinot Noir (★★★★★)

Estate-grown in Chinaman's Terrace Vineyard, at Bendigo, the debut 2009 vintage (★★★★★) was matured for 10 months in French oak casks (55 per cent new). It's a powerful wine, full-coloured, with ripe, spicy aromas and flavours. Weighty and warm, with rich cherry, spice and slight herb flavours, and ripe, supple tannins, it is complex and well-rounded, with excellent cellaring potential.

Vintage	09
WR	6
Drink	11-17

DRY $55 AV

Gibbston Valley Gold River Pinot Noir ★★★☆

This is the Central Otago winery's 'lighter' red, made for 'immediate enjoyment'. The 2008 vintage (★★★☆), harvested at Bendigo and Gibbston, was matured for six months in French oak (30 per cent new). It's a floral, vibrantly fruity red with ripe cherry and plum flavours, a touch of complexity, and lots of drink-young charm.

Vintage	08	07	06
WR	7	6	7
Drink	10-12	P	P

DRY $30 –V

Gibbston Valley Le Mineur d'Orient The Expressionist Series Pinot Noir ★★★★☆

The 2008 vintage (★★★★☆), estate-grown in Chinaman's Terrace Vineyard, at Bendigo, was matured for 11 months in French oak barriques (100 per cent new). Ruby-hued, it is mouthfilling, with ripe cherry and plum flavours, very harmonious, complex and savoury. The 2009 (★★★★) is fullish in colour, with a hint of development. Mouthfilling, it is savoury, spicy and complex, with hints of herbs and liquorice in a forward style, already delicious.

DRY $50 –V

Gibbston Valley Reserve Pinot Noir ★★★★★

At its best, this Central Otago red is mouthfilling and savoury, with superb concentration of sweet-tasting, plummy fruit and lovely harmony. The grapes have been drawn from various sub-regions and vineyards over the years and yields have been very low (under 5 tonnes/hectare). The wine is typically matured in French oak barriques (50 to 70 per cent new). Grown in the School House Vineyard at Bendigo, and matured for 11 months in French oak barriques (60 per cent new), the 2008 vintage (★★★★☆) is full-coloured, scented and supple, with vibrant cherry, plum and spice flavours, ripe, savoury and concentrated. The 2009 (★★★★★) is bold and youthful in colour, with lush cherry and plum flavours. Finely textured, with advanced fruit sweetness and finely integrated oak, it's a very rich and harmonious, beautiful young wine, with a long future.

Vintage	09	08	07	06
WR	7	7	NM	7
Drink	12-20	12-20	NM	10-16

DRY $100 –V

Gibbston Valley School House Central Otago Pinot Noir (★★★★☆)

A 'feminine' style, the debut 2009 vintage (★★★★☆) was estate-grown in the School House Vineyard, at Bendigo. Matured for 10 months in French oak casks (55 per cent new), it is full-coloured, very fragrant and supple, with an array of plum, spice, herb and nut flavours, woven with fresh acidity. An elegant, finely poised wine, it's still very youthful; open 2012+.

Vintage	09
WR	7
Drink	10-17

DRY $55 –V

Giesen Marlborough Pinot Noir ★★★

The 2008 vintage (★★★) is a blend of estate-grown grapes, from the Waihopai Valley, and fruit from Wairau Valley growers. Matured for eight months in French oak barriques (15 per cent new), it is ruby-hued and mouthfilling, with good depth of ripe plum and spice flavours, showing some savoury complexity, and a well-balanced finish.

DRY $22 AV

Giesen Marlborough The Brothers Pinot Noir (★★★☆)

The 2008 vintage (★★★☆) is worth cellaring. Ruby-hued, it is mouthfilling, with ripe, moderately concentrated cherry, plum and spice flavours, showing some savoury, nutty complexity, and fairly firm tannins.

DRY $35 –V

Gladstone Vineyard Wairarapa Pinot Noir ★★★★

Finely scented, the 2008 vintage (★★★★) was hand-picked at Gladstone and matured for 10 months in French oak casks (30 per cent new). A graceful, elegant rather than powerful style, it is intensely varietal, with vibrant, cherryish flavours, hints of herbs and spices, fresh acidity and supple tannins. Showing good, savoury complexity, it's a drink-now or cellaring proposition.

Vintage	08
WR	6
Drink	10-18

DRY $40 –V

Glasnevin Pinot Noir (★★★★☆)

From Fiddler's Green, the 2007 vintage (★★★★☆) was grown at Waipara and matured for 18 months in French oak barriques (30 per cent new). It's a fragrant, ruby-hued red with concentrated plum, spice and slight herb flavours, underlying tannins, good complexity, and the power and structure to mature well.

Vintage	07
WR	7
Drink	10-16

DRY $43 AV

Glazebrook Regional Reserve Martinborough Pinot Noir ★★★☆

From Ngatarawa winery, based in Hawke's Bay, the 2008 vintage (★★★☆) is a supple, ripely flavoured red, based on 11-year-old vines at Te Muna. Bright ruby, it is cherryish, plummy and savoury, with French oak complexity (45 per cent new), very good depth and good cellaring potential.

Vintage	08	07	06	05
WR	6	NM	6	6
Drink	10-14	NM	10-12	P

DRY $27 AV

Goldridge Estate Marlborough Pinot Noir ★★☆

The 2009 vintage (★★★) was grown at three sites in the Wairau Valley and barrique-aged. Ruby-hued, it offers decent depth of cherry, plum, herb and spice flavours, showing some savoury complexity. Priced right.

DRY $19 –V

Goldridge Estate Premium Reserve Marlborough Pinot Noir ★★★

The 2008 vintage (★★★) was hand-picked in the Wairau Valley and matured in oak barriques (25 per cent new). Light ruby, it's a middleweight style with moderately concentrated, ripe cherry, spice and nut flavours. It's drinking well now.

DRY $22 AV

Goldwater Marlborough Pinot Noir ★★★

The 2007 vintage (★★★★) is drinking well now. A floral, full-bodied, soft red, it has ripe, sweet-fruit flavours of cherries, plums and spices, a hint of thyme, and good complexity and density.

Vintage	08	07
WR	6	6
Drink	10-12	10-11

DRY $24 AV

Grasshopper Rock Earnscleugh Vineyard Central Otago Pinot Noir ★★★★

Estate-grown in Alexandra, the 2008 vintage (★★★★★) offers wonderful value. A single-vineyard red, matured in French oak barrels (30 per cent new), it is deep and rich, with ripe cherry, plum, herb and spice flavours, hints of raisins and coffee, and good, savoury complexity. The 2009 (★★★☆) is mouthfilling and full-coloured, with cherry and herb flavours, seasoned with nutty oak, and firm tannins. It shows good concentration, vibrancy and complexity, in a slightly crisper, less ripe style than the 2008.

Vintage	09	08	07	06
WR	7	7	7	6
Drink	10-17	10-16	10-16	10-13

DRY $30 AV

Gravitas Marlborough Pinot Noir ★★★★☆

Estate-grown, hand-picked, fermented with indigenous yeasts and matured in French oak barriques, the refined 2007 vintage (★★★★★) is richly coloured, concentrated and fragrant. It has a core of ripe, sweet fruit, with good complexity, finely balanced tannins and a rich finish.

Vintage	07	06	05
WR	7	6	6
Drink	10-14	10-13	10-12

DRY $34 V+

Greenhough Hope Vineyard Pinot Noir ★★★★★

One of Nelson's greatest reds, at its best powerful, rich and long-lived. It is estate-grown on an elevated terrace of the south-eastern Waimea Plains, where the vines, planted in gravelly loam clays, range up to 28 years old. Yields are very low – 4 to 5 tonnes of grapes per hectare – and the wine is matured for a year in French oak barrels (25 to 50 per cent new). The 2008 vintage (★★★★★) is a lovely, youthful wine, deeply coloured, powerful and concentrated. It has deep, ripe flavours of plums and spices, unusually savoury and complex, and the structure to age well.

Vintage	08	07	06	05	04	03
WR	6	7	6	7	5	7
Drink	10-16	10-15	10-13	10-14	P	P

DRY $45 AV

Greenhough Nelson Pinot Noir ★★★☆

This wine is handled in a similar way to its Hope Vineyard stablemate (above), but without the contribution of as much new oak or fruit from the oldest vines. It is hand-picked from a range of sites and matured for a year in French oak casks (25 per cent new). The 2008 (★★★★), grown at Hope and Upper Moutere, is a ripely scented, supple red with excellent depth of cherry, plum and slight herb flavours, a subtle seasoning of oak, savoury, complex notes and good tannin support. It's a delicious, harmonious wine, for drinking now or cellaring.

Vintage	08	07	06	05	04	03
WR	6	7	6	5	5	6
Drink	10-13	10-13	10-12	10-12	P	P

DRY $26 AV

Greenstone Central Otago Pinot Noir (★★☆)

From Gibbston Valley, the 2008 vintage (★★☆) is ruby-hued, with mouthfilling body and simple, cherry and plum flavours, fresh, ripe and smooth.

DRY $19 –V

Greylands Ridge Central Otago Pinot Noir (★★★☆)

Grown at Alexandra, the 2008 vintage (★★★☆) was very charming in its youth, with cherry and plum flavours, some savoury complexity, gentle tannins and good harmony.

DRY $36 –V

Greylands Ridge Ridgeback Alex Pinot Noir (★★★)

Ruby-hued, the 2008 vintage (★★★) is an enjoyable mid-weight style, with ripe red-berry and spice flavours, fresh and floral.

DRY $25 –V

Greyrock Marlborough Pinot Noir (★★☆)

From Sileni, based in Hawke's Bay, the 2008 vintage (★★☆) is a floral, supple, light red, with gentle strawberry and plum flavours. It's a drink-young style, priced right.

DRY $14 V+

Greystone Waipara Pinot Noir ★★★

Ruby-hued, the 2008 vintage (★★★) was fermented with indigenous yeasts and matured in French oak casks (30 per cent new). Floral and supple, it has cherry and herb flavours in a fruity, fairly light style with good varietal character and drink-young appeal.

Vintage	09	08	07	06
WR	7	5	6	5
Drink	11-17	10-11	10-12	10-12

DRY $39 –V

Grove Mill Grand Reserve Seventeen Valley Vineyard Marlborough Pinot Noir (★★★★)

Built to last, the 2009 vintage (★★★★) is a single-vineyard red, hand-picked and matured for 10 months in French oak barriques. Vibrantly fruity and full-coloured, with a floral, berryish fragrance, it offers strong cherry, plum and spice flavours, ripe and supple, showing excellent depth and harmony.

DRY $43 –V

Grove Mill Marlborough Pinot Noir ★★★

The standard of this winery's red wines in the past rarely matched its whites. The 2007 vintage (★★★) is full-coloured, with firm, nutty flavours, strong but slightly rustic.

Vintage	07	06	05	04	03	02
WR	6	7	7	6	5	6
Drink	10-12	10-11	10	P	P	P

DRY $36 –V

Gumfields Marlborough Pinot Noir (★★★☆)

From West Brook, the ruby-hued 2007 vintage (★★★☆) is fresh and supple, in a charming style with cherry and plum flavours, gently oaked and finely balanced. It shows good varietal character, with drink-young appeal.

DRY $22 V+

Gunn Estate Pinot Noir ★★☆

From Sacred Hill, the 2008 vintage (★★☆) is a blend of Australian and New Zealand wines. Ruby-hued, with a hint of development showing, it offers very easy drinking, with decent depth of ripe cherry and spice flavours, and gentle tannins giving a seductively smooth finish. Ready.

DRY $18 AV

Hans Herzog Marlborough Pinot Noir ★★★★★

This powerful wine needs at least a couple of years to reveal its class. The 2007 vintage (★★★★★) was harvested at 24.2 to 25.1 brix, fermented with indigenous yeasts, matured for a year in French oak barriques (20 per cent new), and bottled unfined and unfiltered. Highly scented, very ripe and silky, it's a top year, with mouthfilling body (14.8 per cent alcohol) and rich cherry, plum and nut flavours, long and lovely.

Vintage	07
WR	7
Drink	10-19

DRY $35 V+

Harwood Hall Central Otago Pinot Noir (★★★☆)

Showing greater complexity than many Pinot Noirs in its price category, the 2008 vintage (★★★☆) is a sweet-fruited wine with good depth of cherry, herb and spice flavours, fresh and supple.

Vintage	09	08
WR	5	5
Drink	10-14	10-13

DRY $24 V+

Hawkdun Rise Central Otago Pinot Noir ★★★☆

This is a single-vineyard, Alexandra red. The ripe-tasting 2008 (★★★★) is deeply coloured and mouthfilling (14.2 per cent alcohol), with generous cherry, plum and spice flavours, and the structure to mature well.

Vintage	07
WR	6
Drink	10-15

DRY $38 –V

Hawkshead Bannockburn Central Otago Pinot Noir (★★★★)

The deeply coloured 2008 vintage (★★★★) was made for this Gibbston-based producer by Steve Davies, using grapes from his vineyard at Bannockburn. Hand-picked at 24.2 to 25.5 brix, it was fermented with indigenous yeasts, matured in French oak barriques (33 per cent new), and bottled unfined and unfiltered. Mouthfilling, warm and supple, it's a deliciously sweet-fruited wine, packed with cherryish, plummy flavour, showing good complexity.

DRY $48 –V

Hawkshead Central Otago Pinot Noir ★★★☆

The 2008 vintage (★★★☆) is a ruby-hued, regional blend of Lowburn (Cromwell Basin) and Gibbston grapes, matured for 11 months in French oak barrels (40 per cent new). It has moderately rich cherry/plum flavours, hints of herbs and tamarillos, well-integrated oak and a very smooth finish.

DRY $39 –V

Hawkshead First Vines Central Otago Pinot Noir ★★★☆

Grown at Gibbston, this wine is based on the oldest vines. Harvested at 24 brix and matured for 11 months in French oak casks (40 per cent new), the 2008 vintage (★★★☆) is a spicy, vibrant, slightly herbal red, with fresh acidity and very good flavour depth.

DRY $43 –V

Hay Maker Marlborough Pinot Noir (★★☆)

From Mud House, the 2008 vintage (★★☆) is a drink-young style, ruby-hued, with raspberryish, slightly spicy flavours, fruity and smooth.

DRY $17 AV

Heart of Stone Marlborough Pinot Noir ★★☆

The 2008 vintage (★★) from Forrest is light and simple, with soft, cherryish flavours, offering easy, no-fuss drinking.

DRY $18 AV

Hell or Highwater Central Otago Pinot Noir (★★★)

Grown in the Cromwell Basin, the 2009 vintage (★★★) is enjoyable young. Ruby-hued, it is mouthfilling and smooth, with ripe berryish fruit flavours, hints of herbs and spices, a touch of complexity and gentle tannins.

DRY $22 AV

Highfield Marlborough Pinot Noir ★★★★☆

The 2008 (★★★★★) is a top vintage. Hand-picked at 24 to 27 brix, it was matured for a year in French oak barrels. Highly scented, with full, youthful colour, it is very generous, savoury and sweet-fruited, with deep cherry, plum and spice flavours, seasoned with nutty oak, gentle acidity, and a soft, rich finish. Best drinking mid-2011+.

Vintage	08	07	06	05	04	03	02
WR	5	6	5	7	6	6	7
Drink	11-15	10-14	P	P	P	P	P

DRY $37 V+

Hinton Estate Vineyard Central Otago Pinot Noir ★★★☆

Maturing well, the 2006 vintage (★★★★) is one of the finest yet. Grown at Alexandra, it is ruby-hued, elegant and vibrantly fruity, with fresh acidity and cherry, plum and spice flavours seasoned with fine-quality oak. Drink now or cellar.

DRY $35 –V

Homer Marlborough Pinot Noir ★★★

From Odyssey, the 2008 (★★★) was hand-picked in the Brancott Valley and aged in seasoned oak casks. Deeply coloured, it is generous and fruity, with strong cherry and plum flavours, ripe and gutsy. The 2009 vintage (★★★) is enjoyable young. Mouthfilling, it is ruby-hued, with cherry, plum and slight herb flavours, showing a touch of complexity, gentle tannins and a smooth finish.

Vintage	08
WR	5
Drink	10-12

DRY $20 AV

Hoppers Crossing Central Otago Pinot Noir (★★☆)

From Auckland-based CPP Wines, the 2008 vintage (★★☆) is a fruity, simple red with a hint of sweet oak and pleasant berry/plum flavours, offering easy, no-fuss drinking.

DRY $20 –V

Hudson John Henry Pinot Noir ★★★

The 2008 vintage (★★★) is a Martinborough red with cherryish, slightly spicy and herbal flavours. It's a middleweight style with good depth, gentle tannins and an attractively perfumed bouquet.

Vintage	07	06
WR	6	4
Drink	10-11	10-12

DRY $34 –V

Huia Marlborough Pinot Noir ★★★☆

The 2007 vintage (★★★☆) was matured for 11 months in French oak. Floral, sweet-fruited and supple, it is moderately concentrated, with cherry, plum and slight herb flavours, showing good complexity.

Vintage	07	06	05	04	03	02
WR	6	6	6	6	6	6
Drink	10-19	10-11	10-11	P	P	P

DRY $36 –V

Huntaway Reserve Central Otago Pinot Noir (★★★☆)

From Pernod Ricard NZ, the 2008 vintage (★★★☆) is a single-vineyard red, grown at Bendigo, in the Cromwell Basin. Ruby-hued, it is mouthfilling and sweet-fruited, with strong cherry, herb and spice flavours, gentle tannins, and some savoury complexity. It should be at its best during 2011.

DRY $24 V+

Hunter's Marlborough Pinot Noir ★★★☆

Typically a very supple, charming red. Recent vintages reflect a change in grape source from Rapaura to the more clay-based soils on the south side of the Wairau Valley. The 2008 (★★★☆) was picked at 24 brix and matured for 10 months in seasoned French oak barriques. Ruby-hued, it's a youthful red with moderately concentrated, ripe flavours of cherries, plums and spices, showing some savoury complexity. Fragrant, full-bodied and smooth, it's still developing, but already highly enjoyable.

Vintage	08
WR	5
Drink	10-13

DRY $27 AV

Hyperion Eos Pinot Noir ★★

Estate-grown at Matakana, north of Auckland, and barrel-matured for a year, this is one of New Zealand's northernmost Pinot Noirs. The 2008 vintage (★★) has slightly developed colour. Mouthfilling and smooth, it is spicy, with hints of herbs and raisins, but lacks real ripeness and richness.

Vintage	08	07	06	05	04	03
WR	7	5	7	6	6	4
Drink	10-14	10-12	10-11	P	P	P

DRY $31 –V

Incognito Pinot Noir (★★★★)

From Gibbston Highgate, the 2008 vintage (★★★★) was grown at Gibbston, in Central Otago, fermented with indigenous yeasts, matured for 11 months in French oak barrels (30 per cent new), and bottled unfined and unfiltered. Floral and ruby-hued, it's a sweet-fruited, supple wine with much more body and depth than its colour suggests. Delicious young, it has rich plum and cherry flavours, subtle oak and gentle tannins. Slightly savoury, with lots of charm and a persistent finish, it's a fragrant, finely textured wine, drinking well now.

DRY $23 V+

Instinct Marlborough Pinot Noir (★★☆)

From C.J. Pask, the 2008 vintage (★★☆) was hand-picked and French oak-aged for 10 months. It's an easy-drinking wine, light ruby, with fresh strawberry and spice aromas and flavours, and a rounded finish. Drink young. (The 2009 is from Martinborough.)

DRY $20 –V

Invivo Central Otago Pinot Noir (★★★)

From an Auckland-based company, the 2008 vintage (★★★) was grown at Lowburn, in the Cromwell Basin, hand-picked and partly barrel-aged. It's a ruby-hued, mid-weight style with ripe sweet-fruit flavours of cherries and plums, gentle tannins, and drink-young charm.

Vintage	09	08
WR	5	5
Drink	10-15	10-13

DRY $30 –V

Isabel Marlborough Pinot Noir ★★★☆

This once-outstanding red was originally grown in the close-planted Tiller Vineyard near Renwick, but is now a multi-site blend, including fruit from the company's Elevation Vineyard in the Waihopai Valley, 300 metres above sea level. It is matured for 10 to 12 months in French oak barriques (15 to 20 per cent new), and bottled without fining or filtering. The 2006 vintage (★★★☆) is full-bodied and smooth, with moderately concentrated plum/spice flavours, showing some savoury complexity.

Vintage	06	05
WR	7	6
Drink	10-16	10-17

DRY $35 –V

Jack's Canyon Waipara Pinot Noir (★★)

The 2009 vintage (★★) was grown in North Canterbury and matured in an even split of tanks and barrels. Ruby-hued, it's an easy-drinking, slightly rustic quaffer, with moderate flavour depth and a smooth finish.

DRY $17 –V

Jackson Estate Gum Emperor Marlborough Pinot Noir ★★★★★

The 2008 vintage (★★★★★) was estate-grown in the Gum Emperor Vineyard, in the Waihopai Valley. Hand-picked, it was fermented with indigenous yeasts, matured in French oak barriques, and bottled without fining or filtering. Richly coloured, it is ripely scented, mouthfilling and supple, with very deep cherry and plum flavours, and hints of liquorice and nuts. Very generous, sweet-fruited and finely textured, with lovely flow across the palate, it's a drink-now or cellaring proposition.

Vintage	08	07	06	05
WR	7	7	NM	6
Drink	10-20	10-18	NM	10-15

DRY $43 V+

Jackson Estate Vintage Widow Marlborough Pinot Noir ★★★★☆

The quality of Jackson Estate's Pinot Noir has shot up since the 2005 (★★★★), the first to be labelled 'Vintage Widow' – a reference to 'our families, often forgotten at vintage'. The 2009 (★★★★★), matured in French oak barriques, is deeply coloured, with a fragrant, complex bouquet. Beautifully rich and sweet-fruited, it has dense cherry, plum and spice flavours and ripe, supple tannins. A powerful, generous wine, with obvious cellaring potential, it's already delicious.

Vintage	09	08	07	06	05	04
WR	6	5	6	5	6	5
Drink	10-20	10-15	10-18	10-12	P	P

DRY $35 V+

John Forrest Collection Pinot Noir (★★★★☆)

From Bannockburn in Central Otago, the 2007 vintage (★★★★☆) is from a season when Forrest harvested no grapes from the Waitaki Valley. Full ruby, it is mouthfilling and very supple, with vibrant cherry, spice and slight herb flavours, showing good concentration, fresh acidity and impressive complexity. Drink now onwards.

Vintage	07
WR	6
Drink	11-20

DRY $70 –V

Johner Estate Gladstone Pinot Noir ★★★

Grown at Gladstone, in the Wairarapa, the 2008 (★★★) has full, slightly developed colour, mouthfilling body, plum, cherry and herb flavours and a smooth finish. The 2009 vintage (★★★) is light ruby, with fresh cherry and spice flavours, a herbal thread and some savoury complexity.

Vintage	09	08	07
WR	6	6	5
Drink	15-20	12-15	P

DRY $37 –V

Johner Estate Gladstone Reserve Pinot Noir ★★★★

The 2009 vintage (★★★★) is a single-vineyard Wairarapa red, grown at Gladstone and French oak-aged. Full-coloured, with a hint of development, it is mouthfilling, with strong cherry, spice and herb flavours, showing good complexity, and a soft, well-rounded finish. Drink now onwards.

Vintage	09
WR	6
Drink	15-19

DRY $50 –V

Johner Estate Moonlight Pinot Noir ★★☆

The 2009 vintage (★★★) is a lightly oaked style, grown in the Wairarapa. Full-bodied and savoury, it has a slightly leafy bouquet, but also plenty of flavour and some complexity. Best drinking 2011.

Vintage	09
WR	6
Drink	11-15

DRY $22 –V

Joseph Ryan Pinot Noir (★★☆)

Still on sale in 2010, the 2006 vintage (★★☆) is a northern Wairarapa red. Fullish in colour, it is green-edged, with some leafy notes, but is still drinking soundly.

DRY $30 –V

Judge Rock Central Otago Pinot Noir ★★★★

The 2008 vintage (★★★★) of this single-vineyard Alexandra wine is mouthfilling and well-structured, with rich, ripe cherry, herb and nut flavours and good, savoury complexity. The 2009 (★★★☆) is scented and supple. A fresh, ruby-hued wine with cherry, plum, spice and herb flavours, and some savoury complexity, it's already enjoyable.

Vintage	09	08	07	06	05	04	03
WR	5	6	6	6	6	4	5
Drink	10-15	10-15	10-14	10-13	10-12	P	P

DRY $39 AV

Judge Rock Venus Central Otago Pinot Noir ★★★☆

The 2008 vintage (★★★☆) from this Alexandra-based producer is a floral, single-vineyard wine with cherry, spice and herb flavours, showing some complexity, elegance and charm. The 2009 (★★★) is ruby-hued, juicy and spicy, with moderately ripe flavours and firm tannins.

Vintage	09	08	07	06
WR	5	6	6	5
Drink	10-12	10-12	10-11	P

DRY $25 AV

Julicher 99 Rows Martinborough Pinot Noir ★★★★☆

The 2009 vintage (★★★★☆) is a great buy. Estate-grown at Te Muna, it was hand-picked at 23 to 26 brix and matured for 10 months in French oak casks (20 per cent new). A robust wine (14.5 per cent alcohol), it is very generous, warm and savoury, with deep cherry, plum and spice flavours and ripe, supple tannins. Showing good complexity, it's already delicious.

DRY $30 V+

Julicher Martinborough Pinot Noir ★★★★☆

Estate-grown on the Te Muna Terraces, the 2008 vintage (★★★★★) was hand-picked at 23 to 24 brix and matured for 11 months in French oak casks (20 per cent new). Very rich and savoury, it has lovely concentration and flow, with brambly, spicy flavours, a hint of herbs, and notable ripeness, depth and complexity. Drink now or cellar.

Vintage	08	07	06	05	04	03	02
WR	7	6	7	6	5	5	5
Drink	10-16	10-14	10-13	10-13	P	P	P

DRY $42 AV

Jumper, The, Marlborough Pinot Noir ★★☆

From Spring Creek Estate, the 2008 vintage (★★☆) was matured for a year in seasoned French oak barriques. Medium-bodied, it's a slightly rustic wine, but shows some flavour depth and complexity.

DRY $18 AV

Kahurangi Estate Nelson Pinot Noir (★★☆)

The 2008 vintage (★★☆) is a light style, but clearly varietal. Pale and light-bodied, it has fresh, straightforward berry and spice flavours, with gentle tannins. A pleasant, drink-young style.

DRY $22 –V

Kaikoura Kaikoura-Marlborough Pinot Noir (★★☆)

Hand-picked at Kaikoura, the 2009 vintage (★★☆) was matured for eight months in seasoned French oak barriques. Light in colour and body, it is smooth, with gentle strawberry and spice flavours. A pleasant, drink-young style.

DRY $25 –V

Kaimira Estate Vintner's Selection Pinot Noir ★★★

Estate-grown at Brightwater, in Nelson, the 2008 vintage (★★★) was matured for 10 months in French oak barriques (30 per cent new). Ruby-hued, it is mouthfilling (14 per cent alcohol), with ripe, moderately concentrated berry and plum flavours, gentle tannins and a smooth finish.

Vintage	08
WR	6
Drink	10-14

DRY $30 –V

Kaituna Valley Canterbury The Kaituna Vineyard Pinot Noir ★★★★★

This arresting Canterbury red flows from a warm and sheltered site on Banks Peninsula, south of Christchurch. Of the total area of Pinot Noir vines, a third was planted between 1977 and 1979; the rest was established in 1997. The wine is matured for over a year in Burgundy oak casks (50 to 70 per cent new). The 2007 vintage (★★★★★) is classy. Deeply coloured, with a ripely scented, slightly peppery bouquet, it has sweet-fruit delights and striking depth of cherry, plum, spice and nut flavours, rich and supple.

DRY $45 AV

Karamea Marlborough Pinot Noir (★★☆)

The 2007 vintage (★★☆) is a middleweight style with green-edged, plum and herb flavours and a smooth finish. Ready.

DRY $20 –V

Kawarau Estate Central Otago Pinot Noir ★★★

Estate-grown organically at Lowburn, the 2008 vintage (★★) was hand-picked and matured for 10 months in French oak barriques (mostly seasoned). Ruby-hued, it's a light style with plum and herb flavours, lacking real ripeness and richness.

Vintage	08	07	06
WR	6	5	6
Drink	10-12	10-11	P

DRY $30 –V

Kawarau Estate Reserve Pinot Noir ★★★☆

Grown organically at Pisa Flats, in the Cromwell Basin of Central Otago, at its best this is a classy, powerful and complex wine. Fermented with indigenous yeasts and matured for 10 months in French oak barriques (30 per cent new), the 2007 (★★★) is earthy and savoury, slightly herbal and nutty, with gentle tannins and some elegance. The 2008 vintage (★★★☆) is ruby-hued, mouthfilling, vibrant and supple, with cherry and spice flavours, showing moderate concentration and good complexity.

Vintage	08	07	06	05
WR	6	7	7	5
Drink	10-14	10-13	10-12	10-11

DRY $43 –V

Kennedy Point Marlborough Pinot Noir (★★★☆)

From a Waiheke Island-based producer, the 2008 vintage (★★★☆) was fermented with indigenous yeasts and matured in French oak for 16 months. It's a supple, fruity wine with ripe plum and spice flavours, showing good varietal character, and some savoury complexity.

DRY $35 –V

Kerner Estate Marlborough Pinot Noir (★★★★)

The stylish 2008 vintage (★★★★) is a single-vineyard, hand-harvested, Wairau Valley red, fermented with indigenous yeasts and matured in seasoned French oak barrels. Floral and supple, it is intensely varietal, with ripe cherry and nut flavours, silky-textured and showing good complexity and charm. Delicious drinking now onwards.

Vintage	08
WR	5
Drink	10-13

DRY $35 AV

Kim Crawford Marlborough Pinot Noir ★★☆

The 2008 vintage (★★☆), aged in tanks and barrels, is a light ruby, pleasant, easy-drinking red, but lacks the richness you'd expect at its price.

DRY $23 –V

Kim Crawford SP Kim's Favourite Marlborough Pinot Noir (★★★★)

Grown mostly in the Waihopai Valley, the 2007 vintage (★★★★) was only partly oak-aged. Delicious young, it's a softly structured wine with deep cherry, plum and spice flavours, showing good richness and roundness.

DRY $34 AV

Kim Crawford SP Rise & Shine Creek Central Otago Pinot Noir ★★★☆

Grown at Bendigo and partly oak-matured, the 2007 vintage (★★★☆) is fruit-packed but only moderately complex. It has strong, ripe plum and spice flavours, with a hint of liquorice, and supple tannins.

DRY $34 –V

Kina Beach Vineyard Reserve Pinot Noir ★★★★

Estate-grown at Tasman, on the Nelson coast, the 2007 vintage (★★★★) was matured for 14 months in French oak barriques (one-third new). Ruby-hued, it's an intensely varietal wine with strong cherry, plum, spice and herb flavours, showing good, savoury complexity. Ready; no rush.

Vintage	07
WR	7
Drink	10-15

DRY $45 –V

Kina Cliffs Nelson Pinot Noir (★★☆)

Estate-grown overlooking Ruby Bay, the 2009 vintage (★★☆) was hand-harvested and French oak-aged for 11 months. Ruby-hued, with a hint of development, it is cherryish, savoury and green-edged, with a distinct herbal thread, but full-bodied, clearly varietal and smooth. Drink young.

Vintage	09	DRY $30 –V
WR	6	
Drink	10-16	

Kina Cliffs Reserve Nelson Pinot Noir (★★★☆)

Grown near the Kina Peninsula, the 2009 vintage (★★★☆) was hand-picked at over 24 brix from very low-cropping vines (2 tonnes/hectare), and matured for 11 months in French oak casks. Mouthfilling, generous, savoury and supple, with very good flavour depth, spicy and slightly herbal, it's a moderately ripe-tasting wine with strong personality, offering good drinking from now onwards.

Vintage	09	DRY $45 –V
WR	7	
Drink	10-19	

Kingsmill Tippet's Dam Central Otago Pinot Noir ★★★★☆

A single-vineyard Bannockburn red, the 2008 vintage (★★★★) is less compelling than the finely scented and flowing 2007 (★★★★★), but still rewarding. Ruby-hued, with a complex bouquet, it is mouthfilling and savoury, with strong cherry, plum, spice and nut flavours and ripe, supple tannins. Drink now or cellar.

Vintage	08	07	06	DRY $45 –V
WR	5	6	5	
Drink	10-14	10-14	10-12	

Konrad Marlborough Pinot Noir ★★★

The 2009 vintage (★★★☆) was estate-grown in the Waihopai Valley and at Foxes Island, in the Wairau Valley. Barrel-aged for 10 months, it is floral and mouthfilling, in a sturdy, sweet-fruited style with ripe plum and spice flavours, showing some savoury complexity.

Vintage	09	08	07	DRY $29 –V
WR	5	4	4	
Drink	11-14	10-14	10-11	

Koru Pinot Noir ★★★★★

This rare, distinguished wine flows from a tiny 1.1-hectare vineyard at the foot of the Wither Hills, near Blenheim, in Marlborough. The intensely varietal 2007 vintage (★★★★★) was French oak-matured and bottled unfined and unfiltered. Full, bright ruby, it is finely scented, mouthfilling, rich and supple. Very sweet-fruited, graceful and flowing, it has ripe cherry/plum flavours, deliciously deep, harmonious and silky-textured, in a lush, 'feminine' style of Pinot Noir, for drinking now or cellaring.

Vintage	07	06	05	04	DRY $78 AV
WR	7	7	7	6	
Drink	10-22	10-20	10-18	10-15	

Koura Bay Blue Duck Awatere Valley Marlborough Pinot Noir ★★★★

The latest vintages have been silky and sensuous. The 2008 (★★★☆) was estate-grown and matured for 11 months in French oak barriques. Floral, sweet-fruited and supple, it's a moderately complex wine with strong, vibrant cherry and plum flavours.

Vintage	08	07
WR	5	6
Drink	10-12	10-14

DRY $25 V+

Kumeu River Estate Pinot Noir ★★★☆

This West Auckland red is different to the floral, buoyant reds grown in the south – less overtly varietal, more savoury and 'red-winey'. The 2008 vintage (★★★☆) is lightish in colour, with earthy, 'forest floor' aromas. Mouthfilling and supple, it is cherryish, slightly spicy, earthy and nutty, with a smooth finish. It's enjoyable now.

Vintage	09	08	07	06	05	04	03	02
WR	7	6	7	7	5	NM	6	4
Drink	10-16	10-15	10-15	10-13	10-11	NM	P	P

DRY $36 –V

Kumeu River Village Pinot Noir ★★★

Estate-grown at Kumeu, in West Auckland, the 2009 vintage (★★★) is bright ruby, fresh, plummy and spicy, in a medium-bodied style, slightly savoury and earthy, with firm tannins. Drink 2011–12.

DRY $18 V+

Kurow Village Waitaki Valley Pinot Noir (★★★☆)

An ideal introduction to the North Otago region's reds, the 2008 vintage (★★★☆) is floral and supple, with good depth of ripe cherry and plum flavours, showing some complexity.

DRY $26 AV

Lake Hayes Central Otago Pinot Noir ★★★★

From Amisfield, the 2008 vintage (★★★★) was matured in French oak casks (20 per cent new). Full ruby, it is floral and vibrantly fruity, with fresh, generous cherry and plum flavours, some savoury complexity, and great drink-young appeal.

Vintage	09	08	07	06
WR	6	6	6	6
Drink	10-13	10-12	P	P

DRY $30 AV

La Strada Marlborough Pinot Noir ★★★★

Made by Fromm, this wine is designed to be ready for drinking upon release, by selecting suitable sites and clones, and 'steering the fermentation towards more fruit expression and moderate tannins and structure'. The 2007 vintage (★★★★) was matured for over a year in French oak barriques (10–20 per cent new). Full-bodied, savoury and supple, it has cherry and spice flavours, showing excellent ripeness, depth, complexity and harmony. It's delicious now.

Vintage	08	07	06	05	04
WR	7	7	7	6	6
Drink	11-15	10-14	10-13	10-12	10-11

DRY $35 AV

Latitude 41 New Zealand Pinot Noir ★★☆
From Spencer Hill, the 2008 vintage (★★☆) is a blend of Marlborough and Nelson grapes, fermented with indigenous yeasts and aged 'on' oak (meaning not barrel-aged). Light and slightly developed in colour, it has cherry, spice and slight herb flavours, with a touch of complexity and firm tannins, but leafy notes detract.

DRY $21 –V

Lawson's Dry Hills Marlborough Pinot Noir ★★★☆
The 2007 (★★★★) was hand-picked in the Brancott and Waihopai valleys, and matured in French oak barriques (25 per cent new). Fragrant, it has strong plum, cherry and spice flavours, showing some savoury complexity, and supple tannins. The 2008 vintage (★★★) is ruby-hued, with cherry, plum and spice flavours, seasoned with nutty oak, a hint of herbs and firm tannins.

Vintage	08	07	06
WR	6	7	5
Drink	10-12	10-12	P

DRY $29 AV

Leaning Rock Central Otago Pinot Noir ★★★☆
Estate-grown at Alexandra, the 2008 vintage (★★★☆) is full-bodied and sweet-fruited, with plummy, spicy flavours, showing some savoury, nutty complexity, and fairly firm tannins. It's still developing; open 2011–12.

DRY $35 –V

Leaning Rock Rise and Shine Central Otago Pinot Noir ★★★☆
Still on sale in 2010, this label is produced only in 'exceptional' years. The 2006 vintage (★★★☆), estate-grown at Alexandra, has earthy, 'forest floor' aromas, leading into a sturdy, sweet-fruited palate. Spicy and earthy, with fairly firm tannins, it's a slightly rustic wine, but full of personality.

DRY $40 –V

Lime Rock Pinot Noir ★★★☆
Grown in Central Hawke's Bay and matured in French oak casks, the 2008 vintage (★★★☆) has strong, fresh plum and spice flavours, showing good complexity and harmony. The 2009 (★★★☆) is similar – vibrant and flavoursome, cherryish and plummy, with good ripeness and roundness.

DRY $29 AV

Lime Rock White Knuckle Hill Pinot Noir (★★★★)
The debut 2007 vintage (★★★★) is Lime Rock's reserve wine, hand-harvested in Central Hawke's Bay from 'the tops of the hills and in the Secret Vineyard, where the soils are shallow'. French oak-aged for eight months, it is boldly coloured and notably powerful, with concentrated, lush, sweet-fruit flavours of plums and spices, some savoury oak complexity and obvious cellaring potential.

Vintage	07
WR	7
Drink	10-14

DRY $40 –V

Lindis River Central Otago Pinot Noir ★★★★

Grown in the Ardgour Valley, 5 kilometres north of Bendigo, the 2007 vintage (★★★★) is full of personality. Matured for 11 months in French oak casks (30 per cent new), it is savoury, supple and finely poised, with concentrated cherry, spice and slight herb flavours, showing good complexity. It's drinking well now.

DRY $35 AV

Lindis River One by One Central Otago Pinot Noir (★★★☆)

Barrel-aged for 18 months (longer than its stablemate, above), the 2006 vintage (★★★☆) is ruby-hued, with a hint of development. Released in April 2009, it's a savoury, spicy, slightly herbal and nutty red, ready now. (There is no 2007 or 2008.)

DRY $40 -V

Lobster Reef Marlborough Pinot Noir (★★★)

From Cape Campbell, the 2009 vintage (★★★) is a medium-bodied style, light ruby, with very smooth, ripe cherry/plum flavours, showing decent depth, and a touch of savoury, spicy complexity. Drink young.

DRY $19 AV

Locharburn Central Otago Pinot Noir ★★★☆

The 2008 (★★★☆) was hand-picked in the Cromwell Basin and matured for 10 months in French oak casks (30 per cent new). Floral and supple, with fresh, ripe sweet-fruit flavours of plums and spices, and a touch of savoury complexity, it's enjoyable now. Tasted prior to bottling (and so not rated), the 2009 is full-coloured, rich and supple, with cherry, plum and herb flavours, showing good density.

Vintage	08	07	06
WR	5	6	5
Drink	10-13	10-13	10-12

DRY $35 -V

Loopline Pinot Noir ★★★

Grown at Opaki, near Masterton, in the northern Wairarapa, the 2008 vintage (★★★☆) is promising. Still youthful, it is fragrant, with good colour depth and fresh cherry, spice and plum flavours, showing good complexity. Open mid-2011+.

DRY $26 -V

Lowburn Ferry Central Otago Pinot Noir ★★★★

Estate-grown at Lowburn, in the Cromwell Basin, the 2008 vintage (★★★★) was matured for 10 months in French oak barriques (20 per cent new). Full-flavoured and firmly structured, it is deeply coloured, with rich, ripe cherryish fruit flavours and a spicy, savoury complexity.

Vintage	08	07	06	05
WR	7	6	5	6
Drink	10-14	10-14	10-12	P

DRY $41 -V

Lowburn Ferry Single Vineyard Home Block Pinot Noir (★★★★)

The 2009 vintage (★★★★) was hand-picked at Lowburn, in Central Otago, and matured for nine months in French oak casks (34 per cent new). Deeply coloured and vibrantly fruity, with very generous plum and slight herb flavours, it shows excellent depth, harmony, structure and length.

DRY $48 –V

Lynfer Estate Wairarapa Pinot Noir (★★☆)

Grown at Gladstone, the 2009 vintage (★★☆) is a single-vineyard red, hand-picked and matured in seasoned barrels. Ruby-hued, it is smooth, with fresh, simple berry/plum flavours in a pleasant, drink-young style.

DRY $23 –V

Mahi Rive Vineyard Marlborough Pinot Noir ★★★★

The 2008 vintage (★★★★) was hand-picked at a relatively warm site at Rapaura, fermented with indigenous yeasts, barrel-aged for 15 months, and bottled unfiltered. Deeply coloured, it is slightly less rich than the highly concentrated 2007 (★★★★☆), but shows good complexity and texture, with mouthfilling body and strong, ripe cherry/plum flavours, smooth and savoury.

Vintage	08	07
WR	6	6
Drink	10-17	10-16

DRY $45 –V

Main Divide Canterbury Pinot Noir ★★★★

A consistently rewarding, drink-young style from Pegasus Bay. The 2008 vintage (★★★★) was fermented with indigenous yeasts and matured for a year in French oak barriques. It is full-coloured, very generous and well-rounded, with strong, ripe plum and spice flavours, oak complexity, and a seductively smooth finish. Fine value.

Vintage	08	07	06	05	04
WR	7	6	7	7	7
Drink	10-13	10-12	10-12	P	P

DRY $25 V+

Main Divide Tehau Reserve Waipara Valley Pinot Noir ★★★★☆

From Pegasus Bay, the 2008 vintage (★★★★) was matured for 18 months in French oak barriques (30 per cent new). A floral, deeply coloured red, it is sturdy, generous and sweet-fruited, with ripe cherry, plum and spice flavours, slightly nutty and savoury, and good complexity. It's already delicious; drink now or cellar.

Vintage	08	07	06
WR	7	6	5
Drink	10-15	10-15	10-13

DRY $33 V+

Main Divide Tipinui Selection Marlborough Pinot Noir ★★★★☆

From Pegasus Bay, the 2008 vintage (★★★★☆) was grown on clay slopes in the Brancott Valley, hand-picked, and matured for 18 months in French oak barriques (30 per cent new).

A fleshy, big-bodied red, it is fragrant and full-coloured, with generous, ripe cherry and plum flavours, a spicy, nutty complexity and lots of personality. Drink now or cellar.

Vintage	08	07	06
WR	7	6	7
Drink	10-16	10-15	10-13

DRY $33 V+

Ma Maison Martinborough Pinot Noir ★★★★☆

This rare wine from Leung Estate is based on close-planted, low-cropped vines planted in 1995. The 2007 (★★★★☆) is dark and fruit-crammed, with sweet-fruit delights and fresh, highly concentrated cherry, plum and slight liquorice flavours. The 2008 vintage (★★★★★) is outstanding. Deep and youthful in colour, it is very rich and sweet-fruited, with a wealth of plum, spice and nut flavours. Sturdy and finely textured, it's already delicious, but well worth cellaring.

DRY $35 V+

Ma Maison Martinborough Pinot Noir Cuvée Sabrina (★★★★☆)

Made from clone 5 Pinot Noir, matured in seasoned French oak barriques, and bottled unfined and unfiltered, the 2007 vintage (★★★★☆) is deeply coloured and fragrant, with very rich, vibrant cherry, plum, herb and slight liquorice flavours, threaded with fresh acidity. It's a classy, very graceful wine, ideal for cellaring.

DRY $70 –V

Ma Maison Martinborough Pinot Noir Cuvée Saffron (★★★★)

Based on the 10/5 clone, the 2007 vintage (★★★★) was matured for 11 months in French oak barriques of mixed ages, and bottled without fining or filtering. It's a concentrated, supple wine, deep and youthful in colour, with fresh, supple plum and slight herb flavours, showing good complexity.

DRY $70 –V

Manu Marlborough Pinot Noir ★★★

From Steve Bird, the 2009 vintage (★★★) was hand-picked on the south side of the Wairau Valley, fermented with indigenous yeasts, and barrel-aged for 10 months. Ruby-hued, floral and supple, with vibrant cherry/plum flavours, hints of herbs and spices, and a light oak seasoning, it's a drink-young charmer.

Vintage	09	08
WR	6	4
Drink	10-14	10-12

DRY $25 –V

Maori Point Central Otago Pinot Noir ★★★☆

Grown at Tarras, north of Lake Dunstan, the 2008 vintage (★★★) was fermented with indigenous yeasts and matured for 10 months in French oak barriques (33 per cent new). Maturing well, it is floral, with concentrated, cherryish, spicy flavours and a well-rounded finish. It's a finely textured wine, with some barnyard notes adding complexity.

Vintage	08
WR	5
Drink	10-14

DRY $29 AV

Map Maker Central Otago Pinot Noir (★★★☆)

From Staete Landt, the ruby-hued 2008 vintage (★★★☆) was grown at Bendigo and Pisa, in the Cromwell Basin, and French oak-matured for 10 months. Fresh strawberry and spice aromas lead into a mouthfilling, supple wine with ripe, moderately rich plum, cherry and spice flavours, showing some complexity, and finely balanced tannins.

Vintage	08
WR	6
Drink	10-12

DRY $29 AV

Marble Point Hanmer Springs Pinot Noir ★★★☆

From a high-altitude site in North Canterbury, the bright ruby 2008 vintage (★★★☆) was matured for 16 months in French oak casks (25 per cent new). Picked at over 24 brix and fermented with indigenous yeasts, it's delicious now – vibrant, cherryish and supple, with moderate concentration and some nutty complexity. The 2009 (★★★★) is a distinct step up, showing greater richness and stuffing. Full-coloured, it has very ripe flavours of plums, cherries, spices and liquorice, oak complexity, and a firm backbone of tannin. A powerful wine, to be released during 2011, it's best opened from 2012 onwards.

Vintage	09	08
WR	6	6
Drink	12-16	11-13

DRY 32 –V

Margrain Home Block Martinborough Pinot Noir ★★★★

Typically an impressive red, based on 'vines from our original plantings which surround the winery'. Matured for a year in French oak barriques, the 2008 vintage (★★★☆) is a mouthfilling, generous red, full-coloured, with strong cherry, plum and spice flavours, a hint of herbs and a firm finish.

Vintage	08	07	06	05	04	03	02
WR	6	7	7	7	7	7	6
Drink	10-16	10-17	10-15	10-14	10-12	P	P

DRY $52 –V

Margrain River's Edge Martinborough Pinot Noir ★★★

Designed for early drinking, the 2008 vintage (★★★), oak-aged for 10 months, was 'barrel selected for its smoothness and charm'. Light ruby, it is fresh and vibrant, with ripe cherry and plum flavours, a touch of oak complexity, and gentle tannins giving a well-rounded finish.

Vintage	09	08
WR	6	5
Drink	10-14	10-13

DRY $28 –V

Martinborough Vineyard Marie Zelie Reserve Pinot Noir ★★★★★
Only 984 bottles exist of the hedonistic 2006 vintage (★★★★★), the first since the arrestingly rich 2003 (★★★★★). From vines up to 26 years old (in 2006), it is a selection of the four best barrels, which were blended in January 2007, returned to older oak casks for a further eight months' aging, and bottled unfined and unfiltered. A very powerful wine, it is also full of charm, with deep colour and great ripeness and richness. Notably concentrated, with an array of plum, strawberry, liquorice and nut flavours, it is silky-textured, inviting current drinking, but still fresh and lively, with obvious potential. (The next vintage of Marie Zelie is 2008.)

DRY $180 –V

Martinborough Vineyard Pinot Noir ★★★★★
This was the first consistently distinguished Pinot Noir made in New Zealand. An intensely varietal wine, it is typically fragrant, with sweet-tasting fruit and cherryish, spicy, complex flavours. In the past, it impressed principally with fragrance and finesse, rather than sheer scale, but in recent years the wine has become markedly bolder. Grown on the shingly Martinborough Terrace, it is made from vines ranging from young to 30 years old, and matured for a year in French oak barriques (30 to 35 per cent new). Already quite open and expressive, the good but not great 2008 vintage (★★★★) has full, fairly youthful colour. It's a fragrant, concentrated wine with cherry and spice flavours, some herb and olive notes, and a savoury, 'forest floor' complexity. Drink now or cellar.

Vintage	08	07	06	05	04	03	02	01	00
WR	6	7	7	7	6	7	6	7	7
Drink	10-19	10-18	10-17	10-15	10-12	10-11	P	P	P

DRY $73 AV

Martinborough Vineyard Te Tera Pinot Noir ★★★★
Te Tera ('the other') is designed for earlier drinking than its famous big brother. Based on 'predominantly younger' vines on the Martinborough Terrace, it is hand-harvested, fermented with indigenous yeasts and matured for eight months in French oak casks (10 per cent new in 2009). The full-coloured 2009 vintage (★★★★) is an invitingly scented, full-coloured, fleshy red with very good depth of ripe plum, spice and herb flavours, and savoury, mushroomy notes adding complexity. It's a drink-young style with plenty of personality.

Vintage	09	08	07	06	05	04
WR	7	7	7	7	7	7
Drink	10-13	10-12	10-11	10-11	P	P

DRY $30 AV

Martinus Estate Martinborough Pinot Noir ★★★★☆
The 2007 vintage (★★★★), released in 2010, was matured for 11 months in French oak casks (25 per cent new). Deep and still fairly youthful in colour, it is full-bodied and concentrated, with fresh cherry, herb and spice flavours, showing good, savoury complexity. The 2008 (★★★★☆) is already delicious. Mouthfilling and sweet-fruited, with deep, youthful colour, it has cherry, plum and spice flavours, showing excellent complexity and richness.

DRY $40 AV

Matahiwi Estate Holly Wairarapa Pinot Noir ★★★☆

Maturing well, the 2008 vintage (★★★★) was grown in the northern Wairarapa and matured in French oak casks (35 per cent new). Still youthful, it's a richly coloured wine with a fragrant, savoury bouquet and good concentration of red-berry, spice and nutty oak flavours. Worth cellaring.

Vintage	08
WR	6
Drink	10-13

DRY $33 –V

Matahiwi Estate Wairarapa Pinot Noir ★★★

The 2008 vintage (★★★☆) has strong drink-young appeal. Bright ruby, with a floral bouquet, it is vibrantly fruity, with good depth of fresh cherry and plum flavours, a subtle twist of oak, gentle tannins and a well-rounded finish.

DRY $25 –V

Matakana Estate Marlborough Pinot Noir ★★★☆

The 2009 vintage (★★★☆) was matured for 10 months in mostly French oak barriques (one-third new). A mouthfilling, ruby-hued, moderately concentrated wine, it's already drinking well, with ripe cherry, plum and spice flavours, savoury and supple.

DRY $32 –V

Matariki Hawke's Bay Pinot Noir ★★★☆

The 2007 vintage (★★★☆) was hand-picked and matured for nine months in French oak barriques (32 per cent new). Ruby-hued and floral, with concentrated, fresh, ripe, spicy flavours and a moderately firm finish, it shows good warmth and complexity.

Vintage	07	06
WR	6	5
Drink	10-12	P

DRY $30 –V

Matua Valley Innovator Central Otago Pinot Noir (★★★)

The ruby-hued, mouthfilling 2007 vintage (★★★) was grown at Gibbston and matured in French oak barriques (35 per cent new). Vibrant, cherryish, plummy and spicy, with fresh acidity, it's a moderately concentrated style, balanced for easy drinking.

DRY $25 –V

Matua Valley Innovator Waimauku Pinot Noir (★★★)

A rare example of Auckland Pinot Noir, the 2007 vintage (★★★) was estate-grown in West Auckland and matured in French oak barriques (20 per cent new). Deeply coloured, it is plummy and spicy, with fresh acidity and a seasoning of toasty oak. A medium to full-bodied style, it's only moderately varietal, but flavoursome and still developing.

DRY $25 –V

Matua Valley Marlborough Pinot Noir ★★☆

The 2009 vintage (★★☆), on sale at less than a year old, is ruby-hued, floral and supple, with fresh, ripe, berryish flavours, skilfully balanced for easy drinking.

DRY $16 AV

Matua Valley Reserve Release Central Otago Pinot Noir (★★★)

Ruby-hued, with good depth of cherry, spice and slight herb flavours, the 2008 vintage (★★★) is a vibrantly fruity, smooth red, with lots of drink-young charm.

DRY $22 AV

Maude Central Otago Pinot Noir ★★★★

The 2008 vintage (★★★★) is bright ruby, with ripe, sweet-fruit characters, very good depth of cherry, plum and spice flavours, showing some nutty complexity, and a firm tannin backbone. The 2009 (★★★★☆) is a blend of grapes from four sub-regions, matured for a year in French oak casks (35 per cent new). Delicious from the start, it is full-coloured, floral and supple, with concentrated plum and spice flavours, sweet-fruited and finely textured. A savoury, very harmonious wine with a silky charm, it's a drink-now or cellaring proposition.

Vintage	07	06
WR	6	5
Drink	10-16	10-15

DRY $32 AV

Maude Mt Maude Family Vineyard Central Otago Pinot Noir ★★★★☆

Developing well, the 2007 vintage (★★★★☆) was based on 16-year-old vines at Wanaka and matured for 18 months in French oak casks (40 per cent new). Dark, with plum and spice flavours, it shows excellent density. A 'serious', savoury, tightly structured wine, starting to round out, it's revealing impressive complexity with bottle-age and drinking well now.

Vintage	07
WR	6
Drink	10-16

DRY $49 –V

Maven Marlborough Pinot Noir ★★★

The 2008 vintage (★★☆) was grown at Rapaura and in the Wairau's southern valleys. Lightish in colour, with a hint of development, it's an easy-drinking style with solid depth of cherry and spice flavours and gentle tannins. Ready.

DRY $24 AV

Michelle Richardson Central Otago Pinot Noir ★★★★☆

The 2007 vintage (★★★★☆) was grown at Cromwell Basin sites, on both sides of Lake Dunstan, fermented with indigenous yeasts and matured for 11 months in French oak barriques (35 per cent new). Enticingly floral, with deep, youthful colour, it has rich, vibrant cherry and plum flavours, with a subtle seasoning of spicy oak. A 'feminine' style, very harmonious, supple and finely textured, it's maturing gracefully; drink now or cellar.

Vintage	07	06
WR	6	6
Drink	10-15	P

DRY $49 –V

Mill Road Hawke's Bay Pinot Noir ★★

From Morton Estate, the non-vintage wine (★★☆) on sale in 2010 is ruby-hued, full-bodied and smooth, with decent depth of moderately youthful, ripe plum and spice flavours. Priced right.

DRY $14 AV

Millton Clos de Ste Anne Naboth's Vineyard Pinot Noir
– see Clos de Ste Anne Naboth's Vineyard Pinot Noir

Millton Gisborne Pinot Noir (★★★)

Grown in the La Cote section of Clos de Ste Anne, the 2008 vintage (★★★) is organically certified. Ruby-hued, it has clearly varietal, strawberry and spice flavours, with a touch of savoury complexity.

DRY $22 AV

Misha's Vineyard The Audition Central Otago Pinot Noir (★★★★☆)

Grown at Bendigo, the 2007 vintage (★★★★☆) is a single-vineyard wine, hand-picked at over 24 brix, fermented with indigenous yeasts, matured in French oak hogsheads (100 per cent new), and bottled without fining or filtration. Deep ruby, it is finely scented and savoury, with sweet-fruit characters and strong cherry, plum and spice flavours, underpinned by fairly firm tannins. A fine debut, it's a complex, harmonious red, for drinking now or cellaring.

DRY $45 –V

Misha's Vineyard The High Note Central Otago Pinot Noir (★★★★)

Estate-grown at Bendigo, the 2008 vintage (★★★★) was hand-picked at 23.5 to 25 brix, fermented with indigenous yeasts and matured in French oak hogsheads (34 per cent new). Ruby-hued, it is savoury and complex, with berry, spice and herb flavours, showing good density, and a rounded finish.

Vintage	08
WR	6
Drink	10-14

DRY $45 –V

Misha's Vineyard Verismo Central Otago Pinot Noir (★★★★☆)

The poised, youthful 2008 vintage (★★★★☆) was estate-grown at Bendigo and matured for 15 months in French oak hogsheads (62 per cent new). Ruby-hued, it is vibrantly fruity, plummy and savoury, very sweet-fruited and supple, in a notably elegant style, worth cellaring to 2012+.

Vintage	08
WR	6
Drink	11-16

DRY $60 –V

Mission Reserve Central Otago Pinot Noir ★★★★

(Note: the word 'Reserve' appears only on the back label.) The 2008 vintage (★★★★) was hand-picked at Pisa, in the Cromwell Basin, and matured in French oak barrels (21 per cent new). Full-coloured, it is mouthfilling, graceful and flowing, with ripe cherry and plum flavours, showing excellent concentration and complexity.

Vintage	09	08	07
WR	6	6	5
Drink	11-17	11-18	10-16

DRY $25 V+

Mitre Rocks Central Otago Pinot Noir ★★★★☆

Estate-grown at Parkburn, in the Cromwell Basin, the 2008 vintage (★★★★★) is polished and refined. Harvested at 25 brix, it was matured for a year in French oak barriques (60 per cent new). Full-coloured and perfumed, with concentrated cherry, plum and nut flavours, beautifully ripe, rich and rounded, it's a skilfully crafted wine, very elegant and age-worthy.

Vintage	08	07	06
WR	7	7	6
Drink	10-17	10-15	10-14

DRY $38 V+

Moana Park Vineyard Tribute Altitude Pinot Noir (★★★)

Grown in Central Hawke's Bay, the 2009 vintage (★★★) was matured in French oak casks (45 per cent new). It's a supple wine with cherry and herb flavours, showing good, savoury complexity.

DRY $30 –V

Momo Marlborough Pinot Noir ★★★☆

A drink-young style from Seresin, the 2008 vintage (★★★) was fermented with indigenous yeasts and matured for 11 months in French oak barriques. Ruby-hued, with moderate depth of cherry, herb and spice flavours showing some savoury complexity and gentle tannins, it shows good varietal character and some muscle.

Vintage	08	07	06
WR	5	7	6
Drink	10-13	10-15	P

DRY $27 AV

Moncellier Central Otago Pinot Noir (★★★)

The softly mouthfilling 2008 vintage (★★★) was harvested at over 24 brix, fermented with indigenous yeasts and matured for 10 months in barrels (25 per cent new). Ruby-hued, it's a very easy-drinking style, with moderately concentrated cherry, plum and spice flavours, ripe and supple.

Vintage	08
WR	5
Drink	10-14

DRY $34 –V

Mondillo Central Otago Pinot Noir ★★★★★

An emerging star. This consistently striking red is grown in a Bendigo vineyard owned by Domenic Mondillo, viticulturist for Gibbston Valley, and made by Rudi Bauer. The 2009 vintage (★★★★★) was matured in French oak barriques (30 per cent new). Invitingly deep in colour, it is beautifully perfumed, mouthfilling, sweet-fruited and supple. An almost hedonistic wine, it has a compelling richness of cherry, plum and spice flavours, finely balanced oak, and silky, ripe tannins.

Vintage	09	08	07	06	05	04
WR	7	7	7	6	7	5
Drink	10-15	10-14	10-13	10-12	10-12	P

DRY $40 V+

Monowai Crownthorpe Pinot Noir ★★★☆

The 2007 vintage (★★★☆) was estate-grown in inland Hawke's Bay, hand-picked, and matured for a year in French (90 per cent) and Hungarian oak barrels. It is full-coloured, fruity and supple, with good depth of strawberry, cherry and plum flavours, and toasty, slightly earthy notes adding complexity. Good value.

DRY $22 V+

Montana Living Land Series Marlborough Pinot Noir (★★★★)

The debut 2009 vintage (★★★★) is a wonderful buy. From vines in conversion to organic production, it was grown on the south side of the Wairau Valley, barrel-matured for nine months (in French and Hungarian oak) and bottled unfined. Fragrant and full-bodied, it has sweet-fruit delights, ripe plum and spice flavours, gentle tannins, and more complexity than you'd expect at its modest price. Already delicious.

DRY $20 V+

Montana Reserve Marlborough Pinot Noir ★★★☆

The 2007 vintage (★★★☆) is immediately appealing, with very good depth of ripe cherry, plum and spice flavours, vibrant and supple.

Vintage	07	06
WR	6	6
Drink	P	P

DRY $28 AV

Montana South Island Pinot Noir ★★★

Since 2006, this multi-region blend has replaced the former Montana Marlborough Pinot Noir. Grown in Marlborough, Waipara and Central Otago, it is matured in stainless steel tanks, large oak cuves and French and European oak barriques. The 2008 vintage (★★★) is enjoyable young, with gentle tannins and good depth of fresh, smooth plum and slight herb flavours.

DRY $21 AV

Montana 'T' Terraces Estate Marlborough Pinot Noir ★★★★☆

Pernod Ricard NZ's flagship Pinot Noir was in 2007 (★★★★★) grown in the Wairau Valley, mostly at Brancott Estate, hand-harvested at over 24 brix, and matured for 10 months in French oak barriques (39 per cent new). A lovely wine, deeply coloured and strikingly perfumed, rich and silky, it has vibrant plum/cherry flavours, showing excellent concentration, warmth, complexity and suppleness. (For the 2008 vintage, see Brancott Estate.)

DRY $41 AV

Montana Terroir Series Forgotten Valley Marlborough Pinot Noir ★★★★★

Forgotten Valley is an offshoot of the Brancott Valley. The 2007 vintage (★★★★★) is a highly attractive red, weighty, with rich cherry and plum flavours, seasoned with toasty oak. It's an impressively dense wine, finely textured and fragrant.

Vintage	07	06
WR	6	6
Drink	P	P

DRY $31 V+

Montana Terroir Series Gabriel's Gully Central Otago Pinot Noir ★★★★

Grown at Bendigo, in the Cromwell Basin, the 2007 vintage (★★★★) is vibrant and supple, with full colour and concentrated, ripe flavours of plums and spices, showing good texture and complexity.

Vintage	07	06
WR	7	7
Drink	P	P

DRY $31 AV

Morton Estate Black Label Marlborough Pinot Noir ★★★

The 2007 vintage (★★★), from the Stone Creek Vineyard, is full-coloured, mouthfilling and supple, with cherryish, nutty, moderately concentrated flavours, fresh and savoury.

Vintage	07
WR	7
Drink	10-14

DRY $35 –V

Morton Estate Stone Creek Marlborough Pinot Noir ★★★

The 2007 vintage (★★★) has strong, moderately ripe, plummy flavours, woven with fresh acidity, and a hint of herbs. Best drinking 2011.

Vintage	07	06
WR	7	6
Drink	10-12	10-12

DRY $22 AV

Morton Estate White Label Hawke's Bay Pinot Noir ★★☆

The 2007 vintage (★★☆) is ruby-hued and mouthfilling (14.5 per cent alcohol) in a relatively warm-climate style, spicy, berryish and firm. Ready.

Vintage	07
WR	6
Drink	10-12

DRY $19 –V

Morton Estate White Label Marlborough Pinot Noir ★★☆

The 2008 vintage (★★☆) has lightish, slightly developed colour. It's an easy-drinking red with plum, spice and herb flavours, fresh and smooth. Ready.

Vintage	08	07
WR	6	7
Drink	10-12	10-12

DRY $19 –V

Mountain Road Taranaki Pinot Noir ★★★

From vines planted near Waitara in 2004, the 2009 vintage (★★★☆) was matured for 11 months in seasoned French oak casks. Already drinking well, it is ruby-hued, sweet-fruited and supple, with fresh, cherryish flavours, some fungal and herbal notes, gentle tannins, and strong drink-young appeal. Well worth discovering.

DRY $30 –V

Mount Dottrel Central Otago Pinot Noir ★★★★

Estate-grown at Parkburn, in the Cromwell Basin, this is the second label of Mitre Rocks. The 2008 vintage (★★★★) was harvested at 25 brix and matured for 10 months in French oak barrels (30 per cent new). Floral and vibrantly fruity, with strong, ripe cherry/plum flavours seasoned with quality oak, a hint of herbs, considerable complexity and a rounded, very harmonious finish, it's drinking well now.

Vintage	08	07	06	05
WR	6	7	6	5
Drink	10-14	10-15	10-12	P

DRY $33 AV

Mount Edward Central Otago Pinot Noir ★★★★☆

The 2007 vintage (★★★★★) is deeply coloured, in a mouthfilling, savoury, complex style with rich, plummy, spicy flavours and a deliciously silky texture.

Vintage	07	06	05	04	03	02
WR	6	6	6	6	6	7
Drink	10-14	10-13	10-12	10-11	P	P

DRY $45 –V

Mount Edward Morrison Vineyard Pinot Noir (★★★★★)

The debut 2007 vintage (★★★★★) of this Central Otago red is deeply coloured and powerful, in a voluptuous style, lush and soft, with deep cherry, plum, spice and liquorice flavours, concentrated and silky. It was grown in the company's vineyard at Lowburn.

DRY $65 AV

Mount Edward Muirkirk Pinot Noir (★★★★★)

From Bannockburn, in Central Otago, the 2008 vintage (★★★★★) is mouthfilling, richly coloured, layered and supple, with very sweet fruit characters and strong cherry, plum and spice flavours, showing lovely texture, complexity and harmony. Savoury and seamless, it's well worth cellaring.

DRY $65 AV

Mount Fishtail Marlborough Pinot Noir ★★★

From Konrad, the 2009 vintage (★★★) was French oak-aged for 10 months. Floral, fruity, ripe and supple, it is ruby-hued, with plum, berry and spice flavours, a touch of savoury complexity and drink-young charm.

Vintage	09	08
WR	5	3
Drink	10-13	10-14

DRY $20 AV

Mount Michael Bessie's Block Pinot Noir ★★★★

A single-vineyard red, grown at Cromwell, in Central Otago, the 2007 vintage (★★★★) is a supple wine with ripe cherry, plum and spice flavours, a subtle oak influence, gentle tannins and some savoury complexity.

DRY $39 AV

Mount Michael Central Otago Pinot Noir ★★★

The 2007 vintage (★★★) is an easy-drinking style, full-coloured, with plum, spice and herb flavours, fresh acidity and a smooth finish.

DRY $29 –V

Mount Riley Limited Release Marlborough Pinot Noir (★★★★)

The 2008 vintage (★★★★) was hand-picked, fermented with indigenous yeasts, and matured in French oak casks (30 per cent new). Sweet-fruited, scented and silky, with cherry, spice and herb flavours, it shows good concentration, complexity and charm.

DRY $25 V+

Mount Riley Marlborough Pinot Noir ★★★

The 2009 vintage (★★★) was matured for nine months in French oak casks. Ruby-hued, it is fresh and supple, with cherry and plum flavours, not concentrated, but offering good varietal character and drink-young appeal.

DRY $22 AV

Mount Riley Seventeen Valley Marlborough Pinot Noir ★★★☆

Hand-picked in the company's Seventeen Valley Vineyard, south of Blenheim, the 2007 vintage (★★★) is full-bodied, spicy, savoury and supple, with a seasoning of nutty French oak. It's a complex style, but green-edged, with considerable development showing. Ready.

Vintage	07	06
WR	5	7
Drink	P	P

DRY $37 –V

Moutere Hills New Zealand Pinot Noir ★★★

The 2007 vintage (★★★☆) is a ruby-hued red, barrel-aged for 11 months. Floral, fruity and supple, it's a mid-weight style with sweet-fruit charm and cherry/plum flavours showing good depth and some savoury complexity.

DRY $40 –V

Mt Beautiful North Canterbury Pinot Noir ★★★☆

The 2008 vintage (★★★☆) was hand-picked in the Cheviot Hills, north of Waipara, and matured for 11 months in French oak barriques (30 per cent new). A medium-bodied, richly varietal wine, it is light ruby, with cherry, plum and slight herb flavours. Supple and savoury, with some earthy complexity, it is already drinking well.

DRY $33 –V

Mt Campbell Nelson Pinot Noir (★★☆)

From Anchorage, the 2009 vintage (★★☆) is a ruby-hued red with fresh cherry, spice and plum flavours. Slightly leafy, with moderate depth, it's a pleasant, early-drinking style.

DRY $18 AV

Mt Difficulty Central Otago Pinot Noir ★★★★

This popular red is grown entirely at Bannockburn. The 2008 vintage (★★★★), matured for a year in French oak barriques, is weighty and supple, with full, ruby colour and a floral, spicy bouquet. It's an instantly appealing wine, savoury, sweet-fruited and supple, with vibrant cherry, plum and spice flavours, showing excellent depth and complexity.

Vintage	08	07	06
WR	6	7	7
Drink	11-16	11-16	10-14

DRY $45 –V

Mt Difficulty Roaring Meg Pinot Noir ★★★☆

Grown in the Cromwell Basin (but not entirely at Bannockburn, unlike its stablemate, above) and French oak-aged for nine months, the 2008 vintage (★★★☆) is floral, supple and sweet-fruited, with fresh, ripe cherry/plum flavours, gently seasoned with toasty oak, and some savoury complexity. It's a delicious drink-young style.

Vintage	08	07	06
WR	6	7	7
Drink	10-13	10-13	P

DRY $28 AV

Mt Difficulty Single Vineyard Long Gully Central Otago Pinot Noir (★★★★☆)

From a vineyard that supplies core fruit for the Mt Difficulty Central Otago Pinot Noir label, this is a more 'feminine' style than its Pipeclay Terrace stablemate (below). The 2007 vintage (★★★★★) matured for 18 months in French oak barriques, is very floral and supple, with lovely, sweet-fruit flavours of cherries and plums, ripe and silky-smooth. It's delicious now.

Vintage	07
WR	7
Drink	10-20

DRY $90 –V

Mt Difficulty Single Vineyard Pipeclay Terrace Pinot Noir ★★★★★

A powerful, lush Central Otago red with densely packed, cherryish, plummy flavours, spicy and long. It is grown on a steep, relatively hot slope at Bannockburn, with bony, gravelly soils. The full-coloured 2007 (★★★★☆), matured for 14 months in French oak barriques, was bottled unfined and unfiltered. Described by the winery as 'distinctively masculine', it is sturdy, very ripe and sweet-fruited, with a strong surge of plum, spice and liquorice flavours, braced by firm tannins.

Vintage	07	06	05
WR	7	NM	7
Drink	10-20	NM	11-17

DRY $90 AV

Mt Hector Wairarapa Pinot Noir (★★★)

From Matahiwi, the 2009 vintage (★★★) is a very attractive, drink-young style. Fragrant and supple, it has fresh, ripe plum and slight herb flavours, showing good depth, and a well-rounded finish.

DRY $17 V+

Mt Rosa Central Otago Pinot Noir ★★★☆

Grown at Gibbston, the 2009 vintage (★★★) is a single-vineyard red French oak-matured. Showing full, slightly developed colour, it has a distinctly leafy streak, but also offers plenty of flavour.

DRY $31 –V

Mt Rosa Reserve Central Otago Pinot Noir ★★★★

Drinking well now, the 2007 vintage (★★★★) is a single-vineyard Gibbston red, matured in French oak barriques (mostly new). Full-coloured, it is weighty and rich, with concentrated cherry, plum and herb flavours, complex, savoury and supple.

DRY $45 –V

Muddy Water Hare's Breath Pinot Noir ★★★★

From 'a block on limestone slopes at the back of the property', the 2008 (★★★★☆) was hand-picked at Waipara, fermented with indigenous yeasts, and matured for 16 months in French oak barriques (40 per cent new). The best vintage yet, it is fragrant and generous, with full, bright ruby colour, rich, ripe plum and spice flavours, complex and savoury, and the tannin structure to age.

Vintage	08	07	06
WR	7	7	7
Drink	10-24	10-15	10-12

DRY $60 –V

Muddy Water Slowhand Pinot Noir ★★★★★

Since 2006 (★★★★★), this label has replaced Mojo as the Waipara winery's top red. Based on the oldest vines (clone 10/5), 'tended by slow hands', it always reveals outstanding personality. Hand-picked at 24.7 to 25.4 brix from ultra low-yielding vines (2.2 tonnes/hectare), and fermented with indigenous yeasts, the outstanding 2007 vintage (★★★★★) was matured for 16 months in French oak barriques (30 per cent new). Rich and youthful in colour, it is dense, savoury and silky, with cherry, spice and herb flavour showing lovely depth, flow and complexity. An exciting mouthful.

Vintage	07
WR	7
Drink	10-15

DRY $65 AV

Muddy Water Waipara Pinot Noir ★★★★☆

The 2008 vintage (★★★★) was hand-picked, fermented with indigenous yeasts and matured for 14 months in French oak barriques (30 per cent new). Ruby-hued, it's a harmonious, very skilfully balanced wine with sweet-fruit delights, cherry, plum and spice flavours, a savoury complexity and silky tannins. Moderately concentrated, it rests its case on finesse rather than power, offering delicious drinking now onwards.

Vintage	08	07
WR	7	7
Drink	10-21	10-15

DRY $40 AV

Mud House Central Otago Pinot Noir ★★★

The 2009 vintage (★★★), grown at Bendigo and partly oak-aged, is a fruit-driven style with fresh cherry and herb flavours, not complex but showing good depth.

DRY $25 –V

Mud House Marlborough Pinot Noir (★★★)

The 2008 vintage (★★★) is a fruit-driven style with vibrant cherry and spice flavours, fresh and supple.

DRY $27 –V

Mud House Swan Central Otago Pinot Noir ★★★★

Grown at Bendigo, in the Cromwell Basin, the fruit-packed, supple 2009 vintage (★★★★) was hand-picked and matured in French oak casks (30 per cent new). Deeply coloured, it has good weight and strong, ripe, youthful flavours of plums and spices.

DRY $29 V+

Murdoch James Blue Rock Martinborough Pinot Noir ★★★☆

Estate-grown south of the township, the 2008 vintage (★★★) has full, slightly developed colour. It shows some nutty, savoury complexity, although green, leafy notes detract.

DRY $34 –V

Murdoch James Fraser Pinot Noir ★★★☆

Earlier vintages were a single-vineyard red, grown on the Martinborough Terrace, but the 2008 (★★★) is a blend of the 'very best barrels'. Matured in French oak casks (80 per cent new), it is full-coloured, with mouthfilling body and plenty of spicy, nutty, slightly leafy flavour.

DRY $65 –V

Murdoch James Pinot Noir ★★★

The 2008 vintage (★★☆) was blended from grapes grown in Martinborough and other parts of the Wairarapa (although the only front-label references are to Martinborough). Oak-aged for 10 months, it has light, slightly developed colour and fresh, simple berry, spice and herb flavours. Drink young.

Vintage	08	07	06	05	04
WR	6	5	5	4	5
Drink	10-12	10-11	P	P	P

DRY $25 –V

Murrays Road Marlborough Pinot Noir (★★★)

Showing some development, the 2008 vintage (★★★) was barrel-aged for 10 months. A fruity, ruby-hued red, it has plum, spice and slight herb flavours, a touch of complexity and a firm finish.

Vintage	08
WR	5
Drink	10-12

DRY $30 –V

Nanny Goat Vineyard Central Otago Pinot Noir ★★★☆

The 2008 vintage (★★★☆) was grown at Gibbston and matured in oak casks (20 per cent new). Floral, ruby-hued and supple, it is moderately concentrated, with ripe cherry and plum flavours, showing some savoury complexity, and lots of drink-young charm.

DRY $32 –V

Nautilus Four Barriques Marlborough Pinot Noir ★★★★★

The 2007 vintage (★★★★★) was made from four casks chosen from over 120 for 'that special magic'. A blend of three barrels, estate-grown in the Clay Hills Vineyard in the Omaka Valley, and one barrel from the company-owned Kaituna Vineyard, on the north side of the Wairau River, it is rich and youthful in colour, beautifully scented and supple, with lovely fruit sweetness, dense cherry and plum flavours, and great harmony.

Vintage	07	06	05
WR	7	7	7
Drink	10-16	10-16	10-15

DRY $60 AV

Nautilus Marlborough Pinot Noir ★★★★

The 2009 vintage (★★★★☆) was sourced mostly from clay slopes on the south side of the Wairau Valley. Hand-picked and matured for 11 months in French oak barriques (30 per cent new), it is deep ruby, savoury and supple, with strong, ripe cherry, spice and nut flavours, showing good complexity and texture. Sweet-fruited and concentrated, it's built to last; open 2012+.

Vintage	09	08	07	06	05	04	03	02
WR	7	6	7	6	7	6	6	5
Drink	11-15	10-14	10-13	10-12	10-11	P	P	P

DRY $39 AV

Ned, The, Marlborough Pinot Noir ★★★☆

Grown in the Waihopai Valley, this is typically a full-coloured, mouthfilling red with plum, spice and slight herb flavours, generous and supple.

DRY $27 AV

Nest, The, Marlborough Pinot Noir (★★☆)

From Lake Chalice, the debut 2008 vintage (★★☆) was estate-grown in the Wairau and lower Waihopai valleys, and matured for eight months in French oak barrels. Ruby-hued, it's a lightweight style, fruity and supple, with drink-young appeal.

DRY $20 –V

Neudorf Moutere Home Vineyard Pinot Noir ★★★★★

Neudorf's flagship red is based principally on a block of clone 5 Pinot Noir vines, over 20 years old, in the original estate vineyard at Upper Moutere, in Nelson. The wine is fermented with indigenous yeasts, matured in French oak barriques (usually 35 to 40 per cent new), and is bottled without fining or filtration. The 2006 vintage (★★★★★) is maturing very gracefully. The bouquet is highly perfumed, savoury and nutty; the palate is sensuous and silky, with an array of cherry, spice, herb and slight dark chocolate flavours, showing considerable backbone and muscle. It's lovely now. (There is no 2007.)

Vintage	07	06	05	04	03	02	01
WR	NM	6	7	NM	7	6	7
Drink	NM	10-15	10-14	NM	10-14	10-12	P

DRY $69 AV

Neudorf Moutere Pinot Noir ★★★★★

Typically a very classy Nelson red. It is hand-picked at Upper Moutere, in the Neudorf home vineyard and the tiny Pomona Vineyard, where the AM 10/5 vines are over 20 years old. The wine is fermented with indigenous yeasts, matured for about 10 months in French oak barriques (20 to 40 per cent new), and is usually bottled without fining or filtering. The 2008 vintage (★★★★★) was hand-picked at 22.7 to 25.2 brix. Fragrant and softly mouthfilling, it is deep and youthful in colour, with a very complex array of strawberry, spice, herb and nut flavours that build to a rich finish. Very generous, savoury and harmonious, it's already drinking well.

Vintage	08	07	06	05	04	03	02	01	00
WR	6	6	7	7	6	7	6	7	6
Drink	10-17	10-16	10-15	10-14	10-12	10-13	10-12	10-11	P

DRY $49 AV

Neudorf Tom's Block Nelson Pinot Noir ★★★★☆

This regional blend offers great value. The 2007 vintage (★★★★★), grown at Upper Moutere and Brightwater, on the Waimea Plains, was hand-harvested, fermented with indigenous yeasts, matured for 11 months in French oak barriques (26 per cent new), and bottled unfined and unfiltered. Floral and finely textured, it is mouthfilling, savoury and supple, with rich, ripe cherry and spice flavours, showing excellent complexity, and lovely harmony.

Vintage	08	07	06	05
WR	6	6	7	7
Drink	10-15	10-14	10-13	10-13

DRY $31 V+

Nevis Bluff Central Otago Pinot Noir ★★★☆

The attractively perfumed 2008 vintage (★★★★) was matured in French oak barriques (25 per cent new). It's a generous wine, already delicious, with full colour and strong plum and spice flavours. Sweet-fruited and savoury, it's a finely textured wine with good complexity and harmony.

Vintage	08
WR	5
Drink	11-15

DRY $48 –V

Nevis Bluff Reserve Central Otago Pinot Noir (★★★★☆)

The debut 2006 vintage (★★★★☆) was based on 14-year-old vines at Gibbston and younger vines at Pisa, in the Cromwell Basin, harvested at an average of 25 brix. Matured for 18 months in French oak barrels (half new), it's a ripe, sweet-fruited red with concentrated cherry and plum flavours, seasoned with nutty oak, good complexity and a well-rounded finish.

Vintage	06
WR	6
Drink	10-15

DRY $85 –V

Ngatarawa Silks Hawke's Bay Pinot Noir ★★☆

This is the least impressive wine in the Silks range. The 2007 vintage (★★★) is enjoyable, with smooth cherry, herb and nut flavours, showing some savoury complexity. The 2008 (★★) is light and plain.

Vintage	07	06	05
WR	6	5	5
Drink	P	P	P

DRY $20 –V

Nga Waka Martinborough Pinot Noir ★★★★

The latest vintages are the best yet. The 2008 (★★★★) is mouthfilling and savoury, with good density of ripe cherry, spice, nut and herb flavours, oak complexity and finely balanced tannins. The instantly attractive 2009 (★★★★☆) is full-bodied, vibrant and sweet-fruited, with lovely depth and texture. Full-coloured, it is very generous and smooth-flowing, offering excellent drinking mid-2011+.

Vintage	09	08	07	06	05
WR	6	7	6	7	NM
Drink	10+	10+	10+	P	NM

DRY $35 AV

Night Owl Central Otago Pinot Noir (★★★)

A drink-young style, the 2008 vintage (★★★) is vibrantly fruity and supple, with fresh cherry and herb flavours, showing satisfying depth, a touch of complexity and a well-rounded finish.

DRY $23 AV

Nobilo Icon Marlborough Pinot Noir ★★★☆

The 2007 vintage (★★★) is vibrantly fruity, with plum, cherry and spice flavours, strong and smooth.

DRY $23 V+

Northburn Station Bill's Blend Lot 2 Pinot Noir (★★★☆)

The 2008 vintage (★★★☆), grown at Northburn, in the Cromwell Basin, in Central Otago, was matured in French oak barrels (15 per cent new). A fruity, drink-young charmer, it shows good depth of very ripe cherry/plum flavours, gentle tannins and a well-rounded finish.

DRY $30 –V

Northburn Station Central Otago Pinot Noir ★★★★

Grown at Northburn, in the Cromwell Basin, the 2008 vintage (★★★★☆) was matured in French oak barriques (35 per cent new). It is full-coloured and fragrant, ripe, spicy and savoury, with a firm backbone of tannin and excellent complexity and density.

DRY $40 –V

Vintage	08	07	06
WR	5	6	6
Drink	11-14	10-13	10-12

Northfield Home Creek Vineyard Waipara Pinot Noir ★★★

Matured for 10 months in French oak barriques (25 per cent new), the 2009 vintage (★★★☆) is ripely fragrant and mouthfilling, with plum and spice flavours showing good depth, fairly firm tannins and considerable complexity. Drink now to 2012.

DRY $25 –V

Odyssey Marlborough Pinot Noir ★★★★

This single-vineyard red is estate-grown and hand-picked in the Brancott Valley and matured in French oak barriques (30 per cent new in 2008). The 2008 vintage (★★★★) is deeply coloured, with a floral, spicy bouquet. Mouthfilling, with sweet-fruit characters and generous cherry/spice flavours, it is still fresh and youthful, with firm tannins, and likely to be long-lived.

DRY $32 AV

Vintage	08	07	06
WR	6	6	7
Drink	10-15	10-13	10-12

Old Coach Road Nelson Pinot Noir ★★☆

From Seifried, the 2009 vintage (★★☆) was matured for eight months in French oak barriques (new to three years old). Ruby-hued, it has moderate depth of cherry and plum flavours, and a green-edged finish. Drink young.

DRY $17 AV

Vintage	09
WR	7
Drink	10-13

Olssen's Jackson Barry Pinot Noir ★★★★

This is the Central Otago winery's middle-tier red, usually impressive. Estate-grown at Bannockburn, the 2009 vintage (★★★★) was matured in French oak barriques (39 per cent new). Deeply coloured, it is concentrated, with ripe cherry and spice flavours, showing excellent texture, complexity and harmony.

DRY $46 –V

Vintage	09	08	07	06
WR	6	5	6	6
Drink	18-20	10-15	10-17	10-17

Olssen's Slapjack Creek Reserve Pinot Noir ★★★★★

The top label from the longest-established Bannockburn, Central Otago winery is 'made from a careful selection of barrels in those years when the wine is of distinctly superior quality'. The

2007 vintage (★★★★★) was matured for 10 months in French oak barriques (37 per cent new). Densely coloured, it is a complex and generous red with sweet-fruit delights, substantial body (over 14 per cent alcohol), and plum, spice and nut flavours showing great depth.

Vintage	07
WR	6
Drink	10-17

DRY $85 –V

Omaka Springs Falveys Marlborough Pinot Noir ★★☆

The rich but slightly rustic 2007 vintage (★★★) was matured for 10 months in French oak barriques (one-third new). It's a generous red, full-coloured, ripe and smooth, with earthy, herbal notes and a well-rounded finish. The ruby-hued 2008 (★★) is solid but plain, with simple, berryish flavours and a very smooth finish.

Vintage	08
WR	6
Drink	10-12

DRY $23 –V

Omihi Road SVR Waipara Fields Pinot Noir (★★★★)

From Torlesse, the 2007 vintage (★★★★) was grown in the Fabris Vineyard and matured for over a year in French oak barriques (50 per cent new). Deep ruby, it's a generous wine with plum, olive and herb flavours, showing good concentration, a savoury, earthy complexity and ripe, supple tannins.

Vintage	07
WR	7
Drink	12-19

DRY $50 –V

Omihi Road Waipara Pinot Noir ★★★

From Torlesse, the 2007 vintage (★★☆) is mouthfilling, with full, slightly developed colour and plenty of flavour, but green-edged and leafy. Ready.

DRY $30 –V

One Tree Central Otago Pinot Noir (★★★)

From Capricorn, a division of Craggy Range, the 2008 vintage (★★★) is ruby-hued, fresh and vibrant, with good body and depth of cherry/plum flavours, a gentle seasoning of French oak, and a rounded finish.

Vintage	08
WR	6
Drink	10-12

DRY $19 AV

Opawa Marlborough Pinot Noir ★★★☆

From Nautilus, the 2009 vintage (★★★☆) was matured in French oak barriques (10 per cent new). It's a very easy-drinking style, ruby-hued, with fresh, ripe berry, plum and spice flavours, showing good depth and some savoury complexity, gentle tannins and a well-rounded finish.

DRY $28 AV

Opihi Vineyard South Canterbury Pinot Noir ★★☆

The 2009 vintage (★★☆) was French oak-aged. Estate-grown and hand-picked, it is light ruby, with smooth, gentle strawberry, herb and spice flavours, and drink-young appeal.

DRY $26 –V

Ostler Caroline's Waitaki Valley Pinot Noir ★★★★

Grown in the Waitaki Valley of North Otago, the fruit-crammed 2009 vintage (★★★★☆) is the best yet. Deeply coloured, it is richly fragrant, with highly concentrated cherry, plum and herb flavours, and gentle tannins. Matured in French oak casks (20 per cent), it's well worth cellaring to 2012+.

Vintage	09	08	07	06	05	04
WR	7	6	NM	6	5	5
Drink	11-20	10-18	NM	10-16	10-13	P

DRY $48 –V

Overstone Marlborough Pinot Noir (★★☆)

From Sileni, the 2008 vintage (★★☆) is ruby-hued, with ripe flavours of cherries and plums. Floral, fresh and supple, it's a fruity, uncomplicated style, with drink-young appeal.

DRY $16 AV

Oyster Bay Marlborough Pinot Noir ★★★☆

From Delegat's, the 2008 vintage (★★★☆) is ruby-hued, with a floral, slightly toasty bouquet. Moderately concentrated, with fresh, ripe plum/spice flavours, it is finely textured, with considerable complexity, and lots of drink-young charm.

Vintage	08	07	06	05
WR	6	6	6	5
Drink	10-13	10-12	10-11	10-11

DRY $25 AV

Palliser Estate Pinot Noir ★★★★★

A richly perfumed, notably elegant and harmonious Martinborough red, concentrated, supple and attractively priced (reflecting its relatively large volume). Most but not all of the grapes come from the company's own vineyards – Palliser, Om Santi, Clouston, Pinnacles and East Base – where the vines range up to over 20 years old. Maturation is for a year in French oak barriques (partly new). The 2008 vintage (★★★★☆) is a fragrant, full-coloured wine, ripe and savoury, with cherryish, spicy flavours showing excellent depth and complexity. Firm and finely balanced, with a lasting finish, it's built to last.

Vintage	08	07	06	05	04
WR	7	6	7	7	4
Drink	10-16	10-15	10-14	10-14	P

DRY $42 V+

Palliser Pencarrow Martinborough Pinot Noir – see Pencarrow Pinot Noir

Paritua Central Otago Pinot Noir ★★★★

The 2008 vintage (★★★★) is a regional blend, grown mostly at Lowburn and blended with grapes from Alexandra and Gibbston. Very scented and supple, it's an intensely varietal wine, ruby-hued, with ripe cherry, plum and spice flavours, showing good complexity.

DRY $37 AV

Parr & Simpson Limestone Bay Pinot Noir ★★★★

A single-vineyard Nelson red, grown at Pohara, Golden Bay, the 2009 vintage (★★★★) was hand-picked and matured for 10 months in French oak barrels (30 per cent new). Ruby-hued, with some fungal, earthy notes in the bouquet, it's an elegant, savoury, intensely varietal wine with strawberry, herb, spice and nut flavours, showing good complexity, and a well-rounded finish. Still youthful, it's priced sharply.

DRY $25 V+

Partington Upper Moutere Pinot Noir (★★★★)

The powerful, concentrated 2008 vintage (★★★★), certified by BioGro, was matured for a year in French oak barriques and bottled unfiltered. Deeply coloured, it is sturdy and tightly structured, with dense plum and spice flavours and a firm backbone of tannin. It's still youthful; open mid-2011+.

Vintage	08	07
WR	6	5
Drink	10-15	10-13

DRY $49 –V

Pasquale Hakataramea Valley Pinot Noir (★★★☆)

Grown in South Canterbury, the 2008 vintage (★★★☆) was fermented with indigenous yeasts, oak-aged for a year, and bottled without fining. It's a medium-bodied red, fresh and vibrant, with cherry, plum, spice and herb flavours, showing good complexity and depth. It's more leafy than its Waitaki Valley stablemate (below), but more concentrated.

DRY $27 AV

Pasquale Waitaki Valley Pinot Noir (★★★☆)

The 2008 vintage (★★★☆) was barrel-aged for a year and bottled without fining. Full-coloured, it has a floral, spicy, attractive bouquet, leading into a youthful wine with moderately concentrated cherry, plum and slight herb flavours, fresh and supple.

DRY $27 AV

Paua Marlborough Pinot Noir (★★★☆)

From Highfield, the 2009 vintage (★★★☆) was barrel-aged for nine months. An attractive drink-young style, it is fresh-scented, with ripe cherry, plum and slight herb flavours, showing good delicacy and harmony.

DRY $23 V+

Paulownia Pinot Noir (★★★☆)

Grown in the northern Wairarapa, the 2009 vintage (★★★☆) is a lightly oaked style. Full of promise, it is sweet-fruited, with very good flavour depth and some savoury complexity.

Vintage	09
WR	6
Drink	11-15

DRY $23 V+

Pegasus Bay Pinot Noir ★★★★★

This Waipara red is one of Canterbury's greatest Pinot Noirs, typically very rich in body and flavour. The close-planted vines, planted in stony, sandy soils, range from 10 to 24 years old. The juice is fermented with indigenous yeasts and the wine is matured for 16 to 18 months in Burgundy oak barrels (40 per cent new). The 2008 vintage (★★★★☆) is deeply coloured and rich. Still very youthful, it is tightly structured, with fresh acidity woven through its generous plum and spice flavours. Highly scented, with good complexity, it needs time; open mid-2011+.

Vintage	08	07	06
WR	6	6	7
Drink	10-16	10-14	10-14

DRY $47 AV

Pegasus Bay Prima Donna Pinot Noir ★★★★★

For its reserve Waipara Pinot Noir, Pegasus Bay wants 'a heavenly voice, a shapely body and a velvety nose'. Only made in favourable vintages (about one in two), it is based on the oldest vines – up to 24 years old – and matured for up to two years in Burgundy barrels (40 to 50 per cent new). The 2006 vintage (★★★★★) is invitingly scented. Deep and youthful in colour, with concentrated, ripe cherry/plum flavours, showing great delicacy and complexity, gentle tannins and a rich, seductively smooth finish, it offers superb drinking from now onwards.

Vintage	06	05
WR	7	6
Drink	10-18	10-16

DRY $84 AV

Pencarrow Pinot Noir ★★★★

This is Palliser Estate's second-tier label, but in top years it is an impressive wine, better than some companies' top reds. The 2008 vintage (★★★★) was grown in Martinborough (76 per cent) and elsewhere (24 per cent), and aged in French oak casks for nine months. A great buy, it is deeply coloured, savoury, warm and spicy, with very good richness, complexity and depth.

DRY $22 V+

People's, The, Pinot Noir (★★★)

From Constellation NZ, the 2008 vintage (★★★) was grown in Alexandra, Central Otago. Ruby-hued, it is smooth, with ripe strawberry and spice flavours, gentle tannins, and a touch of savoury complexity. Drink now.

DRY $22 AV

Peregrine Central Otago Pinot Noir ★★★★★
This typically outstanding red is also a good buy. Grown almost entirely in the Cromwell Basin (2 per cent Gibbston fruit in 2008), it is matured for about 10 months in Burgundy oak barrels (35 to 40 per cent new). The 2008 vintage (★★★★) is very finely scented, with moderately concentrated, sweet-fruit flavours, good complexity and ripe, supple tannins. It's a refined wine, savoury and silky-textured.

Vintage	08	07	06	05	04	03	02
WR	5	6	6	6	5	6	6
Drink	10-14	10-14	10-13	10-12	P	P	P

DRY $39 V+

Peter Yealands Marlborough/Central Otago Pinot Noir (★★★)
A blend of grapes from two regions, the 2009 vintage (★★★) is a vibrantly fruity red with mouthfilling body and fresh, youthful flavours. Cherryish, plummy and supple, with clear-cut varietal characters, satisfying depth and drink-young charm, it should be at its best during 2011.

DRY $20 AV

Pete's Shed Pinot Noir (★★★☆)
From Yealands, the debut 2009 vintage (★★★☆) was harvested in Alexandra at 24 brix and matured in French oak barriques (35 per cent new). Bright ruby, it is mouthfilling and savoury, with fresh acidity and moderately concentrated cherry, plum and herb flavours, fresh, vibrant and firm. Drink 2011–12.

DRY $25 AV

Petit Clos by Clos Henri Marlborough Pinot Noir (★★★)
From young vines, the 2008 vintage (★★★) was mostly aged in tanks, but 10 per cent of the blend was matured for eight months in new French oak casks. It's a medium-bodied red with fresh acidity and satisfying depth of plum, spice and herb flavours, showing some complexity. Drink now.

DRY $23 AV

Pheasant Plucker Martinborough Pinot Noir (★★★)
From mature vines, the 2008 vintage (★★★) was matured in French oak casks (25 per cent new). Bright ruby, with good depth of plummy, spicy flavours, showing fresh acidity, it has a hint of herbs and some complexity.

DRY $28 –V

Pick & Shovel Central Otago Pinot Noir ★★★
From Dry Gully, at Alexandra, the lightly oaked 2009 vintage (★★★) is a drink-young style. Freshly scented and supple, it has fresh, light plum and herb flavours, with a Beaujolais-like charm.

Vintage	09	08
WR	3	5
Drink	10-11	10-12

DRY $20 AV

Picnic by Two Paddocks Pinot Noir ★★★☆

A Central Otago regional blend, the 2009 vintage (★★★) tastes like a second-tier Two Paddocks Pinot Noir, rather than a sort of picnic Beaujolais. Matured in French oak barrels (25 per cent new), it is full ruby, with strong plum, herb and spice flavours, showing some savoury complexity, and fairly firm tannins.

DRY $28 AV

Pisa Moorings Central Otago Pinot Noir ★★★★

Grown in the Cromwell Basin, the 2007 vintage (★★★☆) was fermented with indigenous yeasts and matured for 10 months in French oak barriques (one-third new). It's an elegant, ruby-hued red with moderately concentrated cherry, plum, herb and spice flavours, woven with fresh acidity, and toasty oak adding complexity.

Vintage	07	06	05	04
WR	6	6	5	5
Drink	10-14	10-14	10-11	P

DRY $32 AV

Pisa Range Estate Black Poplar Block Pinot Noir ★★★★★

Grown at Pisa Flats, north of Cromwell, in Central Otago, this is an enticingly scented wine. The 2007 vintage (★★★★★) was hand-picked and matured for a year in French oak barriques (one-third new). A dense, structured style, complex and savoury, it is maturing very gracefully. The 2008 (★★★★★) is another winner. A powerful, deeply coloured wine, it is mouthfilling and rich, with very ripe sweet-fruit characters and lovely depth of cherry, plum, spice and slight liquorice flavours. The 2009 (★★★★★) is again dark, powerful and fruit-packed, with dense cherry and plum flavours. Weighty, savoury and supple, showing lovely richness and harmony, it's well worth cellaring.

Vintage	09	08	07	06	05	04	03
WR	7	7	7	7	6	6	6
Drink	11-18	10-17	10-15	10-14	10-13	10-12	P

DRY $48 AV

Pohangina Valley Estate Pinot Noir ★★☆

Grown in the Manawatu, the 2007 vintage (★★★☆) is the best yet. French oak-aged for nine months, it is deeply coloured, with a spicy bouquet. Mouthfilling, with very good depth of cherry, plum and spice flavours, seasoned with toasty oak, it's a tightly structured wine with fresh acidity and obvious cellaring potential.

Vintage	07	06	05
WR	7	6	5
Drink	10-15	10-13	10-12

DRY $35 –V

Point d'Or Central Otago Pinot Noir (★★★)

From the Aurum winery, the 2008 vintage (★★★) was estate-grown, hand-harvested and barrel-aged. A light style of Pinot Noir, it is ruby-hued, with ripe sweet-fruit characters, decent depth of plum and spice flavours, a touch of complexity, and gentle tannins. A drink-young charmer, priced sharply.

DRY $18 V+

Pond Paddock Martinborough Pinot Noir ★★★☆

Grown in Te Muna Road, the 2007 vintage (★★★☆) was hand-picked at 24.5 brix and matured for 11 months in French oak barrels. Deep ruby, with a slightly leafy bouquet and vibrant cherry, plum and herb flavours showing very good depth, it's a moderately complex style, with an attractively silky texture.

DRY $33 –V

Prophet's Rock Central Otago Pinot Noir ★★★★☆

The 2007 vintage (★★★★★), grown mostly at Bendigo, in the Cromwell Basin, was hand-picked from low-yielding vines (3 tonnes/hectare), fermented with indigenous yeasts, matured for 16 months in French oak barriques (35 per cent new) and bottled unfined and unfiltered. Powerful, weighty and complex, it is deeply coloured, with highly concentrated, ripe cherry, plum and nut flavours. It's a notably complex, dense and savoury wine, delicious now.

DRY $45 –V

Pukeora Estate Pinot Noir ★★★

(Past vintages were labelled San Hill.) The 2009 (★★★) was hand-picked at altitude at Waipukurau, in Central Hawke's Bay, and matured for nine months in French oak barriques. A strapping red (15 per cent alcohol), it is full-coloured, with fresh acidity and strong plum, strawberry, spice and green-herb flavours. It's arguably a bit heavy and jammy, but concentrated, youthful and worth cellaring.

Vintage	09
WR	5
Drink	11-14

DRY $22 AV

Pyramid Valley Growers Collection
Calvert Vineyard Central Otago Pinot Noir (★★★★★)

The delicious 2008 vintage (★★★★★) was grown in a Bannockburn vineyard managed, but not owned, by Felton Road. Hand-harvested, it was fermented with indigenous yeasts, matured for 14 months in French oak barriques (25 per cent new), and bottled without fining or filtering. Richly coloured, it is robust, with highly concentrated, beautifully ripe cherry, plum and spice flavours, and a hint of liquorice. A powerful, lush red, it should flourish with cellaring.

DRY $52 AV

Pyramid Valley Vineyards Angel Flower Pinot Noir (★★★★☆)

Only 22 cases were produced of the 2007 vintage (★★★★☆). Estate-grown at altitude at Waikari, in North Canterbury, it was matured for a year in a one-year-old French oak barrique, and bottled unfined and unfiltered. Deeply coloured, it is mouthfilling, savoury and complex, with generous cherry, plum and spice flavours, fresh and supple. A very graceful wine, harmonious and finely scented, it's still youthful; open 2012+.

DRY $75 –V

Pyramid Valley Vineyards Earth Smoke Pinot Noir ★★★★

Estate-grown on an elevated, east-facing clay slope at Waikari, in North Canterbury, the 2007 vintage (★★★★) is a rare wine – only 22 cases were made. Matured for a year in a single, one-year-old French oak barrique, and bottled unfined and unfiltered, it's a floral, medium-bodied wine (11.8 per cent alcohol), with gentle acidity and strawberry, spice and herb flavours, very savoury and mellow. Ready.

DRY $75 –V

Quartz Reef Bendigo Estate Vineyard Pinot Noir ★★★★★

An emerging Central Otago star. Designed for cellaring, it is estate-grown on a steep, north-facing, 'seriously warm' site at the north-east end of Lake Dunstan, at Bendigo Station. The 2007 vintage (★★★★★) is a serious, savoury red. Highly complex, it has deep, youthful colour and a finely scented bouquet. Powerful, yet also graceful and supple, it has highly concentrated, ripe cherry, spice and nut flavours, with good tannin support, and obvious cellaring potential. The 2008 (★★★★★) is deeply coloured, with dense cherry and spice flavours and ripe, supple tannins giving it early approachability.

Vintage	07	06	05	04	03	02	01
WR	7	6	7	6	7	7	6
Drink	10-13	10-12	10-12	P	10-11	P	P

DRY $77 AV

Quartz Reef Central Otago Bendigo Pinot Noir ★★★★★

A bold, fleshy, generous red. The 2008 vintage (★★★★☆) was estate-grown at Bendigo, hand-picked and matured in French oak barriques. Deeply coloured, it is rich and sweet-fruited, with fresh, strong plum and cherry flavours, a hint of liquorice, subtle oak and fine, supple tannins. Drink now or cellar. The powerful 2007 (★★★★★) is dark, fragrant, sturdy and savoury, with sweet-fruit flavours of cherries, plums and spices, rich and finely textured.

Vintage	08	07	06	05	04
WR	7	7	6	7	6
Drink	10-13	10-12	10-11	P	P

DRY $43 V+

Quest Farm Single Vineyard Central Otago Pinot Noir ★★★★

From Mark Mason, co-founder of Sacred Hill, the 2007 vintage (★★★★) was grown in the Cromwell Basin and matured for a year in French oak casks (30 per cent new). Mouthfilling and supple, it's a savoury, sweet-fruited wine with strong, vibrant cherry and plum flavours, offering excellent drinking now onwards.

DRY $40 –V

Rabbit Ranch Central Otago Pinot Noir ★★★

The early vintages from Chard Farm set out to introduce a 'new breed of Pinot Noir from Central Otago – affordable, early-drinking, fruit-driven'. The 2008 (★★☆) is a light style, with moderate depth of fresh, smooth plum, herb and spice flavours, enjoyable now.

Vintage	08
WR	7
Drink	10-14

DRY $22 AV

Ra Nui Marlborough Pinot Noir ★★★

The 2009 vintage (★★★) was hand-picked and matured for nine months in seasoned French oak barriques. It's an easy-drinking style, ruby-hued, with good depth of cherryish, spicy flavour, fresh, ripe and smooth.

DRY $35 –V

Rapaura Springs Marlborough Pinot Noir ★★★☆

The 2008 vintage (★★★☆) from Spring Creek Vintners is full-coloured, sturdy and sweet-fruited, with good complexity and depth of cherry/plum flavours.

Vintage	08	07
WR	5	6
Drink	10-12	10-12

DRY $25 AV

Rapaura Springs Reserve Central Otago Pinot Noir (★★★☆)

The 2008 vintage (★★★☆), matured for 10 months in French oak barriques (partly new), is mouthfilling and supple. Ruby-hued, with buoyant cherry, plum and spice flavours, showing considerable complexity, it's drinking well now.

Vintage	08
WR	6
Drink	10-12

DRY $27 AV

Red Tussock Central Otago Pinot Noir ★★★

From Quest Farm, the 2008 vintage (★★★) is promoted as a 'bistro wine'. Lightish in colour, it is mouthfilling, with satisfying depth of ripe cherry and herb flavours and gentle tannins, offering enjoyable, early drinking.

DRY $25 –V

Redwood Pass by Vavasour Marlborough Pinot Noir (★★★)

Floral, mouthfilling and supple, the 2008 vintage (★★★) is ruby-hued, with decent depth of ripe cherry, red-berry and spice flavours, and some savoury notes adding a touch of complexity.

Vintage	08
WR	5
Drink	10-12

DRY $21 AV

Renato Nelson Pinot Noir ★★★☆

Drinking well now, the 2007 vintage (★★★★) is full-coloured and weighty, with concentrated, ripe, cherryish, spicy flavours, savoury, nutty and complex. The 2009 (★★★) was grown on the coast, at Kina, and on the Waimea Plains. Hand-picked at 24 brix, fermented with indigenous yeasts and matured for 10 months in French oak barriques (40 per cent new), it's ruby-hued, with good but not great depth of vibrant cherry/plum flavours, threaded with fresh acidity, and some leafy notes.

Vintage	09	08	07	06	05
WR	6	NM	7	5	6
Drink	11-13	NM	10-12	P	P

DRY $27 AV

Ribbonwood Marlborough Pinot Noir ★★★☆

The 2009 vintage (★★★☆) is floral, fresh and supple, with very good depth of cherry and plum flavours, a subtle oak influence (French, 18 per cent new), gentle tannins, and lots of drink-young appeal. (From Framingham.)

Vintage	09				DRY $24 V+
WR	5				
Drink	10-12				

Richmond Plains Nelson Pinot Noir ★★★

Certified organic, the 2009 vintage (★★★) is a floral, supple red with cherry, plum and herb flavours, gentle tannins, and good varietal character and charm. Drink now onwards.

Vintage	09	08	07	06	DRY $23 AV
WR	6	5	6	5	
Drink	10-13	10-12	10-12	P	

Rimu Grove Nelson Pinot Noir ★★★★

Estate-grown near Mapua, on the Nelson coast, this is typically a rich wine with loads of personality. The 2008 vintage (★★★☆) was harvested at 23 to 25.7 brix and matured for 10 months in French oak barriques (23 per cent new). It's a full-flavoured wine, savoury, spicy, nutty and complex, with good texture, but slightly leafy, with some early development showing.

Vintage	08	07	06	05	04	DRY $45 –V
WR	6	7	7	7	6	
Drink	11-22	10-21	10-20	10-15	P	

Rippon Emma's Block Mature Vine Pinot Noir (★★★★☆)

The debut 2008 vintage (★★★★☆) is from an east-facing, lakefront block at Lake Wanaka, in Central Otago. Matured for 17 months in French oak barrels and bottled unfined and unfiltered, it's a very 'feminine', graceful style of Pinot Noir, ruby-hued, spicy and supple, with hints of herbs, and excellent complexity and drive.

DRY $82 –V

Rippon Jeunesse Pinot Noir ★★★★

Made from vines in their youth ('jeunesse'), defined as 'under 12 years old', at Lake Wanaka, in Central Otago, the 2008 vintage (★★★★) was fermented with indigenous yeasts, matured in seasoned French oak barrels, and bottled unfined and unfiltered. Bright ruby, it is very attractively scented, with good weight and depth of cherry, strawberry and spice flavours, fresh and supple. Savoury and slightly nutty, with considerable complexity, it's delicious now, but also worth cellaring.

DRY $39 AV

Rippon Mature Vine Central Otago Pinot Noir ★★★★☆

This scented Lake Wanaka red (labelled 'Mature Vine' since 2008) has a long, proud history and is an elegant, 'feminine' style, rather than a blockbuster. The 2007 vintage (★★★★★), hand-picked from ungrafted vines planted between 1985 and 1991, is deeply coloured, rich, supple and flowing, with strong cherry and plum flavours, savoury and complex. The 2008 (★★★★☆) was French oak-aged for 16 months and bottled unfined and unfiltered. Ruby-hued, with a complex, spicy, earthy, nutty bouquet, it is generous, with an array of cherry, spice, herb and nut flavours, showing excellent complexity and vigour.

Vintage	07	06	05	04	03	02	01	00
WR	7	7	6	6	7	NM	6	6
Drink	10-19	10-15	10-14	10	10-14	NM	P	P

DRY $55 –V

Rippon Tinker's Field Mature Vine Pinot Noir (★★★★★)

From 'the oldest vines on the property', the 2008 vintage (★★★★★) was estate-grown on a north-facing slope at Lake Wanaka, in Central Otago, matured for 17 months in French oak barriques, and bottled without fining or filtering. Described by Rippon as displaying 'unforced masculinity', it is sturdy and full-coloured, with a fragrant, spicy bouquet and generous, ripe, spicy flavours, braced by firm tannins. A powerful, complex wine with strong personality, it's set for a long life.

DRY $95 AV

Riverby Estate Marlborough Pinot Noir ★★★

The 2009 vintage (★★★) is a single-vineyard wine, grown in the heart of the Wairau Valley and matured for a year in French oak casks (20 per cent new). Fruity and supple, it's a ruby-hued, moderately rich style with cherry and slight herb flavours, showing some savoury complexity. It's already enjoyable.

Vintage	09	08
WR	7	7
Drink	10-16	10-15

DRY $28 –V

River Farm Godfrey Road Marlborough Pinot Noir (★★★☆)

The mouthfilling 2009 vintage (★★★☆) was hand-picked in the Wairau Valley at 24.6 brix, fermented with indigenous yeasts, and matured for 11 months in French oak barriques. Sturdy (14.5 per cent alcohol), it is scented and supple, with moderately concentrated cherry/plum flavours and some nutty complexity. It's already quite open and expressive; drink now onwards.

Vintage	09
WR	6
Drink	10-15

DRY $29 AV

Riverstone Marlborough/Canterbury Pinot Noir (★★)

From Villa Maria, the 2008 vintage (★★) is light in body, colour and flavour. Soft and easy, it has fresh, gentle berry and plum flavours. Priced right.

DRY $14 AV

Roaring Meg Pinot Noir – see Mt Difficulty Roaring Meg Pinot Noir

Rochfort Rees Central Otago Pinot Noir (★★★★)

From an Auckland-based company chasing 'the more adventurous, younger drinker', the 2007 vintage (★★★★) is a single-vineyard wine, grown at Gibbston and matured for 10 months in French oak barriques (30 per cent new). Full and youthful in colour, with mouthfilling body, it has strong cherry/plum flavours, herbal notes, silky tannins, and excellent vigour and richness. It's drinking well now.

DRY $29 V+

Rockburn Central Otago Pinot Noir ★★★★

The 2008 vintage (★★★★) is a deeply coloured blend of Parkburn, Cromwell Basin (77 per cent) and Gibbston fruit, matured for 10 months in French oak barriques (30 per cent new). It offers generous cherry, plum and herb flavours, with the finely textured, silky charm that is the hallmark of this label. The 2009 (★★★★) is ruby-hued, sweet-fruited, savoury and smooth. Still very youthful, it shows good weight and texture, with excellent depth and complexity. Open mid-2011+.

Vintage	08
WR	6
Drink	09-14

DRY $45 –V

Rock Face Pinot Noir (★★★)

From Bishop's Head, the 2008 vintage (★★★) is a fresh, fruity, clearly varietal Canterbury red with moderately concentrated cherry/spice flavours, offering very easy drinking.

DRY $22 AV

Rock N Pillar Central Otago Pinot Noir (★★★★)

From the Moffitt family, of Dry Gully, the 2008 vintage (★★★★) was grown in the Rock N Pillar Vineyard, overlooking the Dunstan Basin at Alexandra. Fermented with indigenous yeasts and matured in French oak casks (30 per cent new), it's already delicious. Full-coloured, it is ripe, savoury and supple, with finely textured cherry and spice flavours showing good complexity.

Vintage	08
WR	5
Drink	10-18

DRY $26 V+

Rocky Point Central Otago Pinot Noir ★★★☆

From Prophet's Rock, the youthful 2008 vintage (★★★☆) was grown at Pisa and Bendigo and barrel-aged for 10 months. Ruby-hued, it is vibrantly fruity and attractively scented, with cherry and plum flavours showing some savoury complexity and ripe, supple tannins.

DRY $28 AV

Rose Tree Cottage Marlborough Pinot Noir ★★★☆

From Constellation NZ, the 2007 vintage (★★★☆) was matured for nine months in French oak barriques (new and one-year-old). Enjoyable young, it is vibrantly fruity, with cherry, plum and spice flavours, strong and well-rounded.

DRY $24 V+

Rua Central Otago Pinot Noir ★★★☆

A delicious, drink-young style from Akarua, the 2009 vintage (★★★★) was matured for 10 months in French oak casks (15 per cent new). Generous, with cherry and plum flavours showing very good depth, and a touch of spicy, savoury complexity, it is very fresh and finely balanced, with good harmony and instant appeal.

DRY $25 AV

Ruby Bay Vineyard SV Pinot Noir ★★★

The 2007 vintage (★★★) was hand-picked and matured for 10 months in seasoned French oak barrels. Full-coloured, with herbal notes on the nose and palate, it mingles fresh cherry/plum flavours and subtle oak.

DRY $30 –V

St Jacques Nelson Pinot Noir ★★☆

From Blackenbrook, the 2008 vintage (★★★) was estate-grown, hand-picked and matured for a year in seasoned French oak barrels. Drinking well now, it has good depth of fresh berry, spice and herb flavours, with a hint of oak adding complexity.

Vintage	08
WR	6
Drink	10-11

DRY $23 –V

Sacred Hill Halo Marlborough Pinot Noir ★★★☆

Showing lots of drink-young appeal, the 2009 vintage (★★★☆) was mostly estate-grown and hand-picked in the Waihopai Valley, and 'blended with a touch of Central Otago Pinot for complexity'. French oak-aged, it is full-bodied (14.5 per cent), scented and supple, with fresh strawberry/spice flavours, showing good depth and some savoury complexity.

DRY $26 AV

Sacred Hill Marlborough Pinot Noir ★★★

The 2009 vintage (★★★) was estate-grown in the Waihopai Valley. Ruby-hued and floral, with ripe berry/plum flavours and gentle tannins, it is vibrantly fruity and smooth, with drink-young charm.

DRY $21 AV

Sacred Hill The Wine Thief Series Dry Run Central Otago Pinot Noir (★★★☆)

Offering lots of drink-young charm, the 2008 vintage (★★★☆) is a single-vineyard red, grown at Lowburn, hand-picked and matured for a year in French oak casks (25 per cent new). Bright ruby, it is floral, fresh, vibrantly fruity and supple, with moderately concentrated cherry and plum flavours, finely integrated oak and gentle tannins.

Vintage	08
WR	6
Drink	10-11

DRY $30 –V

Saddleback Central Otago Pinot Noir ★★★☆

From Peregrine, the 2008 vintage (★★★☆) is a skilfully crafted, drink-young style, hand-picked and matured in French oak casks (20 per cent new). Ruby-hued and floral, with very good body and depth of ripe strawberry and spice flavours, showing some savoury complexity and gentle tannins, it's ready to roll. Verging on four-star quality.

DRY $25 AV

Saint Clair Marlborough Pinot Noir ★★★

The 2008 vintage (★★★) was partly fermented with indigenous yeasts and barrel-aged for eight months. Floral, vibrantly fruity and supple, with a touch of complexity and moderate depth of cherry and spice flavours, it's balanced for easy drinking.

Vintage	08	07	06
WR	6	6	6
Drink	10-12	P	P

DRY $25 -V

Saint Clair Omaka Reserve Marlborough Pinot Noir ★★★★

This is Saint Clair's top Pinot Noir. The 2007 vintage (★★★★) was grown mostly in the company's vineyards in the Omaka Valley, and matured for 10 months in French oak barriques (68 per cent new). Deep ruby, it is fresh, vibrant, flowing and supple, with sweet-fruit characters, cherry, plum and olive flavours, gentle tannins and good complexity.

Vintage	08	07	06
WR	NM	6	NM
Drink	NM	10-11	NM

DRY $37 AV

Saint Clair Pioneer Block 4 Sawcut Pinot Noir ★★★☆

Grown in Marlborough's Ure Valley, 40 kilometres south of the Wairau Valley, the Pinot Noirs from this site are deeply coloured and flavoursome, although sometimes a bit crisp and leafy. The 2008 vintage (★★★☆) was matured for 10 months in French oak casks (50 per cent new). Ruby-hued, it has fresh, vibrant cherry, plum and herb flavours, showing good depth and complexity, supple tannins and a leafy edge.

Vintage	08
WR	6
Drink	10-12

DRY $33 -V

Saint Clair Pioneer Block 5 Bull Block Marlborough Pinot Noir ★★★★

From clay-rich soils on the south side of the Omaka Valley, the 2007 vintage (★★★★☆) is a dark, full-bodied red, matured for nine months in French oak casks (new and seasoned). It is powerful and sweet-fruited, with deep cherry, plum and spice flavours, supple and harmonious.

Vintage	07
WR	6
Drink	10-11

DRY $33 AV

Saint Clair Pioneer Block 12 Lone Gum Pinot Noir (★★★★)

The 2007 vintage (★★★★) was grown in the lower Omaka Valley and matured for 10 months in French oak casks (new and older). It has concentrated, ripe flavours of cherries, plums and spices, seasoned with toasty oak, and a firm backbone of tannin.

Vintage	07	DRY $33 AV
WR	6	
Drink	10-11	

Saint Clair Pioneer Block 14 Doctor's Creek Pinot Noir ★★★★

Formerly sold under a Reserve label, the 2008 vintage (★★★★) was estate-grown in the Doctor's Creek Vineyard, south-west of Blenheim. Full-coloured and sturdy, with ripe plum and spice flavours, it is generous and sweet-fruited, with good complexity and moderately firm tannins. Drink now or cellar.

Vintage	08	07	DRY $33 AV
WR	6	6	
Drink	10-12	10-11	

Saint Clair Pioneer Block 15 Strip Block Pinot Noir (★★★★☆)

Full of drink-young charm, the 2007 vintage (★★★★☆) was grown in clay soils in the lower Waihopai Valley, and matured in a mix of tanks and new French oak casks. Full-coloured, it is invitingly fragrant and intensely varietal, with cherry, plum and spice flavours, deliciously fresh, smooth and rich.

Vintage	07	DRY $33 V+
WR	6	
Drink	10-11	

Saint Clair Pioneer Block 16 Awatere Pinot Noir ★★★★

Grown in the Awatere Valley, the 2008 vintage (★★★★) is an elegant red, matured for 10 months in French oak casks (50 per cent new). Bright ruby, it has mouthfilling body, finely integrated oak and strong, ripe cherry, plum and herb flavours, showing good complexity.

Vintage	08	07	DRY $33 AV
WR	6	6	
Drink	10-12	10-11	

Saint Clair Vicar's Choice Marlborough Pinot Noir ★★★

Designed as Saint Clair's 'entry level' Pinot Noir, the 2008 vintage (★★☆) was partly barrel-aged for seven months. It's a pleasant, easy-drinking style with light cherry, herb and nut flavours and gentle tannins.

Vintage	08	07	06	DRY $21 AV
WR	6	6	6	
Drink	10-11	P	P	

Sandihurst Central Otago Pinot Noir (★★★☆)

The vibrantly fruity and supple 2007 vintage (★★★☆) was grown at two sites at Gibbston and matured in French oak barriques (35 per cent new). Ruby-hued, with a floral bouquet, it has cherryish, herbal flavours, showing very good depth.

DRY $30 –V

Sandihurst Waipara Pinot Noir (★★★)

The 2007 vintage (★★★) was grown at two sites in Waipara and matured for 10 months in French oak barriques (35 per cent new). Ruby-hued, it offers good depth of plum, spice and herb flavours, fresh and firm.

DRY $30 –V

Satellite Marlborough Pinot Noir (★★★)

From Spy Valley, the 2008 vintage (★★★) was estate-grown, fermented with indigenous yeasts and French oak-aged for 10 months. Still youthful in colour, mouthfilling, spicy, warm and flavoursome, it's a firmly structured, solid rather than sexy wine, but shows some savoury complexity.

DRY $19 AV

Savée Sea Marlborough Pinot Noir (★★☆)

The 2008 vintage (★★☆) is a light to medium-bodied style with pleasant cherry, spice and herb flavours, green-edged, but with a touch of complexity. It's a forward, well-rounded wine, for no-fuss, early drinking.

DRY $18 AV

Schubert Block B Wairarapa Pinot Noir (★★★★)

This wine is grown near Masterton, hand-picked and French oak-aged. The only vintage I have tasted is the 2006 (★★★★), a deeply coloured wine with a fragrant bouquet of herbs and spices, showing 'forest floor' complexity, mouthfilling body and very generous cherry and plum flavours, with a distinctly leafy streak.

DRY $60 –V

Schubert Marion's Vineyard Wairarapa Pinot Noir ★★★☆

Schubert's lower-priced red is based on clones designed to produce a 'more fruit-driven style with a softer tannin structure'. Hand-picked and French oak-aged, it is typically savoury, spicy and leafy, with herbal notes detracting, but also very good flavour depth and considerable complexity.

DRY $40 –V

Scott Base Central Otago Pinot Noir ★★★☆

From Allan Scott, the 2009 vintage (★★★☆) is a single-vineyard red, grown at Cromwell and matured for a year in French oak casks (25 per cent new). It's a moderately rich wine, ruby-hued, with fresh, vibrant cherry and plum flavours, showing considerable complexity.

Vintage	09	08
WR	6	6
Drink	10-14	10-13

DRY $35 –V

Secret Stone Marlborough Pinot Noir ★★★
From Foster's Group, owner of Matua Valley, the 2009 vintage (★★★☆) was released at less than a year old. Bright ruby, it is mouthfilling and sweet-fruited, with very satisfying depth of plum and spice flavours, showing some oak complexity, gentle tannins, and drink-young appeal.

DRY $22 AV

Seifried Nelson Pinot Noir ★★☆
Matured for 10 months in French oak barriques (new to two-year-old), the 2009 vintage (★★☆) is ruby-hued, with pleasant, light strawberry and spice flavours, a hint of oak and drink-young charm.

Vintage	09	08	07	06
WR	6	6	6	6
Drink	10-15	10-14	10-12	P

DRY $21 –V

Seifried Winemakers Collection Pinot Noir ★★★
The 2009 vintage (★★★) was grown in Nelson and matured for nine months in new and one-year-old French oak barriques. Still very youthful, it is ruby-hued and supple, with ripe plum and spice flavours, showing some savoury complexity.

Vintage	09	08	07	06
WR	5	7	6	6
Drink	10-16	10-15	10-14	10-11

DRY $35 –V

Selaks Winemaker's Favourite Central Otago Pinot Noir (★★★☆)
The 2008 vintage (★★★☆) was harvested at 24.2 brix, fermented partly with indigenous yeasts, and matured in French and American oak barriques. Full-coloured, it is floral, sweet-fruited and supple, with cherry, plum and herb flavours, showing a touch of complexity, and strong drink-young appeal.

DRY $26 AV

Seresin Home Marlborough Pinot Noir (★★★★★)
The debut 2007 vintage (★★★★★) was estate-grown near Renwick, in the central Wairau Valley, hand-picked, fermented with indigenous yeasts, matured for 15 months in French oak barriques (33 per cent new), and bottled unfined and unfiltered. A beautiful wine, it is scented and full-bodied, with deep, youthful colour. Very concentrated and silky, with sweet-fruit delights, it has cherry, spice and nut flavours, notably rich and harmonious. Finely textured, very refined and 'complete', it's one of the greatest Pinot Noirs yet from the valley floor.

Vintage	07
WR	7
Drink	10-18

DRY $50 AV

Seresin Leah Pinot Noir ★★★★

Unlike the single-vineyard reds (below), this immediately appealing, lower-priced wine is grown at three sites – the home vineyard, Raupo Creek and Tatou – and is less new oak-influenced. The 2008 vintage (★★★★) was hand-picked, fermented with indigenous yeasts, matured for 11 months in French oak barriques (25 per cent new), and bottled without filtering. Deeply coloured, it is generous, ripe and spicy, slightly herbal and savoury, with good density and complexity, and excellent drink-young appeal.

Vintage	08	07	06	05	04
WR	6	7	6	6	7
Drink	10-15	10-15	10-12	10-11	P

DRY $37 AV

Seresin Rachel Marlborough Pinot Noir ★★★★

From three company-owned vineyards, the 2007 vintage (★★★★) was hand-picked, fermented with indigenous yeasts, and matured for nine months in French oak barriques (40 per cent new), followed by another six months in barrels. It's a powerful wine, full-coloured, in a 'masculine' style with ripe plum, cherry and spice flavours, deep and firm. It should be long-lived.

Vintage	07	06
WR	7	6
Drink	10-18	10-15

DRY $55 –V

Seresin Raupo Creek Pinot Noir ★★★★

Grown on clay slopes in the Omaka Valley, the 2007 vintage (★★★★) is a single-vineyard wine, fermented with indigenous yeasts, matured for 15 months in French oak barriques (45 per cent new), and bottled unfiltered. Deeply coloured, it is sturdy, with deep cherry and slight herb flavours, showing good, savoury complexity, an earthy streak, and firm underlying tannins.

Vintage	07	06	05	04
WR	7	6	7	6
Drink	10-18	10-15	10-12	10-11

DRY $50 –V

Seresin Sun & Moon Marlborough Pinot Noir (★★★★★)

Only 70 cases were made of the 2007 vintage (★★★★★). Designed for the long haul, it was grown in the hillside Raupo Creek Vineyard (80 per cent) and the home vineyard (20 per cent), fermented with indigenous yeasts, matured for 17 months in French oak barriques, and bottled unfined and unfiltered. Densely coloured, it has a fragrant, very ripe bouquet of plums and liquorice, leading into a powerful, youthful palate. Fresh, with rich plum, spice and slight liquorice fruit flavours to the fore, and supple tannins, it is still quite 'primary', and should be at its best mid-2011+.

Vintage	07
WR	7
Drink	10-18

DRY $120 –V

Seresin Tatou Pinot Noir ★★★★☆

Grown in deep gravels at the upper end of the Wairau Valley, the youthful 2007 vintage (★★★★☆) is certified organic. Hand-picked, it was fermented with indigenous yeasts and matured for 15 months in French oak barriques (50 per cent new). Full ruby, it is rich and silky-textured, sweet-fruited and savoury, with excellent concentration and strong cellaring potential. Best 2012+.

Vintage	07	06	05	04
WR	7	6	7	7
Drink	10-18	10-17	10-14	10-11

DRY $50 –V

Shaky Bridge Central Otago Pinot Noir ★★★☆

Grown at Alexandra, the 2009 vintage (★★★☆) is full-coloured, with a subtle seasoning of oak. It's a slightly herbal style, with very good depth of flavour, cherryish and spicy.

DRY $35 –V

Shingle Peak New Zealand Pinot Noir ★★☆

In the past labelled as Matua Valley Shingle Peak Marlborough Pinot Noir, this is now a country-wide blend. The 2008 (★★☆) is a pleasant, light red with fresh, strawberryish flavours. The 2009 vintage (★★☆) is ruby-hued and mouthfilling, with solid depth of cherryish, plummy flavours, slightly spicy and smooth.

DRY $18 AV

Sileni Cellar Selection Hawke's Bay Pinot Noir ★★★

Top vintages work well as a drink-young proposition. On the market within six months of the harvest, it's a Beaujolais-style red, made with 'minimal' oak handling. The 2009 (★★★) is ruby-hued, fresh and vibrant, in a simple, charming style with raspberry/spice flavours. The 2010 (★★★) is buoyantly fruity, with ripe, cherryish, strawberryish flavours, and gentle acidity and tannins giving a soft, easy finish.

Vintage	09
WR	5
Drink	10-13

DRY $20 AV

Sileni Exceptional Vintage Pinot Noir ★★★★

Grown in the company's elevated, inland vineyard between Maraekakaho and Mangatahi, the 2009 vintage (★★★★) is a youthful Hawke's Bay red with full, ruby colour. Mouthfilling, it has vibrant cherry and spice flavours, fresh and generous, and a nutty, savoury complexity.

Vintage	09
WR	5
Drink	12-15

DRY $60 –V

Sileni Grand Central Central Otago Pinot Noir (★★★☆)

The 2007 vintage (★★★☆) is a single-vineyard, Bendigo wine with deep colour and a freshly scented bouquet, cherryish and spicy. Mouthfilling and supple, with very good flavour depth, gentle tannins and some savoury complexity, it offers highly enjoyable drinking.

DRY $33 –V

Sileni The Plateau Hawke's Bay Pinot Noir ★★★☆

Estate-grown in the inland, elevated Plateau Vineyard at Maraekakaho, the 2008 (★★★) was hand-picked and matured for 10 months in barrels. It is fleshy and soft, with cherry, spice and herb flavours, slightly savoury and toasty. The strongly varietal, ruby-hued 2009 vintage (★★★☆) is already enjoyable, with very good depth of vibrant plum and spice flavours, fresh and smooth.

Vintage	09	08	07
WR	6	6	5
Drink	11-15	11-14	10-13

DRY $30 –V

Soho Marlborough Pinot Noir ★★★☆

From an Auckland-based company, the 2009 vintage (★★★☆) is a single-vineyard, Brancott Valley wine, matured in French oak casks (33 per cent new). Ruby-hued, it has good weight, with ripe-fruit characters and smooth cherry/plum flavours, showing some savoury complexity.

DRY $30 –V

Soho McQueen Central Otago Pinot Noir ★★★☆

The 2009 vintage (★★★★) was grown at Gibbston and Bannockburn, and matured in French oak casks (35 per cent new). Richly scented and deeply coloured, it has cherry, plum and slight herb flavours, vibrant and supple, showing excellent complexity and concentration.

DRY $40 –V

Soljans Barrique Reserve Marlborough Pinot Noir ★★★

Ruby-hued, the 2007 vintage (★★★) is a light to medium-bodied style, hand-picked and 'aged in secondary wood for 10 months'. Easy, enjoyable drinking, it offers cherry, plum, herb and nut flavours, soft and forward.

DRY $29 –V

Soma Nelson Pinot Noir ★★★☆

The 2008 vintage (★★★) was hand-picked in the Avery Vineyard at Hope and matured for 10 months in French oak barrels (one year old). Ruby-hued, it is full-bodied, with cherry and herb flavours showing decent depth, some savoury complexity, and a fairly firm finish.

Vintage	08
WR	6
Drink	10-15

DRY $25 AV

Southbank Estate Marlborough Pinot Noir ★★★

The 2007 vintage (★★★☆), the best yet, was matured for eight months in small French oak barrels (25 per cent new). Full-coloured, it's a fruit-driven style, with very good depth of vibrant, plummy flavour, a subtle seasoning of oak and gentle tannins.

Vintage	07
WR	7
Drink	10-12

DRY $20 AV

Southern Cross Hawke's Bay Pinot Noir ★★

From One Tree Hill Vineyards, a division of Morton Estate, the 2009 vintage (★★) is a drink-young quaffer, with lightish, slightly developed colour. Full-bodied, it has cherry, nut and herb flavours, showing moderate depth. Priced right.

Vintage	09
WR	6
Drink	10-13

DRY $13 AV

Spinyback Nelson Pinot Noir ★★☆

From Waimea Estates, the 2009 vintage (★★☆) is light ruby, with decent depth of plum and herb flavours. It shows some savoury complexity, but also a slight lack of ripeness and roundness.

Vintage	09	08	07
WR	7	6	7
Drink	10-12	10-12	10-11

DRY $18 AV

Spring Creek Estate Marlborough Pinot Noir ★★★

Grown at Rapaura, on the north side of the Wairau Valley, the 2008 vintage (★★☆) is ruby-hued and mouthfilling, with satisfying depth of cherry and spice flavours, some rustic notes and gentle tannins. Ready.

Vintage	08
WR	4
Drink	10-11

DRY $19 AV

Spy Valley Envoy Marlborough Pinot Noir ★★★★☆

The 2008 vintage (★★★★☆) was matured for 18 months in French oak barriques (60 per cent new). Deep ruby, it is robust, with fresh, rich cherry, plum and spice flavours, seasoned with quality oak. Generous, warm, dense and savoury, with a firm foundation of tannin, it's a powerful, sturdy, concentrated wine, with great potential.

Vintage	08	07	06	05
WR	6	7	6	7
Drink	10-14	10-13	10-12	10-11

DRY $56 –V

Spy Valley Envoy Outpost Marlborough Pinot Noir (★★★★☆)

More 'feminine' and 'funky' than its Envoy stablemate (above), the 2008 vintage was French oak-aged for 18 months. Full ruby, it is mouthfilling and youthful, with fresh, vibrant cherry and spice flavours, showing good concentration, and some 'forest floor' notes adding complexity.

Vintage	08
WR	6
Drink	10-14

DRY $56 –V

Spy Valley Marlborough Pinot Noir ★★★★

The 2009 vintage (★★★★☆) was hand-picked at 23.7–26.6 brix, fermented with indigenous yeasts and matured for 10 months in French oak casks. Weighty, rich and supple, it's a very elegant and youthful red. Full ruby, with a floral, scented bouquet, it is muscular (14.5 per cent alcohol) but not heavy, with sweet-fruit delights and concentrated, vibrant cherry/plum flavours. Finely textured, with obvious potential, it is best opened mid-2011+.

Vintage	09	08	07	06	05	04
WR	7	6	7	6	6	6
Drink	10-13	10-12	10-12	10-11	P	P

DRY $35 AV

Staete Landt Marlborough Pinot Noir ★★★☆

This single-vineyard red is typically very fragrant and supple. The 2008 vintage (★★★★) was grown at Rapaura, hand-picked at 24.9 to 26.4 brix, and matured for 18 months in French oak casks (20 per cent new). An elegant wine, ruby-hued, it has ripe plum/spice flavours, showing some nutty complexity. Fresh, youthful and tight-knit, it is finely textured, with good aging potential.

Vintage	08
WR	7
Drink	10-17

DRY $39 –V

Stafford Lane Nelson Pinot Noir ★★☆

The 2008 vintage (★★) was hand-harvested at 23 brix and not barrel-aged. It's a simple, drink-young style, with light strawberry and spice flavours and a smooth finish.

DRY $20 –V

Stockmans Station Central Otago Pinot Noir (★★★☆)

From Wild Earth, the 2008 vintage (★★★☆) is a full-coloured red, estate-grown at Bannockburn and Pisa. Cherryish, spicy and savoury, it has good fruit sweetness and complexity, with ripe, supple tannins. Priced right.

DRY $24 V+

Stoneburn Marlborough Pinot Noir (★★★)

From Hunter's, the 2008 vintage (★★★) is mouthfilling, with a ripe, slightly earthy bouquet. Bright ruby, it is fresh and plummy, with a touch of spicy complexity and decent depth.

DRY $20 AV

Stoneleigh Marlborough Pinot Noir ★★★☆

The 2009 vintage (★★★☆) from Pernod Ricard NZ was grown on the relatively warm, north side of the Wairau Valley, picked at 23.5 to 24.5 brix, matured in French oak casks, and bottled unfined. Floral and supple, it is ruby-hued, with cherry, plum and spice flavours, showing some savoury complexity. Drink now or cellar.

Vintage	09	08	07	06
WR	6	6	6	6
Drink	10-12	10-11	P	P

DRY $24 V+

Stoneleigh Vineyards Rapaura Series Marlborough Pinot Noir ★★★★

The 2008 vintage (★★★★) was hand-picked at 23.8 to 25.2 brix and matured for 10 months in French oak casks (42 per cent new). Mouthfilling and smooth, it has cherry, plum and spice flavours, seasoned with toasty oak, showing very good ripeness, complexity and depth. The 2009 (★★★★) is sturdy (14.5 per cent alcohol), with full, ruby colour. Finely balanced for early drinking, it has strong, vibrant plum, spice and herb flavours, showing excellent varietal character and complexity.

Vintage	09	08	07	06	05
WR	6	6	6	6	5
Drink	10-12	10-11	P	P	P

DRY $32 AV

Stonewall Marlborough Pinot Noir (★★)

From Forrest, the 2008 vintage (★★) is light, simple and smooth, lacking any real depth or appeal.

DRY $19 –V

Stone Paddock Central Otago Pinot Noir ★★★

From Paritua, the 2008 vintage (★★★☆) was hand-picked and matured in French oak barriques (33 per cent new). Attractively scented and mouthfilling, with ripe cherry, plum and spice flavours and gentle tannins, it is fresh, vibrantly fruity and supple, with drink-young charm.

Vintage	07
WR	6
Drink	09-14

DRY $25 –V

Summerhouse Marlborough Pinot Noir ★★★☆

The 2009 vintage (★★★☆) is a single-vineyard red, hand-picked and matured for 11 months in French oak barriques. It's a moderately concentrated wine, ruby-hued and supple, with cherry, plum and nut flavours showing good varietal character and some savoury complexity.

DRY $32 –V

Surveyor Thomson Central Otago Pinot Noir ★★★★

The 2007 vintage (★★★★) from this Lowburn-based producer is savoury, with ripe cherry and spice flavours, showing good complexity. The 2008 (★★★★) is a generous red with excellent ripeness, complexity and depth. It's a graceful, savoury wine, showing good 'pinosity', and likely to be long-lived.

DRY $40 –V

Takutai Nelson Pinot Noir ★★

The 2008 vintage (★★) from Waimea Estates is a quaffer. It's a solid, simple wine with berryish, leafy flavours, lacking a bit of ripeness, richness and roundness, but priced right.

DRY $14 AV

Tarras Vineyards Central Otago Pinot Noir (★★★★)

The youthful, deeply coloured 2008 vintage (★★★★) is an elegant red, grown in The Steppes and The Canyon vineyards. Matured in French oak barriques (30 per cent new), it's a mouthfilling wine with excellent depth of warm, spicy flavour and a backbone of firm, ripe tannins.

Vintage	08
WR	7
Drink	10-16

DRY $32 AV

Tarras Vineyards The Canyon Pinot Noir ★★★★☆

Grown at Bendigo, in Central Otago, and matured in French oak barriques (30 per cent new), the 2008 vintage (★★★★☆) is deeply coloured and beautifully scented. Rich and very vibrant, it has strong, ripe, cherryish flavours, finely integrated oak and supple tannins. A graceful, youthful wine, it should reward cellaring.

Vintage	08	07
WR	7	7
Drink	10-18	10-17

DRY $42 AV

Tarras Vineyards The Steppes Pinot Noir ★★★★☆

The 2008 vintage (★★★★☆) is a single-vineyard red, grown at Tarras (a much cooler site than Bendigo, 10 kilometres away), and matured in French oak barriques (30 per cent new). Deeply coloured, it is sweet-fruited, with strong cherry/spice flavours, warm and savoury. It's a dense, rich Central Otago wine with good presence.

Vintage	08
WR	7
Drink	10-17

DRY $42 AV

Tasman Bay New Zealand Pinot Noir ★★

The 2008 vintage (★★☆) was grown in Nelson and Marlborough, and aged 'on' French oak (meaning not barrel-aged). Ruby-hued, it is enjoyable young, with cherry, herb and spice flavours, light and smooth.

DRY $19 –V

Tatty Bogler Otago Pinot Noir ★★★

From Forrest Estate, the 2007 vintage (★★★) was grown in Bannockburn (Central Otago) and the Waitaki Valley (North Otago). It's an attractive mid-weight, with vibrant cherry and spice flavours, some savoury notes and fresh acidity.

Vintage	09	08	07	06
WR	6	5	6	5
Drink	11-19	11-15	10-15	10-12

DRY $30 –V

Te Henga Premium The Westie Marlborough Pinot Noir (★★☆)

From Babich, the 2008 vintage (★★☆) is pale ruby, in a light style with smooth, cherryish, spicy flavours, balanced for easy, early drinking.

DRY $17 AV

Te Kairanga Estate Martinborough Pinot Noir ★★★☆
The 2009 vintage (★★★☆) is a good-value, drink-young style, oak-matured for eight months. Ruby-hued and floral, it has fresh, strong berry/spice flavours, a hint of herbs and some savoury complexity.

Vintage	09	08
WR	7	7
Drink	10-13	10-12

DRY $21 V+

Te Kairanga John Martin Reserve Pinot Noir ★★★★
The 2007 vintage (★★★★☆) has good weight, sweet-fruit delights and strong cherry, plum and spice flavours. Matured for nine months in French oak casks (35 per cent new), it's a powerful wine, built for cellaring, but showing some maturity and already a pleasure to drink.

Vintage	07	06	05
WR	7	6	5
Drink	10-16	10-15	10-14

DRY $49 –V

Te Kairanga Runholder Martinborough Pinot Noir ★★★☆
This is the middle-tier label. The 2007 (★★★☆), matured for nine months in French oak barriques (35 per cent new), is ready for drinking. Full-coloured, it has plenty of cherryish, spicy, slightly leafy flavour.

Vintage	07	06	05
WR	7	6	5
Drink	10-14	10-12	10-11

DRY $29 AV

Te Mania Nelson Pinot Noir ★★☆
The 2008 vintage (★★☆) was matured in a mix of tanks and barrels. It's a drink-young style, ruby-hued, with light cherry, plum and herb flavours, slightly savoury and very smooth.

Vintage	08	07	06	05
WR	5	7	6	7
Drink	10-13	10-12	10-12	P

DRY $22 –V

Te Mania Reserve Nelson Pinot Noir ★★★☆
Hand-picked and matured for 10 months in French and American oak barrels (30 per cent new), the 2008 vintage (★★★) is sturdy, with satisfying depth of cherry and slight herb flavours, supple and smooth. It's quite forward.

Vintage	08	07	06
WR	5	7	6
Drink	10-13	10-14	10-12

DRY $35 –V

Te Mara Central Otago Pinot Noir ★★★☆

The 2008 vintage (★★★☆) is a scented, supple, mid-weight style. The bouquet is spicy and savoury; the palate is cherryish and plummy, with a hint of herbs and gentle tannins. Drink now or cellar.

DRY $36 –V

Terrace Edge Waipara Valley Pinot Noir ★★★

The 2008 vintage (★★★) was hand-picked, fermented with indigenous yeasts and matured in French oak barriques (25 per cent new). It's a supple, ruby-hued red, with decent depth of cherry and plum flavours, slightly spicy and nutty.

DRY $24 AV

Terrace Heights Estate Marlborough Pinot Noir ★★★☆

The sturdy, warm 2009 vintage (★★★☆) was matured in French oak casks (50 per cent new). Deeply coloured, it has a strong, nutty oak influence, with mouthfilling body, sweet-fruit characters and very good depth of plum and spice flavours.

Vintage	09
WR	6
Drink	11-15

DRY $30 –V

Terrain New Zealand Pinot Noir ★★

The 2008 vintage (★★), sold in a claret-shape bottle, is a drink-young style with light colour and moderate depth of smooth cherry, plum and herb flavours. Ready.

DRY $13 AV

Terravin Eaton Family Vineyard Pinot Noir (★★★★☆)

Estate-grown in Marlborough, the 2009 vintage (★★★★☆) was hand-picked at 23.5 brix, fermented with indigenous yeasts, matured for 11 months in French oak casks (40 per cent new), and bottled unfined and unfiltered. It's a very 'feminine' style, floral and supple, with sweet-fruit delights. Highly perfumed, with ripe cherry, plum and spice flavours, woven with fresh acidity, and good, savoury complexity, it's a graceful wine, still very youthful. Open 2012+.

DRY $78 –V

Terravin Hillside Reserve Marlborough Pinot Noir ★★★★★

Grown on clay slopes in the Omaka Valley, this exceptional red (until recently labelled Hillside Selection) is harvested from the centre of the slope, fermented with indigenous yeasts, matured for 16 to 20 months in French oak barriques (40 to 70 per cent new), and bottled without fining or filtering. The 2008 vintage (★★★★★) is a deeply coloured, masculine style of Pinot Noir, but not tough. Generous, rich and opulent, with a fragrant, warm and spicy bouquet, it is powerful yet supple, with deep, ripe flavours of cherries, plums and spices, and a hint of liquorice. Notably sweet-fruited and complex, it should be long-lived.

Vintage	09	08	07	06	05
WR	7	6	NM	7	6
Drink	12-16	11-15	NM	10-13	11-13

DRY $56 AV

Terravin Pinot Noir ★★★★

The 2009 vintage (★★★★) was grown in Marlborough and matured for 11 months in French oak barriques (35 per cent new). Finely scented, it is full-coloured and mouthfilling, with fresh, vibrant plum, spice and slight liquorice flavours, and supple tannins. A youthful, very floral and elegant wine with rich varietal characters, it should be at its best mid-2011+.

DRY $36 AV

Thornbury Central Otago Pinot Noir ★★★★☆

Typically a great buy. The 2009 vintage (★★★★☆) from Villa Maria was hand-picked at Bannockburn and matured for a year in French oak barriques (35 per cent new). It is deeply coloured and enticingly perfumed, with deliciously strong cherry and plum flavours, very fresh, vibrant and finely textured.

Vintage	09	08	07	06	05
WR	6	7	6	7	6
Drink	10-15	10-15	10-14	10-13	P

DRY $32 V+

Three Miners Earnscleugh Valley Pinot Noir ★★★☆

This single-vineyard red is grown in the Earnscleugh Valley, between Alexandra and Clyde, in Central Otago, and matured in French oak barriques (30 per cent new). The 2008 vintage (★★★☆) is floral, vibrantly fruity, slightly herbal and earthy, with good flavour depth and some savoury complexity.

Vintage	08	07	06	05	04
WR	6	6	6	5	6
Drink	10-16	10-11	10-11	P	P

DRY $27 AV

Three Paddles Martinborough Pinot Noir ★★★☆

From Nga Waka, this second-tier red is a rewarding drink-young style. The 2009 vintage (★★★☆) is medium to full-bodied, with ripe cherry, plum and spice flavours, still very youthful. Sweet-fruited, with some savoury complexity, it is best opened mid-2011+.

Vintage	09	08	07	06
WR	6	7	NM	7
Drink	10+	10+	NM	P

DRY $25 AV

Tiki Central Otago Pinot Noir (★★★★)

The 2008 vintage (★★★★) is enjoyable now. Bright ruby, it is very fresh, sweet-fruited and finely balanced, with rich cherry, plum, spice and slight herb flavours, good, savoury, nutty complexity and ripe, supple tannins.

DRY $45 –V

Tiwaiwaka Martinborough Pinot Noir ★★★☆

The 2007 vintage (★★★☆) is a single-vineyard red, grown on the Martinborough Terrace. Ruby-hued, with a hint of development, it's a mouthfilling and savoury wine with firm, spicy, slightly herbal flavours, showing good complexity.

DRY $38 –V

Tohu Marlborough Pinot Noir ★★★
The 2007 vintage (★★☆) was grown in the Waihopai and Awatere valleys, hand-picked and matured in French oak barriques. It has strong cherry/plum flavours and a smooth finish, but lacks real complexity and fragrance. The 2008 (★★★) is a mid-weight style, ruby-hued, with ripe-fruit flavours to the fore, gentle tannins and drink-young appeal.

Vintage	08	07
WR	5	5
Drink	P	P

DRY $27 –V

Tohu Rore Marlborough Reserve Pinot Noir ★★★★
The 2008 vintage (★★★★) was grown in the Awatere and Waihopai valleys and selected from the 'very best barrels'. Mouthfilling and generous, it is full-coloured and sweet-fruited, with strong cherry, plum and nut flavours, showing good complexity, supple tannins and a well-rounded finish.

DRY $36 AV

Torea Marlborough Pinot Noir (★★★☆)
Offering good value, the 2008 vintage (★★★☆) is a single-vineyard red from Fairhall Downs, hand-picked in the Brancott Valley and made in a 'fruit-driven style' (meaning lightly oaked). Floral and full-bodied, it has gentle tannins and very good depth of plum, spice and slight herb flavours, showing some savoury complexity. It's delicious young.

DRY $20 V+

Torlesse Waipara Pinot Noir ★★☆
The 2009 vintage (★★☆), barrel-aged for a year, is light, cherryish and slightly leafy. The 2008 (★★) is light and green-edged, lacking real ripeness and richness.

Vintage	09
WR	5
Drink	12-15

DRY $20 –V

Torrent Bay Nelson Pinot Noir ★★☆
From Anchorage, the 2009 vintage (★★☆) was grown at Motueka and gently oaked. It's a light style, berryish and slightly herbal, offering smooth, easy drinking.

DRY $17 AV

Tranquillity Bay Nelson Pinot Noir (★★☆)
The 2009 vintage (★★☆) is a light style, ruby-hued, with moderate depth of plum and herb flavours.

DRY $18 AV

Tranquil Valley Marlborough Pinot Noir ★★★
From Huasheng Wines, at Matakana, the 2008 vintage (★★★) is ruby-hued, with a hint of early development. A supple, cherryish red, with good varietal character and a touch of complexity, it's a forward style, enjoyable now.

DRY $25 –V

Trinity Hill Hawke's Bay Pinot Noir ★★★

The 2009 vintage (★★★) was grown at two sites in the cooler hill country to the south and barrel-aged for seven months. Ruby-hued and floral, it has plenty of vibrant, plummy, spicy flavour, some savoury notes and fresh acidity.

DRY $20 AV

Trinity Hill High Country Pinot Noir ★★★★

This impressive wine proves that Hawke's Bay *can* make fine Pinot Noir. Sourced from vineyards in the relatively cool hill country, south of the Heretaunga Plains, it is picked by hand and matured in French oak (with a high percentage of new barriques). The 2008 (★★★★) is floral and sweet-fruited, with the power to age. The colour is full and bright; the palate offers strong, ripe raspberry/spice flavours, with good density, firm tannins and oak complexity. The 2009 (★★★★☆) is deeply coloured, mouthfilling and very rich, with highly concentrated cherry and plum flavours, still very youthful. It's a powerful wine, full of promise.

Vintage	09	08	07	06	05	04
WR	7	6	6	6	6	5
Drink	10-16	10-15	10-14	10-11	P	P

DRY $39 AV

Triplebank Awatere Valley Marlborough Pinot Noir ★★★☆

From Pernod Ricard NZ, the 2008 vintage (★★★☆) was harvested at 26.5 brix, matured in French oak barriques, and bottled unfined. Full-coloured, it is ruby-hued, scented and supple, in a moderately concentrated style with ripe cherry, plum, spice and slight herb flavours, showing some savoury complexity. Verging on four-star quality, it's a drink-now or cellaring proposition.

Vintage	08	07	06
WR	6	6	6
Drink	10-11	P	P

DRY $27 AV

Turning Point New Style Pinot Noir (★★)

From Spencer Hill, the 2008 vintage (★★), grown in Marlborough and Nelson, is based on Pinot Noir (90 per cent), blended with Merlot (5 per cent) and Malbec (5 per cent), to give the 'new style'. Aged 'on' French oak (meaning not barrel-aged), it's a smooth, light dry red with cherry, plum and herb flavours, offering easy, no-fuss drinking.

DRY $16 –V

Tussock Nelson Pinot Noir ★★★

From Woollaston, the 2007 vintage (★★★) was matured for 11 months in French oak barrels (30 per cent new). Full ruby, it is mouthfilling, with plenty of fresh plum, spice and herb flavour. The 2008 (★★★) is light and supple, with cherry and herb flavours, showing some spicy complexity.

Vintage	08
WR	5
Drink	10-15

DRY $24 AV

Twin Islands Marlborough Pinot Noir ★★☆
Negociants' red is a drink-young style. The 2009 vintage (★★☆) is light ruby, with ripe, berryish fruit flavours. A pleasant quaffer.

DRY $18 AV

Two Paddocks First Paddock Pinot Noir ★★★★
Grown in Sam Neill's original Central Otago vineyard, planted at Gibbston in 1993, the 2007 vintage (★★★★★) was matured for 11 months in French oak barriques (30 per cent new). Richly coloured, it is sweet-fruited, savoury and concentrated, with deliciously deep plum and spice flavours, showing excellent complexity. Delicious in its youth, it has the structure to mature well.

Vintage	07	06
WR	6	6
Drink	12-16	12-14

DRY $65 –V

Two Paddocks Picnic Pinot Noir – see Picnic by Two Paddocks Pinot Noir

Two Paddocks Pinot Noir ★★★★
The 2008 vintage (★★★★) is a blend of Alexandra (70 per cent) and Gibbston (30 per cent) fruit, matured in French oak barriques (30 per cent new). Full-coloured, it is drinking well now, with strong cherry, plum, herb and spice flavours, showing excellent complexity. The ruby-hued 2009 (★★★★) is supple and savoury, with good richness and complexity. Scented, it's a mouthfilling wine with deep cherry and herb flavours, vibrantly fruity and flowing.

Vintage	08	07	06
WR	6	7	6
Drink	12-16	12-18	12-14

DRY $50 –V

Two Rivers Marlborough Pinot Noir ★★★☆
Grown and hand-picked at high altitude in the Awatere Valley (333 metres above sea level), the 2009 vintage (★★★☆) was fermented with indigenous yeasts and matured for 11 months in French oak barrels. It's a graceful, ruby-hued, medium-bodied red with fresh, supple cherry and plum flavours, showing very good vibrancy, harmony and drinkability.

DRY $29 AV

Two Sisters Central Otago Pinot Noir ★★★☆
The 2007 vintage (★★★☆) was grown at Lowburn, in the Cromwell Basin, and matured for 14 months in French oak barrels (33 per cent new). Mouthfilling and supple, with cherry, plum and herb flavours showing good complexity and immediacy, it's drinking well now.

DRY $38 –V

Two Tracks Marlborough Pinot Noir (★★★)
A drink-young style from Wither Hills, the 2008 vintage (★★★) is a ruby-hued red with decent depth of cherry, plum and slight herb flavours, showing good varietal character, and a silky-smooth finish.

Vintage	08
WR	6
Drink	10-12

DRY $24 AV

Urlar Gladstone Pinot Noir ★★★☆

Hand-picked at 24.4 brix, matured in French oak barriques (25 per cent new) and bottled unfiltered, the 2008 vintage (★★★★) of this Wairarapa red is mouthfilling, full-flavoured and firmly structured, with strong, ripe cherry, herb and spice notes, underpinned by tight tannins. Earthy and savoury, it has a long finish.

DRY $35 –V

Valli Bannockburn Vineyard Otago Pinot Noir ★★★★☆

The 2008 vintage (★★★★★) is a generous, deeply coloured and sturdy wine with rich, ripe cherry, plum and spice flavours, showing excellent structure and complexity. Fleshy and savoury, sweet-fruited and fragrant, it's already delicious, but a strong candidate for cellaring.

Vintage	08	07	06	05
WR	7	7	7	6
Drink	10-17	10-16	10-16	10-14

DRY $55 –V

Valli Gibbston Vineyard Otago Pinot Noir ★★★★☆

The 2008 vintage (★★★★) is deeply coloured and concentrated, with the cherry, spice and distinctly herbal notes typical of the elevated Gibbston sub-region, fresh, vibrant fruit flavours, good texture, and a lingering finish. It's a finely poised wine, still youthful.

Vintage	08	07	06	05
WR	7	7	7	5
Drink	10-18	10-17	10-16	10-12

DRY $55 –V

Valli Waitaki Vineyard Otago Pinot Noir ★★★☆

Since the first 2004 vintage, this North Otago red has been overshadowed by its Central Otago stablemates. The 2008 (★★★☆) is ruby-hued, floral and supple, with vibrant cherry, plum and dried-herb flavours that flow well. It's still developing.

Vintage	08	07	06
WR	6	4	5
Drink	10-15	10-14	10-12

DRY $55 –V

Van Asch Central Otago Pinot Noir ★★★☆

The 2007 vintage (★★★★) is dark and dense, with rich plum and cherry flavours, showing good complexity.

DRY $45 –V

Vavasour Awatere Valley Pinot Noir ★★★★

The 2008 vintage (★★★★) was hand-picked and matured for nine months in French oak casks (35 per cent new). Youthful, with excellent body and depth of cherry, red-berry and spice flavours, seasoned with toasty oak, it is savoury and complex, with finely balanced tannins.

Vintage	09	08	07
WR	6	5	6
Drink	10-14	10-13	10-12

DRY $30 AV

Vicar's Mistress, The, Pinot Noir ★★★☆

Full and still youthful in colour, the 2007 vintage (★★★☆) was grown at Waipara and matured in French oak casks (25 per cent new). It's a mouthfilling wine with very good depth of plum, spice and herb flavours, showing some savoury complexity.

Vintage	08	07	06	05
WR	7	7	7	6
Drink	10-14	10-13	10-12	10-11

DRY $36 –V

Vidal Marlborough Pinot Noir ★★★★

The 2008 vintage (★★★★) is an elegant style, with full, bright colour and strong cherry and plum flavours. A floral, focused young wine, it is rich, ripe and long, with good complexity and cellaring potential. The 2009 (★★★★) was matured in French oak barrels (21 per cent new). It's a refined, very appealing wine, fragrant and supple, with strong, vibrant, cherryish, plummy flavours.

Vintage	09	08	07	06	05
WR	7	6	7	6	6
Drink	10-14	10-11	10-11	P	P

DRY $26 V+

Vidal Reserve Hawke's Bay Pinot Noir ★★★★

One of the region's best Pinot Noirs, in the past labelled 'Stopbank'. The 2008 vintage (★★★★) was hand-picked in the Keltern Vineyard, at Maraekakaho, and matured in French oak barriques (38 per cent new). It is mouthfilling and concentrated, with rich, ripe plum and spice flavours, showing good complexity. The 2009 (★★★★) is rich and ripe, savoury and complex, in a sturdy, firmly structured style, well worth cellaring.

Vintage	09	08	07	06	05	04
WR	7	7	6	6	6	6
Drink	11-15	10-13	10-12	10-11	P	P

DRY $32 AV

Villa Maria Cellar Selection Marlborough Pinot Noir ★★★★★

Typically a delightful wine, priced sharply, this is often New Zealand's best-value Pinot Noir. Grown in the Awatere and Wairau valleys, it is hand-picked, fermented partly with indigenous yeasts, and matured for nine months in French oak barriques (18 per cent new in 2009). The 2008 (★★★☆) is a lesser vintage. Ruby-hued, it is medium-bodied, with cherry, plum and spice flavours and ripe, supple tannins. Sweet-fruited, it's an intensely varietal wine that should reward moderate cellaring, but lacks the richness of a top year. Tasted before bottling, and so not rated, the 2009 looked promising – fleshy and rich, with strong cherry and plum flavours, finely integrated oak and ripe, supple tannins.

Vintage	09	08	07	06	05	04
WR	6	6	6	7	7	7
Drink	10-14	10-14	10-13	10-12	10-11	P

DRY $32 V+

Villa Maria Private Bin Central Otago Pinot Noir (NR)

The debut 2009 vintage was tasted prior to bottling, so is not rated. Fleshy and smooth, it has good depth of fresh, vibrant cherry, plum and herb flavours, gentle tannins and lots of drink-young charm.

DRY $26 V?

Villa Maria Private Bin Marlborough Pinot Noir ★★★★

Typically an outstanding buy. From a lesser growing season, the 2008 (★★★) was grown in the Awatere and Wairau valleys, and matured for 10 months in French oak barriques (10 per cent new). Ruby-hued, it is vibrantly fruity, with fairly light cherry and plum flavours and a smooth finish.

Vintage	09	08	07	06	05
WR	6	6	6	6	7
Drink	10-13	10-12	10-11	P	P

DRY $26 V+

Villa Maria Reserve Marlborough Pinot Noir ★★★★★

Launched from the 2000 vintage, this label swiftly won recognition as one of the region's boldest, lushest reds. Based on ultra low-yielding vines (2.5 tonnes/hectare) in the Awatere and Wairau valleys, it is matured for over a year in French oak barriques (35 to 50 per cent new), and bottled with minimal fining and filtration. The 2008 (★★★★☆) is mouthfilling and full-coloured, with warm cherry and spice flavours, showing good complexity, and a smooth, long finish. It's a forward vintage, ripe and rounded. The powerful, exceptionally promising 2009 vintage was tasted before bottling, so is not rated. A commanding wine, it is very fleshy, dark and rich, with dense plum/spice flavours that retain vibrancy and suppleness.

Vintage	09	08	07	06	05	04
WR	7	6	7	7	7	7
Drink	10-18	10-18	10-17	10-19	10-18	10-11

DRY $51 AV

Villa Maria Single Vineyard Rutherford Pinot Noir ★★★★★

The 2007 vintage (★★★★★) is based on vines nestled against the Benmorven foothills, on the south side of the Wairau Valley, and was matured for over a year in French oak barriques (25 per cent new). Powerful and full of potential, it's a tightly structured wine with rich colour, sweet-fruit delights, and dense cherry, plum and spice flavours.

Vintage	07	06
WR	7	7
Drink	10-17	10-19

DRY $56 AV

Villa Maria Single Vineyard Seddon Pinot Noir ★★★★★

From an Awatere Valley site even further inland and higher than its stablemate (below), the 2007 vintage (★★★★★) was matured for over a year in French oak barriques (25 per cent new). Richly coloured, it is still youthful and vibrant, with highly concentrated cherry, plum, herb and spice flavours, refined, long and tightly structured. There is no 2008. The 2009 (★★★★★) was matured in French oak barriques (17 per cent new). Weighty and dark, it is vibrantly fruity, with rich plum and spice flavours, deliciously concentrated, savoury and supple.

Vintage	09	08	07	06	05
WR	7	NM	7	7	7
Drink	10-17	NM	10-17	10-19	10-16

DRY $56 AV

Villa Maria Single Vineyard Southern Clays Pinot Noir ★★★★★

Hand-harvested in the Benmorven foothills, on the south side of the Wairau Valley, the richly coloured 2008 vintage (★★★★★) is a lovely, generous, still youthful red with bold, sweet-fruit characters and fresh, plum/spice flavours, showing excellent complexity and density. The 2009 (★★★★★) was matured in French oak barriques (24 per cent new). Deeply coloured, it's an intensely varietal wine, with fresh, densely packed cherry, plum and spice flavours, very refined, supple and long.

Vintage	09	08
WR	7	7
Drink	10-18	10-18

DRY $56 AV

Villa Maria Single Vineyard Taylors Pass Pinot Noir ★★★★☆

Grown in the upper Awatere Valley, the 2007 vintage (★★★★★) was matured for over a year in French oak barriques (25 per cent new). Richly coloured, it reveals intense, cherryish, plummy flavours, fresh and tight, yet deliciously rich and supple.

Vintage	07	06	05	04	03
WR	7	7	7	7	7
Drink	10-17	10-19	10-18	10-11	P

DRY $58 –V

Voss Martinborough Pinot Noir ★★★★☆

Voss is a small winery with a big, instantly likeable Pinot Noir. The 2008 (★★★★☆) was grown at three sites on the Martinborough Terrace, where the vines are up to 21 years old, matured for 10 months in French oak barriques (20 per cent new), and bottled unfined and unfiltered. A classy young red, it is mouthfilling and richly varietal, with deep cherry, plum and spice flavours, fresh, ripe, savoury and supple. Open mid-2011 onwards.

Vintage	08	07	06	05	04	03
WR	6	7	6	7	5	6
Drink	10-14	10-14	10-12	10-13	P	P

DRY $40 AV

Vynfields Martinborough Pinot Noir ★★★☆

Earlier vintages (2003, 2004) were unexciting, but the 2008 (★★★★★), certified BioGro, is a great buy. Hand-picked and matured in French oak barriques (40 per cent new), it is ruby-hued, with an invitingly floral bouquet. Vibrantly fruity, warm and supple, it is notably concentrated, with hints of coffee and spices, and great charm. It should be a five to 10-year wine; open 2012+.

DRY $36 –V

Vynfields Reserve Martinborough Pinot Noir ★★★★

Certified organic, the 2007 vintage (★★★★★) is a lovely red with an enticingly floral bouquet and deep, bright colour. Concentrated and silky, with a spicy, savoury complexity, it has ripe tannins and a long, seductively smooth finish.

DRY $49 –V

Waimea Barrel Selection Nelson Pinot Noir ★★★☆

The 2008 vintage (★★★☆) was harvested at 24 brix and matured for nine months in French and American oak barrels (partly new). Full ruby, it is mouthfilling and supple, with cherry and plum flavours, showing a hint of sweet oak, and good, savoury complexity.

Vintage	08	07
WR	6	7
Drink	10-13	10-12

DRY $24 V+

Waimea Bolitho SV Nelson Pinot Noir ★★★★

The powerful 2007 vintage (★★★★) was estate-grown in the Packhouse Vineyard, on the Waimea Plains, fermented with indigenous yeasts and matured for a year in French oak barriques (50 per cent new). Deeply coloured and sturdy (14.5 per cent alcohol), it is sweet-fruited, with concentrated, cherryish, plummy, slightly herbal flavours, seasoned with toasty oak, and a firm finish. It should be long-lived.

Vintage	07
WR	7
Drink	10-14

DRY $30 AV

Waimea Nelson Pinot Noir ★★☆

The 2009 vintage (★★☆) is ruby-hued and sturdy (over 14 per cent alcohol), with plum, spice and herb flavours, fresh and crisp, that lack real ripeness and richness.

Vintage	09
WR	6
Drink	10-14

DRY $20 -V

Waipara Downs Waipara Pinot Noir ★★☆

The 2008 vintage (★★) of this estate-grown, North Canterbury red is disappointing, with slightly developed colour and green-edged flavours.

DRY $25 -V

Waipara Hills Equinox Pinot Noir (★★★★)

Estate-grown at Waipara, in the Mound Vineyard, the youthful 2009 vintage (★★★★) is full-coloured, mouthfilling, savoury and supple. Sweet-fruited, it has good concentration of cherry and spice flavours, with a hint of herbs, underlying tannins and good varietal character. It should open out well; best drinking mid-2011+.

DRY $30 AV

Waipara Hills Soul of the South Waipara Pinot Noir ★★★

The 2008 (★★★☆) is a fruit-driven style with fresh, ripe, cherryish flavours, lively and supple. The 2009 vintage (★★★), partly oak-aged, is ruby-hued, with buoyantly fruity flavours of plums and spices, woven with fresh acidity.

DRY $21 AV

Waipara Hills Southern Cross Selection Central Otago Pinot Noir ★★★★

Grown and hand-picked at Bendigo, in the Cromwell Basin, and French oak-matured, the 2008 vintage (★★★★☆) is rich and flowing. Finely scented and sweet-fruited, with strong, cherryish, plummy flavours, a subtle seasoning of oak and good complexity, it's a graceful, finely poised red.

DRY $37 AV

Waipara Springs Premo Pinot Noir ★★★★★

Hand-picked from Waipara's oldest Pinot Noir vines, the 2009 vintage (★★★★☆) was fermented with indigenous yeasts and matured for 15 months in French oak barriques (20 per cent new). Full ruby, it is mouthfilling and sweet-fruited, with strong, vibrant cherry, plum and spice flavours, a hint of liquorice, and ripe, supple tannins. It's still very youthful, but already delicious.

DRY $36 V+

Waipara Springs Waipara Pinot Noir (★★★☆)

A very charming, drink-young style, the 2009 vintage (★★★☆) was matured in an even split of tanks and French oak casks (10 per cent new). Ruby-hued, it is mouthfilling, with fresh, vibrant flavours of cherries, plums and spices and gentle tannins.

DRY $22 V+

Waipipi Henry Wairarapa Pinot Noir ★★☆

The 2008 vintage (★★★) was grown at Opaki and French oak-aged. Sweet oak aromas lead into a fresh, cherry and plum-flavoured wine, moderately concentrated, with some savoury complexity, gentle tannins, and plenty of drink-young appeal.

Vintage	08
WR	6
Drink	10-13

DRY $25 –V

Wairau River Home Block Marlborough Pinot Noir ★★★☆

Barrel-aged for a year, the 2007 vintage (★★★☆) is mouthfilling and supple, with ripe cherry, herb and spice flavours, showing good varietal character and some savoury complexity. The 2008 (★★★☆) is full-bodied, with vibrant cherry, plum and spice flavours, seasoned with savoury oak, and very good ripeness, depth and harmony.

Vintage	07
WR	6
Drink	10-11

DRY $32 –V

Wairau River Marlborough Pinot Noir ★★★☆

Estate-grown on the north side of the Wairau Valley, the 2009 vintage (★★★☆) was harvested at over 24 brix and matured for eight months in tanks (30 per cent) and French oak barrels (70 per cent). Enjoyable young, it is mouthfilling, ruby-hued and supple, with fresh cherry, plum and spice flavours, showing a touch of complexity, and a smooth finish.

DRY $25 AV

Wairau River Reserve Marlborough Pinot Noir (★★★★)

The 2009 vintage (★★★★) was estate-grown at Rapaura and matured for 10 months in French oak barriques and puncheons. Savoury and supple, it is ruby-hued, with ripe plum and spice flavours, seasoned with toasty oak, and good complexity. Open mid-2011+.

DRY $40 –V

Waitaki Braids Waitaki Valley Pinot Noir ★★★★

The 2008 vintage (★★★★☆), grown in the Otago Station Vineyard, was hand-harvested, fermented with indigenous yeasts and matured for a year in French oak barriques. Very fragrant, savoury and supple, it is full-coloured, rich and complex, with ripe, sweet-fruit flavours, lovely flow across the palate and a long finish. It's a 'feminine', graceful style, with lots of class.

DRY $60 –V

Waitaki Valley Wines Grants Road Vineyard Pinot Noir (★★★☆)

The 2008 vintage (★★★☆) has a floral bouquet, fresh, ripe, moderately concentrated plum and spice flavours, gentle tannins and lots of drink-young charm.

DRY $40 –V

Waitiri Creek Central Otago Pinot Noir ★★★★

This label has leapt in quality in recent vintages. Grown at Gibbston and Bannockburn, the 2007 vintage (★★★★) was matured in French oak barriques (33 per cent new). It is rich and elegant, with deep colour, strong, plummy, spicy flavours, finely integrated oak and considerable complexity.

DRY $45 –V

Walnut Block Collectables Marlborough Pinot Noir (★★★)

Hand-picked and matured for eight months in French oak barrels, the 2008 vintage (★★★) is sturdy, with ripe flavours of plums, cherries and spices and a touch of nutty, savoury complexity. It's very forward; drink now.

DRY $23 AV

Walnut Block Single Vineyard Marlborough Pinot Noir ★★★★☆

Estate-grown and hand-picked in the Wairau Valley, the 2008 vintage (★★★★☆) was fermented with indigenous yeasts, and matured for 16 months in French oak casks. Full-coloured, it is mouthfilling and supple, with ripe cherry, plum and spice flavours showing excellent complexity and depth.

DRY $30 V+

Weaver Estate Central Otago Pinot Noir (★★★★)

The 2009 vintage (★★★★) is a youthful, tightly structured red with good colour depth and strong, ripe plum, cherry and spice flavours, showing considerable complexity. Well worth cellaring.

DRY $35 AV

Weka River Waipara Valley Pinot Noir ★★★

Mouthfilling and fairly firm, the 2007 vintage (★★★) is ruby-hued, with a leafy bouquet and plum, cherry and herb flavours, only moderately ripe-tasting, but showing very good depth.

Vintage	07
WR	4
Drink	10-13

DRY $33 –V

West Brook Marlborough Pinot Noir ★★★

The 2008 vintage (★★★) was hand-picked at two sites and matured in seasoned oak casks. It's a supple, moderately concentrated wine with cherry and spice flavours, a hint of herbs and some savoury complexity. Ready.

DRY $26 –V

West Brook Waimauku Pinot Noir ★★★

Here's proof that you *can* make good Pinot Noir in Auckland. Estate-grown, hand-picked and matured in French oak casks, the 2008 vintage (★★★) is a ruby-hued, medium-bodied wine with ripe plum/spice flavours, good texture and toasty oak adding complexity. Drink 2011+.

DRY $26 –V

Whitecliff Pinot Noir (★★)

A solid quaffer, the 2008 vintage (★★) is a blend of Australian and New Zealand wines. Full ruby, it is mouthfilling and fruity, with ripe, slightly plummy and spicy flavours, showing moderate varietal character, and a fairly firm finish.

DRY $18 –V

Whitehaven Greg Marlborough Pinot Noir (★★★★☆)

Selected from 'the very best barrels', the 2007 vintage was grown in the Wairau and Awatere valleys and matured in French oak barriques (50 per cent new). Deep and still youthful in colour, it is a powerful red with dense cherry, plum and slight herb flavours. A 'masculine' style, concentrated and firm, with a slightly earthy complexity, it should be at its best 2012+.

DRY $39 V+

Whitehaven Marlborough Pinot Noir ★★★★

The full-coloured 2008 vintage (★★★★) was matured in French oak barriques (40 per cent new). Weighty, dense and silky, with generous, ripe cherry, plum and spice flavours, it has good complexity, supple tannins and the potential to age well.

Vintage	08	07	06
WR	5	7	6
Drink	10-12	10-15	10-11

DRY $30 AV

Whitestone Waipara Pinot Noir (★★★☆)

Maturing well, the 2007 vintage (★★★☆) is ruby-hued and mouthfilling, with cherry, plum and spice flavours, showing considerable complexity. Moderately firm and savoury, with the structure to age, it should be at its best 2010–12.

DRY $25 AV

Wild Earth Vineyards Central Otago Pinot Noir ★★★★☆

The latest vintages are impressive. Grown in the Bannockburn and Lowburn districts, hand-picked and matured in French oak barriques (30 per cent new), the 2008 vintage (★★★★) is a stylish, finely textured red, concentrated and supple, with vibrant cherry, plum, spice and nut flavours, showing excellent ripeness and complexity.

DRY $42 AV

Wild Irishman Bannockburn Central Otago Pinot Noir (★★★★)

From pioneer winemaker Alan Brady, the 2008 vintage (★★★★) is from a block of young vines in the Desert Heart Vineyard, at Bannockburn. Fermented with indigenous yeasts, matured in French oak casks (30 per cent new), and bottled unfiltered, it is ruby-hued, scented and supple, with ripe cherry, plum and spice flavours. It's a buoyantly fruity, lively wine with some muscle and instant appeal.

DRY $32 AV

Wild Irishman Three Colleens Central Otago Pinot Noir (★★★☆)

The 2008 vintage (★★★☆) is from young vines, grown high on the slopes of Mt Rosa, at Gibbston. Fermented with indigenous yeasts, matured for 10 months in French oak barrels (30 per cent new), and bottled unfiltered, it is floral, fruity and soft, with moderately concentrated cherry and herb flavours, showing some savoury, nutty complexity, and a seductively silky texture.

DRY $32 –V

Wild Rock Central Otago Pinot Noir (★★★)

For supermarkets only, the ruby-hued 2008 vintage (★★★) from Wild Rock (a subsidiary of Craggy Range) is a very easy-drinking style, with decent depth of cherry, plum and slight spice flavours, seductively soft and smooth. Drink now.

DRY $19 AV

Wild Rock Cupid's Arrow Central Otago Pinot Noir ★★★☆

From Craggy Range, the 2008 vintage (★★★☆) was harvested at 24 brix and matured in seasoned French oak casks. Drinking well now, it's a ruby-hued red with a fragrant bouquet of spices and dried herbs. Savoury and spicy, it shows good flavour depth and complexity, with a fairly firm finish.

DRY $25 AV

Wild Rock Struggler's Flat Pinot Noir ★★★☆

Drinking well from the start, the top-value 2008 vintage (★★★★) of this Martinborough red is from a subsidiary of Craggy Range. It is bright ruby, mouthfilling and sweet-fruited, with excellent depth of ripe, cherryish, slightly nutty flavours, finely balanced and smooth. The 2009 (★★★☆) was matured for eight months in French oak casks (10 per cent new). Full-bodied, it has ripe cherry, plum and spice flavours, generous, savoury and softly textured.

Vintage	09	08
WR	6	7
Drink	10-15	10-13

DRY $24 V+

Wild South Marlborough Pinot Noir ★★★

From Sacred Hill, the 2009 vintage (★★★☆), grown in the Waihopai Valley, is very easy to like – floral and softly textured. Offering good value, it's a sturdy red, ruby-hued, with very satisfying depth of fresh, ripe cherry, plum and spice flavours, a hint of herbs, and finely balanced tannins. Best drinking 2011–12.

DRY $19 AV

Wild South Reserve Marlborough Pinot Noir ★★★

The 2007 vintage (★★★) was mostly estate-grown in the Waihopai Valley, hand-picked and matured in French oak for a year. Bright ruby, it is floral, supple and sweet-fruited, with moderately concentrated cherry/plum flavours, hints of herbs and some savoury complexity.

Vintage	07
WR	7
Drink	10-13

DRY $32 –V

Wingspan Nelson Pinot Noir ★★☆

From Woollaston Estates and French oak-aged for 11 months, the 2008 vintage (★★☆) is light, crisp and leafy, lacking any real ripeness, depth or charm.

Vintage	08
WR	4
Drink	10-15

DRY $17 AV

Wither Hills Single Vineyard Benmorven Marlborough Pinot Noir (★★★★☆)

Grown in the Benmorven Vineyard, on the south side of the Wairau Valley, the 2007 vintage (★★★★☆) was matured in French oak casks (40 per cent new). Deeply coloured, with slightly toasty aromas and flavours, it is a powerful, ripe, firm style, fleshy (14.5 per cent alcohol), generous, nutty and complex. Best drinking 2011+.

Vintage	07
WR	7
Drink	10-20

DRY $50 –V

Wither Hills Single Vineyard Taylor River Marlborough Pinot Noir (★★★★☆)

From the Taylor River Vineyard, hard against the Wither Hills, the 2007 vintage (★★★★☆) was matured in French oak casks (40 per cent new). Deeply coloured, with 'forest floor' aromas, it is flowing and concentrated, savoury and supple, with cherry, plum and spice flavours showing excellent ripeness and complexity. It's a very graceful wine, built to last.

Vintage	07
WR	6
Drink	10-20

DRY $50 –V

Wither Hills Wairau Valley Marlborough Pinot Noir ★★★★★

Over the past decade, this has been one of the region's most acclaimed reds. It is grown in two company-owned vineyards – Taylor River and Benmorven – on the south side of the Wairau Valley. The wine is matured in French oak barriques, until recently 50 per cent new, but reduced to 20 per cent in 2008, as winemaker Ben Glover is aiming for wines with 'primary, fragrant fruit in their youth, developing complexity, texture and secondary flavours later, after three years'. The 2008 vintage (★★★★) is fragrant and full-coloured, with strong cherry, plum and spice flavours, showing considerable complexity. A graceful, finely balanced wine, very fresh, vibrant and fruity, it should be at its best 2011 onwards.

Vintage	08	07	06
WR	7	7	7
Drink	10-20	10-15	10-14

DRY $34 V+

Wooing Tree Beetle Juice Central Otago Pinot Noir ★★★★

Often a great buy. The 2009 vintage (★★★☆) is a single-vineyard Cromwell red, hand-picked and matured for 11 months in French oak barriques (30 per cent new). Deeply coloured, it has strong cherry, plum and herb flavours, woven with fresh acidity, and mouthfilling body.

Vintage	09	08
WR	6	6
Drink	10-14	10-13

DRY $28 V+

Wooing Tree Central Otago Pinot Noir ★★★★★

The 2009 vintage (★★★★☆) of this single-vineyard Cromwell red was hand-picked at over 25 brix and matured for 11 months in French oak barriques (40 per cent new). Fragrant and deeply coloured, it is powerful (14.5 per cent alcohol), fresh and vibrant, with highly concentrated, ripe flavours of cherries, plums, herbs and liquorice, and a strong new oak influence. It flows smoothly across the palate, but has a good foundation of tannin; open mid-2011+.

Vintage	09	08	07	06	05
WR	6	6	7	6	7
Drink	10-18	10-17	10-16	10-16	10-14

DRY $43 V+

Wooing Tree Sandstorm Reserve Central Otago Pinot Noir ★★★★★

Estate-grown at Cromwell, this wine is hand-picked from especially low-yielding vines and given extended oak aging. All silky charm, the 2008 vintage (★★★★☆) was harvested at nearly 26 brix and matured for 18 months in French oak casks (40 per cent new). Ruby-hued, it is rich, supple and flowing, with an array of cherry, plum, herb, spice and nut flavours, in a very elegant, 'feminine' style. Drink now or cellar.

Vintage	08	07
WR	6	7
Drink	10-18	10-18

DRY $85 –V

Woollaston Estates Nelson Pinot Noir ★★★

Grown at Upper Moutere and matured in French oak barriques (30 per cent new), the 2008 vintage (★★) is disappointing. Light and green-edged, it lacks ripeness and stuffing.

Vintage	08
WR	5
Drink	10-15

DRY $35 –V

Wycroft Forbury Pinot Noir ★★★

Grown near Masterton, in the Wairarapa, the 2008 vintage (★★★) was hand-picked and matured for 10 months in French oak casks (30 per cent new). Ruby-hued, it is fresh, fruity and smooth, with good varietal character and moderate depth of cherry/plum flavours, enjoyable young. The 2009 (★★★) is fresh, berryish and supple, with lively acidity and a touch of complexity.

DRY $30 –V

Wycroft Pinot Noir (★★★☆)

Grown in the northern Wairarapa, the 2009 vintage (★★★☆) is scented and vibrantly fruity, with good depth of cherry, herb and plum flavours, fresh acidity and some savoury complexity.

DRY $45 –V

Yealands Estate Marlborough Pinot Noir (★★★☆)

Estate-grown in the lower Awatere Valley, the 2009 vintage (★★★☆) was hand-picked at 24 brix and matured for a year in French oak barriques (30 per cent new). Floral, it is full-bodied and supple, with fresh berry and plum flavours, crisp acidity and some savoury complexity. It's still very youthful.

DRY $29 AV

Yealands Marlborough Pinot Noir (★★☆)

Light ruby, the 2008 vintage (★★☆) is a drink-young style with gentle raspberry and strawberry flavours, simple and smooth.

DRY $18 AV

St Laurent

This Austrian variety is known for its deeply coloured, silky-smooth reds. It buds early, so is prone to frost damage, but ripens well ahead of Pinot Noir. Judge Rock imported the vine in 2001.

Judge Rock Central Otago St Laurent (★★★)

The 2009 vintage (★★★) is New Zealand's first commercial release of St Laurent. Grown at Alexandra, it's a gutsy, full-coloured red, fresh and fruity, berryish and slightly rustic, with firm tannins.

DRY $40 –V

Sangiovese

Sangiovese, Italy's most extensively planted red-wine variety, is a rarity in New Zealand. Cultivated as a workhorse grape throughout central Italy, in Tuscany it is the foundation of such famous reds as Chianti and Brunello di Montalcino. Here, Sangiovese has sometimes been confused with Montepulciano and its plantings are not expanding – the 2011 area of 6 hectares of bearing vines (mostly in Auckland) will be slightly less than in 2006.

Black Barn Hawke's Bay Sangiovese ★★★★

This Havelock North producer has been producing estate-grown Sangiovese for almost a decade. The 2007 (★★★★) *tastes* like Sangiovese, with good muscle and strong, plummy flavours woven with fresh acidity. So does the 2009 vintage (★★★★), with its full colour, floral bouquet and fresh, concentrated cherry and plum flavours. It's less compelling than Black Barn's 2009 Montepulciano, but still worth discovering.

DRY $32 –V

Matariki Hawke's Bay Sangiovese (★★★☆)

The 2007 vintage (★★★☆), grown in the Gimblett Gravels, was blended with Cabernet Sauvignon (9 per cent), and matured for 17 months in French oak casks (37 per cent new). It's a fruity, spicy, plummy, savoury and nutty red, showing very good flavour depth, although not obviously varietal, in the sense of displaying clear-cut Sangiovese characters.

Vintage	07
WR	6
Drink	10-12

DRY $30 –V

Syrah

Hawke's Bay and the upper North Island (especially Waiheke Island) have a hot new red-wine variety. At *Winestate* magazine's 2009 Wine of the Year Awards in Australia, the trophy for runner-up Shiraz/Syrah of the year was won by Mills Reef Elspeth Hawke's Bay Syrah 2007, and Mission Vineyard Selection Ohiti Road Hawke's Bay Syrah 2008 placed fourth.

The classic 'Syrah' of the Rhône Valley, in France, and Australian 'Shiraz' are in fact the same variety. On the rocky, baking slopes of the upper Rhône Valley, and in several Australian states, this noble grape yields red wines renowned for their outstanding depth of cassis, plum and black-pepper flavours.

Syrah was well known in New Zealand a century ago. Government viticulturist S.F. Anderson wrote in 1917 that Shiraz was being 'grown in nearly all our vineyards [but] the trouble with this variety has been an unevenness in ripening its fruit'. For today's winemakers, the problem has not changed: Syrah has never favoured a too-cool growing environment (wines that are not fully ripe show distinct tomato or tamarillo characters). It needs sites that are relatively hot during the day and retain the heat at night, achieving ripeness in Hawke's Bay late in the season, at about the same time as Cabernet Sauvignon. To curb its natural vigour, stony, dry, low-fertility sites or warm hillside sites are crucial.

The latest national vineyard survey showed that 299 hectares of Syrah will be bearing in 2011 – a steep rise from 62 hectares in 2000. Syrah is now New Zealand's fourth most widely planted red-wine variety, behind Pinot Noir, Merlot and Cabernet Sauvignon, but well ahead of Malbec and Cabernet Franc. Over two-thirds of the vines are in Hawke's Bay, with other significant pockets in Auckland and Northland.

Syrah's potential in this country's warmer vineyard sites is finally being tapped. The top wines possess rich, vibrant blackcurrant, plum and black-pepper flavours, with an enticingly floral bouquet.

Alpha Domus The Barnstormer Hawke's Bay Syrah (★★★)

The 2008 vintage (★★★), grown mostly in the Gimblett Gravels, was matured in seasoned French oak barrels. It's a fruit-driven style, fragrant, full-bodied and smooth, with gentle tannins and fresh, vibrant plum and pepper flavours. It's drinking well now.

Vintage	08
WR	5
Drink	10-17

DRY $25 –V

Artisan Fantail Island Oratia Syrah ★★★

Grown at Oratia, in West Auckland, and barrel-aged (30 per cent new), the 2007 vintage (★★★) is full-coloured, mouthfilling and rounded, with generous, spicy, slightly herbal flavours, enjoyable now.

DRY $27 –V

Ascension The Bandit Reserve Matakana Syrah/Viognier (★★★☆)

The debut 2008 vintage (★★★☆) is a blend of Syrah (95 per cent), picked from first-crop vines, and Viognier (5 per cent), from 13-year-old vines. Co-fermented and matured for nine months in barrels (25 per cent new), it's full-coloured, with a perfumed, peppery bouquet. Generous, with fresh, ripe plum, berry and spice flavours and gentle tannins, it's a vibrantly fruity, soft red with lots of drink-young appeal.

DRY $35 –V

Aspire Hawke's Bay Syrah (★★★☆)

From Matariki, the 2006 vintage (★★★☆) is a Gimblett Gravels red, barrel-aged for over a year. Medium-bodied, with full, bright colour, a floral bouquet, vibrant, gently spicy fruit flavours and some savoury complexity, it's maturing well.

Vintage	07	06
WR	6	6
Drink	10-12	10-11

DRY $20 AV

Aurora Vineyard, The, Bendigo Syrah ★★★★

Syrah is still largely unproven in Central Otago, but this Cromwell Basin red shows what can be achieved. The 2008 vintage (★★★★) was harvested at 24.5 brix and matured for 10 months in French oak casks (40 per cent new). Dark and dense, it has very concentrated blackcurrant, plum, spice and nut flavours. A powerful, rich wine, it is finely structured, with considerable elegance and finesse.

DRY $38 –V

Awaroa Melba Peach Reserve Syrah (★★★★★)

Grown on Waiheke, the 2008 vintage (★★★★★) was one of the stars at a major tasting of the island's wines in mid-2009. It's a powerful red, built to last, with a core of sweet fruit and dense, spicy flavours, complex and firmly structured.

DRY $65 AV

Awaroa Waiheke Island Syrah ★★★★☆

The 2008 vintage (★★★★★) is a rich, boldly coloured Waiheke Island red with concentrated plum and spice flavours. When I tasted it in mid-2009, it looked outstanding – complex, lush and lovely.

DRY $35 AV

Awhitu Greenock Syrah ★★★☆

Grown on the Awhitu Peninsula, flanking the Manukau Harbour in South Auckland, the 2006 vintage (★★★☆) was matured for 14 months in French oak casks (half new). Full but not dense in colour, it's an elegant wine with a peppery fragrance and moderately concentrated cherry, plum and spice flavours, fresh and supple.

DRY $29 –V

Babich Gimblett Gravels Syrah ★★★☆

The 2008 vintage (★★★) was grown in Hawke's Bay and French oak-aged for nearly a year. Medium-bodied, it is fresh and vibrant, with ripe plum, spice and black-pepper flavours, some earthy, savoury notes, and drink-young charm.

DRY $20 AV

Babich Winemakers Reserve Hawke's Bay Syrah ★★★★

Grown in Gimblett Road and matured in French and American oak barriques (partly new), the 2008 vintage (★★★★) was co-fermented with Viognier (5 per cent). Rich and supple, it's a very harmonious wine with fresh, generous plum and black-pepper flavours and a long, spicy finish.

Vintage	08	07	06	05	04
WR	5	7	6	6	6
Drink	10-16	10-15	10-12	P	P

DRY $27 AV

Beach House Hawke's Bay Syrah ★★★★★

The classy, youthful 2007 vintage (★★★★★) offers top value. Estate-grown and hand-picked in The Track Vineyard, in the Gimblett Gravels, it was matured for a year in French and American oak casks. Deeply coloured, it is rich and flowing, with sweet-fruit delights and highly concentrated blackcurrant, plum, spice and liquorice flavours, still fresh and vibrant.

Vintage	07
WR	7
Drink	10-30

DRY $28 V+

Bilancia La Collina Syrah ★★★★★

La collina ('the hill') is grown in the company's steep, early-ripening vineyard on the northern slopes of Roy's Hill, overlooking the Gimblett Gravels district of Hawke's Bay, co-fermented with Viognier skins (but not their juice, giving a 2 per cent Viognier component in the final blend), and matured for up to 22 months in all new (but 'low impact') French oak barriques. A majestic red, it ranks among the country's very finest Syrahs. The 2007 vintage (★★★★★) is dark and youthful in colour. Dense, with very fresh and vibrant, ripe blackcurrant, plum, black-pepper and nut flavours, it is savoury and complex, with firm underlying tannins and obvious long-term potential.

Vintage	07	06	05	04	03	02
WR	7	7	7	7	NM	7
Drink	12-16	10-18	10-17	10-16	NM	10-14

DRY $90 AV

Bilancia Syrah/Viognier ★★★★☆

This Hawke's Bay red is a blend of grapes from vineyards in the Gimblett Gravels district and the company's own block, *la collina*, on Roy's Hill. Co-fermented with Viognier skins and matured in French oak barriques (25 per cent new), the 2007 vintage (★★★★☆) is deeply coloured, with a floral, berryish, spicy bouquet. It is rich and well-ripened, with blackcurrant and spice flavours, a hint of dark chocolate, and excellent density and structure.

Vintage	07	06	05	04
WR	7	7	NM	6
Drink	10-15	10-12	NM	P

DRY $35 AV

Black Barn Vineyards Hawke's Bay Syrah (★★★★)

The graceful, finely textured 2008 vintage (★★★★) is deeply coloured, floral and fruity, with ripe plum, black-pepper and slight liquorice flavours, showing some savoury complexity. Fragrant and supple, it's already highly enjoyable.

DRY $32 –V

Bloody Bay Hawke's Bay Syrah (★★★)

From Federal Geo, a wine distributor, the 2008 vintage (★★★) is full-coloured, with a peppery bouquet. Light but attractive, it's a fruit-driven style with plenty of plummy, spicy flavour, a hint of herbs, and a smooth finish.

DRY $20 –V

Boundary Vineyards Lake Road Gisborne Syrah ★★☆

From Pernod Ricard NZ, the 2008 vintage (★★☆) is strongly peppery, but lacks real richness and roundness. The 2009 (★★★) is a riper style with satisfying depth of plum and spice flavours and a well-rounded finish.

DRY $23 –V

Brookfields Back Block Syrah ★★★☆

Grown in Hawke's Bay, the 2009 vintage (★★★★), matured in French and American oak casks, is a great buy. Deeply coloured, it is mouthfilling and supple, with concentrated plum and black-pepper flavours, richly varietal, fresh and rounded. Drink now or cellar.

Vintage	09
WR	7
Drink	11-19

DRY $19 V+

Brookfields Hillside Syrah ★★★★☆

This distinguished red is grown on a sheltered, north-facing slope between Maraekakaho and Bridge Pa in Hawke's Bay (described by winemaker Peter Robertson as 'surreal – a chosen site'). The 2007 vintage (★★★★★), matured for 18 months in all-new oak casks, is deeply coloured, with a fragrant bouquet mingling spices and sweet oak. Rich and flowing, it's a generous, seductive wine with highly concentrated blackcurrant, spice, chocolate and nut flavours, and ripe, firm tannins. A wine of real power, it should be long-lived.

Vintage	07	06
WR	7	7
Drink	10-18	10-16

DRY $40 –V

Cable Bay Reserve Waiheke Island Syrah ★★★★★

The 2008 (★★★★★) is a bold, very stylish red, enticingly fragrant, with concentrated, spicy flavours, rich, ripe and long. The 2009 vintage (★★★★★), grown at Church Bay, was co-fermented with Viognier (3 per cent) and matured for over a year in French oak barriques. Dark and fragrant, with a well-spiced bouquet, it is mouthfilling and rich, with plum, spice, liquorice and black-pepper flavours, seasoned with toasty oak, and fine-grained tannins. It should be long-lived, but is already delicious.

Vintage	09
WR	7
Drink	10-17

DRY $56 AV

Cable Bay Waiheke Island Syrah ★★★★

The 2009 vintage (★★★★) was matured for over a year in French oak casks. Deep and youthful in colour, it is highly concentrated, with very firm tannins and densely packed plum, pepper, liquorice and nut flavours. It needs time; open 2012+.

Vintage 09
WR 7
Drink 10-16

DRY $33 –V

Cambridge Road Dovetail Syrah/Pinot Noir (★★★★)

Grown in Martinborough, the 2008 vintage (★★★★) was harvested from vines then 22 years old and barrel-aged (12 per cent new). It's a Syrah-dominant style (80 per cent), fresh, elegant, rich and spicy, with good backbone. Worth cellaring.

Vintage 08
WR 4
Drink 10-14

DRY $45 –V

Cambridge Road Martinborough Syrah (★★★★★)

From vines planted in 1986, formerly owned by Murdoch James, the 2008 vintage (★★★★★) is dark and richly scented. A lovely, silky-textured wine with rich, ripe plum and black-pepper flavours, finely integrated oak and a long finish, it offers delicious drinking now onwards.

Vintage 08
WR 6
Drink 10-20

DRY $63 AV

Church Road Hawke's Bay Syrah (★★★★☆)

The debut 2009 vintage (★★★★☆) offers great value. Grown in the Gimblett Gravels (75 per cent) and Pernod Ricard NZ's Redstone Vineyard in The Triangle (25 per cent), it was hand-picked and matured for over a year in French oak barriques (45 per cent new). Weighty and deeply coloured, it has a floral, peppery bouquet. The palate is powerful, with fresh, concentrated plum and spice flavours, savoury, complex and supple. Drink now or cellar.

DRY $27 V+

Church Road Reserve Hawke's Bay Syrah ★★★★☆

The 2008 vintage (★★★★☆) was hand-picked in Pernod Ricard NZ's Redstone Vineyard, in The Triangle, and matured for 16 months in French oak barriques. A powerful, densely coloured red, with concentrated flavours of blackcurrants, plums, dark chocolate and black pepper, seasoned with toasty oak, it's a stylish, complex, rich wine, well worth cellaring.

DRY $37 AV

C.J. Pask Declaration Syrah ★★★★☆

The 2007 vintage (★★★★★), grown in the Gimblett Gravels of Hawke's Bay, has a beautifully floral bouquet, plummy and spicy, with hints of coffee and sweet oak. The palate is bold and rich, with substantial body, deep plum, spice and nut flavours, a silky texture and lovely length.

Vintage	07
WR	7
Drink	10-13

DRY $45 –V

C.J. Pask Gimblett Road Syrah ★★★☆

Top vintages of this Hawke's Bay red offer top value. Estate-grown and matured for a year in French oak casks, the 2008 (★★★) is a middleweight style, deeply coloured, with good depth of blackcurrant, spice and slight herb flavours, braced by tight tannins.

DRY $20 AV

Clevedon Hills Syrah ★★★☆

Grown at Clevedon, in South Auckland, the 2008 vintage (★★★☆) is full-coloured, with a fresh bouquet of plums and pepper. Made in a fruit-driven style, it is vibrant, ripe and supple, showing some savoury complexity and the structure to age. Best drinking mid-2011+. The 2006 (★★★), tasted in mid-2010, is still bright and youthful in colour, with strong plum/spice flavours and fresh acidity. It shows a slight lack of warmth and softness, but is maturing well.

DRY $45 –V

Clos de Ste Anne Syrah The Crucible ★★★★☆

The 2008 vintage (★★★★☆), grown organically in Millton's elevated Clos de Ste Anne vineyard in Gisborne, was matured in large, seasoned oak casks. Perfumed, with a highly spiced, slightly smoky bouquet, it is deeply coloured, mouthfilling and complex, with ripe, spicy, nutty flavours, supple, harmonious, layered and long.

Vintage	08	07	06	05
WR	6	7	6	6
Drink	10-17	10-17	10-15	P

DRY $54 –V

Coney Martinborough Que Sera Syrah ★★★☆

The easy-drinking 2008 vintage (★★★) was matured in oak casks (30 per cent new). Lightish in colour for Syrah, with a fragrant, gently spiced bouquet, it's a medium-bodied wine with satisfying depth of plum/pepper flavours and gentle tannins.

Vintage	08
WR	4
Drink	10-12

DRY $32 –V

Contour Estate Reserve Syrah ★★★★

Launched from the 2007 vintage (★★★★), this rewarding wine has been grown at Matakana, north of Auckland, but the 2009 is the last to be estate-grown – future releases will be made from grapes purchased from Hawke's Bay. Matured in French and American oak barriques, the 2009 (★★★☆) is deeply coloured, with toasty oak aromas leading into a full-flavoured palate, fresh, vibrant and plummy, showing very good depth.

DRY $38 –V

Coopers Creek SV Chalk Ridge Hawke's Bay Syrah ★★★★

The 2008 vintage (★★★★☆) is dark, with rich plum/black-pepper flavours, fresh and long. The 2009 (★★★★) was blended with a splash of Viognier and matured for over a year in French oak casks (50 per cent new). Full-coloured, it is mouthfilling and supple, with ripe plum and spice flavours, showing some savoury, nutty complexity, in a very harmonious style with drink-young appeal.

Vintage	09	08	07	06
WR	7	7	7	6
Drink	11-14	10-13	10-12	P

DRY $28 AV

Corazon Single Vineyard Syrah ★★★☆

Maturing well, the 2008 vintage (★★★★) was hand-picked in Hawke's Bay and matured in French and American oak barriques. Deep and youthful in colour, it is medium to full-bodied, with blackcurrant, plum and spice flavours, showing very good depth, complexity and harmony.

DRY $25 –V

Corbans Cottage Block Hawke's Bay Syrah ★★★★☆

Grown and hand-picked in Pernod Ricard NZ's Redstone Vineyard, in The Triangle, the 2007 vintage (★★★★★) was matured for 18 months in French oak barriques (40 per cent new), and bottled unfined and unfiltered. Dark, powerful and concentrated, it is intensely varietal, with complex plum, black-pepper and toasty oak flavours, tight-knit, strong and youthful, with powerful tannins. The 2008 (★★★★☆) is deeply coloured and scented, with good weight and fresh, intense plum and black-pepper varietal flavours, showing real immediacy.

Vintage	07
WR	7
Drink	10-12

DRY $39 AV

Corbans Private Bin Hawke's Bay Syrah ★★★☆

The 2007 vintage (★★★☆) is dark, with strong, spicy, earthy flavours, showing some complexity, in a slightly more rustic style than its Cottage Block stablemate (above).

DRY $24 AV

Couper's Shed Hawke's Bay Syrah ★★★☆

The 2009 vintage (★★★) is a charming, drink-young style from Pernod Ricard NZ. Full-coloured, vibrantly fruity and supple, it has fresh berry and black-pepper flavours, with a distinctly spicy finish, and a peppery, perfumed bouquet.

DRY $23 AV

Cottle Hill Winery Syrah ★★☆

Grown at Kerikeri, in Northland, the slightly rustic 2006 vintage (★★) was matured for two years in French oak casks. A deeply coloured wine, it lacks real freshness and vibrancy.

DRY $32 –V

Craggy Range Gimblett Gravels Vineyard Syrah ★★★★★

This label (up to and including the 2007 vintage labelled 'Block 14') is overshadowed by the reputation of its stablemate, Le Sol, but further proves the power, structure and finesse that can be achieved with Syrah grown in the Gimblett Gravels of Hawke's Bay. The 2008 (★★★★) is a forward vintage, already drinking well. Hand-picked at 23.7 brix, it was matured for 18 months in French oak barriques (40 per cent new). Deeply coloured and intensely varietal, it has strong cassis, plum and black-pepper flavours, finely integrated French oak and ripe, supple tannins.

Vintage	08	07	06	05	04
WR	6	7	6	7	6
Drink	11-18	10-22	10-20	10-12	10-11

DRY $30 V+

Craggy Range Le Sol Syrah – see Craggy Range Le Sol in the Branded and Other Red Wines section

Crossroads Elms Vineyard Reserve Hawke's Bay Syrah (★★★★☆)

The debut 2007 vintage (★★★★☆) is a single-vineyard red, hand-picked in the Gimblett Gravels and matured for a year in French oak barriques. Densely coloured, it's still extremely youthful, but bursts with ripe plum, spice and liquorice flavours. Firmly structured, with the power to age, it shows great promise; open mid-2010+.

DRY $40 –V

Crossroads Hawke's Bay Syrah ★★☆

The 2008 vintage (★★★) was grown in the Gimblett Gravels and matured for eight months in French oak barriques (18 per cent new). A good drink-young style, it is vibrantly fruity, with clearly varietal aromas and flavours of plums and black pepper, a slightly earthy streak and gentle tannins.

DRY $20 –V

Cypress Hawke's Bay Syrah ★★★★

Estate-grown and hand-picked at Roy's Hill, in the Gimblett Gravels, the 2008 vintage (★★★☆) was matured for four months in seasoned French oak casks. A finely balanced wine, it is full-coloured and supple, with very good depth of plum and black-pepper flavours that build to a well-spiced, rounded finish.

Vintage	08	07
WR	6	6
Drink	10-12	P

DRY $25 AV

Cypress Terraces Hawke's Bay Syrah (★★★★☆)

Estate-grown at Roy's Hill, in the Gimblett Gravels, the classy 2007 vintage (★★★★☆) was matured for 20 months in French oak casks. Dark and generous, it is sweet-fruited, with concentrated plum and spice flavours, showing good complexity, and a firm finish. Drink now or cellar.

Vintage	07
WR	7
Drink	10-13

DRY $40 –V

Dry River Lovat Vineyard Martinborough Syrah ★★★★☆

Top vintages of this rare red, such as the flavour-saturated 2006 (★★★★★), are among the country's best, with strikingly concentrated, tight-knit flavours. The 2008 vintage (★★★★☆) is still very youthful. Deeply coloured, it has a rich, plummy, peppery, slightly smoky fragrance. A medium to full-bodied style (12.5 per cent alcohol), it is fresh and vibrant, with concentrated plum and black-pepper flavours, tight-knit, savoury and supple. Open 2012+.

Vintage	08	07	06	05	04	03	02	01	00
WR	7	6	7	7	6	7	6	7	7
Drink	11-22	10-21	10-20	10-15	10-14	10-17	P	10-11	P

DRY $64 –V

Elephant Hill Hawke's Bay Syrah ★★★★

The 2009 vintage (★★★★☆) is a delicious drink-young style. Hand-picked and matured for 11 months in French oak casks (30 per cent new), it is deeply coloured, with a floral, spicy bouquet, concentrated plum, pepper and spice flavours, showing good complexity, and very supple, ripe tannins. It has great drink-young appeal, but should also age gracefully.

DRY $29 AV

Elephant Hill Reserve Hawke's Bay Syrah ★★★☆

Grown at Te Awanga, the 2008 vintage (★★★☆) was blended with Viognier (1 per cent) and matured for 15 months in French oak casks (100 per cent new). Deeply coloured, it is full-bodied and generous, with concentrated plum and pepper flavours, some herbal and jammy notes, and a rounded finish.

DRY $45 –V

Esk Valley Hawke's Bay Syrah ★★★★

The intensely varietal 2008 vintage (★★★★) was hand-picked and matured for 15 months in French oak barriques. Delicious now, it is deeply coloured, fresh and vibrantly fruity, with strong plum and black-pepper flavours, easy tannins and a smooth, well-spiced finish.

Vintage	09	08	07	06	05
WR	6	6	6	7	6
Drink	11-15	10-12	10-12	10-12	P

DRY $24 V+

Esk Valley Winemakers Reserve Gimblett Gravels Syrah ★★★★★

The 2007 vintage (★★★★★) is the first to be labelled 'Winemakers Reserve' (past releases were sold as 'Reserve'). Grown in the Cornerstone Vineyard, Hawke's Bay, it was matured for 21 months in French oak barriques (35 per cent new). Boldly coloured, it's a powerful wine with deliciously deep, ripe flavours of blackcurrants, plums and spices, showing lovely richness, roundness and harmony. There is no 2008, due to frost.

Vintage	08	07	06	05
WR	NM	7	7	7
Drink	NM	10-17	10-18	10-15

DRY $60 AV

Farmgate Hawke's Bay Syrah (★★★★)

Generous, with loads of personality, the 2007 vintage (★★★★) was made by Ngatarawa for sale via the Farmgate website. Full-coloured, it is sturdy, savoury and spicy, with excellent ripeness, concentration and complexity and a firm foundation of tannin.

DRY $25 AV

Fromm Syrah Fromm Vineyard ★★★★☆

The 2006 vintage (★★★★) was estate-grown in the Wairau Valley, Marlborough, and matured for 16–18 months in French oak barriques (10–20 per cent new). Bold and still youthful in colour, with a spicy, nutty fragrance, it is sturdy, with finely integrated oak and ripe berry and spice flavours, concentrated and supple.

Vintage	08	07	06	05	04	03	02	01
WR	6	6	6	7	7	6	6	7
Drink	11-18	10-17	10-16	10-17	10-16	10-13	10-12	10-13

DRY $51 –V

Georges Michel La Reserve Marlborough Syrah (★★★☆)

Full of drink-young charm, the 2008 vintage (★★★☆) was hand-picked from young vines and French oak-aged for over a year. Vibrant, fruity and supple, it is bright ruby, with fresh plum/spice flavours, gentle tannins and some savoury complexity. Still youthful, it's a very promising debut.

Vintage	08
WR	5
Drink	10-17

DRY $30 –V

Glazebrook Regional Reserve Hawke's Bay Syrah ★★★☆

The 2007 vintage (★★★☆) from Ngatarawa is dark, full-bodied and fresh, with a slightly earthy bouquet and strong plum and spice flavours. It's a sturdy, moderately complex wine, generous and firm.

Vintage	07	06	05
WR	6	6	5
Drink	10-13	10-12	P

DRY $27 –V

Goldridge Estate Premium Reserve Matakana Syrah (★★☆)

The 2008 vintage (★★☆) is solid, showing some spicy, savoury complexity, but also green-edged, lacking a bit of ripeness and roundness.

DRY $19 –V

Greystone Waipara Syrah (★★★☆)

Estate-grown and hand-picked in North Canterbury, the 2008 vintage (★★★☆) is a high-alcohol red (14.5 per cent), matured in French oak casks (65 per cent new). Full-coloured, with a peppery fragrance and gentle tannins, it has very good depth of fresh, spicy, plummy, slightly nutty flavour. Muscular yet supple, it's enjoyable now.

Vintage	09	08
WR	7	6
Drink	10-17	10-16

DRY $46 –V

Gunn Estate Silistria Syrah ★★★★

The 2007 vintage (★★★★) from Sacred Hill was hand-picked in the Gimblett Gravels of Hawke's Bay and matured for a year in French oak barriques (30 per cent new). It is dark and fragrant, with concentrated, ripe blackcurrant, plum and pepper flavours that linger well, and a backbone of fine, silky tannins.

Vintage	07
WR	6
Drink	12-16

DRY $33 –V

Harvest Man Syrah ★★★★☆

From The Hay Paddock, on Waiheke Island, the 2008 vintage (★★★★) was barrel-aged for a year. It's distinctly Rhône Valley-like, with plum and black-pepper flavours, ripe, slightly earthy and savoury, and fine-grained tannins giving early appeal.

Vintage	08	07
WR	5	6
Drink	10-16	10-14

DRY $35 AV

Harwood Hall Marlborough Syrah ★★★☆

Matured for 10 months in seasoned oak barriques, the 2009 vintage (★★★☆) is deeply coloured, floral and supple, in a vibrantly fruity style with good depth of fresh plum and black-pepper flavours. It's a charming, drink-young style, with earthy, savoury notes adding interest.

Vintage	09
WR	6
Drink	10-15

DRY $24 AV

Hyperion Asteria Matakana Syrah (★★☆)

The 2009 vintage (★★☆) was hand-harvested and matured for a year in European oak barriques. Full and youthful in colour, it is mouthfilling, fruity and smooth, with plum and spice flavours, woven with fresh acidity, and a hint of herbs. Moderately ripe-tasting, it shows a slight lack of stuffing and roundness.

Vintage	09
WR	6
Drink	10-18

DRY $32 –V

Instinct Hawke's Bay Syrah (★★★)

From C.J. Pask, the debut 2007 vintage (★★★) has deep colour and mouthfilling body (14 per cent alcohol). Vibrantly fruity, with fresh acidity and vibrant plum and black-pepper flavours, it has lots of drink-young appeal.

DRY $20 –V

Iron Hills Syrah ★★★☆

Grown at Kerikeri, in Northland, the 2007 vintage (★★★☆) was hand-picked at 23 brix and matured in French oak barriques (15 per cent new). Full but not dense in colour, it is supple, with plenty of plummy, spicy flavour, slightly earthy and savoury. An easy-drinking style, it has lots of personality.

Vintage	07
WR	4
Drink	10-12

DRY $25 –V

John Forrest Collection Syrah ★★★★☆

John Forrest views Syrah as Hawke's Bay's 'premier varietal'. Grown in the Cornerstone Vineyard, in the Gimblett Gravels, the 2006 vintage (★★★★☆) has deep colour and a highly fragrant, sweetly oaked bouquet. Mouthfilling (14.5 per cent alcohol) and supple, it has sweet-fruit characters and fresh plum and black-pepper flavours, showing lovely richness and flow.

Vintage	06	05
WR	7	6
Drink	10-15	10-12

DRY $65 –V

Johner Gladstone Syrah ★★★☆

The dark 2009 vintage (★★★☆) was estate-grown in the northern Wairarapa and French oak-aged. It's a sturdy red (14.5 per cent alcohol) with concentrated plum, herb and spice flavours, fresh and strong, and a fragrant, slightly leafy bouquet.

DRY $50 –V

Jurassic Ridge Syrah ★★★★
The 2008 vintage (★★★★) was grown at Church Bay, on Waiheke Island. It's a distinctly savoury and earthy style with good density of blackcurrant and spice flavours and ripe, supple tannins.

Vintage	08
WR	7
Drink	10-14

DRY $35 –V

Karikari Estate Syrah ★★★☆
Estate-grown on Northland's Karikari Peninsula, the 2007 vintage (★★★★) was matured in American and French oak casks (30 per cent new). It's a complex, age-worthy wine with a fragrant, spicy bouquet, concentrated plum, pepper and nutty oak flavours, firm and savoury, and a strongly spicy finish.

Vintage	07
WR	5
Drink	10-12

DRY $29 –V

Kennedy Point Waiheke Island Syrah ★★★★★
A rising star. The refined 2007 vintage (★★★★★) was matured for 18 months in French oak casks. Bold and youthful in colour, with a very fragrant, plummy, peppery, slightly earthy bouquet, it is rich and vibrant, with plum, black-pepper and dark chocolate flavours, highly concentrated and complex. The dark, finely scented 2008 (★★★★★) is powerful, yet very elegant and supple, with a complex array of cassis, spice, liquorice and nut flavours, rich, ripe and flowing. A 'serious' yet seductive wine, it's already delicious, but should mature well for a decade.

Vintage	08	07
WR	7	7
Drink	10-16	11-18

DRY $39 V+

Kidnapper Cliffs Hawke's Bay Syrah (★★★★★)
From Te Awa, the boldly coloured 2009 vintage (★★★★★) is very elegant, finely poised and age-worthy. Estate-grown in the Gimblett Gravels, it's not a blockbuster, but youthful and tightly structured, with fresh, highly concentrated plum and black-pepper flavours, deeply spicy, supple and long. Potentially very complex, it's well worth cellaring to 2014+.

DRY $55 AV

Lammastide Wairarapa Syrah (★★★)
The bargain-priced 2007 vintage (★★★) is drinking well now. Full-coloured, with a slightly leafy bouquet, it is mouthfilling, with generous plum, spice and green-leaf flavours, and a rounded finish.

DRY $14 V+

La Strada Marlborough Syrah ★★★★

The 2008 vintage from Fromm (★★★★) shows again just how enjoyable the region's Syrah can be. Co-fermented with Viognier (5 per cent), it was matured for 16 months in oak barriques. A distinctly cool-climate style, it is densely coloured, with rich, peppery aromas and fresh, vibrant berry and spice flavours, pure and lingering.

Vintage	09	08	07	06	05	04
WR	6	6	7	7	6	6
Drink	10-15	10-14	10-13	10-12	10-11	P

DRY $34 –V

Mahurangi River Winery Companions Syrah/Viognier ★★

The 2008 (☆) is an unoaked style, very light and unripe-tasting. The 2009 vintage (★★☆), matured briefly in French oak casks (50 per cent new), is fullish in colour, in a middleweight style with a spicy, peppery bouquet and fresh, supple, green-edged flavours.

DRY $39 –V

Maimai Creek Hawke's Bay Syrah ★★★

The 2008 vintage (★★★) has fullish, youthful colour. Perfumed, with sweet oak aromas, it is smooth, with plum and black-pepper flavours, in a very easy-drinking style.

DRY $28 –V

Man O' War Waiheke Island Dreadnought Syrah ★★★★☆

Grown on Waiheke Island and matured in French and American oak barriques (20 per cent new), the 2008 vintage (★★★★★) is a fragrant, bold, highly complex red with deep plum, cassis, spice and nut flavours and a very long finish. Deeply coloured, it's a very classy and concentrated wine, built for the long haul. Open 2012+.

Vintage	08	07
WR	6	5
Drink	11-18	10-12

DRY $46 –V

Man O' War Waiheke Island Syrah ★★★★

The 2008 vintage (★★★★) was grown at the eastern end of the island and matured in French and American oak casks. It's a densely packed wine with plum, blackcurrant and spice flavours, a hint of sweet oak, and a firm finish. Powerful and youthful, it should reward cellaring.

Vintage	08	07
WR	6	5
Drink	10-15	10-11

DRY $28 AV

Marsden Bay of Islands Syrah ★★★

The 2009 vintage (★★★☆) was grown at Kerikeri, in Northland, and matured for 15 months in oak casks. Fresh and vibrantly fruity, with full, bright colour, it's a sweet-fruited wine with ripe plum/pepper flavours and drink-young appeal.

Vintage	09
WR	6
Drink	10-14

DRY $35 –V

Matariki Aspire Syrah – see Aspire Syrah

Matariki Hawke's Bay Syrah ★★★★

Estate-grown and hand-picked in the Gimblett Gravels and matured for 18 months in French oak casks (56 per cent new), the 2006 vintage (★★★★) is floral, supple and intensely varietal, with fragrant plum/spice aromas and flavours, gentle tannins, earthy, savoury notes adding complexity and a lengthy finish.

Vintage	06
WR	6
Drink	10-12

DRY $27 AV

Matua Valley Innovator Syrah/Viognier (★★★☆)

An attractive mid-weight, the 2007 vintage (★★★☆) was grown in the Bullrush Vineyard, hand-picked, and matured for 18 months in French oak casks (20 per cent new). It's deeply coloured, with vibrant, ripe, brambly, plummy, spicy flavours, showing some complexity.

Vintage	07
WR	7
Drink	10-12

DRY $25 –V

Matua Valley Reserve Release Hawke's Bay Syrah (★★☆)

Grown in the Matheson Vineyard, in Hawke's Bay, the 2008 vintage (★★) was French oak-aged for 15 months. Light in colour, it has fresh plum and spice flavours, showing moderate depth.

DRY $22 –V

Mills Reef Elspeth Syrah ★★★★★

One of Hawke's Bay's greatest Syrahs. The classy 2007 vintage (★★★★★) was estate-grown and hand-picked at 24 brix at two sites in the Gimblett Gravels – the Mere Road Vineyard (70 per cent) and the Trust Vineyard (30 per cent). Fermented with indigenous yeasts and matured for a year in French oak barriques (65 per cent new), it's a rich, full-bodied style, dark, with ripe sweet-fruit characters, strong, intensely varietal plum, spice and liquorice flavours, showing good complexity, and silky tannins.

Vintage	07	06	05	04	03	02
WR	7	7	7	7	NM	7
Drink	10-17	10-15	10-16	10-15	NM	10-14

DRY $40 AV

Mills Reef Elspeth Trust Vineyard Syrah (★★★★★)

The distinguished 2007 vintage (★★★★★) is an estate-grown, single-vineyard Hawke's Bay red, hand-picked in the Gimblett Gravels, fermented with indigenous yeasts, and matured for 14 months in French oak barriques (50 per cent new). Dark and sweet-fruited, it has a peppery fragrance and dense blackcurrant, plum and pepper flavours, firm and structured. Drink now to 2015.

DRY $40 AV

Mills Reef Reserve Hawke's Bay Syrah ★★★★

The 2007 vintage (★★★★), grown in the Gimblett Gravels, Hawke's Bay, was co-fermented with 2 per cent Viognier. Matured for a year in American oak casks (30 per cent new), it's an intensely varietal wine with deep colour and a fresh, spicy bouquet. Mouthfilling, vibrant and supple, it has blackcurrant, plum and pepper flavours, smooth and strong.

Vintage	07	06	05	04
WR	7	6	7	6
Drink	10-12	P	P	P

DRY $25 AV

Mills Reef Reserve Hawke's Bay Syrah Unfiltered (★★★★)

Bottled unfined and unfiltered 'to retain its full complexity and texture', the 2007 vintage (★★★★) was estate-grown in the Gimblett Gravels, Hawke's Bay, co-fermented with Viognier (2 per cent), and matured for a year in a 4:1 mix of French and American oak barrels (50 per cent new). Full-coloured, it has a ripe, peppery bouquet and flavours, showing good, savoury complexity, and supple tannins.

DRY $25 AV

Miro Syrah (★★★★☆)

Grown on Waiheke Island, the 2008 vintage (★★★★☆) is a blend of Syrah (97 per cent) and Viognier (3 per cent). It's an elegant wine, still very youthful, with concentrated, very fresh and vibrant plum and black-pepper flavours, showing good, savoury complexity. Drink 2012+.

DRY $55 –V

Mission Hawke's Bay Syrah ★★★

The 2009 vintage (★★★), partly oak-aged, is fresh, vibrant and smooth, in a fruit-driven style with good depth of plum, spice and slight herb flavours. It's enjoyable young.

DRY $17 AV

Mission Jewelstone Syrah ★★★★☆

The 2008 vintage (★★★★) was grown in Mere Road, in the Gimblett Gravels of Hawke's Bay, and matured for 17 months in French oak barriques (50 per cent new). A sturdy red, built to last, it is densely coloured, with sweet-fruit characters, strong berry and spice flavours and firm, ripe tannins.

Vintage	08	07
WR	5	7
Drink	11-20	10-20

DRY $35 AV

Mission Reserve Hawke's Bay Syrah ★★★★

The 2009 vintage (★★★☆) is a blend of Gimblett Gravels (89 per cent) and Ohiti Road grapes, matured in French oak casks (17 per cent new). Deeply coloured, it has fresh blackcurrant, plum, spice and nut flavours, showing good ripeness, complexity and length.

Vintage	09	08	07	06
WR	5	5	7	5
Drink	10-16	10-12	10-15	10-11

DRY $24 V+

Mission Vineyard Selection Ohiti Road Syrah ★★★☆

Grown at Ohiti, in Hawke's Bay, the 2009 vintage (★★★☆) was French oak-matured for eight months. Deeply coloured, it has a floral, spicy bouquet. It's enjoyable young, with strong, fresh plum/spice flavours, a subtle oak influence and gentle tannins.

DRY $20 AV

Moana Park Vineyard Selection Gimblett Road Syrah ★★★

The 2009 vintage (★★★) was grown in the Gimblett Gravels and French oak-aged. Full-coloured, it is fruity and smooth, with vibrant, berryish flavours, gentle tannins and a spicy finish.

DRY $22 –V

Moana Park Vineyard Tribute Syrah/Viognier ★★★★

Very rich and soft, the 2008 vintage (★★★★☆) is a dark, powerful Gimblett Road, Hawke's Bay red. Harvested at over 24 brix, matured for a year in French oak barriques (45 per cent new), and bottled unfined and unfiltered, it is perfumed and spicy, with an earthy streak and highly concentrated plum, black-pepper and nut flavours. Worth cellaring.

DRY $32 –V

Morton Estate Black Label Hawke's Bay Syrah ★★★

The 2007 vintage (★★★☆) is full-flavoured, plummy and spicy. It shows good density and complexity, with a fairly firm finish, but some herbal and rustic notes detract slightly.

Vintage	07
WR	7
Drink	10-16

DRY $35 –V

Morton Estate White Label Hawke's Bay Syrah ★★☆

The 2007 vintage (★★☆) has fullish, moderately youthful colour. It's a fruit-driven style, peppery, fresh and supple, for drinking now.

Vintage	07
WR	6
Drink	10-15

DRY $19 –V

Mount Tamahunga Matakana Syrah (★★★☆)

Grown at the property previously called The Antipodean, the 2008 vintage (★★★☆) was matured for 15 months in French oak casks (two-thirds new). Full-coloured, it is mouthfilling and youthful, with very good depth of plum and spice flavours, fresh acidity and considerable complexity. Worth cellaring.

Vintage	08
WR	6
Drink	10-16

DRY $39 –V

Mudbrick Vineyard Reserve Syrah ★★★★☆

Grown on Waiheke Island, the outstanding 2008 vintage (★★★★★) was matured in American oak casks (50 per cent new). Hand-picked, it is finely scented, with deep, purple-flushed colour, mouthfilling body (14.4 per cent alcohol), a core of sweet fruit, lovely density of blackcurrant, plum and black-pepper flavours, nutty and complex, and fine-grained tannins. It's already delicious, but should be long-lived.

Vintage	08	07	06	05
WR	7	7	7	7
Drink	10-15	10-14	10-12	P

DRY $50 –V

Mudbrick Vineyard Shepherds Point Syrah (★★★★☆)

A single-vineyard red, grown at Onetangi, on Waiheke Island, the 2008 vintage (★★★★☆) is dark and powerful (14.5 per cent alcohol), with bold blackcurrant, plum and pepper flavours, seasoned with French oak. The 2009 (★★★★) is an elegant, finely textured wine with good density of plum and black-pepper flavours, ripe and smooth.

Vintage	09	08
WR	6	7
Drink	10-12	10-12

DRY $42 –V

Murdoch James Saleyards Syrah ★★★

The 2008 vintage (★★★) is a Martinborough red, ruby-hued, with a peppery bouquet and silky-smooth palate, showing a hint of herbs and some nutty complexity.

DRY $40 –V

Newton/Forrest Estate Gimblett Gravels Hawke's Bay Syrah (★★★★★)

The powerful, fruit-packed 2006 vintage (★★★★★) is closer to Australian than Rhône styles of Syrah. Grown in the Cornerstone Vineyard and matured in French (70 per cent) and American (30 per cent) oak casks, it is bold and richly coloured, with dense blackcurrant, plum, spice and black-pepper flavours, seasoned with toasty oak, and an underlay of ripe, firm tannins.

Vintage	07	06
WR	7	7
Drink	11-15	11-15

DRY $40 AV

Ngatarawa Silks Syrah ★★★☆

The 2008 vintage (★★★) of this Hawke's Bay red is full-coloured and firm, with good depth of plummy, peppery flavour, fresh and youthful.

Vintage	08	07	06
WR	6	6	6
Drink	10-13	10-12	P

DRY $20 AV

Ngatarawa Stables Reserve Syrah (★★★☆)

The debut 2009 vintage (★★★☆) is youthful, with deep, purple-red colour and fresh cassis, plum and pepper flavours, showing some earthy, savoury notes. It's a well-balanced, vibrantly fruity wine with very satisfying depth.

DRY $22 AV

Nikau Point Hawke's Bay Syrah ★★☆

From Morton Estate, the 2007 vintage (★★★) is a good, gutsy quaffer, with fairly full colour and plenty of firm, spicy flavour.

Vintage	07		DRY $17 –V
WR	7		
Drink	10-14		

Obsidian Waiheke Island Syrah ★★★★★

The dense, serious 2008 (★★★★★) is powerful, tightly structured and built to last. Deep and youthful in colour, it is fragrant, with highly concentrated plum, cassis, black-pepper and nutty oak flavours and a rich, smooth finish. The 2009 vintage (★★★★★) is a beauty. Co-fermented with Viognier (2.5 per cent), it was matured for 10 months in French oak barriques (40 per cent new). Floral, rich and supple, it is very elegant, with deep plum, spice and nut flavours, gentle tannins and a finely poised, silky-smooth finish. It's already delicious, but has obvious cellaring potential.

Vintage	08		DRY $53 AV
WR	7		
Drink	10-20		

Ohinemuri Estate Gimblett Gravels Syrah ★★★☆

Drinking well now, the 2007 vintage (★★★☆) of this Hawke's Bay red has full, bright colour. Barrel-aged for a year, it has strong plum and black-pepper flavours, subtle oak and some nutty complexity.

Vintage	07	06	DRY $25 –V
WR	6	6	
Drink	10-12	P	

Okahu Syrah ★★★★

The 2007 vintage (★★★★) of this Northland red was matured in French and American oak casks (partly new). It's a medium-bodied style (12.5 per cent alcohol), full-coloured and sweet-fruited, fresh and vibrant, with ripe plum and spice flavours, very supple tannins and lots of drink-young appeal.

DRY $30 –V

Omaha Bay Vineyard Huapai Syrah ★★☆

The 2007 vintage (★★) from this Matakana winery was grown in the Papa Vineyard at Huapai, in West Auckland. Full-coloured, with plum and green-leaf flavours, it is earthy and slightly medicinal, and clearly overshadowed by its Matakana stablemate of the same vintage (below).

Vintage	07	06	05	04	DRY $27 –V
WR	6	5	5	6	
Drink	10-15	10-14	10-11	P	

Omaha Bay Vineyard Matakana Syrah (★★★★)

The 2007 vintage (★★★★) is dark and fruit-crammed, with rich, vibrant plum and black-pepper flavours, a sweet oak influence and a long, spicy finish. It's a concentrated wine, worth cellaring.

Vintage	07
WR	6
Drink	10-19

DRY $30 –V

Paritua Hawke's Bay Syrah ★★★★

Already delicious, the 2008 vintage (★★★★☆) was estate-grown in The Triangle. Sweet-fruited and finely textured, it has a fragrant, nutty, complex bouquet, leading into a rich and silky palate with plum, spice and slight liquorice flavours, very generous and harmonious.

Vintage	07
WR	7
Drink	10-14

DRY $37 –V

Passage Rock Reserve David's Syrah (★★★★★)

The rare 2008 vintage (★★★★★) was grown on Waiheke Island and matured in French oak barriques (100 per cent new). Densely coloured, it's a classy, seamless wine, powerful (14.5 per cent alcohol) but not heavy, with beautifully ripe cassis and spice flavours, showing notable density, roundness and harmony.

DRY $100 AV

Passage Rock Reserve Syrah ★★★★★

Waiheke Island's most awarded wine of late is partly estate-grown and fully matured in American and French oak barriques, mostly new. A powerful, opulent red, it is seductively rich and well-rounded. Big, black and beautiful, the 2008 (★★★★★) is a great vintage of a classic label. Densely coloured, with a beautifully fragrant, peppery bouquet, it has highly concentrated plum, cherry and spice flavours, rich, finely textured and flowing.

DRY $50 AV

Passage Rock Syrah ★★★★★

This Waiheke Island red is consistently rewarding. Partly estate-grown and fully matured in American (mostly) and French oak barriques, the 2008 vintage (★★★★★) has bold, bright colour and highly concentrated plum and black-pepper flavours, firm and very youthful. Beautifully ripe and rich, with a solid underlay of tannin and good complexity, it's well worth cellaring.

DRY $35 V+

Providence Matakana Syrah ★★★★

Tasted in 2009, the 2002 vintage (★★★) was savoury and mellow, and the 2004 (★★★☆) was still fresh, with considerable complexity, but the 2005 (★★★★★) is the first distinguished Syrah from this small, highly regarded producer. Richly coloured, it is generous, with ripe cassis and black-pepper flavours, showing lovely texture, complexity and depth.

DRY $130 –V

Ra Nui Cob Cottage Reserve Marlborough Limited Release Syrah (★★☆)

A light style, the 2007 vintage (★★☆) is a single-vineyard wine, matured for 20 months in French oak barriques. Full in colour, with leafy aromas and flavours, it offers smooth, easy drinking.

DRY $30 –V

Sacred Hill Deer Stalkers Syrah ★★★★☆

Less striking than the memorable 2007 vintage (★★★★★), the 2008 (★★★★) was hand-picked in the Gimblett Gravels, Hawke's Bay, and matured for 16 months in French oak barriques. Dark and dense, it has fresh, concentrated cassis, plum and black-pepper flavours, firm, ripe tannins and good cellaring potential.

Vintage	08	07	06
WR	6	7	7
Drink	10-16	10-15	10-16

DRY $50 –V

Sacred Hill Halo Hawke's Bay Syrah (★★★☆)

Very enjoyable in its youth, the debut 2008 vintage (★★★☆) of this Hawke's Bay red was mostly grown in The Triangle, with 'a touch of Gimblett Gravels'. Full-coloured, with a floral bouquet, it is fresh and vibrant, with plum and pepper flavours showing some savoury complexity and gentle tannins.

DRY $26 –V

Sacred Hill The Wine Thief Series Hawke's Bay Syrah ★★★★

The 2007 vintage (★★★★) was harvested in the Gimblett Gravels and matured for a year in French oak (30 per cent new). It's an intensely varietal, boldly coloured wine with a strong surge of blackcurrant, plum and spice flavours, a delicate seasoning of toasty oak, and finely balanced tannins.

Vintage	07	06
WR	7	7
Drink	10-11	10-12

DRY $30 –V

Saltings Estate Matakana Vineyard Syrah ★★★

Hand-picked from a sloping site overlooking the Sandspit estuary, the 2007 vintage (★★★) was matured for 16 months in seasoned French oak casks. Deeply coloured, it's a medium to full-bodied wine with plenty of flavour, an earthy streak, leafy notes and some complexity.

DRY $31 –V

Salvare Hawke's Bay Syrah (★★★)

Grown in Gimblett Road and barrel-aged for a year, the fruity 2007 vintage (★★★) is a mid-weight style with bright colour and vibrant flavours of plums and black pepper, fresh and smooth.

DRY $25 –V

Sears Road Syrah (★★☆)

Grown in Hawke's Bay, the 2008 vintage (★★☆) is a solid quaffer. Fullish in colour, it is medium-bodied, with fresh plum/spice flavours, a hint of sweet oak and a smooth finish.

DRY $14 AV

Seifried Nelson Syrah ★★★

Grown at Brightwater, on the Waimea Plains, and matured in French oak barriques, the 2008 vintage (★★★) is a light style, with lots of drink-young appeal. Ruby-hued, it has plummy, distinctly spicy aromas and flavours, some oak complexity and a peppery, smooth finish.

Vintage	08
WR	6
Drink	10-15

DRY $21 –V

Selaks Winemakers Favourite Hawke's Bay Syrah ★★★★

Grown partly in the company's Corner 50 Vineyard, in The Triangle, and in the Gimblett Gravels, the 2008 vintage (★★★☆) was matured for nearly a year in French and American oak barriques (new and one-year-old). It's an easy-drinking style, fruity and supple, with clearly varietal plum/black-pepper flavours, showing good complexity and depth.

DRY $21 V+

Shipwreck Bay Syrah ★★★☆

From Okahu Estate, the 2008 vintage (★★★) is a blend of estate-grown, Northland (70 per cent) and Te Hana (north of Auckland) grapes. Full-coloured, with cherryish, plummy, slightly earthy flavours, seasoned with sweet oak, and gentle tannins, it's an enjoyable mid-weight.

DRY $18 V+

Sileni Cellar Selection Hawke's Bay Syrah ★★★

The floral, easy-drinking 2008 vintage (★★★) was French and American oak-aged. Full-coloured, it has black-pepper and slight herb flavours, a touch of savoury complexity and gentle tannins.

Vintage	08
WR	5
Drink	10-12

DRY $20 –V

Sileni The Peak Hawke's Bay Syrah (★★★☆)

A single-vineyard red, grown in The Triangle and French and American oak-matured for over a year, the 2007 vintage (★★★☆) is full-coloured, fresh, ripe, plummy and supple, with gentle black-pepper notes and good fruit sweetness, complexity and depth.

Vintage	07
WR	5
Drink	10-14

DRY $30 –V

Soho Valentino Waiheke Island Syrah (★★★★)

The 2009 vintage (★★★★) is deeply coloured, with a nutty, spicy bouquet. It's a rich, ripe, concentrated red with plum, spice and liquorice flavours, strongly seasoned with toasty oak. Showing good warmth and density, it needs time; open 2012+.

DRY $38 –V

Soland Syrah ★★★

Grown in the tiny (0.8-hectare) Fat Pig Vineyard at Kerikeri, in Northland, the 2007 vintage (★★☆) is fresh, vibrant, crisp and peppery, but lacks a bit of ripeness and roundness.

DRY $25 –V

Southbank Estate Hawke's Bay Syrah ★★★

The 2007 vintage (★★☆) is dark, gutsy and firm, with plum and black-pepper flavours, but slightly rustic.

DRY $20 AV

Squawking Magpie The Chatterer Hawke's Bay Syrah ★★★☆

The 2007 vintage (★★★★) is a deeply coloured Gimblett Gravels red with a floral, peppery bouquet. Mouthfilling, it has firm tannins and strong blackcurrant and spice flavours, showing good complexity.

DRY $25 –V

Squawking Magpie The Stoned Crow Syrah ★★★★

Densely coloured, the 2007 vintage (★★★★) was grown in the Gimblett Gravels, Hawke's Bay. Well worth cellaring, it has firm tannins and blackcurrant, pepper and nut flavours, showing excellent concentration.

DRY $40 –V

Staete Landt Marlborough Syrah ★★★☆

The 2008 vintage (★★★☆) was hand-harvested at Rapaura and matured for 17 months in French oak barriques (40 per cent new). Full-coloured, it is sturdy and firm, with fresh plum and spice flavours, showing a hint of tamarillo, lots of toasty oak, and good concentration and complexity.

Vintage	08
WR	6
Drink	11-17

DRY $55 –V

Stonecroft Hawke's Bay Crofters Syrah ★★★☆

The non-vintage wine (★★★☆) on the market in early 2010 tastes like a decent Côtes-du-Rhône. Blended mostly from 2007 wine, estate-grown in the Gimblett Gravels and barrel-aged, it is plummy, nutty and spicy, in a flavoursome, savoury, earthy style with considerable complexity. Drink now.

DRY $20 AV

Stonecroft Serine Syrah ★★★★

The 2008 vintage (★★★★) was estate-grown in the Gimblett Gravels and matured for 18 months in French oak casks (33 per cent new). It's an elegant, vibrantly fruity red, full-coloured, with plummy, distinctly spicy flavours, good savoury complexity and fairly firm tannins. Worth cellaring.

Vintage	08	07	06
WR	6	5	5
Drink	10-15	10-15	10-15

DRY $25 AV

Stonecroft Syrah ★★★★★

This Hawke's Bay winery was the first to consistently produce a top-flight Syrah in New Zealand. The early vintages were grown entirely in Stonecroft's stony, arid vineyard in Mere Road, west of Hastings, but the 1998 introduced grapes from the newer Tokarahi Vineyard at the foot of Roy's Hill, which is contributing 'denser, more intense flavours'. Maturation is for 18 months in French oak barriques (one-third to 50 per cent new). The 2008 vintage (★★★★☆) is refined, with good density of youthful, plum and black-pepper flavours, and ripe, supple tannins. Full-coloured, it's a complex, finely textured wine, likely to be at its best 2012+.

Vintage	08	07	06	05	04	03	02
WR	7	6	6	5	NM	7	5
Drink	13-20	12-20	10-20	10-20	NM	10-15	10-12

DRY $45 AV

Stone Paddock Hawke's Bay Syrah ★★☆

From Paritua, the 2008 vintage (★★☆), matured for nine months in barrels (30 per cent new), is fullish in colour, with spicy, slightly earthy flavours, offering pleasant, easy drinking.

Vintage	08
WR	6
Drink	10-14

DRY $23 –V

Stonyridge Pilgrim Syrah/Mourvedre/Grenache ★★★★★

The 2008 vintage (★★★★★) of this Rhône-style blend was estate-grown at Onetangi, on Waiheke Island, and matured for a year in French oak barriques (50 per cent new). Still youthful, it is floral and dark, dense, savoury, complex and finely textured, with a well-rounded, very harmonious finish. The 2009 (★★★★) is highly refined. Fleshy, it is deeply coloured, rich and supple, with sweet-fruit delights and deep blackcurrant, plum and spice flavours. A muscular wine with real power and complexity, it's well worth cellaring.

Vintage	09
WR	7
Drink	11-18

DRY $80 AV

Te Awa Left Field Hawke's Bay Syrah (★★★☆)

Designed for early drinking, the 2009 vintage (★★★☆) was estate-grown in the Gimblett Gravels, blended with a small amount of Viognier, and matured for nine months in old oak hogsheads. It's a fruit-driven style, deeply coloured, with very good depth of strongly varietal, plummy, peppery flavour, fresh, vibrant and youthful.

DRY $26 –V

Te Awa Syrah ★★★★

The boldly coloured 2009 vintage (★★★★) of this estate-grown, Gimblett Gravels, Hawke's Bay red is mouthfilling and sweet-fruited, with rich plum and black-pepper flavours, and a hint of liquorice. Finely textured and vibrantly fruity, it's likely to be at its best 2012+.

DRY $35 –V

Te Kairanga Runholder Syrah (★★★☆)

The debut 2008 vintage (★★★☆) was grown in Hawke's Bay and matured for 17 months in French oak casks (42 per cent new). Richly coloured, with a fresh, spicy bouquet, it is mouthfilling, with plum, spice and black-pepper flavours, showing some savoury complexity, and good tannin backbone. Drink now or cellar.

Vintage	08
WR	7
Drink	10-18

DRY $29 –V

Te Mania Nelson Syrah ★★☆

The 2008 vintage (★★★) was hand-picked and matured for 10 months in seasoned French and American oak casks. It has fragrant, strongly peppery aromas, leading into a full-flavoured, spicy wine, with soft tannins giving an easy-drinking appeal.

Vintage	08	07	06
WR	5	6	5
Drink	10-12	P	P

DRY $22 –V

Te Mata Estate Bullnose Syrah ★★★★★

Grown in the Bullnose Vineyard, in The Triangle inland from Hastings, in Hawke's Bay, this classy red is based on 12 to 20-year-old vines, hand-picked and matured for 15 to 16 months in French oak barriques (35 per cent new). Unlike its Woodthorpe stablemate (below), it is not blended with Viognier, and the vines for the Bullnose label are cropped lower. The 2008 (★★★★★) is highly refined, with a lovely fragrance and deep plum, black-pepper and dark chocolate flavours, very fresh, supple and rich. It's a forward vintage; drink now or cellar.

Vintage	08	07	06	05	04	03	02
WR	7	7	7	7	7	6	7
Drink	10-16	10-17	10-16	10-15	10-12	P	P

DRY $44 AV

Te Mata Estate Woodthorpe Syrah ★★★☆

The good-value 2009 vintage (★★★☆) was made by co-fermenting Syrah, estate-grown in the Woodthorpe Vineyard, in Hawke's Bay, with a small amount of Viognier. French oak-aged for 13 months, it has a floral, peppery bouquet, leading into a fresh, supple wine with very good depth of plum/spice flavours, a touch of complexity and lots of drink-young appeal.

Vintage	09
WR	7
Drink	10-13

DRY $19 V+

Te Puna Mountain Landing Syrah (★★★)

Grown on the Purerua Peninsula, in Northland, the 2009 vintage (★★★) was picked at over 25 brix from first-crop vines and matured for a year in seasoned oak casks. Full-coloured, it has a peppery fragrance, with plummy, spicy, slightly raisiny flavours and substantial body.

DRY $40 –V

Terrace Edge Waipara Valley Syrah ★★★

The 2008 vintage (★★★☆) was hand-picked, fermented with indigenous yeasts and matured for 10 months in French oak barriques (25 per cent new). It's a spicy and flavoursome red with fresh acidity, but also green-edged, showing a slight lack of ripeness and roundness.

DRY $23 –V

Te Whau Vineyard Waiheke Island Syrah ★★★★★

The superb 2008 vintage (★★★★★) was hand-harvested from young, hill-grown vines, trained on stakes with no wires, fermented with indigenous yeasts and matured for over a year in two French oak barrels (one new). Dark and highly scented, it is rich and supple, with great fruit sweetness and complexity. The 2009 (★★★★☆) is rare – only 24 cases were produced. It has a very fragrant bouquet of spices, earth and olives, showing excellent complexity. The palate is very full-bodied, firm and savoury, with deep spice, plum, herb and dark chocolate flavours, and a rounded finish. Highly concentrated, it impresses as a forward vintage, to enjoy now onwards.

Vintage	09	08	07
WR	7	7	7
Drink	10-15	10-15	10-13

DRY $85 –V

Ti Point Hawke's Bay Syrah (★★★☆)

The 2008 vintage (★★★☆) is a buoyantly fruity Gimblett Gravels red, hand-picked and French oak-aged for a year, with very good depth of plum and black-pepper flavours. It's a deeply coloured, mouthfilling wine with gentle tannins.

DRY $22 AV

Tinpot Hut Hawke's Bay Syrah (★★★☆)

The 2007 vintage (★★★☆) is a single-vineyard red, grown in the Dartmoor Valley and matured in tanks and barrels. Fragrant plum and pepper aromas lead into a vibrant, fruit-driven style, moderately complex, with plenty of flavour, gentle tannins and good harmony and immediacy.

DRY $29 –V

Trinity Hill Gimblett Gravels Syrah ★★★★☆

Winemakers John Hancock and Warren Gibson are pursuing a 'savoury, earthy Rhône style'. Grown in the Gimblett Gravels, the 2008 vintage (★★★★☆) was hand-picked, co-fermented with Viognier (8 per cent), and matured for over a year in French oak barriques (25 per cent new). Fleshy and fruity, with excellent depth through the palate, it's a highly approachable, warm and supple red with deep colour and ripe blackcurrant, plum and spice flavours, showing excellent complexity. It's still youthful; open mid-2011+.

Vintage	08	07	06	05	04	03	02
WR	6	6	6	5	6	NM	6
Drink	12-20	10-17	10-18	10-15	10-12	NM	10-15

DRY $35 AV

Trinity Hill Hawke's Bay Syrah ★★★☆

The 2009 vintage (★★★☆) was hand-picked and partly barrel-aged. Fleshy and fruity, it is deeply coloured and floral, with plenty of peppery, plummy flavour, a hint of dark chocolate and a well-rounded finish.

DRY $20 AV

Trinity Hill Homage Gimblett Gravels Hawke's Bay Syrah ★★★★★

One of the country's most distinguished – and expensive – reds. Harvested by hand from ultra low-cropped (2.5 tonnes/hectare), mature vines, and matured for 18 months in French oak barriques (mostly new), the 2007 vintage (★★★★★) is a densely coloured, majestic red, still very youthful. Blended with Viognier (9 per cent), it has a commanding mouthfeel (14.5 per cent alcohol), with highly concentrated flavours of plums, spices and liquorice, and a foundation of ripe, fine-grained tannins. It's still years away from revealing its full personality; open 2012+.

Vintage	07	06	05	04	03	02
WR	6	7	NM	5	NM	6
Drink	10-17	10-17	NM	10-14	NM	10-14

DRY $120 –V

Two Gates Hawke's Bay Syrah (★★★★)

Certified organic, the 2007 vintage (★★★★) is a Gimblett Gravels red with dark colour and dense, spicy flavours. A single-vineyard wine, it was harvested from six-year-old vines and matured for 18 months in French oak barriques (50 per cent new). Powerful, with a strong seasoning of smoky oak, it has loads of rich, ripe fruit and a long finish.

DRY $55 –V

Unison Hawke's Bay Syrah ★★★★☆

The 2008 vintage (★★★★) was hand-picked in the Gimblett Gravels and barrel-aged for 16 months. Deeply coloured, with a peppery fragrance, it is still very youthful, with fresh plum, spice and dark chocolate flavours, showing good concentration. Open 2012+.

DRY $39 AV

Vidal Hawke's Bay Syrah ★★★★

The 2007 vintage (★★★★☆) was grown in the Gimblett Gravels (93 per cent) and matured for 18 months in French oak barriques (39 per cent new). Dark and youthful in colour, it is mouthfilling, with highly concentrated plum, black-pepper and nutty oak flavours, and lovely texture. The 2008 (★★★☆) is fresh and aromatic, with deep, bright colour and very good depth of plum/spice flavours, showing some savoury complexity.

Vintage	08	07	06
WR	7	7	7
Drink	10-13	10-14	10-11

DRY $26 AV

Vidal Reserve Hawke's Bay Syrah ★★★★★

Grown in the Gimblett Gravels, this is typically a dark, opulent wine with dense plum, spice and liquorice flavours, lush and long. A powerful, very ripe style, it needs about four years to show at its best. The 2007 vintage (★★★★☆), matured for 20 months in French oak barriques (25 per cent new), is densely coloured, with highly concentrated plum and black-pepper flavours. (There is no 2008.)

Vintage	08	07	06	05	04
WR	NM	7	7	7	7
Drink	NM	10-15	10-13	10-15	10-12

DRY $55 AV

View Estate Syrah (★★★★)

The instantly appealing 2008 vintage (★★★★) was grown on Waiheke Island, hand-picked at 23.7 brix and oak-aged for 10 months. It has strong, ripe plum/spice flavours, seasoned with sweet American oak, and a well-rounded finish. Ready to roll.

DRY $39 –V

Villa Maria Cellar Selection Hawke's Bay Syrah ★★★★★

A great buy. The 2008 vintage (★★★★☆), estate-grown and hand-picked in the Gimblett Gravels (mostly), was matured for 20 months in French oak barriques (45 per cent new). It's a beautifully fragrant wine with concentrated, ripe plum and spice flavours, and gentle tannins giving drink-young appeal.

Vintage	08	07	06	05	04
WR	7	7	6	6	7
Drink	11-15	10-15	10-16	10-12	10-12

DRY $32 V+

Villa Maria Private Bin Hawke's Bay Syrah ★★★☆

The 2008 vintage (★★★★) is a full-flavoured, distinctly spicy blend of Dartmoor Valley (60 per cent) and Gimblett Gravels grapes, including Viognier (2 per cent). Matured in French and American oak barriques (30 per cent new), it has a peppery bouquet, showing good complexity. The palate is mouthfilling and generous, with blackcurrant, plum and spice flavours, fresh, ripe and rounded.

Vintage	08
WR	6
Drink	10-12

DRY $26 –V

Villa Maria Reserve Hawke's Bay Syrah ★★★★★

The 2007 vintage (★★★★★) is a densely coloured, power-packed Gimblett Gravels red, matured for 20 months in French oak barriques (56 per cent new). It should be long-lived, with a notably fragrant bouquet of dark berries, tar, anise and violets, bold plum, black-pepper and liquorice flavours, very fine tannins and good complexity.

Vintage	07	06	05
WR	7	7	7
Drink	10-19	10-18	10-19

DRY $56 AV

Waimata Cognoscenti Syrah (★★★★)

The attractively perfumed 2008 vintage (★★★★) is a Gisborne red, co-fermented with Viognier (2 per cent) and matured in French (mostly) and American oak (30 per cent new). Full-coloured, with concentrated, ripe, spicy flavours, showing good complexity and length, it is elegant, vibrantly fruity and tightly structured, with aging potential.

DRY $25 AV

Waimea Nelson Syrah ★★★

The 2008 vintage (★★★) is a single-vineyard red, American oak-aged. It's a mouthfilling wine with perfumed oak aromas and satisfying depth of plum and spice flavours, fresh, vibrant and supple.

Vintage	08	07
WR	6	6
Drink	10-12	10-11

DRY $24 –V

Waitapu Estate Reef Point Syrah (★★★)

The full-coloured 2008 vintage (★★★) was grown at Ahipara, in Northland. Still fresh and vibrantly fruity, with plenty of plummy, spicy flavour, seasoned with cedary French oak, it is floral and supple, with some aging potential.

DRY $28 –V

Weeping Sands Waiheke Island Syrah ★★★★☆

From Obsidian, the 2009 vintage (★★★★) was grown at Onetangi, blended with Viognier (2.5 per cent), and matured in French (principally) and American oak casks (25 per cent new). Dark, with a fragrant, spicy bouquet, it is very youthful, with deep blackcurrant, plum and black-pepper flavours, finely integrated oak and ripe, supple tannins. Best drinking mid-2011+.

Vintage	09	08	07	06
WR	6	7	6	5
Drink	10-18	10-16	10-15	10-12

DRY $31 AV

Wild Rock Angel's Dust Hawke's Bay Syrah ★★★☆

Still youthful, the 2008 vintage (★★★☆) is a blend of Syrah (98 per cent) and Malbec (2 per cent), matured for over a year in French oak barriques (16 per cent new). It's an intensely varietal wine, with accentuated, spicy aromas. Full-coloured, it has mouthfilling body and strong, vibrant plum and black-pepper flavours.

Vintage	08
WR	7
Drink	10-14

DRY $25 –V

Tempranillo

The star grape of Rioja, Tempranillo is grown extensively across northern and central Spain, where it yields strawberry, spice and tobacco-flavoured reds, full of personality. Barrel-aged versions mature well, developing great complexity. The great Spanish variety is starting to spread into the New World, but is still very rare in New Zealand, with 7 hectares of bearing vines in 2011 (mostly in Hawke's Bay).

Black Barn Hawke's Bay Tempranillo (★★★★☆)

Hand-picked at Havelock North, the 2009 vintage (★★★★☆) is deeply coloured, generous, full-bodied (14.5 per cent alcohol) and supple, with deep plum and spice flavours, hints of raisins and liquorice, power through the palate and good, savoury complexity. Full of personality, it should be at its best mid-2011+.

DRY $48 –V

Hawkes Ridge Tempranillo (★★★)

Hand-picked in Hawke's Bay, the 2008 vintage (★★★) has fullish colour, with some early development showing. Slightly leafy, it's a smooth, middleweight red with fresh acidity and cherry/plum flavours that show some savoury complexity, but it lacks real ripeness and stuffing. Drink now.

DRY $36 –V

Pete's Shed Tempranillo ★★☆

From Yealands, the 2009 vintage (★★☆) was estate-grown in the Awatere Valley, Marlborough, hand-picked at 25 brix, and matured for eight months in seasoned French oak casks. It's a lightweight style with plum/spice flavours and hints of herbs and tamarillos, but lacks any real stuffing.

DRY $23 –V

Rock Ferry Central Otago Tempranillo (★★★☆)

Grown at Bendigo – as far from Rioja, Spain, as anyone has planted the famous red-wine grape – the debut 2008 vintage (★★★☆) is a hand-picked, single-vineyard red, matured for a year in seasoned oak casks. Full-coloured and sweetly oaked, it's a promising debut – plummy and spicy, showing some savoury complexity and a smooth finish. Drink now.

Vintage	09	08
WR	5	6
Drink	11-16	10-13

DRY $39 –V

Trinity Hill Gimblett Gravels Tempranillo ★★★★★

This is a consistently impressive red, full of personality. The 2008 vintage (★★★★★), grown in the Gimblett Gravels, Hawke's Bay, was matured for 10 months in French (90 per cent) and American oak casks (25 per cent new). A blend of Tempranillo (87 per cent), Touriga Nacional (10 per cent), Malbec (2 per cent) and Viognier (1 per cent), it's a generous, serious, age-worthy red with full, youthful colour and fresh, deep plum and spice flavours, complex, savoury, finely balanced and lingering.

Vintage	08	07	06	05	04
WR	6	6	6	5	5
Drink	11-14	11-14	10-14	10-12	10-11

DRY $35 V+

Zinfandel

In California, where it is extensively planted, Zinfandel produces muscular, heady reds that can approach a dry port style. It is believed to be identical to the Primitivo variety, which yields highly characterful, warm, spicy reds in southern Italy. There are only 4 hectares of bearing Zinfandel vines in New Zealand, clustered in Hawke's Bay, with no expansion projected between 2004 and 2011. Alan Limmer, founder of the Stonecroft winery in Hawke's Bay, believes 'Zin' has potential here, 'if you can stand the stress of growing a grape that falls apart at the first sign of a dubious weather map!'

Stonecroft Zinfandel ★★★☆

The 2008 vintage (★★★☆) was estate-grown in the Gimblett Gravels of Hawke's Bay and matured for over 18 months in American oak casks. Ruby-hued, it's a fresh, lively, medium-bodied red with spicy, slightly peppery aromas and flavours and a firm finish, but lacks real richness.

Vintage	08	07
WR	4	7
Drink	10-15	10-20

DRY $27 –V

Zweigelt

Austria's most popular red-wine variety is a crossing of Blaufränkisch and St Laurent. It's a naturally high-yielding variety, but cropped lower can produce appealing, velvety reds, usually at their best when young. Zweigelt is extremely rare in New Zealand, with 3 hectares planted. (See also Seifried Sylvia, in the Branded and Other Red Wines section.)

Hans Herzog Marlborough Zweigelt (★★★★)

The debut 2008 vintage (★★★★) was hand-picked at 23.8 brix and matured for a year in French oak barriques (50 per cent new). Boldly coloured, it has concentrated, berryish flavours, fresh and rich, with a slight medicinal note that is presumably characteristic of the variety.

Vintage	09
WR	7
Drink	10-21

DRY $53 –V

Index of Wine Brands

This index should be especially useful when you are visiting wineries as a quick way to find the reviews of each company's range of wines. It also provides links between different wine brands made by the same producer (for example, Grove Mill and Sanctuary).

3 Stones 42, 159, 266
3 Terraces 159, 514
25 Steps 514
36 Bottles 159, 514
1769 515
1912 515
12,000 Miles 160, 267, 515

Abbey Cellars 219, 372, 453, 470, 474
Akarua 42, 160, 219, 515
  (*see also* Rua)
Ake Ake 42, 160, 411, 468, 474
Alana 42, 219, 372, 516
alex.gold 516
Alexander 474, 516
Alexandra Wine Company 42, 516
  (*see also* alex.gold)
Alexia 43, 160, 220, 267, 411, 475, 517
Allan Scott 43, 133, 160, 220, 267, 372, 395, 396, 517
  (*see also* Scott Base)
Alluviale 34, 373, 429
  (*see also* Redd Gravels)
Alpha Domus 34, 43, 44, 267, 361, 373, 411, 429, 475, 630
  (*see also* Bell Bird Bay)
Alpine Valley 268
Amisfield 161, 220, 268, 373, 374, 412, 517, 518 (*see also* Lake Hayes)
Anchorage 44, 133, 161, 220, 221, 268, 361, 374, 518
  (*see also* Little Black Shag, Mt Campbell, Southern Lighthouse, Torrent Bay, Tranquillity Bay)
Anthem 518
Ant Moore 161, 221

Aquila 396
Ara 268, 269, 518, 519
Arcadia 396
Archangel 519
Arrow Rock 269
Artisan 34, 44, 132, 133, 161, 221, 269, 374, 412, 429, 450, 519, 630
Ascension 44, 132, 361, 412, 450, 475, 511, 630
Ash Ridge 269
Ashwell 45, 270, 453, 519, 520
Ashwood 161
Askerne 45, 134, 162, 270, 359, 361, 374, 412, 454, 475, 520
Aspire 45, 270, 454, 520, 631
Astrolabe 45, 134, 162, 221, 270, 271, 520 (*see also* Durvillea)
Ataahua 46, 134, 476, 521
Ata Rangi 46, 163, 271, 374, 412, 430, 520, 521
Auburn 222
Auntsfield 46, 271, 521
Aurora 163, 222, 375, 522, 631
Aurum 163, 222, 375, 522
  (*see also* Point d'Or)
Awaroa 412, 454, 476, 631
Awatere River 163, 272, 523
Awa Valley 470, 476, 522
Awhitu 631

Babich 48, 134, 163, 222, 272, 362, 430, 454, 476, 477, 511, 523, 631, 632 (*see also* Cheeky Little, Rongopai, Te Henga)
Bald Hills 164, 223, 523
Bannock Brae 223, 413, 523, 524
Barking Hedge 273, 524

Bascand 48, 164, 223, 273, 413, 524
Beach House 48, 135, 223, 375, 450, 454, 477, 508, 632
Bel Echo 273, 524
Bell Bird Bay 477
Bellbird Spring 34, 164, 273, 424
Bell Hill 525
Belmonte 273, 525
Benfield & Delamare 430
Bensen Block 48, 164, 273, 477
Bernadino 396
Big Sky 274, 525
Bijou 164
Bilancia 164, 165, 525, 832
Bird 135, 165, 274, 525
Bishop's Head 165, 223, 525 (*see also* Rock Face)
Black Barn 48, 49, 165, 224, 274, 477, 508, 526, 629, 632, 659
Black Cottage 165, 274, 526
Blackenbrook 49, 135, 156, 165, 224, 274, 508, 526 (*see also* St Jacques)
Black Estate 49, 224, 526
Black Quail 526
Black Ridge 526
Black Stilt 166
Bladen 135, 166, 224, 275, 477, 527
Blairpatrick 527
Blind River 275
Bloody Bay 49, 166, 527, 633
Blue Ridge 49, 527
Boatshed Bay 50, 527
BorehamWood 166, 224, 275
Borthwick 50, 224, 275, 527
Boulder Bank Road 276
Boulders 225
Bouldevines 50, 135, 166, 225, 276, 528 (*see also* Sprig)
Boundary 50, 166, 276, 528, 633
Bracken's Order 157, 528
Brams Run 276, 528
Brancott 50, 136, 166, 167, 276, 397, 528

Breakers Bay 277
Breaksea Sound 528
Brennan 136, 167, 529
Brick Bay 167, 430, 431
Brightside 50, 167, 225, 277, 529
Brightwater 51, 167, 225
Brodie 529
Bronte 168, 529
Brookfields 51, 136, 168, 225, 277, 362, 375, 455, 470, 478, 633
Brunton Road 52, 136, 168, 478
Burnt Spur 168, 277, 530
Bushmere 52, 136, 362
Butterfish Bay 168, 362, 413

Cable Bay 136, 278, 362, 413, 431, 530, 633, 634 (*see also* Culley)
Cable Station 53, 530
Cadwalladers 53
Cambridge Road 413, 530, 634
Camshorn 169, 226, 278, 530
Canadoro 455
Cape Campbell 53, 169, 278, 531 (*see also* Cable Station, Lobster Reef)
Carrick 53, 54, 169, 225, 278, 531
Castaway Bay 169, 278
Catalina Sounds 54, 169, 278, 531
Cathedral Cove 54, 278, 478
Cellar 9 532
Central Schist 532
Charcoal Gully 532
Chard Farm 54, 169, 279, 532 (*see also* Rabbit Ranch)
Chardon 397
Charles Wiffen 54, 137, 170, 226, 279, 376, 478, 532
Cheeky Little 54, 279, 431
Church Road 55, 170, 279, 362, 376, 455, 456, 473, 478, 479, 533, 634
Churton 279, 533
Cicada 280
C.J. Pask 56, 280, 456, 470, 479, 635 (*see also* Instinct)

Clark Estate 170, 227, 280
Clayfork 280
Claylaur 280
Clayridge 157, 170, 227, 280, 363, 533
Clearview 35, 56, 57, 137, 281, 359, 376, 414, 431, 432, 450, 456, 479, 533
Clevedon Hills 32, 534, 635
Cliff Edge 480
Clifford Bay 171, 281 (*see also* Pebble Row)
Clos de Ste Anne 57, 363, 534, 635
Clos Henri 281, 534 (*see also* Bel Echo, Petit Clos)
Clos Marguerite 281, 534
Clos St. William 171, 227
Cloudy Bay 35, 57, 137, 171, 227, 282, 376, 534 (*see also* Pelorus)
Coal Pit 282, 414, 535
Cockle Bay 282
Coney 171, 227, 535, 635
Coniglio 58
Contour 636
Cooks Beach 282
Coopers Creek 32, 58, 59, 137, 154, 171, 228, 282, 283, 363, 376, 414, 432, 456, 457, 470, 480, 535, 636
Corazon 59, 172, 283, 480, 636
Corbans 59, 60, 137, 155, 172, 228, 283, 284, 377, 457, 480, 636
Cottle Hill 637
Couper's Shed 60, 172, 284, 480, 636
Crab Farm 60, 138, 228, 284, 481, 536
Cracroft Chase 172
Craggy Range 35, 60, 61, 173, 228, 229, 284, 363, 433, 434, 481, 536, 537, 637 (*see also* One Tree, Wild Rock)
Crater Rim, The 173, 229, 285, 377, 537
Crawford Farm 61, 173, 285, 481, 537

Crazy by Nature 61, 435
Croft 61, 285, 538
Croney 61, 285, 538
Crossings, The 285, 538
Crossroads 61, 138, 173, 229, 285, 435, 481, 538, 637
Crowded House 62, 173, 286, 538
Culley 62, 173, 230, 538
Curio 138, 173, 286, 538
Cuvée 397, 398
Cypress 62, 174, 364, 481, 637, 638

d'Akaroa 230
Dada 36
Daisy Rock 286
Dancing Water 230, 286, 539
Daniel Le Brun 398
Darjon 230
Darling, The 138, 174, 286, 287, 539
Dashwood 62, 174, 287, 539
Dawn Ghost 174, 539
Day Break 287
Deep Cove 539
Delegat 62, 63, 287, 457, 482, 539, 540 (*see also* Oyster Bay)
Delta 540
Desert Heart 174, 230, 414, 540
Destiny Bay 435, 436
Deutz 398, 399
Devil's Staircase 174, 541
Discovery Point 63, 230, 287
Distant Land 63, 175, 288, 458, 482, 541
Divine Daughter, The 231
Doctors', The 32, 154, 231, 288, 377, 399
Dog Point 36, 63, 288, 541
Dolbel 63, 288, 399, 414, 482
Domaine Georges Michel 64, 414
Domaine Jaquiery 541
Domain Road 175, 231, 288, 415, 541
Doubtless 458

Drumsara 175, 415, 542
(*see also* Dawn Ghost)
Dry Gully 138, 175, 542
(*see also* Pick & Shovel)
Drylands 64, 232, 289, 542
Dry River 64, 139, 175, 232, 364, 377, 378, 542, 638
Dunleavy 458
Durvillea 176, 289

East Coast 64
Edge, The 176, 542
Elephant Hill 65, 289, 364, 415, 482, 543, 638
Eliot Brothers 289, 543
Ellero 139, 543
Elstree 399
Emeny Road 65
Eradus 176, 289
Escarpment 65, 176, 543, 544
(*see also* Edge The, Kiwa, Kupe, Pahi, Te Rehua)
Esk Valley 65, 66, 130, 176, 232, 290, 360, 415, 435, 482, 544, 638, 639
Eve 544

Fairbourne 290 (*see also* Two Tails)
Fairhall Downs 66, 176, 290, 544
(*see also* Torea)
Fairmont 290, 544
Fallen Angel 232, 290, 378, 399, 545
Fall Harvest 66, 483, 544
Farmers Market 66, 177, 291, 483, 545
Farmgate 66, 130, 139, 291, 378, 639
Felton Road 67, 233, 378, 545, 546
Fiddler's Green 67, 177, 233, 291, 546
(*see also* Glasnevin)
Fisherman's Bite 291
Five Flax 67, 177, 233, 291, 483
Folding Hill 546
Forrest 67, 131, 139, 177, 234, 291, 292, 378, 379, 400, 547 (*see also* Belmonte, Doctors' The, Heart of Stone, John Forrest, Newton/Forrest, Stonewall, Tatty Bogler)
Fossil Ridge 68, 140, 415, 547
Foxes Island 68, 234, 292, 547
(*see also* Fox Junior, Seven Terraces)
Fox Junior 292
Framingham 68, 140, 177, 235, 292, 364, 379, 380, 415, 508, 548
(*see also* Ribbonwood)
Freefall 178, 548
Frizzell 68, 178, 293, 400, 483, 548
Fromm 68, 69, 235, 380, 471, 548, 549, 639 (*see also* La Strada)
Full Circle 293

Gem 69, 293, 484
Georges Michel 293, 364, 400, 549, 550, 639
Georgetown 550
Gibbston Highgate 69, 178, 550
(*see also* Incognito)
Gibbston Valley 69, 140, 157, 178, 235, 236, 381, 416, 550, 551
(*see also* Greenstone)
Gibson Bridge 140, 178, 179, 294, 381, 416, 436
Giesen 70, 236, 381, 551, 552
Gillman 416, 436
Gladstone 179, 294, 364, 416, 436, 552 (*see also* 3 Terraces, 12,000 Miles)
Glasnevin 179, 236, 552
Glazebrook 70, 179, 295, 365, 381, 484, 552, 639
Golden Hills 180, 295
Goldridge 70, 180, 236, 295, 484, 552, 553, 640
Goldwater 71, 295, 436, 484, 553
Grass Cove 180, 295
Grasshopper Rock 553
Gravitas 71, 381, 382, 553
Great Red 437
Greenhough 71, 140, 157, 236, 296, 553, 554

Greenstone 72, 180, 554
Greylands Ridge 554
Greyrock 296, 484, 554
Greystone 72, 140, 180, 237, 296, 382, 416, 554, 640
Greywacke 181, 237, 296, 382
Grove Mill 72, 181, 237, 296, 554, 555 (*see also* Sanctuary)
Gumfields 555
Gunn 72, 181, 297, 555, 640

Hans Herzog 36, 72, 181, 238, 297, 365, 485, 509, 555, 660
Harvest Man 640
Harwood Hall 181, 297, 365, 555, 640
Hawk's Nest 451
Hawkdun Rise 555
Hawkesby 471
Hawkes Ridge 365, 659
Hawkshead 181, 238, 297, 556
Hay Maker 73, 182, 238, 297, 485, 556
Hay Paddock, The 437 (*see also* Harvest Man)
Heart of Stone 298, 556
Hell or Highwater 182, 238, 556
Highfield 73, 238, 298, 556 (*see also* Elstree, Paua)
Hihi 485, 511
Himmelsfeld 298
Hinchco 73, 400, 416, 485
Hinton 557
Hitchen Road 73, 416, 469, 471, 511
Homer 298, 557
Hoppers Crossing 557
Hudson 238, 239, 298, 382, 557
Huia 74, 141, 182, 239, 298, 400, 417, 557
Huntaway 74, 141, 182, 299, 485, 557
Hunter's 40, 74, 141, 239, 299, 400, 401, 417, 437, 558 (*see also* Stoneburn)
Hurunui River 239, 299

Hyperion 74, 182, 458, 471, 485, 558, 641

Incognito 183, 558
Instinct 74, 299, 558, 641
Invivo 300, 558 (*see also* Bram's Run)
Iron Hills 641
Isabel 75, 183, 239, 300, 559
Isola 459, 486
Italiano Bianco 401
Ivicevich 75
Jack's Canyon 239, 300, 559
Jackson Estate 75, 300, 559
Johanneshof 141, 183, 301, 382, 401
Johner 75, 183, 240, 301, 383, 417, 459, 560, 641
John Forrest 36, 75, 240, 383, 459, 560, 641
Joseph Ryan 365, 401, 560
Judge Rock 417, 560, 561, 629
Jules Taylor 301, 417
Julicher 183, 301, 417, 561 (*see also* 99 Rows)
Jumper, The 301, 561
Jurassic Ridge 184, 418, 452, 509, 642

Kahurangi 76, 561 (*see also* Trout Valley)
Kaikoura 561
Kaimira 76, 141, 184, 240, 302, 359, 401, 562 (*see also* Brightside)
Kaipara 37, 76
Kaituna Valley 76, 184, 302, 562
Kakapo 302
Karamea 302, 562
Karikari Estate 76, 437, 511, 642
Kawarau Estate 76, 184, 302, 562
Kemblefield 77, 302
Kennedy Point 77, 302, 459, 486, 563, 642
Kerner 158, 563
Kerr Farm 77, 303, 418, 460, 512
Kidnapper Cliffs 37, 77, 438, 512, 642

Kim Crawford 77, 78, 185, 303, 366, 486, 563 (*see also* Crawford Farm)
Kina Beach 78, 303, 418, 563
Kina Cliffs 303, 564
Kingsmill 240, 564
Kirkpatrick 78, 142, 282, 418, 471, 487
Kiwa 543
Kono 78
Konrad 142, 240, 304, 383, 384, 564 (*see also* Mount Fishtail)
Koru 564
Koura Bay 185, 304, 565 (*see also* Whalesback)
Kumeu River 78, 79, 80, 185, 304, 418, 487, 565
Kupe 80, 543
Kurow Village 241, 565

Lake Chalice 80, 185, 241, 304, 401, 487 (*see also* Nest, The)
Lake Hayes 185, 565
La Michelle 401
Lammastide 642
La Strada 80, 305, 418, 565, 643
Latitude 41 186, 305, 566
Lawson's Dry Hills 81, 142, 186, 241, 305, 418, 566 (*see also* Mount Vernon)
Leaning Rock 142, 156, 241, 566
Lime Rock 186, 306, 566
Lincoln 384 (*see also* Distant Land)
Lindauer 402, 403
Lindis River 567 (*see also* 1912)
Little Black Shag 306
Lobster Reef 186, 306, 567
Locharburn 186, 241, 306, 419, 567
Lochiel 81, 419, 472, 487
Lonestone 81, 187
Longbush 81, 142, 143, 187, 306, 487
Longridge 82, 187, 306, 487
Longview 82, 460, 472
Loopline 242, 306, 567

Lowburn Ferry 419, 567, 568
Lynfer 306, 568

Mahana 403
Mahi 82, 143, 187, 307, 568
Mahurangi River 82, 83, 419, 488, 643
Maimai Creek 83, 143, 187, 242, 308, 419, 488, 643
Main Divide 83, 187, 242, 308, 384, 488, 568
Ma Maison 569
Manaia 438
Man O' War 83, 188, 308, 419, 438, 451, 460, 488, 643 (*see also* Road Works)
Mansion House Bay 308
Manu 188, 308, 569
Maori Point 188, 420, 569
Map Maker 83, 308, 570
Marble Point 84, 242, 309, 384, 570
Margrain 84, 131, 188, 242, 309, 384, 385, 420, 570
Marisco 309
Marsden 37, 84, 188, 309, 420, 438, 468, 512, 643
Martinborough Vineyard 84, 189, 243, 309, 385, 420, 571 (*see also* Burnt Spur)
Martinus 571
Massey Dacta 310
Matahiwi 85, 310, 420, 488, 572 (*see also* Mt Hector)
Matakana Estate 85, 189, 310, 451, 489, 572 (*see also* Goldridge)
Matariki 85, 86, 310, 438, 460, 572, 629, 644 (*see also* Aspire)
Matawara 310, 489
Matawhero 32, 86, 143, 189, 311, 366, 489
Matua Valley 86, 87, 189, 311, 366, 385, 403, 420, 421, 489, 490, 572, 573, 644 (*see also* Secret Stone, Shingle Peak)

Maude   87, 190, 243, 311, 385, 573
Maven   190, 312, 573
   (*see also* Castaway Bay)
Maximus   472
McNaught & Walker   312
Mebus   461
Messenger, The   439
Metis   312
Michael Ramon   190
Michelle Richardson   87, 312, 573
Mill Road   87, 312, 490, 574
Mills Reef   87, 88, 190, 243, 312, 313, 461, 490, 644, 645
Millton   37, 88, 131, 156, 243, 366, 385, 421, 574 (*see also* Clos de Ste Anne, Crazy By Nature)
Mimi   403
Miro   421, 462, 472, 645
Misha's Vineyard   143, 190, 244, 313, 574
Mission   88, 89, 143, 190, 191, 244, 366, 386, 421, 462, 463, 491, 575, 645, 646
Mitre Rocks   575 (*see also* Mount Dottrel)
Moana Park   89, 144, 191, 313, 366, 463, 491, 575, 646
Momo   89, 191, 244, 314, 575
Moncellier   191, 314, 575
Mondillo   244, 576
Monkey Bay   90, 191, 314, 491
Monowai   314, 576
Montana   33, 90, 144, 192, 244, 245, 314–316, 358, 367, 404, 421, 491, 492, 576, 577
Morepork   192
Morton   91, 145, 192, 193, 245, 316, 317, 367, 386, 404, 405, 421, 439, 492, 509, 577, 578, 646 (*see also* Coniglio, Mill Road, Mimi, Nikau Point, Penny Lane, Southern Cross)
Mother Clucker's   92
Mountain Road   317, 578

Mount Dottrel   193, 421, 578
Mount Edward   245, 578
Mount Fishtail   193, 318, 579
Mount Maude   92
Mount Michael   92, 579
Mount Nelson   318
Mount Riley   92, 193, 318, 405, 579
Mount Tamahunga   646
Mount Vernon   193, 318
Moutere Hills   92, 580
Mt Beautiful   194, 245, 319, 580
Mt Campbell   319, 580
Mt Difficulty   194, 245, 246, 319, 580, 581
Mt Hector   92, 194, 319, 581
Mt Rosa   158, 194, 246, 319, 422, 581
Mudbrick   93, 367, 439, 463, 464, 492, 646, 647
Muddy Water   93, 246, 247, 320, 386, 422, 439, 512, 581, 582
Mud House   93, 145, 194, 247, 319, 320, 493, 582 (*see also* Curio, Hay Maker)
Murdoch James   93, 195, 247, 320, 582, 647
Murray's Barn   320
Murray's Road   320, 583

Nanny Goat   583
Nautilus   94, 195, 320, 405, 583
   (*see also* Opawa, Twin Islands)
Navrina Cove   321
Ned, The   195, 321, 583
Nest, The   94, 321, 493, 583
Neudorf   94, 195, 247, 321, 584
Nevis Bluff   196, 584, 585
Newton Forrest   440, 464, 472, 493, 647
Ngatarawa   94, 95, 321, 322, 386, 387, 464, 493, 494, 585, 647
   (*see also* Farmgate, Glazebrook)

Nga Waka 95, 96, 322, 585
 (*see also* Three Paddles)
Night Owl 585
Nikau Point 96, 196, 322, 422, 494, 648
No. 1 Family Estate 405
Nobilo 96, 323, 405, 494, 585
Northburn Station 247, 248, 422, 585, 586
Northfield 96, 323, 422, 586

Oak Hill 96, 196, 422
Obsidian 96, 367, 440, 648
 (*see also* Weeping Sands)
Odyssey 97, 196, 323, 422, 586
 (*see also* Homer)
Ohau Gravels 196, 323
Ohinemuri 97, 145, 248, 323, 648
Okahu 97, 468, 512, 648
 (*see also* Shipwreck Bay)
Old Coach Road 98, 145, 197, 248, 324, 586
Olssen's 98, 145, 197, 248, 324, 423, 440, 586
Omaha Bay 132, 197, 423, 451, 648, 649
Omaka Springs 98, 197, 324, 494, 587
Omihi Road 98, 145, 197, 249, 324, 587
Omori 197
One Tree 99, 198, 324, 494, 587
Onyx 99
Opawa 198, 325, 587
Open House 198, 325
Opihi 99, 155, 198, 249, 588
Orinoco 99, 249, 325
Ostler 198, 249, 588
O:TU 325
Overstone 325, 588
Oyster Bay 99, 325, 588

Pahi 543
Palliser 99, 199, 249, 326, 387, 406, 588 (*see also* Pencarrow)
Paritua 37, 100, 249, 387, 441, 589, 649 (*see also* Red Wire, Stone Paddock, White Wire)
Parr & Simpson 100, 199, 589
Partington 326, 589
Pasquale 199, 589
Passage Rock 100, 146, 199, 326, 367, 423, 441, 464, 649
Paua 326, 589
Paulownia 199, 387, 423, 590
Peacock Sky 100, 423, 464
Peak 326
Pebble Row 326
Pegasus Bay 100, 101, 146, 250, 327, 388, 441, 590 (*see also* Main Divide)
Pelorus 406
Pencarrow 101, 327, 590
Penny Lane 101, 327
People's, The 327, 590
Peregrine 101, 199, 250, 327, 591
 (*see also* Saddleback)
Pete's Shed 591, 659
Peter Yealands 199, 250, 327, 591
Petit Clos 328, 591
Pheasant Plucker 591
Pick & Shovel 591
Picnic 251, 592
Pisa Moorings 200, 592
Pisa Range 592
Poderi Crisci 101, 200, 423, 441, 496
Pohangina Valley 592
Point d'Or 592
Pond Paddock 251, 593
Poverty Bay 424, 496
Prophet's Rock 200, 251, 593
 (*see also* Rocky Point)
Providence 496, 650
Pruner's Reward, The 328
Pukeora 101, 200, 593
Puriri Hills 442
Pyramid Valley 146, 158, 251, 388, 452, 593, 594

Quartz Reef 200, 406, 594
Quest Farm 594

Rabbit Ranch 201, 594
Rannach 496
Ransom 442, 468
Ra Nui 102, 146, 201, 328, 595, 650
Rapaura Springs 102, 328, 595
Recession 443
Redd Gravels 443
Redmetal 102, 496
Redoubt Hill 201, 252, 328
Red Tussock 201, 595
Red Wire 443
Redwood Pass 328, 595
Renato 102, 201, 328, 497, 595
Revington 102, 146
Ribbonwood 201, 252, 329, 596
Richmond Plains 103, 252, 329, 388, 424, 596
Rimu Grove 103, 202, 252, 596 (*see also* Bronte)
Rippon 38, 252, 253, 596, 597
Riverby 103, 202, 253, 329, 389, 597
River Farm 103, 147, 202, 329, 497, 597
Riverstone 103, 407, 497, 597
Road Works 103, 202, 330, 497
Rochfort Rees 330, 598
Rockburn 104, 147, 202, 253, 330, 424, 598 (*see also* Devil's Staircase)
Rock Face 104, 598
Rock Ferry 203, 330, 368, 389, 407, 659
Rock N Pillar 598
Rocky Point 598
Rongopai 104, 330, 497
Rose Tree Cottage 389, 598
Rua 599
Rua Whenua 330, 443, 497
Ruben Hall 104
Ruby Bay 104, 203, 253, 330, 599

St Jacques 599
St Jerome 465
Sacred Hill 104, 105, 203, 331, 465, 498, 599, 650 (*see also* Gunn, Whitecliff, Wild South)
Saddleback 203, 253, 600
Saint Clair 105, 106, 107, 147, 203, 204, 254, 331–333, 498, 499, 600, 601
Saints 107, 147, 204, 334, 389, 465, 499
Saltings 650
Salvare 107, 368, 499, 651
Sanctuary 148, 204, 334
Sandihurst 602
San Hill 443
Satellite 334, 602
Saveé Sea 334, 602
Schubert 602
Scott Base 108, 204, 254, 602
Sea Level 334
Sears Road 108, 204, 334, 499, 651
Secret Stone 108, 204, 334, 603 (*see also* Matawara)
Seifried 108, 148, 154, 205, 254, 335, 371, 389, 444, 465, 603, 651 (*see also* Old Coach Road)
Selaks 109, 148, 205, 335, 368, 390, 407, 424, 499, 603, 651
Sentinel 335
Seresin 38, 109, 148, 205, 255, 336, 390, 603–605 (*see also* Momo)
Seven Terraces 336
Shaky Bridge 109, 149, 205, 206, 255, 424, 605
Shepherd's Ridge 110, 337
Sherwood 206 (*see also* Clearwater)
Shingle Peak 110, 206, 337, 407, 605 (*see also* Matua Valley)
Shipwreck Bay 110, 255, 337, 500, 651
Sileni 110, 206, 255, 337, 338, 390, 407, 408, 424, 452, 500, 605, 606, 651 (*see also* Greyrock, Overstone)
Sisters, The 339

Sliding Hill 339
Soho 111, 206, 339, 424, 425, 444, 606, 652
Soland 652
Soljans 111, 149, 206, 339, 390, 408, 501, 513, 606
Soma 256, 606
Southbank 111, 206, 339, 425, 606, 652
Southern Cross 111, 207, 339, 501, 607
Southern Lighthouse 256, 340
Spinyback 111, 207, 256, 340, 607
Sprig 340
Spring Creek 256, 340, 607 (*see also* Jumper, The)
Spy Valley 111, 112, 149, 207, 256, 257, 340, 341, 390, 391, 408, 501, 607, 608 (*see also* Satellite)
Squawking Magpie 112, 341, 501, 652
Staete Landt 112, 207, 257, 341, 368, 391, 608, 652 (*see also* Map Maker)
Stafford Lane 112, 149, 208, 257, 341, 509, 608
Stanley Estates 341
Starborough 208, 341
Stockman's Station 608
Stone Bridge 112, 113, 150, 208, 368, 501
Stoneburn 342, 608
Stonecroft 113, 150, 342, 425, 444, 502, 652, 653, 660
Stoneleigh 113, 208, 257, 342, 425, 502, 608, 609
Stone Paddock 114, 342, 391, 425, 444, 609, 653
Stonewall 343, 609
Stonyridge 444, 445, 472, 653 (*see also* Fallen Angel)
Stop Banks 114, 343
Sugar Loaf 343
Summerhouse 114, 150, 257, 343, 408, 609
Surveyor Thomson 609

Takatu 208, 425, 502
Takutai 343, 609
Tama 502
Tarras 425, 426, 610
Tasman Bay 114, 209, 343, 610
Tatty Bogler 209, 426, 610
Te Awa 114, 343, 392, 445, 465, 503, 513, 653, 654 (*see also* Kidnapper Cliffs)
Te Hana 408
Te Henga 115, 209, 426, 446, 610
Te Kairanga 115, 150, 209, 257, 344, 426, 452, 466, 503, 611, 654
Te Mania 116, 209, 258, 344, 392, 426, 503, 611, 654 (*see also* Richmond Plains)
Te Mara 209, 258, 612
Te Mata 116, 344, 368, 446, 466, 469, 503, 654
Te Motu 466 (*see also* Dunleavy)
Te Puna 655
Te Rehua 543
Terrace Edge 210, 258, 612, 655
Terrace Heights 210, 345, 369, 612 (*see also* Murray's Barn)
Terrain 116, 210, 258, 345, 610
Terravin 38, 117, 210, 345, 504, 610, 613
Te Whare Ra 38, 151
Te Whau 117, 426, 446, 655
Thornbury 117, 210, 258, 345, 504, 613
Three Miners 211, 613
Three Paddles 117, 258, 346, 613
Tiki 211, 346, 613 (*see also* Alpine Valley)
Timara 117, 258, 346
Tinpot Hut 211, 346, 655
Ti Point 118, 211, 347, 369, 426, 504, 655
Tiritiri 118
Tiwaiwaka 613
Tohu 118, 211, 259, 347, 614 (*see also* Kono)

Toi Toi   118, 211, 259, 347
Tolaga Bay   118, 156
Tom   446
Torea   211, 347, 614
Torlesse   119, 151, 212, 259, 347, 392, 427, 614 (*see also* Omihi Road)
Torrent Bay   119, 212, 347, 614
Tranquillity Bay   119, 348, 614
Tranquil Valley   212, 348, 614
Tresillian   212, 259
Trinity Hill   33, 119, 212, 348, 369, 392, 409, 427, 447, 509, 615, 655, 656, 659 (*see also* Metis)
Triplebank   213, 348, 615
Trout Valley   213
Tukipo River   120
Tupari   213, 348
Turanga Creek   213, 369, 392, 447
Turning Point   348, 615
Tussock   213, 349, 427, 615
TW   120, 392, 473
Twin Islands   120, 349, 409, 616
Two Gates   447, 656
Two Paddocks   616 (*see also* Picnic)
Two Rivers   213, 259, 349, 616 (*see also* Black Cottage, Navrina Cove)
Two Sisters   213, 260, 616
Two Tails   349
Two Tracks   120, 214, 349, 616

Unison   349, 427, 448, 504, 656 (*see also* Recession)
Urlar   214, 260, 349, 393, 617

Valli   260, 617
Van Asch   214, 617
Vavasour   121, 214, 350, 617 (*see also* Dashwood, Redwood Pass)
Verde   409
Vicar's Mistress, The   618
Vidal   121, 214, 260, 350, 369, 370, 504, 505, 618, 656, 657

View Estate   657
Villa Maria   33, 122–124, 151, 214, 215, 260, 261, 350–352, 360, 370, 393, 409, 427, 467, 505, 506, 618–620, 657 (*see also* Esk Valley, Vidal, Riverstone, Ruben Hall, Thornbury)
Vin Alto   448, 449
Vinoptima   151
Voss   124, 261, 620
Vynfields   38, 261, 427, 620

Waimarie   124
Waimata   124, 658
Waimea   39, 125, 152, 215, 262, 352, 371, 393, 428, 469, 506, 507, 621, 658 (*see also* Spinyback, Takutai)
Waipara Downs   394, 621
Waipara Hills   125, 152, 215, 216, 262, 353, 409, 621, 622
Waipara Springs   125, 126, 152, 262, 263, 353, 622
Waipara West   126, 353
Waipipi   126, 263, 353, 410, 449, 622
Wairau River   126, 152, 216, 263, 353, 354, 371, 622, 623
Waitaki Braids   216, 623
Waitaki Valley Wines   623
Waitapu   371, 513, 658
Waitiri Creek   623
Walnut Block   354, 623
Weaver   623
Weeping Sands   216, 428, 467, 507, 510, 658
Weka River   263, 354, 624
West Brook   127, 152, 216, 264, 354, 473, 624 (*see also* Blue Ridge, Gumfields, Ivicevich)
Whalesback   354
Whitecaps   355
Whitecliff   127, 216, 355, 507, 624
White Cloud   39, 410
White Gold   217

Whitehaven   127, 152, 217, 264, 355, 624 (*see also* Mansion House Bay, Whitecaps)
Whitestone   158, 217, 355, 625
White Wire   39
Wicked Vicar, The   127
Wild Earth   217, 264, 625 (*see also* 25 Steps, 1769, Deep Cove, Eve, Stockman's Station)
Wild Irishman   625
Wild Rock   127, 128, 217, 356, 428, 507, 625, 626, 658
Wild South   128, 218, 264, 356, 626
William Thomas   356

Wingspan   356, 626
Wishart   128, 449
Wither Hills   129, 218, 264, 356, 626, 627 (*see also* Open House, Shepherd's Ridge, Two Tracks)
Wooing Tree   39, 129, 218, 394, 428, 627, 628
Woollaston   218, 264, 356, 628 (*see also* Tussock, Wingspan)
Woven Stone   356
Wycroft   628

Yealands   153, 218, 265, 356, 371, 628 (*see also* Full Circle, Pete's Shed)